DATE DUE

DE 16 '97		
MY 11 '9		
MY 28 '9		
JE 7 06		

DEMCO 38-296

PURSUING POWER
Latinos and the Political System

PURSUING POWER
Latinos and the Political System

F. Chris Garcia, editor

UNIVERSITY OF NOTRE DAME PRESS
NOTRE DAME, INDIANA 46556

Copyright 1997 by
University of Notre Dame Press
Notre Dame, IN 46556

Manufactured in the United States of America

Library of Congress Cataloging-in-Publication Data

Pursuing power : Latinos and the political system / edited by F. Chris
    Garcia.
        p.   cm.
    Includes bibliographical references.
    ISBN 0-268-01312-8 (alk. paper). — ISBN 0-268-01313-6 (pbk. :
alk. paper)
    1. Hispanic Americans—Politics and government.   2. Political
participation—United States.   I. Garcia, F. Chris.
E184.S75.P87   1997
327′.042′08968073—dc20   96-26440
                                                                    CIP

The paper used in this publication meets the minimum requirements
of the American National Standard for Information Sciences—
Permanence of Paper for Printed Library Materials, ANSI Z39.48-1984.

Composed primarily in 1995, fifty years after the end of World War II, this book is dedicated to the World War II Generation—assuredly one to which we are most indebted and thankful—and particularly to the Hispanic Americans, male and female, of that remarkable generation. Their sacrifices, their valor, their patriotism, and their collective responsibilities for and to this country are unsurpassed. Not yet commensurably recognized nor appreciated, half a century later Latinos are still engaged in struggles for full acceptance and equality.

Contents

Contents

Preface

THE PURPOSE OF THIS volume is to provide a systematic overview of and perspective on the involvement of Latinos in the politics of the United States. It is even more obvious now than it was in 1988 when *Latinos and the Political System* was published,[1] that this country is being greatly affected by its burgeoning Hispanic population.[2] Inevitably, Latinos will become more and more significant players in the political, social, and economic arenas. Our public and private sectors will increasingly recognize and reflect this change. Indeed, to the extent that there is an American core culture, it will continue to become more Latinized at the same time as Latinos become more Anglicized.

The major institutions of our society—including private enterprise, the media, educational and religious institutions, and government—now at least are aware of the large and growing Hispanic presence. Scholars, including political scientists, have turned more of their attention to Latinos. In short, in the 1990s, Latinos have been *recognized,* if not completely appreciated or accommodated.

Over the past decade, a noticeably increased amount of information has been generated about Latinos. Of note is the special attention paid by government agencies in their reports, including the 1990 Census. The turn of the decade also witnessed the first nationally representative opinion survey—the Latino National Political Survey[3]—which focused on the political orientations of the three largest Hispanic groups. Byproducts of that project included a bibliographic documentation of research on Latinos and politics which revealed an astonishingly large number of entries.[4] Other major national surveys either included a significant subsample of Latinos or included items about Latinos in them. These and other reports over the past several years underscored the great and increasing *diversity,* and little understood complexity, of the Latino community. Especially noteworthy are the variations related to national origin, the geographic dispersion and sociodemographic profiles, including immigration patterns and generational status.

It is hoped that this volume will add to the understanding of the status of the Latino political situation in the mid-1990s. Every effort has been made to select writings which are particularly important or insightful regarding some of the most salient aspects of Latino politics. Of course, there are many more fine articles than could be included here. Contained in these pages are several articles written especially for this volume as well as reprints of previously published work which are "classic" in that they are especially significant or interesting expositions on a topic and thereby deserve further dissemination. My own exposition has been expanded in order to fill in some of the gaps which are inevitable in any anthology and to provide continuity and context for the individual selections.

This volume includes less material on political history and demography and more on public policies, especially in relation to prominent issues facing the American public as the twentieth century draws to a close. Moreover, we have brought out some little noticed dimensions of Latino politics, for example, the essential role of Hispanic women in politics, and included more articles on community mobilization and interest-group activities.

The readings have been placed in a "systems" framework to help readers conceptualize and place in context the relationships and interrelationships among the major components of the American political system. The use of the Eastonian system model as an organizing framework should not be interpreted as a bias toward any particular style or strategy of politics nor a preference towards any model of the distribution of power in this system.[5]

This volume is the product of many hardworking and dedicated individuals. First and foremost, my sincerest gratitude goes to the scholars and colleagues who produced the articles. Next, I am grateful to those copyright holders which graciously allowed us to reprint their works (with special gratitude to Dr. Felix M. Padilla for his graciousness). Another major debt of thanks is extended to the competent and conscientious staff of Notre Dame University Press whose interest in Latino publications and support for my work over more than two decades is greatly appreciated. Special appreciation is extended to Carole Roos for her skillful editing, her supportive attitude, and her perceptive suggestions for improving the manuscript. Also making major contributions of time, skill, interest, and support to the preparation of this work were Sandy Garcia, Gina Adam, Loyola Chastain, Scotty Shea, and Robin Tropper.

NOTES

1. *Latinos and the Political System,* ed. F. Chris Garcia (Notre Dame, Ind. : University of Notre Dame Press, 1988).

2. While realizing that some activists and academics make a great deal of the different semantic connotations and implications of the labels "Latino" and "Hispanic," and that group labels are significant in many ways, in this volume they are used interchangeably as an umbrella term encompassing those residents of the United States whose ancestry is derived from the Spanish cultural regions of the Western hemisphere.

3. The first comprehensive report of the results of the Latino National Political Survey is contained in Rodolfo O. de la Garza, Louis DeSipio, F. Chris Garcia, John Garcia, and Angelo Falcon, *Latino Voices: Mexican, Puerto Rican and Cuban Perspectives on American Politics* (Boulder, Colo.: Westview Press, 1992).

4. Compiled and edited by F. Chris Garcia, John A. Garcia, Rodolfo O. de la Garza, Angelo Falcon, and Cara Abeyta, *Latinos and Politics: A Select Research Bibliography* (Austin, Tex.: Center for Mexican American Studies, University of Texas at Austin, 1990).

5. A recent overview of Latino politics which posits several theories of the distribution of power in the United States and proposes a new variation of one theory, pluralism, as it applies to Latinos is Rodney E. Hero, *Latinos and the U.S. Political System: Two-Tiered Pluralism* (Philadelphia: Temple University Press, 1992).

Introduction

IF THE 1980s were the "Decade of the Hispanics," the 1990s appear to be the decade of Hispanic "recognition and diversity." The major institutions of American society—governments, businesses, schools, the media, and others—as well as much of the general populace, finally recognize the presence and major impact of Latinos. Moreover, the increased numbers of Hispanics coming from different countries, the dispersion of Hispanics throughout all regions of the U.S., and Latinos' use of every form and style of political strategy and tactics (all within a setting of an increased public discourse and awareness about multiculturalism) emphasize the complex diversity within this population.

Perhaps the most dramatic force leading to the increased recognition of Latinos was the tremendous growth in the number of Latinos reported by the 1990 census. The Hispanic population increased by approximately 53 percent from 1980 to 1990, that is, from about 14 million to at least 22 million. The Hispanic population grew five to seven times as fast as the non-Hispanic population. In March 1995, the U.S. Census Bureau reported that between 1990 and 1994 the Hispanic population had continued to grow to 26 million. Such a dramatic increase in numbers could not help but be noticed by policy makers as well as by many members of the general public.

Immigration became one of the major items on the public agenda—an issue which would remain visible and even intensify as the 1990s progressed. Earlier debate had resulted in the Immigration Reform and Control Act (IRCA) of 1986. It is not clear whether this national statute had the net effect of improving Latinos' situation or of being less than beneficial. The continued immigration of Latinos, with estimates of up to a million additional Latino immigrants coming into the country each year both legally and illegally, caused alarm among some segments of the non-Hispanic population and provided a basis for optimism among some Latino leaders. Anxious and ethnocentric spokes-

1

persons with anti-Latino biases spoke about "brown hordes" with foreign values and a lack of loyalty to the United States destroying the American way of life and all that it stands for. Several movements to limit or ban completely the use of the Spanish language swept the United States. Several states (up to twenty-three in 1996) actually passed legislation which restricted the use of Spanish. Organizations and movements such as US English and English First continued to lobby for the exclusive or official use of English. National legislation to this effect was introduced and passed the U.S. House of Representatives in 1996.

In addition to the huge increase in the number of Latinos, related demographic trends increased their recognition and diversity. For one, although the majority of Latino immigrants continued to come from Mexico, there was a very noticeable increase in the number of immigrants from other countries of Latin America including Central and South America and the Caribbean. In fact, the growth of the population of "Central and South Americans" and "other Hispanics" over the decade was 67 percent or about 5 million new Latinos. This posed new challenges as well as opportunities for Latino politics and for the way that the American political system would respond. Additionally, the long-time concentration of Latinos in the Southwest, the Midwest, and a few urban centers in the Northeast and Florida changed rapidly as the Latino population dispersed throughout the country. The 1990 Census indicated Latinos in every state of the Union, even in such areas as the Deep South and the Plains states. Moreover, the 1990 Census reported that the number of Hispanics living in the suburbs of the nation's metro areas grew by 69 percent over the decade. Almost half (48%) of Latinos resided in the suburbs, rather than in the central cities or rural areas.

The demographic and political trends of the 1980s fostered the search for and the use of an appropriate supranational or pan-ethnic term for the rapidly diversifying populations from Latin America. Bolstered by increasing numbers and other impressive demographic trends, Latino spokespersons stressed the rapidly increasing *potential* of this collection of 22 million individuals. It was to the strategic advantage of Latino leaders and activists to use a collective term, since the use of a single label implied a certain amount of cohesion and unity in that population. It was strategically clever to emphasize the commonalties among the various Latino national-origin groups and to de-emphasize their differences. Some political analysts, although cognizant of the strategic importance of unity, were more critical and attempted to analyze and specify areas of common cultural and political concern as well as to understand the variations. At the turn of the decade, a major national survey of the three largest Latino groups—Mexican Americans, Puerto Ricans, and Cubans—provided empirical evidence that although there were some areas of consensus and commonality, particularly in relationship to these groups' cultural heritage and political value system, there was less political cohesion than some activists and scholars had contended.[1]

One of the challenges of Latino leadership may be how to mobilize the diverse national-origin groups to support common "Latino" causes. A rethinking of Latino politics at the national level may be warranted to focus on coalitions among various national-origin groups. *Coalitional* politics may offer the optimal opportunities for success, particularly at the higher levels of government. Strategies could include both coalitions of various Latino groups and coalitions which included Latinos and other sectors of the population, such as other ethnic or racial minorities or some segment of the core-cultural population such as liberals, women, or white working-class people.

The intense political activity by Latinos in the 1960s and early 1970s was regarded with some understanding and support by the general American public.[2] In the late 1970s the mood of the American public grew less open to "progressive" movements. The 1980s have been characterized as "the decade of greed" because of the purported emphasis on material advancement and a relative lack of concern for, or responsibility towards, community and public affairs. Most would characterize the decade as a "conservative" one, since conservative Republican presidents were elected and served from 1980 (Ronald Reagan) through 1992 (George Bush). Those administrations seemed to be concerned with issues other than racial and ethnic equality, assisting the disadvantaged, or improving the common good through direct government participation. It was an era of an emphasis on the privatization of programs and a more laissez-faire or even "survival of the fittest" philosophy. From a liberal perspective, it seemed that governments backed away from their commitment to directly concern themselves with or assist the lower socioeconomic levels of our society. Indeed the more stringent critics of that era charged the national administration with being insensitive to the plight of racial and ethnic groups at best and at worst outwardly elitist or even racist.

Major economic trends became apparent at the end of the 1980s as data demonstrated that the wealthiest Americans became much more prosperous and the lower, lower-middle, and middle socioeconomic classes either did not improve their status or actually lost ground to inflation in relationship to the upper-middle and upper socioeconomic classes. Latinos, the overwhelming proportion of whom are working class or lower-middle class, shared the plight of these lower strata of society. The 1990 Census and other economic data showed that the relative position of Latinos along various socioeconomic dimensions had changed only a little over the ten years from 1980 to 1990. At best, some very slight progress had been made in a few areas.

In the 1990s, Latinos used every political tactic available to Americans: elections and political parties; interest-group activities with the executive, legislative, and judicial branches, including several successful lawsuits; grassroots lobbying through the media; and involvement in direct, even confrontational, actions, including boycotts, marches, protests, and other demonstrations, especially on college campuses. Some Latinos sought alliances with other national-origin Latino, as well as non-Latino, groups; some went it alone with emphasis on their own national-origin compatriots.

Some advances in representation were made as Latinos increased their numbers in Congress and in state and local governments, most specifically on community school boards. So there was at least some "descriptive" representation, which is minimally one kind of recognition of the growing significance of the Latino population. It is not as clear that substantive representation embodied in policies made similarly notable advances, with perhaps two noteworthy exceptions being the Civil Rights Act of 1991 and the extension of the Voting Rights Acts in 1992 to further promote the representation of language minorities.

In any case, in the 1990s, there was a great emphasis on the potential of Latino politics underlying the national level of electoral politics. This potential was stressed in the 1980, 1984, 1988, and 1992 elections. However, the potential was not fully realized, and this observation has also been true more generally in almost all areas of Latino politics.

To help the reader make sense of Latino politics in the United States, a well-known and much-used conceptual framework is employed to structure our information. This framework is modeled on the political system paradigm conceptualized by David Easton.[3] The political system can be schematized as follows:

THE POLITICAL SYSTEM

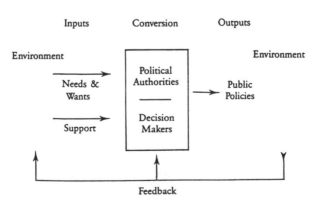

Four basic elements of the system include: 1) the setting or environment in which the political system operates, i.e., the contextual factors, 2) inputs into the system, 3) conversion, and 4) system outputs or outcomes. The political system is one of many systems, such as the economic and social systems, operating in any society. It is distinctive in that it allocates values and goods authoritatively, that is, it makes binding decisions by choosing from among many possible policies and legitimizing some into laws or other forms of public policy.

Understanding how the political system operates is not possible if one is ignorant of its history, the condition of other coexisting systems, the prevailing mood of the system's populace, and other major contextual factors. Therefore, to understand Latino politics, one must have some familiarity with the *setting* in which Latinos are interacting with the political system. A brief overview is presented in Part One.

The *input* side of the system is the area where most Latino political activity takes place as Hispanics attempt to engage the system by presenting their needs and wants. Latino desires are aggregated into some kind of a collective form and must be communicated to the authorities; that is, articulated to the political system decision makers. The variety of tactics currently in use is presented by the articles in Part Two.

The *conversion* process is the point where the authoritative decision makers or public authorities decide which interests shall be legitimized by government; that is, which shall become binding public policy. The question of Latino representation at all levels of government including positions in the bureaucracy is one of continuing interest. Part Three considers some aspects of conversion.

The *outputs* of the system come in the formulation and promulgation of public policy: laws, regulations, and the policy outcomes that ensue from those. From the viewpoint of a socioeconomically depressed ethnic group, most of the desired outcomes revolve around the topics of exclusion, inequality, socioeconomic deprivation, and a related cluster of issues such as education, employment, housing, health, the lack of public services, crime, and drug abuse. More Latino-specific issues include the protection or promotion of the Spanish language (including bilingual education), affirmative action, immigration, and to a lesser extent, United States foreign policy towards Latin America. Policy outputs and outcomes are examined in Part Four.

Policies and issues on the public agenda are always changing—taking new forms and involving new publics. Although the future configurations of Latino politics cannot be predicted, it is possible to project some possibilities and speculate about what is to come. In the final section of this volume, several scholars of Latino politics give us their insightful assessments of future possibilities.

This volume should provide an opportunity to the reader to assess the current state of Latino politics in the "decade of Hispanic recognition and diversity" and perhaps formulate a prognosis, at least for the immediate future, of Latinos in the United States political system.

It is hoped that not only will this volume lead to increased awareness and understanding of Latino politics, but that it might also encourage even more attention to and research on the continuing disadvantaged position of Latinos in the United States and the implications for them and for this nation of the increased Latinization or "browning" of this nation.

NOTES

1. Rodolfo O. de la Garza, Louis DeSipio, F. Chris Garcia, John A. Garcia, and Angelo Falcon, *Latino Voices: Mexican, Puerto Rican, and Cuban Perspectives in American Politics* (Boulder, Colo.: Westview Press, 1992).

2. For an inside perspective on the Chicano Movement, see Carlos Munoz, *Youth, Identity, Power: The Chicano Movement* (New York: Verso, 1989).

3. David Easton, *A Framework for Political Analysis* (Englewood Cliffs, N.J.: Prentice Hall, 1965) and *A Systems Analysis of Political Life* (New York: Chauncy Wiley and Sons, 1965). The schematic diagram used here is a slightly modified and greatly simplified version of the Eastonian political system model.

PART I

The Setting: Sociodemographic and Attitudinal

THIS SECTION BRIEFLY INTRODUCES the setting in which Latinos engage in politics. The status of any group in a polity is the product of many forces and circumstances, including its physical environment, its developmental history, the economic system, the major philosophies and ideologies, and its beliefs and values. Some of the most salient threads of experience common to many Latinos are 1) the rapidly expanding Latino populations in the United States, 2) historical and socioeconomic experiences which in some ways are diverse but in other ways include some significant commonalties among these groups, and 3) the racism and prejudice which these groups have encountered and to some extent still are experiencing.

One of the most touted demographic projections is that Latinos will become the largest distinctive ethnic minority group in this country early in the twenty-first century. The projections for this significant milestone range from 2005 to 2045 with the most recent and responsible estimates putting that date between 2006 and 2013. Becoming the largest distinctive ethnic minority group (surpassing African Americans who have so long been the largest) is deemed by many to be crucially significant. Latinos have for generations, if not centuries, been the "invisible minority." Ethnic relations, civil rights activities, and in general the attention of United States policy makers have been cast in black and white terms. With some exceptions, the other distinctive ethnic minorities such as Asian Americans, Native Americans, and especially Hispanic Americans have been relegated to secondary roles, if not entirely ignored. Latino activists base many of their hopes for political success on Latinos becoming the largest group, implying that one kind of demographic primacy will also lead to corresponding importance in the political, social, and economic spheres. Certainly the implications are immense; the *potential* is tremendous.

A Census Bureau update in March 1995 placed the number of Latinos at about 26 million in 1994, about 10 percent of the total U.S. population. Immigration contributed to about half of this growth. Revised 1990 Census estimates placed the Mexican-American population at 13.5 million, an increase of 7.7 million (54%) over the decade. Puerto Ricans increased to 2.7 million, a 35 percent increase. The Cuban-American population was estimated to be about 1.1 million, a 34 percent increase. In addition to the notably high growth rate of Mexican Americans, the next most rapid was that of "Central and South Americans." This group from about twenty countries comprised about 3 million new residents. "Other Hispanic origin" accounted for a total of 5 million residents and grew by 67 percent.

Not only the absolute size of the Latino population, but its concentration and distribution are significant for Latino politics. Areas of Latino concentration have the greatest potential for greatly increased political influence, particularly at the state and local governmental level. By 1990, Latinos were present in every one of the fifty states. Although widely distributed, this dispersion is still light in some areas and very concentrated in others. In 1990, about nine out of ten Hispanics lived in ten states. The state with the largest Hispanic population was California, where 25.8 percent of the population was Latino, comprising 7.7 million residents. California was followed by Texas with 4.3 million Latinos (25.5% of its residents); New York, 2.2 million (12.3%); Florida, 1.6 million (12.2%); Illinois, 900 thousand (7.9%); New Jersey, 740 thousand (9.6%); Arizona, 688 thousand (18.8%); New Mexico, 579 thousand (38%); Colorado, 424 thousand (12.9%); and Massachusetts, 288 thousand (4.8%). The trend towards a pattern of dispersion throughout the country also has significant implications for national politics. Obviously, numbers are a major political resource in the political arena, and that one resource alone seems to be increasingly significant for the politics of Latinos in the United States.

Socioeconomic and sociodemographic characteristics other than population are very significant for Latinos in U.S. politics. Not only are these indicators of well-being, and as such allow measurement of the socioeconomic standing of Latinos, but they also are indicators of other potential political resources which Latinos can bring to bear in politics. However, Latinos as a whole (and each national-origin group with a few exceptions) exhibit a general pattern of socioeconomic characteristics that indicates their disadvantage. The general pattern is that Latinos tend to have lower incomes than do non-Latino Whites, suffer higher rates of unemployment and poverty, have a lower level of educational attainment, live in more dilapidated housing, and are disproportionately concentrated in the service and labor sectors of the economy rather than occupying professional and managerial occupational positions. The relative paucity of these resources puts Latinos at a disadvantage in employing their socioeconomic resources for political purposes. On the other hand, they are graphic indicators of Latinos' relatively unequal status and as such can serve to heighten the political goals of socioeconomic parity, for example.

Before we examine additional socioeconomic data that will give us some objective measurement of the status of Latinos, it is crucial that two caveats be heeded. First, very little of the data available for the "Latino" or "Hispanic" group is broken out by *national origin;* most of the data lumps together Cubans, Puerto Ricans, Mexicans, Central and South Americans and "others." Second, very seldom is the country of birth or the number of *generations* in the U.S. reported or used in analysis. This means that Hispanics whose ancestors have been in the United States for several generations are averaged into these statistics with those who are first-generation native born and with those who are foreign born and who may have resided in this country for only a short time. Since the patterns of immigration for various Latinos is very diverse and extends over centuries, statistics which lump all national-origin groups and all generations together can obscure considerable variation. From the viewpoint of those who think that Latinos are basically an immigrant ethnic population, one would expect that those who have been here the longest will have advanced socioeconomically and politically more than will have the more recent immigrants. This has been the pattern typical of voluntary immigrants to the United States. Those who feel that Latinos are more similar to an oppressed racial group for whom immigration is relatively less important and who have been subjected to extremely severe discrimination, such as the African or Native Americans, might expect very minimal advancement regardless of length of residence in this country.

Keeping the above cautions in mind, there is some evidence, albeit indirect, that Latino job holders have increased their very slow movement into higher prestige and income occupations, including white-collar, managerial, and professional positions. It is clearer that they are constituting a smaller proportion of the "operators, fabricators and laborers" in this society. In 1983, 32 percent of Hispanic males were in this lowest occupational category; in 1993, 28 percent were in these positions. Nevertheless, in the 1990s the largest proportion of Latinos were still in the less desirable, lower-paying positions. For example, the proportion of Hispanic men employed in managerial and professional occupations in 1993 was 12 percent compared to 28 percent for non-Hispanic men. In contrast, among "operators, fabricators, and laborers" 28 percent of Latino males were in this category compared to 19 percent of non-Hispanic male workers.

A 1993 government report allows some further analysis of these general statistics by national origin.[1] For example, in the higher-paying managerial and professional ranks, 20 percent of Cubans are situated here compared to 16 percent of the Puerto Ricans and 9 percent of those of Mexican origin. The Latino National Political Survey (LNPS) provides us with generational information, which unfortunately is lacking from many other sources. The LNPS nativity and generational data are most meaningful for the large Mexican-American sample with analysis showing dramatic and highly significant statistical changes among four generations. Only 6 percent of the foreign-born Mexicans reported holding a managerial or professional position; 12 percent of those born in the United States were in this category, as were 16 percent of those whose parents were born here and 18 percent of those who were at least the third generation U.S. born. The generational progression was even more marked for movement out of the laboring class—37 percent of the foreign born, 25 percent of the first U.S.-born generation, 20 percent of the second generation, and 16 percent of the third were in that category.

The overall relatively depressed labor position was reflected in income statistics. The median income of Latino households in the 1960s was only about 60 percent of the median family income of all Americans. By the late 1970s, that percentage had climbed to almost 70 percent where it seemed to level off. By 1992, the median income of Hispanic households was still about 70 percent of that of non-Hispanic households—$22,859 for Latinos and $33,355 for non-Latinos. Only 16 percent of Hispanic households had incomes of $50,000 or more in 1993, compared to 30 percent of non-Hispanic white households. Moreover, Hispanic households are larger and have more income contributors than non-Hispanic white households.

The diversity among national-origin groups is reflected in household income statistics. In 1993, 14 percent of Mexican households earned $50,000 or more, compared to 13 percent of Puerto Rican households, 25 percent of Cubans, 10 percent of Central and South Americans, and 21 percent of "other" Hispanics. The LNPS allows us a look at possible generational influences. A majority of foreign-born and first-generation U.S.-born Mexicans had household incomes below $20,000. Among second and third U.S.-born generations, slight majorities were above $20,000.

Twenty-eight percent of Mexican Americans were in the poverty category in 1969, compared to 13 percent of majority Americans. By 1974, these figures were down to 24 and 9 percent respectively, but in 1985, poverty rates were back up to 25 percent for Hispanics, 14 percent for all Americans, and 11 percent for Anglos (Whites). In 1992, those rates were back up to 29 percent for Hispanics and 11 percent for Anglos. The poverty rates were highest for Puerto Ricans (33%) and lowest for Cubans (15%) with Mexican Americans at 26 percent.

Throughout the past three decades, unemployment among Latinos also remained higher than that for Anglo Americans. The unemployment rate for Hispanics in 1992 was 12 percent compared to 7 percent for the total non-Latino work force. Therefore, there was some statistical improvement, but again, expectations of equity fell short of realization.

Related to occupation and income is the educational level of the worker. In 1970, only three of ten Hispanics 25 years and older had completed at least four years of high school. By 1980, about four of ten Hispanics had graduated. By 1990, this increased to about half. In 1993, among Hispanics 25 years old and over, 53 percent had completed high school compared to 84 percent of non-Hispanics. And young Hispanics were significantly more educated than were their elders. Yet even in this overall picture of improvement, a nagging problem remains—that of dropouts—Hispanic dropout rates continue to be disturbingly high. For example in 1991 the high school dropout rate for Hispanics was 35 percent compared to 9 percent for Whites.

Another one of the most important shared characteristics of Latinos in this country is their perception and treatment by non-Hispanic Americans. Discriminatory treatment and negative stereotyping may be a critically important common experience which tends to unite otherwise diverse Latinos as well as to provide them with a common political goal of equality. Some major studies in the late 1980s and early 1990s provided scientific, quantitative evidence to confirm the negative view of Latinos held by a large proportion of the American population. A new analysis of existing polling data which was sponsored by the American Jewish Committee in 1989 and conducted by the National Opinion Research Center measured the "social standing" of various groups in the United States. Americans were asked to rate the social position of several groups in the United States. Native white Americans and Americans of western European descent were accorded the highest social standing. Those clustering near or at the bottom of the social status scale included Latin Americans, Mexicans, and Puerto Ricans. An analysis of the 1990

General Social Survey data by its director, Dr. Tom Smith, focused on
Americans' stereotypes toward six distinctive groups as compared to
Whites. "Hispanics" were characteristically perceived as negative stereotypes. Hispanics were perceived as significantly more likely to be lazier,
more violence prone, more likely to live off welfare, less intelligent, and
less patriotic than the average white American. A third major study, conducted by LH Research in 1993 and reported in 1994, found that many
Whites continued to hold negative views of Latinos. For example, a significant proportion (21%) of Americans felt that Hispanics "lacked ambition and drive to succeed." (By the way, this study also found negative
racial stereotyping and biases among distinctive ethnic minorities, including Hispanics, as well as by white Americans.) These studies only
serve to lend empirical confirmation to what has been known to be a
central feature of American society—racism and prejudicial perceptions
of distinctive ethnic and racial minorities continue into the end of the
twentieth century. Latinos thus have the added burden of being devalued
by the American society and being resisted in their attempts to elevate
their political as well as their socioeconomic standing.

    While some of the American political cultural values such as equal-
ity and liberty have provided a favorable atmosphere for Latinos' perse-
vering attempts toward parity and justice, other aspects of the political
culture such as racism have worked against those attempts. In addition
to the attitudes and values of the dominant culture, another important
consideration when examining the context in which Latino politics takes
place is the cultural values of Latinos themselves. Certainly the attitudes,
beliefs, and values of Latinos, particularly those which are politically
relevant, have an important effect on Latino politics. However, the effects
attributed to Latino cultural values, and even the existence and configu-
ration of those values, are subject to a great deal of uncertainty and disagreement.

    The major national study of Latino political orientations, the Lat-
ino National Political Survey, attempted to empirically measure many
Latino political orientations. Among other findings, it reported that
many of the values of the three groups studied—Mexican Americans,
Puerto Ricans, and Cuban Americans—were surprisingly similar to
those of core-culture, non-Latino Americans. For example, support of
basic American political values such as equality and liberty, levels of patriotism, and political ideology were found to be quite similar to those of
the white Americans in the survey. Very little, if any, evidence was found
that the cultural values of Latinos are dysfunctional to participation in
American politics, a claim which some observers have made to explain
the subordinate status of Latinos. The survey also found some dissimi-

larities between the orientations of these three largest Latino groups. These distinctive opinions and attitudes call into question the current level of claimed cohesion among national-origin groups subsumed under the umbrella term "Latino" or "Hispanic." This could pose a challenge for leaders and activists attempting to pursue strategies based upon the concept of a generalized and unified Latino political community. While there is no doubt that the concept of "Latino" has had some utility,[2] certainly symbolic and sometimes pragmatic, would-be leaders must also be aware of the differences among the national-origin groups in order to tailor political goals and strategies accordingly. A transnational-origin, pan-ethnic Latino political force of 27 million certainly has important implications different from that of several different national-origin groups operating under a loose nomenclature rubric, or united in primarily ad hoc coalitions focusing on particular issues or situations, or sharing a similar discriminatory treatment by Whites.

In his article Peter Skerry digs into some of the dilemmas and paradoxes facing Hispanics in the United States and explores the political implications of these. In his view, one of the primary dilemmas distinctive to Hispanics is tied to their diversity and their somewhat ambiguous status in a racially divided and racially conscious society. He raises two major questions both of which have great importance for Latinos in general and for Latino politics specifically. The first is the use of the generic umbrella term "Hispanic" or "Latino." Demographically, there is no doubt that the people called Latinos or Hispanics are an extremely heterogeneous group with regard to national origin, experiences in their homelands and in the United States, and varying socioeconomic characteristics. However, the terms "Hispanic" or "Latinos" used as a pan-ethnic description can both be advantageous in implying strength and solidarity, as well as a liability in leading to a misunderstanding of the particular needs and strengths of each group. There are some class similarities, but even more cultural ones, including such things as the Spanish language, relationship with the Catholic Church, and some debatable cultural values. While these socioeconomic, cultural, and historical differences and similarities are important, Skerry's focus is on the political significance of a pan-ethnic designation, particularly in light of important, politically relevant differences. The political interests of Latino groups often vary, as does their power. An examination of the three largest Hispanic groups illustrates that, and the differences among another twenty or so national-origin groups further complicates the picture. Is it likely that a pan-Hispanic coalition will operate effectively in mobilizing to support or oppose issues of common interest to them? It is in the Midwest, which in many ways is a kind of microcosm of the Latino situation nationally, where coalition politics have led to the most effective and united Latino mobilization. There the term "Latino" with its more political connotations is often used to connote a cohesive and effective political bloc, and this tactic may have the same implications nationally. In essence one finds in the Midwest virtually all the features that could apply to Latinos on a national basis. It may well be that lessons learned from the Latino political microcosm in the Midwest will be most important in developing Latino political strategies and tactics in the national political arena.

The second major perceptual dilemma pointed out by Skerry, which he greatly elaborates and makes the theme of his controversial book, *Mexican Americans: The Ambivalent Minority*,[3] is which of two contrasting political strategies Hispanics should follow. Should Hispanics follow the political route blazed by African Americans, that is, one pushed by a victimized racial minority with a history of severe racial discrimination, and pursue power primarily as a relatively homogeneous national racial minority? Or alternatively, are Hispanics more like white ethnic Catholic immigrant groups such as the Italians, who through eventual incorporation into the core American culture, emphasizing educational and economic success, and focusing on community and local levels, eventually will take their place after a few generations alongside other ethnic minority groups? This ambivalence is a major dilemma for Hispanics, one which has significant effects on Latinos' self-perceptions, the way they are viewed and treated by non-Hispanics, and of prime concern, their goals, tactics, and strategies for pursuing political power. Skerry feels that the transnational identification of Hispanics/Latinos promoted by political leaders and academics designed to emulate the black political strategies for such programs as affirmative action may seem to resolve short-term problems, but in the long term may work against Hispanics and their incorporation as full-fledged Americans.

Part One should provide the reader with an overview of some of the salient characteristics of the setting in which Latinos participate and pursue power within the political system in the United States. Their experiential development explains much about the current situation in which Latinos find themselves as well as the strategies they may adopt to pursue their goals.

Likewise, socioeconomic conditions, particularly the disadvantaged status of Latinos, speak loudly to Latinos' political strategies and goals. The attitudinal and cultural setting is characterized primarily by core-culture resistance to Latinos' incorporation; by the supportive political orientations of many Latinos; and also by some distinctive views between Latino national-origin groups. These perceptions and attitudes also have a major impact on Latino politics.

How these contextual factors affect political inputs into the system, what form these inputs take, and how they are communicated, form the rationale for the subsequent section.

NOTES

1. Patricia Montgomery, "The Hispanic Population of the United States, March, 1993," *Current Population Reports,* Series P20–475 (Washington, D.C.: U.S. Department of Commerce, Bureau of the Census).

2. For an insightful exposition of the political basis of the term 'Latino' and its relationship with political mobilization, see Felix M. Padilla, *Latino Ethnic Consciousness: The Case of Mexican Americans and Puerto Ricans in Chicago* (Notre Dame, Ind.: University of Notre Dame Press, 1985).

3. Peter Skerry, *Mexican Americans: The Ambivalent Minority* (New York: Free Press, 1993). For critical views by a number of Latino politics scholars and the response of the author, see the critiques and replies in "Mexican Americans: Are They an Ambivalent Minority?" (Claremont, Calif.: Tomas Rivera Center, 1994).

1. E Pluribus Hispanic?

Peter Skerry

IN THE SUMMER OF 1987, the surprise success of *La Bamba,* a film about teenage singer Ritchie Valens (born Valenzuela), inspired a news media celebration of the role of Hispanics in our national life. But several ironies surrounding the film went unnoted. For example, the writer and director of this commercial success was Luis Valdez, former director of the agitprop-inspired Teatro Campesino and professor of Chicano studies at Berkeley. Valdez had once denounced "the subversive onslaught of the 20th-century neon *gabacho* [gringo] commercialism that passes for American culture" and rejected "efforts to make us disappear into the white melting pot, only to be hauled out again when it is convenient or profitable for *gabacho* . . . politicians." Yet *La Bamba* paints a very typical picture of American life, one of aspiration and assimilation. It is a bittersweet success story of a clean-cut Mexican-American kid who loved his family and his Anglo girlfriend, sang his way to rock 'n' roll stardom, and died young in a 1959 plane crash. And this young man who grew up in a migrant labor camp, whose big hit was a Mexican folk song, *La Bamba,* in fact spoke little Spanish.

To complicate matters, in the film Valens was played not by a Mexican American but by a young actor, Lou Diamond Phillips, who was born in the Philippines and raised in Texas, and who describes his background as a mixture of Filipino, Hawaiian, Chinese, Scotch-Irish, and Cherokee. A Puerto Rican, Esai Morales, played Valens's half brother. The next year Phillips again portrayed a Mexican American, in *Stand and Deliver,* a film about Jaime Escalante, the math teacher acclaimed for his work with East Los Angeles high-school students. Bolivian-born Escalante was played by Mexican-American actor Edward James Olmos,

From the *Wilson Quarterly,* Summer 1992. Copyright © 1992 by Peter Skerry.

who grew up in East Los Angeles. The film was co-written and directed by Ramon Menendez, a Cuban-born graduate of the UCLA film school.

This tale of two films suggests how problematic the term "Hispanic" can be. Both movies, which brought so much positive attention to Hispanics, were actually about Mexican Americans. At the same time, they were projects on which Hispanics of diverse backgrounds collaborated, suggesting the possibility of an emergent pan-ethnic Hispanic culture. In these ways, the films raise the question: Does the term "Hispanic" have any real substance to it, or is it merely the creation of media moguls and political entrepreneurs?

Alejandro Portes, a Cuban-born sociologist who teaches at Johns Hopkins, is one of those who takes the latter view. He argues that " 'Hispanic' ethnic solidarity is quite fragile because it is ultimately a political creation, rather than one based on the real experiences of the groups so labelled." Yet the difficulty with this formulation is that what begins as "a political creation" often ends up defining "real experiences." Earlier in this century hundreds of thousands of European peasants left their villages thinking of themselves as Sicilians, Calabrians, and the like, but after arriving here they gradually came to regard themselves as they were regarded by Americans—as Italians and, eventually, as Italian Americans. As Greek philosophy long ago taught, the essence of politics is the shaping and perfecting of "natural" social ties through human artifice and convention. It would therefore be a mistake to dismiss the term "Hispanic" as a mere political contrivance. A closer look at it tells us as much about the conventions of contemporary American politics as it does about Hispanics themselves.

More precisely, the term reflects the pervasive tendency in the United States to encourage members of these groups to define themselves in divisive—and not wholly appropriate—racial terms. At the same time, the vagueness of a term that subsumes Indian peasants from Central America and the grandchildren of Portuguese immigrants may moderate these divisive tendencies, enabling Hispanics to stake a claim on our nation's immigrant ethnic tradition. The substantial historical, social, and economic differences among the various Hispanic groups are continually played out in the media, in marketing, and in politics. Nevertheless, the very ambiguity of the pan-ethnic term serves to blur these distinctions, making it politically useful and assuring its longevity.

Puerto Rican, Mexican, and Cuban[1] leaders often denounce the term "Hispanic" as a stereotypic label concocted during the 1970s by ignorant government bureaucrats intent on cramming diverse groups into one ill-fitting category. And one is tempted to agree, since only eight percent of "Hispanics" use the label to identify themselves. Yet these same leaders resort to "Hispanic" when it suits their purposes. Bureaucrats did not found the Congressional *Hispanic* Caucus in 1976. Nor did bureaucrats stretch the term to include then-Representative Tony Coelho (of Portuguese descent) and the non-voting congressional delegates from the Virgin Islands and Guam.

Nor have bureaucrats encouraged the debate among these leaders over which pan-ethnic term is preferable, "Hispanic" or "Latino." Wading through arcane analyses of these terms, one despairs of finding any meaningful distinction. At the moment, "Latino" is in the ascendancy among those seeking the least "Eurocentric" designation. As Berkeley social scientists Charles Henry and Carlos Munoz write, "The term ['Hispanic'] implicitly underscores the white European culture of Spain at the expense of the nonwhite cultures that have profoundly shaped the experiences of all Latin Americans . . . " Yet the same could be said of "Latino," which is after all a Spanish word meaning "Latin." Indeed, for much of this century "Latin American" was the euphemism used by assimilationist Mexicans to obscure their ties to Mexico (as when Mexicans in Corpus Christi, Texas, in 1929 formed the League of United *Latin American* Citizens). But circumstances change, and today the animus against "Hispanic" undoubtedly stems from the perception that it was coined by federal officials. Finally, because it is Spanish, "Latino" is felt to be the more politically assertive word.[2]

Whatever the term used and however strained its interpretation, there *are* significant similarities among the various national-origin groups. The first and most obvious is socioeconomic status: Whether they are Mexicans and Puerto Ricans in Chicago, or Salvadoran, Guatemalan, and Mexican immigrants in Los Angeles, or Dominicans and Puerto Ricans in New York City, most Hispanics belong to the lower or working classes.

Yet class similarities are less striking than cultural ones. For most Hispanics, the Spanish language is the most visible and charged symbol of their common cultural heritage. This is true even though about one-fourth of all Hispanics do not speak the language of their forebears.

Latinos also share a long and ambivalent relationship with the Catholic Church. In part, the ambivalence reflects the Church's history of alliances with European-oriented Latin American elites and its distance from the concerns of the indigenous populations. Because Hispanics generally have not brought their own clergy with them to the United States, this gap has persisted in this country, particularly since the American Catholic Church has been dominated by Irish clergy with very different notions of the faith. Hispanic cultures also emphasize *personalismo,* which in the religious context translates into a reliance more on ties to individual clerics or patron saints than to the institutional Church. Among Puerto Ricans and Mexicans in particular, this longstanding ambivalence has led to steady defections to various Protestant churches, especially small fundamentalist sects. Sociologist Andrew Greeley estimates that the defections amount to about 60,000 individuals each year. One can sit in any barrio rectory and hear rumors flying about who has "turned Protestant." Today, only about 70 percent of Hispanics are Catholics.

Finally, Hispanics share an emphasis on family life. For example, while 70 percent of non-Hispanic households are maintained by families, more than 80 percent of Hispanic households are. To be sure, as researchers Frank Bean and Marta Tienda note, Hispanics experience separation and divorce as frequently as non-Hispanic whites. Moreover, a higher proportion of Hispanic than non-Hispanic families are female-headed (23.8 versus 16.4 percent). Yet Hispanics (with the exception of Cubans) also have larger families than non-Hispanics. Furthermore, two-parent Hispanic families are much more likely than their non-Hispanic white counterparts to include a grandparent or other adult relative. Social scientists debate whether these family characteristics reflect cultural values or social and economic forces. What is not debatable is that Hispanics see themselves as much more family-oriented than non-Hispanics.

All of these cultural similarities do not mean, however, that a cohesive Hispanic identity is emerging in the United States. Often, these shared characteristics lead to friction among the groups. Strong family ties, for example, can hinder development of the impersonal, instrumental relationships needed to forge stable political organizations. As a result, the national-origin groups are often factionalized internally, and such problems will likely afflict organizational efforts among groups.

A common religion is likewise no guarantee of cohesion, especially since Latinos from different countries often worship different saints and manifestations of the Virgin. Nor is the Spanish language the unifying force it is typically assumed to be. "The way we speak Spanish" tops the list of items that Hispanics polled by Daniel Yankelovich said are significant differences among them; fully one-third cited it. In Los Angeles's Pico-Union district, for example, the director of a childcare center serving Mexican and a variety of Central American immigrants notes that the idiomatic differences among them are so great that composing Spanish-language materials acceptable to parents and staff usually requires heated negotiations.

The question of whether Hispanics are one group or several also arises in the marketplace. In the 1980s, McDonald's launched a successful pan-Hispanic campaign featuring a celebration which to non-Hispanics looked like a birthday party, but which all Hispanics recognized as a *quinceañera,* a party marking a young woman's coming-of-age on her 15th birthday. On the other hand, an insecticide company blundered badly when it mounted a pan-Hispanic campaign promising that its product would kill all *"bichos"*—which means bugs to Mexicans, but the male genitals to Puerto Ricans. Other problems have arisen, literally, from differences in taste. Goya Foods, one of the largest Hispanic-owned firms in the nation, grew with the post-World War II influx of Puerto Ricans, and has since developed a loyal customer base among them and other Caribbean Hispanics in the Northeast. But its recent effort to develop a line of Mexican foods for the Southwestern market failed miserably. As an embarrassed Goya executive admitted to the *Wall Street Journal,* "Nobody here knew anything about Mexican food."

Such episodes reflect not just cultural differences among Hispanics but social and economic ones as well. Cubans are, by virtually all socio-economic indicators, the most successful Hispanics. (See table, p. 22.) They have the most education, the lowest unemployment, the highest family and household income, the lowest proportion of individuals and families living below the poverty level, the highest rate of home ownership, and the lowest proportion of female-headed households. Puerto Ricans, by contrast, have fared least well and are by some measures worse off than blacks. Mexicans generally fall between the Cubans and Puerto Ricans.

Such socioeconomic differences reflect the distinctive history of each group and the circumstances of its arrival in the United States. Cubans have come here in the wake of Castro's revolution, and even though (with the exception of the Marielitos) they have arrived relatively well endowed with financial and educational resources, they have, as refugees, received substantial help from the federal government. Puerto Ricans, on the other hand, have come to the mainland with fewer advantages, having been pushed off the land and out of the cities by rapid post-World War II industrialization on the island.

Mexicans present a more complicated story. Many are longtime U.S. residents, and some can trace their ancestry back not only to the time when the American Southwest was part of Mexico, but to the millennia before the arrival of Europeans on the continent. Nevertheless, the overwhelming majority of Mexicans in the United States today are recent immigrants, most of whom arrived illegally. This complicated group profile is highlighted by the fact that Mexicans are the Hispanic group with the highest proportion of illegals, as well as the highest proportion of individuals born in the United States.

Following separate paths to the United States, these groups settled in different regions. Almost two-thirds of all Cubans live in Florida; more than two-thirds of Puerto Ricans live in the Northeast; about three-fifths of Mexicans live in the West. Even in cities that are home to several Hispanic groups, each tends to live in distinct neighborhoods. In Chicago, for example, Mexicans are concentrated in the Little Village and Pilsen districts, while Puerto Ricans are clustered in Logan Square and Humboldt Park. Intermarriage among Hispanic groups similarly appears to be infrequent, except perhaps among Puerto Ricans, Dominicans, and other Central or South Americans in New York City.

Such historical and socioeconomic differences are obviously important, but their *political* significance is not readily apparent. Each group certainly has its own unique relationship to the American political system. The Cubans are the smallest group (constituting less than five percent of all Hispanics), but they are the most powerful politically. As refugees, they have long dreamed of overthrowing Castro and returning home. Yet at a time when this dream seems closer to realization than ever, its appeal has begun to diminish, particularly among younger Cubans born and raised here. It is in any event striking that Cubans have a significantly higher naturalization rate than Mexicans, whose long and complex history in the Southwest has translated into one of the lowest such rates among all groups in the United States. This helps explain why Mexicans have yet to wield political power commensurate with their numbers, which make them the largest Hispanic group (accounting for 63 percent of all Hispanics). Puerto Ricans, by contrast, are U.S. citizens at birth, but their circular migration between the island and the mainland, along with the fact that they constitute only about 11 percent of Hispanics, helps make them the weakest of these three groups.

The political interest of the three groups are as varied as their power, as can be seen in the Congressional Hispanic Caucus. Founded with five members in 1976, the Caucus has grown to 13 members (10 voting and three non-voting), of which all but two are Democrats. Most of the members are Mexicans; two are Puerto Ricans; one Cuban. Congressional Quarterly's *1991 Guide to Congress* contrasts the Hispanic Caucus with its black counterpart and notes that the former "rarely took a unanimous position." The Caucus's high point came in 1983–1984, when it succeeded in blocking action on the controversial Simpson-Mazzoli immigration reform legislation. Yet as then-Representative Manuel Lujan (R.-N.M.) observed, "Everyone [in the Caucus] is opposed to the Simpson-Mazzoli bill, but each of us has different reasons." In fact, the Caucus was unable to agree on alternative legislation, and Simpson-Mazzoli ultimately passed, albeit in altered form.

Hispanics Compared

	Non-Hispanics	Blacks	Hispanics	Mexicans	Puerto Ricans	Cubans	Cent. & S. Americans
Population (in millions)	227.4	30.9	21.4*	13.4	2.4	1.1	3.0
Median household income (in dollars)	30.513	18.676	22.330	22.439	16.169	25.900	23.568
Percent households with income of $50,000 or more	25.4	11.9	13.4	11.6	11.9	19.8	15.7
Percent households maintained by families	69.6	70.0	80.1	81.7	77.8	78.8	82.5
Percent female-headed households	11.4	47.8	19.1	15.6	33.7	15.3	21.5
Percent urban households	72.8	N/A	91.8	90.5	95.2	95.7	97.0
Percent households owning or buying home	65.8	42.4	39.0	43.5	23.4	47.3	22.2
Percent completed high school	80.5	66.7	51.3	43.6	58.0	61.0	60.4
Percent with four or more years of college	22.3	11.5	9.7	6.2	10.1	18.5	15.1
Percent unemployed	6.9	12.4	10.0	10.7	10.3	6.4	10.3
Percent of individuals below poverty level	12.1	31.9	28.1	28.1	40.6	16.9	25.4

*Not shown in the table are 1.5 million people in the category "other Hispanic."
Source: Various Current Population Reports, 1991 (U.S. Bureau of the Census).

Bilingual education and the Voting Rights Act are two issues around which the Caucus has been able to come together. Yet there are plenty of other issues where Hispanic interests do not very neatly converge: Cubans have focused on anti-Castro initiatives; Puerto Ricans have been preoccupied with the statehood question; and Mexicans and Central Americans (the fastest growing Hispanic group, having increased by more than 250 percent from 1980 to 1990) have emphasized immigration issues.

Any convergence of interests among Hispanic groups is equally difficult to find at the local level. At one extreme is Washington, D.C., unique among American cities in that none of the three principal Hispanic groups—Mexicans, Cubans, Puerto Ricans—predominates numerically. The largest group, Salvadorans, has only recently arrived, during the 1980s. The capital's Hispanic population is small—only six percent of the city's total, and barely one percent of the electorate. It is also extremely diverse—the metropolitan area sustains no fewer than 17 Spanish-language newspapers. This demographic fragmentation, along with the refugee and illegal status of many newcomers, has stymied efforts at political organization and hindered the emergence of effective leadership. These problems were highlighted in the aftermath of a riot in the city's Mount Pleasant neighborhood that made national headlines in the spring of 1991.

Washington Latinos, still in a largely "pre-political" mode, flex their organizational muscles planning for the annual Hispanic Festival, which has in recent years been marked by intense bickering over the management of the event. One such dispute—between a Panamanian building contractor, a Spanish newspaper publisher, and a Puerto Rican radio-station owner—got so heated that the League of Women Voters was brought in to resolve it. Until very recently, this acrimony has benefited Puerto Ricans from New York, who, as citizens and Anglophones, enjoyed an advantage in negotiating festival arrangements with city and federal officials.

Puerto Ricans—with leaders like Herman Badillo, Robert García, Fernando Ferrer, and José Serrano—have also dominated Hispanic politics in New York City, but for different reasons. There they are the most established and largest Hispanic group, constituting about 50 percent of all Hispanics. With Cubans and Mexicans each accounting for only three percent, Dominicans are the other major Hispanic group in New York. They share with Puerto Ricans both Caribbean origins and a racial mixture that includes many blacks. Residential and intermarriage patterns also suggest that the two groups are in much closer contact with each other, and with black Americans, than with other Latino groups in

New York. Politically, Puerto Ricans and Dominicans have at times cooperated but at other times competed. The severe fragmentation of Washington is generally not apparent. But neither is a pan-Hispanic coalition. One reason is that, while Puerto Ricans are U.S. citizens, many other New York Hispanics are not, and the latter remain more focused on the politics of their homelands.

Then there is Miami, where Cubans today constitute about 62 percent of the city's Hispanic population, with Nicaraguans and "other Hispanics" from Central and South America accounting for another 32 percent. Yet the city's first Hispanic mayor, Maurice Ferré, was a Puerto Rican, elected in 1973 by an anti-Cuban coalition of Anglos, blacks, and Puerto Ricans (who constitute only five percent of the city's Hispanics). Miami's first Cuban mayor, Xavier Suarez, was elected in 1985, when Ferré lost his black support. The Hispanics of Miami are a long way from the pre-political state of their counterparts in Washington, but, like former San Antonio mayor Henry Cisneros, Suarez has been the beneficiary not of any pan-Hispanic political coalition but of the overwhelming predominance of a single group.

As in Miami, Latino politics in Los Angeles has been dominated by a single group—not Cubans, who constitute about one percent of the city's Latinos, but Mexicans, who account for about 67 percent. Most of the remaining Hispanics (31 percent) are "other Hispanics," which in this instance means Salvadorans, Guatemalans, and Nicaraguans who flooded into the city during the 1980s. Aside from whatever attention was sporadically paid to them by activists criticizing U.S. foreign policy in Central America, these predominantly poor and illegal immigrants have had no visible presence in Los Angeles politics.

Yet in the immediate aftermath of the recent riots in Los Angeles, signs of change were evident. Mexican leaders, who up to then had been quite willing to represent Central Americans as part of one enormous and growing Latino constituency, were quick to contrast the destruction in the Pico-Union district, just west of downtown, where Central Americans have crowded into dilapidated apartment buildings, with the calm that prevailed in the Mexican neighborhoods of East Los Angeles. At the same time, these leaders, always concerned that blacks get attention and resources at the expense of Latinos, expressed outrage that the riots were being defined in black and white terms, and could be heard claiming, "These were our riots, too."

The one city with some signs of an Hispanic coalition is Chicago, where Mexicans constitute about 65 percent of Hispanics, and Puerto Ricans about 22 percent. Through efforts like the Latino Institute, a nonprofit advocacy and research institute founded in 1974, and the *Lat-*

ino Studies Journal at DePaul University, local Hispanic leaders have tried to forge a unified Latino political agenda. But such efforts seem to reflect the long-term goals of activists and intellectuals more than on-the-ground realities. Not only do Puerto Ricans and Mexicans live in distinct neighborhoods, the latter are more likely than Puerto Ricans to live among Anglos. These residential patterns are reflected, not surprisingly, in politics. Puerto Ricans, for example, have been much more supportive of Harold Washington's and Jesse Jackson's electoral bids than Mexicans. As one Latino community activist says about efforts to build a Latino-black coalition in Chicago: "Mexicans have been passing [as whites] for years. They have lived in white neighborhoods. There are more black Puerto Ricans, so there is much stronger support [for the coalition]."

If the outlines of an emergent Hispanic identity or agenda are not obvious in politics, they might be more evident in the mass media. After all, immigrant Latinos do not become citizens or voters immediately, but they do become consumers. Latino markets are among the fastest-growing in the nation, and three Spanish-language television networks—Galavision, Telemundo, Univision—have emerged to serve them, recently joined by a Spanish-language version of CNN. The rise of these networks now presents the possibility of these different groups coming together in a way that was not possible for earlier, European immigrant groups.

Yet one problem with this scenario is that Spanish-language television generally is ignored by young Hispanics, who overwhelmingly prefer to tune in to CBS, MTV, and other mainstream offerings. As Henry R. Silverman, then president of the Telemundo Group, told the *New York Times,* "There is no question that teen-age Hispanics are not watching Spanish-language programs." The continuing influx of immigrants undoubtedly helps these networks offset this generation gap. But this same influx also further complicates pan-Hispanic marketing strategies. Guillermo Martinez, executive news director for the Univision Network offers this explanation: "The only power we [Spanish-language broadcasters] have now is at the local level. We know that. But it is difficult to influence three different groups—Cubans, Mexicans, and Puerto Ricans—in the same way."

Sergio Munoz of Los Angeles's Spanish-language daily, *La Opinion,* is among those who have faulted Univision and Telemundo for trying "to appeal to a hypothetical homogeneous Latin American community." But such criticisms are the least of it. The Spanish-language media have also been the stage for rancorous disagreements among Hispanic groups. In 1990, for example, Carlos Alberto Montaner, a Cuban-born commentator on Univision, caused a furor by pointing to the high incidence of female-headed families among Puerto Ricans as a cause of the group's disastrous poverty rate. Angry Puerto Rican leaders were further outraged when the president of Univision, the Chilean American Joaquin Blaya, refused to fire Montaner.

There have also been conflicts over who controls, and profits from, the Spanish-language media. Here Cubans are frequent targets, for two reasons. First, they have the education and resources necessary to take advantage of the growing Hispanic market. Second, Spanish-language production facilities have become concentrated in Miami, which is the nation's second largest Hispanic market and, unlike Los Angeles, has low, non-union production costs.

Mexicans in particular tend to resent Cuban influence. Apparently in response to such discontents, Los Angeles-based Galavision recently established itself as a national network; yet it does not even plan to have outlets in Miami and New York. The president of the network's parent company puts it forthrightly: "You cannot satisfy all Hispanic tastes. Ours is not a smorgasbord programming menu like that of the two other networks. Our fare caters to the growing Mexican and Central American population, while the Caribbean and Cuban migration is basically over."

Although seldom reported, similar tensions are evident among Hispanics in the political arena. In Chicago, for example, a Mexican activist who advocates a Latino political agenda nevertheless cautions:

> [W]e need to be concerned with the term Latino or Hispanic because that includes everybody. It includes the Cubans, the Central and South Americans, and I have always felt the struggle has been a Chicano-*Boricua* [Puerto Rican] struggle. I have worked with the city in other capacities and I've always seen how they like to impose upon us a Cuban or a South American to positions of power to keep the Chicanos and the *Boricuas* divided.

Within the Republican Party, there have been debilitating tensions between Cubans and Mexicans. Possessing considerable organizational skills and financial resources, Cubans have attained leadership positions within the party without playing the Hispanic card. In the early 1980s, for example, a Cuban surgeon from Los Angeles, Dr. Tirso del Junco, became state party chair on the basis of his fund-raising efforts. When del Junco subsequently focused his efforts on the Republican National Hispanic Assembly, he encountered stiff opposition from Mexican Republicans who did not share his ideological conservatism and resented his domination of Republican Hispanic politics. The Cubans, in turn, regard the small businessmen and struggling entrepreneurs who typify Mexican Republicans as poor relations, embarrassments among affluent

Anglo colleagues, and ideological weaklings with all-too-recent ties to Democrats. Mexicans who ally themselves with Cubans are reviled by fellow Mexicans as "stooges." The resulting battles within Hispanic Republican circles have hindered the party's efforts to reach out to Mexicans, the largest and one of the fastest growing Hispanic groups.

Tensions among Hispanic groups are not usually so acrimonious. Puerto Ricans and Mexicans, for example, have not experienced the class and ideological animosities rife among Latino Republicans. But the ever-present possibility of ill feelings encourages efforts to de-emphasize or even ignore differences and to emphasize the similarities among Hispanics. This tendency is especially strong among non-Hispanics. As one education administrator explained to me, the "Hispanic" category is indispensable to foundation executives who, by setting up programs designated broadly for Hispanics, avoid the problems that would arise if they targeted specific groups. Better to establish an umbrella program, the thinking goes, and let the various groups fight it out among themselves. Government bureaucrats and politicians apply the same logic, and so do Hispanics themselves. A Chicana activist accustomed to dealing with colleagues from different parts of the nation uses the term "Latino" and explains, "It avoids problems."

For such leaders, though, the strongest reasons for adopting the "Latino" label are not merely defensive. Those most likely to refer to themselves or others as Latino or Hispanic are the most cosmopolitan and nationally oriented politicos. In Washington, "Hispanic" has certainly been the term of choice for some time, as suggested by the names of many Washington-based efforts: the Hispanic Caucus; *Hispanic Link*, a weekly newsletter culling news of interest to all Hispanics; *Hispanic* magazine, a general interest English-language monthly; or the National Coalition of Hispanic Health and Human Services Organizations. Former Congressman Robert García, a New York-born Puerto Rican, put it well: "When I first came to Washington I saw myself as a Puerto Rican. I quickly realized that the majority society saw me as a member of a larger group called Hispanic."

As García suggested, being "Hispanic" allows these leaders to increase the size of the constituencies they represent. It also helps specific groups reposition themselves in the political marketplace. Cubans, for example, constitute a small and steadily shrinking proportion of all Hispanics, but as "Hispanics" they become part of a rapidly expanding national presence. As *Los Angeles Times* editorial writer Frank Del Olmo (a Mexican) writes: "The term 'Hispanic' allowed other Latinos to use a large and growing Mexican-American population to increase *their* influence." Given Cuban foreign-policy concerns and the consequent role they seek to play in Washington, this factor has been critical to their political aspirations.

Mexicans have become "Hispanics" for different reasons. Historically, they have felt ignored and isolated in the Southwest, at the farthest possible remove from the centers of the nation's economic and political power. But as "Hispanics," Mexicans are part of a group spread all over the United States, including Puerto Ricans in the Northeast and Cubans in Florida. Though hardly oblivious to the importance of their growing numbers, Mexican leaders are keen to avoid having their interests and problems dismissed as those of a regional group and understand the importance of being regarded as a *national* minority group.

The same goal of raising themselves above the status of a regional group also induces Cubans and Puerto Ricans to adopt the "Hispanic" label. And as with Cubans, becoming Hispanic allows Puerto Ricans to tap into whatever clout accompanies the huge and still growing Mexican population. Yet more to the point, Puerto Rican leaders embrace the pan-ethnic label to moderate the popular impression that Puerto Ricans have sunk into the underclass. Manuel A. Bustelo, former executive director of the National Puerto Rican Forum, makes the point in the negative: "The use of 'Hispanic' rather than specific ethnic groups has distorted realities. In many instances, this has served to convey a more positive picture of overall advancement, while concealing the fact that the Puerto Rican communities in the mainland are worse off than in previous years."

Complex though these dynamics are, they comprise only half of what is encouraging these leaders to call themselves "Hispanics." For if becoming "Hispanic" allows each group to become a *national* minority, it also allows each to become a national *minority*—that is, a group that has experienced racial discrimination and is therefore in need of special help and programs. As "Hispanics," each group can stake a stronger claim of this kind on the nation's conscience than it could on its own. Clearly, the path being followed is that of black Americans, who (as Hispanic leaders continually remind themselves) captured the nation's attention in the 1950s and '60s by making racial discrimination more than just a "Southern problem." By shifting the source of redress to Washington, blacks gained the help of more sympathetic, nationally oriented elites, particularly the media. But the black struggle for equality fundamentally altered American politics. It hastened the demise of states' rights and the consequent nationalization of American politics. This new framework substantially limits the political options now available to Hispanics.

Therefore, the phrase *national minority* captures two sides of a very

important coin. Only by trading on that coin can otherwise locally oriented and disparate Hispanic groups hope to compete politically with
blacks, their only rival for the attention of national political elites. Thus,
in contemporary discourse "Hispanic" has come to be used as a non-
white racial designation corresponding to "black." Think for a moment
how accustomed we are to hearing, and repeating, the phrase "whites,
blacks, and Hispanics," which is routinely used in newspapers, government reports, opinion polls, and scholarly journals. The litany rolls so
readily off our tongues that we forget that these are not in fact mutually
exclusive categories. While white and black have generally come to be
accepted as distinct racial categories, Hispanic—at least until quite recently—has been regarded as an ethno-cultural designation. Yet today,
the Census Bureau is virtually alone in maintaining this distinction: The
small print at the bottom of its tables continually reminds us that "Hispanics can be of any race."

Even as the transformation of "Hispanic" into a non-white racial
category proceeds in Washington, individual Hispanics offer a more
complicated picture of themselves. On the one hand, about 52 percent of
all those belonging to Hispanic groups told the 1990 census they were
"white." About three percent defined themselves as "black." On the
other hand, most of the remaining Hispanics—about 43 percent—designated themselves as "other race." Moreover, this "other race" category
has grown since 1980. In other words, these figures challenge the ready
assumption that *all* Hispanics are non-white. But at the same time, they
point to the emergence of a distinct non-white racial identity among
some Hispanics.

This confusion, or ambivalence, over racial identity is at the core
of the emergent "Hispanic" category. In emulating the political example
of blacks and claiming status as a racial minority group, Hispanics run
the risk of being stigmatized as a group beyond help or hope. In fact, this
may already be happening to Puerto Ricans in the United States. Yet as
"Hispanics," Puerto Ricans can also identify themselves (and be identified) with a more positive aspect of the American experience—immigrant aspiration and upward mobility. For this is how, to varying degrees, Cubans and Mexicans are perceived. Yet many Mexicans also see
themselves as members of a racial minority deserving of the same extraordinary help that has, despite much controversy, been afforded black
Americans. Even Cubans, who despite their evident prosperity qualify
(as Hispanics) for affirmative action benefits, find it useful to be part of
a group which includes Puerto Ricans and others who fit the profile of
an impoverished urban minority. Thus, depending on the specific context, Hispanics can claim to be an immigrant ethnic group in the classic

American pattern, or, alternatively, a minority group suffering racial discrimination.

To observers such as Alejandro Portes, this confusion underscores the artificiality of the term "Hispanic." Yet the complaint misses the point: Imprecision is what makes the term so politically useful. On the most mundane level, it gives activists the option of throwing their opponents off-guard by insisting on the inappropriateness of the "label." More fundamentally, "Hispanic" speaks to the critical concerns of any disadvantaged group that seeks support from the modern welfare state. On the one hand, all such claimants must establish the legitimacy of their demands on the public sector. Largely because they follow in the wake of the black civil-rights movement, Hispanics today must base this legitimacy on claims of racial disadvantage and discrimination. On the other hand, claims must also be based on evidence that the group is worthy of help and yet not so disadvantaged that it is beyond hope. The old distinction between the "worthy" and "unworthy" poor endures in today's welfare state. The two facets of "Hispanic"—immigrant ethnic group and racial minority—meet the divergent requirements.

Despite the many social, cultural, and economic differences among these national-origin groups, the term "Hispanic" does have political substance. Today much of that substance derives from the notion of a nonwhite racial identity. Not without grounding in the way Hispanics see themselves, this identity is nevertheless exaggerated by leaders encouraged by our post-civil rights regime to compete with blacks as a racial minority. This strategy clearly solves short-term political problems for these leaders, but if it works and Hispanics begin to see themselves exclusively as a minority group, America's racial problems will have acquired a new and troubling dimension.

NOTES

1. Precision would seem to require the use of terms such as "Mexican American" and "Cuban American." But even these are not precise, because they typically refer to aggregates that include both the assimilated members of the group and recent immigrants for whom the suffix "-American" is, arguably, inappropriate. For the sake of conciseness, therefore, I use the terms "Mexicans" and "Cubans."

2. In this article, I follow the lead of the Washington-based advocacy group, the National Council of La Raza, and use the two terms interchangeably.

PART II

Input to the Political System: Participation

IN ORDER TO AFFECT A political system, Latinos must have effective input to governmental decision makers. Latino interests and needs must somehow be aggregated and effectively communicated to governments. In the American political system, this is often done through a variety of participative activities and organizations.

During the "Decade of the Hispanic" in the 1980s, most Latino political energy and attention were focused on conventional activities, mainly electoral and litigational. The pace of these traditional forms of electoral politics continued into the 1990s. However, a manifest change is the increased diversity of participation styles and strategies. Latinos more and more are using multiple forms of political activity to exert influence, including more organizational activity and a noticeable increase in some of the political tactics of the 1960s and 1970s—protests, marches, demonstrations, and boycotts.

A great deal still remains unknown about the voting behavior and related political activities of Latinos. We know that in general Latinos participate at a lower rate than do Anglos, typically lagging some 10–30 percent in voter registration and turnout. This varies considerably depending on the particular place and circumstances. There is also considerable variation among the various national-origin groups. For example, Puerto Ricans on the mainland and Mexican Americans, but not Cuban Americans, generally are registered to vote in lower proportions than are majority culture citizens. There is some disagreement about whether or not once they are registered Hispanics vote in the same proportion as do non-Hispanics, but the weight of evidence is towards a lower level of voting participation. The major confounding factor in examining Latino electoral participation is citizenship status. It is estimated that some 35–40 percent of voting age Latinos are non-citizens, thus automatically ex-

31

cluding them from possible participation in the franchise. When non-citizens are excluded from the calculations of those eligible to vote, registration and voting levels approach, but are still significantly below, those of non-Latinos. Some analyses, such as that by Rosenstone and Wolfinger[1] report that when socioeconomic characteristics such as income, education, and age are held constant, Latinos vote at about the same rate as do non-Latinos. However, other studies, such as those by Calvo and Rosenstone[2] and by Arvizu and Garcia,[3] modify this generality and elaborate on several variations to this theme.

With the exception of the Cubans, Latinos strongly identify with the Democratic party in general. When they do turn out to vote, Latinos' voting preferences exhibit a tendency towards supporting the Democratic party (again with the notable exception of the strong Republicanism of the Cubans). For example, in the presidential election of 1976, Jimmy Carter received about 76 percent of the Latino vote. Ronald Reagan made some inroads into the Latino vote, but his Democratic opponents still received 61 percent Latino support in 1980 (Carter) and 62 percent in 1984 (Walter Mondale). In 1988 Democrat Michael Dukakis won the vote of about 69 percent of Latinos in a losing cause to George Bush. In 1992 when Bill Clinton won the presidency with only 43 percent of the nation's popular vote, Latinos gave him 62 percent of their votes. Latinos also have supported Democratic candidates for Congress at the 60–80 percent level over the past several decades. Latinos were even more Democratic in voting for federal offices in 1996. Bill Clinton received 72 percent of the Hispanic vote and about 84 percent of Latinos voted for Democratic candidates for Congress.

Although Latinos comprise about 10 percent of the nation's populace, the Latino electorate constitutes only about 5 percent of the total, because their voting rates are relatively low. Calvo and Rosenstone examined the participation of Hispanics between 1974 and 1986. Using a variety of sources, including the 1984 Current Population Survey of the U.S. Census Bureau, national election surveys of the Center for Political Studies, and Roper Poll data, they reinforced the general observation that "Hispanics are less likely to participate in politics than are other Americans." Examining thirteen forms of political expression, both electoral and non-electoral, they found that Hispanics participate at significantly lower levels. Most of their study was centered on voting participation. In the 1984 presidential election, Hispanic turnout was 25 percent lower than that of non-Hispanics. It must be remembered that between a third and 40 percent of Hispanics are non-citizens, and this greatly influences all these statistics. In terms of voting population, Hispanics were 5.7 percent of the voting age population, 4.0 percent of the citizen voting age population, and only 3.1 percent of those who actually cast a ballot. In other words, the "citizenship barrier produced two-thirds" of the drop in relative voting rate. Over the years studied by these authors, Hispanic voter turnout averaged 15 percentage points lower than the turnout of other Americans.

These authors made the crucial point that overall statistics conceal significant differences among various national-origin Hispanic subgroups. The 1984 pattern is typical, with Puerto Ricans being the least politically involved, Mexican Americans being slightly more active, and Cubans having very high electoral participation rates—very comparable to those of non-Hispanics. The authors looked for differences in voter turnout rates by examining those sociodemographic characteristics which usually contribute to lower voter turnout among all population groups, including education, income, and occupation—the major three variables comprising objective socioeconomic class. For the general population, correlations have been reported between older age, male gender, and higher levels of formal education and greater participation in electoral politics. In general this also held true for the Hispanic population, although it varied by nationality group. The same positive association held for the combined Hispanic group, for Mexican Americans, and for Puerto Ricans but again, not for Cubans. Increased education did increase voter turnout for Hispanics, but less so than for other Americans. Income also had relatively less impact on Hispanic voter turnout than on non-Hispanic participation. So in general, the class bias in voter turnout was present but smaller for Hispanics than for other Americans. It had its greatest impact on Mexican Americans and an almost negligible effect on the likelihood of Cuban Americans' voting. Gender seemed to make little difference in turnout, and age had its usual impact on both Hispanics and non-Hispanics; that is, turnout was lowest among the very young then increased until it declined in old age. When other demographic variables were held constant, aging increased turnout steadily until people were well into their 70s. So, class and age biases were less for Hispanics than for non-Hispanics; among Latinos they were generally larger for Mexicans and for Puerto Ricans and had hardly any effect on Cubans. Arvizu and Garcia have brought the analysis of Latino national voting behavior up to the 1988 election with their analysis of the Latino National Political Survey data. The diminution of voting is again found to be related to the "class" variables of education and income levels. Factors which tend to increase people's vested interest in society such as age, years in the United States, and home ownership were additionally found to have significant ("life cycle") effects. Again differing patterns exist for each Latino national-origin group.

Since demographic measures seemed to have less of an impact on Hispanic voter participation rates than for non-Hispanics, Calvo and Rosenstone examined the effect of political mobilization by organizations such as political parties and community political and civic groups and found generally that their impact was significant. However, since none of these fully explained the differential rate of voter participation, the authors speculated that perhaps it was *language* that is a barrier to effective Hispanic participation; they also speculated that "some Hispanic immigrants do not hold a kind of social, psychological, and political attachment to the U.S. that they maintain for their country of origin." Cubans were seen as an exception because of their political refugee status and their high rate of naturalization. (However, the Latino National Political Survey found that these groups' attitudinal attachments to the United States and its values are comparable to that of non-Hispanic Whites, and their political attachments to their homelands are secondary.) Finally, the authors suspected that for many Puerto Ricans and Mexicans, the benefits of participating in politics may have been perceived as minimal, or at least were unclear, but they concluded by noting that the trend in Hispanic turnout between 1976 and 1984 was one of increasing participation in elections. Very recent analysis of the LNPS data on non-voting political participation by Hero and Campbell and by Wrinkle et al. elaborates on the complexity of Latino participation. The former find that in some circumstances Latinos' rate of participation is greater than previously thought.[4] The latter authors reinforce the importance of mobilization, socioeconomic variables, and distinctive cultural backgrounds.[5]

With the huge increase in the number of Latinos in the United States, it becomes increasingly important for Latinos to use effectively their enhanced numbers at the ballot box. Organizations such as the National Association of Latino Elected Officials (NALEO) have been very active in drives to naturalize immigrants. The Southwest Voter Registration Education Project also continued its efforts through the 1980s and 1990s in registration drives. Such efforts by Latino organizations seem to be particularly important, since core culture political organizations such as political parties and individuals such as candidates for office seem to ignore disproportionately the Latino potential, depriving them of an important source of voter interest and mobilization and power.[6]

Underlying the forms and the content of inputs to the political system are the political attitudes which Latinos hold. Increasingly, a likely inference is that over and above sociodemographic variables, psychological factors may account for a substantial amount of the yet not fully explained voter gap between Latinos and Anglos. Such orientations include their attitudes towards political participation. Conventional psychological reasons given for lower participation include such explanations as the cultural values of Hispanics; feelings of cynicism and alienation toward a hostile government; a feeling of disinterest or apathy due to a history of exclusion; a relatively greater lack of cognitive knowledge about public and political affairs; and other such speculations. There have been few representative, scientific surveys which investigate the political attitudes, values, and beliefs of Hispanic adults. However, the Latino National Political Survey has provided some significant information about the political participation of the three largest national-origin groups of Latinos both attitudinally and behaviorally.[7] It may very well be that it is not greater attachment to home countries or national-origin cultural characteristics that are the most significant psychological states as much as it is overcoming a legacy of discouragement and exclusion. Once Latinos have been able to have a stake in this society—material and emotional— over a period of several generations, the resultant acceptance and attachment likely will lead to very comparable participation rates.

Before Latino political interests can be communicated to political decision makers via their participation, some consensus on those interests must be discerned. It is likely that those interests will vary from locale to locale, from one time to another, and also among the various Latino communities, including national-origin communities. What is the Latino political agenda, or more precisely, what are some of the items on Latino political agendas? At the national level, early in 1990, the Latino National Political Survey helped to cast some light on Latinos' preferences for public policies. In a question measuring attitudes towards increased government spending on public policy areas, there were major similarities between the preferences of Mexicans, Puerto Ricans, and Cubans. Crime control and drug prevention measures topped the list for all three groups, closely followed by public education and then by health care. A nationwide exit poll, taken by Voter Research and Surveys of Hispanics exiting the polling places in 1990, asked them which were the "issues that mattered the most." The top two concerns of Hispanics at that time were education (39 percent) and crime/drugs (38 percent). One should note that these policy agenda items are very similar to those expressed by non-Hispanics and very well could serve as a basis for coalitions of common concerns.

The Latino National Political Survey also revealed a few public policy areas that were distinctively different for Latinos and non-Latinos. Latinos were extremely supportive of policies protecting or promoting the Spanish language (for example, bilingual education and anti-official English policies) while Whites tend to favor the opposite position on these. There is also a notable difference on an affirmative action/quota item. Mexicans, and especially Puerto Ricans, tended to be more in favor of preferential admission and hiring for their groups than did Cubans and much more so than did non-Hispanic Whites. Surprisingly to some, immigration did not seem to be a major concern of Hispanics nationwide at the turn of the decade (although it is becoming increasingly salient); and those taking a position on the issue tended to favor a restrictive immigration policy rather than a more liberal one at that time.

While it is often convenient or even necessary to speak of Latinos as a homogeneous group, studies of participation, among others, indicate that there may be considerable variation between national-origin groups. The Latino National Political Survey found that in national electoral participation, Cubans are most participative, Puerto Ricans the least, and Mexican Americans in between, with many variations among the latter group. However, in non-voting activities, a different pattern emerges. For example, Mexican Americans are the most likely to sign a petition, attend a public meeting, be involved in school activities, and participate in boycotts.

In his article, "Political Participation: Resources and Involvement among Latinos in the American Political System," John A. Garcia uses the LNPS data in order to present and analyze some of the latest and most comprehensive data about Latino political participation. Again, the relatively lower rate of voting participation by Latinos is confirmed. Mexicans and Puerto Ricans have voted at the lowest rates; among Latinos, Cubans are distinctively high in their voting participation, and it is the Anglos in these geographical areas who register and vote at the highest levels. When it comes to other, non-electoral types of political participation, Puerto Ricans and Mexicans display a higher rate of participation in such activities as signing petitions and attending public meetings than do the Cubans. On measures of political participation in political activities specifically involving Latino causes, the rate for all groups is lower, probably due to more limited opportunities.

Garcia looks for the reasons for relatively lower levels of participation in the three Latino groups in terms of their (1) socioeconomic characteristics, (2) resources and opportunities, especially those which are directly related to their occupational experiences, and (3) mobilization activities. The most significant demographic variable is citizenship. One of the major reasons for the low rate of Hispanic voting is the significant proportion of them who are not citizens—approximately one-third of Mexican Americans for example, as well as a substantial proportion of Cubans. Since all Puerto Ricans are citizens, this boosts their electoral index. About 40 percent of eligible Hispanics are in fact registered, and those generally are almost as likely to vote as are non-Hispanics. Politically relevant attitudes among Latinos seem to be supportive of electoral norms. (This is most well established for Chicanos).[8] Both positive civic attitudes and collective action orientations seem to exist in significant proportions among many Latinos. Yet these orientations do not seem to be directly translated into a correspondingly high level of actual political participation. Demographic variables such as comparatively lower education, lower occupational status, lower age, and foreign-born nativity combine to have a depressing effect on participation. Education is seen to be the single most important sociodemographic variable related to all forms of participation. Job-related skills which can be transferred to political participation are associated with higher levels of non-electoral activities, particularly for Cubans and Puerto Ricans. Mobilization by leaders and organizations needs renewed emphasis in order to boost participation rates. The rate of Latino political participation may well increase in the 1990s as the socioeconomic status of many Latinos improves, and if catalytic individuals or issues promote mobilization. However, additional reliable data as well as the tremendous influx of immigrants makes it difficult to be precise about this.

When the Calvo-Rosenstone study was published in the late 1980s, the authors felt that voter registration procedures were still an obstacle to electoral participation. However, later reforms such as the extensions of the Voting Rights Act and "motor voter registration" at the national and state levels have greatly ameliorated this situation over the past decade. In fact, a more recent (1993) analysis of Latino electoral participation holds that legislation and litigation based on those laws have had a cumulative major and positive effect on Latino electoral influence and "have been integral to Latino electoral empowerment." Rodolfo de la Garza and Louis DeSipio ("Save the Baby, Change the Bathwater, and Scrub the Tub: Latino Electoral Participation after Twenty Years of the Voting Rights Act Coverage") structure their exposition around the federal Voting Rights Acts. The initial and basic Voting Rights Act, designed primarily to remedy the vote exclusion of African Americans, was passed in 1965. With a succession of amendments it was extended to some language minorities, including Hispanics in 1970, and was increasingly expanded to Hispanics in 1975, 1982, and 1992, with the latest extension to the year 2007. In the article, first the historical circumstances surrounding the legislative constructions of these statutes are described. Next presented are the concurrent, and in many ways more effective, interpretations and decisions of the courts to overcome historical institutional impediments. Provisions of the VRA prohibiting minority vote dilution have provided the courts with a statutory basis for intervening against acts of intimidation against Latinos, prohibiting English literacy tests and ballots, and ordering single-member electoral districts and favorable districting patterns. The 1975 amendments were especially useful in empowering the federal courts to invalidate many state and local statutes and practices which had served as barriers to electoral participation by "language minorities."

Historically, there had not existed widespread exclusion of Mexican Americans from most electorates to any great extent, certainly not comparable to that of African Americans. In fact the authors conclude that the VRA itself has had little effect on increasing Latino registration and voting rates. However, because of their growing population, Latinos have become a larger share of the national electorate, and their spatial concentration (in conjunction with the VRA reforms) have given Latinos unprecedented potential to elect the officials their communities prefer. That potential has been somewhat realized, as the number of elected Hispanic officials has shown a steady incremental growth. However, registration and turnout rates continue to lag by about 15 points even after being adjusted for citizenship status. Their analysis of the LNPS data revealed that the traditional demographic correlates of low voting—age, education, and income—probably have greater effects than language usage, perceptions of discrimination, cynicism, or alienation from non-Latino candidates or officials. Factors which probably have greater depressing effects on turnouts are the results of a vicious cycle of socialization towards non-participation which may not likely be broken under current circumstances that in general are decreasing voter participation in the U.S.

Even the VRA may have inadvertently contributed to the perpetuation of non-participatory behavior by contributing to safe, non-competitive electoral districts. These tend to almost guarantee the re-election of incumbents, usually Democratic and Hispanic, and to discourage challengers, competition, and the consequent mobilization of voters. The authors conclude that the Voting Rights Act ("The Baby") was and is important as a symbol to Latinos of importance and inclusion and as a preventative against old-style overt discrimination. Ethnic gerrymandering on behalf of Latinos should be modified to produce not only districts that guarantee Latino victories but also more competitive "Latino influence" districts that would encourage competition for the Latino vote as one essential element in an electoral coalition. And finally, their "most important" suggestion is for the federal government to exercise some strong leadership in promoting several approaches towards naturalizing citizenship for the approximately 40 percent of Latino non-citizens.

In late June 1995, the U.S. Supreme Court ruled in a Georgia case (*Miller v. Johnson*) that race should not and could not be the "predominant" consideration in drawing legislative districts. In a 5–4 vote, the Court held that such racial gerrymandering was contrary to the Constitution and the Voting Rights Act. Although all the implications of the decision were not clear, it did seem that the Court might have begun to roll back some of the extensions of the Voting Rights Act, at least limiting the extent to which districting could be used to guarantee the election of racial minorities (and perhaps ethnic minorities such as Latinos). However, at the same time the Court issued an order sustaining a 1992 California redistricting plan that gave Black or Hispanic voters a majority in several districts.

Voting may be necessary but it certainly is not sufficient to have a major impact on the ongoing decisions of public officials. Effective organizational work is also needed. In addition to electoral participation and participation through political parties, interest-group activities are a major form of political input. The Latino National Political Survey found that there was little awareness among the Latino people of major national organizations reflecting their interests, with only the League of United Latin American Citizens (LULAC) being mentioned by a notable proportion of the Latino population. Yet, the activities of Latino organizations have been extremely important to advancing the political causes of Latinos. Much of this activity has been at the local and state level; it has been much less obvious at the national level.

Probably the most visible and effective organizations in the pursuit of power over the past decade have been the Mexican American Legal Defense and Education Foundation (MALDEF), the Southwest Voter Registration and Education Project (SWVREP), the National Association of Latino Elected Officials (NALEO), and the National Council for La Raza (NCLR). MALDEF has been most influential in its litigational activities, as it has represented Latino interests in the areas of affirmative action, minority vote dilution, and redistricting. SWVREP has made its primary contribution in the area of voter registration. The National Council is the most visible association lobbying in Washington and also serves as a coordinating body and clearinghouse for information on Latinos. NALEO strives to increase the number and efficacy of Latinos holding public office.

Interest-group activity arguably is more important than participation in elections as a means of influencing government policy through political action. From a conventional perspective, organizational membership has been low among Latinos (even lower than it is for the general

American population); and activity in strictly political organizations is minimal, especially at the state and national levels.

The importance of organizational mobilization at the local level is featured in the article by Benjamin Marquez, "The Industrial Areas Foundation and the Mexican-American Community in Texas: The Politics of Issue Mobilization." It illustrates how relatively powerless people may mobilize, organize their interests, get on the public agenda, exert political pressures, and win many local victories. In this process, the community gains in self-esteem and efficacy, that is, builds empowerment. The IAF style is confrontational in style, but its goals are not; its guiding principles are pragmatic rather than ideological. Thus, although local victories can be won, and their immediate effects improve the quality of life in poor Mexican communities, this approach is not likely to have significant impact on the basic distribution of economic and political power nationally.

If one adopts a less conventional definition of "political organization," Latinos have a long history of rich and vital participation in the collective activities of their communities. Throughout the history of Hispanics in the U.S., there has been the formation of mutual help associations (*mutualistas*) in the communities. Latinos have also been major participants in the struggles of labor unions. But the political aspects of these have seldom been recognized.[9] Mary Pardo gives an account of community mobilization focused against the implementation of some public policies of the state of California which would have adverse effects on the Latino community in East Los Angeles. Mexican-American women have often been the primary "activists" in the family-related and school-related activities that involve the communication of their interests, networking and organizing. Such behind the scenes "support" activities have not been recognized as political, although many of the same activities are utilized in conventional politics. In describing the "Mexican American Women Grassroots Community Activists: 'Mothers of East Los Angeles'," Pardo pointedly destroys many of the conventional wisdom myths about the non-roles of Mexican-American women in politics. In contradiction to the common mythology which asserts that they have a depressing effect on participation, Mexican-American cultural values, such as familism, gender role differentiation, and deference to authority, Latinos' relationship to the Catholic Church, and even lower socioeconomic status are used in this case to support successful grassroots activism, mobilization, and coalition building.

As this society finds more and more of its communities becoming multi-ethnic, it is through *coalitional* politics that the pursuit of power will be most successful. In Regalado's article on "political incorporation" or true empowerment of excluded minorities, he offers several thoughtful critiques of others' writings on minority empowerment, particularly the narrow perspective that many have presented on the "successes" of Latinos pursuing power. Often, ad hoc or "after the fact" electoral coalitions are attributed a level of significance which is exaggerated. The importance of the private sector, the critical significance of economic class and structures, the incorporation of the grassroots community rather than just the elite, and the importance of coalitions in addition to those involving elections are often overlooked.

Regalado's example is the fragmented city of Los Angeles, the southern California minority-majority megalopolis, with its 65 percent distinctive minority population (including 40 percent Latino), its rapidly changing social and economic structures, and its stubbornly persistent lack of Latino empowerment. The political process lags well behind the cultural and economic changes that are rapidly occurring in the area. Some of the new Latino leadership realize the necessity of building community power coalition, often using labor unions as their base. However, considerable animosity and competition still continue to exist, especially among Latinos, Blacks, and Whites. The coalitions within Los Angeles city government's administration and council are problematic and still in a state of flux. Even current coalitional activities within decision-making bodies are those of relatively disconnected elites, primarily reflecting the past demographic composition of the city.

Regalado suggests that pursuing power should take place "not so much with electoral coalitions but with community coalitions to empower communities and their families." Coalitions must be community based, ought to include realistic proportions of the community's demographic groups, and should coalesce around (primarily local) issues which unite rather than divide people. Electoral coalitions primarily have enhanced the representation of tenuously accountable governing elites and has scarcely represented the incorporation of the city's most populous communities of color (e.g., Latinos).

A continued focus on electoral coalitions, and the resulting elite incorporation misdirects attention and activities away from the more significant coalition building that must occur among multiracial communities of depressed socioeconomic status between elections. The most effective coalitions center around mobilization and organization building to pursue power for the purpose of solving common community problems.

The alleged passive, submissive, and apolitical stereotype of Latinas is further belied by Carol Hardy-Fanta as she analyses and describes "Latina Women and Politics in Boston." Boston Latinas of several national-origin backgrounds have participated in the full range of political roles—formal and informal. As in the Los Angeles example, their most important role has been as the organizers and communicators—in short the mobilizers—at the community level. These are activities that, while they are behind the scene, are absolutely essential for the more visible "surface" politics which have long been perceived as male prerogatives, especially in the traditional Hispanic culture. The Latinas are termed "connectors" who are the bridge between the power structure and the grassroots and among the communities' peoples. Their perception of politics is different than that of the men who participate in (and many who study) politics. Less emphasis is placed on obtaining and holding visible governmental positions and more on involvement in the process of acting on behalf of protecting and promoting the family and community's interests in what women are more likely to call "problem solving" than political participation. In Fanta-Hardy's terms, women are more concerned with "relational" or participatory rather than "positional" or structural aspects of politics.

The chances of successful input—that which exerts maximum influence on public policy in a manner favorable to those seeking government support for their needs or wants—is maximized when participation is intense and comprehensive. Among Latinos, it is the Cubans who typically are pointed out as being the most politically successful. Dario Moreno elaborates on this in "The Cuban Model: Political Empowerment in Miami." Cubans had an auspiciously favorable start in this country, unlike other Hispanics. They were welcomed by the government and given preferential treatment. A relatively homogeneous group, they brought with them a large population with education and skills which quickly led to socioeconomic power. They suffered relatively little discrimination from the larger society, especially within their "institutionally complete" enclave. Cubans have used every political vehicle available to control government and politics in the Miami–Dade County locale— successful court challenges to increase their power, elections featuring high turnout and pro-Cuban candidate bloc voting, taking over one of the two political parties in that area while playing one party off against the other in other arenas, uniting around a common ideology and a major policy issue, effectively organizing a strong interest group in the national arena with its corresponding political action committee, and even controlling their own media. Moreno concludes that the Cuban success is *not* transportable to other Hispanic communities because of the very special and unique circumstances of their historical, demographic, and socioeconomic situation. However, although the total model may not be applicable as a whole to many other Latino communities, it does provide some insights into the several elements comprising successful politics, each of which can be studied as an ideal example of how to pursue and increase political power

NOTES

1. Raymond Wolfinger and Steve Rosenstone, *Who Votes?* (New Haven, Conn.: Yale University Press, 1980).

2. Maria A. Calvo and Steven J. Rosenstone, "Hispanic Political Participation," Latino Electorates Series (San Antonio, Tex.: Southwest Voter Research Institute, 1989).

3. John R. Arvizu and F. Chris Garcia, "Latino Voting Participation: Explaining and Differentiating Latino Voter Turnout," *Hispanic Journal of Behavioral Sciences* 18, no. 2 (May 1996): 104–28.

4. Rodney F. Hero and Anne G. Campbell, "Understanding Latino Political Participation: Exploring the Evidence from the Latino National Political Survey," *Hispanic Journal of Behavioral Sciences* 18, no. 2 (May 1996): 129–41.

5. Robert D. Wrinkle, Joseph Stewart, Jr., J. L. Polinard, Kenneth J. Meier, and John R. Arvizu, "Ethnicity and Non-Electoral Participation," *Hispanic Journal of Behavioral Sciences* 18, no. 2 (May 1996): 142–53.

6. This is a major hypothesis based on several case studies presented and analyzed in Rodolfo de la Garza et al., *Barrio Ballots: Latino Politics in the 1990 Elections* (Boulder, Colo.: Westview Press, 1994).

7. An overall description of the project and presentation of the overall findings from the Latino National Political Survey is found in *Latino Voices: Mexican, Puerto Rican, and Cuban Perspectives on American Politics,* by Rodolfo O. de la Garza, Louis DeSipio, F. Chris Garcia, John A. Garcia, and Angelo Falcon (Boulder, Colo.: Westview Press, 1992).

8. This is a major paradox reported by John Garcia and Carlos Arce in their article "Political Orientations and Behaviors of Chicanos: Trying to Make Sense Out of Attitudes and Participation," in *Latinos and the Political System,* ed. F. Chris Garcia (Notre Dame, Ind.: University of Notre Dame Press, 1988).

9. A recent exception is a study examining the relationship between organizational membership and political participation among Latinos. Generally a strong and positive relationship is found. See William Diaz, "Latino Participation in America—Associational and Political Roles," *Hispanic Journal of Behavioral Sciences* 18, no. 2 (May 1996): 154–174.

2. Political Participation: Resources and Involvement among Latinos in the American Political System

John A. Garcia

THE DISCUSSION OF POLITICAL participation in America has been grounded in theoretical discourses of democracy involving individual rights, responsibilities, and institutional responsiveness and policies. While individual participation is the norm for a democratic society, there is clear evidence that uneven rates of participation exist among different population subgroups (Conway 1991; Verba and Nie 1972). Who gets involved in politics and why some get more involved than others is the focus of this paper. Also, it is clear that individuals are in and out of politics over the course of their life span, with very few individuals continually involved. There is a substantial research literature that examines and tries to explain rates and modes of political participation (Milbrath and Goel 1977; Bennett and Bennett 1989). Yet the knowledge base for Latino participation in the U.S. is virtually nonexistent. According to the 1990 census this group exceeds 22.4 million which represents slightly less than 10 percent of the total population and is developing into a growing presence in the American political arena. Our attention will be directed to Latinos in the U.S.

There is a growing concern about the political potential of this group and how their political involvement is impacting the American political system. The growth of the Latino population has resulted from a higher fertility rate and youthful age structure, as well as continuous migration from Mexico and Latin America. For our purposes, Latinos include individuals from Mexico, Central and South America, the Spanish Carribean, and the Iberian peninsula. The limited evidence on Latino political participation suggests lower than average participation rates, as well as involvement in a limited range of activities. Socioeconomic status is viewed as the major determinant of an individual's political participation (Brady et al. 1995). In addition, cultural factors such as Spanish language maintenance, foreign-born origin, and value systems are also cited as salient contributors to participatory patterns (Verba et al. 1993; McClain and Garcia 1993). Thus this paper will explore both the arenas of political participation for Latinos as well as explanatory variables for individual participation.

POLITICAL PARTICIPATION: INDIVIDUAL RESOURCES, INVOLVEMENTS, AND MOBILIZATION

Citizen activism is an expected norm for a democratic society, yet the actual level of individual involvement is minimal. Citizen involvement is seen as a source of policy benefits and political advantage for leaders. The articulation and advocacy of individual and group policy preferences onto political institutions and processes serve to define the policy agenda and the policy choices of various constituencies. This interaction of citizenry and political institutions and leaders places pressure on the system to respond. At the same time, there are costs and resources involved for individual political participation. In terms of resources, the demands can be requests to work on campaigns, contribute to organizations and/or campaigns, signing petitions, or writing letters on behalf of concerns or issues. The individual costs are time, financial resources, communication and organizational skills, and personal orientations that include self-confidence, efficacy, and trust.

Some individuals are better able to absorb the costs of participation than others. Thus the difference in participation levels among individuals is due partially to the choices one makes with his or her available time and resources. Obviously the inclination to participate and available resources enable individuals to make the choice to be involved.

The crux of individually related factors associated with political participation can be categorized as resources, rewards, interests, and beliefs. The traditional base for individual resources fall within the rubric of socioeconomic resources—education, income, and occupation. Education fosters democratic values such as individual rights and responsibilities, involvement, political expressions, and freedoms. It also nurtures a sense of citizen competence, as well as providing skills for political learning. The latter point involves political information and understanding of issues, institutions, and processes, as well as the requisite communication and organizational skills to impact the political system. Usually, more educated and "experienced" individuals can understand and work with complex, abstract, and intangible subject matters. Also greater levels of education are generally associated with exposure to extensive and politically useful related information.

The other two legs of the socioeconomic triangle—occupation and income—contribute to resource accumulation and political conversion. That is, higher occupational status provides an organizational setting for exposure to relevant information, social networks, opportunities to exercise leadership and develop politically relevant skills. In addition, higher status jobs are generally associated with higher income levels and greater exposure to political stimuli (Verba et al. 1993). The latter point refers to the interaction between individuals and political interests that seek to mobilize persons for specific causes and issues. Income levels affect participation in terms of economic resources, time, and opportunities. Individuals who have a direct stake in political outcomes, as well as policy preferences, will be involved politically (Leighley 1990; Huckfeldt and Sprague 1987). Thus, persons in higher occupational status positions and higher income levels are directly motivated and invested in political involvement.

Our discussion connects resources with rewards for participation. Political participation can result in material benefits in terms of policy benefits and access (Rosenstone and Hansen 1993). Additional rewards could include solidarity benefits by interactions with like-minded persons and positive personal social networks. Beliefs in certain values such as moral issues (i.e., religious practices and beliefs, prayer, inception of life, etc.) motivate a person to engage in purposive actions. There are collective rewards as well as selective rewards which serve to involve individuals. Individuals who identify closely with political leaders and aspirants are more likely to participate and act as more committed partisans.

This discussion of individual political participation entails a cluster of resources, motivations, and opportunities. The accumulation of resources affords an individual the ability to participate, as well as serving as the target of strategic mobilization. In addition to personal resources, time, money, and skills provide the conversion of individual resources to specific participatory modes and arenas (Rosenstone and Hansen 1993). The motivation dimension deals with such attitudinal factors as political interest, efficacy, group consciousness (Verba and Nie 1972; Miller et al. 1981), and trust. Individuals with a positive sense of personal and political efficacy, self-confidence, and political trust are more likely to have preferences, motivations, and apply their resources toward political actions.

The other part of the participation equation lies with mobilization. Mobilization is the process whereby persons are induced to participate and are directly mobilized by organizations and leaders. The mobilization process can occur indirectly through the use of an individual's associates (Huckfeldt and Sprague, 1992). Direct forms of mobilization would involve rallies, meetings, petition drives, requests for money. The benefits of direct mobilization for individuals is the subsidization of political information which facilitates activism. The strategy for political mobilization involves targeting persons with sufficient resources and maximizing the returns from the organization's perspective by successfully receiving the desired support.

Prime targets for mobilization are persons who are knowledgeable, centrally positioned in social networks, and likely to respond by participating and producing outcomes (Rosenstone and Hansen 1993). In sociodemographic terms, these individuals would be employed, belong to organizations, are in leadership positions in business organizations and local government, as well as being affluent, educated, and partisan. Thus the connection between resources and involvement entails the abilities and inclinations to participate with the opportunity to use one's resources in a focused activity and arena.

The arenas of political participation have been identified as primarily electoral, governmental, and organizational. Another realm of participation deals with one-on-one interactions of political discourse and informational exchange. The electoral arena would include registering to vote, voting, volunteering on campaigns, donating money to campaigns and organizational efforts, and contacting public officials. The non-electoral arenas and activities include involvement in local issues, participating on governing and advisory boards and commissions, contacting public officials and bureaucrats, and protest activity. An individual's participation in non-political secondary institutions like employment-related groups, church, and voluntary associations serves to expose one to political messages and information, interactive and focused discussions, and interpersonal networks. Finally, the development of politically relevant skills such as making presentations, conducting meetings, managing group efforts, fund raising, and public speaking is associated with greater levels of political participation in all arenas (Brady et al. 1995).

THE LATINO COMMUNITY AND POLITICAL PARTICIPATION

Our discussion about political participation represents the extant literature and major findings. As we indicated earlier, the research on reasons for political participation by Latinos is very limited. Overall, levels of participation among Latinos are lower than the general population, the majority (i.e., Anglos), and African Americans (Hero 1991). In the areas of electoral participation, Latinos both register and vote at lower rates than their Anglo counterparts (Garcia and Arce 1988; Welch and Sigelman 1993). The primary explanations lie with lower socioeconomic status, nativity, and Spanish language maintenance. Membership and participation in organizations (political as well as non-political secondary groups) are significantly lower for Latinos (Garcia and de la Garza 1985; Uhlaner et al. 1989). Excluding Puerto Ricans, the other Latino subgroups have a substantial proportion of their community that are foreign-born. With such a sizable foreign-born segment, rates of participation are significantly affected (Garcia 1982; Pachon and DeSipio 1994). The issues of political integration and socialization become important factors for the foreign-born segment of the Latino community. The youthful character of the Latino population also contributes to lower rates of participation as their median age is seven to ten years younger than the general population (with the exception of the Cubans) (Calvo and Rosenstone 1989). Participation rates increased among the over thirty-five age group of individuals with greater investments and stakes in the economic and political system.

In addition, it is important to distinguish between the various national-origin groups under the Latino umbrella (i.e., Cubans, Puerto Ricans, Mexican origin, El Salvadoran, etc.). Each group's history in the U.S., their demographic profiles, the extent of foreign-born residential population, cultural maintenance, regional concentration, and political and economic status all influence the specific character of each group's political participatory modes (Jennings 1994; Boswell and Curtis 1984). While it is useful to identify and speak about a national Latino community, it is equally important to be cognizant of inter-group differences.

Relatively speaking, data and analysis are most available for the Mexican-origin population in terms of voting behavior, electoral activities, organizational behavior, and partisan behavior. One of the frequently used descriptors, electorally, for Mexican Americans is "if they vote they count." Even after the advent of the Voting Rights and extended "protection" for linguistic minorities, Mexican-American voter registration and turnout levels trail Anglos and African Americans by 10 to 20 percentage points (Grofman and Davidson 1992; McClain and Garcia 1993; Regalado and Martinez 1991). There is also evidence of their lesser direct involvement in campaigns as workers, canvassers, or financial contributors (de la Garza et al. 1992; Uhlaner et al. 1989). In terms of secondary association membership and activities, Mexican

Americans do not join organizations compared to other groups and much less frequently join more politically oriented groups. This pattern is more pronounced among the foreign-born segment (Garcia and de la Garza 1985; Pachon and DeSipio 1994).

Attitudinally, Mexican Americans express support for participatory norms and behavior, while feeling less efficacious and confident in their understanding of the political process (Garcia and Arce 1988). Levels of political trust tend to fall in the mid-range. Similar findings are minimally available for other Latino subgroups. Issues of anti-communism, embargo of Cuba, immigration and refugee admission policy, and, to a limited sense, domestic areas of taxation, spending, and social welfare issues serve as major policy foci for the Cuban community (Moreno and Warren 1992; Portes and Mozo 1985). Partisan-wise, the Cuban community has supported the Republican party and its candidates (F. C. Garcia et al. 1991; de la Garza and DeSipio 1992). The balance of the extant research on Cubans has been focused in southern Florida and the integration of the community into the economic and political system (Moreno and Warren 1992; Portes and Mozo 1985).

The third largest Latino subgroup is Puerto Rican, located in the northeast and the Chicago metropolitan area. Works by Jennings (1994; 1977) and Falcon (1988) have focused upon their particular political status, i.e., U.S. citizens connected by commonwealth status. Puerto Ricans, the most urbanized Latino population, also are the most economically disadvantaged. While electoral and governmental activities among Puerto Ricans on the "island" have active participation levels, the extant knowledge about Puerto Rican participation in the mainland shows it is significantly lower (Falcon 1988). Registration and turnout rates are generally 10 to 20 percentage points lower than for the majority population. There is evidence of Puerto Rican involvement in local New York City politics, particularly the educational arena (Falcon et al. 1994; Jennings, 1994). Some findings from the Latino National Political Survey (LNPS) indicate moderate to slightly more conservative self-placement by Puerto Ricans on a seven-point ideology scale (de la Garza et al. 1992).

It is only recently with the completion of the LNPS that baseline political data is available for the three major Latino groups—Mexicans, Puerto Rican, and Cubans. The book, *Latino Voices* (de la Garza et al. 1992) provides some new information on political orientations, behaviors, and policy preferences. Rates of political participation are generally lower for each of these three groups relative to the majority population, although there are some intergroup variations. That is, voter registration and self-reported turnout is higher among eligible Cubans than for Mexican-origin and Puerto Rican respondents. Mexican-origin respondents identify most strongly with the Democratic party (about two-thirds); while Cubans are the most Republican in affiliation. Both Mexican-origin and Puerto Rican respondents are more likely to be engaged in non-electoral political activities than their Cuban counterparts (de la Garza et al. 1993). As we have suggested at the beginning of this paper, our focus lies with the portrait of modes of participation for Latinos and the contributing factors. The LNPS will serve as the data medium to examine the political participation of Latinos.

THE LATINO NATIONAL POLITICAL SURVEY

The Latino National Political Survey represents the first national probability survey of persons of Spanish origin living in the U.S. Eligibility for this survey were persons of Mexican, Puerto Rican, and Cuban origin. These three national-origin groups constitute four-fifths of the Latino population in the U.S. A total of forty primary sampling units (PSU's) were designated for the national sample with twenty-eight SMSA's (Standard Metropolitan Statistical Areas) as self-representing sites. The other twelve sites were stratified based on geography (i.e., state), metro vs. non-metropolitan status, and concentration of Latinos in the PSU's. Adults were randomly selected and a face-to-face interview was conducted. The approximately ninety-minute interviews were conducted during July 1989 to March 1990.

A total of 2,816 persons of Mexican, Puerto Rican, and Cuban origin completed the interview schedule. Of that total, 1,546 were Mexican origin, 589 Puerto Rican, and 679 Cuban. In addition the research design included a sample of non-Latinos from the same PSU's as the selected Latinos. A total of 598 non-Latinos were interviewed in an abbreviated version of the LNPS instrument. The survey sample represents population coverage for each of the three Latino subgroups of 90.2 to 91.5 percent.

A critical aspect of the sample design was a sample selection that included low-density Latino residential areas (particularly at the secondary and tertiary sampling stages). This enabled one-fourth of the Latino respondents to come from low-density areas (less than 20 percent), and another 25 percent from areas of 25 to 49 percent Latino concentration. Extensive pre-testing, use of bilingual and bi-cultural interviewers, and post-1980 demographic updates from planning departments at the PSU's helped to improve the coverage and response rates.

The characteristics of the respondents parallel those of each of the national-origin groups when compared with the 1989 Current Popula-

tion Report on Hispanics (see table 1). Slightly greater numbers of females were represented in the sample (57.6%) and over three-fifths of
the sample were foreign-born. Cubans constituted the greatest percentage of foreign-born at 86.7 percent. Approximately 60 percent of the respondents completed the interview in Spanish with almost 80 percent of
the Cubans responding in Spanish. The balance of the demographic
characteristics (i.e., education, income, occupation, age, etc.) is presented
in Appendix A.

The Electoral Arena: Exploring Voting Activities among Latinos

Our discussion of individual political participation centers around involvement in a number of political arenas. The more visible arena is that
of elections and electorally related activities (i.e., campaigns, contributing money, volunteering, etc.). In the LNPS, a series of questions were
asked about Latinos' electoral behavior. These activities included: current and ever-registered status; if voted in 1988; and voting record for the
1986 and 1984 Congressional elections. One of the prime requirements
for voting is meeting the age and citizenship requirements. A significant

TABLE 1

Voting Activities among Latinos

Voting Activity	Mexican origin	Puerto Rican	Cuban	Anglos[1]
Ever been registered to vote in U.S.	76.0%[2]	73.0%	82.0%[3]	89.0%
Currently registered to vote in U.S.	65.0%	63.0%	77.0%	86.0%
Voted in November 1988 elections	49.0%	50.0%	67.0%	89.0%
Voted for U.S. representative in 1986	36.0%	32.0%	51.0%	61.0%

1 The term 'Anglo' is used to describe the non-Latino respondents in the LNPS who are racially self-
identified as white.
2 This percentage represents the portion of the Mexican-origin persons who are eligible to be registered
to vote (i.e., citizens and over eighteen). The non-citizens were not included in the base.
3 This percentage represents the portion of Cuban-origin persons who are eligible to be registered to
vote (i.e., citizens and over eighteen). The non-citizens were not included in the base.

number of the Mexican and Cuban-origin respondents are ineligible (45.5% and 54% respectively) due to foreign-born and non-citizen status.

Among the eligible Latinos, a significant portion have been registered voters at one time (see table 1). For Mexican origin, 76.0 percent of the eligibles have ever been registered, with similar percentages for Puerto Ricans (73.0%) and higher for Cubans (82.0%). While the Cuban proportion is greater, a larger percentage of their total are foreign-born. We do have responses from the Anglo sample of the LNPS which is significantly higher than all of the Latino subgroups. If we limit our profile of currently registered Latino voters, there is a noticeable drop-off from the "ever-registered" voter group. For the Mexican-origin and Puerto Rican respondents, approximately 15 percent fewer respondents are currently registered than the ever-registered group. Whereas almost nine-tenths of the Anglo respondents indicated that they had voted in the 1988 presidential election, only one-half of Mexican origin and Puerto Rican and two-thirds of the Cubans had voted. Going back to previous elections, the gap between Latino and Anglo voters is even greater. Previous research has indicated an electoral gap between Latinos, and the margin continues (Calvo and Rosenstone 1989; Wolfinger and Rosenstone 1980; Welch and Sigelman 1993). Yet the gap has been closing and with the increasing rates of naturalization and growth of the adult-age population, higher rates of registration and voting should follow.

POLITICALLY RELATED ACTIVITIES AMONG LATINOS

In addition to the acts of registering and voting, there are a number of other politically related activities that reflect modes of political participation (Calvo and Rosenstone, 1988; Milbrath and Goel 1977). From the LNPS, a battery of questions was asked. They included: signing a petition on an issue or problem; communicating with a public official regarding issues of concern; attending a public meeting; going to political rallies; working for a political party or candidate; and contributing money for a campaign. The general public is much less involved in these activities than in voting.[1] In table 2, we see the extent of Latino involvement in these activities. There are similarities across the three subgroups in petition signing, communicating with officials, and going to rallies. The groups are comparable at the levels of participation that involved less than 10 percent of the respondents. The only exception lies with signing a petition which is usually the result of mobilization efforts by an organization or ad hoc group. While there are common levels of politically related activities among the three groups, Cubans participate appre-

TABLE 2

General Politically Related Activities among Latinos

GENERAL POLITICALLY RELATED ACTIVITIES	MEXICAN ORIGIN	PUERTO RICAN	CUBAN	CALVO AND ROSENSTONE[1]
Signed a petition regarding an issue or problem that concerns you	20.0%	20.0%	14.0%	26.6%
Written a letter, telephoned or sent a telegram to an editor or public official regarding issues that concern you	8.0%	8.0%	9.0%	7.5%
Attended a public meeting	12.0%	16.0%	6.0%	18.9%
Gone to any political meetings, rallies, speeches, or dinners in support of a particular candidate	5.0%	7.0%	5.0%	5.4%
Worked either for pay or on a volunteer basis for a party or candidate running for office	4.0%	4.0%	2.0%	2.1%
Contributed money to an individual candidate, a political party, or an issue in an election	5.0%	6.0%	4.0%	3.3%

1 The percentages in this column are drawn from Table 1 of the Calvo and Rosenstone article on Hispanic political participation. Their data sources were the U.S. Bureau of Census Current Population Studies, the American National Election Studies, and Roper polls from 1980–86.

ciably less in attending meetings and working on political campaigns. Some previous research on Cubans in southern Florida has suggested that members of this Latino subgroup are more voting specialists and less involved in other facets of electoral or politically related activities.

A unique feature of the LNPS is a battery of participation items placed in a specific context of politically related activities on behalf of the respondents' own national-origin group and their issues and concerns. They parallel the conventional battery of items on "generic" politically related activities. In this case, the Latino-focused activities include: attending a meeting or demonstration; contributing money to a candidate or group; signing a petition in support of national-origin concerns; writing a letter or contacting in some other way a public official; working as a volunteer; and working with a group to get people to vote for Latinos. Generally speaking, their levels of participation in their national-origin political activities relative to the generic activities is lower

TABLE 3

*Latino Group-Based Non-Voting
Governmental Political Activities*

NON-VOTING ACTIVITIES	MEXICAN ORIGIN	PUERTO RICAN	CUBANS
Attended a public meeting or demonstration regarding one's group	6.0%	10.0%	6.0%
Contributed money to a candidate from one's group, to an organization of one's group, or to support other activities related to one's group	5.0%	7.0%	7.0%
Signed a petition in support of one's concerns	9.0%	9.0%	7.0%
Wrote a letter, telephoned, or sent a telegram to an editor or public official regarding issues concerning one's group	3.0%	3.0%	8.0%
Worked as a volunteer or for pay for a candidate endorsed by groups or leaders from one's group	3.0%	4.0%	1.0%
Worked with people from one's group to get people from one's group to vote as a group	6.0%	5.0%	2.0%

(see table 3). For example, 14 to 20 percent of the Latino respondents had signed a petition; while 7 to 9 percent had signed a petition in support of a Latino concern. A similar pattern was the case for attending a public meeting. As we have mentioned earlier, individual involvement is also influenced by directed mobilization efforts.

On the other hand, comparable levels of participation were evident in the other categories. One partial explanation for a seemingly lower rate of participation for Latino-focused activities is the limited opportunities to engage in such activities. Our earlier discussion of political participation includes both individual resources and involvement as well as mobilization efforts by leaders and organizations to activate individuals. In the case of Latinos, the mobilization dimension may be even more crucial to an "under-resourced" community. For the most part, there is little variation between the three subgroups, except that Cubans contact public officials at twice the rate than either Mexican-origin or Puerto Rican respondents (i.e., 8.0% vs. 3.0%). On the other hand, Mexican origin and Puerto Ricans are twice as likely to be involved in get out the vote efforts or volunteering on Latino campaigns. Finally, Puerto Ricans are two-thirds more likely to attend public meetings than their Mexican-origin and Cuban counterparts.

TABLE 4

Politically Related Activities on the Job
(Respondents with jobs only, excluding don't knows)

JOB-RELATED ACTIVITY	MEXICAN ORIGIN	PUERTO RICAN	CUBAN
Wrote a letter	17.0%	23.0%	30.0%
Took part in a meeting where decisions were made	30.0%	38.0%	35.0%
Gave a presentation or talk	15.0%	24.0%	17.0%
Got in touch with a government official	9.0%	10.0%	12.0%
Made a telephone call to someone you don't know personally	28.0%	38.0%	38.0%

RESOURCE ENHANCEMENT: SKILL-BUILDING

Our preliminary profile of the participation rates among the three Latino subgroups indicates relatively lower rates of participation than Anglos (when comparable data is available) and quite limited involvement in Latino-focused political activities. The primary contributors for individual political participation lie with higher levels of socioeconomic status (i.e., education, income, and occupation). At the same time, recent research by Verba et al. (1993) has posited the importance of job-related skills that significantly enhance proclivity and opportunities for participation. That is, being employed and developing skills which require managing and prioritizing time and responsibilities, and developing communicative skills are directly transferable to political situations and activities.

The recent work by Verba et al. (1993) illustrates how individuals with job-related skills are much more likely to belong to and be involved in organizations, as well as politically specific activities. Such individuals have the interest, exposure to political issues and information, and abilities to participate effectively. The LNPS included a battery of items that asked the Latinos if they had performed any of the following activities: 1) wrote a letter on the job; 2) made a telephone call to someone that he or she did not know personally; 3) gave a presentation or talk; or 4) got in touch with a public official. For the most part, greater percentages of Cubans have exercised those job-related skills (see table 4). Over one-third of the Cuban respondents have taken part in a meeting where decisions were made and communicated over the telephone. A similar level

TABLE 5

Summary of Political Participation Activities
for the Latino Subgroups

PARTICIPATION SUMMARIES	MEXICAN ORIGIN	PUERTO RICAN	CUBAN
Electoral Index			
None	55.9%	26.8%	60.4%
One	15.0	22.5	8.5
Two	29.1	50.8	31.8
Electoral Index for Latino Campaigns			
None	89.5	87.2	90.6
One	6.4	9.2	7.4
Two/Three	4.1	3.4	1.9
Governmental			
Activities Index			
None	72.6	70.3	80.7
One	16.8	17.3	10.6
Two/Three	10.7	12.4	8.8
Politically Relevant			
Job Skills Index			
None	68.4	70.5	67.4
One	11.4	7.4	9.1
Two	8.0	7.7	7.7
Three	4.3	3.9	5.6
Four/Five	7.9	10.5	10.2
No. of Respondents	1,546	589	679

of involvement in decision-making meetings and telephone communication were evident for Puerto Rican respondents.

At the same time, similar percentages of Mexican origin and Puerto Ricans have participated in decision-making meetings. Almost one-fourth of the Puerto Rican respondents have given a presentation or talk. For the most part, Mexican-origin respondents had the lowest rates of job-related skills relative to the other Latino group members. Clearly, employment and occupational status will be determining factors by which Latinos acquire the job-related skills.

In order to present a composite profile of the rate of political participation among Latinos, we have constructed a series of indices for the various modes of participation (see table 5). The five indices are : a) a general electoral index; b) electoral index for Latino-specific campaigns; c/d) governmental activities index (for general and Latino-specific activities); and e) a job-related skills index. All of the indices are the summation of the specified variables in tables 1–4. The combined electoral index indicates that Puerto Rican residents are the most active as 50.8 percent are both registered and active voters. Little difference is evident between the Mexican origin and Cubans.

This finding does challenge some conventional wisdom about the Cuban community's voting levels. Again, the high percentage of Cubans that are foreign-born does "undercut" the size of their voting bloc. While the percentage of eligible Cubans who do vote is higher than the other Latino groups, the population base is smaller. A key factor for these latter two groups is the substantial portion of the population that is foreign-born and non-citizens. Much higher rates of non-participation are evident for the Latino-specific electoral activities as close to nine-tenths of all of the respondents have not participated. Again exploring the additional reasons why higher rates of non-participation exist within the Latino electoral arena would also incorporate attitudinal and structural factors. Our analysis in this paper serves as a first stage into a multifaceted phenomenon.

The level of participation in governmentally related activities is lower for Cubans than for Mexicans and Puerto Ricans as about 10 percent had not engaged in any governmental activities. For governmental activities on specifically Latino issues and concerns, lower rates of participation were evident for all three groups in comparison to any type of governmental activity. There was virtually no variation between the three groups. Finally, an index was constructed for the job-related skills; little variation exists. That is, approximately two-thirds of all Latino respondents had not exercised any of the job skills. At the other end of the index (four or five activities accomplished), only one-tenth of the respondents fell into that category. Thus our composite indices of different modes of political participation indicate low to somewhat moderate levels of participation relative to levels for other racial/ethnic groups in the U.S. (Rosenstone and Hansen 1993). Now the more challenging aspect of this research paper lies in determining some *explanations* for Latino participation. Our earlier reference to the extant literature has strongly suggested that socioeconomic status is the major contributor, along with participatory orientations and job-related skills.

CAUSES OF PARTICIPATION IN ELECTORAL POLITICS AMONG LATINOS

In attempting to explain important contributing factors for modes of political participation, we will specify a model. The primary core of the specified independent variables are socioeconomic factors. The two key variables are educational attainment and household income. The former variable is measured by the number of years of schooling completed by each respondent. Our measure of income is that of the total household in fifteen income categories (i.e., $5,000 or less to over $75,000). Both variables were recoded to have a range of 0 to 1 with intervals of either .25 or .33. In lieu of occupational status, the respondent employment status (Verba and Scholzman 1979) was added to the independent variable list.[2] The other background variables incorporated into the multivariate analysis are: age of respondents; gender; nativity; home owner status, and Latino national-origin group. The latter variable was introduced as a dummy variable with Cubans serving as the reference group.

Two additional variables were included in the analysis to deal with participatory skills and experiences. The first is our job-related skills index and the other is whether the respondent has worked in a group situation to solve a local problem. Thus our model specification identifies individual resource and involvement-related factors. The series of dependent variables are the specific participation activities rather than the summary indices. The inclusion of the nativity variables serves as a "cultural" variable which is closely associated with English/Spanish language use. The variable specification of each of the three Latino subgroups enables us to examine if intergroup differences are pertinent for possible explanations of political participation rather than the aggregated Latino category.

Electoral Participation

Our multivariate approach is logistic regression with four nominal electoral variables — 1) registered to vote or not; 2) voted in 1988; 3) donated money or not to a campaign; and 4) worked on a campaign. The 0 and 1 value for each of these dependent variables lends itself to logistic regression. The independent variables are coded with a 0 or 1 value or from 0 to 1.[3] With registered to vote status as the first dependent variable, educational attainment, nativity, and being Puerto Rican proved to have significant beta coefficients. The method of variable inclusion for the listed independent variables meant that not all of the variables met the entry criteria. For the first set of significant variables, more years of schooling, being U.S. born, and of Puerto Rican origin proved to increase the probability of being a registered voter.

Some additional variables had significant beta coefficients. They were: age (positive); household income (positive); gender (negative); job-related skills (positive); and collective efforts to work on a local problem (positive). Another way of characterizing these sets of variables is that older, higher income, enhanced skilled, and involved Latinos are more likely to be registered to vote. The negative coefficient for gender (female is coded 0) indicates that there is a lower probability that Latinas are registered to vote. The overall goodness of fit measure and Chi-square value with the included independent variables were statistically significant. In addition, 77.9 percent of the cases were correctly classified.

The results of the logistic regression with the other electoral variables produced very similar results (see table 6). That is, educational attainment, income, nativity, and being Puerto Rican had significant beta coefficients. In addition, age, job-related skills, and collectively working

TABLE 6

*Causes of Participation
in Electoral Politics among Latinos
Forms of Electoral Participation*

VARIABLES	REGISTERED TO VOTE	VOTED IN 1988	DONATED MONEY	WORKED ON A CAMPAIGN
Educational attainment	1.74 (.16)[1]	1.42 (.16)*	1.54 (.29)*	1.63 (.34)*
Household income	.53 (.21)*[2]	1.13 (.20)*	1.27 (.40)*	
Age of respondent	.06 (.004)*	.06 (.004)*	.02 (.007)*	.03 (.007)*
Gender	-.26 (.10)*			-.54 (.21)*
Nativity	2.39 (.13)*	1.45 (.12)*	.45 (.18)*	.76 (.22)*
Participatory skills	.27 (.04)*	.16 (.04)*	.23 (.05)*	.30 (.06)*
Latino national- origin group:	*	*		
Mexican origin	.20 (.14)	.14 (.14)		
Puerto Rican	2.18 (.16)*	1.34 (.15)*		
Worked in a group to solve a local problem	.18 (.08)*	.32 (.07)*	.32 (.08)*	.42 (.08)*
Employment status	------[3]			
-2 Log likelihood	2331.66	2502.78	945.9	760.0
Goodness of fit	2773.39	2330.77	2516.4	2246.87
Chi-square	1197.97*	775.77*	176.37*	139.60*
% of cases correctly classified	77.9%	75.4%	94.3%	95.6%

1 The standard error term is reported in parenthesis.
2 The * indicates that the coefficient for this variable was significant at the .05 level or less.
3 If the column is blank, then the variable did not meet the criteria for inclusion in the equation.

on local problems increased the probability of voting, donating money, and working on a campaign. For electoral activities, the importance of acquired and accumulated individual resources clearly distinguishes Latino political participants from non-participants. In addition, the acquisition of job-related skills and local community involvement also play a key role. In this paper, our multivariate analysis has not integrated the possible interaction or association between the identified independent variables in explaining further the contributions of these variables with electoral participation. Our classification of cases for the other electoral dependent variables was significantly higher for predicting who donates money or has worked on a campaign (94.3% and 95.6% respectively).

Governmental Activities

The second series of logistic regression focused on governmental activities such as writing Congress, attending public meetings, and signing a petition. Each of the dependent variables were coded as 0 or 1 and the same set of independent variables was introduced into the logistic regression equations. Fewer variables met the criteria for inclusion than the results of the electoral participation analysis. Educational attainment, age, nativity, job-related skills, and working on local problems have statistically significant coefficients (see table 7). Gains in educational attainment, particularly beyond high school, appreciably increased the probability that a Latino would have written Congress. There were no subgroup effects for this equation; although being Puerto Rican increased the probability that he or she would sign a petition. Again, appropriate petition "signatures" are limited to registered voters. For writing Congress, 90.3 percent of the cases were correctly classified. Again the goodness of fit and the Chi-square were significant. An overview summary of these results would suggest that the educational investment and accumulated time in the system (i.e., native born and older) are key resources, in addition to experiences with collective efforts. Gains in education can provide greater knowledge, information, and interest in involvement with political institutions and actors. In addition, more educated and older Latinos may have a more vested stake in the actions of government with the skills to be effective.

Attending public meetings or not is affected by the same set of independent variables as the previous analysis with the addition of household income and Latino subgroup status. Relative to Cuban respondents, both Mexican origin and Puerto Ricans have a higher probability of at-

TABLE 7

Latinos' Participation in Governmental Activities:
A Multivariate Analysis

Variables	Wrote Congress	Attended Meeting	Signed Petition
Educational attainment	1.15 (.22)[1]*[2]	1.12 (.21)*	1.25 (.17)*
Household income	[3]	.69 (.28)*	.74 (.23)*
Age of respondent	.03 (.005)*	.02 (.005)*	
Gender			
Nativity	.44 (.15)*	.39 (.15)*	1.04 (.11)*
Participatory skills	.32 (.04)*	.28 (.04)*	.21 (.04)*
Latino national-origin group:			
Mexican origin		.76 (.21)*	
Puerto Rican		1.16 (.21)*	
Worked in a group to solve a local problem	.38 (.07)*	.58 (.22)*	.43 (.08)*
Homeowner status			
Employment status			
-2 Log likelihood	1388.06	1562.11	2087.48
Goodness of fit	2611.08	2320.64	2600.57
Chi-square	193.04*	300.62*	437.40*
% of cases correctly classified	90.3%	88.7%	81.9%

1 The standard error term is reported in parenthesis.
2 * represents a significant coefficient at or below the .05 level for this variable in the logistic regression equation.
3 If the column is blank, then the variable did not meet the criteria for inclusion in the equation.

tending public meetings. Again the socioeconomic variables including income proved to be significant positively, as well as U.S.-born origin. Our job skills and local involvement variables continue to be salient contributors for increased probabilities of governmental participation. The percentage of correctly classified cases was 88.7 percent.

Finally, the same set of factors were significant in influencing whether Latinos signed petitions or not. Educational attainment, nativity, and household income are the key factors involved in this governmental activity. Job skills and local involvement variables are significant as well. As in the case of the other variables, the goodness of fit and Chi-square were significant and 81.9 percent of the cases were correctly classified.

Latino-Specific Political Activities

A unique feature of the LNPS was the battery of Latino-specific electoral and governmental activities with reported levels of participation for each of the Latino groups. In the multivariate analysis, we included both types of activities. The five dependent variables were: worked for a Latino candidate; signed a petition regarding Latinos; tried to persuade voters to support a Latino candidate; donated money to a Latino campaign; and wrote a letter on behalf of Latino concerns. Again we included the same set of independent variables in the analysis. Overall, the summary statistics were significant and a relatively high percentage of the cases (90% plus) were correctly classified. At the same time, fewer independent variables were significant contributors (see table 8).

Only educational attainment and age proved to be significant among the sociodemographic variables. Throughout our multivariate analysis, education is the primary factor affecting higher probabilities for all types of political participation explored. Consistency is the case for the job-related skills and local involvement variables. That is, individuals with politically transferable job-related skills are more involved in all kinds of participation modes. For every Latino-specific participation variable, these two variables were statistically significant. The Latino national-origin variables were significant for working for a Latino candidate, signing a petition, and persuading prospective voters. That is, relative to Cuban respondents, both Mexican origin and Puerto Ricans had higher probabilities of engaging in these types of activities. It is important to note that our analysis is focusing on contributing factors and how rates of participation can be affected rather than a direct cause and effect relationship.

The importance of specific Latino subgroup status is not evident with the dependent variables of donating money to Latino candidates or writing a letter on behalf of Latino concerns. For these modes of participation, there is no significant effect of being Cuban or Puerto Rican or Mexican origin.

As we have noted in the previous analyses, the job-related and involvement variables were statistically significant for all of the Latino-specific variables. The consistency of these two variables has a direct association with socioeconomic status, particularly educational attainment. That is, more years of schooling is associated with income level and occupational and employment status. As a result of these interrelationships, the development of job-related skills is much more likely.

As with the other analyses, the goodness of fit and Chi-square

TABLE 8

Summary of Factors Influencing Participation in Electoral Politics Involving Latino Electoral Activities

Variables	Worked for a Latino Candidate	Signed a Petition for Latino Concerns	Tried to Persuade Voters for a Latino Candidate	Donated Money to a Latino Campaign	Wrote Letter on Behalf of Latino Concerns
Educational attainment	1.36 (.34)[1]*[2] [3]	1.30 (.21)*	1.24 (.27)*	.90 (.24)*	1.16 (.30)*
Household income					
Age of respondent	.04 (.008)*	.01 (.005)*	.01 (.006)*		.02 (.007)*
Nativity			-.39 (.19)*		
Gender				.46 (.16)*	.70 (.21)*
Participatory skills	.32 (.06)*	.16 (.04)*	.22 (.05)*	.26 (.05)*	.32 (.07)*
Latino national-origin group:	*	*	*		
Mexican origin	1.32 (.35)*	.58 (.19)*	1.32 (.29)*		
Puerto Rican	1.31 (.38)*	.75 (.21)*	1.05 (.31)*		
Worked in a group to solve a local problem	.35 (.08)*	.25 (.07)*	.31 (.07)*	.35 (.07)*	.34 (.08)*
Homeowner status					
Employment status					-.63 (.27)
-2 Log likelihood	707.70	1505.92	1032.40	1188.29	839.04
Goodness of fit	2564.95	2562.08	2495.42	2459.47	2514.21
Chi-square	98.39*	107.23*	89.12*	108.05*	87.78*
% of cases correctly classified	96.3%	90.4%	94.2%	93.0%	95.6%

1 The standard error term is reported in parenthesis.
2 * represents a significant coefficient at or below the .05 level for this variable.
3 If the column is blank, then the variable did not meet the criteria for inclusion in the equation.

measures had significant coefficients, and over 90 percent of the cases were correctly classified for each of the dependent variables. Our examination of the contributors to participatory modes included individual resource-related variables and important skills and involvement. In the case of Latinos, the role of education, particularly, and other sociodemographic variables do influence rates of political participation. At the same time, accumulated job skills and experiences have a direct and positive transference to modes of political participation. The implications of these results will be discussed in the conclusion section.

Latino Political Participation: Patterns and Future Directions

Our initial query regarding the political participation of Latinos was twofold. The first was to develop a profile of the levels of participation for the three major Latino subgroups (i.e., Mexican, Puerto Rican, and Cuban) in several arenas of political activity. The second query was to explain the contributing factors that affect their participation rates. The extant literature on Latinos has indicated lower rates of participation relative to other groups in American politics. In an earlier version of an article on Mexican-American political participation (Garcia and Arce 1988), the low rates of electoral participation were reconfirmed. At the same time, Mexican Americans seemed to hold participatory orientations while seeing the American political system as complex and removed. As a result there is certain irony that lower socioeconomic status among Mexican Americans serves to limit rates of participation while there is some internalization of the values about the importance of voting and involvement. The irony lies in the void between the orientation and the political behavior.

This article uses the Latino National Political Survey which expands the scope of political participation to include Puerto Rican and Cubans. In addition, our approach to political participation examines the important resources for individuals that create the interest, motivation, and opportunities for political involvement. At the same time, the combination of individual resources and mobilization work to influence rates and modes of political participation. That is, persons with critical resources are much more likely to be contacted by leaders/activists and organizations to engage in particular political activities. Their social networks and status equips them with skills, information, and exposure to political issues and policies.

The incorporation of this perspective on participation serves as our framework to examine the state of participation for Latinos in the U.S. We identified three arenas of participation which included electoral, governmental, and Latino-specific political activities. The breadth of the LNPS allowed us to analyze self-reported political behaviors. The results of our analysis produced a profile of Latinos that still have relatively lower rates of participation than the majority population in all modes of participation. At the same time, the variation of participation is not always as extreme for particular activities such as signing petitions or attending public meetings.

Electorally, a significant proportion of eligible Latinos have been registered at some time, yet there was a drop-off with current registration levels and votes in the 1988 and 1986 elections. While the percentage of Cuban voters is higher than for Mexican origin and Puerto Ricans, the strength of voting is diluted by a significant segment that is foreign-born and non-citizen. This element is slightly more pronounced for the Mexican-origin community. Despite U.S. citizenship for Puerto Ricans, their electoral rates are comparable to the Mexican-origin respondents. This is in direct contrast with voter registration and turnout levels among Puerto Ricans in Puerto Rico.

For governmental participation, there was some intergroup variation as both Mexican origin and Puerto Ricans had greater levels of participation than Cubans when it comes to attending public meetings and signing petitions, and, to a lesser extent, volunteering on a campaign. Overall, the level of governmental participation is not appreciably high for Latinos. Fortunately, the LNPS included a battery of items that asked Latinos about their involvement with specific Latino political activities. In these areas (which paralleled the general electoral and governmental items), the levels of Latino participation were even lower than for the general activities. There were some modest intergroup variations as more Cubans had contacted a public official, while more Mexican origin and Puerto Ricans had worked to persuade voters and volunteered than their Cuban counterparts.

As we moved from establishing a profile of Latino rates of political participation to possible explanatory factors, our analysis incorporated the idea of critical job skills. There are several job-related experiences that can be transferred to enhance participation levels by expanding individual resources, motivations, and opportunities. The extent of job skills acquired by Latinos is notable with intergroup variation. A greater percentage of Cuban respondents have written job-related letters. For the rest of job-related activities, all three groups are similar.

Our multivariate analysis also incorporated both education and household income levels as the expected critical factors affecting participation, in addition to several other sociodemographic variables (i.e., gender, age, employment status, nativity, and homeowner status). The inclusion of nativity was expected to introduce the potential impact of foreign-born status. We also included the job-skills summary index and whether the respondent had worked with a group on a local problem. Tables 6 through 8 deal with the analysis of these independent variables on a number of electoral, governmental, and Latino-directed political activities. Our focus was self-reported political behaviors rather than participatory orientations.

Our analysis reinforced previous participation research showing that gains in educational attainment significantly impact greater rates of political participation. This finding was consistent for every logistic regression equation. At the same time, household income proved to be an important factor for most of the political activities. In addition to the expected impact of education and income, age and nativity (older and U.S. born) proved to increase the probability of higher Latino participation rates. The national-origin subgroup variation was reflected in the electoral arena as Puerto Ricans, enjoying U.S. citizenship, increased the probability that they were registered and voting more than Cubans and Mexican origin. Being Puerto Rican or Mexican origin does increase the participation rates for many Latino-specific political activities. These group members are more likely to work for a Latino candidate, sign a petition on a Latino issue, and persuade voters to vote for a Latino than their Cuban counterparts.

As education proved to be a consistently positive influence on participation levels, so did the acquisition of relevant job skills. That is, for every logistic equation, the job-skills index was statistically significant. The rationale of increased information, raised interests, and transferable skills to the political arena that are associated with these variables appears to be confirmed through this analysis. Similarly, Latinos who have worked in a group setting to deal with some local problem were more likely to have participated in political activities. Again, the motivation and, more than likely, social networks among these individuals serve to seize opportunities for resolving salient problems.

With the examination of political participation among Latinos, what are the implications for the near future? The growth rate among Latinos continues to exceed the national rate and the largest minority "standing" is expected in ten to fifteen years. Perhaps more importantly, Latino demographics regarding age structure and citizenship status will be critical aspects for political participation. In the case of the former, there will be a greater percentage of Latinos over twenty-one and their median age is approaching thirty. The association of age with political participation should result in higher participation rates. Recent data from the Immigration and Naturalization Service indicates much higher naturalization rates among all Latino subgroups. Thus the political base for Latinos will increase due to these demographic patterns.

At the same time, the improvement of human capital (i.e., education, income, and occupational status) is problematic. Latinos continue to lag in these three areas with a slower rate of progress to close the gap. As our analysis indicated, gains in educational attainment are critical to raise the probability of greater Latino political participation. The benefits of education, politically, lie with information, interest, understanding, and self-confidence to engage in political activities. In addition, social networks provide and expose individuals to political information, leaders, and organizations. Gains in socioeconomic status, particularly in occupation, enable Latinos to acquire and develop job skills that enhance communication, organizing, and decision-making. These transferable skills will serve Latinos well in various political arenas.

We are identifying developments among activist/participants rather than necessarily expanding significantly the growth of the Latino leadership. An accompanying factor for the future of Latino political participation is that of mobilization activities. The actions and strategies of leaders and organizations are crucial for the direction and effectiveness of active Latinos. Mobilization of Latinos will increase levels of voting and campaign involvement and will inspire actions for social and political change. Latino leaders and organizations can subsidize the costs of political participation by providing information, analysis, voter registration forms, naturalization assistance, etc. to facilitate individual involvement. The use of social networks enables leaders and organizations to tap friendships, social obligations, and belief systems among Latinos. At the same time mobilizers focus their efforts on Latinos with the resources to participate.

Thus it is the combination of the willingness of Latinos who have the resource accumulation and transferable political skills and the ability of leadership to mobilize that will define the levels of political participation for Latinos. One final piece of the equation lies with external events and political climate. The rise of nativism, affirmative action backlash, and social welfare program cutbacks/elimination can serve as catalysts for the Latino communities to attenuate their participation efforts and directions.

APPENDIX A

Sociodemographic Characteristics of the
Latino National Political Survey

Variables	Mexican origin	Puerto Rican	Cuban
Gender			
% Female	56.7	63.5	56.8
Age (mean = 41.3)			
17–24	389 (23.9%)	107 (18.2%)	56 (8.2%)
25–34	509 (31.3%)	166 (28.2%)	107 (15.7%)
35–50	427 (26.2%)	167 (28.4%)	175 (25.7%)
50+	303 (18.6%)	149 (25.3%)	344 (50.4%)
Race			
White	747 (51.1%)	327 (58.2%)	618 (92.0%)
Black	4 (.3%)	23 (4.1%)	22 (3.3%)
Spanish origin	711 (48.6%)	212 (37.7%)	32 (4.8%)
Education			
Mean years	9.04	10.04	10.56
Range of years	0–17	0–17	0–17
Religion			
Catholic	1195 (77.4%)	384 (65.2%)	527 (77.7%)
Protestant	183 (11.9%)	131 (22.2%)	93 (13.7%)
Other	165 (10.7%)	74 (12.6%)	58 (8.6%)
Work status			
Employed	1004 (65.1%)	294 (50.1%)	414 (61.0%)
Unemployed	169 (11.0%)	71 (12.1%)	48 (7.1%)
Not in work force	370 (24.0%)	222 (37.8%)	217 (32.0%)
Household income			
0–$10,000	319 (22.2%)	214 (39.4%)	140 (22.8%)
$10,000–20,000	244 (17.0%)	93 (17.1%)	107 (22.8%)
$20,000–34,999	396 (27.6%)	126 (23.2%)	166 (27.0%)
> $35,000	475 (33.1%)	110 (20.3%)	201 (32.7%)

Notes

1. For the same set of political activities used in the LNPS, the Calvo and Rosenstone article on Hispanic participation identifies Hispanic rates for 1984.

2. The occupational variable in the LNPS uses the census listing of occupational codes. In many cases, these specific occupations are recoded into white collar, clerical, and other types of categories. Given the relatively narrow range of occupation and N's in each type, the decision was to use employment status as the exploratory vehicle for labor market involvement.

3. With the use of logistic regression, the dependent and independent variables need to be dichotomous and/or have a range between 0 and 1. In the case of education and income, the original categories were recoded to have values be-

tween 0 and 1. For example, education was recoded: 0 years = 0; 1–8 years = .25; 9–11 years = .50; 12 years = .75; 13 years or more = 1.

References

Boswell, Thomas, and J. Curtis. 1984. *The Cuban American Experience: Culture, Images and Perspectives*. Totoma, N.J.: Rowman and Allahend.

Bennett, Linda, and Stephen Bennett. 1989. "Enduring Gender Differences in Political Interest: The Impact of Socialization and Political Dispositions." *American Political Quarterly* 17: 102–22.

Brady, Henry, Sidney Verba, and Kay Schlozman. 1995. "Beyond SES: A Resource Model of Political Participation." *American Political Science Review* 89 (June): 271–94.

Calvo, Maria Antonia, and Steve Rosenstone. 1989. *Hispanic Political Participation*. San Antonio: Southwest Voter Research Institute.

Conway, Margaret. 1991. *Political Participation in the United States*. 2nd ed. Washington, D.C.: Congressional Quarterly Press.

de la Garza, Rodolfo, Martha Menchaca, and Louis DeSipio. 1994. *Barrio Ballots: Latino Politics in the 1990 Elections*. Boulder, Colo.: Westview Press.

de la Garza, Rodolfo, L. DeSipio, F. C. Garcia, J. A. Garcia, and A. Falcon. 1992. *Latino Voices: Mexican, Puerto Rican, and Cuban Perspectives on American Politics*. Boulder, Colo.: Westview Press.

de la Garza, Rodolfo, and Louis DeSipio. 1992. *From Rhetoric to Reality: Latino Politics in the 1988 Elections*. Boulder, Colo.: Westview Press.

Falcon, Angelo. 1988. "Black and Latino Politics in New York City: Race and Ethnicity in a Changing Urban Context." In *Latinos and the Political System*, ed. F. Chris Garcia. 2nd ed. Notre Dame, Ind.: University of Notre Dame Press.

Falcon, Angelo. 1984. "A History of Puerto Rican Politics in New York City, 1860–1945." In *Puerto Rican Politics in Urban America*, ed. James Jennings and Monte Rivera. Westport, Conn.: Praeger.

Garcia, F. Chris. 1991. "The Effects of Partisanship on Electoral Behavior: An Analysis and Comparison of Latino and Anglo Voting in the 1988 Presidential Election." Paper presented at the annual meeting of the American Political Science Association, Chicago.

Garcia, John A. 1981. "Political Integration of Mexican Immigrants: Explorations into the Naturalization Process." *International Migration Review* 15 (Winter): 608–26.

Garcia, John A., and Carlos Arce. 1988. "Political Orientations and Behaviors: Trying to Make Sense Out of Attitudes and Participation." In *Latinos and the Political System*, ed. F. Chris Garcia. 2nd ed. Notre Dame, Ind.: University of Notre Dame Press.

Garcia, John A., and R. de la Garza. 1985. "Mobilizing the Mexican Immigrant:

The Role of Mexican American Organizations." *Western Political Quarterly* 38: 551–64.

Garcia, John A., F. C. Garcia, A. Falcon, and R. de la Garza. 1991. "Ethnicity and National Origin Status: Patterns of Identity among Latinos in the U.S." Paper presented at the annual meeting of the American Political Science Association, Washington, D.C.

Grofman, Bernard, and Chandler Davidson (eds.). 1992. *Controversies in Minority Voting: The Voting Rights in Perspective.* Washington, D.C.: Brookings Institution.

Hero, Rodney. 1991. *Latinos and the U.S. Political System.* Philadelphia: Temple University Press.

Huckfeldt, Robert. 1979. "Political Participation and the Neighborhood Context." *American Journal of Political Science* 23 (June): 579–92.

Huckfeldt, Robert, and John Sprague. 1987. "Networks in Context: The Social Flow of Political Information." *American Political Science Review* 81 (December): 1198–1216.

Huckfeldt, Robert, and John Sprague. 1992. "Political Parties and Electoral Mobilization: Political Structure, Social Structure, and Party Canvasses." *American Political Science Review* 86 (March): 70–86.

Jennings, James. 1994. *Blacks, Puerto Ricans and Asians in Urban America: Status and Prospects for Politics and Activism.* Westport, Conn.: Praeger.

Jennings, James. 1988. "Future Directions for Puerto Rican Politics in the U.S. and Puerto Rico." In *Latinos and the Political System,* ed. F. Chris Garcia. 2nd ed. Notre Dame, Ind.: University of Notre Dame Press.

Jennings, James. 1977. *Puerto Rican Politics in New York City.* Washington D.C.: University Press of America.

Leighley, Janet. 1990. "Social Interaction and Contextual Influences on Political Participation." *American Politics Quarterly* 18 (October): 458–75.

McClain, Paula, and John A. Garcia. 1993. "Expanding Disciplinary Boundaries: Black, Latino and Racial Minority Group Politics in Political Science." In *Political Science: The State of the Discipline II,* ed. A. Finifter. Washington, D.C.: American Political Science Association.

McManus, Susan, and C. Cassel. 1984. "Mexican Americans in City Politics: Participation, Representation and Policy Preferences." *Urban Interest* 4: 57–69.

Milbrath, Lester, and M. L. Goel. 1977. *Political Participation.* 2nd ed. Chicago: Rand McNally.

Miller, Arthur, Patricia Gurin, Gerald Gurin, and Okasana Malanchuk. 1981. "Group Consciousness and Political Participation." *American Journal of Political Science* 25 (August): 494–511.

Moreno, Dario, and Christopher Warren. 1992. "The Conservative Enclave: Cubans in Florida." In *From Rhetoric to Reality: Latino Politics in the 1988 Elections,* ed. R. de la Garza and Louis DeSipio. Boulder, Colo.: Westview Press.

Pachon, Harry, and Louis DeSipio. 1994. *New Americans by Choice: Political Perspectives of Latino Immigrants.* Boulder, Colo.: Westview Press.

Portes, Alejandro. 1984. "The Rise of Ethnicity: Determinants of Ethnic Perceptions among Cuban Exiles in Miami." *American Sociological Review* 49: 383–97.

Portes, Alejandro, and R. Mozo. 1985. "The Political Adaptation Process of Cubans and Other Ethnic Minorities in the United States: A Preliminary Analysis." *International Migration Review* 19: 35–63.

Regalado, J., and G. Martinez. 1991. "Reapportionment and Coalition Building: A Case of Informal Barriers to Latino Empowerment in Los Angeles County." In *Latinos and Political Coalition for the 1990's,* ed. R. Villareal and N. Hernandez. New York: Greenwood Press.

Rodriguez, Clara. 1989. *Puerto Ricans Born in the USA.* Boston: Unwin-Hyman.

Rosenstone, Steve, and John Hansen. 1993. *Mobilization, Participation, and Democracy in America.* New York: Macmillan.

Scholzman, Kay, and Sidney Verba. 1979. *Insult to Injury: Unemployment, Class, and Political Response.* Cambridge, Mass.: Harvard University Press.

Uhlaner, Carole Jean. 1991. "Political Participation and Discrimination: A Comparative Analysis of Asians, Blacks and Latinos." In *Political Participation and American Democracy,* ed. William Crotty. New York: Greenwood Press.

Uhlaner, Carole Jean, Bruce Cain, and Roderick Kiewet. 1989. "Political Participation of Ethnic Minorities in the 1980's." *Political Behavior* 11 (September): 195–221.

Verba, Sidney, and Norman Nie. 1972. *Participation in America: Political Democracy and Social Equality.* New York: Harper and Row.

Verba, Sidney, Kay Schlozman, and Henry Brady. 1993. "Citizen Activity: Who Participates? What Do They Say?" *American Political Science Review* 87: 303–18.

Villareal, Robert, and Norma Hernandez (eds.). 1991. *Latinos and Political Coalitions.* New York: Greenwood Press.

Welch, Susan, and Lee Sigelman. 1993 "The Politics of Hispanic Americans: Insights from National Surveys, 1980–1988." *Social Science Quarterly* 74:76–94.

Wolfinger, Raymond, and Steve Rosenstone. 1980. *Who Votes?* New Haven, Conn.: Yale University Press.

3. Save the Baby, Change the Bathwater, and Scrub the Tub: Latino Electoral Participation after Twenty Years of Voting Rights Act Coverage

Rodolfo O. de la Garza and Louis DeSipio

THE RECENT EXTENSION OF THE Voting Rights Act (VRA) until 2007 offers Congress and voting rights activists the opportunity to stop and reflect on their accomplishments since 1965 (*Public Law 102–344*). The Act unquestionably changed the construction of American politics at a profound level. The VRA has abolished formal structures of intimidation and exclusion of blacks in the South so that once-excluded Southern blacks are now integral parts of Democratic coalitions throughout the region.

The effect has been dramatic but less profound on Mexican Americans and other Latinos.[1] Congress debated Mexican-American exclusion less actively, but VRA-induced changes—the elimination of anti-Mexican voter dilution efforts, the provision of bilingual election materials, and the creation of many districts that routinely elect Mexican Americans and other Latinos to office—are integral to increased Latino electoral empowerment.

Despite the elimination of formal barriers and the creation of new electoral opportunities, Latinos and African Americans continue to participate in electoral politics at levels significantly below those of the white population. Congress did not explicitly address this issue in 1965 or in any of the subsequent extensions of the bill.

Published originally in 71 *Texas Law Review* 1479 (1993). Copyright 1993 by the Texas Law Review Association. Reprinted by permission.

In this paper, we examine the history of the VRA and Latino communities. As we will suggest, little debate went into the needs of Mexican Americans or other Latinos when Congress extended the provisions of the Act to them. Had Congress engaged in this debate, it might have developed voter empowerment strategies to meet the unique needs of this population.

In the second section, we discuss the effect of the Act on Latinos in three key areas: reducing structural barriers and intimidation, increasing co-ethnic elected officials, and increasing electoral turnout. In the third section, we examine Latino electoral participation in greater depth. In addition to presenting data on noncitizenship and Latino electoral turnout, we look at four sets of characteristics related to voting and VRA protections—sociodemographic characteristics of the population, perceptions of discrimination, use of voting protections offered by VRA, and non-electoral political and community activity. We then discuss several possible explanations for continuing low levels of registration and voting. Finally, in the fifth section we suggest several possible strategies to increase electoral involvement. Overall, we seek to initiate the debate over what is needed to raise Latino participation rates, a debate that Congress did not undertake in 1975, 1982, or 1992.

I. Congress, the Courts, and the Construction of the VRA

The original impetus for the VRA was the exclusion of the African-American community from voting in the South. The exclusion of Latinos and other language minorities was not debated either in 1965 or 1970. Instead, the Act and its first extension targeted practices that limited political participation among Southern blacks. Because our focus is the Latino community, we do not discuss the 1965 Act (de la Garza and DeSipio 1990).

The extension of the Act in 1970 began a progressive liberalization of the types of electoral participation covered by the VRA (*Public Law 91–285*). However, the extension failed to establish criteria for the inclusion of language minorities. The 1970 Act extended the threshold for coverage to jurisdictions using a literacy test and in which less than 50 percent of the voting-age residents were registered on November 1, 1968 or voted in the 1968 presidential election. With these changes, the Act for the first time extended to four counties with significant Latino populations (Apache County, Arizona; Imperial County, California; Kings and New York Counties, New York).

Although the original provisions of the VRA were amended and its scope and coverage broadened, the bill was crafted without input from the Mexican-American and Puerto Rican communities. No Latino testified before Congressional committees in either 1965 or 1969–1970, and the participants in the Congressional debates voiced no concern about low Mexican-American or Latino voting rates.

Congress and the Extension of the VRA to Language Minorities

This inattention to Latino electoral participation changed with the debate over the extension of the Voting Rights Act in 1975 (*Public Law 94–73*). In addition to extending the VRA and its jurisdictional coverage for seven years, the 1975 Amendments extended the basic protections of the Act to specific language minorities.[2] Preclearance and federal observer protections were extended under Title 2 of the Act to any jurisdiction in which 1) the Census Bureau determined that more than 5 percent of the voting-age citizens were of a single language minority; 2) election materials had been prepared only in English in the 1972 presidential election; *and* 3) less than 50 percent of the voting-age citizens had registered for or voted in the 1972 presidential elections. Bilingual election materials were mandated under Title 3 in jurisdictions where the Census Bureau determined that a single language minority constituted more than 5 percent of the voting-age population and the literacy rate among the language minority was higher than the national English illiteracy rate.[3]

Other provisions of the 1975 Amendments made permanent the previously temporary ban on the use of literacy tests in voter registration. Congress also empowered individuals to bring suit to impose preclearance requirements on a jurisdiction, a role previously reserved solely for the Justice Department.

Supported by Mexican-American elected officials, leaders of national and local Mexican-American organizations and one national Puerto Rican organization testified in favor of the 1975 extension of the Act to language minorities (U.S. House of Representatives 1975; U.S. Senate 1975). They also were supported by Mexican Americans who had unsuccessfully sought elective office and contended that their failure to be elected was the result of electoral discrimination. Two patterns emerge from their testimony. First, the situation described is similar to the experience of blacks prior to 1965. Second, the most serious violations of Mexican-American voting rights occurred in Texas.

Vilma Martínez, president and general counsel of the Mexican American Legal Defense and Education Fund (MALDEF), for example, began her testimony with a description of the "pattern of abuse in Uvalde County," Texas. Uvalde County, she noted, "is strikingly reminiscent of the Deep South in the early 1960s" (U.S. Senate 1975, 756–770). Among the abuses she reported were the refusal to place registered Mexican-American voters on voting lists, election judges' deliberate invalidation of ballots cast by minority voters, the refusal to name minority group members as deputy registrars, and election judges' refusal of aid to minority voters illiterate in English.

After providing background in the techniques of de facto and de jure voter exclusion, Martínez also noted the techniques used to exclude or dilute Mexican-American electoral participation. In Texas and in the other states of the Southwest, she identified educational segregation, at-large elections, anti-minority gerrymanders, and stringent third-party ballot access requirements as tools for excluding minorities from the political process.

Other testimony focused also on the exclusion of the Mexican-American population from the political process. For example, Congressman Edward Roybal, a Democrat from California, testified that rural Mexican Americans in California faced obstacles, including intimidation, in trying to register to vote (U.S. Senate 1975, 255–268). Leonel Castillo, Controller of the City of Houston, recounted a pattern of Texas laws designed to exclude Mexican-American voters, including a poll tax, annual registration (nine to eleven months before the next general election), and English-language registration and reregistration notifications (U.S. Senate 1975, 738–756).

These patterns are illustrative of the testimony offered by Mexican-American witnesses. The witnesses focused on combating state and local government efforts to exclude and intimidate Mexican-American voters. The need for bilingual voting materials and the problem of at-large elections and malapportionment were mentioned but were not the focus of testimony. Qualitative judgments were offered with minimal quantitative evidence.

From the committees' perspectives, perhaps, no more than generalizations were required. Committee members asked these witnesses little about the specifics of the 1975 Amendments to the Act. The eventual success or failure of the effort to extend the Act to language minorities does not appear from the testimony to have depended on evidence of unique problems faced by Mexican Americans or other Latinos based on their status as a language minority. Instead, general overt discrimination, particularly in Texas, seems to have earned Latinos nationwide the special protection extended to blacks ten years before (Thernstrom 1987, chapter 3).

Congress consciously excluded "language minorities" other than
the Latinos, Asian Americans, Alaskan natives, and Native Americans
from the protections of the Act. Two amendments to the House bill in
the House by Biaggi and Solarz, both New York Democrats, attempted
to expand the definition of "minority group" to include all persons whose
principal language was other than English. Both amendments were defeated by large margins. Another effort to delete all of Title 2 was defeated 305 to 104. Congress consciously included Texas Mexican Americans under Title 2. Henry B. González, a Texas Democrat, proposed an
amendment to limit application of Title 2 to states *currently* maintaining tests or devices. In a close vote, the Senate rejected this amendment,
which would have exempted Texas from coverage. The Senate also tabled
an amendment proposed by Senator Peter Domenici, a Republican from
New Mexico, to establish a higher threshold (25 percent) for the percentage of language minorities in the jurisdiction.

The 1975 Amendments to the VRA passed by large margins in
both houses of Congress. In the Senate, the bill passed seventy-seven to
twelve. Of the twelve votes against, only one came from a Senator—John
Tower of Texas—from one of the states with jurisdictions newly covered
by Title 2. The House vote was a similarly lopsided 341 to 70. As a percentage, more of these opposition votes came from Representatives of
the states newly covered by Title 2 than from Representatives from the
South. Twenty-five of the seventy votes in opposition came from the
seven states with Latino populations including ten of forty-one of those
voting from California and six of twenty from Texas.

1982 Extension

Congress again extended and amended the VRA in 1982 (*Public Law
97–205*). The 1982 Amendments extended until 1992 the requirement
for bilingual election materials and extended preclearance provisions for
twenty-five years. A jurisdiction could bail out of coverage under the Act
by proving to a three-judge court in the D. C. Circuit that it had had a
clean voting record for ten years. Finally, the 1982 Amendments reestab-
lished a "results" test for discrimination under the Act, overruling the
Supreme Court's ruling in *City of Mobile v. Bolden* (1980). In *Mobile,*
the court ruled that an intent to discriminate must be documented to
prove a violation of the Act. With the passage of the 1982 extensions,
Congress liberalized this standard, requiring only documentation of discriminatory effect.

Much of the debate over the 1982 extension focused on whether discriminatory intent or effect should be required to establish a violation. Congress heard testimony from a larger number of witnesses than in any of the previous congressional visits to this topic. The House of Representatives held eighteen days of hearings and heard from 156 witnesses (compared to thirteen days of hearings and 48 witnesses in 1975) (U.S. House of Representatives 1981). Again, the Latino witnesses represented a wide range of organizations and elective offices. Although views varied, two themes recurred. The first was a continuation of the discussion from 1975 regarding overt discrimination against Latinos seeking to register and vote. Again, many of these examples came from Texas (U.S. House of Representatives 1981, 102–129). The second major theme raised by Latino witnesses concerned the deleterious effect of malapportionment and at-large districting on the election of Mexican Americans and other Latinos to public office (U.S. House of Representatives 1981, 929–1009). While many witnesses acknowledged that bilingual election materials are a tool to empowerment, defending their continued need was not the focus of testimony.

Again, Congress strongly endorsed the extension of the Act. This high degree of support also was evident among the congressional delegations from the seven states with significant Latino populations (those with jurisdictions covered by Title 2). The Senate passed the extension eighty-five to eight, with only one Senator—S. I. Hayakawa of California—from the seven states among those voting against it. The House passed the extension by a vote of 389 to 24. Among the no votes, only five were from those seven states.

1992 Extension

The effort to extend and expand the Voting Rights Act in 1992 faced greater opposition within Congress than it had in 1982 (Dumas 1992). The proposed legislation extended the bilingual voting assistance for fifteen years (until 2007) and extended bilingual voting assistance to localities with populations of at least 10,000 of any one of the covered language minorities. This added several major cities, including Los Angeles, San Francisco, and Philadelphia, to the sixty-eight counties that provided bilingual voting materials under the pre-existing threshold of 5 percent of the population using one of the languages covered by the Act.

Despite extensive efforts to amend the bill to make it unpassable, its advocates prevailed. The vote in the House, 237 to 125, was much closer than in 1982. Among those who opposed the bill, ninety-seven were Republican, many of whom helped generate the failed amendments.

The amendments included reducing the fifteen-year extension to five years, forcing the federal government to pay the costs of bilingual voting materials, and eliminating the bilingual provisions altogether. One of the leaders of these efforts at amendment was Southern California Republican Dana Rohrbacher, who was joined by several other Southern California Republicans. The sole Republican Hispanic in Congress, Ileana Ros-Lehtinen, opposed all of the amendments and supported passage of the final bill. Interestingly, considering his opposition to the Voting Rights Act Amendments of 1975, Congressman Henry B. González opposed the amendments and voted in favor of the 1992 extension.

The Courts and Minority Voting Rights

Congressional efforts to design voting rights policy have not been the only arena for debate and change. Since the passage of the original Act in 1965, the federal courts have been active in interpreting Congressional intent and setting the terms of the popular debate. The two major areas of court involvement in the VRA are review of Justice Department activities under the preclearance provisions of Section 5 for jurisdictions directly covered by the Act and Section 2 claims that a jurisdictional procedure or practice (after the 1982 amendments) results in racial discrimination. The second area for court involvement applies to all jurisdictions nationwide. Because its scope is broader and individuals can directly litigate, more case law had developed on Section 2 issues. As will be suggested below, these two issues merged in the late 1980s.

Only the District Court for the District of Columbia and the Supreme Court have jurisdiction over Section 5 claims. This jurisdictional limitation has been a bone of contention among members of Congress from states covered by the Act. However, in the first three extension debates, Congress has refused to divest control to the district courts for the states requiring preclearance.

Appeals of Justice Department rejections of electoral law changes numbered 2,167 between 1965 and 1988. Approximately half of these Justice Department actions (1,088) were rejections of annexations that were perceived to dilute minority votes. Another 472 involved methods of election. Only 248 involved rejections of redistricting efforts (Parker 1989, 59).

Critics of the Act contend that this process of preclearance grants excessive discretionary authority to the Justice Department, exacts too high a cost on the jurisdictions and, perhaps most disturbingly, undermines local control over issues that have minimal impact on minority voter participation (Grofman 1985; Thernstrom 1987, chapters 7 and 8). We recognize that the threat of expensive litigation undoubtedly has been used to induce jurisdictions to act as they otherwise would not. Nonetheless, the small number of actual Justice Department rejections of voting law changes suggests that Section 5 has not created undue burdens. The 2,167 rejections amount to less than 100 each year.

In the 1970s and early 1980s, the courts narrowed their interpretation of the discriminatory effect under Section 5. In *City of Lockhart v. United States,* the Supreme Court held that a plan did not have a discriminatory effect unless, compared with the previous plan, it diminished the voting strength of minority voters. New Justice Department regulations adopted in 1987 tried to bring Section 5 standards for voting-law changes more into line with the results test for Section 2 litigation.

Although the courts have had a relatively minor role in the elaboration of Section 5, their role has been central to the process of developing Section 2 of the Act. Section 2 prohibits the use of any device that serves to dilute the minority vote. Initially, the definition of these devices was limited to literacy tests. The focus of much of the litigation arising out of Section 2, however, is now on types of elections and districting procedures (Thernstrom 1987, chapters 3, 7, and 8).

Through the late 1960s and 1970s, the Supreme Court looked to the *effect* of electoral practices. However, in *City of Mobile v. Bolden* (1980) and later in *Rogers v. Lodge* (1982), the Court held that minority vote dilution had to be the *intent* of the jurisdiction for a violation of Section 2 to exist. The *City of Mobile* ruling made challenges to at-large districting efforts more difficult. Where before the Court had accepted circumstantial evidence of discrimination such as the failure to elect minorities, discriminatory electoral rules, or discrimination in employment or services, the standard established in *City of Mobile* required plaintiffs to offer proof of discriminatory intent. Perhaps anticipating Congress' effort to return statutorily to the earlier de facto standard, the ruling in *Rogers* allowed the intent standard to be satisfied, in the absence of direct evidence, by some of the circumstantial evidence that previously had been accepted by the courts.

After the passage of the 1982 amendments and the return to the effect standard, the Supreme Court established a new, somewhat easier standard to prove violation under Section 2. In *Thornburg v. Gingles,* the Court established a three-part test for evaluating the legality of election systems. At-large election systems were illegal if: (1) the minority population was sufficiently compact to create a single-member district with a majority of the minority group; (2) minority voters were politically cohesive and had a history of voting for the same candidate; and (3) the candidates preferred by the minority community were usually defeated by cohesive voting in the white community. Under this standard, where bloc voting has occurred, localities must establish single-member districts (Parker 1989, 55–60).

This new "results" standard has widened the number and location of jurisdictions subject to suit under Section 2 of the Act. It also has added pressure to jurisdictions to account for group voting patterns in the districting process after the 1990 Census. Despite the more liberal standard established in *Gingles,* however, minority political empowerment is far from assured simply through the drawing of single member districts. Mexican Americans in Watsonville, California, for example, brought suit to eliminate multimember districts (*Gomez v. City of Watsonville* 1988). Latinos constituted almost 50 percent of the city's population according to the 1980 Census, yet had been able to elect only one of the six at-large city council members (and that election of a Latino came only after the suit had been initiated). Basing its holding on *Gingles,* the court rejected an at-large city council voting scheme in favor of single-member districts. Despite this victory, the first election after the establishment of single-member districts resulted in the election of only one Latino council member (though not the incumbent).

Conclusion: Congress, the Courts, and Voting Rights

Over the past twenty-seven years, Congress has considered the VRA five times. Each of these considerations has expanded the original scope of the legislation to encompass more protections for minorities. Congress began by providing a relatively narrow protection from overt forms of discrimination, such as literacy tests, against African Americans in the South, and has expanded the VRA to recognize ever-wider ranges of voting discrimination, including those affecting Latino populations. Among the most important provisions for the purposes of this paper are the extension of preclearance to portions of the Southwest, South Florida, and New York City, the establishment of bilingual election materials to assure voting access to citizens with limited proficiency in English, the development of the "results" test for violations of Section 2, and the empowerment of individuals as well as the Justice Department to bring suit to effect electoral changes.

While each of these changes was debated in Congress, a reading of the testimony and debates does not suggest that these changes, though fundamental to minority electoral empowerment, were considered or debated anywhere as thoughtfully or deeply as the original enactment of the VRA in 1965. Instead, a perception that overt discrimination against Mexican Americans, and by extension all Latinos, was comparable to that experienced by blacks in the South seemed to underlie the debate. Testimony presented suggests that at least in the case of Texas this perception was grounded in reality. The language use and illiteracy thresholds for coverage under the Act represent more of a means to a desired end—inclusion of all significantly Latino areas—than well-considered tools in and of themselves. The reasons behind the seemingly widespread acceptance of this end by Congress, if the final vote on the bill is any judge, are harder to evaluate.

At some level, though, the Amendments to the VRA must be understood in terms of Congress's righting a historical wrong and attempting to equalize levels of political participation among groups in society during a period of progressive social change. Unfortunately, the absence of a conscious goal, other than the relatively general elimination of impediments to electoral participation, has created a debate over means. In the remainder of this paper we discuss some of the current impediments faced by the Latino community in the electoral process and some tentative strategies to achieve those ends. These strategies attempt to further the steady expansion of electoral empowerment mandated by Congress through the extensions to the VRA.

II. The Voting Rights Act and Latino Electoral Participation

The extension of the VRA to language minorities in 1975 changed the nature of the debate over voting and non-voting in the Mexican-American and the larger Latino communities. Prior to the Act many states and localities erected statutory barriers to Mexican-American voter participation. The 1975 extension of the Act undermined many of these structural barriers and introduced the federal courts as an arena for debate on other impediments to full electoral participation. Further, the law and the courts established many districts that were able to elect Latinos to office.

Despite these accomplishments, the Act has not overcome the economic and citizenship barriers that limit Latino electoral participation. As we will describe, Mexican Americans were electorally active prior to 1975. Although data are scarce, the few studies from before 1975 suggest that Mexican Americans, or at least those in the several urban areas studied, participated at rates equal to or higher than today. In this section, then, we examine three measures for evaluating the VRA's utility to the Latino community: 1) eliminating structural barriers and intimidation; 2) increasing the numbers of "safe" districts that can elect Latinos to office; and 3) increasing levels of Latino electoral participation.

Structural Barriers and Intimidation

In the testimony before Congress in both 1975 and 1982, Latino leaders offered many examples of the deliberate exclusion of Mexican Americans from the vote. Techniques reminiscent of the pre-VRA South spiced the testimony. Overt intimidation, capricious changes in voting rules, English language registration and voting requirements, lengthy residential requirements, and the manipulation of the Mexican-American vote by non–Mexican-American political leaders were discussed as tools used to exclude Mexican Americans. As we have indicated, these experiences disproportionately came from Texas, but they were representative of the shared experiences of Mexican Americans in most of the Southwest.

The history of the manipulated vote is long and well documented (Weeks 1930; Anders 1979). Mexican Americans in Texas's Rio Grande Valley, for example, provided the foundation of the conservative Wells machine in the 1900s and 1910s and, thereafter continued to be controlled by various bosses into the 1940s. The vote of Texas's urban Mexican Americans, mostly concentrated in San Antonio, also was not free. The combination of these rural and urban machines offered Lyndon Johnson his narrow victory in the 1948 Senate race (Caro 1990). The Mexican-American vote in Northern New Mexico also was machine controlled. While these machines had largely disappeared before the extension of the VRA to Latinos, their legacy was a perception among many—both within and outside the Latino community—of a manipulated vote.

When the Mexican-American vote was unmanipulated, it was often subject to intimidation. The economically dependent position of many Mexican Americans made economic threats very powerful. Explicit threats often were not necessary. Registration requirements excluded many migrant laborers from participation. Literacy tests created the opportunity to exclude those to whom the election official chose to apply the rules. The poll tax in Texas excluded many poor people. English-language ballots excluded still more.

Once Mexican Americans were able to register and vote, districting strategies often prevented them from electing candidates of their choice. Racial gerrymandering divided Mexican-American communities to prevent candidates preferred by them from being elected. At-large elections diminished or eliminated the impact of sizable Mexican-American minorities in the larger jurisdictions.

The New York Puerto Rican vote was subject to manipulation as well. New York established a literacy test in 1922 for potential voters who could not present a certificate that they had completed eighth grade in a school in which "English is the official language of the institution." Inspectors routinely denied certificates from schools in Puerto Rico despite the fact that English was the official language of instruction in Puerto Rican schools until 1946 (Meyer 1989, chapter 7). Polling places were also moved and reduced in number just prior to the 1948 elections.

The VRA has, in our judgment, successfully addressed each of the structural barriers faced by Latino voters. In the 1988 election, Latino monitors documented two examples of attempted voter intimidation (Pachon et al. 1992). The effort in Texas was blocked well before election day and received national press attention bringing some embarrassment to the Republican party officials who initiated the efforts. Thus, overall, the pervasiveness of intimidation has been replaced by sporadic, unsuccessful, and even embarrassing efforts to keep Mexican Americans from the polls.

Similarly, other structural barriers that kept many Mexican Americans from the polls have disappeared. A few, such as the poll tax, ended before 1975. The VRA, however, ensured that all of the remaining barriers—lengthy residence requirements for registration, English-language ballots, changes in registration or polling places, and anti-minority districting schemes—have either been eliminated or made subject to federal scrutiny (Cotrell and Polinard 1986).

Perhaps as importantly, by freeing the Mexican-American vote, the parties—particularly the Democrats in the Southwestern states—have become dependent upon Mexican-American votes for victory. As a result, efforts to limit the Mexican-American vote have become partisan as well as civil rights issues. Thus, the advocates for Mexican-American voting rights include more than just Mexican Americans. In the attempted voter intimidation case in Texas in 1988, for example, in response to the involvement of the Republican Secretary of State, the U.S. Justice Department joined the Mexican-American Legal Defense and Education Fund to block the effort.

Latino Elected Officials

Unlike African Americans in the South, Mexican Americans and other Latinos were never absolutely excluded from elective office.[4] Prior to the

1960s, many of these elected Latinos participated in and contributed to the manipulation and structural exclusion that characterized voting in the Southwest (Anders 1979). Their inclusion suggests that Mexican Americans never faced the absolute racial and ethnic prejudice faced by African Americans.

Further, a handful of Mexican Americans and other Latinos have served at the state level and in major cities throughout the country's history. In addition to Florida's Hernandez, several Mexican Americans served in California's first constitutional convention and one served as Governor in the 1870s. Riverside County Supervisor Miguel Estudillo served in the Assembly from 1905 to 1908 and in the Senate from 1909 to 1912. Texan J. T. Canales served in the Texas legislature in the 1900s and 1910s. Though referred to on the floor of the legislature as the "Greaser from Brownsville," he manipulated the system sufficiently both to serve and to oppose the Wells machine in South Texas and to lead an embarrassing investigation into the Texas Rangers. Chicago's first "Latino" alderman, William Emilio Rodriguez, served from 1915 to 1918. In New Mexico, the native Hispanics had a long tradition of relatively unobstructed political participation that produced Mexican-American elected officials at all levels of elective office, including U.S. Senators and members of the U.S. House of Representatives. New York's first Puerto Rican elected official, Oscar García Rivera, served for one term in the state legislature beginning in 1937 (Falcón 1984).

Despite these exceptions, Latino office holders prior to 1975 were rare, even in areas with large numbers of Latinos. In 1973, there were 1,280 Latino elected officials in the six heavily Latino states (Arizona, California, Florida, New Mexico, New York, and Texas) (Lemus 1973). By 1991, the number of Latino elected officials in these states had nearly tripled to 3,677 (NALEO Educational Fund 1991). In the six states for which pre-VRA data exist, the number of Latino elected officials since the passage of the VRA has increased more rapidly than either the Latino population or the number of elective offices (Pachon and DeSipio 1992). Increases of this magnitude suggest that an exogenous factor such as the VRA and the new electoral climate it inspired are responsible (García 1986).

Many of the new VRA districts contain high concentrations of Latinos. In a 1987 survey of Latino elected officials nationwide, the National Association of Latino Elected and Appointed Officials (NALEO) Educational Fund found that the constituency of the average district represented by a Latino is 55 percent Latino. In Texas, the state with the largest number of Latino office holders, the median constituency is 73 percent Latino (NALEO Educational Fund 1990, table 11).[5] We will return to this topic in Part IV.

Latino candidates are also increasingly nominated and, in some cases, elected to citywide and statewide office without the benefit of VRA-mandated districts. Mexican Americans in New Mexico have a long history of service in statewide and federal office and Arizona elected Raul Castro governor in 1974. In addition to these pre-VRA electoral accomplishments, the late 1980s have seen an increase in the frequency and diversity of electoral offices for which Latinos compete and, frequently, win. Denver elected Federico Peña mayor in 1983 and 1987. In Florida, Bob Martínez was elected governor in 1986. In Texas, the Republican Party nominated Roy Barrera for attorney general in 1986. Texas elected Raul González to the State Supreme Court in 1986 and elected Dan Morales attorney general in 1990. Lena Guerrero ran for (and lost) a position on the Texas Railroad Commission in 1992. In Chicago, Puerto Rican Miriam Santos was elected to serve as the city treasurer.

Latino Voting

While the VRA has successfully reduced, if not eliminated, structural barriers to Latino voting and anti-Latino voter intimidation while influencing an increase in the range of seats available to Latino candidates, it has not been as successful in increasing the percentage of Latinos going to the polls. A discussion of this topic is complicated by the unreliability of pre-1975 Latino electoral turnout data. What we present, then, must be seen merely as an indicator of some aspects of the pre-1975 vote. We hypothesize that data from rural areas, which were subject to both intimidation and manipulation, would look quite different from these data and show lower overall levels of participation. We also suspect that these data represent a more unfettered Mexican-American vote than would have existed in the 1950s or before.

Latino Voting before 1975. Several city-level examinations explore Mexican-American voting levels in the 1960s. A study of Mexican-American voting patterns in the 1964 presidential race documents registration rates of 46 percent and 56 percent and voter turnout rates of 38 percent and 50 percent for San Antonio and Los Angeles, respectively. The study looks only at these cities and includes only U.S. citizens in its pool of eligible voters (Grebler, Moore, and Guzman 1970, 564). The Mexican-American registration rates for Los Angeles were somewhat lower than the rates for the city's general population (77 percent). Although San Antonio's Mexican-American registration rates were lower than those of Los Angeles, they exceed the rate for the population as a whole in San Antonio (43 percent).

A study of Texas "Mexican-American" counties from throughout the 1960s indicates that their overall registration rates exceed the registration rates for the state as a whole in five of six elections (with 1960 as the exception) (McCleskey and Merrill 1973). The Mexican-American counties, however, show lower levels of voting in all but one of the elections (1962 as the exception). The authors define Mexican-American counties as those with Mexican-American majorities. As a result, the relatively high overall levels of registration in these counties may suggest high Anglo registration to maintain electoral dominance over the larger Mexican-American population. Registration rates increase steadily throughout the decade in both the Mexican-American counties and the state as a whole (from 47 percent in 1960 to 63 percent in 1970 for the state as a whole and from 47 percent to 70 percent for Mexican-American counties). Voter turnout as a percentage of those registered, on the other hand, declined in the 1960s. The statewide voter turnout rates dropped from 89 percent to 76 percent from 1960 to 1968. For Mexican-American counties, turnout dropped from 79 percent to 61 percent.

A third study from the 1960s looked at Harris County (Houston), Texas. It finds that while the Spanish surnamed made up 5.6 percent of the potential electorate (adults who had paid the poll tax), they made up only 3.1 percent of the actual electorate (McCleskey and Nimmo 1968). Poll taxes and registration requirements impeded the movement from the potential to the actual electorate, according to the authors. Among the actual electorate, the Spanish surnamed had nearly the highest levels of non-voting of any of the gender, age, race, ethnic, or occupational groups studied. They also had the lowest rates of "maximum participation" voting in the two primaries and general elections studied. Just 3.9 percent of Mexican Americans who were qualified and registered to vote actually voted in all three elections. This accumulative turnout rate compares to 11.3 percent for the survey population as a whole and 13 percent or more for respondents over 40 and for professionals and managers.

While these studies are somewhat contradictory, they strongly indicate that prior to the VRA Mexican Americans were not excluded from the Texas and Los Angeles electorates. In some specific cases, their registration and turnout levels actually exceeded those of Anglos. These data are confirmed by the first national sample of Latino electoral participation. In the 1972 presidential election (prior to the extension of the VRA to the Latino community), approximately 44 percent of the "Spanish-surnamed population" registered and 37 percent voted (U.S. Bureau of the Census 1973, Table One). Unlike the data we will present from the 1980s, these figures do not exclude non-U.S. citizens from the pool of Latino adults. As a result, the 1972 figures underestimate actual rates of Latino registration and voting.

Latino Voting after 1975. Despite the protections of the VRA, Latino registration and voting rates have not increased significantly since 1975. The registration and voting rates among U.S.-citizen Latinos in 1988, for example, were 56.6 percent and 45.9 percent, respectively (U.S. Bureau of the Census 1989). While these seem and may actually be higher than the comparable figures from 1972, the inclusion of noncitizens in the 1972 data probably makes the actual figures for that year somewhat higher. The 1988 data also are lower than the findings from Los Angeles and from the "Mexican-American counties" in the 1960s reported earlier. As we have suggested, the weakness of pre-1975 data makes such comparisons risky. Our point is evident even if the 1988 registration and voting rates are the same as those from before 1975—the VRA may not have significantly boosted Latino voter turnout.

Further, the 1988 data, adjusted as they are for citizenship, mask a steadily increasing number of noncitizen adult Latinos. The unadjusted registration and voting rates for 1988 were 35.5 percent for registration and 28.8 percent for voting. The number of noncitizen adult Latinos has increased from 1.7 million in 1976 to 5.2 million in 1990 (Pachon et al. 1992, Figure 5).

Latino registration and turnout rates also lag behind those of both the population as a whole and of the African-American population. In 1988, for example, Latino registration rates trailed the overall registration rate by 31 percentage points and voter turnout rates lagged by 29 percentage points. When adjusted for the higher rates of noncitizenship in the Latino community, registration and voting rates lag by 14 percentage points and 15 percentage points respectively (U.S. Bureau of the Census, Table 1). Adjusted Latino registration and voting rates were approximately 10 and 7 percentage points lower than those for African Americans in 1988.

While the VRA has not increased Latino registration and voting, the picture is not altogether bleak. The natural increases in Latino population relative to that of the population as a whole and small increases in Latino electoral participation have increased the overall participation of Latinos relative to that of the national population. In the 1980s, for example, turnout among all Latino U.S. citizens increased slightly; relative to 1980, turnout among all U.S. citizens declined.

In relative terms, Latino voters have become an increasing share of the national electorate. Between 1976 and 1988 not only did the Latino share of the national electorate grow from 2.4 percent to 3.6 percent, it also grew to the level where it influenced statewide results in several states (Pachon et al. 1992, 18–21). This 50 percent increase in Latino share of the national electorate in presidential elections did not keep up with the 100 percent increase in the Latino adult population in this twelve-year period.

The Latino electorate also has the advantage of spatial concentration in just nine states (including four of the five most populous states). In the 1992 elections, for example, Latino voters constituted 26 percent of the actual voters in New Mexico, 14 percent in Texas, 10 percent in California, 7 percent in Florida, and 5 percent in New York. State-level significance masks the Latino concentration within states. South Texas and Northern New Mexico—as well as such cities as Los Angeles, Houston, Miami, and New York—all have large active Latino populations able, under the right circumstances, to influence local elections and elect Latinos to city-wide and state legislative offices (Guerra 1992; Guerra and Fraga 1995). Also, in some areas, particularly New Mexico and Miami, Latinos vote at rates comparable to those of non-Hispanic whites in many elections (Hain and García 1981, 54; Grenier et al. 1994). Despite these demographic strengths—the potential for state-level electoral significance, regional concentration, and local electoral strength—aggregate measures of Latino electoral participation continue to lag behind those of other populations.

Conclusions

At a fundamental level, then, the extension of the VRA to Latinos is an important symbol. After over a hundred years of exclusion, it assured that Latinos were welcome in the electorate. Despite significant improvements in eliminating structural barriers to participation and in electing Latinos to office, however, Latino registration and voting rates nationally have not increased beyond pre-1975 levels. Further, the gap between Latinos and other electoral groups remains. In Part IV, we examine some of the causes of this persistent gap between Latino and non-Latino electoral participation.

III. Insights from the Latino National Political Survey

The census data used to examine national voting patterns obscure salient characteristics of the Latino electorate. Until recently, however, these data and exit polls (which tend to have high sampling errors [Balz 1987]) were the only national sources of data on Latino registration and voting patterns. More importantly, there were no reliable national data on the factors that influence Latino voting and non-voting. The recent completion of the Latino National Political Survey (LNPS) begins to rectify these deficiencies in the data.

The LNPS is a national probability sample of the three largest Latino national origin groups—Mexican Americans, Puerto Ricans, and Cuban Americans.[6] Consequently, in this discussion of the LNPS, when we use the collective ethnic identity term "Latino," we are referring to these three groups. The survey, conducted in 1989 and 1990, includes interviews with more than 2,800 Latinos and a comparison group of nearly 450 Anglos who reside in the same Standard Metropolitan Statistical Areas (SMSAs) as the sampled Latinos. The survey consisted of more than 200 questions. Weighted frequencies for the answers to most survey questions are reported for each of the three national-origin groups in *Latino Voices: Mexican, Puerto Rican, and Cuban Perspectives on American Politics*. This book also includes a discussion of the survey's methodology (de la Garza et al. 1992).

In the analysis presented here, we report selected findings from the LNPS related to the questions directly addressing Latino electoral participation and the VRA. The survey offers a rich lode of material on the determinants of political participation; what is presented here is only the most brief of summaries.

Overview of the LNPS Data

On the most straightforward question relating to Latino electoral participation, the LNPS reports higher levels of noncitizenship among Latinos and higher levels of registration and voting among both U.S.-citizen Latinos and Anglos than do other national sources of data. As indicated in table 1, more than one half of the Mexican-origin respondents and almost all of the Puerto Rican and Anglo-origin respondents are U.S. citizens. Slightly less than half of the Cuban-origin respondents are citizens (hereafter we will refer to these groups as Mexican Americans, Puerto Ricans, Cuban Americans, and Anglos).[7]

Among the U.S. citizen respondents to the LNPS, approximately 65 percent of the Mexican Americans and Puerto Ricans and 78 percent of the Cuban Americans and Anglos were registered to vote when the survey was conducted (see table 2). These rates are significantly higher, both for Latino and for Anglos, than those reported by the Census Bureau.

Turnout rates vary by national-origin group. Approximately 49

TABLE 1

Citizenship Status of LNPS Respondents, by National Origin

U.S. CITIZENSHIP STATUS	MEXICAN	PUERTO RICAN	CUBAN	ANGLO
U.S. citizen	878	587	312	446
	56.8%	99.6%	45.9%	97.7%
Not U.S. citizen	668	2	367	10
	43.2%	0.4%	54.1%	2.3%

Source: Latino National Political Survey

percent of Mexican Americans, 50 percent of Puerto Ricans, 67 percent of Cuban Americans, and 70 percent for Anglos voted in 1988 (see table 3).[8] As we have suggested, the Anglos in the sample are residents of the SMSAs (and the neighborhoods) included in the LNPS sample. They are not, then, necessarily representative of Anglos nationwide.

Characteristics of the Latino Adult Population According to the LNPS

We use the LNPS to examine the components of the Latino electorate in a manner that suggests the relevance of the VRA to Latino voters. Our discussion disaggregates four groups within the Latino adult population. The first is the noncitizens, who are (for the most part) statutorily excluded from electoral participation. The remaining three groups are eligible to participate in American politics: the nonregistered, the registered

TABLE 2

Citizen Voter Registration Status in 1988, by National Origin

RESPONDENT REGISTERED TO VOTE IN 1989-1990	MEXICAN	PUERTO RICAN	CUBAN	ANGLO
No	303	211	69	99
	34.6%	36.0%	22.0%	22.2%
Yes	574	375	243	347
	65.4%	64.0%	78.0%	77.8%
Total	877	585	312	446
	100.0%	100.0%	100.0%	100.0%

Source: Latino National Political Survey

TABLE 3

Voting in 1988 Election Among U.S. Citizens, by National Origin

Did Respondent Vote in the 1988 Elections	Mexican	Puerto Rican	Cuban	Anglo
Yes	431	290	210	313
	49.3%	49.9%	67.2%	70.2%
No	141	81	34	34
	16.1%	13.9%	10.7%	7.6%
Not registered	303	211	69	99
	34.6%	36.2%	22.0%	22.2%
Total	875	581	312	446
	100.0%	100.0%	100.0%	100.0%

Source: Latino National Political Survey

nonvoters, and the voters. First, we examine several sociodemographic factors of these four groups. Second, we explore several factors that induced the extension of the VRA to Latinos. Finally, we look at some of the by-products of the Act.

Demographics by Citizenship and Voting Status. The effect of demographics and socioeconomic status on American voting has been analyzed extensively. Wolfinger and Rosenstone (1980), for example, analyzed national-level voting patterns for whites, blacks, and Mexican Americans. They found that when they statistically controlled for four factors—citizenship, age, education, and income—African Americans voted at higher rates than the national average and Mexican Americans voted at comparable rates to the national average.

As would be expected from Wolfinger and Rosenstone's findings, age, education, and income of LNPS respondents are positively correlated to voting. The nonregistered in the LNPS are younger than the registered nonvoters and the nonvoters tend to be younger than the voters (see table 4). For Latinos as a whole, just 2.2 percent of the nonregistered and 4.7 percent of the registered nonvoting populations have more than a high school education. It should be noted that the data for Latinos as a whole strongly reflect the Mexican-American respondents' experiences. Language is, however, a less useful indicator to distinguish between voters and nonvoters among the eligible. While the nonregistered are the most likely to be Spanish dominant, there is virtually no difference in the language competence of the registered nonvoters and the voters.

TABLE 4

Demographic Characteristics of Latino National Political Survey Respondents

| | NON-CITIZENS | | | CITIZEN NOT REGISTERED | | | |
AGE	M	C	L	M	PR	C	L
18–24	156	31	223	88	53	26	170
	23.4%	8.7%	22.0%	43.6%	34.2%	47.3%	41.3%
25–34	248	65	373	58	43	14	117
	37.2%	17.9%	35.3%	28.7%	28.2%	25.5%	28.4%
35–50	195	116	313	36	39	5	81
	29.3%	31.9%	29.6%	18.1%	25.1%	9.5%	19.6%
51–65	54	84	101	16	7	7	31
	8.1%	23.1%	9.5%	8.2%	4.7%	13.5%	7.4%
66+	13	67	38	3	12	2	13
	2.0%	18.4%	3.6%	1.5%	7.8%	4.1%	3.3%
Median	32 yrs	48 yrs	32 yrs	27 yrs	30 yrs	25 yrs	27 yrs
Education Completed							
0–8 years	435	164	669	44	43	7	95
	65.2%	45.0%	63.2%	22.0%	28.0%	12.6%	23.2%
9–12 years,	56	58	96	65	49	10	131
no degree	8.4%	15.9%	9.1%	32.7%	32.0%	17.3%	31.9%
H.S. Degree	146	107	240	85	51	32	166
	21.9%	29.4%	22.6%	42.5%	33.2%	58.5%	40.7%
Post-	30	35	53	6	10	6	17
H.S.Education	4.6%	9.7%	5.0%	2.8%	6.8%	11.5%	2.2%
Language Used at Home							
Spanish	571	314	907	39	79	34	121
	85.5%	85.9%	85.5%	19.4%	51.4%	61.8%	29.4%
English or	97	52	153	162	75	21	290
Bilingual	14.5%	14.1%	14.5%	80.6%	48.9%	38.2%	70.6%

Key:
M: Mexican origin   PR: Puerto Rican origin   C: Cuban origin   L: Latino origin
Latino column is a combined sample of Mexicans, Puerto Ricans, and Cubans nationwide (of which
Mexican-origin peoples compose 78 percent). It is not the sum of the Mexican, Puerto Rican, and Cuban
responses.

Perceptions of Discrimination in the Latino Community. As we
have suggested, the major justification for extending the VRA to Latinos
was the testimony describing the widespread discrimination against Mexican Americans in the Southwest and, to a lesser degree at least in terms
of testimony, Puerto Ricans in the continental United States. To the ex-

REGISTERED NOT VOTING				VOTING			
M	PR	C	L	M	PR	C	L
54	32	6	101	53	34	22	106
22.8%	24.5%	13.0%	22.9%	12.1%	11.5%	10.6%	11.9%
76	43	16	143	100	81	33	209
32.3%	32.7%	33.7%	32.4%	22.7%	27.5%	15.6%	23.4%
54	35	13	105	134	109	50	282
22.9%	27.0%	27.3%	23.9%	30.5%	37.0%	23.8%	31.6%
36	15	9	65	101	51	63	198
15.5%	11.1%	19.5%	14.7%	23.1%	17.3%	29.8%	22.2%
15	6	3	27	51	20	42	98
6.5%	4.7%	6.5%	6.1%	11.6%	6.7%	20.1%	11.0%
33 yrs	33 yrs	36 yrs	33 yrs	40 yrs	38 yrs	50 yrs	40 yrs
42	37	7	88	91	94	47	209
17.9%	28.2%	14.6%	20.0%	20.8%	32.0%	22.3%	23.5%
64	30	5	113	73	48	19	144
27.0%	22.7%	10.1%	25.7%	16.8%	16.2%	9.1%	16.1%
122	56	18	219	201	106	64	381
51.9%	42.8%	39.8%	49.7%	46.2%	36.1%	30.9%	42.8%
7	8	16	21	71	46	78	156
3.1%	6.3%	35.4%	4.7%	16.3%	15.7%	37.6%	17.6%
32	53	23	89	59	124	133	209
13.5%	40.7%	49.3%	20.1%	13.6%	42.2%	63.3%	23.4%
204	78	23	353	379	171	77	684
86.5%	59.3%	50.7%	79.9%	86.4%	57.8%	36.7%	76.6%

Data reported here are weighted. As a result, cells with a value of zero can have a percentage value other than zero. For an explanation of this phenomenon, see de la Garza et al. (1992), Chapter 1.
Source: Latino National Political Survey

tent that discrimination persists, the original justification of the VRA remains.

The LNPS found contradictory patterns regarding discrimination. Between 20 and 40 percent of respondents, regardless of citizenship or voting status, national origin, or language used at home, feel that they have personally experienced discrimination. Regardless of these feelings about their personal experience, however, the majority feel that their co-ethnics face "a lot" or "some" discrimination. By substantial majorities, Cuban Americans are the least likely to perceive personal or group discrimination. Interestingly, overall the respondents who speak Spanish at home are less likely to perceive that they have been discriminated against than are those who speak English or are fully bilingual at home (see tables 5 and 6). Citizenship status, voter registration, and voting have a slight impact on the perception of personal discrimination for English speakers. Latino registered nonvoters and voters are slightly more likely to perceive that they have been discriminated against than are the non-registered and the noncitizens.

Voting Protections Assured by the VRA. The VRA explicitly assured Latinos access to bilingual voting materials and sought to end voter intimidation and to increase governmental responsiveness. Increasingly, it has also offered Latinos the option to elect co-ethnics to office. The LNPS offers several measures of the degree to which Latinos feel government officials are responsive, how the presence of a co-ethnic on the ballot influences their decision about whether to vote and for whom to vote, and how useful bilingual election materials are to voters.

Overwhelmingly, LNPS respondents believe that they were treated fairly by the last public official with whom they interacted (see tables 7 and 8). Also, although many report no interactions with public officials (perhaps representing some latent distrust of public services), large majorities of those who did report interaction find that both Latino and non-Latino public officials treat them fairly. Surprisingly, perceptions of governmental fairness are even stronger among Spanish speakers.

Advocates of the VRA insist that the opportunity to elect candidates of their choosing (for example, co-ethnics) is central to Latino political incorporation (Fuchs 1990; Cain 1992). Nonetheless, substantial majorities of LNPS respondents report that the presence of a co-ethnic on the ballot makes no difference in their likelihood of voting (see tables 9 and 10). This finding may reflect the fact that majorities of registered nonvoters and of Puerto Rican voters have not had the opportunity to vote for co-ethnics. This may be why, despite their assurances that the presence of a co-ethnic on the ballot makes no difference, respondents who have had the opportunity to choose between a co-ethnic and a non–co-ethnic overwhelmingly have chosen the co-ethnic. These findings may indicate that VRA advocates are right—that is, the positive correlation between voting and having a co-ethnic on the ballot may indicate that the latter increases the former.

Although the VRA did not provide for such measures, its enactment stimulated voter registration drives among Latinos. Indeed, it is fair to argue that more resources have been devoted to voter registration than to any other political activity. Nevertheless, the great majority of respondents have not been contacted to register and vote (see tables 11 and 12). Considering the intense effort and financial commitment to voter registration among Hispanic influentials, this finding is surprising. Moreover, the Spanish-speaking nonregistered—the group least likely to be involved in politics—are also the least likely to have been contacted. It does seem that such contacts spur voting, since 57 percent of all Latinos contacted voted.

The VRA's most explicit achievement for Latinos was mandating the availability of Spanish-language voting materials. The LNPS asked respondents if they used Spanish materials only if they answered the Spanish-language questionnaire and reported that they had voted in 1988.[9] Very few reported that they used Spanish ballots.

Interestingly, although the VRA was designed to rectify educational and other forms of discrimination against Mexican Americans and Puerto Ricans, Cuban respondents were the most likely to report access to the Spanish language ballots. Puerto Rican respondents were the most likely to use the Spanish ballots when available. The Spanish-speaking Cuban voters were more likely than the Spanish-speaking Mexican voters to use the Spanish ballots. As we would expect, the respondents who speak English or are bilingual at home (and answered the LNPS in Spanish) were less likely to use Spanish-language ballots and other Spanish voting assistance than were the Spanish speakers.

The VRA from the Perspective of LNPS Respondents. These data offer several insights into how the VRA has affected Latino voting. Several focus on sociodemographic characteristics of the Latino population that were not the focus of the 1975 extension of the VRA. Others were a central focus of the Act and of judicial interpretations of its meaning.

Latinos, particularly Latino nonvoters, are young, and few have education beyond the high school level. These factors lower registration and voting rates. Among the citizens, however, the majority of Mexican Americans and Puerto Ricans speak English at home. Thus, the characteristic that was most important to policymakers in 1975, language, is less an impediment to participation than are education and age.

Latinos also are a population with very high levels of noncitizenship. Regardless of whether one uses the LNPS noncitizenship rates or those of the Census Bureau, a minimum of nearly 40 percent of Latino adults cannot participate in electoral politics because of nationality. Although the share of Latino noncitizens was smaller in 1975, this too was unaddressed in the 1975 VRA debates.

Finally, the gap between registration and voting is larger among Latinos than among other electoral groups. Ironically, this perhaps may

TABLE 5

Perceptions of Discrimination among Latinos Who Speak English or English and Spanish at Home

	Non-citizens			Citizen Not Registered			
	M	C	L	M	PR	C	L
Respondent Faced							
Discrimination	29	8	44	51	22	5	91
	29.8%	14.7%	28.4%	31.8%	30.0%	24.5%	31.3%
Level of Discrimination Faced by Respondents' National-Origin Group							
A Lot	32	4	47	41	26	0	78
	33.2%	7.4%	30.8%	25.6%	36.2%	0.0%	26.9%
Some	38	18	59	82	33	11	144
	39.0%	35.2%	38.6%	50.9%	45.9%	53.3%	50.1%
A Little	19	10	30	33	5	3	52
	19.6%	19.2%	19.6%	20.4%	7.1%	15.5%	18.0%
None	8	20	17	5	8	7	15
	8.1%	38.2%	10.9%	3.1%	10.8%	31.2%	5.0%

Key:
M: Mexican origin   PR: Puerto Rican origin   C: Cuban origin   L: Latino origin

Latino column is a combined sample of Mexicans, Puerto Ricans and Cubans nationwide (of which Mexican-origin peoples compose 78 percent). It is not the sum of the Mexican, Puerto Rican, and Cuban responses.

be viewed as a success of the VRA, whose goal was to ensure registration and voting opportunities. Unfortunately for Latinos, although the VRA facilitated registration and spurred registration drives among other groups, the efforts have reached few Latinos. More importantly, Latino nonvoters still outnumber voters by substantial numbers.

The LNPS suggests that some of the factors that led to the extension of the VRA to Latinos have diminished in importance. Relatively few respondents report that they have faced discrimination themselves, even though many more report that their national-origin group faces significant discrimination. Their contacts with public officials, both Latino and non-Latino, result in fair treatment. They also report that having co-ethnics on the ballot is of little importance, but they vote for co-ethnics when given the opportunity.

Finally, the most tangible result of the 1975 extension of the VRA, bilingual election assistance, is used by relatively few respondents. The original targets of the Act—Mexican Americans—are less likely to use this benefit than are Cuban Americans. This is ironic, given that nowhere in the congressional debate is there a suggestion that the bilingual ballot

REGISTERED NOT VOTING				VOTING			
M	PR	C	L	M	PR	C	L
89	24	4	145	159	63	20	277
43.4%	31.2%	17.4%	41.1%	41.9%	36.7%	25.3%	40.5%
77	31	4	133	118	53	7	209
37.6%	40.1%	15.7%	37.6%	31.2%	31.1%	9.6%	30.5%
100	31	7	167	192	82	39	343
48.9%	39.9%	30.0%	47.2%	50.7%	47.9%	49.9%	50.2%
22	11	4	41	53	30	17	101
11.0%	13.5%	19.2%	11.6%	13.9%	17.3%	22.2%	14.8%
5	5	8	13	16	6	14	31
2.5%	6.4%	35.1%	3.7%	4.2%	3.6%	18.3%	4.5%

Data reported here are weighted. As a result, cells with a value of zero can have a percentage value other than zero. For an explanation of this phenomenon, see de la Garza et al. (1992), Chapter 1.
Source: Latino National Political Survey

provisions were intended as a tool for immigrant acculturation or political empowerment. In fact, Congress explicitly rejected the amendment in 1975 by Representatives Biaggi and Solarz to extend bilingual ballots to all language minorities (for example, to European immigrants).

The contradiction highlighted in these data—between a citizen population that continues to participate at lower than average levels yet despite the specific protections assured by the VRA—is the focus of the remaining two sections of this paper. In Section IV, we offer some explanations for the continued low levels of electoral participation among Latinos. In Section V, we offer some possible remedies that need to be incorporated into a new-generation VRA if the goal of the Act is to assure comparable levels of participation regardless of ethnicity.

IV. EXPLANATIONS FOR LOW LEVELS OF LATINO ELECTORAL PARTICIPATION

Low levels of Latino electoral participation have a tendency to be self-perpetuating. Once the perception arises that Latinos do not vote, can-

TABLE 6

Perceptions of Discrimination among Latinos Who Speak Spanish at Home

	NON-CITIZENS			CITIZEN NOT REGISTERED			
	M	C	L	M	PR	C	L
Respondent Faced							
Discrimination 146		32	218	10	24	4	32
25.6%		10.3%	24.1%	24.9%	30.7%	11.0%	26.4%
Level of Discrimination Faced by Respondents' National-Origin Group							
A Lot	175	22	256	10	29	1	36
	30.7%	7.0%	28.4%	26.6%	37.1%	3.8%	29.6%
Some	200	79	309	17	23	16	45
	35.1%	25.4%	34.2%	44.1%	28.6%	47.4%	37.2%
A Little	146	40	221	8	17	8	25
	25.7%	12.8%	24.5%	19.3%	21.0%	24.1%	20.4%
None	48	171	117	4	11	8	15
	8.4%	54.8%	12.9%	10.0%	13.4%	24.6%	12.7%

Key:
M: Mexican origin   PR: Puerto Rican origin   C: Cuban origin   L: Latino origin

Latino column is a combined sample of Mexicans, Puerto Ricans, and Cubans nationwide (of which Mexican-origin peoples compose 78 percent). It is not the sum of the Mexican, Puerto Rican, and Cuban responses.

didates, campaigns, and parties have no reason to reach out to these communities. Without outreach, the many "new" voters in these communities are not socialized into the political system and become chronic nonvoters.

While this vicious cycle could occur in any community, we argue that the effect is greater on Latinos because they have a higher share of "new" voters. Who are the Latino new voters? They fall into three groups. The first is those newly turned eighteen each election year. All electorates have such voters, but Latinos, as a younger population, have a higher share of the newly adult. Unlike other populations, many of these young adults are the children of nonvoters. The second category of "new" voters are those who have been formally excluded from American politics. Included in this group are those who were victims of the discrimination, intimidation, and exclusion that we have discussed. These are the people who were never socialized into electoral politics and whom the 1975 VRA extension was designed to serve. Both the African-American and Latino communities have many of this type of new electorate. The third group includes newly naturalized citizens (and permanent resi-

	Registered Not Voting				Voting			
M	PR	C	L	M	PR	C	L
11	7	0	21	18	35	23	57
35.5%	12.6%	0.0%	23.4%	30.3%	28.2%	17.2%	27.1%
13	15	1	29	21	46	7	64
41.5%	27.4%	2.4%	32.8%	36.0%	37.8%	5.0%	31.2%
7	19	8	26	19	39	46	66
22.2%	35.7%	36.0%	28.8%	32.0%	31.7%	34.2%	32.3%
5	14	0	16	11	24	26	40
14.8%	26.1%	0.0%	18.5%	19.0%	19.5%	19.6%	19.3%
7	6	14	18	7	13	55	35
21.6%	10.8%	61.6%	19.9%	12.9%	11.0%	41.1%	17.2%

Data reported here are weighted. As a result, cells with a value of zero can have a percentage value other than zero. For an explanation of this phenomenon, see de la Garza et al. (1992), Chapter 1.
Source: Latino National Political Survey

dents in areas that permit noncitizen voting). Latinos have a much higher share of this type of new electorate than either African Americans or whites.

Some would argue that something in their cultural heritage makes Latinos less likely to participate (Lewis 1959). While not wanting to dignify this perspective with a lengthy response, we would remind the reader of the high levels of voting in both Miami and New Mexico that we have already discussed. Further, in specific elections, Latinos have organized and turned out in record numbers. The election of Federico Peña as Mayor of Denver is an example (Hero 1992, chapter 7). Further, as the Wolfinger and Rosenstone findings suggest, Mexican Americans may actually vote at higher rates than non-Hispanic white citizens of similar age, class, and education.

How, then, can we explain low levels of Latino electoral turnout? The first explanation is the sociodemographic factors that Wolfinger and Rosenstone examine. The second is the effect of high and growing rates of immigration and noncitizenship. High rates of noncitizenship depress community-wide electoral impact and create large constituencies with few votes. The third is a series of structural characteristics of the elec-

TABLE 7

Perception of Fair Treatment by Government Officials among Latinos Who Speak English or English and Spanish at Home

| | NON-CITIZENS | | | CITIZEN NOT REGISTERED | | | |
	M	C	L	M	PR	C	L
Treatment by Public Officials							
A) Treatment by Non-Latinos							
Fair	12	2	18	21	16	7	43
	75.0%	100.0%	75.0%	91.3%	80.0%	100.0%	89.6%
Not Fair	4	0	6	2	4	0	5
	25.0%	0.0%	25.0%	8.7%	20.0%	0.0%	10.4%
B) Treatment by Latinos							
Fair	7	3	11	4	2	0	7
	63.6%	100.0%	64.7%	80.0%	100.0%	0.0%	87.5%
Not Fair	4	0	6	1	0	1	1
	36.4%	0.0%	35.3%	20.0%	0.0%	100.0%	12.5%

TABLE 8

Perception of Fair Treatment by Government Officials among Latinos Who Speak Spanish at Home

| | NON-CITIZENS | | | CITIZEN NOT REGISTERED | | | |
	M	C	L	M	PR	C	L
Treatment by Public Officials							
A) Treatment by Non-Latinos							
Fair	94	47	148	8	6	5	16
	94.9%	95.9%	94.9%	100.0%	100.0%	100.0%	100.0%
Not Fair	5	2	8	0	0	0	0
	5.1%	4.1%	5.1%	0.0%	0.0%	0.0%	0.0%
B) Treatment by Latinos							
Fair	65	25	101	3	5	0	7
	97.0%	96.2%	97.1%	75.0%	100.0%	–	77.8%
Not Fair	2	1	3	1	0	0	2
	3.0%	3.8%	2.9%	25.0%	0.0%	–	22.2%

Key:
M: Mexican origin   PR: Puerto Rican origin   C: Cuban origin   L: Latino origin

Latino column is a combined sample of Mexicans, Puerto Ricans, and Cubans nationwide (of which Mexican-origin peoples compose 78 percent). It is not the sum of the Mexican, Puerto Rican, and Cuban responses.

	Registered Not Voting				Voting		
M	PR	C	L	M	PR	C	L
34	7	4	55	76	23	18	131
81.0%	87.5%	100.0%	82.1%	95.0%	85.2%	90.0%	93.6%
8	1	0	12	4	4	2	9
19.0%	12.5%	0.0%	17.9%	5.0%	14.8%	10.0%	6.4%
20	0	0	29	16	4	3	27
100.0%	–	–	100.0%	100.0%	100.0%	100.0%	100.0%
0	0	0	0	0	0	0	0
0.0%	–	–	0.0%	0.0%	0.0%	0.0%	0.0%

	Registered Not Voting				Voting		
M	PR	C	L	M	PR	C	L
2	13	1	11	4	23	18	26
66.7%	92.9%	50.0%	84.6%	100.0%	92.0%	94.7%	92.9%
1	1	1	2	0	2	1	2
33.3%	7.1%	50.0%	15.4%	0.0%	8.0%	5.3%	7.1%
1	5	0	5	5	11	11	19
100.0%	100.0%	–	83.3%	100.0%	91.7%	91.7%	95.0%
0	0	0	1	0	1	1	1
0.0%	0.0%	–	16.7%	0.0%	8.3%	8.3%	5.0%

Data reported here are weighted. As a result, cells with a value of zero can have a percentage value other than zero. For an explanation of this phenomenon, see de la Garza et al. (1992), Chapter 1.
Source: Latino National Political Survey

TABLE 9

Significance of a Co-ethnic on the Ballot, Opportunity to Vote for a Co-ethnic, and Vote in Election with a Co-ethnic among Latinos Who Speak English or English and Spanish at Home

	NON-CITIZENS			CITIZEN NOT REGISTERED			
	M	C	L	M	PR	C	L
Likelihood of Voting When a Co-Ethnic Runs For Office							
More Likely to Vote	–	–	–	–	–	–	–
	–	–	–	–	–	–	–
Less Likely to Vote	–	–	–	–	–	–	–
	–	–	–	–	–	–	–
Makes No Difference	–	–	–	–	–	–	–
	–	–	–	–	–	–	–
Has Respondent Had the Opportunity to Vote for a Co-Ethnic							
No	–	–	–	–	–	–	–
	–	–	–	–	–	–	–
Yes	–	–	–	–	–	–	–
	–	–	–	–	–	–	–
Vote in an Election between a Co-Ethnic and an Anglo							
For Co-Ethnic	–	–	–	–	–	–	–
	–	–	–	–	–	–	–
For Anglo	–	–	–	–	–	–	–
	–	–	–	–	–	–	–
For Another Candidate	–	–	–	–	–	–	–
	–	–	–	–	–	–	–

Key:

M: Mexican origin   PR: Puerto Rican origin   C: Cuban origin   L: Latino origin

Latino column is a combined sample of Mexicans, Puerto Ricans, and Cubans nationwide (of which Mexican-origin peoples compose 78 percent). It is not the sum of the Mexican, Puerto Rican, and Cuban responses.

toral system that affect all electorates, but that limit new electorates most seriously. Finally, the fourth limiting factor is an unintended by-product of the VRA itself: the creation of VRA-mandated, strongly partisan Latino districts has reduced electoral competition in high-concentration Latino areas. As a result, there is little competition in the Latino barrios that would serve as a focus for mobilizing any type of vote. Unfortunately, the new electorates tend to reside in exactly those districts.

REGISTERED NOT VOTING				VOTING			
M	PR	C	L	M	PR	C	L
45	17	4	78	110	52	8	196
22.4%	21.4%	16.0%	22.1%	29.0%	30.7%	10.8%	28.7%
9	5	3	17	5	4	3	11
4.5%	6.2%	12.1%	4.9%	1.5%	2.3%	3.7%	1.7%
148	56	17	257	263	114	66	474
73.1%	72.4%	71.9%	73.0%	69.5%	67.0%	85.5%	69.6%
148	58	17	257	127	88	29	252
75.7%	75.3%	72.2%	75.5%	34.8%	53.9%	38.1%	38.3%
48	19	6	83	237	76	47	406
24.3%	24.7%	27.8%	24.5%	65.2%	46.1%	61.9%	61.7%
32	10	2	53	159	59	31	278
74.1%	56.3%	41.7%	70.5%	75.2%	84.5%	70.6%	76.3%
6	1	2	10	29	9	8	50
15.0%	3.5%	30.3%	13.4%	13.7%	12.9%	18.3%	13.8%
5	7	2	12	23	2	5	36
10.9%	40.2%	28.0%	16.1%	11.0%	2.6%	11.1%	9.9%

Data reported here are weighted. As a result, cells with a value of zero can have a percentage value other than zero. For an explanation of this phenomenon, see de la Garza et al. (1992), Chapter 1.

Source: Latino National Political Survey

Traditional Sociodemographic Explanations

In Section III, we introduced the findings of Wolfinger and Rosenstone. Their study of the relationship of socioeconomic status and citizenship to voting strongly indicates that all populations, regardless of race and ethnicity, share a class, education, and age bias in voting. Higher income people vote more than those with lower incomes. Those with more education vote more than those with less. Older people vote more than young adults. Each of these factors affects Latinos disproportionately.

The Hispanic population is younger than the non-Hispanic popu-

TABLE 10

Significance of a Co-ethnic on the Ballot, Opportunity to Vote for a Co-ethnic, and Vote in Election with a Co-ethnic among Latinos Who Speak Spanish at Home

| | NON-CITIZENS | | | CITIZEN NOT REGISTERED | | | |
	M	C	L	M	PR	C	L
Likelihood of Voting When a Co-Ethnic Runs For Office							
More Likely to Vote	–	–	–	–	–	–	–
Less Likely to Vote	–	–	–	–	–	–	–
Makes No Difference	–	–	–	–	–	–	–
Has Respondent Had the Opportunity to Vote for a Co-Ethnic							
No	–	–	–	–	–	–	–
	–	–	–	–	–	–	–
Yes	–	–	–	–	–	–	–
	–	–	–	–	–	–	–
Vote in an Election between a Co-Ethnic and an Anglo							
For Co-Ethnic	–	–	–	–	–	–	–
	–	–	–	–	–	–	–
For Anglo	–	–	–	–	–	–	–
	–	–	–	–	–	–	–
For Another Candidate	–	–	–	–	–	–	–

Key:
M: Mexican origin   PR: Puerto Rican origin   C: Cuban origin   L: Latino origin

Latino column is a combined sample of Mexicans, Puerto Ricans, and Cubans nationwide (of which Mexican-origin peoples compose 78 percent). It is not the sum of the Mexican, Puerto Rican, and Cuban responses.

lation (U.S. Bureau of the Census 1991; Pachon et al. 1992). In 1991, for example, the median age for Latinos was 26.2 years; the median for the total population was 33. Accordingly, young adults make up a larger percentage of the Latino population. While young adults are statutorily able to vote, they are much less likely in practice to exercise the franchise. Older people, on the other hand, are quite likely to vote. The difference is stark. Among Latinos between the ages of 18 and 20, just 16 percent voted in 1990. Almost 40 percent of Latinos over the age of 45 voted in

REGISTERED NOT VOTING				VOTING			
M	PR	C	L	M	PR	C	L
13	25	5	37	28	64	41	97
42.7%	46.1%	21.7%	42.6%	47.6%	51.6%	31.4%	46.5%
0	0	1	0	1	0	11	5
0.0%	0.0%	2.4%	2.3%	2.0%	0.0%	8.4%	2.3%
18	29	17	50	30	60	79	107
57.3%	53.9%	75.9%	57.2%	50.4%	48.4%	60.3%	51.3%
21	37	13	59	13	58	27	66
67.7%	73.8%	55.7%	69.3%	22.9%	50.7%	21.2%	34.0%
10	13	10	26	42	56	102	128
32.3%	26.2%	44.3%	30.7%	77.1%	49.3%	78.8%	66.0%
9	10	7	21	32	45	77	99
94.7%	76.7%	70.8%	85.8%	87.2%	80.7%	83.2%	84.2%
0	1	1	1	1	4	12	8
0.0%	10.1%	10.8%	4.7%	3.5%	6.8%	13.0%	6.7%
0	2	2	2	3	7	4	11
5.3%	13.2%	18.3%	9.5%	9.3%	12.5%	3.8%	9.2%

Data reported here are weighted. As a result, cells with a value of zero can have a percentage value other than zero. For an explanation of this phenomenon, see de la Garza et al. (1992), Chapter 1.
Source: Latino National Political Survey

the same election. While 29 percent of Latino U.S. citizens were 45 or older in 1990, 43 percent of the national population was in this category.

Low levels of formal education have effects similar to those of youth on voting. Unlike youth, however, adults rarely grow out of low levels of education. Less than one-quarter of Latinos with four or fewer years of education voted in 1990. Among those with five or more years of education beyond a high school diploma, more than 62 percent voted. Among Latino adults, 6.5 percent fall into the former category and 4 percent fall into the latter. Again, a comparison with the population as a whole is instructive. In the general population, those with four or fewer

TABLE 11

Registration and Voting among Latinos Who Speak English or English and Spanish at Home

	NON-CITIZENS			CITIZEN NOT REGISTERED			
	M	C	L	M	PR	C	L
Did Someone Talk to Respondent about Registering to Vote?							
No	–	–	–	108	54	18	197
	–	–	–	67.2%	71.8%	84.0%	68.3%
Yes	–	–	–	53	21	3	91
	–	–	–	32.8%	28.2%	16.0%	31.7%
Use of Spanish Election Materials and Assistance[1]							
Spanish Ballots-	–	–	–	–	–	–	–
Available	–	–	–	–	–	–	–
Used Spanish or Spanish							
and English	–	–	–	–	–	–	–
Ballots	–	–	–	–	–	–	–
Spanish Ballots Helped							
Respondent Vote	–	–	–	–	–	–	–
	–	–	–	–	–	–	–
Election Assistance in							
Spanish	–	–	–	–	–	–	–
Available	–	–	–	–	–	–	–

Key:
M: Mexican origin   PR: Puerto Rican origin   C: Cuban origin   L: Latino origin

[1]The LNPS only asked interviewees who used the Spanish language questionnaire if they had access to Spanish language voting materials. Most of the respondents who speak English or are bilingual at home did not request the Spanish language questionnaire. For more complete information on use of Spanish language voting materials, see table 8.

[2]Denominator is the number of people who answered the question (the number of Spanish speakers and bilinguals who used the Spanish language questionnaire and voted in the 1988 elections (Mexicans n = 75, Puerto Ricans n = 162, Cubans n = 143, Latinos n = 257).

[3]Denominator is total number of respondents with access to Spanish language voting assistance.

years of education vote at the same rate as Latinos. At the other extreme, among those with five or more years of post-high school education, turnout is approximately 9 percentage points higher in the general population than the Latino population. More important than this gap in turnout is the share of the population in each category. Just over 1 percent of the non-Latino citizen population has four or fewer years of education; more than 8 percent have five or more years of education beyond a high school diploma.

	Registered Not Voting				Voting		
M	PR	C	L	M	PR	C	L
128	42	20	219	189	101	59	358
64.5%	53.6%	86.0%	63.2%	50.6%	59.0%	76.1%	52.9%
71	36	3	128	185	70	18	319
35.5%	46.4%	14.0%	36.8%	49.4%	41.0%	23.9%	47.1%
–	–	–		24	25	19	57
–	–	–	–	32.0%	15.4%	13.2%	22.2%[2]
–	–	–	–	13	9	4	27
–	–	–	–	54.2%	36.0%	21.1%	47.4%[3]
–	–	–	–	16	12	6	33
–	–	–	–	66.7%	48.0%	31.6%	57.9%[3]
–	–	–	–	3	11	4	13
–	–	–	–	4.0%	6.8%	2.8%	5.1%[2]

Latino column is a combined sample of Mexicans, Puerto Ricans, and Cubans nationwide (of which Mexican-origin peoples compose 78 percent). It is not the sum of the Mexican, Puerto Rican, and Cuban responses.

Data reported here are weighted. As a result, cells with a value of zero can have a percentage value other than zero. For an explanation of this phenomenon, see de la Garza et al. (1992), Chapter 1.

Source: Latino National Political Survey

Income follows the same pattern as age and education. Latinos with high incomes vote at rates lower than non-Latinos with comparable incomes and at rates higher than Latinos (and non-Latinos) with low incomes. Latino incomes are, on average, much lower—mean family incomes of $23,400 compared to $36,000 for the population as a whole—putting more Latinos in the income categories least likely to vote.

No single factor assures that Latinos participate at rates lower than the general population. Instead, they mutually depress Latino participation. All populations face the same limits. Latinos, however, are more likely to have higher numbers in the categories that are least likely to participate.

TABLE 12

Registration and Voting among Latinos Who Speak Spanish at Home

	NON-CITIZENS			CITIZEN NOT REGISTERED			
	M	C	L	M	PR	C	L

Did Someone Talk to Respondent About Registering to Vote?

No	–	–	–	37	71	20	108
	–	–	–	95.1%	89.7%	59.0%	89.8%
Yes	–	–	–	2	8	14	12
	–	–	–	4.9%	10.3%	41.0%	10.2%

Use of Spanish Election Materials and Assistance[1]

Spanish Ballots-	–	–	–	–	–	–	–
Available	–	–	–	–	–	–	–
Used Spanish or Spanish							
and English	–	–	–	–	–	–	–
Ballots	–	–	–	–	–	–	–
Spanish Ballots Helped							
Respondent Vote	–	–	–	–	–	–	–
	–	–	–	–	–	–	–
Election Assistance in							
Spanish	–	–	–	–	–	–	–
Available	–	–	–	–	–	–	–

Key:
M: Mexican origin   PR: Puerto Rican origin   C: Cuban origin   L: Latino origin

[1]The LNPS only asked interviewees who used the Spanish language questionnaire if they had access to Spanish language voting materials. Most of the respondents who speak English or are bilingual at home did not request the Spanish language questionnaire. For more complete information on use of Spanish language voting materials, see table 7.

[2]Denominator is the number of people who answered the question (Spanish speakers and bilinguals who voted in 1988 and who used the Spanish language questionnaire) (Mexicans n = 75, Puerto Ricans n = 162, Cubans n = 143, and Latinos n = 257).

[3]Denominator is total number of respondents with access to Spanish language voting assistance.

Noncitizenship and Continuing High Levels of Immigration

High levels of immigration and the concomitant growth in the number of noncitizens exacerbates the sociodemographic limitations on voting in two ways. First, immigrants tend to have the age, education, and income characteristics of the electoral nonparticipants. Second, even if they were to overcome these limitations because of a greater attachment to the United States or a greater desire to participate, they are statutorily excluded from most electoral participation.[10]

REGISTERED NOT VOTING				VOTING			
M	PR	C	L	M	PR	C	L
24	40	19	68	31	72	111	126
78.1%	75.8%	85.4%	77.7%	53.7%	58.8%	84.0%	61.2%
7	13	3	19	27	50	21	80
21.9%	24.2%	14.6%	22.3%	46.3%	41.2%	16.0%	38.8%
–	–	–	–	28	52	87	101
–	–	–	–	37.3%	32.1%	60.9%	39.3%[2]
–	–	–	–	19	47	63	78
–	–	–	–	67.9%	90.4%	72.4%	77.2%[3]
–	–	–	–	21	47	63	80
–	–	–	–	75.0%	90.4%	72.4%	79.2%[3]
–	–	–	–	12	29	18	42
–	–	–	–	16.0%	17.9%	17.0	16.3%[2]

Latino column is a combined sample of Mexicans, Puerto Ricans, and Cubans nationwide (of which Mexican-origin peoples compose 78 percent). It is not the sum of the Mexican, Puerto Rican, and Cuban responses.
Data reported here are weighted. As a result, cells with a value of zero can have a percentage value other than zero. For an explanation of this phenomenon, see de la Garza et al. (1992), Chapter 1.
Source: Latino National Political Survey

It is not possible to provide an exact count of the number of Latino permanent resident aliens in the United States. Census data includes an indeterminate number of undocumented immigrants; Immigration and Naturalization Service data on legal immigration do not account for emigration. Instead, we can suggest the magnitude of Latino noncitizenship. The Census Bureau estimated that there were 5.2 million Latino noncitizens in 1990. This number exceeded the number of Latinos who voted that year (an off-year election). From 1981 to 1991, approximately 4.7 million Latinos legally immigrated to the United States, including approximately 2.3 million who received legal status under the provisions of the Immigration Reform and Control Act of 1986 (U.S. Immigration and Naturalization Service 1994). Naturalization does not keep pace with immigration. In the 1980s, slightly more than 500,000

Latinos naturalized. Most of these had immigrated in the 1960s and 1970s; on average, Latinos reside in the United States for fourteen to fifteen years prior to naturalization.

This discussion of the Latino immigrant population indicates why the characteristics of immigrants tend to shape the characteristics of all Latinos. Between 40 and 50 percent of Latino adults are foreign born. Thus, what Latino immigrants bring to the country in terms of age, education, and skills plays an important role in defining the demographic characteristics of the Latino population. An indication of the characteristics they bring can be seen in table 4. They tend to be young adults who speak Spanish at home and have low levels of formal education. While the growing body of research into Latino immigrant acculturation demonstrates that legal immigrants adopt many traditionally American values and behaviors, the constant influx of new immigrants assures that the lower categories of the sociodemographic indicators will continue to fill with new immigrants.

Naturalization rates among Latino immigrants are somewhat lower than those among the other two regions providing large numbers of immigrants—Asia and Europe. While this may be slowly changing, for the present the number of eligible Latino immigrants who are not naturalized and cannot vote grows significantly each year. Thus, Latino electoral participation rates will continue to be lower than the community's raw population size should suggest.

Newly Emerging Structural Characteristics of the Electoral System

Seven major structural changes are occurring throughout the American political system.[11] These do not uniquely impact the Latino community or the states where Latinos reside. Instead, they are systemic and, at least partially, explain the steady decline in electoral participation of all electorates throughout the 1960s, 1970s, and 1980s. Although they have been analyzed extensively elsewhere, we want to introduce them briefly into this discussion. We will discuss one of these items, the fourth, in greater depth in the next section. These changes include:

1. The decline of political parties and, at the community level, of local partisan ethnic clubs or organizations.
2. The decline of partisan competition in many races, which reduces partisan mobilization efforts, the consequences of which are felt particularly by those less familiar with the American

electoral system (i.e., the naturalized immigrant and the traditionally marginalized native-born citizen).

3. The rise of candidate-centered campaigns run by consultants independent of the parties.

4. The increase in VRA-produced, safe, uncompetitive, ethnically homogeneous districts. These districts usually produce intense competition only when they are initially established or when they become vacant.

5. The increasing reliance on campaign technology that allows candidates to target their message so that it reaches only those registered voters most likely to vote and reduces outreach to communities that have not voted at high rates in the past.

6. The use of direct-democracy ballot strategies such as initiatives, referenda, constitutional amendments, and bond authority, which make the vote increasingly complex, combined with the increase in the number of elective offices, particularly for ambiguously titled special districts.

7. The increasing diversification of the electorate, accompanied by extending ethnic-specific voting protections, including bilingual electoral information and districting guarantees to traditionally excluded groups such as Asians, Native Americans, and Latinos.

While these changes affect the electorate as a whole, we are convinced that their impact is particularly felt among the new electorates that we have described. More to the point, only the last of these enhances minority participation. This positive effect is surely overwhelmed by the dampening effect on electoral participation of the other six, which together may account for much of the decline in electoral turnout that the nation has experienced in recent decades.

VRA Districts

Each of the newly emerging structural characteristics discussed in the previous section has the effect of diminishing the link between the electorate and the electoral system. The VRA, however, was intended to establish and strengthen just this link. The Act was intended primarily to increase minority electoral participation, regardless of race or ethnicity. Once enabled to vote freely, Latinos would be able to elect representatives of their choosing. Yet, unintentionally perhaps, VRA districts may have weakened the link between Latino voters and electoral institutions by emphasizing who gets elected over who votes.

As the VRA moved from ensuring individual voting rights to ensuring implicitly communities' rights to elect their own to office, districting strategies that formerly had been used against minorities came to be used to their benefit. Congress and the courts mandated that when drawing districts, jurisdictions had to assure minorities of "safe" districts. While the definition of safe districts and the lengths to which jurisdictions had to go to draw them is not the focus of this paper, their effect is. Safe districts have to have a sufficient number of the minority population to ensure that it can elect a fellow minority member. Because minorities tend to vote at lower rates than whites, these districts often must contain the targeted minority at more than 50 percent of the voting-age population. In the case of Latinos, the districts have to be even more overwhelmingly Latino. High rates of noncitizenship in high density Latino areas mean that to have a majority or strong plurality of voting-age population, Latino districts must contain a lot of young Latinos and noncitizens. Thus, one characteristic of Latino districts is a lower number of voters than in other districts (de la Garza and DeSipio 1995).

What is the effect of districts drawn to ensure the election of Latinos? The most obvious is the election of Latinos. As we noted, the increase in the number of Latino elected officials has been dramatic. This achievement had its price, however. These majority Latino districts are highly partisan. In Mexican-American and Puerto Rican areas, the partisanship is Democratic; in Cuban areas, Republican. As a result, these districts are essentially uncontested in the general election. Unfortunately, there is also little competition in the primaries; even with the current anti-incumbent fever, incumbents have many advantages that are hard for challengers to overcome, particularly in relatively poor districts with more marginalized electorates. As a result, incumbents can assure primary and general-election victories with a small cadre of strong supporters, comfortable in the awareness that much of the district is uninterested, unaware, or unable to participate.[12]

A fair criticism of this argument is that many incumbents run in safe districts. Yet, these Latino districts were designed to help mobilize new electorates into American politics. Unless they are mobilized, the new electorates will not be socialized into the political system and are condemned to political limbo: they are neither formally excluded nor included. Thus, VRA districts may have the unintended effect of distancing all but the most committed voters from elections even while they assure that Latinos (and African Americans) are elected to office. The goal of electing minorities is seen as equal to the goal of mobilizing new electorates; the former may even obscure the latter. As it has evolved, in other words, the original objective of the VRA has been de-emphasized in favor of what must be recognized as a secondary, if important, goal.

Conclusions

We want to emphasize that the lack of electoral competition in many VRA districts is just one of the factors that maintains low levels of electoral participation in the Latino community. In fact, it may well explain less than the sociodemographic factors, including noncitizenship and the structural changes in the American political system that are numbing political participation in general. Yet, the districts are part of a system that does little to mobilize voters.

Since its original passage in 1965, the VRA has been amended several times. Each amendment has broadened the coverage of the Act. Each has also moved away from the original narrow effort to eliminate obstacles to participation (Issacharoff 1992). In our concluding section, we propose three strategies that could be incorporated to encourage electoral participation.

V. Recommendations for a New Voting Rights Act

Twenty years after the VRA's extension to Latinos, we must ask where we are in terms of Latino electoral empowerment. Our findings indicate that the VRA has been successful in making a symbolic statement of Latino inclusion and in discouraging and largely eliminating the overt electoral discrimination faced by Mexican Americans in the Southwest prior to 1975. It has failed, however, to address the core problems keeping many potential Latino voters from the polls.

At a deeper level, our findings indicate the danger in viewing American minorities through a single lens. Many of the solutions offered to Latinos more appropriately meet the needs of the African Americans for whom the solutions were originally designed. Although there is overlap in the communities' needs, as we have shown, there are also important differences. The most important among these is the VRA districts, which, considering the composition of the Latino adult population and the diffuse electoral discrimination faced by Latinos prior to 1975, may serve to exacerbate nonparticipation among many Latino adults.

We propose, then, three sets of strategies to assure that the electorate (both potential and current) is a more central focus of both the VRA and Latino community discussions of electoral empowerment. The first is a commitment to maintaining the Act's bilingual electoral provisions. Despite our findings that these are little used, there is both a practical and a symbolic need to maintain bilingual ballots. Second, we would suggest that although time will ameliorate some of the sociodemographic limitations that we have discussed, the increasingly dynamic Latino electorate itself needs to establish a community-wide commitment to new voter mobilization. This should not be just a conventional effort at voter registration, but instead a full range of activities from naturalization to get-out-the-vote campaigns. Finally, we develop two suggestions around the question of noncitizens: that the federal government promote nationalization among eligible noncitizens, and that limited noncitizen voting eligibility for new permanent resident aliens be used as a tool to integrate these new immigrants into the civic and electoral culture. Since they constitute nearly 40 percent of the Latino adult population, noncitizens need to be a central focus of any discussion of Latino community empowerment.

The Symbolic and Practical Need
to Maintain Bilingual Voting Assistance

As we noted, few Latino voters report that they have had access to bilingual voting materials. Even fewer report that they rely on this assistance. Yet, the availability of such material inflames many critics of the VRA and galvanizes both Latino and non-Latino critics as evidence of a desire among Latinos to be somehow separatist (Chavez 1991). Despite the recent extension of bilingual provisions until 2007, some may see this is the time to move away from this form of voter protection.

We would argue that the elimination of bilingual ballots is not appropriate for two reasons. First, at a symbolic level, the bilingual provisions still serve as a signal that Latinos are welcome in the American political system. Few may use the bilingual ballots, but their presence reminds voters that Spanish speakers are a part of the nation and were consciously excluded from participation for more than 100 years. Congress did not extend bilingual assistance to all language minority groups, but instead only to those that had faced discrimination. The symbolism of the rectification of this wrong remains important.

Second, the bilingual provisions continue to serve the purpose for which they were designed (though, we acknowledge, an ever smaller share of those using the bilingual assistance were the original beneficiaries). Many native-born Mexican Americans who went to school as late as the early 1970s were the product of a discriminatory education system that denied them education in English. Some need bilingual assistance. Further, many Puerto Ricans, especially those raised in Puerto Rico who migrated to the United States as adults, are not functional in English. Their right to participate as U.S. citizens is abridged unless they have access to election materials in the language of their state-provided education. Thus, for symbolic and practical reasons, we argue that bilingual ballots need to be preserved. As this paper indicates, however, these alone are not enough to assure equal levels of participation.

Not all Latinos faced the exclusion that Mexican Americans faced in the Southwest prior to 1975. Nor do many have the unique relationship that Puerto Ricans have with the United States. Some would argue that other Latinos, particularly Cuban Americans and new immigrants from Central and South America, should not, as a normative matter, benefit from this program designed to rectify past discrimination. We do not find this argument convincing for two reasons. First, Congress specifically included all Spanish "language minority" residents of the United States (assuming the jurisdictions met the 5 percent threshold). It could have limited the coverage of the act to Mexican Americans or to the Southwest but did not. Second, the elimination of coverage for Cuban Americans, Central and South Americans, and Latinos from the Caribbean would create an undue and perhaps impossible bureaucratic burden. Thus, again for symbolic as well as practical reasons, we oppose the narrowing of the bilingual election material provisions to exclude non-Mexican and non–Puerto Rican Latinos.

Overcoming Sociodemographic Limits
on Latino Voting through New Voter Mobilization

The limits of age, education, and income will be with the Latino community for many years to come. They are themselves self-reinforcing and are further reinforced by continuing immigration

Yet, at the same time, they are less relevant for an increasing share of the Latino population. Latinos are aging. Also, increasing numbers are obtaining higher levels of education and earning higher incomes. We do not present these generalizations as Pollyannas. Instead, the emergence of a growing core of Latinos who have all the characteristics associated with higher levels of voting should steadily increase turnout among Latinos. As turnout increases, so should the impetus among candidates, campaigns, and parties to reach out to Latinos.

The burden of mobilization cannot fall solely on campaign institutions, however. As we indicated in Section IV, the potential for mobilization from these organizations has steadily declined over the past three decades. Instead, Latino leaders, including elected officials and nonelective community leaders, must galvanize this community into participation. The neglect that characterizes many noncompetitive races must be replaced by an ethos of involvement and participation. Where the battle has evolved to emphasize proportionate representation, the battle must return to its original objective: proportionate participation.

As we have indicated, one obstacle to equal participation is the impact of VRA districts on Latino voter mobilization. To remedy this, we would suggest that the focus during redistricting shift from maximizing the number of Latino districts to designing districts of varied Latino population densities, some that Latinos will be assured of representing (majority Latino districts) and others that Latinos will grow into representing in the period before the next redistricting (Latino influence districts).

This combination of district densities would have a series of beneficial effects. First, the majority Latino districts would assure that Latino voices are heard in the elected body. Second, the influence districts would assure that there is active competition for Latino votes and mobilization of new voters. If these districts elect Latinos soon after redistricting, they will have been elected through new voter mobilization or through coalitions between Latinos and non-Latinos. If they elect non-Latinos, these elected officials will have to be accountable to their large (but not majority) Latino constituency or face the possibility of strong competition from a Latino in the next election. An example would be the Florida district represented by Claude Pepper (Moreno and Rae 1992).

This recommendation might seem to foster ethnic divisiveness. We would argue, however, that long-term effects of competition and new voter mobilization would be better for the system than a demobilization and exclusion of a majority of the potential electorate, even if the effects included some ethnic tensions. Although it was not the intent of the state legislators, we would argue that congressional redistricting in both 1982 and 1992 has followed the pattern we recommend in several states (Cain and Kiewet 1985; Falcón 1992).

Studies of the African-American population indicate that the civil rights movement had a long-term effect on the black community. The fight for basic rights ensured that participants remained involved politically long after the rights had been won (Verba and Nie 1972). By earning coverage under the VRA without a similar level of community-wide demand making, Latinos may have lost out on some of the long-term benefits that African Americans won. Thus, while until now the battle has been focused on protections that have already been realized, we increasingly must focus on energizing the community from within. This sort of community-wide electoral mobilization has occurred at different times in different places. We have mentioned the examples of Miami, northern New Mexico, and Denver. Community leaders must draw on these models to assure that the beneficial provisions of the VRA are not lost to sociodemographic factors or to the general malaise of modern American politics.

Noncitizen Voting and Naturalization Drives

Our final suggestions focus on the approximately 40 percent of the Latino population excluded from participation on the basis of their citizenship status. Although we discuss this last, we would argue that it is the most important dilemma facing Latino leaders, and one whose magnitude is unique to Latinos (Duarte 1985). We make two suggestions. The first addresses naturalization and the second noncitizen voting (Levinson 1989).

The federal government has traditionally abjured any responsibility for encouraging immigrants to naturalize. Its justification is that naturalization is viewed as a voluntary act and should be both desired and earned. From the 1870s to the 1910s, however, local governments and political machines moved immigrants to citizenship with hardly a second thought. The federal government was able to maintain its distance while millions of immigrants passed to citizenship (DeSipio 1993).

During the current wave of large-scale immigration, the federal government has until recently maintained its hands-off position, and no other public or private organization has filled the gap. Indeed, an effort, during the Carter Administration by Immigration and Naturalization Service Commissioner Leonel Castillo to promote naturalization in immigrant communities led to a congressional rebuke of Castillo. The current INS Commissioner, Doris Meissner, has indicated a willingness to change this policy and to use INS resources to promote naturalization among eligible immigrants (Pachon and DeSipio 1994). While budget constraints may doom this proposal, the INS is currently seeking ways to privatize some aspects of nationalization applicant processing and to streamline the processing in addition to more nascent efforts to promote naturalization (DeSipio 1995).

We advocate that these proposals and endeavors be expanded. This suggestion is based on two factors. First, immigration is a federal function; yet, once immigrants come to the United States, there is no follow-through on the part of the federal government. Immigration policy needs a concomitant settlement policy. Second, naturalization is bureaucratically complex. A recent study of Latino immigrants found that almost all plan to remain in the United States permanently and most desire U.S. citizenship, yet many do not know where to turn to get assistance and to find out what is required of them (NALEO Educational Fund 1989; DeSipio and Alegre 1992). Specifically, we advocate the establishment of a grant program to community organizations and local governments to promote the value of naturalization and to assist applicants with the bureaucratic requirements of citizenship. We also advocate the use of the public schools as a training ground not only for being a good American (citizenship), but also for how to become an American (naturalization).

Our second suggestion is a modified form of the current effort to make noncitizens eligible to vote. We would add two twists. First, we would allow noncitizens to vote only for the five-year period during which they are statutorily ineligible to naturalize. Under this system, recently immigrated permanent residents would be able to obtain a five-year voter registration card (transferable across jurisdictions, but not extendable). After the five years, they would no longer be eligible for permanent resident voting privileges, but would be able to naturalize. Recognizing that the INS suffers from frequent backlogs, we would allow some provision for extending the temporary privileges while the application is on file. Although the authors of this discussion do not fully agree on whether voting should be limited to local elections (de la Garza) or should include all elections (DeSipio), we both advocate the extension of noncitizen voting privileges to local elections at a minimum.

The second twist is that naturalization applicants who can show that they voted in most primary and general elections during the five-year period of noncitizen voter registration would be exempt from the naturalization exam. The exam is designed to test good citizenship through indirect measures such as knowledge of American history and civics. We propose that voting is an equally good measure of commitment to and understanding of the American system.

VI. RENEWED CHALLENGE TO THE VRA: *SHAW V. RENO* AND ITS AFTERMATH

Over the past two years, the Supreme Court has indicated that it might be reexamining the constitutionality of minority-districting strategies. Although a subsequent ruling indicated the court's basic support for the

VRA, its ruling in *Shaw v. Reno* (1993) indicates that VRA advocates cannot assume that future courts will continue to hold the VRA and, particularly, the results test to be constitutional. Our article does not address the central issue in that case—the limits of districting design strategies. Nevertheless, *Shaw* raises several issues that could influence Latino districting strategies under the Voting Rights Act. Thus, the ruling is relevant to our discussion of Latino electoral participation and the VRA.

The Court's concern about creating oddly shaped districts in order to increase the likelihood of electing minority representatives calls into question two newly designed Congressional districts that elected Latinos in 1992 (New York's 12th and Illinois's 4th) and one in which a Latino was expected to win, but did not (Texas's 29th). The construction of these districts could now be challenged. The impact of this new judicial caution will probably be much greater in state legislative and local districting where there are many more districts. It could force advocates of districting plans designed to increase the number of Latino elected officials to spend extra time and resources justifying their plans before the courts. If the courts respond negatively to these pleas, the steady increase in the number of Latino officeholders will probably slow.

Justice O'Connor's majority opinion potentially raises a more significant dilemma for Latino coverage under the Voting Rights Act. She is implicitly concerned about community. Specifically, she questions whether designers of districts can assume a commonality among African Americans despite residence in different parts of the state. As we have indicated, the existence of community is even more difficult to assume among Latinos. Thus, the introduction of "community" into the judicial lexicon for evaluating the appropriateness of districting strategies raises the possibility that the courts could respond favorably to a challenge of the VRA's categorization of all "Spanish-surnamed" peoples as being a community for the purposes of designing VRA districts.

We present evidence of this weak Latino claim to community when discussing the political histories of the various Latino national-origin groups. Adding to these different experiences is the absence of a self-perceived common political agenda among Latinos themselves (de la Garza et al. 1992, Table 9.22). This absence has begun to manifest itself in areas in which more than one Latino national-origin group resides. Recent political history, such as the Los Angeles riots, demonstrates that Latinos of different national origins can have very different political interests despite their residence in the same jurisdiction or geographic area. This ruling increases the already existing possibility that one Latino national-origin group could challenge a districting plan that used its numbers to create a district likely to elect a member of another group. For example, Dominicans in New York could object to the use of their numbers to construct a district that would be likely to elect a Puerto Rican.

Underlying the Court's ruling is a concern that we share and that we have discussed in this analysis. Specifically, the Court notes that legislatures and courts can go too far in creating majority-minority districts. This is not a new concern. Courts, legislatures, and minority-districting advocates have long resisted efforts to "pack" minorities—placing all Latinos or blacks into as few districts as possible. The *Shaw* decision potentially raises judicial concern about majority-minority districts to a new level.

As we have indicated, majority-minority districts run the risk of harboring safe incumbents who do not need to mobilize voters. Without mobilization, the negative impact of class, education, and age on Latino and black voting are further reinforced. Moreover, removing minorities from Anglo-represented districts reduces the need for Anglo elected officials to respond to minority community needs or to build coalitions with minority elected officials. The *Shaw* ruling does not address this concern. By placing advocates of minority districts on notice that maximizing the number of minority districts is not the only standard against which a VRA districting plan will be evaluated by the courts, however, *Shaw* opens the possibility that questions such as how to develop districts that expand minority participation as well as minority representation will be raised.

Finally, the majority opinion in *Shaw* raises an issue that we find disturbing and empirically unfounded. The call for judicial scrutiny of race-based districting raises the possibility that the fundamental underpinnings of the Voting Rights Act and of black- and Latino-sensitive districting schemes may be subject to constitutional challenge. As we have demonstrated, Mexican Americans and Puerto Ricans experienced true exclusion (as did African Americans). The specific type of remedies needed for Latinos may well have differed from those designed for blacks, but in both cases the solution involved a sensitivity to race and ethnicity and a remedial provision of districts likely to elect blacks and Latinos. Thus, we call for saving the baby—maintaining the Voting Rights Act and its coverage of Latinos—while changing the bathwater and scrubbing the tub—redesigning the Act so as to assure that it maximizes Latino interaction with government and participation in the selection of community representatives. We, then, are concerned that *Shaw* might be used to challenge the underlying need for the VRA or to raise what we consider to be an insidious claim that non-Hispanic whites today face exclusion comparable to that experienced by African Americans, Mexican Americans, and Puerto Ricans prior to the enactment of the VRA.

CONCLUSION

Although the extension of the VRA to language minorities, particularly Latinos, was not very deeply considered by Congress, its effects have been overwhelmingly positive, but limited. In one area—voter mobilization—however, much more needs to be done. We suggest three broad areas for action. First, the protections of the current Act must be maintained. Until 2007, this seems certain. Second, Latino community leaders must look beyond solely electing Latinos to office and instead mobilize all Latinos, regardless of age, education, or income, to participate in electoral politics. Finally, the high rate of noncitizenship must be recognized as an especially important problem for Latinos. To address this, we advocate a limited form of noncitizenship voting. This noncitizen voting, though, is a means to an end—to promote the transition from immigrant to citizen.

NOTES

An earlier version of this article appeared in the *Texas Law Review* (V 71 #7: 1479–1539).

1. We use the terms 'Latino' and 'Hispanic' interchangeably to refer to residents of the United States who can trace their ancestry to the Spanish-speaking regions of Latin America or the Caribbean.

2. In addition to "Spanish heritage," the covered language minorities were: Native Americans, Asian-Americans, and Alaskan natives.

3. Title II protections were extended to the following areas with Spanish-heritage language minorities: Arizona (10 counties), California (6 counties), Colorado (1 county), Florida (6 counties), New Mexico (3 counties), New York (3 counties) and all of Texas. Spanish bilingual ballots were required in 14 counties in Arizona, 38 counties in California, 1 town in Connecticut, 34 counties in Colorado, 6 counties in Florida, 1 county in Idaho, 1 county in Kansas, 1 county in Louisiana, 7 counties in Nevada, 32 counties in New Mexico, 3 counties in New York, 1 county in Oregon, 148 counties in Texas, 2 counties in Utah, 4 counties in Washington and 4 counties in Wyoming.

4. The first documented "Latino" elected official was Joseph M. Hernandez, a Whig from Florida in the 1822–1823 Congressional term. By way of comparison, the first African Americans did not appear in Congress until 1870 (Voting Rights Review 1992a; 1992b).

5. Rates for other states are: Arizona 60 percent, California 45 percent, Florida 43 percent, Illinois 56 percent, New Mexico 50 percent and New York 55 percent (NALEO Educational Fund 1990, Table 11).

6. We use these three national origin–focused terms (as well as Anglos) to identify the respondents to the LNPS. The survey was careful to allow respon-

dents to select their own preferred identity term, including American or a pan-ethnic term.

7. These rates of noncitizenship are somewhat higher than the national average of Latino adult noncitizenship of 37.7 percent (U.S. Bureau of the Census 1991a, Table 2).

8. Although these reported voting rates exceed the levels reported in other national data sources, they follow the national patterns. Indeed, the Mexican and Puerto Rican turnout rates are quite close to the national figures for all Latinos. Mexican Americans and Puerto Ricans constitute approximately 75 percent of Latinos (63 and 11 percent, respectively). The higher figures for Cuban Americans are in keeping with studies of the Florida Cuban population that show that Cuban Americans tend to vote at higher rates than do other Latinos and, after accounting for U.S. citizenship, at rates exceeding the Florida Anglo population (Moreno and Warren 1992).

9. The total weighted n for respondents who answered the questions about Spanish language voting materials is 380; the total number of weighted responses for all Latinos (which overrepresents Mexican Americans relative to Puerto Ricans and Cuban Americans) is 257.

10. Several jurisdictions allow noncitizens to vote in some elections. Among areas with significant Latino populations, New York allows noncitizen voting for its community school boards and Chicago for its school-based school boards. Until the 1920s, many states allowed noncitizens who had declared their intention to naturalize to vote (Rosberg 1977). It should be noted that this state decision to allow noncitizen voting was instrumental; the states that offered noncitizens the franchise wanted new residents during a period of competition for immigrants.

11. These seven characteristics of the modern electoral system emerged during a post-project meeting of a five-city ethnographic study of political participation in core Latino barrios (de la Garza, Menchaca, and DeSipio 1994). Bruce Cain (1991) has developed a similar typology.

12. In the five-city study, only one barrio, Calle Ocho in Miami, saw high levels of candidate-voter interaction. The other four research sites—Magnolia in Houston, Pilsen in Chicago, Boyle Heights in Los Angeles, and El Barrio in New York—saw few efforts by candidates to reach out to barrio residents, as voters or otherwise (de la Garza, Menchaca, and DeSipio 1994).

REFERENCES

Anders, Evan. 1979. *Boss Rule in South Texas.* Austin: University of Texas Press.
Balz, Daniel. 1987. "Polling and the Latino Community: Does Anybody Have the Numbers?" In *Ignored Voices: Public Opinion Poll and the Latino Community,* ed. Rodolfo O. de la Garza. Austin, Tex.: Center for Mexican American Studies Press.

Cain, Bruce. 1990. "Voting Rights and Democratic Theory: Toward a Color Blind Society?" In *Controversies in Minority Voting: The Voting Rights Act in Perspective,* ed. Bernard Grofman and Chandler Davidson. Washington, D.C.: Brookings Institution.

Cain, Bruce. 1991. "The Contemporary Context of Racial and Ethnic Politics in California." In *Racial and Ethnic Politics in California,* ed. Bryan O. Jackson and Michael Preston. Berkeley: Institute for Governmental Studies Press.

Cain, Bruce, and D. Roderick Kiewet. 1985. "Ethnicity and Electoral Choice: Mexican American Voting Behavior in the California 30th Congressional District." In *The Mexican American Experience: An Interdisciplinary Anthology,* ed. Rodolfo O. de la Garza et al. Austin, Tex.: University of Texas Press.

Caro, Robert. 1990. *Means of Ascent.* New York: Knopf.

City of Mobile v. Bolden. 446 U.S. 55, 1980.

Chavez, Linda. 1991. *Out of the Barrio: Toward a New Politics of Hispanic Assimilation.* New York: Basic Books.

Cotrell, Charles L., and Jerry Polinard. 1986. "Effects of the Voting Rights Act in Texas: Perceptions of County Election Administrators." *Publius: The Journal of Federalism* 16 (Fall): 67–80.

de la Garza, Rodolfo O., and Louis DeSipio. 1990. "The Voting Rights Act and Latino Electoral Participation." Paper prepared for presentation at the "Key to Empowerment? The Voting Rights Act of 1965" Conference, the American University, April 7.

de la Garza, Rodolfo O., and Louis DeSipio. 1995. *Ethnic Ironies: Latino Politics in the 1992 Elections.* Boulder, Colo.: Westview Press.

de la Garza, Rodolfo O., Louis DeSipio, F. Chris García, John A. García, and Angelo Falcón. 1992. *Latino Voices: Mexican, Puerto Rican, and Cuban Perspectives on American Politics.* Boulder, Colo.: Westview Press.

de la Garza, Rodolfo O., Martha Menchaca, and Louis DeSipio, eds. 1994. *Barrio Ballots: Latino Politics in the 1990 Elections.* Boulder, Colo.: Westview Press.

DeSipio, Louis. 1993. "Counting on the Latino Vote: Latinos as a New Electorate." Doctoral dissertation, University of Texas at Austin [forthcoming from the University Press of Virginia].

DeSipio, Louis. 1995. "Are We Incorporating the Next Generation? Citizenship and Naturalization Among U.S. Immigrants." Paper prepared for presentation at the Western Political Science Association, March.

DeSipio, Louis, and Juan-Carlos Alegre, eds. 1992. *NLIS Research Notes* 1–11. Washington, D.C.: The NALEO Education Fund.

Duarte, E. B. 1985. "Role of INS in Naturalization Outreach." In *First National Conference on Citizenship and the Hispanic Community, Proceedings.* Washington, D.C.: NALEO Education Fund.

Dumas, Kitty. 1992. "Bilingual Voting Help Extended After Partisan Scrap in House." *Congressional Quarterly* (July 25): 2179.

Falcón, Angelo. 1984. "A History of Puerto Rican Politics in New York City: 1860s to 1945." In *Puerto Rican Politics in Urban America,* ed. James Jennings and Monte Rivera. Westport, Conn.: Greenwood Press.

Falcón, Angelo. 1992. "Time to Rethink the Voting Rights Act?" *Social Policy* (Fall/Winter).

Fincher, Ernest B. 1974. *Spanish Americans as a Political Factor in New Mexico.* New York: Arno Press.

Fuchs, Lawrence. 1990. *The American Kaleidoscope: Race, Ethnicity, and the Civic Culture.* Hanover, N.H.: University Press of New England.

García, John A. 1986. "The Voting Rights Act and Hispanic Political Representation in the Southwest." *Publius: The Journal of Federalism* 16 (Fall): 49–66.

Gomez v. City of Watsonville. 863 F 2nd. 1407, 1988.

Grebler, Leo, Joan W. Moore, and Ralph C. Guzman. 1970. *The Mexican American People: The Nation's Second Largest Minority.* New York: The Free Press.

Grenier, Guillermo, with Fabiana Invernizzi, Linda Salup, and Jorge Schmidt. 1994. "Los Bravos de la Política: Politics and Cubans in Miami." In *Barrio Ballots: Latino Politics in the 1990 Elections,* ed. Rodolfo O. de la Garza, Martha Menchaca, and Louis DeSipio. Boulder, Colo.: Westview Press.

Grofman, Bernard. 1985. "Criteria for Districting: A Social Science Perspective." *UCLA Law Review* 33.

Guerra, Fernando. 1992. "Conditions Not Met: California Elections and the Latino Community." In *From Rhetoric to Reality: Latino Politics in the 1988 Elections,* ed. Rodolfo O. de la Garza and Louis DeSipio. Boulder, Colo.: Westview Press.

Guerra, Fernando, and Luis Fraga. 1995. "Theory, Reality, and Perpetual Potential: Latinos and the 1992 California Elections." In *Ethnic Ironies: Latinos Politics in the 1992 Elections,* ed. Rodolfo O. de la Garza and Louis DeSipio. Boulder, Colo.: Westview Press.

Hain, Paul, and Jose C. García. 1981. "Voting, Elections and Parties." In *New Mexico Government,* ed. F. Chris García and Paul L. Hain. Albuquerque: University of New Mexico Press.

Hero, Rodney E. 1992. *Latinos and the U.S. Political System: Two Tiered Pluralism.* Philadelphia, Penn.: Temple University Press.

Holmes, Jack E. 1967. *Politics in New Mexico.* Albuquerque: University of New Mexico Press.

Issacharoff, Samuel. 1992. "Polarized Voting and the Electoral Process: The Transformation of Voting Rights Jurisprudence." *Michigan Law Review* 90.

Lemus, Frank. 1973. *National Roster of Spanish Surnamed Officials.* Los Angeles: Aztlan Publications.

Levinson, Sanford. 1989. "Suffrage and Community: Who Should Vote?" *Florida Law Review* 41: 545–562.

Lewis, Oscar. 1959. *Five Families: Mexican Case Studies in the Culture of Poverty.* New York: Basic Books.

McCleskey, Clifton, and Bruce Merrill. 1973. "Mexican American Political Behavior in Texas." *Social Science Quarterly* 53, no. 4 (March): 785–798.

McCleskey, Clifton, and Dan Nimmo. 1968. "Differences between Potential, Registered and Actual Voters: The Houston Metropolitan Area in 1964." *Social Science Quarterly* 49: 103–114.

Meyer, Gerald. 1989. *Vito Marcantonio: Radical Politician 1902–1954.* Albany, N.Y.: State University of New York Press.

Moreno, Dario, and Christopher Warren. 1992. "The Conservative Enclave: Cubans in Florida." In *From Rhetoric to Reality: Latino Politics in the 1988 Election,* ed. Rodolfo O. de la Garza and Louis DeSipio. Boulder, Colo.: Westview Press.

Moreno, Dario, and Nicol Rae. 1992. "Ethnicity and Partisanship: The Eighteenth Congressional District in Miami." In *Miami Now! Immigration, Ethnicity, and Social Change,* ed. Guillermo Grenier and Alex Stepik III. Gainesville, Fla.: University Press of Florida.

NALEO Educational Fund. 1989. *The National Latino Immigrant Survey.* Washington, D.C.: The NALEO Educational Fund.

NALEO Educational Fund. 1990. *1989 National Roster of Hispanic Elected Officials.* Washington, DC: NALEO Educational Fund.

NALEO Educational Fund. 1991. *1991 National Roster of Hispanic Elected Officials.* Washington, D.C.: NALEO Educational Fund.

Pachon, Harry, and Louis DeSipio. 1992. "Latino Elected Officials in the 1990s." *PS: Political Science and Politics.* 25, no. 2. (June): 212–217.

Pachon, Harry, and Louis DeSipio. 1994. *New Americans by Choice: Political Perspectives of Latino Immigrants.* Boulder, Colo.: Westview Press.

Pachon, Harry, Louis DeSipio, Juan-Carlos Alegre, and Mark Magana. 1992. *The Latino Vote in 1992.* Washington, D.C.: NALEO Educational Fund.

Parker, Frank R. 1989. "Changing Standards in Voting Rights Law." In *Redistricting in the 1990s: A Guide for Minority Groups,* ed. William P. O'Hare. Washington, D.C.: The Population Reference Bureau.

Rogers v. Lodge. 458 U.S. 613, 1982.

Rosberg, Gerald. 1977. "Aliens and Equal Protection: Why Not the Right to Vote?" *Michigan Law Review* (April-May): 1092–1136.

Shaw v. Reno. 1993. 113 S. Ct. 2816.

Thernstrom, Abigail M. 1987. *Whose Votes Count? Affirmative Action and Minority Voting Rights.* Cambridge, Mass.: Harvard University Press.

Thornburg V. Gingles. 476 U.S. 30, 1986.

U.S. Bureau of the Census. 1973. *Voting and Registration in the Election of November 1972.* Current Population Reports P-20 #253. Washington, D.C.: U.S. Government Printing Office.

U.S. Bureau of the Census. 1989. *Voting and Registration in the Election of November 1988.* Current Population Reports P-20 #440. Washington, D.C.: U.S. Government Printing Office.

U.S. Bureau of the Census. 1991. *Voting and Registration in the Election of November 1990.* Current Population Reports P-20 #453. Washington, D.C.: U.S. Government Printing Office.

U.S. House of Representatives. 1975. *Hearings on H.R. 939, H.R. 2148, H.R. 3247 and H.R. 3501 Extension of the Voting Rights Act.* Washington, D.C.: U.S. Government Printing Office.

U.S. House of Representatives, Committee on the Judiciary, Subcommittee on Civil and Constitutional Rights. 1981. *Hearings on Extension of the Voting Rights Act.* Washington, D.C.: U.S. Government Printing Office.

U.S. Immigration and Naturalization Service. 1994. *1993 Statistical Yearbook of the Immigration and Naturalization Service.* Springfield, Va.: National Technical Information Service.

U.S. Senate, Committee on the Judiciary, Subcommittee on Constitutional Rights. 1975. *Hearings on S. 407, S. 903, S. 1297, S. 1409 and S. 1443 Extension of the Voting Rights Act of 1965.* Washington, D.C.: U.S. Government Printing Office.

Verba, Sidney, and Norman Nie. 1972. *Participation in America: Political Democracy and Social Inequality.* Chicago: University of Chicago Press.

Voting Rights Review. 1992a. "Chronological Listing of Hispanic Members of Congress Throughout U.S. History." Summer-Fall: 22.

Voting Rights Review. 1992b. "Chronological Listing of African American Members of Congress Throughout U.S. History" Summer-Fall: 21.

Weeks, O. Douglas. 1930. "The Texas Mexican and the Politics of South Texas." *American Political Science Review* 606–627.

Wolfinger, Raymond E., and Steven J. Rosenstone. 1980. *Who Votes?* New Haven, Conn.: Yale University Press.

4. The Industrial Areas Foundation and the Mexican-American Community in Texas: The Politics of Issue Mobilization

Benjamin Marquez

NEIGHBORHOOD ORGANIZATIONS, THEIR MEMBERSHIP, and their ability to create change at the local level have long concerned political scientists. The potential for minority political organizations to achieve lasting social change through the public sphere is an important issue as they pressure city government, enter biracial coalitions, or capture important local political offices (Eisinger 1980, Browning et al. 1984, Preston 1987:chs 7–11; Browning et al. 1990). This chapter examines the political agenda and activities of the Industrial Areas Foundation (IAF) in Mexican-American barrios in Texas, the current locus of Alinsky-style organizing. Representing communities throughout Texas, the IAF has revitalized Saul Alinsky's organizing principles and activist style to gain concessions on issues ranging from street paving to utility rate hikes and property taxes.

The two major questions addressed in this chapter concern the Alinsky style of organizing and whether or not that program can empower minorities to create lasting social and economic change. First, we ask whether the Industrial Areas Foundation network has been able to articulate the needs of the poor and translate them into a viable public policy agenda. In other words, has the IAF brought a set of policy proposals to the formal decision-making stage, received active consideration by public officials, and succeeded in receiving concessions from those public officials? Second, we ask whether or not any of the political successes they have enjoyed can eventually lead to changes in the economic problems facing the Mexican-American community such as poverty and unemployment.

The analytical approach to neighborhood mobilization which has dominated U.S. political science has been the group theory of politics, or pluralism. According to the pluralist school, individuals are independent decision makers who are free to participate in local politics whenever they judge it in their interests to do so. Group membership is overlapping and follows no rigid class pattern, and organizations usually dissipate once the issues that brought the group together are resolved. Even traditionally excluded groups like the poor or racial minorities who are willing to organize, invest their resources in the political process, and are prepared to compromise can have a decisive impact on local policy. Since social inequalities are said to be dispersed and not cumulative, poverty should not be an insurmountable obstacle since readily available political resources such as the vote, intelligence, and commitment can be utilized successfully by insurgent groups.

Political events, most notably the racial conflicts of the 1960s, not only called into question the major tenets of pluralist theory, but spawned a series of radical critiques of pluralism's interpretation of social conflict and political change. The general thrust of these critiques is that pluralist theory takes the capitalist political economy for granted and ignores vast inequalities in power and income in the United States. The elitist school of community power argues that a closed circle of elites have a far-reaching ability to constrain community mobilization efforts. Their social network, access to resources, and allies in decision-making centers give them an advantage rarely matched by neighborhood groups. Furthermore, the reputed power of local elites acts to demoralize the poor, thereby making the initiation of urban insurgency less likely. Neo-Marxist approaches to community decision making expand the critique of pluralism by arguing that the political and economic order is a power relationship in itself, one that works against the initiation of political demands which call for a redistribution of power and wealth. Because of the city's dependence on privately generated wealth, local authorities are predisposed to cooperate with upper-class interests and resist those who challenge the existing order.

For radical urban analysts concerned with minority political power, the relevant task is not only to critique the "apologetic" nature of U.S. pluralism (Kesselman 1983), but to understand the extent to which urban political organizations can increase the political participation of the poor as well as improve their lives. Recent studies of grassroots organizing from this perspective have argued that not only are community organizations growing in strength, but that they hold the potential to democratize local politics. Some authors see community organizations as the primary instruments through which political struggles with the state are waged and the class interests of poor neighborhoods are articulated (Delgado 1986:213). Given this hopeful outlook, the critical question is whether or not that participation can lead to real changes in local economic decision making (Boyte and Evans 1984).

The most far-reaching assertion concerning the power of urban political movements to turn political gains into economic change has been made by Manuel Castells. He argues that urban social movements hold the potential to radically change local and, ultimately, national life. Based on his crossnational study of urban political movements, he found two common trends among urban political groups. First, these insurgent movements challenged local business investment decisions and land use plans which promoted the notion of a city as a place for profit, and where services and space were distributed according to income level. Second, they sought to replace hierarchical political decision making with neighborhood self-management. For him, these groups were reacting to economic and political trends, and proposed an alternative to the interests and values of the dominant classes (1983:318–320). What makes his work unique in urban studies is his insistence that these goals constitute an imperative, a demand that political and economic democracy be implemented if the needs of the poor are to be resolved. He argues that anything less than democratic control of economic decision making would constitute reformism, a mere cosmetic change in a system that needs radical restructuring (ibid.:299).

This chapter demonstrates that, in the relatively short period of time the IAF has been active in Texas, it has successfully introduced a number of political initiatives on the public policy agenda. Since its first organization was established in 1974, the IAF network has confronted local power structures throughout the state and established a reputation as a formidable and aggressive player in local and state politics (Reitzes and Reitzes 1987:119). The network has also scored a number of impressive public policy victories in the areas of public works, education, and water service delivery. However, while it appears that the IAF is slowly altering the political character of the state, it will be argued that their potential to radically alter the economic problems that plague the Mexican-American community is problematic. Not only are the problems facing poor Mexican-Americans tied to national and international economic trends, but Alinsky's (1971) theory of community organizing is based on a conservative political philosophy designed to achieve piecemeal reform. Although Alinsky and his followers advance a populist vision of politics and economic deprivation in the United States, they fail to formulate an explicit political strategy which would counteract economic processes and market-driven decisions in economics.

The IAF's efforts represent a new chapter in the history of political organizing in the Mexican-American community and a departure from the cultural nationalism of the 1960s (Gomez-Quiñones 1978; Barrera 1979, 1985; Muñoz 1989). The IAF network is composed of eleven organizations in eight different cities in Texas including Houston, Fort Worth, San Antonio, El Paso, Austin, and communities in the Rio Grande Valley. Although the network has organized a wide range of neighborhoods throughout the state, the group's membership is largely Mexican-American, the bulk of the poor and powerless in Texas. With their statewide network, organizational skills, and record of success, the IAF represents an important new form of political activism in the Mexican-American community in a state that has a long history of racial conflict (Montejano 1987).

Utilizing the organizing principles of Alinsky (1971), the Industrial Areas Foundation has mobilized the poor and their limited resources in a renewed fight for social justice in Texas. They have brought with them all the earmarks of traditional Alinsky organizations: detailed research on community concerns, the development of umbrella organizations, the involvement of local churches, and the use of full-time professional organizers (Reitzes and Reitzes 1987:238–239). Alinsky-style groups inspire the poor to become involved in politics by organizing around issues that directly affect their lives, issues that the residents themselves have identified as important. A large part of an organizer's job is taken up in interviews with people in neighborhoods to find out who the potential leaders are, what concerns the community, and what will motivate them to act (Boyte 1990). The pattern of political action is to identify a target, a concretely defined embodiment of the causes of a neighborhood problem, and then attack that target with all the resources at the community's disposal (McKnight and Kretzmann 1984). To gain a response from public and private officials, the IAF makes ample use of the harsh confrontational style of politics that gained Saul Alinsky notoriety in the 1950s and 1960s. The acidic denunciations of public or corporate officials who oppose them also serve to involve their members emotionally in the group and to place their opposition in a defensive position (Levine 1973).

Has the Texas IAF network successfully initiated a policy agenda for poor Mexican-Americans? If the minority community is to create successful strategies for social change, it is important to understand how their issues can be translated into formal consideration by public officials (Polsby 1984; Nelson 1984). If the media attention they have received in recent years is a valid indicator, they have clearly articulated the social needs of Mexican-Americans in Texas. However, as Roger Cobb and Charles Elder (1972:85–86) have noted, the "systemic" agenda of legitimate social issues is distinct from the formal agenda, issues which are being given active and serious consideration by authoritative decision makers.

Cobb, Jennie Keith-Ross, and Marc Ross have developed a model through which one can understand the agenda-building process and through which the IAF's political platform and record of achievements can be assessed. They argue that there are four stages which shape all issue careers: initiation, specification, expansion, and entrance. Initiation is where grievances are articulated; specification is where grievances are translated into specific demands; expansion is where widespread support is rallied in order to attract the attention of decision makers; and finally, entrance is where there is movement to the formal agenda, where serious consideration of the issue takes place (1976:127–130).

The IAF's philosophy is one which accepts the challenge of moving their concerns through these stages. Indeed, they claim to prepare their members for a lifetime of political participation. A crucial aspect of IAF politics is the process by which the poor are urged to think about their problems and identify specific solutions to those problems and act upon them. IAF activists see their organizations as training grounds through which democratic principles are learned and practiced. One leader observed that the organization has a commitment to political literacy and that each organization in the IAF network was like a "mini-university" where people learn to participate in the policy-making process (Cortes 1988). Organizers see one of the network's main functions as helping people become part of public life by becoming directly involved in community decision making (Valle 1987). One IAF organizer observed that his organization provided a vehicle "where people learn about public debate and participation . . . politics in its highest form. We agitate and teach people how to act in their interests. Where else does that happen? It doesn't happen in the universities. It doesn't happen in the churches. I don't know where else it occurs. People love it" (Holler 1988).

Although Alinsky recognized the tendency for a political and economic elite to usurp power in U.S. communities, he believed it was within the power of grassroots insurgency to counterbalance their structural advantages. He held a deep faith in political pluralism and the need to protect a multigroup, competitive political system. In other words, established interests are entrenched and powerful, but with the proper organizing efforts, their power could be curbed, and poor people's lives could be transformed. In a classic pluralistic fashion, Alinsky defined power as the ability to act, the successful participation in local, citywide, or national decision making (Reitzes and Reitzes 1987:41). Alinsky-style groups in Texas endorse this approach as they seek to manipulate the political system through use of intelligence, persuasion, confrontation, and the vote. The relevant skill is learning how to hold public officials accountable, how to negotiate.

The IAF's strategy of involving the poor in the political process begins with a consciousness-raising process, one by which individuals are taught to think about their problems and act upon them. A central element of the IAF's organizational strategy is to raise people's expectations about themselves, their families, and their communities (Fisher 1984:149). Through the process of consciousness raising, individuals broaden their concept of the possible and cast off any self-imposed restraints (Obregon 1987). As Maria Luisa Vasquez of The Metropolitan Organization (TMO) in Houston noted, "you sort of relate power to what politicians do to the people, to what the rich do to the poor. I now know darned well that I'd better act on my self interest, politicians and corporations act on theirs all the time" (Boyer 1985). Furthermore, they learn to see themselves as part of a wider community. They are encouraged to look beyond their narrow economic interests and embrace community values such as the well-being of their neighbors and friends, their traditions, and their feelings of dignity and worth (Boyte and Evans 1984:94). "We have been united in one voice," notes one activist. "And when I speak on behalf of the organization. And it's not for me that I speak, but for all the poor people" (Obregon 1987).

Organizers spend a great deal of time speaking with residents of poor neighborhoods before they begin asking individuals to attend meetings or to volunteer their time. Once information about community conditions and resident concerns is collected, then a group is organized around the issues that neighborhood residents have identified. The focus on participation and the need for citizens to become involved in local affairs is part of the IAF's appeal. They try to politically re-educate the people they work with so that they not only see the possibility for social change, but see the necessity for them to become actively involved in the process. One activist recalled that it was the style of persuasion used by IAF activists that involved him in his local organization: "[When it was pointed out] . . . what was happening in the country as far as the family, the condition of American values, what we could do to maintain those values that were being attacked, that was sort of the spark" (Reed 1986).

Saul Alinsky's broad and sweeping vision of social change was designed to create a society where people's potentials would be realized, where they could "live in dignity, security, happiness, and peace" (Alinsky 1969:15). The Texas IAF's rhetoric adopts the same tone of alarm and moral condemnation. In a recent statement of their political agenda they argued that

> The situation that the IAF Network organizations find today in Texas is one of economic decline that is eating away at the social fabric of our communities. The quality of life is deteriorating for families throughout the state as unemployment grows, school drop out rates soar, neighborhoods deteriorate for lack of public investment, medical care and health resources move beyond the reach of more and more people. Our agenda calls for investment in Texas; in human capital, in social capital, and in technological capabilities. (IAF 1988)

Once Alinsky-style groups have motivated their members to understand their common problems, the next step is to advance to Cobb, Keith-Ross, and Ross's final stages of agenda setting and attract the attention of decision makers and move their demands to the formal decision-making agenda. This is by no means a simple process, but the underlying premise of the IAF's political strategy is that the U.S. political system is malleable enough to accommodate the demands of grassroots groups. The record reveals that they have done quite well in the governmental sphere. With the skills of their professional organizers and a core of dedicated activists, the IAF network has been able to influence local public policy through a combination of unconventional political tactics and an accurate mapping of neighborhood and local power patterns. In San Antonio, Communities Organized for Public Service (COPS) is the oldest IAF organization with the longest record of success. It has won millions of dollars in capital improvement monies, housing, new jobs, and other material benefits for the barrios of San Antonio. Between 1974 and 1981 San Antonio received $178.7 million in federal Community Development Block Grants, where $86 million went to COPS districts and 91 percent of the money was spent on projects favored by the group (Reitzes and Reitzes 1987:123).

The first joint action of the Texas IAF network demonstrated their political clout. In 1984, they acted to pressure the Texas governor to call a special session of the legislature to equalize the distribution of funds for education in the state. In 1984 the legislature passed an appropriations bill which stated that 70 percent of the total state appropriation to education will be distributed equally to all districts. As Donald and Dietrich Reitzes (1987:125) note, their skills and influence were formidable:

> COPS and Texas Interfaith leaders spend hundreds of hours in meetings with the governor, lieutenant governor, and key members of the House and Senate. After winning the battle for a special session, Texas Interfaith had thirty days, the maximum legal length of a special session, to "educate the legislators about the issue and its impact on the community." Delegations of Texas Interfaith organizations converged on Austin for rallies and to lobby representatives. Careful planning and coordination brought more than a thousand people to a mass rally to show popular support for the bill and generate favorable public opinion. Later, the rally broke up into small groups to lobby hometown lawmakers. During the period of crucial deliberations, key legislators were visited four or five times a day by Texas Interfaith delegations.

Similar successes have been recorded in other issue areas. In El Paso, the Inter-Religious Sponsoring Organization (EPISO) was instrumental in securing the passage of nine bond issues in El Paso in 1987 which brought $93 million worth of capital improvements to the city, much of which would be spent in Mexican-American areas of the city (EPISO 1987). In 1988, EPISO successfully fought for the creation of the Lower Valley Water District to provide water and sewer service to the growing number of *colonias* (unincorporated subdivisions) outside of El Paso, where an estimated 28,000 Mexican-Americans live without running water and about 53,000 have no sewer service (Applebome 1988; Cook 1988). Activists from the Texas IAF network of organizations spearheaded a drive to obtain state funding to extend water and sewer services throughout Texas. In June 1989, this effort resulted in the passage of the "*colonias* bill," which provided $30 million in general appropriations and cleared the way for bond sales to more than 2,000 Mexican-Americans, and forced the Environmental Protection Agency to cancel its plan to allow private firms to dispose of toxic waste by burning it in ships off the Gulf of Mexico (Acuña 1988:436). While other IAF organizations cannot claim the same degree of success, they too have won concessions from local government and corporations on issues as diverse as insurance premiums, utility rate increases, roads, and property taxes.

More established groups like EPISO, COPS, and Valley Interfaith have attracted the attention of the media and forced local politicians to make them part of the regular decision-making process. IAF groups have also sought to elect public officials sympathetic to their issue agenda. The network has been able to regularly mobilize hundreds and, on occasion, thousands of people for public meetings and voter mobilization drives. Since 1977, in three elections in the five districts served by COPS in San Antonio, thirteen of fifteen candidates most in accord with the group's positions have won election. Henry Cisneros, in his first election to the mayor's office, although not formally endorsed by the organization, benefited from the mobilization of the Latino vote (Lind 1984). In 1984, Valley Interfaith claimed to have registered 25,000 new voters for that year's presidential election (ibid.). That same year, approximately 21,000 Mexican-Americans were registered to vote through a registration drive conducted by EPISO. The drive produced the largest number of voters registered in the history of El Paso and increased the Mexican-American registration by over 4 percent (Navarro 1986:8). EPISO's fight for the extension of water to the outlying areas of El Paso was only one part of a larger struggle for empowerment of the Mexican-American community, a struggle that the IAF network has taken to the Texas state legislature. The statewide network has sponsored rallies in Austin that have attracted as many as 3,000 people to lobby the legislature on their social service agenda which included education, indigent health care, and aid to families with dependent children (*The Texas Observer,* "Levantando" 1987).

Following Alinsky's dictum that public officials respond to political strength rather than moral appeals, the Texas IAF has won praise from some and grudging respect from others. TMO in Houston has had a pact with mayor Kathy Whitmire committing her to meet with the group on a monthly basis to review progress on their issue agenda (Reitzes and Reitzes 1987:127). In San Antonio, where COPS has established a long record of working both with and against mayor Henry Cisneros, he has always acknowledged their power and influence. In 1988, he stated: "I can say unequivocally, COPS has fundamentally altered the moral tone and the political and physical face of San Antonio. It has also confirmed the judgment of the U.S. Catholic bishops' pastoral letter Economic Justice for All—that one way to overcome poverty is to empower the poor to participate more fully in decisions that affect their lives."

THE LIMITS OF PRESSURE GROUP REFORM

As specified by Cobb, Keith-Ross, and Ross (1976), the Texas IAF network has effectively articulated problems in several Mexican-American communities in Texas, translated them into specific grievances, and brought a number of policy initiatives to the formal decision-making stage. While they have successfully ushered through a number of important public policy initiatives, at this point it is important to ask to what extent these policy initiatives can lead to success in the area of economic development and a redistribution of resources.

Although Cobb, Keith-Ross, and Ross (1976:130–131) try to predict how the characteristics of a group's issue agenda affect its eventual success on the formal policy-making agenda, they do not distinguish between the policy initiatives the IAF has won thus far (public works, education, and water delivery) and the more global issues that concern them such as unemployment and poverty (see Polsby 1984:165–166). There is a growing literature which questions the ability of insurgent organizations to institute populist or redistributive politics through conventional means (Peterson 1981; Swanstrom 1985). These authors argue that the forces shaping the conditions under which low-income minority people live are not under the control of local governments, even governments run by minority regimes. They note the change in the U.S. economy from manufacturing and distribution activities to administration, information, and services has increased the number of problems minorities face and made their resolution prohibitively difficult without a nationally coordinated political and economic program (Browning et al. 1990:226–227; Wilson 1987).

The preceding argument speaks to the problems involved in political organizing and coalition building, but the more relevant critique contained in this literature asserts that it is the free market itself that victimizes minorities and isolates the poor (Logan and Molotch 1987). If insurgent politics is to be ultimately successful in counteracting poverty and powerlessness, a specific program designed to counteract market-driven decisions must be formulated. One charge leveled against Alinsky-style groups is that they are conservative in nature because they do not advocate a restructuring of the economy through political means (Levine 1973). Although Saul Alinsky has been recognized as an organizational genius, his political theorizing has been interpreted as one that leads to compromise and limited social reform. His philosophy of organizing has been criticized as a variation of pluralism that does not prescribe methods by which economic structures that dominate the poor and perpetuate their status can be transformed (Fisher 1984; McKnight and Kretzmann 1984).

At first glance, this criticism seems unfounded. The difficulty of overcoming adverse economic trends and structures presents the single most difficult problem insurgent groups face, and the IAF's political pronouncements are highly critical of the economic status quo. As one member of Valley Interfaith stated: "I want to see enough jobs for everybody that wants to work. I want jobs to be in the [Rio Grande] Valley, not welfare. . . . I want people on assistance to regain their dignity" (Lerma 1988). The lack of a generally accepted position on the political economy by the IAF network of groups is troubling since activists agree on the issues and their severity. One activist summarized the concern of the Texas IAF network when he argued that the United States was becoming "a two tiered society, a lower class and an upper class. We have families where the husband and wife don't see each other. They are working more and more and getting less and less" (Korcsmar 1988).

Social movement could pose a threat to the existing class order by working to restructure the social relations of production by challenging the right of free enterprise to set wages as well as make autonomous production and investment decisions (Wright 1985:ch. 1). However, in the case of the IAF, the biting critique of social institutions implied in its rhetoric does not reflect a radical vision of a future society. Indeed, an elimination or restructuring of the free enterprise system is explicitly rejected by the group. Alinsky himself was a virulent anti-socialist and shunned political ideologies that mapped out specific goals or had clearly articulated theories of economic processes—a central concern if anything other than reform is to be sought. Constructing elaborate theories about the workings of industrial capitalism and the inequalities it generates is not part of the IAF's consciousness-raising process.

The IAF's reformist stance toward the modern industrial state is one reason Alinsky-style groups have worked well with religious institutions. In Texas, it is the Roman Catholic Church that provides a set of moral values as well as spiritual and political guidance to the IAF network (IAF 1978). Activists cite their commitment to Christian principles as one of the major reasons they participate in the IAF network of organizations: "For me it is almost a ministry. . . . We do a lot of scriptural readings, our work is centered on the gospel" (Petry 1988). Some borrow from liberation theology in their analysis of poverty and injustice, but the connection to a more materialist interpretation of economic oppression is not made. Occasionally activists defined the problem in class terms. One organizer asserted: "If you are underprivileged because someone wants to make a profit, you are being oppressed" (Rodriguez 1988). Nevertheless, such views are not widely articulated among Texas IAF activists.

Formal links between local groups and churches are an essential aspect of the Alinsky form of organizing since they provide community organizations with experienced leaders as well as other resources, such as money and office space (Reitzes and Reitzes 1987:52). But the acceptance of these resources can act as a constraint on political activity. As

Lawrence Mosqueda (1986:ch. 4) has argued, the historical role of the Catholic Church in the Mexican-American community has been to control or restrain any radical political activity. Isidro Ortiz (1984), in a study of the Alinsky-style group United Neighborhood Organization (UNO), found that not only were the resources of the Catholic Church essential for the survival of the East Los Angeles group, but that the church exerted considerable control over the group's activities. The degree to which the church would support the activities of UNO depended on the political orientation of local bishops as well as the outcome of bureaucratic struggles within the Catholic hierarchy. Even the strong links Alinsky himself established with the Catholic Church were broken because of these disputes. The IAF national headquarters itself was moved from Chicago to New York because of a conflict over goals and tactics between the organizers and a newly installed, conservative Catholic administration in Chicago (Finks 1984).

The question of the church's restrictions on the radical potential of the Texas IAF is academic. The IAF's goals are construed within a tradition of social conservatism and its demands vis-à-vis the question of private property and the market are limited. The first assumption made by the Alinsky school is not that the poor are victims of a class hierarchy or economic imperatives. Rather they assert that people can be motivated by their immediate self-interest and it is the job of the organizer to identify those interests and use them to develop political agendas (Alinsky 1969:13). Alinsky saw neighborhoods as units of "collective consumption" and building effective political groups was, in effect, the building of consumer-oriented interest groups defined by geography (McKnight and Kretzmann 1984:15). Ernesto Cortes, lead organizer for the IAF network, pursues the same line of reasoning when he asks: "What are most of us interested in? Our everyday lives and our families and the schools that our kids go to and the quality of those schools and how much money we have and our real estate and our property" (1986:15). Organizing efforts in the Mexican-American community by IAF organizers begin with this premise, and thousands of hours of one-on-one interviews with residents of barrios in Texas precede any effort to bring individuals into active participation in an Alinsky-style group. While the specific issues found in Texas barrios and poor neighborhoods may vary, the general themes are constant. IAF organizers find that people identify issues such as drainage, utility rates, traffic problems, and other concerns that blight their daily lives as issues that concern them the most. Following Alinsky's admonition to avoid theoretical analysis or debates, IAF organizers do not attempt to make causal links to economic processes that lack immediate importance to their followers or coalition partners (Sekul 1983:176).

Levine (1973) has argued that Alinsky-style organizations get their radical reputation from their confrontational style rather than the content of their political agenda. That is, they demand access to decision-making arenas, vilify public officials who disagree with them, and identify with the plight of the poor all while seeking limited goals. For example, IAF activist Father Armand Matthew notes that "the ministry of the church is to liberate in the name of Jesus Christ." Likewise, the Reverend Virgilio Elizonso appeared to accept the charge that his political philosophy was socialist in nature by stating: "I'd consider it an honor if someone called me [a Marxist] because that would mean I'm doing my job" (Obregon 1987). Nevertheless, other sponsors of the IAF are closer to the mark when they emphasize the limited nature of their goals. Bishop John McCarthy, explaining the support the Galveston-Houston Roman Catholic Archdiocese has given to their local IAF organization, noted that "there is nothing more conservative, nothing more American than these types of organizations" (del Olmo 1983). By conservative, the bishop was arguing that their organization was not questioning the basic social and economic basis of society, but rather was seeking to become an active participant in the decision-making process and to eventually redirect its public policy priorities. Ernesto Cortes, director of the Texas IAF network, observed that "being a radical in the American tradition is about making that framework work" (1988).

Making the system work does not involve questioning its foundations. Edward Chambers, national director of the IAF, has eliminated references to the IAF being "radical" or to "radicalism" of any kind in its program. The network appeals to church or family values and the need for citizens to defend their beliefs actively through participation in local community organizations. Their appeal to traditional values is a strategy designed to broaden the base of community support and allay the fear of middle-class or conservative residents. The IAF clearly supports the free enterprise system, and today the IAF organizations are not fighting for community control but for a broader participation in decision making and an expansion and improvement of city services (Reitzes and Reitzes 1987:115).

Framing political objectives in terms of people's immediate needs limits the universe of the possible. The first question IAF activists ask themselves before deciding to concentrate on a social problem is whether or not it can be changed through the political process. Defining winnable issues is done by making a distinction between what are called "issues or problems." Issues are those problems which can be corrected through conventional pressure group politics. Problems are those structures or processes that are beyond the immediate influence of individual political groups. As one activist put it, "world hunger is a problem, not an issue" (Ceasar 1988). While these terms are open to various interpretations, the IAF defines problems as social trends or economic processes that cannot be resolved through pressure group politics while issues are those concerns which can be resolved through government action. Although Alinsky's legacy is one of forcing local institutions to respond to the needs and concerns of the poor, the processes and assumptions of a free market economy were never brought into question (Boyte and Evans 1984:86). In the end, politics and economics are distinct. As one IAF activist remarked: "You fight issues that are winnable. You have to let some things go. I know that it's hard" (Petry 1988).

DISCUSSION

In the fall of 1988 the IAF network in Texas initiated a campaign to register as many voters as possible in low-income areas for the upcoming presidential election. The campaign was called "sign up and take charge," and eight of the eleven organizations that are part of the network mobilized over 1,950 activists to canvass Mexican-American barrios and get their constituents to vote on election day. The theme was popular sovereignty. The network wanted to strengthen local organizations in order to force the federal government to give a higher priority to such issues as education, health care, and employment. The network was also preparing its members to gain experience so that they could develop leaders who would become involved in politics at the national level. This organizing drive was but one in a series of campaigns that the network has sponsored over the years to gain control of the decision-making process in the Southwest. Thus, Castells's first claim that neighborhood organizations represent a move toward democratization and can successfully acquire a larger say in local policy making is correct. Their efforts are motivated by a recognition that powerful forces opposed them, that government had always been biased toward monied interests, and that politics had been corrupted by money and unaccountable power.

    Still, there is a tension in the IAF's analysis of political economy. IAF activists recognize the wide range of economic problems facing the Mexican-American community, yet they do not argue that they are rooted in the imperatives of the free market. Indeed, very little time is spent building theories of politics and the economy. Saul Alinsky rejected ideological schemes because, for him, theoretical understanding implied a belief in basic and immutable truths (Alinsky 1969:xii–xv). Alinsky was action oriented and believed that it was immediate needs, not an appeal to abstract values, that would motivate people to act (Alinsky 1972:72). Furthermore, Alinsky believed his organizers should avoid the dangers of theory and have no more than a blurred vision of a better world. It should be up to the communities they organize to define their own future (Finks 1984:255). To the extent that the IAF network remains true to Alinsky, theory building will not become a central part of their agenda.

The lack of concern with theory is not unique to Alinsky-style organizations. Mark Kann (1983:371) argues that the new urban movements in the United States as yet have no theoretical solutions to concrete problems they face. He characterizes contemporary populist movements as "pioneers in ambivalence" who oppose corporate capitalism but in turn support "human scale" accumulation and ownership, exchange value, and market relations. However, drawing on ambiguous human or community values leaves too much unsaid and many urban organizations may carry conservative or counter-progressive baggage. As Robert Fisher notes, "it is not always clear whose traditions, whose hopes, whose community the new populism supports. Whose traditions are supported for example, when new populist organizations refuse to take a stand on busing, school integration, or abortion?" (1984:140–141). If these problems are ever to be worked out, urban neighborhood organizations must eventually develop long-range goals which address imbalances in a class society, whether they are fighting for a stop sign or for eviction blockage. Otherwise, group victories that win concessions from local government or corporations may deflect more radical possibilities by proving that the existing system "works" by being responsive to poor and working people and, therefore, is in no need of fundamental change (ibid.:162).

The economic dominance of business in any community is a structural feature of the local political economy that the IAF has not adequately addressed. As John McKnight and John Kretzmann (1984:17) have observed, the most difficult challenge to community building is to devise ways to insert local concerns into the equations by which businesses make decisions. In San Antonio, COPS found itself battling economic trends by attempting to pressure local businesses into paying higher wages. COPS fought the local Economic Development Foundation and its campaign to attract business to San Antonio by promoting the city's low wage scales and unorganized labor force. They asked that businesses coming into the city pay a "decent wage" of $15,000 a year for a family to support itself (Boyte 1984:151–152). However admirable this political crusade was, the enormity of the economic problems poor Mexican-Americans face may lie beyond such political pressure. Their economic vulnerability was dramatized in 1983 when a freezing storm put 20,000 farm workers out of work in the Rio Grande Valley, an IAF stronghold. Robert Marel (1989:57) summarized the impact of the storm:

> It is estimated that more than 7,000 jobs have been lost for the next several years, and that 3,000 to 4,000 jobs have been permanently lost because the new, smaller groves will require less manual labor. Prior to the Big Freeze the Valley's unemployment rates were among the highest in the United States, but after the Freeze unemployment soared even higher. The McAllen-Edenburg Pharr MSA site of the majority of citrus groves, registered the highest unemployment rate (19%) of any area in the United States in 1984. Cameron County was only a few rankings behind Hidalgo County.

Valley Interfaith lobbied the Reagan Administration for a $66.7 million public works project to provide jobs in the hardest hit areas, but despite the crisis atmosphere and their efforts to sway the president, their request was denied (Lind 1984).

The political victories and public recognition achieved by the IAF have galvanized the network in Mexican-American barrios throughout Texas. Yet there are limits to social change through IAF-sponsored tactics and political maneuvering. Carl Boggs, a political activist who has worked with groups like the Texas IAF, observes that the main failing of insurgent neighborhood groups is that they fail to spell out the class content and political form of the challenge they pose to corporate structures. There is no critical or transformative approach to power relations or domination, and neither the workings of the free market nor the legitimacy of existing institutions is questioned. He further argues that the aggressive new populist critique of the free market's excesses never questions the logic of accumulation itself (1983:359).

By confining political activity to legitimate institutions, the new populism is forced to define what is possible strictly in conventional normative terms. This observation is a critical one since Boggs asserts that, without a concrete plan to challenge material interests embedded in capitalist property relations, they are likely to fail in their efforts to permanently transform the lives of the poor. This theme is echoed by Henry Flores (1989), who found that, in San Antonio where the IAF has experienced its most spectacular successes, the relationship between business and government has always been an unequal one. In this activist city, where grassroots organizing had yielded millions of dollars in projects for Mexican-American neighborhoods, private interests continue to exercise a free hand when making investment and production decisions.

CONCLUSION

The record reveals that the IAF has articulated the needs of the poor and translated them into a successful public policy agenda. Following the pattern outlined by Cobb, Keith-Ross, and Ross (1976), IAF-affiliated organizations have brought a series of crucial problems to the formal decision-making stage of government and can claim credit for policy changes in a wide range of issue areas. Public works, property taxes, and education are areas in which the IAF network has had a profound influence. Although the network has focused on smaller, more manageable issues, it has won many political victories on behalf of the Mexican-American community and improved the lives of thousands of people in Texas. Thus, the ability of the IAF to expand the participation of the poor in the democratic process is real. The IAF network has fought its way into the policy-making agenda following the traditional pluralist criteria of organization, resource mobilization, and coalition building.

While the IAF has experienced a degree of success in the governmental field, can these reforms lead to changes in the larger economic problems that Mexican-Americans face? On this count there is reason to doubt that it can. First, one must take into account the extraordinary effort the poor must exert when participating in the policy process in the first place. The constant uphill political battles the IAF has fought on behalf of poor Mexican-Americans have mired them in years of conflict and compromise. Even when local IAF affiliate groups have established themselves as a force to contend with in local politics, they have not been accepted as part of the local political establishment. For example, El Paso mayor Jonathan Rogers did not acknowledge the role that EPISO played in bringing water to the *colonias* and publicly stated that "in my opinion, they were not a factor at all" (Cook 1988).

Even in IAF strongholds, local politicians have successfully rebuffed the network's demands. San Antonio mayor Henry Cisneros fought COPS over the issue of a domed stadium which would be paid for with an increase in the sales tax. Cisneros took the position that the sports stadium would promote economic growth in the city, while COPS felt that the poor would be paying for the project while other needs such as housing and education were neglected (Hagerty 1987). The debate reached such an acrimonious level that Cisneros openly declared he was ending his relationship with the group because of the "personal abuse" they heaped on him when fighting the proposal (Martinez 1987). That break from their former ally cost COPS much of their political capital when the mayor eventually prevailed and the referendum on the domed stadium won in the 1989 referendum. With the backing of the business community, whose extensive media campaign promoted the initiative, Cisneros was able to hand the IAF a major defeat. Ironically, it was the Mexican-American precincts, heavily canvassed by COPS, that carried the vote for the mayor (Flores 1989).

There is also reason to believe that lobbying local governmental officials and business elites may yield palpable reforms, but long-term structural change may lie beyond the grasp of neighborhood insurgency. Issues such as educational reform will pay long-term economic benefits to the Mexican-American community, but the issues addressed by the IAF have not confronted the fundamental economic disadvantages minorities must confront on a day-to-day basis. As the radical school of community power suggests, the economic order itself is a power relationship, one that works against the redistribution of wealth and power. Indeed, the depressed economic system along the Texas-Mexico border continues to generate new economic hardships faster than the IAF has been able to generate solutions for them.

A case in point is the issue of water service delivery. The campaign that EPISO initiated to bring water to El Paso's *colonias* was accomplished by an entire decade of laborious effort, a period in which their problems grew exponentially. An estimated 185,000 poor Mexican-Americans live in *colonias* from California to the lower Rio Grande Valley of Texas (Applebome 1988). Poverty, substandard housing, and a lack of water are manifestations of economic processes along the U.S.-Mexico border which generate low incomes, a labor market glut, and high unemployment (Briggs 1984:ch. 7). By the late 1970s, the *colonias* in El Paso were growing at a ten-year rate of 200 percent, exceeding the rate of such subdivisions across the border in Juarez (Maraniss 1987). These settlements were so unregulated that when an engineering firm was hired by the state in 1987 to assess water needs, six weeks were needed to find and list the 435 *colonias* in three counties (Morris 1989). Although the new water and sewer services will dramatically improve the health and well-being of the *colonias'* residents, poverty and the underlying processes that create it have continued unabated. Even the redistributive effects of the water plan are minimal. The ten-year battle created a water district which would have to fund between $60 and $70 million in water and sewer pipe construction, as well as legal and environmental requirements in one of the most property-poor districts in Texas. And once construction is completed, each family will be charged an average of $1,500 for a first-time hookup (Rocha 1989).

The link between such issues as water service delivery and the task of influencing the market in matters such as jobs, wages, training programs, and investment has not been explored by the new Alinsky organizations. IAF activists and liberal public officials claimed that extension of water and sewer services to the *colonias* would help residents "pull themselves out of the cycle of poverty," but it is not clear what steps would have to be taken in order for that change to occur (Applebome 1988; Morris 1989). In fact, the reforms initiated by the IAF network have resulted in some negative consequences for their low-income constituents. The El Paso County government had to adopt strict new subdivision rules that govern sewage and water supply systems, paved roads, curbs, and gutters in order to be eligible for a portion of the $100 million in help state legislatures earmarked to aid the *colonias*. These regulations, designed to ensure sanitary conditions in the *colonias* and protect residents from unscrupulous developers, will result in driving the price of land up and thereby crowding the poor out of another source of low-cost housing. As Maureen Hilton, a lawyer for the county, commented, "it's really a choice between two evils. Are you going to have a clean environment and not have people dying of hepatitis, or are you going to stop giving housing to the poor? You can't win either way" (Bezick 1990).

Freeing people from the daily burden of securing clean water will allow them to focus their energy on self-improvement, but the economic constraints that pushed them to live in the substandard unincorporated areas continue unabated. For all their strident rhetoric, the Texas IAF network has yet to directly confront the question of private property and a free market economy and how its functioning relates to the problem of poverty. If the political and economic system directs the IAF from one issue to another without confronting its source, Saul Alinsky's strategy of community mobilization methods may be inadequate to counteract national and international trends that are creating unemployment and a declining standard of living in the United States. The network's faith in political pluralism is strong, but it is not evident what the limits of interest group politics may be or how one may distinguish between solvable "issues" and unsolvable "problems."

In sum, the IAF's success in the world of pressure group politics has not translated into the ability to alter their constituents' structural disadvantages. What has been revealed in this chapter is that the successful initiation of an issue agenda can be accomplished without threatening existing hierarchies of wealth and power. Pluralism's prescriptions for agenda setting and social change poorly reflect the problematic nature of politics among the poor and dispossessed. Likewise, Castells's (1983) claim that insurgent organizations represent a force that will eventually transform local politics takes few of these barriers into account. A more likely interpretation of the IAF record is one which reveals the limits of urban political change. The network will continue to organize in communities throughout the state and it is likely that they will experience further successes in the public arena. However, the widespread changes anticipated by scholars and activists alike will be difficult to achieve. The barriers to fundamental social change are firmly entrenched and the resources the poor are able to mobilize are meager in the face of the market's ability to make investment and production decisions that have far-reaching implications for the Mexican-American community. In the end, the activities of the IAF in Texas may lead to a more pluralistic public order, but it will be one "whose future is stamped by the logic, rules, and legally protected power of capitalism" (Plotkin 1983:157).

Saul Alinsky himself offered no solution to these questions, yet implicitly recognized that real change in the lives of the poor required far more than increased political democratization. As he wrote: "The Back of the Yards Council at the zenith of its power could not deal with its most pressing problem of its time, the issue of widespread unemployment, until our whole economy boomed as a result of world developments" (Alinsky 1969:225). Luther Jones, an El Paso County executive, who has worked extensively with EPISO on the issue of water for the *colonias,* has noted the same dilemma facing IAF activists and their reform style of politics: "There are immense problems along the border that El Paso didn't cause and can't control. We can get these people water, but we're not going to solve poverty" (Applebome 1988).

REFERENCES

Acuña, Rodolfo. 1988. *Occupied America: A History of Chicanos.* New York: Harper and Row.
Alinsky, Saul. 1969. *Reveille for Radicals.* New York: Vintage.
———. 1971. *Rules for Radicals.* New York: Random House.
———. 1972. "A Candid Conversation with the Feisty Radical Organizer." *Playboy,* March.
Applebome, Peter. 1988. "Along U.S. Border, a Third World is Reborn." *New York Times,* 27 March.
———. 1989. "At Texas Border, Hopes for Sewers and Water." *New York Times,* 28 December.

Barrera, Mario. 1979. *Race and Class in the Southwest.* Notre Dame, IN: University of Notre Dame Press.

———. 1985. "The Historic Evolution of Chicano Ethnic Goals." *Sage Race Relations Abstracts* 10:1–48.

Bezick, Denise. 1990. "It's Health vs Cheap Housing in Colonia Flap." *El Paso Times,* 1 July.

Boggs, Carl. 1983. "The New Populism and the Limits of Structural Reforms." *Theory and Society* 12:343–363.

Boyer, Edward J. 1985. "Group Strength." *Los Angeles Times,* 8 September.

Boyte, Harry C. 1980. *The Backyard Revolution.* Philadelphia: Temple University Press.

———. 1981. "Community Organizing in the 1970s: Seeds of Democratic Revolt." In *Community Organization for Urban Social Change,* eds. Robert Fisher and Pater Romanofsky. Westport, CT: Greenwood Press.

———. 1984. *Community is Possible.* New York: Harper and Row.

———. 1990. "The Growth of Citizen Politics." *Dissent* 37:513–518.

Boyte, Harry C., and Sara Evans. 1984. "Strategies in Search for America: Cultural Radicalism, Populism, and Democratic Culture." *Socialist Review* 14:73–101.

Briggs, Vernon M. 1984. *Immigration Policy and the American Labor Force.* Baltimore: Johns Hopkins University Press.

Browning, Rufus P., Dale Rogers Marshall, and David H. Tabb. 1984. *Protest is not Enough: The Struggle of Blacks and Hispanics for Equality in Urban Politics.* Berkeley, CA: University of California Press.

———. 1990. *Racial Politics in American Cities.* New York: Longman.

Castells, Manuel. 1983. *The City and the Grassroots.* Berkeley, CA: University of California Press.

Ceasar, Paul, Sr. 1988. Interview with Benjamin Marquez. 18 July.

Cobb, Roger W., and Charles D. Elder. 1972. *Participation in American Politics: The Dynamics of Agenda Building.* Boston: Allyn and Bacon.

———. 1981. "Communications and Public Policy." In *Handbook of Political Communication,* eds. Dan D. Mimmo and Keith R. Sanders. Beverly Hills, CA: Sage Publications.

———. 1983. *Participation in American Politics: The Dynamics of Agenda-Building.* Baltimore: Johns Hopkins University Press.

Cobb, Roger W., Jennie Keith-Ross, and Marc Howard Ross. 1976. "Agenda Building as a Comparative Political Process." *American Political Science Review* 70:126–138.

Cook, Allison. 1988. "Just Add Water." *Texas Monthly* 16:70–74.

Cortes, Ernesto, Jr. 1986. "Organizing the Community." *Texas Monthly,* 11 July.

———. 1988. Interview with Benjamin Marquez. 1 October.

Delgado, Gary. 1986. *Organizing the Movement: The Roots and Growth of ACORN.* Philadelphia: Temple University Press.

del Olmo, Frank. 1983. "Two Latino Activists Travel Separate Paths." *Los Angeles Times,* 29 July.

Eisinger, Peter K. 1980. *The Politics of Displacement: Racial and Ethnic Transition in Three American Cities*. New York: Academic Press.

EPISO. 1987. *1987 4th Annual Friends of EPISO Ad Book*. Unpublished article in the author's possession.

Finks, David. 1984. *The Radical Vision of Saul Alinsky*. New York: Paulist Press.

Fisher, Robert. 1984. *Let the People Decide*. Boston: Twayne Publishers.

Flores, Henry. 1989. "You Can't Win for Winning: Hispanic Mayoral Politics in San Antonio Texas." Presented at the annual meeting of the Western Political Science Association, Salt Lake City, UT.

Garcia, F. Chris, and Rudolfo de la Garza. 1977. *The Chicano Political Experience*. North Scituate, MA: Duxbury Press.

Gomez-Quiñones, Juan. 1978. *Mexican Students Por La Raza*. Santa Barbara, CA: Editorial La Causa.

Hagerty, Vaughn. 1987. "COPS Puts Stadium Vote on Hold; Says it Won't Back Tax Funds Use." *San Antonio Light,* 26 October.

Hero, Rodney C. 1992. *Latinos and the American Political System: Two Tiered Pluralism?* Philadelphia: Temple University Press.

Holler, Tom. 1988. Interview with Benjamin Marquez. 12 July.

Industrial Areas Foundation. 1978. *Organizing for Family and Congregation*. Franklin Square, NY: Industrial Areas Foundation.

———. 1988. "Sign-up and Take Charge Campaign." Unpublished leaflet in possession of the author.

Kann, Mark E. 1983. "The New Populism and the New Marxism." *Theory and Society* 12:365–373.

Kesselman, Mark. 1982. "The Conflictual Evolution of American Political Science: From Apologetic Pluralism to Trilateralism and Marxism." In *Public Values and Private Power in American Politics,* ed. J. David Greenstone. Chicago: University of Chicago Press.

———. 1983. "From State Theory to Class Struggle and Compromise: Contemporary Marxist Political Studies." *Social Science Quarterly* 64:826–845.

Korcsmar, Reverend John S. 1988. Interview with Benjamin Marquez. 2 October.

Lerma, Amalia. 1988. Interview with Benjamin Marquez. 30 September.

"Levantando La Voz." 1987. *The Texas Observer,* 17 July.

Levine, Charles F. 1973. "Understanding Alinsky: Conservative Wine in Radical Bottles." *American Behavioral Scientist* 17:279–284.

Lind, Scott. 1984. "Reagan ACTION Chief Attacks Valley Interfaith and Public Works." *The Texas Observer,* 6 April.

Logan, John R., and Harvey M. Molotch. 1987. *Urban Fortunes: The Political Economy of Place*. Berkeley, CA: University of California Press.

McKnight, John, and John Kretzmann. 1984. "Community Organizing in the 80's: Toward a Post-Alinsky Agenda." *Social Polity* 14:15–17.

Maraniss, David. 1989. "El Paso's Perimeter of Policy." *Washington Post,* 17 August.

Marel, Robert Lee. 1989. *Poorest of Americans: The Mexican Americans of the Lower Rio Grande Valley of Texas*. Notre Dame, IN: University of Notre Dame Press.

Marquez, Benjamin. 1989. "The Politics of Race and Assimilation: The League of United Latin American Citizens, 1929–1949." *Western Political Quarterly* 42:355–373.

———. 1990. "Organizing the Mexican-American Community in Texas." *Policy Studies Review* 9:355–373.

Martinez, Gebe. 1987. "Cisneros Slams His Door on COPS for its 'Abuse'." *San Antonio Light,* 28 November.

Montejano, David. 1987. *Anglos and Mexicans in the Making of Texas, 1836–1986.* Austin: University of Texas Press.

Morris, Julie. 1989. "The Third World in Texas." *Gannett News Service,* 10 October.

Mosqueda, Lawrence J. 1986. *Chicanos, Catholicism, and Political Ideology.* New York: University Press of America.

Muños, Carlos, Jr. 1989. *Youth, Identity, Power: The Chicano Movement.* New York: Verso.

Navarro, Cecilia. 1986. "Understanding the Mexican American Voter: Legacy and Potential of the Mexican American Community." Master's Thesis, University of Texas at El Paso.

Nelson, Barbara. 1984. *Making an Issue of Child Abuse.* Chicago: University of Chicago Press.

Obregon, Enedelia J. 1987. "Ministry Battling Poverty." *Austin American Statesman,* 7 September.

Ortiz, Isidro. 1984. "Chicano Urban Politics and the Politics of Reform in the Seventies." *Western Political Quarterly* 37:564–577.

Peterson, Paul E. 1981. *City Limits.* Chicago: University of Chicago Press.

Petry, Alcie. 1988. Interview with Benjamin Marquez. 18 July.

Plotkin, Sidney. 1983. "Democratic Change in the Urban Political Economy: San Antonio's Edwards Aquifer Controversy." In *The Politics of San Antonio,* eds. David R. Johnson, John A. Booth, and Richard J. Harris. Lincoln, NE: University of Nebraska Press.

Polsby, Nelson W. 1980. *Community Power and Political Theory.* New Haven, CT: Yale University Press.

———. 1984. *Political Innovation in America.* New Haven, CT: Yale University Press.

Preston, Michael B., Lenneal J. Henderson, and Paul L. Puryear. 1987. *The New Black Politics: The Search for Political Power,* 2nd. ed. New York: Longman.

Reed, Steve. 1989. "Austin Interfaith Quietly Taking Root in Politics." *Austin American Statesman,* 9 February.

Reitzes, Donald C., and Dietrich C. Reitzes. 1987. *The Alinsky Legacy: Alive and Kicking.* Greenwich, CT.: JAI Press.

Rocha, Elisa. 1989. "Fledgling Entity Faces Uphill Battle to Hook Up Lower Valley 'Colonias'." *El Paso Herald Post,* 30 December.

Rodriguez, Elisa, Sr. 1988. Interview with Benjamin Marquez. 2 October.

Sekul, Joseph D. 1983. "Communities Organized for Public Service: Citizen

Power and Public Policy in San Antonio." In *The Politics of San Antonio,* eds. David R. Johnson, John A. Booth, and Richard J. Harris. Lincoln, NE: University of Nebraska Press.

Swanstrom, Todd. 1985. *The Crisis of Growth Politics: Cleveland, Kucinich, and the Challenge of Urban Populism.* Philadelphia: Temple University Press.

Valle, Isabel. 1987. "Minister: COPS Deals with Poor." *San Antonio Express News,* 28 December.

Wilson, William J. 1987. *The Truly Disadvantaged.* Chicago: University of Chicago Press.

Wright, Eric O. 1978. *Class, Crisis, and the State.* London: New Left Books.

———. 1985. *Classes.* London: Verso.

5. Mexican American Women Grassroots Community Activists: "Mothers of East Los Angeles"

Mary Pardo

THE RELATIVELY FEW STUDIES OF Chicana political activism show a bias in the way political activism is conceptualized by social scientists, who often use a narrow definition confined to electoral politics.[1] Most feminist research uses an expanded definition that moves across the boundaries between public, electoral politics and private, family politics; but feminist research generally focuses on women mobilized around gender-specific issues.[2] For some feminists, adherence to "tradition" constitutes conservatism and submission to patriarchy. Both approaches exclude the contributions of working-class women, particularly those of Afro-American women and Latinas, thus failing to capture the full dynamic of social change.[3]

The following case study of Mexican American women activists in "Mothers of East Los Angeles" (MELA) contributes another dimension to the conception of grassroots politics. It illustrates how these Mexican American women transform "traditional" networks and resources based on family and culture into political assets to defend the quality of urban life. Far from unique, these patterns of activism are repeated in Latin America and elsewhere. Here as in other times and places, the women's activism arises out of seemingly "traditional" roles, addresses wider social and political issues, and capitalizes on informal associations sanc-

"Mexican American Women Grassroots Community Activists: 'Mothers of East Los Angeles'," by Mary Pardo, *Frontiers*. Vol. XI, No. 1. pp. 1–7. Frontiers Editorial Collective Women's Studies Program, University Press of Colorado, Boulder, CO.

tioned by the community.[4] Religion, commonly viewed as a conservative force, is intertwined with politics.[5] Often, women speak of their communities and their activism as extensions of their family and household responsibility. The central role of women in grassroots struggles around quality of life, in the Third World and in the United States, challenges conventional assumptions about the powerlessness of women and static definitions of culture and tradition.

In general, the women in MELA are longtime residents of East Los Angeles; some are bilingual and native born, others Mexican born and Spanish dominant. All the core activists are bilingual and have lived in the community over thirty years. All have been active in parish-sponsored groups and activities; some have had experience working in community-based groups arising from schools, neighborhood watch associations, and labor support groups. To gain an appreciation of the group and the core activists, I used ethnographic field methods. I interviewed six women, using a life history approach focused on their first community activities, current activism, household and family responsibilities, and perceptions of community issues.[6] Also, from December 1987 through October 1989, I attended hearings on the two currently pending projects of contention—a proposed state prison and a toxic waste incinerator—and participated in community and organizational meetings and demonstrations. The following discussion briefly chronicles an intense and significant five-year segment of community history from which emerged MELA and the women's transformation of "traditional" resources and experiences into political assets for community mobilization.[7]

THE COMMUNITY CONTEXT:
EAST LOS ANGELES RESISTING SIEGE

Political science theory often guides the political strategies used by local government to select the sites for undesirable projects. In 1984, the state of California commissioned a public relations firm to assess the political difficulties facing the construction of energy-producing waste incinerators. The report provided a "personality profile" of those residents most likely to organize effective opposition to projects:

> middle and upper socioeconomic strata possess better resources to effectuate their opposition. Middle and higher socioeconomic strata neighborhoods should not fall within the one-mile and five-mile radii of the proposed site. Conversely, older people, people

with a high school education or less are least likely to oppose a facility.[8]

The state accordingly placed the plant in Commerce, a predominantly Mexican American, low-income community. This pattern holds throughout the state and the country: three out of five Afro-Americans and Latinos live near toxic waste sites, and three of the five largest hazardous waste landfills are in communities with at least 80 percent minority populations.[9]

Similarly, in March 1985, when the state sought a site for the first state prison in Los Angeles County, Governor Deukmejian resolved to place the 1,700-inmate institution in East Los Angeles, within a mile of the long-established Boyle Heights neighborhood and within two miles of thirty-four schools. Furthermore, violating convention, the state bid on the expensive parcel of industrially zoned land without compiling an environmental impact report or providing a public community hearing. According to James Vigil, Jr., a field representative for Assemblywoman Gloria Molina, shortly after the state announced the site selection, Molina's office began informing the community and gauging residents' sentiments about it through direct mailings and calls to leaders of organizations and business groups.

In spring 1986, after much pressure from the 56th assembly district office and the community, the Department of Corrections agreed to hold a public information meeting, which was attended by over 700 Boyle Heights residents. From this moment on, Vigil observed, "the tables turned, the community mobilized, and the residents began calling the political representatives and requesting their presence at hearings and meetings."[10] By summer 1986, the community was well aware of the prison site proposal. Over two thousand people, carrying placards proclaiming "No Prison in ELA," marched from Resurrection Church in Boyle Heights to the 3rd Street bridge linking East Los Angeles with the rapidly expanding downtown Los Angeles.[11] This march marked the beginning of one of the largest grassroots coalitions to emerge from the Latino community in the last decade.

Prominent among the coalition's groups is "Mothers of East Los Angeles," a loosely knit group of over 400 Mexican American women.[12] MELA initially coalesced to oppose the state prison construction but has since organized opposition to several other projects detrimental to the quality of life in the central city.[13] Its second large target is a toxic waste incinerator proposed for Vernon, a small city adjacent to East Los Angeles. This incinerator would worsen the already debilitating air quality of the entire county and set a precedent dangerous for other communities throughout California.[14] When MELA took up the fight against the toxic waste incinerator, it became more than a single-issue group and began working with environmental groups around the state.[15] As a result of the community struggle, AB58 (Roybal-Allard), which provides all Californians with the minimum protection of an environmental impact report before the construction of hazardous waste incinerators, was signed into law. But the law's effectiveness relies on a watchful community network. Since its emergence, "Mothers of East Los Angeles" has become centrally important to just such a network of grassroots activists including a select number of Catholic priests and two Mexican American political representatives. Furthermore, the group's very formation, and its continued spirit and activism, fly in the face of the conventional political science beliefs regarding political participation.

Predictions by the "experts" attribute the low formal political participation (i.e., voting) of Mexican American people in the U.S. to a set of cultural "retardants" including primary kinship systems, fatalism, religious traditionalism, traditional cultural values, and mother country attachment.[16] The core activists in MELA may appear to fit this description, as well as the state-commissioned profile of residents least likely to oppose toxic waste incinerator projects. All the women live in a low-income community. Furthermore, they identify themselves as active and committed participants in the Catholic Church; they claim an ethnic identity—Mexican American; their ages range from forty to sixty; and they have attained at most high school educations. However, these women fail to conform to the predicted political apathy. Instead, they have transformed social identity—ethnic identity, class identity, and gender identity—into an impetus as well a basis for activism.

TRANSFORMATION AS A DOMINANT THEME

From the life histories of the group's core activists and from my own field notes, I have selected excerpts that tell two representative stories. One is a narrative of the events that led to community mobilization in East Los Angeles. The other is a story of transformation, the process of creating new and better relationships that empower people to unite and achieve common goals.[17]

First, women have transformed organizing experiences and social networks arising from gender-related responsibilities into political resources.[18] When I asked the women about the first community, not necessarily "political," involvement they could recall, they discussed experiences that predated the formation of MELA. Juana Gutiérrez explained:

Well, it didn't start with the prison, you know. It started when my kids went to school. I started by joining the Parents Club and we worked on different problems here in the area. Like the people who come to the parks to sell drugs to the kids. I got the neighbors to have meetings. I would go knock at the doors, house to house. And I told them that we should stick together with the Neighborhood Watch for the community and for the kids.[19]

Erlinda Robles similarly recalled:

I wanted my kids to go to Catholic school and from the time my oldest one went there, I was there every day. I used to take my two little ones with me and I helped one way or another. I used to question things they did. And the other mothers would just watch me. Later, they would ask me, "Why do you do that? They are going to take it out on your kids." I'd say, "They better not." And before you knew it, we had a big group of mothers that were very involved.[20]

Part of a mother's "traditional" responsibility includes overseeing her child's progress in school, interacting with school staff, and supporting school activities. In these processes, women meet other mothers and begin developing a network of acquaintanceships and friendships based on mutual concern for the welfare of their children.

Although the women in MELA carried the greatest burden of participating in school activities, Erlinda Robles also spoke of strategies they used to draw men into the enterprise and into the networks:[21]

At the beginning, the priests used to say who the president of the mothers guild would be; they used to pick 'um. But, we wanted elections, so we got elections. Then we wanted the fathers to be involved, and the nuns suggested that a father should be president and a mother would be secretary or be involved there [at the school site].[22]

Of course, this comment piqued my curiosity, so I asked how the mothers agreed on the nuns' suggestion. The answer was simple and instructive:

At the time we thought it was a "natural" way to get the fathers involved because they weren't involved; it was just the mothers. Everybody [the women] agreed on them [the fathers] being president because they worked all day and they couldn't be involved in a lot of daily activities like food sales and whatever. During the week, a steering committee of mothers planned the group's activities. But now that I think about it, a woman could have done the job just as well![23]

So women got men into the group by giving them a position they could manage. The men may have held the title of "president," but they were not making day-to-day decisions about work, nor were they dictating the direction of the group. Erlinda Robles laughed as she recalled an occasion when the president insisted, against the wishes of the women, on scheduling a parents' group fundraiser—a breakfast—on Mother's Day. On that morning, only the president and his wife were present to prepare breakfast. This should alert researchers against measuring power and influence by looking solely at who holds titles.

Each of the cofounders had a history of working with groups arising out of the responsibilities usually assumed by "mothers"—the education of children and the safety of the surrounding community. From these groups, they gained valuable experiences and networks that facilitated the formation of "Mothers of East Los Angeles." Juana Gutiérrez explained how preexisting networks progressively expanded community support:

> You know nobody knew about the plan to build a prison in this community until Assemblywoman Gloria Molina told me. Martha Molina called me and said, "You know what is happening in your area? The governor wants to put a prison in Boyle Heights!" So, I called a Neighborhood Watch meeting at my house and we got fifteen people together. Then, Father John started informing his people at the Church and that is when the group of two to three hundred started showing up for every march on the bridge.[24]

MELA effectively linked up preexisting networks into a viable grassroots coalition.

Second, the process of activism also transformed previously "invisible" women, making them not only visible but the center of public attention. From a conventional perspective, political activism assumes a kind of gender neutrality. This means that anyone can participate, but men are the expected key actors. In accordance with this pattern, in winter 1986 an informal group of concerned businessmen in the community began lobbying and testifying against the prison at hearings in Sacramento. Working in conjunction with Assemblywoman Molina, they made many trips to Sacramento at their own expense. Residents who did not have the income to travel were unable to join them. Finally, Molina, commonly recognized as a forceful advocate for Latinas and the community, asked Frank Villalobos, an urban planner in the group, why there were no women coming up to speak in Sacramento against the prison. As he phrased it, "I was getting some heat from her because no women were going up there."[25]

In response to this comment, Veronica Gutiérrez, a law student who lived in the community, agreed to accompany him on the next trip to Sacramento.[26] He also mentioned the comment to Father John Moretta at Resurrection Catholic Parish. Meanwhile, representatives of the business sector of the community and of the 56th assembly district office were continuing to compile arguments and supportive data against the East Los Angeles prison site. Frank Villalobos stated one of the pressing problems:

> We felt that the Senators whom we prepared all this for didn't even acknowledge that we existed. They kept calling it the "downtown" site, and they argued that there was no opposition in the community. So, I told Father Moretta, what we have to do is demonstrate that there is a link (proximity) between the Boyle Heights community and the prison.[27]

The next juncture illustrates how perceptions of gender-specific behavior set in motion a sequence of events that brought women into the political limelight. Father Moretta decided to ask all the women to meet after mass. He told them about the prison site and called for their support. When I asked him about his rationale for selecting the women, he replied:

> I felt so strongly about the issue, and I knew in my heart what a terrible offense this was to the people. So, I was afraid that once we got into a demonstration situation we had to be very careful. I thought the women would be cooler and calmer than the men. The bottom line is that the men came anyway. The first times out the majority were women. Then they began to invite their husbands and their children, but originally it was just women.[28]

Father Moretta also named the group. Quite moved by a film, *The Official Story*, about the courageous Argentine women who demonstrated for the return of their children who disappeared during a repressive right-wing military dictatorship, he transformed the name "Las Madres de la Plaza de Mayo" into "Mothers of East Los Angeles."[29]

However, Aurora Castillo, one of the cofounders of the group, modified my emphasis on the predominance of women:

> Of course the fathers work. We also have many, many grandmothers. And all this IS with the support of the fathers. They make the

placards and the posters; they do the security and carry the signs; and they come to the marches when they can.[30]

Although women played a key role in the mobilization, they emphasized the group's broad base of active supporters as well as the other organizations in the "Coalition Against the Prison." Their intent was to counter any notion that MELA was composed exclusively of women or mothers and to stress the "inclusiveness" of the group. All the women who assumed lead roles in the group had long histories of volunteer work in the Boyle Heights community; but formation of the group brought them out of the "private" margins and into "public" light.

Third, the women in "Mothers of East L.A." have transformed the definition of "mother" to include militant political opposition to state-proposed projects they see as adverse to the quality of life in the community. Explaining how she discovered the issue, Aurora Castillo said,

> You know if one of your children's safety is jeopardized, the mother turns into a lioness. That's why Father John got the mothers. We have to have a well-organized, strong group of mothers to protect the community and oppose things that are detrimental to us. You know the governor is in the wrong and the mothers are in the right. After all, the mothers have to be right. Mothers are for the children's interest, not for self-interest; the governor is for his own political interest.[31]

The women also have expanded the boundaries of "motherhood" to include social and political community activism and redefined the word to include women who are not biological "mothers." At one meeting a young Latina expressed her solidarity with the group and, almost apologetically, qualified herself as a "resident," not a "mother," of East Los Angeles. Erlinda Robles replied:

> When you are fighting for a better life for children and "doing" for them, isn't that what mothers do? So we're all mothers. You don't have to have children to be a "mother."[32]

At critical points, grassroots community activism requires attending many meetings, phone calling, and door-to-door communications—all very labor-intensive work. In order to keep harmony in the "domestic" sphere, the core activists must creatively integrate family members into their community activities. I asked Erlinda Robles how her husband felt about her activism, and she replied quite openly:

> My husband doesn't like getting involved, but he takes me because he knows I like it. Sometimes we would have two or three meetings

a week. And my husband would say, "Why are you doing so much? It is really getting out of hand." But he is very supportive. Once he gets there, he enjoys it and he starts in arguing too! See, it's just that he is not used to it. He couldn't believe things happened the way that they do. He was in the Navy twenty years and they brainwashed him that none of the politicians could do wrong. So he has come a long way. Now he comes home and parks the car out front and asks me, "Well, where are we going tonight?"[33]

When women explain their activism, they link family and community as one entity. Juana Gutiérrez, a woman with extensive experience working on community and neighborhood issues, stated:

> Yo como madre de familia, y como residente del Este de Los Angeles, seguiré luchando sin descanso por que se nos respete. Y yo lo hago con bastante cariño hacia mi comunidad. Digo "mi comunidad," porque me siento parte de ella, quiero a mi raza como parte de mi familia, y si Dios me permite seguiré luchando contra todos los gobernadores que quieran abusar de nosotros. (As a mother and a resident of East L.A., I shall continue fighting tirelessly, so we will be respected. And I will do this with much affection for my community. I say "my community" because I am part of it. I love my "raza" [race] as part of my family; and if God allows, I will keep on fighting against all the governors that want to take advantage of us.)[34]

Like the other activists, she has expanded her responsibilities and legitimated militant opposition to abuse of the community by representatives of the state.

Working-class women activists seldom opt to separate themselves from men and their families. In this particular struggle for community quality of life, they are fighting for the family unit and thus are not competitive with men.[35] Of course, this fact does not preclude different alignments in other contexts and situations.[36]

Fourth, the story of MELA also shows the transformation of class and ethnic identity. Aurora Castillo told of an incident that illustrated her growing knowledge of the relationship of East Los Angeles to other communities and the basis necessary for coalition building:

> And do you know we have been approached by other groups? [She lowers her voice in emphasis.] You know that Pacific Palisades group asked for our backing. But what they did, they sent their powerful lobbyist that they pay thousands of dollars to get our support against the drilling in Pacific Palisades. So what we did was

tell them to send their grassroots people, not their lobbyist. We're suspicious. We don't want to talk to a high-salaried lobbyist; we are humble people. We did our own lobbying. In one week we went to Sacramento twice.[37]

The contrast between the often tedious and labor-intensive work of mobilizing people at the "grassroots" level and the paid work of a "high salaried lobbyist" represents a point of pride and integrity, not a deficiency or a source of shame. If the two groups were to construct a coalition, they must communicate on equal terms.

The women of MELA combine a willingness to assert opposition with a critical assessment of their own weaknesses. At one community meeting, for example, representatives of several oil companies attempted to gain support for placement of an oil pipeline through the center of East Los Angeles. The exchange between the women in the audience and the oil representative was heated, as women alternated asking questions about the chosen route for the pipeline:

> "Is it going through Cielito Lindo [Reagan's ranch]?" The oil representative answered, "No." Another woman stood up and asked, "Why not place it along the coastline?" Without thinking of the implications, the representative responded, "Oh, no! If it burst, it would endanger the marine life." The woman retorted, "You value the marine life more than human beings?" His face reddened with anger and the hearing disintegrated into angry chanting.[38]

The proposal was quickly defeated. But Aurora Castillo acknowledged that it was not solely their opposition that brought about the defeat:

> We won because the westside was opposed to it, so we united with them. You know there are a lot of attorneys who live there and they also questioned the representative. Believe me, no way is justice blind. . . . We just don't want all this garbage thrown at us because we are low-income and Mexican American. We are lucky now that we have good representatives, which we didn't have before.[39]

Throughout their life histories, the women refer to the disruptive effects of land use decisions made in the 1950s. As longtime residents, all but one share the experience of losing a home and relocating to make way for a freeway. Juana Gutiérrez refers to the community response at that time:

> Una de las cosas que me caen muy mal es la injusticia y en nuestra comunidad hemos visto mucho de eso. Sobre todo antes, porque creo que nuestra gente estaba mas dormida, nos atrevíamos menos.

En los cincuentas hicieron los freeways y así, sin más, nos dieron la
notica de que nos teníamos que mudar. Y eso pasó dos veces. La
gente se conformaba porque lo ordeno el gobierno. Recuerdo que
yo me enojaba y quería que los demás me secundaran, pero nadia
quería hacer nada. (One of the things that really upsets me is the
injustice that we see so much in our community. Above everything
else, I believe that our people were less aware; we were less challenging. In the 1950s—they made the freeways and just like that
they gave us a notice that we had to move. That happened twice.
The people accepted it because the government ordered it. I remem-
ber that I was angry and wanted the others to back me but nobody
else wanted to do anything.)[40]

The freeways that cut through communities and disrupted neighborhoods are now a concrete reminder of shared injustice, of the vulner-
ability of the community in the 1950s. The community's social and
political history thus informs perceptions of its current predicament;
however, today's activists emphasize not the powerlessness of the community but the change in status and progression toward political empowerment.

Fifth, the core activists typically tell stories illustrating personal
change and a new sense of entitlement to speak for the community. They
have transformed the unspoken sentiments of individuals into a collective community voice. Lucy Ramos related her initial apprehensions:

I was afraid to get involved. I didn't know what was going to come
out of this and I hesitated at first. Right after we started, Father
John came up to me and told me, "I want you to be a spokesperson." I said, "Oh no, I don't know what I am going to say." I was
nervous. I am surprised I didn't have a nervous breakdown then.
Every time we used to get in front of the TV cameras and even
interviews like this, I used to sit there and I could feel myself shak-
ing. But as time went on, I started getting used to it.

And this is what I have noticed with a lot of them. They were
afraid to speak up and say anything. Now, with this prison issue, a
lot of them have come out and come forward and given their opinions. Everybody used to be real "quietlike."[41]

She also related a situation that brought all her fears to a climax, which
she confronted and resolved as follows:

When I first started working with the coalition, Channel 13 called
me up and said they wanted to interview me and I said OK. Then
I started getting nervous. So I called Father John and told him,

"You better get over here right away." He said, "Don't worry, don't worry, you can handle it by yourself." Then Channel 13 called me back and said they were going to interview another person, someone I had never heard of, and asked if it was OK if he came to my house. And I said OK again. Then I began thinking, what if this guy is for the prison? What am I going to do? And I was so nervous and I thought, I know what I am going to do!

Since the meeting was taking place in her home, she reasoned that she was entitled to order any troublemakers out of her domain:

If this man tells me anything, I am just going to chase him out of my house. That is what I am going to do! All these thoughts were going through my head. Then Channel 13 walk into my house followed by six men I had never met. And I thought, Oh, my God, what did I get myself into? I kept saying to myself, if they get smart with me I am throwing them ALL out.[42]

At this point her tone expressed a sense of resolve. In fact, the situation turned out to be neither confrontational nor threatening, as the "other men" were also members of the coalition. This woman confronted an anxiety-laden situation by relying on her sense of control within her home and family—a quite "traditional" source of authority for women—and transforming that control into the courage to express a political position before a potential audience all over one of the largest metropolitan areas in the nation.

People living in Third World countries as well as in minority communities in the United States face an increasingly degraded environment.[43] Recognizing the threat to the well-being of their families, residents have mobilized at the neighborhood level to fight for "quality of life" issues. The common notion that environmental well-being is of concern solely to white middle-class and upper-class residents ignores the specific way working-class neighborhoods suffer from the fallout of the city "growth machine" geared for profit.[44]

In Los Angeles, the culmination of postwar urban renewal policies, the growing Pacific Rim trade surplus and investment, and low-wage international labor migration from Third World countries are creating potentially volatile conditions. Literally palatial financial buildings swallow up the space previously occupied by modest, low-cost housing. Increasing density and development not matched by investment in social programs, services, and infrastructure erode the quality of life, beginning in the core of the city.[45] Latinos, the majority of whom live close to the center of the city, must confront the distilled social consequences of development focused solely on profit. The Mexican American community in East Los Angeles, much like other minority working-class communities, has been a repository for prisons instead of new schools, hazardous industries instead of safe work sites, and one of the largest concentrations of freeway interchanges in the country, which transports much wealth past the community. And the concerns of residents in East Los Angeles may provide lessons for other minority as well as middle-class communities. Increasing environmental pollution resulting from inadequate waste disposal plans and an out-of-control "need" for penal institutions to contain the casualties created by the growing bipolar distribution of wages may not be limited to the Southwest.[46] These conditions set the stage for new conflicts and new opportunities, to transform old relationships into coalitions that can challenge state agendas and create new community visions.[47]

Mexican American women living east of downtown Los Angeles exemplify the tendency of women to enter into environmental struggles in defense of their community. Women have a rich historical legacy of community activism, partly reconstructed over the last two decades in social histories of women who contested other "quality of life issues," from the price of bread to "Demon Rum" (often representing domestic violence).[48]

But something new is also happening. The issues "traditionally" addressed by women—health, housing, sanitation, and the urban environment—have moved to center stage as capitalist urbanization progresses. Environmental issues now fuel the fires of many political campaigns and drive citizens beyond the rather restricted, perfunctory political act of voting. Instances of political mobilization at the grassroots level, where women often play a central role, allow us to "see" abstract concepts like participatory democracy and social change as dynamic processes.

The existence and activities of "Mothers of East Los Angeles" attest to the dynamic nature of participatory democracy, as well as to the dynamic nature of our gender, class, and ethnic identity. The story of MELA reveals, on the one hand, how individuals and groups can transform a seemingly "traditional" role such as "mother." On the other hand, it illustrates how such a role may also be a social agent drawing members of the community into the "political" arena. Studying women's contributions as well as men's will shed greater light on the networks dynamic of grassroots movements.[49]

The work "Mothers of East Los Angeles" do to mobilize the community demonstrates that people's political involvement cannot be predicted by their cultural characteristics. These women have defied stereotypes of apathy and used ethnic, gender, and class identity as an impetus, a strength, a vehicle for political activism. They have expanded their—and our—understanding of the complexities of a political system, and they have reaffirmed the possibility of "doing something."

They also generously share the lessons they have learned. One of the women in "Mothers of East Los Angeles" told me, as I hesitated to set up an interview with another woman I hadn't yet met in person,

> You know, nothing ventured nothing lost. You should have seen how timid we were the first time we went to a public hearing. Now, forget it, I walk right up and make myself heard and that's what you have to do.[50]

NOTES

On September 15, 1989, another version of this paper was accepted for presentation at the 1990 International Sociological Association meetings to be held in Madrid, Spain, July 9, 1990.

1. See Vicky Randall, *Women and Politics, An International Perspective* (Chicago: University of Chicago Press, 1987), for a review of the central themes and debates in the literature. For two of the few books on Chicanas, work, and family, see Vicki L. Ruiz, *Cannery Women, Cannery Lives, Mexican Women, Unionization, and the California Food Processing Industry, 1930–1950* (Albuquerque: University of New Mexico Press, 1987), and Patricia Zavella, *Women's Work & Chicano Families* (Ithaca, N.Y.: Cornell University Press, 1987).

2. For recent exceptions to this approach, see Anne Witte Garland, *Women Activists: Challenging the Abuse of Power* (New York: The Feminist Press, 1988); Ann Bookman and Sandra Morgan, eds., *Women and the Politics of Empowerment* (Philadelphia: Temple University Press, 1987); Karen Sacks, *Caring by the Hour* (Chicago: University of Illinois Press, 1988). For a sociological analysis of community activism among Afro-American women see Cheryl Townsend Gilkes, "Holding Back the Ocean with a Broom," *The Black Woman* (Beverly Hills, Calif.: Sage Publications, 1980).

3. For two exceptions to this criticism, see Sara Evans, *Born for Liberty, A History of Women in America* (New York: The Free Press, 1989), and Bettina Aptheker, *Tapestries of Life, Women's Work, Women's Consciousness, and the Meaning of Daily Experience* (Amherst: The University of Massachusetts Press, 1989). For a critique, see Maxine Baca Zinn, Lynn Weber Cannon, Elizabeth Higginbotham, and Bonnie Thornton Dill, "The Costs of Exclusionary Practices in Women's Studies," *Signs* 11, no. 2 (Winter 1986).

4. For cases of grassroots activism among women in Latin America, see Sally W. Yudelman, *Hopeful Openings, A Study of Five Women's Development Organizations in Latin America and the Caribbean* (West Hartford, Conn.: Ku-

marian Press, 1987). For an excellent case analysis of how informal associations enlarge and empower women's world in Third World countries, see Kathryn S. March and Rachelle L. Taqqu, *Women's Informal Associations in Developing Countries, Catalysts for Change?* (Boulder, Colo.: Westview Press, 1986). Also, see Carmen Feijoó, "Women in Neighbourhoods: From Local Issues to Gender Problems," *Canadian Woman Studies* 6, no. 1 (Fall 1984) for a concise overview of the patterns of activism.

    5. The relationship between Catholicism and political activism is varied and not unitary. In some Mexican American communities, grassroots activism relies on parish networks. See Isidro D. Ortiz, "Chicano Urban Politics and the Politics of Reform in the Seventies," *The Western Political Quarterly* 37, no. 4 (December 1984): 565–77. Also, see Joseph D. Sekul, "Communities Organized for Public Service: Citizen Power and Public Power in San Antonio," in *Latinos and the Political System,* edited by F. Chris Garcia (Notre Dame, Ind.: University of Notre Dame Press, 1988). Sekul tells how COPS members challenged prevailing patterns of power by working for the well-being of families and cites four former presidents who were Mexican American women, but he makes no special point of gender.

    6. I also interviewed other members of the Coalition Against the Prison and local political office representatives. For a general reference, see James P. Spradley, *The Ethnographic Interview* (New York: Holt, Rinehart and Winston, 1979). For a review essay focused on the relevancy of the method for examining the diversity of women's experiences, see Susan N. G. Geiger, "Women's Life Histories: Method and Content," *Signs* 11, no. 2 (Winter 1982): 334–51.

    7. During the last five years, over 300 newspaper articles have appeared on the issue. Frank Villalobos generously shared his extensive newspaper archives with me. See Leo C. Wolinsky, "L.A. Prison Bill 'Locked Up' in New Clash," *Los Angeles Times,* 16 July 1987, sec. 1, p. 3; Rudy Acuña, "The Fate of East L.A.: One Big Jail," *Los Angeles Herald Examiner,* 28 April 1989, A15; Carolina Serna, "Eastside Residents Oppose Prison," *La Gente UCLA Student Newspaper* 17, no. 1 (October 1986): 5; Daniel M. Weintraub, "10,000 Fee Paid to Lawmaker Who Left Sickbed to Cast Vote," *Los Angeles Times,* 13 March 1988, sec. 1, p. 3.

    8. Cerrell Associates, Inc., "Political Difficulties Facing Waste-to-Energy Conversion Plant Siting," Report Prepared for California Waste Management Board, State of California (Los Angeles, 1984): 43.

    9. Jesus Sanchez, "The Environment: Whose Movement?" *California Tomorrow* 3, nos. 3 & 4 (Fall 1988): 13. Also see Rudy Acuña, *A Community Under Siege* (Los Angeles: Chicano Studies Research Center Publications, UCLA, 1984). The book and its title capture the sentiments and the history of a community that bears an unfair burden of city projects deemed undesirable by all residents.

    10. James Vigil, Jr., field representative for Assemblywoman Gloria Molina, 1984–1986, Personal Interview, Whittier, Calif., 27 September 1989. Vigil stated that the Department of Corrections used a threefold strategy: politi-

cal pressure in the legislature, the promise of jobs for residents, and contracts for local businesses.

11. Edward J. Boyer and Marita Hernandez, "Eastside Seethes over Prison Plan," *Los Angeles Times,* 13 August 1986, sec. 2, p. 1.

12. Martha Molina-Aviles, currently administrative assistant for Assemblywoman Lucille Roybal-Allard, 56th assembly district, and former field representative for Gloria Molina when she held this assembly seat, Personal Interview, Los Angeles, 5 June 1989. Molina-Aviles, who grew up in East Los Angeles, used her experiences and insights to help forge strong links among the women in MELA, other members of the coalition, and the assembly office.

13. MELA has also opposed the expansion of a county prison literally across the street from William Mead Housing Projects, home to 2,000 Latinos, Asians, and Afro-Americans, and a chemical treatment plant for toxic wastes.

14. The first of its kind in a metropolitan area, it would burn 125,000 pounds per day of hazardous wastes. For an excellent article that links recent struggles against hazardous waste dumps and incinerators in minority communities and features women in MELA, see Dick Russell, "Environmental Racism: Minority Communities and Their Battle against Toxics," *The Amicus Journal* 11, no. 2 (Spring 1989): 22–32.

15. Miguel G. Mendívil, field representative for Assemblywoman Lucille Roybal-Allard, 56th assembly district, Personal Interview, Los Angeles, 25 April 1989.

16. John Garcia and Rudolfo de la Garza, "Mobilizing the Mexican Immigrant: The Role of Mexican American Organizations," *The Western Political Quarterly* 38, no. 4 (December 1985): 551–64.

17. This concept is discussed in relation to Latino communities in David T. Abalos, *Latinos in the U.S., The Sacred and the Political* (Indiana: University of Notre Dame Press, 1986). The notion of transformation of traditional culture in struggles against oppression is certainly not a new one. For a brief essay on a longer work, see Frantz Fanon, "Algeria Unveiled," *The New Left Reader,* edited by Carl Oglesby (New York: Grove Press, Inc, 1969): 161–85.

18. Karen Sacks, *Caring by the Hour.*

19. Juana Gutiérrez, Personal Interview, Boyle Heights, East Los Angeles, 15 January 1988.

20. Erlinda Robles, Personal Interview, Boyle Heights, Los Angeles, 14 September 1989.

21. Mina Davis Caulfield, "Imperialism, the Family, and Cultures of Resistance," *Socialist Revolution* 29 (1974): 67–85.

22. Erlinda Robles, Personal Interview.

23. Ibid.

24. Juana Gutiérrez, Personal Interview.

25. Frank Villalobos, architect and urban planner, Personal Interview, Los Angeles, 2 May 1989.

26. The law student, Veronica Gutiérrez, is the daughter of Juana Gutiérrez, one of the cofounders of MELA. Martín Gutiérrez, one of her sons, was a

field representative for Assemblywoman Lucille Roybal-Allard and also central to community mobilization. Ricardo Gutiérrez, Juana's husband, and almost all the other family members are community activists. They are a microcosm of the family networks that strengthened community mobilization and the Coalition Against the Prison. See Raymundo Reynoso, "Juana Beatrice Gutiérrez: La incansable lucha de una activista comunitaria," *La Opinion*, 6 Agosto de 1989, Acceso, p. 1, and Louis Sahagun, "The Mothers of East L.A. Transform Themselves and Their Community," *Los Angeles Times*, 13 August 1989, sec. 2, p. 1.

27. Frank Villalobos, Personal Interview.

28. Father John Moretta, Resurrection Parish, Personal Interview, Boyle Heights, Los Angeles, 24 May 1989.

29. The Plaza de Mayo mothers organized spontaneously to demand the return of their missing children, in open defiance of the Argentine military dictatorship. For a brief overview of the group and its relationship to other women's organizations in Argentina, and a synopsis of the criticism of the mothers that reveals ideological camps, see Gloria Bonder, "Women's Organizations in Argentina's Transition to Democracy," in *Women and Counter Power*, edited by Yolanda Cohen (New York: Black Rose Books, 1989): 65–85. There is no direct relationship between this group and MELA.

30. Aurora Castillo, Personal Interview, Boyle Heights, Los Angeles, 15 January 1988.

31. Aurora Castillo, Personal Interview.

32. Erlinda Robles, Personal Interview.

33. Ibid.

34. Reynoso, "Juana Beatriz Gutiérrez," p. 1.

35. For historical examples, see Chris Marín, "La Asociación Hispano-Americana de Madres Y Esposas: Tucson's Mexican American Women in World War II," *Renato Rosaldo Lecture Series 1: 1983–1984* (Tucson, Ariz.: Mexican American Studies Center, University of Arizona, Tucson, 1985) and Judy Aulette and Trudy Mills, "Something Old, Something New: Auxiliary Work in the 1983–1986 Copper Strike," *Feminist Studies* 14, no. 2 (Summer 1988): 251–69.

36. Mina Davis Caulfield, "Imperialism, the Family and Cultures of Resistance."

37. Aurora Castillo, Personal Interview.

38. As reconstructed by Juana Gutiérrez, Ricardo Gutiérrez, and Aurora Castillo.

39. Aurora Castillo, Personal Interview.

40. Juana Gutiérrez, Personal Interview.

41. Lucy Ramos, Personal Interview, Boyle Heights, Los Angeles, 3 May 1989.

42. Ibid.

43. For an overview of contemporary Third World struggles against environmental degradation, see Alan B. Durning, "Saving the Planet," *The Progressive* 53, no. 4 (April 1989): 35–59.

44. John Logan and Harvey Molotch, *Urban Fortunes* (Berkeley: Univer-

sity of California Press, 1988). Logan and Molotch use the term in reference to a coalition of business people, local politicians, and the media.

45. Mike Davis, "Chinatown, Part Two? The Internationalization of Downtown Los Angeles," *New Left Review*, no. 164 (July/August 1987): 64–86.

46. Paul Ong, *The Widening Divide, Income Inequality and Poverty in Los Angeles* (Los Angeles: The Research Group on the Los Angeles Economy, 1989). This UCLA-based study documents the growing gap between "haves" and "have nots" in the midst of the economic boom in Los Angeles. According to economists, the study mirrors a national trend in which rising employment levels are failing to lift the poor out of poverty or boost the middle class; see Jill Steward, "Two-Tiered Economy Feared as Dead End of Unskilled," *Los Angeles Times*, 25 June 1989, sec. 2, p. 1. At the same time, the California prison population will climb to more than twice its designed capacity by 1995. See Carl Ingram, "New Forecast Sees a Worse Jam in Prisons," *Los Angeles Times*, 27 June 1989, sec. 1, p. 23.

47. The point that urban land use policies are the products of class struggle—both cause and consequence—is made by Don Parson, "The Development of Redevelopment: Public Housing and Urban Renewal in Los Angeles," *International Journal of Urban and Regional Research* 6, no. 4 (December 1982): 392–413. Parson provides an excellent discussion of the working-class struggle for housing in the 1930s, the counterinitiative of urban renewal in the 1950s, and the inner city revolts of the 1960s.

48. Louise Tilly, "Paths of Proletarianization: Organization of Production, Sexual Division of Labor, and Women's Collective Action," *Signs* 7, no. 2 (1981): 400–17; Alice Kessler-Harris, "Women's Social Mission," *Women Have Always Worked* (Old Westbury, N.Y.: The Feminist Press, 1981): 102–35. For a literature review of women's activism during the Progressive Era, see Marilyn Gittell and Teresa Shtob, "Changing Women's Roles in Political Volunteerism and Reform of the City," in *Women and the American City*, edited by Catharine Stimpson et al. (Chicago: University of Chicago Press, 1981): 64–75.

49. Karen Sacks, *Caring by the Hour*, argues that often the significance of women's contributions is not "seen" because they take place in networks.

50. Aurora Castillo, Personal Interview.

6. The Political Incorporation of L.A.'s Communities of Color: A Critical Assessment

Jaime A. Regalado

COMMUNITIES OF COLOR ARE NOT incorporated into the day-to-day politics and policymaking of Los Angeles and throughout the modern history of the city, they never have been. If by incorporation we are referring to a sustained presence in, and influence on, either the dominant coalition of the city council or, more broadly, the city's governing regime (coalition), grassroots communities on the Eastside, Southside, and Central City West (home to large concentrations of Latinos, African Americans, and Koreans) are not well represented. If, however, we are referring to the incorporation of African American and, to a lesser degree, Latino and Asian elites[1] and the organizations they represent, then incorporation has occurred.

Sonenshein (1986, 1989, 1993) persuasively argues that the city's African-American community became incorporated in and through the Bradley era (1973–1993) of the city's history. More specifically, he contends that such incorporation was the intended result of biracial electoral coalition formation and activity joining the largely African-American Southside with the largely Jewish Westside. A successfully sustained coalition begat incorporation and empowerment for the city's Southside while strengthening incorporation and the fruits thereof for the Westside. However, in Sonenshein's discussions of incorporation and empowerment, he is almost entirely silent on the city's large Latino and Asian populations as well as on the major roles played by corporate and labor communities.

Several questions are prompted largely by omission in Sonenshein's

169

work. First, is political empowerment the exclusive province of electoral participation and influence over formal political structures? Second, does incorporation beget empowerment or is it much the same condition, as Sonenshein seems to imply? Third, can we adequately assess relations of power and incorporation by restricting our focus to two of the city's four predominant racial/ethnic clusters and also ignoring structural relations and roles played by private sector institutions?

In the pages that follow I will contend that political incorporation is a significant piece of the community empowerment puzzle, the formal electoral piece. But in and of itself, it does not constitute community empowerment. Any assessment of community empowerment must include:

- the empowerment circumstances and conditions of all major populations of the city/area,
- the nature of the private sector and its interactions with public and community sectors, and
- the coalition and/or partnership interactions of these populations and sectors, electoral or otherwise.

THE POLITICAL INCORPORATION THESIS

The pioneering work by Browning, Marshall, and Tabb (BMT), in 1984 and 1989, defined the model of political incorporation and guided subsequent applications used widely by political scientists to assess degrees to which communities of color have become empowered politically in formal structures of local governance. In brief, BMT found that processes of community mobilization led to political incorporation in their original study of Northern California cities (1984) and in subsequent applications to other cities by a number of scholars. In identifying qualitatively different patterns of coalitions and corresponding levels of incorporation, the authors concluded that the cities in which communities of color gained sustained councilmanic influence had governments more responsive in four areas of resource allocation: commission, board, and department appointments; city contracts; city employment; and establishment of a civilian police review board. These areas of resource allocation would become the litmus test for those communities which achieved sustained political influence (incorporation).

According to the BMT model, incorporation was achieved only through a sustained electoral coalition effort on the part of a community of color (predominantly African American) and another community, predominantly liberal and white, which I have previously called the "wild card" of incorporation dependency (1991). On this and other counts, there have been criticisms of the model (see Regalado 1991; Hero 1992; Schmidt 1996; Geron 1996). Hero has criticized the extent to which the model strictly relies on resource allocation measures as testimony to a community's incorporation "arrival" while Schmidt has faulted its relative omission of structural institutions and relations from incorporation and empowerment assessments. Geron implies that political incorporation as defined in the BMT model might, unintentionally, best assess forms of political co-option of leadership levels in communities of color.

INCORPORATION APPLICATIONS IN L.A.: THE SONENSHEIN THESIS

The political incorporation of African Americans was oversold by Sonenshein (1989, 1990, 1993) as he applied the Browning, Marshall, and Tabb model to Los Angeles. By relying on the model's strict adherence to bi-racial electoral coalition efforts, Sonenshein's definition of racial politics and the pursuit of political power became narrow and wanting. Struggles for empowerment and incorporation scenarios are limited to the electoral arena, the bi-racial components of the coalition and definitions of political influence defined by public sector resource allocation. There is little discussion of class and economic structures and powers. Similarly, non-electoral coalitions and movements are ignored even though they may help to determine intra- and inter-community power bases for communities of color (Regalado 1995). (Several coalition formations come to mind: the Community Coalition Against Substance Abuse, South Central Organizing Committee, United Youth on the Move, United Neighborhoods Organization, Mothers of East Los Angeles, the Empowerment Congress, the New Majority Task Force of Los Angeles, and the MultiCultural Collaborative.) Electoral coalitions and the political incorporation of select fragments of communities or individuals of middle-class background do not by themselves define the political empowerment of a community or its political influence. During the Bradley years, when the incorporation of African Americans was widely touted (Sonenshein 1986, 1989, 1992, 1993), the questions should have been, as always, who became incorporated in the African-American community and at what cost? The following section contains a discussion of contemporary demographic and economic realities and relations in Los Angeles.

THE NEW DEMOGRAPHY OF LOS ANGELES

Los Angeles has changed considerably since the mid-1970s. Demographically, the city houses extremes of growing wealth and poverty, more Latinos and Asians and fewer whites and African Americans. Latino and Asian growth has been dramatic in this period (see Modarres 1994, 1995). By the mid-1990s, the city's residents had become approximately 40 percent Latino, 35 percent white, 12 percent Asian, 11 percent African American, and 2 percent other. For this period, corresponding percentages of ethnic/racial representation on the city's legislative body are 20 percent Latino (3 seats), 60 percent white (9 seats), 0 percent Asian (no seats), and 20 percent African American (3 seats).

By comparing population and representation figures, it is easy to conclude that although Latinos have made significant council gains, they continue to be significantly underrepresented. Whites are significantly overrepresented, Asians unrepresented, and African Americans overrepresented. However, when controlling for factors such as who is registered to vote and who actually votes, the numbers on representation become even more illuminating. For example, in typical city-wide elections, Latinos make up approximately 8–10 percent of the vote, whites approximately 65 percent, Asians approximately 6–8 percent and African Americans approximately 15 percent (Sonenshein 1995; Regalado 1994; *Los Angeles Times* 1995).

Most of both Latino and Asian/Pacific Islander growth has occurred among the working class and poor socioeconomic sectors, approximately 40 percent fueled by immigration (both legal and illegal) (Teixeira 1995; Modarres 1995). Unlike previous patterns of immigration found among Latinos and Asians, in the 1980s Central American as well as Mexican immigrants began moving massively into southern Los Angeles, an area predominantly of African-American residency since the 1950s (Modarres 1995). This "repopulation" of South Los Angeles has fueled a number of situations over the past five years: racial and cultural tension, negative perceptions of competition for scarce jobs and dwindling city and county resources, political competition and fear, as well as largely hidden examples of cooperation and coalition-building (see Wakabayashi 1996). Asian in-migration into South L.A., largely but not exclusively of family merchant–class Koreans, has become a familiar, if oversimplified, story of racial tension and class conflict through the Rodney King and LAPD episode, the Latasha Harlings killing and the riots and rebellions of 1992 (see Baldassare 1994).

Since the relaxation of federal laws restricting Asian immigration in the 1970s, the numbers of Asians (predominantly Chinese, Koreans,

Vietnamese, and Cambodians) moving into the city and the municipalities which border Los Angeles have increased at a rate faster than any other group in the Metropolitan Area (see Modarres 1995; La 1995; Ong 1994). Although most of the newly arrived affluent Chinese moved into municipalities of the west San Gabriel Valley (such as Monterey Park, San Marino, San Gabriel and Alhambra), many in poorer economic circumstances moved into less wealthy areas of the San Gabriel Valley (such as El Monte and Pico Rivera) and into the sweatshop areas of L.A.'s Chinatown, Little Tokyo, and Koreatown. Koreans moved to different parts of the city but set up many of their shops and stores in the Koreatown/South Central Los Angeles corridor as well as in East Los Angeles. Since the unrest of 1992, this population and its advocates have decried its lack of political representation and influence (incorporation). The Koreatown section of Los Angeles exists in the 10th Council District presided over by Nate Holden, an African-American widely viewed as being accessible for Korean merchant campaign funds but less accessible and accountable on issues most significant to their community.

The Restructuring of L.A.'s Economy and Social Relations

The repercussions of the new global economy on the local economy and body politic are still unraveling in Los Angeles. The economic restructuring taking place mirrors the demographic restructuring, with which it is inextricably linked, in many ways. Part of the new post-manufacturing, information industry restructuring has resulted in a number of sobering realities for the nation and western region (Rifkin 1966) as well as for the Southland (see Merl and Rivera-Brooks 1996; Peltz 1996; Silverstein 1996; and Rabin 1996). Corporate mergers have cost Los Angeles thousands of jobs with, for example, the loss of the last two banking headquarters (Security Pacific and First Interstate Banks) and significant restructuring in remaining corporate employers such as Pacific Enterprises, Pacific Telesis, Pacific Bell, Southern California Edison, and the Southern California Gas Company, to name a few, threaten thousands of additional jobs and careers. Merger-inspired business and individual tax losses for the city, coupled with the near-decimation of the L.A.-based aerospace industry has resulted in a serious tax (revenue) and service disequilibrium which is becoming more severe, as Pagano and Bowman (1995) noted in a number of American cities.

The predominant economic vision of the city's governing regime in the Bradley era (1973–1993), which underscored development strategy and implementation, was to create a Los Angeles that would be the western center of finance in the United States as well as the business and shipping gateway to the Pacific Rim. In this vision, the massive revitalization of the downtown's Central Business District (CBD)—the arena in which to locate corporate headquarters—and corollary multiplier expectations in outlying communities, and the creation of a state-of-the-art rail to port transportation system running from the Alameda section of Los Angeles to the Port of Los Angeles were to be the crown jewels. This was consistently presented to communities of color as a vision of "trickle down" benefits as a result of multiplier business expansion, in the form of community investment, jobs, increased salaries, and purchasing power (see Regalado 1992).

STRUCTURAL DIMENSIONS OF POLITICS

Los Angeles is governed in a strong council form. Fifteen councilmembers are elected for four-year terms in single member district elections. Although much has been made, both before and especially since the 1992 L.A. riots and rebellions, of strengthening the office of mayor vis-à-vis that of the city council, even those councilmembers closest to Mayor Riordan (such as Richard Alatorre) balk at either relinquishing power and/or providing the mayor with additional powers (Regalado 1995). The socially balkanized and racially/ethnically segregated nature of the city has been exacerbated over the years by a political segregation frequently referred to as council fiefdoms.

This is not meant to suggest that the position of mayor in Los Angeles is powerless or that the city council is all-powerful. This is not the case, for the mayor (1) has widespread appointment authority (largely reserved for those loyal to his campaign treasury as well as his policy and ideological outlooks) to the many commissions which govern the departments running the city, (2) sets annual policy (including budgetary) agendas for the city as a whole, (3) has veto authority over measures passed by the council, including the budget, and (4) is broadly perceived to be the city's preeminent public figure, booster, and spokesperson. Perhaps the most important of the mayor's formal powers revolve around his commission appointments, and among the most notable are the revenue ("juice") commissions, such as the Airport, Public Works, Harbor, and Water and Power (see Erie 1996, 1992). (Whereas the mayor both nominates and replaces commissioners, he appoints department heads but cannot, by himself, fire them.) The mayor has made these revenue departments a central piece of his budgetary puzzle and wizardry, frequently drawing on their resources over the past three years to close deficits and pay for cherished projects. Although Riordan's actions diverge from the previous relations of fiscal autonomy between the city and these departments, his appointed commissioners have routinely obliged him. However, recently threatened legal action by the State of California to secure some of this revenue for the state presents the mayor with potentially severe obstacles to continuing this practice in the future (see Merl 1996a). Additionally, federal officials have ordered Riordan to cease diverting revenue from the Department of Airports, a key to the mayor's plan and promise to expand the Los Angeles Police Department. Thirty million dollars are at stake (see Wilgoren and Bornemeier 1996).

Term limits now prevent all of the city's elected officials from remaining in the same office for more than two consecutive terms. A significant question to ponder, especially for political incorporation theorists, is whether the incorporation of communities of color will be more difficult to achieve, as well as sustain, under term limits. It seems likely that, at the outset, since mass-based electoral and community coalitions have historically been difficult to maintain over time, it would be difficult to consistently sustain electoral coalitions to replace "termed" councilmembers.

Mayor Riordan came into office (in 1993) in the midst of a severe recession and an atmosphere of business anxiety and some business exodus, severe racial and ethnic conflict and community explosion (the riots and civil unrest of the previous year). In great part due to these conditions, the governing regime which Riordan nominally heads got off to a very slow start in defining its economic vision of and economic development goals for the city.

The mayor's specific visions and strategies tied to such visions remain elusive. Over the first three years of his inaugural term, Riordan has been increasingly judged by his pledge to create a safer city by hiring and deploying 7,000 police, a pledge to create a process and environment more friendly to doing business in L.A., and a Riordan-inspired massive public relations campaign to attract new business (the New Los Angeles Marketing Partnership) promoting "L.A. as the Place." He has also been judged by intentions to prevent businesses from moving headquarters and satellites away from the city, commitments obtained to infuse capital streams into South Central Los Angeles (in a similar vein as the original Rebuild L.A.), and his efforts to reduce racial and community tension (see Merl and Rivera-Brooks 1996). In this context, the mayor's most recent "State of the City" address indicated that continued police hiring and expansion, overhaul of the city's business tax structure, and steps to spur community revitalization and development would be the highlights of the coming year (see Merl 1996b).

On this question of bringing revitalization and economic development to inner city communities, Riordan's primary hope is that L.A.'s
new Community Development Bank, funded largely through HUD to
the tune of $430 million as a consolation prize for "runner-up" empow-
erment zone status, and private banking interests will provide the base
for his Los Angeles Neighborhoods Initiative, the designated vehicle for
community development (defined primarily as economic development
and human capacity building). The Bank, which recently announced its
first loan, is expected to work with community, public, and private
sources to provide low-interest loans, venture capital, and technical assistance in inner city communities falling within L.A.'s Supplemental Empowerment Zone and Enterprise Communities (including Watts and
portions of South Central L.A. represented by Councilmembers Mark
Ridley Thomas and Rita Walters, portions of East L.A. represented by
Richard Alatorre, a sliver of the Pico Union portion of Mike Hernandez'
First District and the Pacoima area of the San Fernando Valley represented by Richard Alarcon).

This is a picture of communities in need, but of combustible political relations as well. Much of that combustion was responsible for the
long delays and, ultimately, the poorly drafted Empowerment Zone Proposal rejected in Washington, D.C. However, the jolt of rejection, as well
as the subsequent and significant consolation prize to be realized through
the Bank, have forced a certain amount of pragmatism among frequently divided councilmembers (namely Alatorre and Ridley-Thomas)
and among councilmembers and the mayor. Still, the lead evaluator of
L.A.'s Supplemental Empowerment Zone and, therefore, the Bank, informed me that the community capacity building expectation of HUD
and Bank directives has been discarded in favor of a strict focus on economic development.

Riordan, who is already campaigning for next year's mayoral election, has little to show for his first term. With the exception of privatization, on which Riordan has been increasingly silent, the areas mentioned above were priorities raised by Riordan during the campaign of
1993. Thus, in terms of "the vision thing," it seems to be more of the
same. What is not suggested in Riordan's public comments is how to get
along better with the city council in order to ensure that his visions for
the city become translated into public policy.

Riordan's relations with the city's business communities (large and
small) are, as might be expected, quite good. However, his relations with
organized labor are very much in transition. The construction trades and
other elite units of organized labor headquartered in the leadership of the
Los Angeles County Federation of Labor (L.A. County Fed) had become

a firm part of the city's governing coalition and growth regime under Bradley (Regalado 1991). Bradley and Bill Robertson, former Executive Secretary Treasurer of the L.A. County Fed, shared a close personal and political relationship. The latter was largely based on a common vision of massive building projects in the central city core of the downtown area (Regalado 1992). With the joint retirements of Bradley and Robertson in 1993, a new regime partnership developed, joining incoming Mayor Riordan with Robertson's hand-picked successor, James Wood. Wood had long served Robertson as the political director of the L.A. County Fed and Bradley as his appointed chairman of the powerful Community Redevelopment Agency's Board of Commissioners, which underscored the symbiotic relationship between Bradley and labor's highest leadership, almost entirely white and old guard.

However, the house of local labor is going through a period of intense difficulty and restructuring, reflecting the demographic, political, and economic realities of the city, region, and nation. As the power of the politically conservative construction trades has eroded with California's long recession and bitter jurisdiction infighting, progressive and member-diverse service unions (such as the United Food and Commercial Workers Local 770, Service Employees International Union Local 660, and Hotel Employees and Restaurant Employees Union Local 11) have grown in strength and stature. These unions are, for the first time in the history of the city, served by a younger generation of Latino leadership stressing active organizing and community coalition-building (see Regalado 1995).

An intense power struggle that divided both leaders and rank and file along racial and ideological lines (Latinos and progressive whites in the one corner and older-guard whites and African Americans in the other) developed in the wake of the death of James Wood in February (see Silverstein 1996). To Riordan, Wood went from being an architect of Bradley's growth machine to a close confident of the new mayor, initially through Riordan's Chief of Staff, Bill Wardlow. (Wardlow and Wood had long been the best of friends.) In Wood's absence, no obvious labor link exists to share in the mayor's vision and regime. Wood's successor, Miguel Contreras, served H.E.R.E. (Hotel Employees and Restaurant Employees) International before becoming affiliated with H.E.R.E. Local 11 in Los Angeles. He is married to Local 11 President Maria Elena Durazo, an active and progressive labor leader. Both come from the fields and backgrounds with the United Farm Workers, hardly the substance of political inclusion in the Riordan regime.

Reflecting raw divisions in the city at large, labor has much internal mending to accomplish before it can present a strengthened and unified front to wage political and economic battle. Particularly severe is the degree of discord and distrust of the emerged Latino leadership and its growing membership on the part of the older white leadership and rank and file as well as the African-American trade unionists (Sickler 1996; Silverstein 1996). On a more optimistic note, strong and supportive relations have developed among Latino and Asian-Pacific union leaders and members, the fastest growing segments of the population and workforce in Los Angeles. This has been particularly evident in the full-scale battle to organize downtown's New Otani Hotel, the focus on organizing new workforce L.A. on the part of AFL-CIO Region VI under its Director, David Sickler, and the frequently joined activities of the Labor Council on Latin American Advancement (LCLAA) and the Asian Pacific Alliance for Los Angeles (APALA), the Latino and Asian organizational arms of the L.A. County Fed. This is a story largely unknown and "untold" outside labor circles.

Finally, both the Community Redevelopment Agency (CRA) and RLA (the former Rebuild L.A.) are going through phases of confusion and relative idleness (CRA) consistent with the mid-90s regime change and vision on the one hand, and of selected smallness of scale (RLA) on the other. Whereas the CRA mobilized public capital and merged efforts with private sector partners virtually unrestricted by city council control under Bradley, under Riordan rule and incomplete vision, the council commands more control of the agency's budget and agenda. Today it is an agency in search of vision and direction, much like the mayor.

CONTEMPORARY MAYORAL-COUNCILMANIC REALITIES

The L.A. city council has historically ratified mayoral commission appointments, routinely in most cases. However, because the management style of Richard Riordan, which seldom involves informing or lobbying members before council voting, has irked many a councilmember, several of Riordan's commission choices have been denied by the council. His top-down corporate style of managing city affairs, in which he delegates almost all inter-personal actions and interactions with councilmembers to staffers, has prevented Riordan from creating or engineering a dominant and supportive council coalition. Such a predominant council coalition, ideologically moderate-to-conservative and predominantly white, seemed to be forming in Riordan's inaugural year (1993–4) under the leadership of Richard Alatorre and including Council President John Ferraro (mid-Wilshire and points west of downtown) and San Fernando Val ley representatives Joel Wachs, Hal Bernson, and Laura Chick. There was even the potential for involvement of the other two Latino councilmembers. However, the mayor's aloof and condescending style of attempting to command city business and policy from afar, with little effort offered toward personal communication with council members (as had been the case in the Bradley Administration), has resulted in a mayoral support system on the council that seldom rises above individual personalities and issues. Thus, unlike the Bradley years, in which there was an emphasis on personal relations and "stroking," there is no substantial coalition of mayoral support on the council.

Significantly, the city's legislative body is instead divided into rival political and racial/ethnic orbits with a large swing body of councilmembers uncommitted to either extreme. On most revenue, economic development and land use matters, Riordan has generally been able to count on the moderate Alatorre, the conservative Ferrero, and fellow Republicans Wachs and Bernson, conservatives both, to be supportive. The rival camp is centered around the council's three African-American members, preeminently Mark Ridley-Thomas (along with Rita Walters and Nate Holden). On most policy matters, Jewish Councilmember Marvin Braude joins this liberal group. In the gray middle sit the council's other seven members, the majority of whom have increasingly sided with the liberal faction in resisting the mayor on such issues as affirmative action, privatization, police deployment, department personnel review and commission appointments. Thus, the city council under Riordan does not have a dominant central coalition or orbit. In some ways it is a throwback to the city council in pre-Bradley days, one divided among itself and frequently warring with a "citizen mayor."

For incorporation theorists then, there is not at present a predominate council coalition to join or lead. Rather, the council is characterized by shifting orbits and coalitions around specific issues motivated, in part, by personalities, ideology, and racial/ethnic considerations.

COMMUNITY ISSUES AND POLICY CONCERNS

Andranovich and Riposa (1995) contend that seldom do issues and concerns defined at inner-city community levels successfully meet public policy outcomes, even when the process is understood. They suggest that it is not the result of a lack of knowledge on the part of the policymakers, but rather is due to different interpretations and, perhaps, priorities. Similarly, Jackson (1990) and, to a lesser extent, Pachon (1991) argue that policymakers have long known the needs and concerns of the city's poorest communities. However, Jackson argued that African-American electoral victories, anchored by Bradley's twenty-year reign, could have translated into policy outcomes better serving the needs of L.A.'s Southside communities. He contends that the loyalties of the Bradley coalition, in spite of the Southside's alleged incorporation (Sonenshein 1989), were elsewhere. Where Jackson implied that the spoils of Bradley's electoral coalition victories went primarily to the city's Westside, Regalado (1991, 1992) suggested that many of the spoils remained downtown, as well. Davis (1990) and Mann (1989) argued that it could not have been different inasmuch as Bradley was merely the symbolic headstone, not Sonenshein's progressive visionary, of a governing coalition dominated by downtown and westside corporate and financial interests.

When asked to name the most salient issues for their communities, the vast majority of the city's Latino and African-American respondents cite jobs, economic security, crime, gangs and youth violence, race relations, better services, affordable housing, inferior schools, and economic development (Adelante Eastside Study 1995; Bobo et al. 1992; Pachon 1991; Jackson 1990). These issues, along with a general category of creating and enhancing "livable communities," correlate strongly with conclusions reached and recommendations made by the LA 2000 Committee, a select group of economic, political, and multi-cultural elites representing the city's governing coalition under Bradley, in its LA 2000 Report on preparing for and building the city's future (Los Angeles 2000 1988). While schools do not come under the city's control or political purview and job growth and provision is increasingly dependent upon international, national, and regional economies and market trends as well as visions of changing governing coalitions (Rifkin 1996; Pagano & Bowman 1995; Stone 1989), the other issues are part of what cities are empowered to address. It might, then, be expected that an "incorporated" community would be able to move many of these issues and identified problems to the "front-burner" and have them addressed by policymakers.

However, although Sonenshein has long contended that the city's African-American community, in coalition partnership with a Jewish liberal community, was politically incorporated during Bradley's mayoral reign, not only did the vast majority of the city's African Americans not believe themselves to be empowered as a community (Jackson 1990), but issues of concern were not seriously addressed, much less acted upon, during the Bradley era (Davis 1990). On the political incorporation scale, city resources were allocated to gain jobs, contracts, and appointments for many African Americans who were already considered elites within their communities. Beyond this relatively small circle benefitting from the fruits of incorporation, African Americans received few tangible "empowerment benefits" redistributed during their "incorporation period."

Browning, Marshall, and Tabb point out that communities of color need to become internally organized around galvanizing issues, coalesce with at least another strategic community (preeminently white and liberal), select candidates, and elect representatives of the coalition's choice on the city council to maintain an organized vigil to keep their councilmembers "in line," witness their elected representatives becoming part of the council's governing coalition, and gain policy influence on the city's legislative body. Lacking these attributes, Southside African-American communities, Eastside and Central West Latino communities, and Mid-City Asian communities are not politically incorporated.

Perhaps the answer lies not so much with electoral coalitions but with community coalitions to empower communities and their families. Kayden (1996) reports on one such inter-district coalition (The Empowerment Congress) in the Eighth Council District of Mark Ridley-Thomas, formed to deal with issues as defined by grassroots communities from the bottom-up. The Eighth District includes many neighborhoods in South Central Los Angeles. Although the District contains an African-American resident majority, Latinos are expected to become the majority by the time of the next city-wide redistricting in 2001. However, the Congress is predominantly comprised of African Americans. It might be anticipated that the long-term viability of the Congress as a community coalition will be more secure only after it becomes more inclusive of Latinos at all levels. Be that as it may, the coalition is unique in that it reaches into neighborhood and block levels to define issues of community significance, develop strategies to deal with such issues, and work with local elected officials to gain public and private sector support for programs and remedies connected with these defined issues, problems, and strategies (Kayden 1996). The practical goal which guides the coalition is to pick issues carefully and focus on what unites people. Kayden argues that term limits will not mean much for this district since it is the unanimous opinion of the Congress that Ridley-Thomas' successors must gain the support of the coalition or they will not be elected. For those theorists who place their entire incorporation thesis on bi-racial electoral coalition development and sustainment, how is this example to be explained, an example not ostensibly of an electoral coalition?

INCORPORATION IN L.A. REVISITED

For African-American elites, access to city hall and representation on the city council's predominant policy coalition peaked during the Bradley mayoral years (1973–1993). However, even prior to Bradley's first term as mayor, the political incorporation of some African Americans into elite status and the politics of city hall influence had already begun. The vehicles involved in this process were the three council districts in which African Americans had been elected (one of whom was Bradley himself) by the mid-1960s and the developing African-American and Jewish council coalition (see Sonenshein 1989, 1993) of mutual support. The Bradley years also marked the beginning of such incorporation for a smaller number of Latino and Asian elites.

Although public sector perks for Latinos were few and far between from 1973 to the mid-1980s, Richard Alatorre's election in 1985 as only the second Latino city council member in this century brought an incorporation boost to Latino contractors, financiers, lawyers, builders, planners, and consultants. Alatorre's immediate entree to a declining, though still predominant, coalition of Bradley supporters on the council during Mayor Tom's fourth term brought immediate benefits to a core of Latino professionals. Although some Latino elites operated in a city hall that had opened more widely during the Bradley years, Alatorre's presence opened the door even more for a number of Latinos connected with him in his days as a key member of Willie Brown's inner circle in the California Assembly (his council district covers much of the same area as his former assembly district).

The election to the council of two additional Latino representatives, Mike Hernandez and Richard Alarcon in 1989 and 1993, was historic; for the first time in more than 100 years, Latinos controlled three of fifteen council seats. However, their elections were neither significant in expanding the pool of "incorporated Latinos," nor did they result from significant bi-racial or multi-racial coalition activity. The limited nature of their "incorporation pull" was partially due to the limited networks that the two former political neophytes had cultivated prior to their elections. It also had much to do with the content and context of their respective council districts. Hernandez' district, although overwhelmingly Latino, is the poorest of the council's fifteen districts and contains the largest concentrations of immigrants and non-registered voters. It is a district rife with crime, gang activity and youth violence, poorly performing and poorly maintained schools. Alarcon, on the other hand, was elected to a San Fernando Valley district containing a majority of white voters. Whites as well as Latinos in "the Valley" have never felt they were part of, much less politically incorporated into, Los Angeles and the downtown elites who govern the immense city. There were few "ready to ride" to incorporated status on Alarcon's coat-tails. In a similar vein, Flannigan (1996) contends that the Valley's predominant populations (whites and Latinos) vote primarily on the basis of class background and interest, not on the racial or ethnic background factors that seem to galvanize voting preferences in the rest of Los Angeles. Flannigan argues that this can clearly be seen in the Valley's movement to secede from the city.

In spite of formal councilmanic gains, respected observers contend that the very same Latinos remain "plugged" into the politics of influence and privilege in city hall. For them, as well as former and current office holders, this amounts to a relatively closed "circulation of (the very same) elites" (Molina 1991).

Asian elites, comprised in the majority of Japanese and Chinese bankers, venture capitalists, merchants, business managers, financiers, builders, contractors, and restauranteurs, were also more broadly incorporated into the city's predominant governing coalition under Bradley than at any other time in the city's history. The attraction was mutual. For Bradley, Asian capital investment into the city's downtown core became a cornerstone of financing his public-private partnerships and his vision of redeveloping the central business district—which dominated his economic development agenda through four of his five terms in the mayor's office (see Regalado 1992; Pastor and Hayling 1990). For Asian elites, the investment and management of capital in an area becoming more strategic to serving the Pacific Rim, aided by public sector inducements (largely through the Community Redevelopment Agency), promised relatively "safe" investment strategies.

The incorporation of Asian elites, both foreign and domestic, was at least symbolically accelerated, to a degree, with the seating of the city's first and only Asian councilmember, Mike Woo (whose father is a Chinatown banker), from the mid-1980s to 1993. However, because Bradley had already made key elite connections within the Asian community, Woo's influence on further Asian political incorporation was not substantial. Furthermore, his 13th councilmanic district, which included the communities of Hollywood, Silverlake, and Echo Park, contained a majority of white voters, while Asians and Latinos constituted but small "ripples" of electoral prowess. Woo was exceedingly careful not to appear as the Asian "torchbearer" on the council, a role that the Asian grassroots community clearly wanted of him (Kwoh 1991). In sum, although it would be unfair to suggest that only those Asians with capital to invest or manage became incorporated under Bradley, they nonetheless became the cornerstone of the Asian community's politically incorporated.

However, it may be argued that these electoral victories, far from representing the political incorporation of the city's most populous communities of color, amounted to little beyond a circulation of "community elites," that is, of predominantly middle class individuals who may or may not have represented constituencies other than their personal businesses or private interests. This is not meant to suggest that scores of individuals of color did not become incorporated into the city's structural politics because of African-American and Latino electoral gains. This surely did take place, primarily for African Americans. However, the degree to which those of working class and poor backgrounds became incorporated in the process was very slight (Jackson 1990; Davis 1990; Regalado 1992). Perhaps there were many expectations of what electoral representation would bring for inner city communities. Such expectations could never be realized through the structures of electoral participation (Peterson 1981; Davis 1993, 1990).

COALITION-BUILDING, INCORPORATION, EMPOWERMENT

At least beginning with the L.A. riots and unrest of 1992, Los Angeles has been symbolically viewed as containing a mix of the conditions which bedevil urban America. Most specifically, L.A.'s consistent self-boostering during the Bradley era frequently misled the nation and world about the degree to which mixed ethnic and racial communities got along and how each such community had a voice in city hall and the politics of the city. However, since 1992, prognoses on race relations, cooperative bi-racial or multi-racial coalition-building opportunities (electoral, community, and professional), and the political incorporation of communities of color are not especially optimistic, by most accounts.

Since the unrest of 1992, many have written of racial and ethnic relations in the city (see Baldassare 1994; Sonenshein 1993; Regalado 1994, 1992; Totten and Schockman 1995). Most do not have rosy predictions for proactive bi-racial or multi-racial electoral coalition-building. Far fewer write of non-electoral community-based efforts to empower grassroots communities of color (MultiCultural Collaborative 1996; Calderon and Wong 1995; Negrete and Taira 1995; Chang and Yu 1995; Regalado 1994). Even though inter-community and intra-community divisiveness and conflict are broadly evident, and are even growing in some instances, most public sector officials seemingly pretend either that the problem does not exist or that it will go away of its own volition. For example, even though Bradley was broadly praised in many quarters as

a "great healer" and "bridge builder" among the many cultural and social communities comprising Los Angeles, his commitment and that of
his coalition majority on the council to the city's lone agency charged
with improving social and cultural relations (the Human Relations Commission) was almost totally ignored, continuously underfunded, and
condemned to a two-person office.

In this pointed example, the Bradley Coalition's commitment to
improving relations seemed largely symbolic. This was even more telling
in his extremely limited use of redistribution policy, which could have
helped to empower working poor communities of color on the city's
southern and eastern sides (Jackson 1990; Mann 1989; Davis 1990).
RLA was the most significant gesture of near-total public sector capitu-
lation on questions of race relations, human and structural capital ero-
sion in inner cities and community empowerment. However, under Riordan, even the symbolism of the city's commitment and efforts to improve
community and human relations is gone. A focused reliance on electoral coalitions, incorporation into the corridors of legislative power,
and the resulting expectations of and commitments from the public sector has been misguided for students of urban power strategies and realities.

The real work to empower communities of color and build coalitions of color in the process has been taking place at community and
grassroots levels between and during election cycles. An absolute focus
on the electoral arena not only diminishes non-electoral community and
coalition efforts but, in the process, also dismisses community histories
which provide a broader (and more complete) context in which to understand struggles for empowerment as well as struggles against bigotry,
persecution, and oppression. Thus, the examples of contemporary multi-
racial coalitions such as the New Majority Task Force of Los Angeles,
the Coalition Against Substance Abuse, and The MultiCultural Collaborative, as well as those of bi-racial coalitions of the recent past such as
the Black-Latino Roundtable and the Black-Korean Alliance, become important (see Regalado 1995, 1994). However, outside of an electoral coalition format, these are little recognized and much less important to political incorporation theorists who, in the time-tested fashion of all
pluralists, ascribe questions of empowerment almost exclusively to the
electoral arena.

NOTE

1. For the purposes of this paper, 'elites' refer to individuals who own
their own businesses, control and direct community organizations that operate

with significant public and private sector contracts, religious leaders, lawyers (primarily business and corporate), builders and contractors, financiers, and lobbyists-political consultants.

REFERENCES

Acuna, Rodolfo F. 1996. *Anything But Mexican: Chicanos in Contemporary Los Angeles*. London: Verso Press.

Adelante Eastside Study. 1995. *Final Report: Summary of Recommendations, Opportunities and Findings*. Los Angeles: Barrio Planners Collaborative Team.

Andranovich, Gregory, and Gerry Riposa. 1995. "Urban Policy Issues and the 1994 Mid-Term Election: A Grassroot Perspective." *Journal of California Politics and Policy*: 5–13.

Baldassare, Mark (ed). 1994. *The Los Angeles Riots: Lessons for the Urban Future*. Boulder, Colo.: Westview Press.

Bobo, Lawrence, Camille L. Zubrinsky, James H. Johnson, Jr., and Melvil L. Oliver. 1992. "Public Opinion before and after a Spring of Discontent." In *The Los Angeles Riots: Lessons for the Urban Future*, ed. Mark Baldassare. Boulder, Colo.: Westview.

Browning, Rufus, Dale Rogers Marshall, and David Tabb. 1984. *Protest is Not Enough: The Struggle of Blacks and Hispanics for Equality in Urban Politics*. Berkeley: University of California Press.

Browning, Rufus, Dale Rogers Marshall, and David Tabb. 1989. *Racial Politics in American Cities*. New York: Longman.

Calderon, Jose, and Gay Yuen Wong. 1995. "Combating Coalitions in the San Gabriel Valley." *Journal of California Politics and Policy*: 55–60.

Chang, Edward, and Eui Young Yu. 1995. *Multi-Ethnic Coalition-Building in Los Angeles*. Claremont: Regina Press.

Cohen, Mara A. 1996. "Public Sector Autonomy in Los Angeles: The Development of Redevelopment." Paper presented at the Annual Meeting of the Western Political Science Association, San Francisco.

Davis, Mike. 1990. *City of Quartz: Excavating the Future of Los Angeles*. London: Verso Press.

Davis, Mike. 1993. "Who Killed L.A.? The War against the Cities." *Crossroads* (June): 2–19.

Erie, Steven P. 1992. "How the Urban West Was Won: The Local State and Economic Growth in Los Angeles, 1880–1932." *Urban Affairs Quarterly* 27 (June): 519–54.

Erie, Steven P. 1996. "A Budget That Pays Today's Bills with L.A.'s Future Growth." *Los Angeles Times* (May 19): M6.

Flannigan, James. 1996. "City Hall, Airlines Need to Work on Reving LAX Economic Engine." *Los Angeles Times* (June 12): D1, 5.

Geron, Kim. 1996. "The Political Incorporation of Latinos: Symbolic or Substantive Representation at the Local Level?" Doctoral dissertation. University of California, Riverside.

Hero, Rodney E. 1992. *Latinos and the U.S. Political System: Two-Tiered Pluralism*. Philadelphia: Temple University Press.

Jackson, Byran O. 1990. "Black Political Power in the City of Angels: An Analysis of Mayor Tom Bradley's Electoral Success." *National Political Science Review* 2: 169–75.

Jackson, Byran O. 1991. "Racial and Ethnic Voting Cleavages in Los Angeles Politics." In *Racial and Ethnic Politics in California*, ed. Byran O. Jackson and Michael B. Preston. Berkeley: IGS Press.

Kayden, Xandra. 1996. "A Political Machine That Creates a Sense of Belonging." *Los Angeles Times* (March 10): M6.

Kwoh, Stewart. 1991. Personal interview. Los Angeles.

La, Carolyn. 1995. "Beyond the Bashing: Realities of Asian Immigration in California." *Journal of California Politics and Policy*: 53–54.

Los Angeles 2000 Committee. 1988. *L.A. 2000: A City for the Future*.

Mann, Eric. 1989. "New Coalitions for L.A.'s Future." *LA Weekly* 11 (February 24-March 2): 49.

Merl, Jean. 1996a. "City Reliance on Profitable Departments Threatened." *Los Angeles Times* (May 25): B1, 3.

Merl, Jean. 1996b. "Riordan Upbeat in Assessing State of the City." *Los Angeles Times* (April 17): A1, 4.

Merl, Jean, and Nancy Rivera-Brooks. 1996. "Riordan Sets Goals for L.A.'s Economy." *Los Angeles Times* (March 7): B1, 3.

Modarres, Ali. 1994. *The Racial and Ethnic Structure of Los Angeles County: A Geographic Guide*. Los Angeles: PBI Publications.

Modarres, Ali. 1995. "The Demographic Reality of Immigration in the 1980s." *Journal of California Politics and Policy*: 37–51.

Molina, Gloria. 1991. Personal interview. Los Angeles.

MultiCultural Collaborative. 1996. *Race, Power and Promise in Los Angeles: An Assessment of Responses to Human Relations Conflicts*. Los Angeles.

Negrete, Edward, Jr., and Susan Shimizu Taira. 1995. "The Voices of Blacks and Latinos: Understanding Racial Conflict." *Journal of California Politics and Policy*: 65–73.

Ong, Paul (ed). 1994. *The State of Asian Pacific American Economic Diversity, Issues and Policies*. Los Angeles: LEAP and UCLA Asian American Studies Center.

Pachon, Harry. 1991. "U.S. Citizenship and Latino Participation in California Politics." In *Racial and Ethnic Politics in California*, ed. Byran O. Jackson and Michael B. Preston. Berkeley: IGS Press.

Pagano, Michael A., and Ann O'M. Bowman. 1995. *Cityscapes and Capital: The Politics of Urban Development*. Baltimore: John Hopkins University Press.

Pastor, Manuel, and Crystal Hayling (eds). 1990. *Economic Development: The New Majority in Los Angeles*. Los Angeles: Occidental College.

Peltz, James. 1996. "Aerospace Job Losses Putting L.A.'s Middle Class at Risk, Survey Warns." *Los Angeles Times* (March 8): D1, 5.

Peterson, Paul. 1981. *City Limits*. Chicago: University of Chicago Press.

Rabin, Jeffrey. 1996. "State and L.A. County Have Begun a Comeback, Economist Says." *Los Angeles Times* (March 6): B3.

Regalado, James A. 1991. "Organized Labor and Los Angeles City Politics: An Assessment in the Bradley Years, 1973–1989." *Urban Affairs Quarterly* 27: 1, 87–108.

Regalado, James A. 1992. "Political Representation, Economic Development Policymaking, and Social Crisis in Los Angeles, 1973–1992." In *City of Angels*, ed. Gerry Riposa and Carolyn Dersch. Dubuque: Kendall/Hunt.

Regalado, James A. 1994. "Community Coalition-Building." In *The Los Angeles Riots: Lessons for the Urban Future*, ed. Mark Baldassare. Boulder, Colo: Westview Press.

Regalado, James A. 1995. "Creating Multi-Cultural Harmony in Los Angeles? A Critical Perspective." In *Multi-Ethnic Coalition-Building in Los Angeles*, ed. Edward Chang and Eui Young Yu. Claremont: Regina Press.

Rifkin, Jeremy. 1996. "Civil Society in the Information Age." *The Nation* (February 26): 262, 11–16.

Schmidt, Ronald, Sr. 1996. "Politics in Black and White." A book review in *National Political Science Review* (September).

Sickler, Carole. 1996. Personal interview. Los Angeles County Federation of Labor.

Silverstein, Stuart. 1996. "Layoffs' Pace Slows in February." *Los Angeles Times* (March 7): D1, 7.

Sonenshein, Raphael. 1986. "Biracial Coalition Politics in Los Angeles." *PS* (Summer): 19, 582–90.

Sonenshein, Raphael. 1989. "The Dynamics of Biracial Coalitions: Crossover Politics in Los Angeles. "*Western Political Quarterly* (June): 105, 333–53.

Sonenshein, Raphael. 1990. "Biracial Coalition Politics in Los Angeles." In *Racial Politics in American Cities*, ed. R. Browning, D. R. Marshall, and D. Tabb. New York: Longman.

Sonenshein, Raphael. 1992. "Politics in the Ashes: Los Angeles after the Violence." In *City of Angels*, ed. Gerry Riposa and Carolyn Dersch. Dubuque: Kendall/Hunt.

Sonenshein, Raphael. 1993. *Politics in Black and White: Race and Power in Los Angeles*. Princeton: Princeton University Press.

Sonenshein, Raphael. 1995. "Minority Politics at the Crossroads: Voting Patterns in the 1993 Los Angeles Mayoral Election." Paper presented at the meeting of the Western Political Science Association (March 16–18), Portland.

Sonenshein, Raphael. 1996. "Urban Conservatism in an Age of Diversity: A Comparative Analysis of the Mayoralties of San Francisco's Frank Jordan and Los Angeles' Richard Riordan." Paper presented at the meeting of the Western Political Science Association (March 14–16), San Francisco.

Stone, Clarence N. 1989. *Regime Politics*. University of Kansas Press.

Teixeira, Steve. 1995. "Immigration: Old Problem in the New Transnational Economy." *Journal of California Politics and Policy*: 33–37.

Totten III, George O., and H. Eric Schockman (eds). 1994. *Community in Crisis: The Korean American Community after the Los Angeles Civil Unrest of April 1992.* Los Angeles: University of Southern California.

Wakabayashi, Ronald. 1996. "Managing Inter-Group Relations in Los Angeles." *Journal of California Politics and Policy* (forthcoming).

Wilgoren, Jodi, and James Bornemeier. 1996. "U.S. Officials Vow to Bar Use of LAX Funds." *Los Angeles Times* (May 2): B1, 3.

7. Latina Women and Politics in Boston: *Somos La Vida, La Fuerza, La Mujer*

Carol Hardy-Fanta

> We are life, strength, women.
> *Julia de Burgos*
> *Puerto Rican poet*

STUDIES OF LATINO POLITICS generally ignore the role of Latina women as political actors or view women as constrained from political participation by cultural or gender-based oppression. Cultural values of *machismo* and its female correlate, *marianismo,* appear to create a submissive and passive role for Latina women that suppresses political participation (Guzmán, 1976; Melville, 1980; Mirandé and Enríquez, 1979; and Barragán, 1980). These cultural values supposedly exacerbate gender-based attributes that "leave politics to the men" (Rinehart, 1986; Holtzman and Williams, 1991). Structural obstacles and gender-based power relations, according to the political science literature, also stifle the political aspirations of women in general (Rule, 1981; Welch and Secret, 1981).

GENDER AND POLITICS IN LATINO COMMUNITIES: IGNORED VOICES

A major flaw in current scholarship on Latino political participation is the lack of attention to the political life of Latina women. Foley et al. (1977) do not mention women except in tangential ways: women are

From *Latino Studies Journal,* May 1992, pp. 38–54. Used by permission of the publisher.

wives of candidates, for example. In Jennings and Rivera's book on Puerto Rican politics, again, there is no attention to Latina women in politics, or to issues specifically related to women (Jennings and Rivera, 1984). Guzmán identifies Chicana women as important reputational leaders within Mexican American communities, but devotes only two paragraphs in his book to this subject (1976). He concludes: "The role of women as community leaders among minority groups has been neglected by scholars" (Guzmán, 1976:165). Even books based on more recent research, such as Villarreal et al. (1988) and Gómez-Quiñones (1990), include no mention of women in the index or chapter titles (Villarreal et al.) and reduce Latina women's political contribution to a few sentences and paragraphs dispersed throughout the entire presentation (Gómez-Quiñones). Garcia's edited collection on Latinos in the political system, contains not one entry which focuses on Latina women in political roles (Garcia, 1988).

While there have been occasional writings on the life experiences of Latina women following migration (e.g., Sánchez Korrol, 1983:85–117), some mention of Latina community leaders or elected officials (Pachon, 1987:xvi; Falcón, 1988:183), and some recent attention to Mexican American women in community organizing efforts (Rose, 1990; Pardo, 1990; and Carrillo, 1986), there has been little research that explicitly explores Latina women and politics. Current research in mainstream journals seems to focus on the health, illness, maternal roles, and labor market characteristics of Latino women (e.g. Castillo-Speed, 1990.)

Thus, much is missing about Latina women and political life. What are their political views, opinions, attitudes and, most importantly, their experiences in the political world? What do they think politically, and what is the nature of their political activities? Do Latina women differ from Latino men and from traditional models of women's political participation? Research on Latino political participation seems to follow the mainstream model of being a male preserve of knowledge.

My study of Latino politics in Boston explicitly challenges the previous invisibility of Latina women as political actors, illustrates the impact of gender on the definition of politics, and demonstrates how Latina women overcome many of the structural and gender-based constraints on Latino political participation.

I used qualitative methods to study political participation in the Latino community in Boston during a two year period, 1988 to 1990 (Hardy-Fanta, 1991). The study went beyond the more easily measured voting rates commonly used in political surveys. I conducted in-depth, semi-structured, interviews with 31 influential Latinos (*la gente profesional*) and 22 common folk (*la gente del pueblo*). The interviews were conducted in English or in Spanish and each lasted between two and three hours. Influential Latinos were selected using a combination of reputational and snowball sampling. The common folk Latinos (*la gente del pueblo*) were selected using three methods: (1) snowball referrals from the influential group, (2) volunteers from community events, and (3) referrals from staff at Latino community centers located in the three main Latino neighborhoods in Boston. In addition, over one hundred hours of participant observation of community organizing and other political events added context and richness to the interview data. The interviews and field notes were analyzed using a text base computer program, *The Ethnograph*.

Throughout the article I use the term *Latino* for persons from the following groups: Puerto Ricans, Dominicans, Central and South Americans, Mexican Americans, and Cubans. The term *Latino* replaces *Hispanic* and *Spanish-Speaking*, and, like the term *Chicano* for Mexican Americans, replaces an Anglo-chosen designation with a self-chosen ethnic identity. For a discussion of the development of *Latinismo* and its political implications, see, for example, Padilla (1985). I specifically use the feminine version *Latina* when I refer to Latina women. All names of interviewees are fictitious; the names of public or elected officials are true names.

Contrary to the image of the passive and apolitical Latina women, I discovered that, at least in Boston and I suspect elsewhere as well, Latina women play an important role in the political mobilization of Latino communities. From the first interview to the last, and throughout the observations I conducted at community events, what emerged was that (1) Latina women are political actors, (2) Latina women and Latino men view politics in very different ways, (3) the gender of the political mobilizer has a direct impact on mobilization style, and (4) gender differences then either constrain or stimulate political participation.

LATINA WOMEN AS POLITICAL ACTORS

Latina women are active in Boston's politics and demonstrate the full range of political roles: running for office, mobilizing voters, mobilizing communities for concrete benefits, and providing political education for new members of the community.

Latina women in Boston have run for office more than their white female counterparts and in equal numbers to Latino men. Three of the six Latino candidates who have run for office in Boston were women. In fact, the first Latino person to run for mayor of Boston was not a man but a woman: Diana Lam in 1991. While her candidacy was extremely short-lived, the *Boston Globe* declared that she would have presented the most serious challenge to the incumbent.

Latina women also participate in party politics (almost exclusively the Democratic Party) and have attended and been elected to state party caucuses. They take on leadership roles in the Latino Democratic Committee. They are also active in voter registration drives. Rosa López, for example, is a Mexican American woman who runs a major (non-Latino) government program. She, like other women, is very active in ward politics. When she names people who organized a local voter registration ward drive, half of the people are women. One Puerto Rican candidate recalls: "I think that women have participated in politics in terms of being active and registering more voters than men in the Latino community."

In addition to the more formal aspects of organized politics, Latina women in Boston provide the crucial link in drawing non-participators (including illegal residents and non-citizens) into political participation at the grass-roots level. Even Latino men recognize the vital role of Latina women in political mobilization. Julio Rojas, for example, is a Puerto Rican man who is extremely active in Latino politics. He firmly states that:

> Women have been a major force at the grass-roots level in the Hispanic community—from the day we came here, from the day we came to the United States. *At the grass roots, the community level, women have been the major force for change* (emphasis added).

Nelson Merced, a Puerto Rican elected official, ties Latina women's political skills to their connectedness within the community:

> I think more than anything else, women have a lot more potential, the Hispanic women have a lot more potential for getting elected. [I ask: Why is that? and he replies:] Because they're more involved in the community, they're organized—they're better organizers . . . they communicate better with people, they're there in the community, they're in the trenches all the time, they deal with the household, and they may work, but they have—I think they have a stronger network, where men have—sort of—these networks, but I think they're weaker, whereas the women have a stronger network.

Even Tito Morales, an elderly Puerto Rican man who was called sexist by others in the community, revealed the long-standing contribution of Latina women to political mobilization. Morales, who spent over

forty years organizing protests and voter participation, described a picket
at Boston City Hall to increase the allotment of public housing units to
Latinos. Who was the person he identified as having brought the protesters?—Doña Petra, a Puerto Rican woman. And what was the gender of
the protesters? He explains: "We forced our way in—*there were like fifty
women,* you understand, with Doña Petra, and we forced our way in,
and they had to receive us and an apartment turned up for everybody"
(emphasis added).

Latina women activists also acknowledge the predominance of Latina women as political mobilizers at the community level. These women
activists identify other Latina women as the driving force for pulling Latinos into political participation. Tamara González, a Puerto Rican activist, says, for example, "If you look at our community, you will see—if
you look through the gamut and count numbers, there are more women
working in the politics of empowerment of the community than there are
men." And Teresa Andrade, a woman from Brazil, gives testament to the
strong presence of Latina women, despite the male struggles for power
and turf:

> The pecking order is such that it takes women a while to get in-
> volved, but, usually when they get involved, they get more involved
> [than men]. But around community-based struggles, I have *never*
> seen one where the women were not *extremely* involved (emphasis
> in original).

One of the important roles for Latina women is that of *connec-
tor*—or bridge—between the power structure and the community. When
politicians want a Latino presence at a rally, they call on certain key Latina women. Marta Correa, a 50 year old woman from South America,
explains how it works:

> There have been meetings at the State House, and Juan [the
> Mayor's Hispanic Liaison] called me . . . and also, when they were
> going to honor [Mayor] Flynn and they wanted—there was going
> to be a group—we had a group of many Hispanics—they called
> me.

These women do not necessarily have titles and are not identified in
the media as "leaders." In fact, men and women I interviewed acknowledged that many of the "leaders" who do have titles within the Anglo
political structure, are not actually well-known within the Latino community itself. Julio Rojas, for example, blames the lack of connectedness
between many of the male leaders and the community residents for the

decline in participation by *la gente del pueblo* since the mass mobilizations of the 1970s. He describes what he told a Latino elected official:

> I told him to go back to your own district, that's where you were elected, because you're doing like most of us do, we come from the community and we forget to go back to that community. We forget to go to the grocery store, to the barber shop, we lose touch with that community.

Latina women are also connectors in another way: I found that the independent leaders—the connectors—the people who actually draw Latinos into politics at the grass-roots level, are Latina women. Tamara González, for example, describes Latina women who are intimately tied to the community: the *alcadezas del barrio* or *cacicas. Alcadezas* is the female form of Mayor (*alcalde*); *cacica* is the female form of the original Taino Indian rulers of Puerto Rico. She describes the community empowerment role of these women:

> Where we come to the community level is what we call the *alcadezas del barrio, o cacicas*—these are women that within their own little geographical area know everything that goes on . . . We don't know a lot of those women [but] they do exist and they hare an incredible role of empowerment within the community.

Between the sheer numbers of Latina women who participate in politics in Boston, and the multitude of political roles they play in community mobilization, it is clear that Latina women are not passive and submissive as characterized in the political science and sociological literatures. These Latinas run for office, are active in party politics, work indefatigably to increase voter participation, and play a key role in community mobilization. What are the differences between Latina women and Latino men in how they conceive of politics and political mobilization?

LATINA WOMEN, LATINO MEN: DIFFERENT IMAGES OF POLITICS

Gender differences that affect Latino political participation revolve around the different images Latina women and Latino men have about politics. When I asked Andrea Del Valle, a 34 year old Puerto Rican community activist, "Tell me what you do politically," she replied, "It depends on what you mean by politics." Latina women talk more about making connections—connections between personal problems and social policy, and connectedness among people within the community.

They talk more about struggling together and they see politics in the Latino community as a type of survival politics rather than the attainment of appointed or elected office. Latino men, in contrast, are much more likely to discuss politics in terms of gaining positions in government.

The difference in the number of times Latino men talked about *positions* and *status* compared to women was striking. Thirteen of the eighteen influential men discussed politics in terms of positions and status for a total of 55 times; the average number of mentions was 3.0. Only six of twenty influential women, in comparison, discussed positions and status. They mentioned this theme only 12 times in total and the average was thus 0.6. In other words, the men were, on the average, five times more likely to define politics in terms of positions and status than the women. (Averages are the number of mentions divided by the total number of individuals in the group).

If the women I interviewed did not describe politics in terms of positions and status, what did they focus on? The women talked about the *process* of becoming political—the process of making internal connections between private problems and public issues, the emergence of political consciousness, and the personal connections that brought them into political forays. The twenty influential women spontaneously described the ways they became political a total of 67 times for an average of 3.4. The men, on the other hand, were less likely to discuss their politicization process (only twelve men discussed it), and they did so less often (a total of only 31 mentions, for an average of 1.7). Thus, *the men talked about positions and status five times more than the women, but about their politicization process only half as much.*

Compare these two quotes, the first from a woman talking about Nelson Merced's first campaign, the second from a Puerto Rican man describing his recollections of Latino political history in Boston:

Carla Gardner:

Survival is politics. Struggling with DSS to keep your kids, the landlord about your rent, keeping your kids safe from drugs, dealing with the trash and abandoned cars—it's everyday politics—trying to get control. Even if you look at the campaign, for all the men who worked on the scene, there were women who made it possible. You saw women who pooled the kids, took care of each others kids so someone could vote or work on the campaign. . . . How just surviving is political, to support your family, get support from each other, where do you get the energy to keep going? Also, what's important is what will follow the campaign, pulling people into a community effort, making people feel a part of politics, that they count and can affect the outcome, affect the process, affect their lives. *Hispanics vote when there's something to vote for, but there's more to politics than voting* (emphasis added).

Juan Maldonado:

We're talking—first, the beginning of 1983. [Mayor] Flynn, on the other side, quickly incorporates and starts looking for some of the supporters of [Governor] King and at the same time starts recruiting Latinos from state government, because it was not only [Governor] Dukakis, it was [Secretary of State] Michael Connolly, who decided to do the same thing and it was Lieutenant Governor Kerry who decides to do the same thing so that for the first time ever when you walk into the State House, you go to the Lieutenant Governor's office, there's at least one or two Latinos, you go to the Governor's office, you go to state government, you go to Michael Connolly's office and you start seeing Latinos. Then the mayor gets in the same thing, but he has to recruit some from state government and then he recruits some from King's administration. So then you start seeing Latinos coming into Mayor's Flynn administration of which there are a number. Edwin Colina, he used to be at the Secretary of State's office, moves over to Flynn's administration. Russ Lopez used to be at Lieutenant Governor's office, moves over to the Flynn administration. Let me think, some of the folks—Juanita Fonseca, who used to be at MCAD, not MCAD, the MDC, moves over to the Flynn administration. Phyllis Barajas, who used to be at DSS moves over to the Flynn administration. Juan Vázquez, who used to be at DYS moves over to the Flynn administration. Now some of these people moved on, like Vázquez is no longer there, but just gives you examples of people who move into the Flynn administration.

Men such as Juan Maldonado of the second quote, in essence, *define* political participation as achieving positions and operating within formal political organizations. Women such as Carla Gardner talk about connecting the problems of poverty to political action. She also defines politics as "pulling people into a community effort."

The Latina women and Latino men I interviewed also differed when they recalled the political history of Boston's Latino community. Latina women overwhelmingly focused on grass-roots political struggles and community mobilization whereas the men described politics in terms of elections, redistricting, and formal, organized political structures such as the Latino Democratic Committee. Latina women recalled the mass mobilization and the integration of large numbers of *la gente del pueblo* into the political process during the 1970s; they focused on *participatory* politics. Latino men framed politics in terms of organizational or electoral efforts.

Seven of twenty influential women specifically used the term "grass-roots organizing" to describe Latino political history. Only three men mentioned the term. Over half the women described the mass mobilization efforts against urban renewal during the 1970s whereas only one man did so. Thirteen of the eighteen influential men discussed elections a total of 43 times (a male average of 2.4). Twelve of the Latina women discussed elections a total of 19 times (a female average of 1.0); in other words, Latina women discussed elections less than half as much as men. The redistricting data are even more striking: men discussed redistricting sixteen times as often as women. Nine men discussed redistricting a total of 14 times (an average of 0.8); only one woman mentioned redistricting as part of political history (an average of 0.05).

Nevertheless, the Latina women actually discussed *voting* more than men. Sixteen of the 20 influential women discussed voting a total of 48 times (an average of 2.4); 12 of the 18 influential men discussed voting a total of 34 times (an average of 1.9). Voting generally is a more participatory activity (involves more people), than the politics of redistricting and managing election campaigns. In addition, the women talked about participation and less about power. Only 8 women, compared to 11 men, discussed power and the number of mentions of power by women was half that of men (17 to 34).

The male emphasis on positions as politics may explain, in part, the prior invisibility of Latina women in politics. When mainstream political scientists study political life, they tend to count and interview people holding appointed or elected positions. If women tend to work more in relational rather than positional aspects of politics—efforts more directly tied to increasing the participation of non-participators—then what women do may be less visible.

The concern for positions versus relations as a gender-based trait has been discussed at length by Chodorow (1974) and Kathlene (1989). In addition, Pardo (1990) examined the political organizing of Mexican American women in Los Angeles and found that the Latina women mobilized Latino men

> by giving them a position they could manage. The men may have held the title of 'president,' but they were not making day-to-day decisions about work, nor were they dictating the direction of the group. . . . *This should alert researchers against measuring power*

and influence by looking solely at who holds titles (Pardo 1990, 3; emphasis added).

I found a similar process in Boston. For example, when I asked Andrea Del Valle (a Puerto Rican activist) if I should speak to Tomás Pachón, whom I heard was the president of a Latino organizing center, she said, "I don't know how people got the idea that it's [a man]. I think it's more in people's minds how they perceive things. You can have ten women, but if there's a man, 'Oh, he must be the president!' "

CONNECTEDNESS: GENDER AND POLITICAL MOBILIZATION
IN THE LATINO COMMUNITY

Latina women and Latino men in Boston agreed that "staying in touch" and building networks play a critical role in increasing political participation within the community. Almost everyone I interviewed stressed the need to "stay connected." Leaders need to stay in touch with their constituencies to bridge the gap between the activist and la gente, between people of different classes and countries of origin, and between officials and the common folk. However, Latino men and Latina women differed in two important ways: (1) the Latina women discussed the need for personal connections for mobilization success much more frequently than men, and (2) Latina women described specific examples of how they stayed connected—and then built on these connections—to the people they were trying to mobilize.

Latina women talked about connectedness and collectively organized activities twice as often as men: a total of twenty-four mentions for an average of 1.2. Only seven men (compared to thirteen women) discussed connectedness a total of eleven times for an average of 0.6. Latina women also mobilized around and through issues and relationships tied to their daily lives. The use of "strong ties" (Granovetter 1973, 1982), i.e., personal ties, to draw others into politically- or community-oriented networks overcomes many of the constraints that suppress Latino political participation in the United States. Boneparth (1981) and Aviel (1981) see Latina women mobilizing others through everyday relationships:

Patterns of female political participation across Latin America reveal that women's roles in the family, although typically perceived as obstacles to participation, also serve as rationalizations for leadership roles as well as catalysts for mobilization (Boneparth 1981, 3–4).

For Latinos, and new immigrants in general, migration causes a disruption of communal and social ties. The development of a sense of political efficacy hinges on being familiar with political facts about government institutions, people, and issues, where to go for community and personal problem-solving, and who is receptive to Latino issues. Mobilization methods that build on personal relationships provide democratic experiences and increase social integration, thus leading the way for participation in politics.

Many of the barriers that Latinos face in general (e.g., language, residential dispersion, a lack of legal status or citizenship, lack of familiarity with the U.S. political system, barriers to registration and voting, and leadership failures) are overcome by Latina women in Boston. I will provide three illustrations of Latina women who typify the way personal connectedness leads to collective action.

Example #1: Marina Acevedo is a caseworker at a local Latino agency. She runs an elderly Latino support group. This group of *ancianos* ("old folks") serves two purposes: the group provides social opportunities for the individual members and the group performs typical Puerto Rican songs at local cultural events. In the melding of culture and politics, Marina Acevedo brings this group of men and women to many of the political events that I observed during my two years of fieldwork. The group members were active participants in a workshop on how to organize the community. I also heard them give eloquent testimony about the effects of proposed budget cuts at the "Hispanic Town Meeting" held at Boston City Hall. The constraint of residential dispersion is overcome as Marina Acevedo brings people together from various neighborhoods, transports the group physically and emotionally to Anglo power centers, and provides much needed political information and access. It is the personal connection between Marina Acevedo and these men and women that brings them to political events and enables them to become participators.

Example #2: Juana Oviedo is a 63 year old Puerto Rican woman who has lived in the United States for decades. On the surface, she epitomizes the stereotype of the passive, submissive, Latina woman. She is poor, has only a 6th grade education, speaks little English, has little political information, and is confused by the Anglo political system and candidates. She also expresses a low sense of affiliation with the United States. Nevertheless, Juana Oviedo was part of a group effort to lobby the State Legislature and spoke out on a videotape made for the express purpose of lobbying the legislature. What caused this "apolitical" woman to participate in a relatively sophisticated political effort? She participated because the leader of a woman's group at a local Latino agency organized the group for political action. Participation in political lobbying is thus generated by the appeal of a Latina woman and by being part of a group.

Throughout the hours of my interviews with Juana Oviedo she makes it clear that, as an individual, it would never have occurred to her to join a protest, let alone speak on a videotape destined for public officials. She recalls her testimony:

> *Quieren quitar esa ayuda—y ¡es imposible que quiten eso! Porque imagínese tanta gente pobre y los viejitos—como ahora misma yo, que no tengo a nadie, y yo voy y me oriento con ellas . . . Si quitan eso, los pobres viejitos que no tienen quien les ayuda. . . . Yo le digo, yo voy a todo. Yo no sé hablar bien, pero yo digo, "¡No!"*

> They want to take away that help—and it's impossible that they should take it away! Because, imagine how many poor people—and the little old people—look at me, even, I who don't have anyone, and I go [to the group] and they help me . . . If they take that away, those poor old folks who don't have anyone to help them. . . . I tell you, I go to everything. I don't know how to speak well, but I say, "No!"

The combination of social connectedness and collectively sponsored activities pulled Juana Oviedo into political participation, translated her message into the language of the politicians and government officials, and involved her in influencing public policy through political action.

Example #3: Participatory experiences developed by Latina women in Boston also tackle the barrier of non-citizenship and lack of legal status. I found that the Latina women I interviewed were more likely than the Latino men to describe strategies they used to mobilize Latino non-citizens and undocumented residents. María Ramírez, for example, is a Puerto Rican woman who is active in election campaigns. She values the vote but also sees a role in the political process for non-voting, non-citizen, Latinos. María Ramírez works with Latinos in her neighborhood—Latinos who cannot vote, are not citizens, and are here illegally—to solve community problems. She feels that her personal investment in her neighborhood creates change. Personal *caring* is communicated to people who then are more willing to get involved in solving community problems. She first focuses on the need to connect neighbor to neighbor, whether the people involved are citizens from Puerto Rico or legal or illegal residents from Santo Domingo and Central America:

I've called a couple of people and said, "Look, these are our kids, we either see them get their heads beat in, put away for life, get shot up or we go out there and we help them." They're not my children *personally,* but they are *our* kids and we all get labeled the same and they [the police] don't care if they [the kids] are Puerto Rican, if they're from Santo Domingo, if they're from El Salvador, they don't care, they speak Spanish, they're Hispanic, that's all they know. So we either *do* something about it or we don't. We're trying to talk to the parents and I have neighbors talking to neighbors, talking saying "Look, let's not have a riot this weekend, let's try to talk—What's the problem?" but that's the only way to do it (emphasis in original).

María Ramírez then described how she succeeded in mobilizing undocumented immigrants in a Latino neighborhood to tackle the problem of drugs:

We had this drug house and I told the people on Boylston Street— they could not vote, *the majority of those people could not vote.* And they weren't Puerto Ricans either. I said, "You live on this street, you want it to be good, you take responsibility." [I ask: And what did they do?] They first thought I was *crazy!* They said, "What do you mean?! I mean—Some of these people were even—*illegal,* and I said "I don't care, if you're legal or not, you want responsibility, you do something about it." We have to decide what we want and go after it. [Me: And so what did they do?] They did. We put this march together, we had the New England Telephone Company donate the BAD shirts—Boston Against Drugs—we had buttons, we made banners, they cooked, we rallied in front of the drug houses with the cops and everything. We pointed the people out. *They* did that—I mean, I was there, but *they* did it. And every time there was an incident, they came out to the streets and they said "*No more,*" and it took us a year, but they [the drug dealers] aren't there anymore. The elected official was there, the police were there and these are people who do not vote! (emphasis in original).

Working with neighbors helps to overcome both the disinclination to get involved associated with poverty, not being able to speak English, and the inhibitions imposed by illegal status. Here, in this example, are Latinos who are *illegal* residents working *side by side* with the police in the city of Boston—and they are being led by a Latina woman.

How do these examples differ from the male concern for positions and status? Pantoja and Martell (1989–1990) confirm my findings about the relational-positional gender difference and demonstrate that this difference is not limited to a unique community in Boston. They describe Latina women's leadership patterns in New York during the 1970s:

> We would meet a lot in each other's home and we'd eat together . . . it was that type of environment. We arrived collectively at decisions and helped one another . . . , which is pretty much the way women go about things. You might have the baby in one hand and you're talking on the phone to some politician and then you put it [the phone] down and go tend to the baby (Pantoja and Martell, 1989–1990:49).

Latina women responded to the needs of the community and became leaders of the people. Despite this fact, or perhaps because of it, "a group of Puerto Rican men went about in a deliberate manner to remove women from leadership positions" (1989–90, 50). Pantoja recalls: "Later on some of the women who I talked to told me, 'I killed myself out there organizing, and then when they hired a paid organizer it was a man' " (Pantoja and Martell, 1989–1990:50). Pantoja and Martell corroborate my findings that Latino male concerns for positions once the men move into directorships reflect a difference in male and female leadership styles:

> The coming of a male leadership made a difference in organizational objectives and philosophy. The main characteristic of functioning [in the male-led organizations] has been a *one-person, hierarchical and closed-system leadership style, concern[ed] with personal and career goals* (Pantoja and Martell, 1989–1990:50; emphasis added).

And Aracelis Guzmán, a 47 year old Mexican American activist in Boston, declares that male leaders constrain participation by their efforts to dominate group events:

> They—when they become leaders [she slaps her hands together sharply] they go off on their own. They get on their horse and you *cannot* get them down from there. And this is very divisive, very harmful . . . [because] everyone is there, like this,—saying, "Yes, yes," when, in reality, they do not agree with him. And it's the mental set that the man—the macho—has all the answers (emphasis in original).

Many women I spoke with gave examples of Latino male designated or self-appointed leaders who either inadvertently or deliberately obstructed community organizational efforts because the efforts were initiated by others. Control over the agenda (Bachrach and Baratz, 1962; Lukes, 1974) may be more of a gender-based trait than is commonly discussed in the literature.

CONCLUSION

Contrary to the traditional image of the passive, submissive, and apolitical Latina woman, Latina women play an important role in the mobilization of Latino communities. Through connectedness and collectively organized networks Latina women overcome many of the constraints on Latino political participation in Boston.

I found strong support for the view that there are also intrinsic differences between the way women conceive of or practice politics. According to this view, women—not just Latina women—blend private and public politics (Evans, 1980; Sapiro, 1983), consider politics to be about connectedness and interpersonal relations (Flammang, 1984; Kelly and Burgess, 1989), and see political life in more relational rather than positional terms (Chodorow 1974; Kathlene 1989; Pardo 1990). Feminist research on black women in politics leads to similar conclusions. Dill (1988), for example, presents the private efforts of black women domestic servants as evidence of resistance politics. Private actions and informal networks provided support for lower-class black women to achieve major social changes (Sacks, 1988; Garland, 1988).

Thus, the differences I found between Latina women and Latino men, confirm the importance for women of the interpersonal process of politics, the emphasis on connectedness, and the importance of grassroots, personal politics—a politics tied to individual, family, friendship networks, and community relationships. The political mobilization of Latino communities represents a critical challenge for the coming decade; failing to recognize the contribution of Latina women as political mobilizers can only retard the mobilization process. It is time for the voices of Latina women as political actors to be heard. To achieve our goal of increasing Latino political participation we must begin to learn from the experiences of Latina women in politics.

REFERENCES

Aviel, J. F. 1981. "Political Participation of Women in Latin America." *The Western Political Quarterly*, (34):156–173.

Bachrach, P., and M. S. Baratz. 1962. "Two Faces of Power." *American Political Science Review,* (56):947–952.

Barragán, P. B. 1980. "The Lack of Political Involvement of Hispanic Women as it Relates to their Educational Background and Occupational Opportunities," in National Institute of Education, *Conference on the Educational and Occupational Needs of Hispanic Women.* (Washington, DC: National Institute of Education):39–46.

Bonoparth, E. 1981. "Women and Politics: Introduction." *The Western Political Quarterly,* (34):3–4.

Carillo, T. 1986. "The Women's Movement and the Left in Mexico: The Presidential Candidacy of Doña Rosario Ibarra," in T. Córdova, N. Cantú, G. Cardenas, J. García, and C. M. Sierra, eds., *Chicana voices: Intersections of Class, Race, and Gender.* (Austin, TX: University of Texas at Austin, Center for Mexican American Studies):96–113.

Castillo-Speed, L. 1990. "Chicana Studies: A Selected List of Materials since 1980." *Frontiers,* (11):66–84.

Chodorow, N. 1974. "Family Structure and Feminine Personality," in M. Z. Rosaldo and L. Lamphere, eds., *Woman, Culture and Society.* (Stanford: Stanford University Press).

Dill, B. T. 1988. " 'Making Your Job Good Yourself': Domestic Service and the Construction of Personal Dignity," in Ann Bookman and Sandra Morgen, eds., *Women and the Politics of Empowerment.* (Philadelphia: Temple University Press):33–52.

Evans, S. 1980. *Personal Politics.* (New York: Vintage Books).

Falcón, A. 1988. "Black and Latino Politics in New York City: Race and Ethnicity in a Changing Urban Context," in F. C. García, ed., *Latinos and the Political System.* (Notre Dame: University of Notre Dame Press):171–194.

Flammang, J. A. 1984. "Introduction: Reflections on Themes of a Women's Politics," in Janet A. Flammang, ed., *Political Women: Current roles in State and Local Government.* (Beverly Hills: Sage Publications).

Foley, D. E., C. Mota, D. E. Post, and I. Lozano. 1977. *From Peones to Políticos: Ethnic Relations in a South Texas Town, 1900–1977.* (Austin, TX: The University of Texas at Austin, Center for Mexican American Studies).

Garland, A. W. 1988. *Women Activists: Challenging the Abuse of Power.* (New York: The Feminist Press).

Garcia, F. C., ed. 1988. *Latinos and the Political System.* (Notre Dame: University of Notre Dame Press).

Gómez-Quiñones, J. 1990. *Chicano Politics: Reality and Promise 1940–1990.* (Albuquerque: University of New Mexico Press).

Granovetter, M. S. 1973. "The Strength of Weak Ties. *American Journal of Sociology,* (78):1360–1380.

———. 1982. "The Strength of Weak Ties: A Network Theory Revisited," in P. V. Marsden and N. Lin, eds., *Social Structure and Network Analysis.* (Beverly Hills, CA: Sage): 105–130.

Guzmán, R. 1976. *The Political Socialization of the Mexican American People.* (New York: Arno Press, Inc).

Hardy-Fanta, C. 1991. "Latina Women, Latino Men, and Political Participation in Boston: *La Chispa que Prende.*" Ph.D. diss., Brandeis University. (Philadelphia: Temple University Press, forthcoming).

Holtzman, E., and S. Williams. 1991. "Women in the Political World: Observations," in J. K. Conway, S. C. Bourque, and J. W. Scott, eds., *Learning about Women: Gender, Politics, and Power.* (Ann Arbor: University of Michigan Press):25–33.

Jennings, J., and M. Rivera, eds. 1984. *Puerto Rican Politics in Urban America.* (Westport, CT: Greenwood Press).

Kathlene, L. 1989. "Uncovering the Political Impacts of Gender: An Exploratory Study." *The Western Political Quarterly,* (42):397–421.

Kelly, R. M., and J. Burgess. 1989. "Gender and the Meaning of Power and Politics," *Women and Politics* (9):47–82.

Lukes, S. 1974. *Power: A Radical View.* (London: Macmillan Education, Ltd.).

Melville, M. B., ed. 1980. *Twice a Minority: Mexican American Women.* (St. Louis: C. V. Mosby).

Mirandé, A., and E. Enríquez. 1979. *La Chicana: The Mexican American Woman.* (Chicago: University of Chicago Press).

Pachon, H. P. 1987. "An Overview of Hispanic Elected Officials in 1987," in NALEO, *1987 National Roster of Hispanic Elected Officials.* (Washington, DC: National Association of Latino Elected and Appointed Officials [NALEO]):iv–xxvi.

Padilla, F. M. 1985. *Latino Ethnic Consciousness: The Case of Mexican Americans and Puerto Ricans in Chicago.* (Notre Dame: University of Notre Dame Press).

Pantoja, A., and E. Martell. 1989–1990. "Mi Gente," *Centro de Estudios Puertorriqueños Bulletin,* (2):48–55.

Pardo, M. 1990. "Mexican American Women Grassroots Community Activists: 'Mothers of East Los Angeles'," *Frontiers,* (11):1–7.

Rinehart, S. T. 1988. "Toward Women's Political Resocialization: Patterns of Predisposition in the Learning of Feminist Attitudes," in R. M. Kelly, ed., *Gender and Socialization to Power and Politics.* (New York: Haworth Press):11–26.

Rose, M. 1990. "Traditional and Nontraditional Patterns of Female Activism in the United Farm Workers of America, 1962 to 1980," *Frontiers,* (11):26–32.

Rule, W. 1981. "Why Women Don't Run: The Critical Contextual Factors in Women's Legislative Recruitment," *The Western Political Quarterly,* (34):60–77.

Sacks, K. B. 1988. "Gender and Grassroots Leadership," in A. Bookman and S. Morgen, eds., *Women and the Politics of Empowerment.* (Philadelphia: Temple University Press):77–94.

Sánchez Korrol, V. 1983. *From Colonia to Community: The History of Puerto Ricans in New York City, 1917–1948.* (Westport, CT: Greenwood Press).

Sapiro, V. 1983. *The Political Integration of Women: Roles, Socialization and Politics.* (Urbana: University of Illinois Press).

Villarreal, R. E., N. G. Hernandez, and H. D. Neighbor. 1988. *Latino Empowerment: Progress, Problems, and Prospects.* (Westport, CT: Greenwood Press).

Welch, S., and P. Secret. 1981. "Sex, Race and Political Participation," *The Western Political Quarterly,* (34): 5–16.

8. The Cuban Model: Political Empowerment in Miami

Dario Moreno

THE POLITICAL EMPOWERMENT OF CUBAN AMERICANS

CUBAN AMERICANS HAVE MADE extraordinary gains in politics during the last decade. Since 1982 Cuban candidates won three U.S. Congressional Seats, ten Florida state house seats, three Florida state senate seats, the mayorship of Miami, Coral Gables, Hialeah, and other communities in Florida and Northern New Jersey. In close statewide elections, Florida's Latin voters have demonstrated that their bloc voting can alter the outcome. Both Senator Connie Mack in 1988 and former President George Bush in 1992 were able to win in Florida largely due to overwhelming support among Cuban American voters (Moreno and Warren 1996). Nationally, the election of three Cuban Americans to the U.S. House combined with the ongoing lobbying efforts of such groups as the Cuban American National Foundation and the Valladares Foundation has resulted in an expanded role for Cuban Americans in Washington, especially with regard to U.S. Cuban policy.

All political, demographic, and social indicators point to the probability that the 1990s will be another decade of dramatic political gains for Cuban Americans. Cuban Republicans were nothing short of catalytic during Florida's reapportionment debate in dramatically modifying the Democratic majority's plans for Congressional and state legislative district lines. Cubans not only gain an additional Congressional district but also two more seats in the Florida House of Representatives. Locally, within Dade County, Cuban politicians have also used the Voting Rights Act to increase Latino political power. In 1986 a group of Hispanic and Black plaintiffs led by State Senator Carrie Meek brought suit against

Metro Dade's at-large electoral system. The plaintiffs in *Meek v. Metro-Dade* claimed that at-large elections led to a condition where minorities were grossly under-represented on the county commission. Indeed with one Black and one Latino commissioner in 1990, minorities accounted for only 22 percent of the commission, while together constituting over 70 percent of the population of Dade County. In December 1992, Federal District Judge Donald Graham declared Metro-Dade's electoral system to be in violation of the Voting Rights Act, and ordered the commissioners to come up with a new plan based on single-member districts in time for fresh elections in February 1993 (Moreno and Rae 1994).

The 1993 Metro-Dade elections drastically altered the political balance in Dade County. The county commission went from one in which non-Hispanic Whites controlled seven out of the nine seats to one in which Blacks and Hispanics controlled ten out of the thirteen seats. In the 1993 election, non-Hispanic Whites went from controlling 78 percent of the seats in the county commission to controlling only 23 percent of the seats. Hispanics, who in the old at-large system controlled only 11 percent of the commission despite the fact that they made up 49 percent of the county's population, were able to capture six seats (five Cuban Americans and a Puerto Rican) in the new single-member districts system. African Americans also dramatically increased their representation from 11 to 30 percent of the commission (Moreno and Rae 1994). The shift in power at county hall led the Dade County School Board to abandon its at-large electoral system in 1994 as it too was faced with a lawsuit under the Voting Rights Act.

These political accomplishments occurred in a general context of Hispanic ascendancy in culture and business. The 1980s should be viewed as a transitional decade in Dade as Miami moves from being a tripartite city (Anglo, Blacks, and Hispanics) to becoming a largely "Hispanic city" in the 1990s. The political and socioeconomic success of Cuban Americans in Dade County raises several important questions for Latino politics: Is the "Cuban model" of political and economic empowerment a model that is unique to conditions in Miami or is it a model that could be replicated by other Latino populations?

THE CUBAN MODEL

The "Cuban model" for political empowerment does not fit the pattern followed by other minority groups. The Cuban political experience in the United States is significantly different from that of African Americans and other Latinos. As journalist Earl Shorris wrote, "Cubans identify with the conquerors, not the conquered, the subject, not the object" (Shorris 1992, 333). Cubans as recent arrivals in the United States have not suffered the historical discrimination and oppression envisioned in most of the literature on racial and language minorities. Moreover, as political exiles they entered the United States voluntarily and not in a forced process as did African Americans and many Latinos. The unique historical experience of the Cuban community in Miami had led many scholars to conclude that the minority model used in Mexican-American and African-American studies is not appropriate for Cubans. Rodney Hero suggests that the traditional pluralism model might be better suited for Cubans than his two-tiered pluralism theory or the internal colonialism model (Hero 1992, 27). Some even suggest that the Cuban-American model for political incorporation more closely resembles those of ethnic groups such as the Irish and the Italians.

However, the traditional pluralism approach understates both formal and informal discrimination against Cuban Americans. Cubans face racism and discrimination because of their racial background, language, and national origin. Even the most privileged white Cuban immigrants of 1961 confronted racism in the United States. In Miami in the early 1960s, it was common to find signs posted in apartment buildings that read: "No Pets, No Kids, No Cubans" (Torres 1986). Public resentment against Cuban Americans is reflected in a 1993 *USA Today*/CNN/Gallup poll which found that only 19 percent of the respondents believed that immigration from Cuba has benefitted the United States (Sharp 1993). Moreover, during the 1960s and 1970s, due to the urging of local Anglo politicians, new Cuban refugees were relocated outside of Dade County in an effort to prevent the political empowerment of Cubans. A resettlement program was established through which families arriving from Cuba were given assistance if they immediately relocated away from Miami. The assistance included transportation costs to the new destination, help in finding housing and employment, and financial assistance until such time as employment was secured. More than 300,000 persons were resettled away from Miami between 1961–1978 under this program (Perez 1992, 87).

In understanding the role of Cuban Americans in the U.S. political system it is useful to view them as a stigmatized class—in other words, as vulnerable to the same types of discrimination as other Hispanics and Blacks while at the same time not suffering from the historical legacy of slavery or the conquest of the Southwest. The Cuban model is a unique mixture of official privilege and official discrimination, a combination of not experiencing the legacy of oppression which Blacks and Chicanos suffered but at the same time facing the language, political, and economic barriers erected by the dominant society. The Cuban-American strategy for overcoming the stigma of discrimination is also unique. The critical factor in explaining the political empowerment of Cuban Americans is geopolitical. The interaction of Cuban talent and ambition with the opportunity provided by Miami's political and economic underdevelopment allowed Cubans to overcome the obstacles created by the city's Anglo establishment. It was the interaction of the middle-class Cuban migration and the city of Miami that produced the Cuban success story. Through an examination of the conditions that prevail in Miami, specifically, patterns of migration, socioeconomic conditions, and the existence of a self-sustained Cuban enclave, we can begin to explain why the Cuban experience is unique to Miami.

THE CUBAN ENCLAVE

Standing in a city that has been described as "the capital of Latin America" (Levine 1985), it is difficult to appreciate that thirty years ago Hispanic influence in Miami was practically nonexistent. The Hispanic community in Dade traces its modern roots to Fidel Castro's revolutionary victory on January 1, 1959. During the ensuing thirty years, more than 750,000 Cuban refugees arrived in the United States, most passing through Miami. Cuban immigration was aided by favorable U.S. government policy, which viewed Cuban refugees as U.S. allies in the cold war against Soviet-style communism.

During this period Congress approved "The Cuban Adjustment Act of 1966" which granted Cuban immigrants special status, allowing them to enter the United States without the restrictions imposed on other groups. The law gives automatic residency to any Cuban who comes to the United States, be it a tourist who overstays his visa or someone who sneaks in. People fleeing any other country, even other communist countries, must submit clear proof that they are persecuted. For Cubans, escape is usually enough to guarantee permanent resettlement in the United States. No other group has benefitted from such an exception for so long. The act, passed during the height of American-Cuban hostility, endured in large part because of the political clout of Cuban Americans. More than 500,000 immigrated to the U.S. under the Cuban Adjustment Act (Perez 1992, 85).

Most Cuban exiles settled in Miami or returned to the city after first settling in the North. Another large Cuban community of about

80,000 was established in the area around Union City, New Jersey, while smaller communities exist in Chicago and Los Angeles. By the 1992 Census 56 percent of the 1.1 million Cubans in the United States lived in the greater Miami area (Dade County). Miami now ranks third in the nation, behind only Los Angeles and New York, in the size of its Hispanic population. When one considers that Miami has a substantially smaller overall population than either of these other two cities, and that almost all of the Hispanic population has settled in the city since 1960, it is not unreasonable to suggest that Miami has undergone the single most dramatic ethnic transformation of any major American city in this century.

This settlement pattern has facilitated the development of the Cuban enclave in Miami. The basis of the enclave is highly differential entrepreneurial activity. Alejandro Portes and Robert L. Bach define an ethnic enclave as "a distinctive economic formation, characterized by the spatial concentration of immigrants who organize a variety of enterprises to serve their own ethnic market and the general population" (Portes and Bach 1985, 203). They argue that the two fundamental conditions necessary for an economic enclave are in existence in Cuban Miami.

The Cuban community in Miami has both the presence of immigrants with sufficient capital, either brought from Cuba or accumulated in the United States, to create new opportunities for economic growth and an extensive division of labor. An important source of capital was the estimated $4 billion of aid that the U.S. government provided to Cuban exiles. After locating in Miami, the Cuban middle class developed an elaborate network of successful small enterprises. These small and middle-size enterprises served as a source of employment for ensuing waves of Cuban immigrants. Travel writer David Rieff captured the dynamic of Cuban exile economics when he wrote, "the first wave of immigrants (those who came to Miami in the first year after the revolution) founded the businesses that employed the second wave (those who came to Miami between the mid–sixties and the mid-seventies); in turn both groups employed the third wave" (Rieff 1987, 46).

The proliferation of small businesses, primarily serving Latin tastes, is the foundation of Cuban economic and political power in Miami. Miami ranks first in terms of the number of Hispanic-owned businesses relative to the size of the Latino population. Miami has an estimated 55,712 Hispanic-owned businesses. Some 7,700 of minority firms were large enough to have paid workers, and those employed 34,504 people. These Hispanic-owned firms in the enclave also generated nearly $3.8 billion in receipts in 1987 or about 15 percent of all receipts generated by Hispanic-owned firms in the United States. Among Hispanics,

Cubans have by far the highest business ownership rates, at 63 businesses for every 1,000 Cuban Americans. This rate is more than three times that of Mexicans (19) and nearly six times that of Puerto Ricans (11).

The high rate of business ownership among Cubans is due to the selective migration of former business owners and better-educated adults following the Cuban Revolution. Another reason is the heavy concentration of Cubans in the Miami area, which had a booming economy during the 1980s. That large, prosperous ethnic enclave provides Miami's Cubans with a potent small business incubator. Cubans have also been successful in the founding of larger corporations. With about 5 percent of the country's Hispanic population, Miami has almost a third of the largest Hispanic-owned businesses in the United States. Thirty-one of the top 100 Hispanic businesses in the U.S. are located in Dade County. The Cuban presence and their economic success has also attracted Latin American tourists and capital and resulted in scores of multinational corporations locating their Latin American offices in Miami.

Sociologist Lisandro Perez pointed out that the strong and diversified entrepreneurial activity is responsible for the enclave's most important overall feature: institutional completeness (Perez 1992, 90–91). Cubans in Miami can, if they wish, live out their lives within the community. The wide range of sales and services, including professional services, available within the community makes possible its completeness. There are thirty Latino-owned banks, 1,500 Latino lawyers, eight Spanish radio stations, two Spanish television stations. Cubans can work in a Cuban-owned business, shop in a Cuban supermarket, visit a Cuban doctor or dentist, eat at Cuban restaurants, and avoid all interaction with the dominant society. Clearly, the success of Cubans in Miami was, to begin with at least, almost independent of that of the larger community.

Thus the Latino penetration into Dade County was not only a demographic revolution, but a socioeconomic transformation. The Cuban immigrants of the early 1960s were not the dispossessed under-class of that country, but included many accomplished professionals who combined personal effort with an "open-armed" immigration policy and substantial federal economic assistance in establishing themselves in Miami. Subsequent groups of Cuban entrants throughout the 1960s brought a large portion of the Cuban middle class as well as an upwardly mobile working class to Miami. While a myth of the "Golden Cuban" (i.e., that all Cubans are wealthy) persists even in the face of a somewhat modest standard of living for many of the most recently arrived Cuban refugees (especially those who came during the Mariel boatlift), Cuban immigration in general has been accompanied by rapid economic incor-

TABLE 1

ECONOMIC INDICATORS FOR LATINOS IN THE U.S. WORK FORCE

	CUBAN	PUERTO RICAN	MEXICAN
Per Capita Income	$13,787	$ 8,403	$ 7,447
% Poverty	14.9 %	31 %	26.9 %
% Professionals	22.1 %	21.5 %	12.4 %
% Laborers	18.0 %	25.4 %	21.5 %

Source: U.S. Census Bureau, 1990 Census of the Population

poration. Overall, national census figures show that Cuban Americans fared better in terms of income than other Hispanic groups (see table 1). Cuban Americans also have higher occupational status than other Hispanic Americans. About 20 percent of the Cuban labor force is employed in high-level white-collar occupations, which are a combination of the executive, administrative, managerial, and professional classes. Only about 18 percent are employed as low-paid operators, fabricators, and laborers.

Thus the poverty that is so frequently associated with new immigrant groups has been conspicuously absent in the Cuban immigrant experience. Only about 15 percent of the Cuban-American population lives below the poverty level, substantially fewer than for other Latinos. Ultimately, it is a combination of the numerical, economic, and political force of the middle- and upper-class Cuban community that has the greatest impact on Miami politics.

The relative prosperity of the Cuban community and their large numbers in cohesive and contiguous neighborhoods have safeguarded the Cuban-American community to a large extent from the prejudice and discrimination that has plagued other Latino groups in the United States. Miami, in the view of many in the Cuban community, is essentially a Cuban city. Indeed, the only city in the world where more Cubans live is Havana itself. This image of Hispanics making Miami uniquely "theirs" is reflected in public opinion surveys which show that Anglos in Miami feel as much or more discrimination than do Hispanics.

CUBAN POLITICAL POWER

The demographic, socioeconomic, and cultural conditions described above created unique political opportunities for Hispanics in Miami.

These favorable conditions have led to the acceleration of the process of ethnic empowerment in Miami. The Cuban pattern of political empowerment is characterized by the following five factors, some of which are common to other ethnic groups, while others are unique to Miami.

Ethnic Mobilization

Miami's Cubans, like most ethnic groups in the U.S., tend to follow the mobilization theory of ethnic voting that Raymond Wolfinger posited:

> The strength of ethnic voting depends on both the intensity of ethnic identification and the level of ethnic relevance in the election. The most powerful and visible sign of ethnic political relevance is a fellow-ethnic's name at the head of the ticket, evident to everyone who enters the voting booth. (Wolfinger 1965, 905)

The 1989 special elections in Florida's 18th Congressional district—held for twenty-eight years by Representative Claude Pepper—is one of the clearest examples in recent years of a campaign and election in which ethnic factors predominated over all others (Moreno and Rae 1992). This election largely corroborates Wolfinger's mobilization theory by demonstrating the capacity of ethnicity to override partisanship and all other issues in a particular context.

This congressional election saw Gerald Richman and the Democratic party defeated by a large and monolithic Cuban-American vote. Richman's "American seat" slogan which was the key to victory in the Democratic runoff proved to be a two-edged sword. Cuban Americans, offended by the perceived racism of the Democratic candidate, voted for Ros-Lehtinen by the remarkable margin of 94 to 6 percent (*Miami Herald*, August 30, 1989). The mobilization of the Cuban community around the Republican candidate was overwhelming and impressive. Local Cuban media, five radio and two television stations, bombarded the airwaves on election day with anti-Richman propaganda including the dubious claim that Fidel Castro himself had endorsed the Democratic candidate. Richman carried all of the other blocs of voters: Jewish, Anglos, and Blacks but they represented only 47 percent of the electorate. High Cuban turnout—some Little Havana precincts reported 70 percent turnout—provided Ros-Lehtinen with the margin of victory, 53 percent of the votes. The Republicans won simply because more Cubans voted and almost all of them voted for Ros-Lehtinen.

The heavy Cuban-American vote and the high turnout for the Republican candidate was undoubtedly aided by the fact that Ros-Lehtinen was Cuban. However, the support for Ros in the congressional election must be put in the context of a dramatic trend toward the GOP among Dade County Cubans. In recent elections Dade's Hispanics have given lopsided victories to such conservative Republican candidates as President George Bush with 83 percent of the vote in 1988 and 73 percent in 1992, Senator Connie Mack with 79 percent in 1988, and Governor Bob Martinez with 77 percent in 1990 (Moreno and Rae 1992; Moreno and Warren, 1996).

This pattern of ethnic bloc voting among Cuban Americans is pervasive in all levels of Miami politics. Indeed, the 1992 election reflected the degree to which the Dade County Republican Party has become little more than a "front organization" for the interests of the Cuban community (Moreno and Rae 1992, 201). While not always united on every issue, Cuban Republicans are now the most politically coherent and potent force in the Dade delegation to the state legislature. Moreover, three Cuban Republicans defeated strong Anglo Democrat opponents on the strength of Latino bloc voting.

It seems clear that there has been a genuine secular realignment (Key 1959) of partisan forces in South Florida, which has taken place on the basis of both local and national concerns. However in this process, the Democratic and Republican parties in Dade County have become little more than "front organizations" for the interests of particular ethnic groups. If this assessment is correct, then ethnicity will likely remain the most important factor determining electoral outcomes in South Florida for some time to come.

Ideological Consistency

The "Cuban model" of ethnic mobilization is unique because of its ideological dimension. Although it is no longer the "singular" Cuban issue it once was, preoccupation with Latin American communism generally and Castro specifically still stands as a core political issue in the community. The Republican party, with its reliance on hard-line foreign policy rhetoric, became their natural home.

Although one has to be cautious about overgeneralizing Cuban foreign policy attitudes, voting and poll data reflect a strong Cuban-American consensus on the broad outline of an anti-Castro policy (see table 2). The centerpiece of this policy is the maintenance of the U.S. economic embargo against the island. Although some exile groups have articulated a more progressive U.S. policy, these groups are frequently characterized by a lack of popular support within the community.

TABLE 2

CUBAN-AMERICAN FOREIGN POLICY BELIEFS

Issue	% in Agreement	
	1995	1991
Favor current U.S. policy (no diplomatic relations and no trade)	73	80
Favor tightening the U.S. trade embargo	81	86
Favor military action by the exile community against Cuba	73	76
Favor a U.S. invasion of Cuba	57	63
Favor U.S. support for an internal rebellion to overthrow the Castro government	73	75
Favor increasing international economic pressure on Cuba	84	85
Favor negotiations with the Cuban government to allow family members to travel to the United States	83	75
Favor negotiations with the Cuban government to allow regular phone communications with the island	67	62
Favor starting negotiations with the Cuban government to facilitate a democratic transition	69	62
Favor a national dialogue between the exile community, the Cuban government, and Cuban dissidents	46	40

Source: Florida International University Florida Poll, July 1993 and March 1991.

The Cuban-American consensus for a hard-line policy toward Cuba is especially evident in public opinion polls. The polls not only show that 73 percent of Cuban Americans support maintaining the current U.S. policy of no diplomatic relations with Castro, but also that 81 percent are in favor of tightening the U.S. trade embargo, and 84 percent support increasing international economic pressure on the island (see table 2). Indeed, many view the indirect pressure of the embargo as not going far enough. Poll data also reflect the still evident militancy of the Cuban exile community, with 57 percent supporting a U.S. invasion of Cuba, and 73 percent favoring military raids by exiles against the Castro regime. Moreover, in direct contradiction to the many press accounts and scholarly articles that speak of a new moderation among Cuban Americans, the poll numbers have been relatively stable over the last few years (see table 2). The polls do show that a majority of Cuban Americans favor negotiations with the Castro regime on specific issues such as family visits, phone communications, and other forms of humanitarian aid, and there is evidence of some willingness to negotiate the political future of Cuba with the Castro regime, but clearly only if negotiations lead to a democratic transition on the island, which is to say the total relinquishing of power by Castro and the Communist party.

Also indicative of the consensus on the parameters of U.S.-Cuba policy was the 1992 House race between Ileana Ros-Lehtinen and Cuban Democrat Madga Davis. Davis advocated a more progressive U.S. Cuban policy and openly opposed the Torricelli Bill. Ros-Lehtinen was a House sponsor of the legislation. The Davis campaign was well financed, raising over $200,000, and she had broad support from a coalition of moderate and liberal Cuban organizations in addition to significant support from non-Cuban Democrats. Despite the money and support, Davis lost the election to Ros-Lehtinen 69 to 31 percent, and among Cuban voters she lost by an overwhelming margin of 82 to 18 percent. The unpopularity of Davis and her policy stand among Cuban voters was reflected when fellow Democrat Conchy Bretos refused to take a $100 campaign contribution from Davis in Bretos's campaign for the non-partisan county commission.

The foreign policy conservatism of the Cuban community has created a litmus test for candidates. This conservatism, especially as it is applied to presidential and senate races, helps to explain the community's support for Bob Graham during the governor's race in 1982, followed by his rejection in the Hispanic precincts in his 1986 senate election. In the governor's contest, Graham ran extremely well in the Cuban neighborhoods. However, in 1986 when Graham challenged conservative Republican Paula Hawkins for her senate seat, Graham lost these very same Cuban neighborhoods by a three-to-one margin. Foreign policy stands also explain the disproportionate support in those same precincts for Connie Mack in the 1988 senate race. Democratic contender Buddy McKay was viewed by most as a moderate, as he had been a consistent opponent of Contra aid.

Notwithstanding some moderation on domestic issues, in many ways anti-communism has become a form of ethnic self-identification in the Cuban community—resulting in this foreign policy conservatism being carried over to the next generation of Cuban Americans. During the two-year period between January 1992 and December 1994 over 67 percent of the newly registered Cubans under thirty registered Republican.

Incorporation into the Republican Party

Cuban political empowerment can also be attributed to their incorporation into the Republican party which historically has been the under-utilized party in Florida. As with many of the immigrant groups who came to the U.S. in the late 1800s, the party of opportunity frequently is the party which is the weakest in the region. Like the Irish in Boston who seized control of the Democratic party's local machinery in the face of "Yankee Republicanism," the Cubans have become dominant in Dade County's Republican party, providing an "entree" for Cuban political activists and candidates. In the late 1970s, facing significantly less competition for party nominations, Cubans soon became a common fixture on the ballot in offering Republican opposition in what had formerly been one-party contests.

The GOP has made historic gains in South Florida through the incorporation of Cuban Americans into their party. In 1980 the entire Dade delegation to the state legislature, with one exception, was composed of Democrats. By 1994 nine of the nineteen state representatives and three of the six state senators were Republicans, all of these were Cuban Americans. The GOP in Dade has become the leading political organization serving the interests of the Cuban community.

In contrast to the success the Republican party has had in attracting Cuban support is the poor record of the Democrats. As late as 1979, 49 percent of the Hispanics in Dade County registered as Democrats, compared to only 39 percent for the GOP. However the Democrats were unable to provide entree for Cuban-American candidates. Lincoln Diaz-Balart provides a case in point: in 1982 he ran for the state house as a Democrat but after a bloody primary campaign against an Anglo opponent, he lost the general election to a Cuban Republican. In 1986 he ran for the state house, this time as a Republican. Facing no competition in the primary, he easily won the seat against an Anglo Democrat. He later succeeded Ileana Ros-Lehtinen to the State Senate and is currently Dade's second Cuban-American Republican Congressman.

The Democratic party's difficulty in recruiting Cuban Americans was also reflected in the 18th Congressional District election. The logic of the 18th's demographics led the state Democratic chairman—a Cuban—Simon Ferro to conclude that the strongest Democratic contender was likely to be a Cuban Democrat who could win the election by cutting into Republican support among Cubans and holding on to the traditional Democratic constituencies of elderly Jews and Blacks. The leading Cuban Democrat in South Florida, Hialeah Mayor Rail Martinez, was uninterested in a race which he appeared unlikely to be able to win.

That left Miami City Commissioner Rosario Kennedy, a powerful vote-getter in municipal elections, as the leading Cuban Democratic alternative, and Kennedy was eventually cajoled into running by Ferro. However, Kennedy was easily defeated in the Democratic primary by political neophyte Gerald Richman.

Kennedy's labor and Black endorsements were insufficient to withstand the groundswell of Democratic support for Richman, whose campaign benefitted from the surprising degree of Anglo discontent with Miami's increasingly dominant Cuban-American political establishment (Moreno and Rae 1992, 192).

However, Richman's defeat was assured in the general election when the GOP candidate Ileana Ros-Lehtinen was able to successfully exploit the division created by the primary campaign. The Democratic candidate failed to get the endorsement of an embittered Rosario Kennedy, and Dade's only other prominent Cuban Democrat—Hialeah Mayor Raul Martinez—was forthright in his condemnation of Richman's campaign tactics:

> If you really care about the community, you cannot vote for this man. I do not think that his campaign is what the Democratic party stands for. (*Miami Herald*, August 18, 1989)

Richman's primary election victory added to the perception of many Cuban Americans that the Democratic party is anti-Cuban. The Democratic problems have left the party without any prominent Cubans. Kennedy lost her city commission seat to Miriam Alonso, and Rail Martinez is currently under federal indictment on racketeering charges. This is reflected by the fact that today over 68 percent of Dade's Hispanics are Republicans.

The Cuban American Foundation

Cuban-American empowerment has been aided by the creation of political institutions to articulate their concerns. Of greatest importance has been the advent of the Cuban American National Foundation (CANF) as one of the more powerful Hispanic organizations in the country. The foundation, founded in 1981, has quickly replaced the militant, sometimes violent Alpha-66 and Omega-7 groups as the principal Cuban political organization in the U.S. The foundation's founders, mostly affluent younger Cuban Americans who had been active in Republican politics, were far more sophisticated than their predecessors. They organized a U.S.-style political action committee in Washington to articulate the principal objectives of the foundation—namely, providing information on Cuba to Washington policy makers and providing information to Cubans still living in Cuba (Fernandez 1987, 125).

Radio Marti, the foundation's project to broadcast radio programs to Cuba, was the first noteworthy policy achievement of the foundation. In the wake of heavy CANF lobbying, the bill to create the USIA-run radio station received broad bipartisan support. Reagan actively supported Radio Marti and Florida Senators Paula Hawkins and Lawton Chiles sponsored the bill. Moreover, all the Democratic Congressmen from Dade County (Pepper, Fascell, Lehman, and Smith) actively supported the radio station. Congressional approval of Radio Marti reflected not only the effectiveness of the foundation's lobbying effort and the president's active advocacy of the project, but the electoral clout of Cubans in Florida whose support was actively cultivated by Reagan and other Republican leaders. In 1989, the foundation successfully lobbied for the expansion of the broadcast project with the creation of T.V. Marti.

CANF's most important success to date was the passage in 1992 of the Cuban Democracy Act. The Act which tightened the U.S. economic embargo against Cuba was passed over the objection of the U.S. State Department. The State Department was particularly concerned that the legislation's mandated sanctions on countries that give aid or provide favorable terms of trade to Cuba would prevent Washington from helping Russia and Eastern Europe (Robbins 1992, 166). In addition, the Bush Administration expressed concern that the ban on U.S. foreign subsidiaries trading with Cuba would strain Washington's foreign relations by imposing American values outside the United States (Robbins 1992, 166).

Ultimately, the State Department's Latin American office was outmaneuvered by the Cuban American community. Angered by the Bush Administration's reluctance to embrace the Torricelli Bill, the foundation and even some prominent Cuban Republicans arranged for Bill Clinton to visit Little Havana and endorse the bill during the 1992 presidential campaign. Cuban Americans wanted to pressure Bush to endorse the Cuban Democracy Act, and the open overtures to a Democratic presidential candidate demonstrated both tactically and substantively that CANF was quite willing to play the parties off against each other in pursuit of a policy goal. Bill Clinton's visit to Miami in April was a triumph and was used as a platform for endorsing the Torricelli Bill. By endorsing the bill before Bush, Clinton scored a public relations coup in the very heart of the then-president's political base. Bush reacted quickly to the political threat by overruling his own State Department and announcing his support for the legislation, even interrupting a Kennebunkport weekend to announce that he was tightening the embargo by requiring that ships carrying Cuban goods obtain special licenses to enter U.S. ports.

The White House agreed to the Torricelli Bill after its sponsors consented to modify the legislation. The final compromise addressed the State Department's concerns that the bill would create a diplomatic backlash against the United States by softening some of the bill's harshest provisions. The compromise bill urged, rather than required, the president to impose sanctions on countries that aid Cuba, and urged, rather than required, the administration to lobby allies to "sign on" to the embargo. However, the ban on foreign subsidiary trade with Cuba stayed in. Bush ceremoniously came to Miami to sign the Torricelli Bill into law.

Money from the foundation's political action committee has helped buy congressional influence. The Free Cuba Political Action Committee, which is the foundation's vehicle for campaign contributions, contributed twice as much to Democratic candidates for office nationwide than Republicans during the 1990–92 election cycle (Falk 1992). During the past decade, foundation members have donated $1.3 million in campaign contributions; Mas Canosa himself is the biggest Hispanic contributor nationwide. In 1992, more than $200,000 has gone to lobbying efforts and campaign contributions for sympathetic congressmen (Booth 1992). According to Federal Election Commission records, the Free Cuba PAC gave $182,897 in campaign contributions in 1987–88 and $114,127 in 1989–90 (Robinson 1992). The PAC's war chest comes largely from the directors of the foundation, who must contribute $10,000 a year for a seat on the foundation board. A pledge of $5,000 a year is required for membership in the PAC (Nichols 1988).

Campaign contributions to influential congressmen has made CANF a key player on Capitol Hill. Especially important to the foundation is Representative Robert Torricelli, the New Jersey Democrat who sponsored the embargo-tightening Cuban Democracy Act of 1992. Torricelli has few Cuban Americans in his congressional district, but New Jersey has a large Cuban-American constituency, 85,000 strong, mostly in nearby Union City, who could provide a solid base of support if Torricelli decides to run for governor or senate (Robbins 1992, 166). Moreover, Torricelli was instrumental in the election of Robert Menendez (the first Cuban Democratic Congressman) in the neighboring congressional district and has advocated a Democratic party out-reach to the Cuban-American community. Torricelli's political ambitions are supported by CANF, which provides the New Jersey Democrat with large political contributions from its coffers. In 1992 alone, Torricelli received $26,750 from the foundation's Free Cuba PAC. Moreover, Mas Canosa has gone out of his way to support New Jersey Democrats, including campaigning for Governor Jim Florio in 1993, at least partly due to his symbiotic relationship with Torricelli.

Another important supporter of CANF in Congress is the senior Democratic Senator from Florida, Robert Graham. He was the Senate sponsor of the Torricelli Bill. Graham was easily re-elected in 1992 with overwhelming Cuban-American support. Graham's showing in the predominately Hispanic precincts frequently approached Bush's 70 percent margin (Moreno and Warren 1996). Even measured against a weak opponent, the vote constituted a remarkable turnaround in Graham's fortunes among Cuban voters (see table 2). Although he had received a much smaller majority of the votes in Hispanic precincts in his 1982 gubernatorial re-election (again, against comparatively weak opposition), in his 1986 Senate election against Republican incumbent Paula Hawkins, he only received 24 percent of the Cuban vote (Moreno and Warren 1992, 134). Graham's sponsorship of the Cuban Democracy Act combined with his politically low-keyed service orientation toward his Hispanic constituents seems to have converted uneven support among Cubans in the past into a more solid and predictable base. Graham is unlikely to risk this political base by offending his anti-Castro Cuban-American supporters.

Media

Cuban-American political mobilization has been aided by the power of the Hispanic-owned radio and television stations. The five radio and two television stations have a clear ethnic agenda. They are a key source of support for Hispanic causes and have played an important role in the political activity of the community. For example, it was the Cuban radio stations that mobilized the Hispanic crowd that attacked the anti-Contra demonstrators at the Torch of Friendship. Cuban stations have also led campaigns against the Cuban Museum for selling works of a pro-Castro artist and Florida International University for refusing to accept the establishment of a Cuban Institute run by the Cuban American National Foundation, and they participated in the banning of entertainers that perform in Cuba from the famed Calle Ocho festival.

They have also rallied the community against perceived acts of discrimination. For example, in the aftermath of the passage of Proposition 11 (the English Only initiative), a supermarket clerk was suspended for speaking Spanish in front of customers. The Hispanic stations' reaction was swift and effective in informing the citizenry. The store in which the incident occurred received over twenty bomb threats, picket lines were set up, and the radio stations began organizing a boycott of the supermarket chain. Less than forty-eight hours after the incident the company announced that the clerk would be reinstated, the offending manager transferred out of Dade County, and the store issued a public apology to their Spanish-speaking customers. The chain then conducted an extensive campaign in the Spanish-speaking media to regain their share of the Hispanic market.

CONCLUSION

Cuban Americans translated their numbers and their economic strength into political power in the first generation after arriving in the United States. In Miami, the Cuban community accomplished in thirty years what it took the Irish Americans of Boston five generations to accomplish. The success of the Cubans is not due to some Cuban political strategy which can be replicated by other ethnic groups. In fact, the Cuban model of empowerment was made possible by special conditions which favored quick empowerment. The circumstances that existed in Miami—specifically, demographic and socioeconomic conditions and the existence of a self-sustained Cuban enclave—are simply unique to the Cuban experience.

However, the uniqueness of the Cuban experience offers a competing model for minority group empowerment in the United States. The lesson from Miami is that group cohesiveness, both economically in the enclave and ideologically in the anti-Castro struggle, was the building block for Cuban political empowerment. This cohesiveness combined with the favorable conditions that Cubans found when they arrived in the United States to create the Cuban success story. Cubans not only found a relatively weak political establishment and benefitted from federal policy which favored Cuban immigration, but Cubans also benefitted from generous federally funded programs that aided the newly arrived refugees. Thus in explaining the political empowerment of Cuban Americans one needs to examine the interaction of Cuban talent and ambition with the opportunity provided by Miami's political and economic underdevelopment.

The Cuban model is not only a fascinating one in its own right, but it also raises important questions about such long-standing issues as the nature of ethnic or minority group political identity, empowerment, discrimination, assimilation, adaptation, agenda-setting, mobilization, and incorporation, as well as offers new insights into the diversity of Latino politics.

References

Booth, Cathy. 1992. "The Man Who Would Oust Castro." *Time,* October 26.

Carter, Tom. 1993. "94 funds approved for Radio, TV Marti: Move called 'victory against Castro'." *Washington Times,* October 14.

Falk, Pamela. 1992. "Exiles Set Policy Agenda on Cuba for Next Administration." *Wall Street Journal,* October 16, A15.

Fernandez, Damian. 1987. "From Little Havana to Washington, D.C.: Cuban Americans and U.S. Foreign Policy." In *Ethnic Groups and U.S. Foreign Policy,* ed. Mohammed E. Ahrari. Westport, Conn.: Greenwood Press.

Gannon, Michael V. 1984. "A History of Florida to 1900." In *Florida's Politics and Government,* ed. Manning J. Dauer, 2nd ed. Gainesville: University Presses of Florida.

Glazer, Nathan, and Daniel P. Moynihan, eds. 1975. *Ethnicity: Theory and Experience.* Cambridge, Mass: Harvard University Press.

Hero, Rodney E. 1992. *Latinos and the U.S. Political System: Two-Tiered Pluralism.* Philadelphia: Temple University Press.

Key, V. O., Jr. 1959. "Secular Realignment and the Party System." *Journal of Politics* 21:198–219.

Levine, Barry B. 1985. "The Capital of Latin America." *Wilson Quarterly* (Winter): 46–69.

Malone, Joseph J. 1988. "Change Patterns: 1986–1987 Registration, Dade County, Florida." Metro-Dade Elections Department.

Malone, Joseph J. 1985. "Hispanics in the Electoral Process of Dade County, Florida: The Coming of Age." Metro-Dade Elections Department.

Metro-Dade Planning Department. 1986. *Hispanic Profile: Dade County's Hispanic Origin Population.*

Moreno, Dario, and Nicol Rae. 1994. "District Elections and Minority Empowerment: The Evidence From Dade County." Paper presented at Western Political Science Association, Albuquerque, New Mexico, March.

Moreno, Dario, and Nicol Rae. 1992. "Ethnicity and Partisanship: The Case of the 18th Congressional District in Miami." In *Miami Today,* ed. Guillermo Grenier and Alex Stepick. Miami: Florida International Press.

Moreno, Dario, and Christopher L. Warren. 1996. "The Conservative Enclave Revisited." In *Ethnic Ironies: Latino Politics in the 1992 Elections,* ed. Rodolfo O. de la Garza and Louis DeSipio. Boulder, Colo.: Westview Press.

Moreno, Dario, and Christopher L. Warren. 1992. "The Conservative Enclave: Cubans in Florida." In *From Rhetoric to Reality: Latino Politics in the 1988 Elections,* ed. Rudolfo de la Garza and Louis DeSipio. Boulder, Colo.: Westview Press.

Nichols, John Spicer. 1988. "Cuba: The Congress; the Power of the Anti-Castro Lobby." *Nation Enterprises,* October 24.

Nielsen, Francois. 1985. "Toward a Theory of Ethnic Solidarity in Modern Societies." *American Sociological Review* 50: 133–149.

Olzak, Susan. 1983. "Contemporary Ethnic Mobilization." *Annual Reviews of Sociology* 9: 355–374.

Perez, Lisandro. 1992. "Cuban Miami." In *Miami Today,* ed. Guillermo Grenier and Alex Stepick. Miami: Florida International Press.

Portes, Alejandro, and Robert L. Bach. 1985. *Latin Journey: Cuban and Mexican Immigrants in the United States.* Berkeley: University of California.

Richardson, Bill. 1985. "Hispanic American Concerns." *Foreign Policy* 60: 30–39.

Rieff, David. 1987. *Going to Miami: Exiles, Tourists, and Refugees in the New America.* Boston: Little, Brown.

Robbins, Carla Ann. 1992. "Dateline Washington: Cuban American Clout." *Foreign Policy* 88 (Fall): 162–182.

Robinson, Linda. 1992. "After Castro Moves Out." *U.S. News and World Report* 112 (no. 17): 42, 44.

Sharp, Deborah. 1993. "For Cubans, Success, Conflict," *USA Today,* July 15.

Strategy Research Corporation. 1988. *The 1989 South Florida Latin Market.*

Torres, Maria. 1986. "Cuban Exiles Are Not a Bit Golden," *Chicago Tribune,* November 15.

Warren, Christopher L. 1984. "Hispanics." In *Florida's Politics and Government,* ed. Manning J. Dauer, 2nd ed. Gainesville: University Presses of Florida.

Warren, Christopher L., John G. Corbett, and John F. Stack, Jr. 1989. "Hispanic Ascendancy and Tripartite Politics in Miami." In *Racial Politics,* ed. Rufus P. Browning, Dale Rogers Marshall, and David H. Tabb. New York: Longman.

Warren, Christopher L., John F. Stack, Jr., and John G. Corbett. 1986. "Minority Mobilization in an International City: Rivalry and Conflict in Miami." *PS* 3: 626–634.

U.S. Bureau of the Census. 1982. *General Population Characteristics, Florida: Table 16.* Washington, D.C.: U.S. Government Printing Office.

Wolfinger, Raymond E. 1965. "The Development of Ethnic Voting." *American Political Science Review* 59: 896–908.

PART III

The Conversion Process: Representation and Decision Making

CONVERSION IS AT THE HEART of the policy-making process. Persons in positions of authority—legislators, executives, administrators, judges—convert the inputs which they receive from individuals, interest groups, political parties, and others from their constituencies and others from outside their electoral constituencies into binding policy decisions, that is, into laws and regulations. The needs, desires, and wants of the citizenry are not automatically and mechanistically converted into public policy. First, persons and groups wanting the government to act on their behalf must engage the attention of the officials and have their issue concerns placed onto the public policy agenda. Then *conversion* or the policy-making process begins.

As decision makers consider these individual or group inputs, giving them a greater or lesser degree of attention, many factors come into play. In addition to the many institutional and situational factors which impact on decision making, who these public authorities are plays a role. Their backgrounds and other personal characteristics have an impact on the kinds of decisions they make or do not make. Latinos have been greatly underrepresented in these positions. The assumption has been that Latino representatives, if elected, would make decisions which are more favorable to the Hispanic community.

Historically, one of the reasons for the paucity of Latino legislative representation has been the practice of gerrymandering by the people in power. Legislative district boundaries have been drawn to eliminate or at least minimize the number of Latino representatives in Congress. In his article "Hispanics in the 103rd Congress: The 1990 Census, Reapportionment, Redistricting and the 1992 Elections," Maurilio Vigil describes the background and the processes by which the 1992 Congressional elections, proscribed by the 1990 Census count, produced a dramatic increase in the number of Hispanic U.S. Representatives. The foundations for this gain included the large increases in the Hispanic population between 1980 and 1990; a favorable electoral climate provided by the Voting Rights Acts and subsequent court decisions giving minorities some advantages in reapportionment and redistricting, and to a lesser extent Hispanic activism, including effective campaigning, interest-group activities, and coalition formations. In addition to the increase in their numbers, especially notable is the increased diversity among Congressional Hispanics with the addition of representatives from additional states, more women, more non-Mexicans, and more Republicans. Based on their increased numbers and visibility and their recognition by the receptive Democratic administration, Vigil speculates about the possibility of increased effectiveness by the Hispanic Congressional Caucus, while recognizing that unified action is made more difficult by the increased diversity.

The Hispanic Congressional Caucus maintained its existence during the 1980s and into the 1990s. Even though it was bolstered by the addition of several members, it seemed to be minimally effective, other than in a symbolic manner. One of the reasons for its minimal impact on policy was its continued internal divisions along ideological, partisan, and national-origin lines. What could not be foreseen was the Republican takeover of the 104th Congress through the sweeping Republican victories in the 1994 elections. With the coming to power of the Republican-led Congress in 1995, the Hispanic Congressional Caucus' potential seemed to be diminished even more. There were no changes in the composition of the voting members of the Hispanic contingent, which meant that the fourteen Democrats lost their positions of organizational influence. All but three of the Caucus members were Democrats, now the minority party, and the Republican House leadership expressed a desire to abolish funding for several "special interest" legislative caucuses, including the Hispanic Caucus.

Regardless of the policy efficacy of the Congressional Hispanic Caucus, an important question to consider is whether increased representation of Hispanics in Congress necessarily results in more favorable national policies being enacted. Research by Welch and Hibbing,[1] reported in *Latinos and the Political System,* began to answer this extremely important but little-researched question. That study concluded that liberal policy representation of Hispanics can be correlated with Hispanic representation in Congress and with the proportion of Hispanics in Congressional constituencies. These authors did find a significant correlation between the voting patterns of the Hispanic representatives on 1,740 votes over a nine-year period (1972–80) and liberal (or at least less conservative) positions as evidenced by roll call voting. There was a positive correlation, although not nearly as strong, between larger populations of Hispanic voters in the Congressional districts and a more liberal voting record of the non-Hispanic representatives from those districts.

In the more recent study included here, "Latinos and Substantive Representation in the U.S. House of Representatives: Direct, Indirect, or Nonexistent?" Rodney Hero and Caroline Tolbert examine the extent of substantive representation of Latinos in the 100th U.S. House of Representatives (1987–88). They initially hypothesize that the increased numbers of Latinos in the United States and also in the United States House of Representatives during the 1980s have led to an increase in direct or "dyadic" substantive representation of Latinos. They utilize pro-Hispanic issue "scores" (as determined by the Southwest Voter Research Institute) of Congressional voting patterns and analyze these by the ethnic background of Representatives and the percent of Latino constituent House districts. As with the Welch and Hibbing study and others of similar nature, Hero and Tolbert find little direct substantive representation of Latinos. Representatives who are of Latino origin have somewhat distinct voting patterns, but Latino constituencies seem to have little impact on how representatives vote. Nevertheless, during the period studied, legislation deemed salient to Latinos was enacted, indicating that perhaps some "collective" or "partisan" substantive representation does seem to occur through some yet unspecified process.

While the focus of most concern over Latino representation in government seems to be on the legislative branch, this underestimates the great impact which appointed as well as elected administrative officials have on the formulation and implementation of public policy. Harry Pachon has asserted that the Latino communities have not been influential in the policy-making process at the national governmental level largely because of the lack of representation of Hispanics in the federal bureaucracy.[2] Pachon also blames the lack of Latino influence in the policy-making process on the absence of major, national political interest groups of Latinos and on the bi-racial, that is "Black and White," perspective of most public policy makers. For these two reasons, he believes that Hispanic representation in the bureaucracy is particularly important.

Pachon's projection in 1983 that "Hispanic underrepresentation in the federal government will continue—most likely through the upcoming decade"—is supported by the results of a study by Antonio Sisneros published in 1993, "Hispanics in the Public Service in the Late Twentieth Century."[3] Very slight increases have occurred. For example, the percentage of Hispanics in the federal executive branch public service increased from 4.5 percent in 1982 to 5.2 percent in 1988. Among all the Hispanics employed in the federal public service, the percentage in the two highest policymaking levels, Grades 13–15 and the Senior Executive Service, increased in the years 1982 to 1989 from 7.19 to 8.52 percent and from 0.11 to 0.15 percent, respectively.

Often in the past, the system has either co-opted Latinos or appointed Latinos to "token" positions. In either case, the effect on policy making is minimal. Perhaps catalyzed by the Chicano Movement of the 1960s, presidential appointments to relatively high positions in the federal bureaucracy increased dramatically beginning with the Nixon Administration, and continuing through the Ford, Carter, Reagan, Bush, and Clinton Administrations. However, often these appointments were mainly symbolic, since the positions in question either were in special Latino or minority-oriented agencies or they offered the appointee little or no significant influence in policy formulation. President George Bush appointed two Hispanics to Cabinet positions—Manuel Lujan to head the Interior Department and Lauro Cavazos (who had been appointed by Reagan) as Secretary of Education. He also named Antonia C. Novello as U.S. Surgeon General and Catalina Vasquez Villapando as Treasurer of the United States. The latter succeeded Kathleen Davalos Ortega, appointed by Ronald Reagan, who in turn had succeeded Ramona Acosta Banuelos. President Bill Clinton appointed Latinos to two Cabinet positions of substantial importance to Hispanics: Federico Pena as Secretary of the Department of Transportation and Henry Cisneros as Secretary of the Department of Housing and Urban Development. Such appointments are doubly useful in that, in addition to providing opportunities for policy leadership, the appointees serve as high profile public role models to which other Latinos, especially the young, can relate. No Hispanic has yet been appointed to the United States Supreme court.

Even if Latinos are represented by co-ethnics in the legislative and executive branches, to be responsive to Hispanic needs they must perceive their role as a special one, that is as having a special responsibility to represent the Latino community, among others. Alternatively, they must attempt to exert influence on their colleagues on behalf of Latinos in order to impact policy favorably. One of the few studies casting light on this aspect of representation is by Rodolfo de la Garza who has inquired extensively and intensively into the perceived roles of Chicano political elites. His hypothesis was that truly "active" representation of Hispanics in legislative as well as executive/administrative positions would help to impact public policy in a positive direction for Hispanics. Attempts were made to distinguish the representatives of each Chicano political generation from those that preceded it, and most importantly, to determine if those representatives perceived themselves as having a special responsibility to represent the interests of Hispanics. Some evidence was found of expressions of a special duty to represent the interests of their ethnic group. This was especially so among members of those socialized during the Civil Rights era of the 1950s and 1960s and also was more evident among appointed administrators and Hispanic organizational leaders than among elected officials. In some of his related research, de la Garza had found that not only were Chicano elites different from their Anglo counterparts (in that they were more likely to come from families of lower socioeconomic status) but also that their experiences of discrimination constituted a very important political socialization experience that affected their perception of their decision-making roles and responsibilities.[4]

There is considerable evidence that Latinos are more concerned with problems and policies at the state and local levels than with national issues. Overall, from 1984 to 1993, there was an average gain of 41 percent in the number of Hispanic elected office (HEOs) holders throughout the country, from 3,128 to 4,420.[5] In 1995, the *National Roster of Hispanic Elected Officials* (compiled annually by NALEO) reported an increase over the past two years, subsequent to the 1994 election, of 214 Hispanic elected officials, an increase of 45. This increase was attributed to the redistricting of 1991 and 1992 plus the increase in the naturalization of Hispanic immigrants. Most of these were at the local level—municipalities, counties, and school boards; in fact, these account for more than three-fourths of all HEOs. Particularly in the late 1970s and early 1980s, this increase had been abetted by litigation which produced single-member, districted electoral constituencies from previous at-large, multi-member districts. Groups such as MALDEF and SVREP were in the forefront of these challenges to the courts. Reapportionments fairer to previously excluded groups following the 1980 and 1990 censuses had also promoted Latino electoral successes.

More Latinos were elected to positions in state and local governments in the 1970s and 1980s than had been elected in the previous 100 years. State legislatures evidenced an increasing Latino representation. For example, only thirty-eight Latinos were elected to the California state legislature between 1860 and 1979 (out of more than 4,000 persons who were members of the legislature during that century); twelve were serving in 1993. In Texas, Latino representation improved from six legislators in 1962, to twenty-five in 1984, to thirty-two in 1993. In Arizona, Latino representation in the legislature went from three to eleven between 1962 and 1984 and to ten in 1993. The number of Latinos in the Colorado legislature increased from zero to eight in the period 1962 to 1978 and then to six in 1984, and to eight in 1993. In New Mexico, the total number of Hispanic legislators increased from twenty-three in 1962 to forty-five in 1993, although the proportion in the legislature remained relatively unchanged in the same period. Overall then, while Latino representation in the Southwestern state legislatures remained small and fairly constant from 1932 to 1962, after the "reapportionment revolution" of the 1960s it more than doubled between 1962 and 1978 from a total of thirty-two legislators in the five Southwestern states to a total of eighty legislators in 1978. Over the next fifteen years it grew to 117 in 1993. Although there were major gains for Latinos in these years, it should be noted that in all the states of the Southwest, the proportion of Latino lawmakers in the state legislatures (except for one) remains far below the proportion of Latinos in the total population of each state.

An attempt to discover the impact of increased Hispanic representation in a state legislature was conducted by Tatcho Mindiola and Armando Gutierrez for the state of Texas.[6] Their research addresses the general question of how important it is for Latinos to have Latino legislators in representative bodies and also the auxiliary question as to how effective Latino legislators actually are in passing the legislation which they have introduced.

In the first half of the 1970s two of the five Southwestern governorships were held by Latinos, with Raul Castro serving as governor in Arizona and Jerry Apodaca as the governor of New Mexico. In 1984, there was one Latino governor and four other Latino elected state governmental executives, all in New Mexico. Hispanic state officials increased by 31.5 percent from 1984 to 1993. Texas elected its first statewide executive in 1992 with the election of Dan Morales to the post of State Treasurer.

Political gains for Latinos at other levels of government were also much in evidence. Municipal officials have increased by 45 percent and county officials by 41 percent from 1984 to 1993. In the past two decades some gains also have been made in the larger cities of the United States, with Latinos gaining a seat or two on city councils in El Paso, San Antonio, Houston, Denver, and other cities. Mayorships have been gained in Denver (Pena), San Antonio (Cisneros), Santa Fe (Jaramillo), Albuquerque (Chavez), and Sacramento (Serna). Still, in most of the larger and more populous metropolitan areas, Latinos generally remain badly underrepresented. Of the 19,300 municipalities in the United States, only 196 (about 1%) had Hispanic mayors in 1993.

Especially notable was the increase in female (Latina) office holders. Their numbers increased over the decade from 376 in 1984 to 1,049 in 1993, a 179 percent increase. There is a greater proportion of female officeholders in the purportedly "macho" Hispanic population (33%) than there is among the general U.S. population (20%).

Yet even with these steady and significant increases, Latino elected officials still represented less than one percent of the nation's elected officials. Overall, it seems that increased Latino representation in public policy-making bodies does have a favorable impact on policies which are helpful to the Latino political community. The exact conditions for favorable conversions of needs and wants into positive governmental policies are not yet clearly delineated, but additional research should elucidate further this critical process of conversion.

NOTES

1. Susan Welch and John R. Hibbing, "Hispanic Representation in the U.S. Congress," *Social Science Quarterly* 65, no. 2 (June 1984): 328–35; reprinted in *Latinos and the Political System,* ed. F. Chris Garcia (Notre Dame, Ind.: University of Notre Dame Press, 1988), 291–99.

2. Harry P. Pachon, "Hispanic Underrepresentation in the Federal Bureaucracy: The Missing Link in the Policy Process," in *Latinos and the Political System,* 306–27.

3. Antonio Sisneros, "Hispanics in the Public Service in the Late Twentieth Century," *Public Administration Review* 53, no. 1 (January February 1993). 1–6.

4. Rodolfo de la Garza and Davis Vaughn, "The Political Socialization of Chicano Elites: A Generational Approach," *Social Science Quarterly* 65 (June 1984): 290–307.

5. Most of these statistics on Hispanic office holders are derived from the various reports of the National Association of Latino Elected and Appointed Officials, especially "An Overview of Hispanic Elected Officials in 1993," by Harry P. Pachon and Juan Carlos Alegre, in the *1993 National Roster of Hispanic Elected Officials.*

6. Tatcho Mindiola, Jr., and Armando Gutierrez, "Chicanos and the Legislative Process: Reality and Illusion in the Politics of Change," in *Latinos and the Political System,* 349–62.

9. Hispanics in the 103rd Congress: The 1990 Census, Reapportionment, Redistricting, and the 1992 Elections

Maurilio E. Vigil

THE *Congressional Quarterly* in 1992 described the 103rd Congress as one of the most diverse in Congressional history. "The class of 1992," said CQ, "also includes many more women, Blacks and Hispanics. So the 103rd will set records for the number of women and minorities" (C.Q., November 7, 1992).

Among the record number of minorities were eight new Hispanic Congresspersons who increased Hispanic representation to 17 full-fledged members of Congress (two other Hispanics serve as delegates from Puerto Rico and the Virgin Islands), the largest delegation ever. The eight new Hispanic Congresspersons represented the largest single increase ever recorded by Hispanics since the first Hispanic, Joseph Hernandez, was elected to represent the Territory of Florida in 1822. Indeed, the increase was greater than the five who entered Congress in the 1960's and six who entered in the 1980's (Vigil, 1984). However, even with the increased numbers Hispanics still remain underrepresented with only 4.4 percent of the membership of Congress while they constitute about nine percent of the U.S. population.

The increase of Hispanic Congresspersons is due directly to the increased population of Hispanics reported in the 1990 U.S. Census and the subsequent congressional reapportionment and redistricting process. But, while benefitting Hispanics, the census and the redistricting process also cost Hispanics additional seats. Nonetheless, the increased numbers

From *Latino Studies Journal,* Volume 5, No. 2, May 1994, pp. 40–76. Used by permission of the publisher.

promise to revitalize and enhance the status and power of the Congressional Hispanic Caucus. As one new Congressman Frank Tejada said, "The Hispanic Caucus will become more visible and will have a louder voice because of the increased numbers" (C.Q., January 2, 1993).

This paper describes how the Congressional reapportionment and redistricting process following the release of the 1990 census resulted in additional seats for Hispanic Congresspersons. It will also examine the electoral circumstances that enabled Hispanics to capture those seats. Finally, it will speculate on the implications of the increased representation for the Congressional Hispanic Caucus and for Hispanics in general.

HISPANICS IN CONGRESS: HISTORY AND RECENT TRENDS

Hispanics have been represented in Congress since the 1820's and almost continuously since the middle of the 19th century. Joseph Marion Hernandez was the first Hispanic ever to serve in Congress. He was a delegate from the Florida Territory in 1822–1823. In 1853, José Manuel Gallegos, a priest, became the first of nine Hispanics who represented New Mexico as delegates of the Territory between 1852 and 1911. Rumualdo Pacheco from California was the first Hispano to be elected as a regular member of Congress. He entered Congress in 1879 and served until 1883. Louisiana became the third state to elect an Hispano to Congress with the election of Ladislas Lazaro in 1913. Lazaro served until his death in 1827. Joachim Octave Fernandez next represented Louisiana in Congress, serving four terms between 1930 and 1940.

When New Mexico became a state in 1912, it did not immediately elect an Hispano to Congress despite the many who had served during the territorial period. But in 1914, Benigno "B.C." Hernandez was elected to New Mexico's single seat in the U.S. House. Hernandez served from 1915 to 1916 and 1919 to 1920. Nestor Montoya replaced Hernandez as Congressman from New Mexico and served from 1921 to 1923 when he died in office.

Octaviano Larrazolo, a former New Mexico Governor, became the first Hispanic United States Senator in 1929 following his election in 1928 to fill the unexpired term of Senator A. A. Jones who had died in office. Larrazolo served one year before ill health forced him to retire in 1930.

The election of Dennis Chavez as Congressman from New Mexico in 1930 ushered in the modern era for Hispanics in Congress. Chavez served two terms in the U.S. House and in 1935 was appointed to the U.S. Senate to replace Senator Bronson Cutting who had died in a plane crash. Chavez had challenged Cutting in the 1934 senatorial election and contested the outcome of a close election. Chavez went on to serve a total of 27 years in the U.S. Senate before his death in 1962.

New Mexico qualified for a second seat in the U.S. House following the 1940 census and Antonio M. Fernandez was elected to the second seat in 1943 and retained it until his death in 1956. Joseph M. Montoya replaced Fernandez in 1957 and retained the seat until 1964 when he was elected to the U.S. Senate. Montoya thus became with Dennis Chavez the only Hispanic to hold seats in both houses of Congress. Montoya in fact, was elected to Chavez' seat, having defeated the Republican, Edwin L. Mechem, who was appointed Senator following Chavez' death. Montoya went on to serve two terms before his defeat by former astronaut Harrison Schmitt in 1976.

The decade of the 1960's was an important turning point for Hispanics in Congress. Prior to this, Hispanic representation had been limited to the Congressmen from New Mexico and a few isolated cases from Florida, California and Louisiana. This changed in the 1960's as Hispanos benefitted from reapportionment and redistricting brought about by the 1960 census. Henry B. Gonzales was elected to Congress in 1961 from a district encompassing the San Antonio, Texas area. Eligio "Kika" de la Garza was elected to the House in 1964 from another district encompassing the South Texas cities of Mission, McAllen and Edinburg. Gonzales and de la Garza remain in Congress at this writing as the most influential Hispanic Congressmen. Gonzales serves as Chair of the House Banking, Business and Industry Committee and de la Garza as Chair of the House Agriculture Committee.

Edward Roybal was elected to the 88th Congress from a district in Los Angeles, California in 1962. In New Mexico, Manuel Lujan restored parity for Hispanos in the New Mexico Congressional delegation when he was elected to the U.S. House in 1968. Lujan remained in Congress until 1990 when he retired and was subsequently appointed as Secretary of Interior under President George Bush. Herman Badillo became the first Puerto Rican elected to Congress in 1970, representing a district from New York's South Bronx. Badillo retired after three terms and was replaced by Robert Garcia, also a Puerto Rican, who represented the South Bronx district from 1978 until his resignation in 1990.

The decades of the 1980's witnessed further developments which doubled the size of the Hispanic Congressional delegation. The 1980 census of population revealed new population growth and shifts which transferred a number of Congressional seats from the "rustbelt" (Northeast and Midwest) to the sunbelt states. The Congressional redistricting process, carried out in the shadow of the 1975 Voting Rights Act resulted in the creation of several new congressional seats with Hispanic concentrations. In California, Matthew "Marty" Martinez and Esteban Torrez were elected from newly created U.S. House districts in the Los Angeles metropolitan area in 1982. In Texas, Solomon Ortiz was elected in 1982 to a newly created Congressional district in the Brownsville/Corpus Christi area. Albert Bustamante was elected in 1984 to another new district from the San Antonio area. New Mexico qualified for a third seat in Congress following the 1980 census and Bill Richardson (who claims Hispanic origins through his mother) was elected to a newly created district in 1982.

Further developments in the late 1980's brought in other Hispanic faces to Congress. In 1989, Ileana Ros-Lehtinen became the first Cuban and Hispanic woman elected to the U.S. House when she was elected to a Miami, Florida, seat vacated by the late Congressman Claude Pepper. In 1990, José Serrano was elected to the South Bronx seat vacated by the resignation of Robert Garcia. Ed Pastor became Arizona's first Hispanic Congressman in 1991 when he was appointed then elected to the U.S. House seat vacated by the ailing Congressman Morris K. Udall. Thus, the dawn of the decade of the 1990's saw ten Hispanos as regular members of Congress and two as delegates from American territories and they were poised to reap the benefits from the 1990's reapportionment and redistricting process.

THE 1990 CENSUS

The U.S. Census is more important today than it ever was. Given the laws, court decisions and administrative actions that require information about the numbers and nature of the population, the importance of the census cannot be overstated.

The enumeration done by the U.S. Census is more important for its reporting of the geographic distribution of the population than for its total count for the nation as a whole. The Census is used for sharing or distributing our fixed resources whether measured in fiscal (public funds) or political (seats in Congress) terms. Thus if one jurisdiction (state, county or municipality) gets more, another receives less. Thus an undercount and any adjustment resulting therefrom deprives one entity and rewards another.

When the 1990 Census results were released in early 1991, there was an immediate outcry from state and municipal officials and representatives of ethnic groups challenging the accuracy of the enumeration. The worst fears of Census officials were affirmed when the Census Bureau released a Post-Enumeration Survey (PES) which revealed a substantial undercount of the population. In the PES, (mandated by federal court order), the Census Bureau surveyed 156,000 households to measure how thoroughly the census had counted the population, to calculate the extent of the inaccuracy and make necessary corrections. According to the PES released on June 13, 1991, the national undercount was estimated to be 5.2 million or 2.1 percent of the total U.S. population. The figures would translate into an approximate undercount of 1.2 million or 5.2 percent for Hispanics, 1.5 million or 4.8 percent for Blacks and 99 thousand or 5.0 percent for Native Americans.

For Hispanics, the PES undercount results were particularly important. In addition to being the most undercounted group, the PES showed that the states with the largest Mexican-American populations, New Mexico (4.7%), California (3.8%), Arizona (3.4%), and Texas (3.3%), were the states with the largest percentage of undercount in the nation. Corrections of the undercount in fact would result in the states of California and Arizona receiving one additional seat in Congress each, while the states of Pennsylvania and Wisconsin would each lose one seat (N.Y. Times, June 14, 1991).

On July 15, 1991, U.S. Commerce Secretary Robert Mosbacher announced that the U.S. Census Bureau would not adjust the census figures and that those originally reported would stand.

While the economic and social impact of the Census undercount are difficult to calculate, the consequences for future political empowerment of Hispanics can be estimated. Census figures are used for two distinctly political processes, reapportionment and redistricting. As the reapportionment and redistricting affects representation in the U.S. Congress, state legislatures, state boards of education and judicial districts, and various local governing bodies, the widespread impact of the Census will be felt.

IMPACT ON RE-APPORTIONMENT

The first and most direct political result of the Census undercount for Hispanics is in the apportionment of congressional seats. One of the primary purposes of the Census is to re-apportion 385 seats in the U.S. House of Representatives according to the population changes that occurred in the previous ten years. Because of population shifts documented by the 1990 Census, nineteen house seats, primarily from the northeast and midwest states were redistributed to sunbelt states. Even before the Census undercount was announced, Hispanic leaders and activists expressed hopes for and openly claimed some of the new congressional seats allocated to California (7), Florida (4), Texas (3), and Arizona (1), after the 1990 Census. Arturo Vargas, Director of Outreach Policy for the Mexican American Legal Defense Fund and Education Fund (MALDEF) argued that, "there's a direct correlation . . . half the population gain in California, for example, is Hispanic." Therefore, reasoned California Congressman Esteban E. Torres, "three of the seven seats should be Hispanic" (Russell, 1991). Noting high Hispanic population increases in all these states, Hispanics expressed hopes of increasing the numbers of Hispanic Congresspersons from 10 to as many as 19. Those expectations increased when news of the undercount revealed that an adjusted census would give California and Arizona an additional seat each. The argument of Hispanic leaders was bolstered by the fact that Hispanics were the most undercounted group.

Although 15 seats were allocated to states with large Hispanic populations and two more would have been added with the census adjustment, there is no assurance that the state legislatures in those seats would have created "Hispanic Congressional Districts" (or seats with Hispanic majorities). Nor is it possible to ascertain how many of those 15 or 17 seats would have been contested by Hispanic candidates successfully. It is possible to speculate, however, that the undercount cost Hispanics at least one and possibly two seats and that they stood to gain anywhere from one to seventeen seats from the new census.

EFFECT ON REDISTRICTING

The most widespread political effect of the Census undercount was on the process of redistricting of Congressional seats throughout the country. As many of the states had begun the redistricting process using the initial Census reports, the undercount revelations created a chaotic situation which was not resolved by Secretary Mosbacher's decision. The City of New York along with other cities and minority group organizations filed a lawsuit citing the unfairness of it. New York Mayor David Dinkins called Mosbacher's decision "nothing less than statistical grand larceny" (N.Y. Times, July 16, 1991). In California, Democrats filed a Freedom of Information Act request for the block by block adjusted totals calculated by the census.

In June 1991, the Texas State Legislature in regular session released a new state legislative redistricting plan that was immediately criticized by a coalition of Blacks and Hispanics. The coalition argued that since the greatest state population growth had been among minorities, that the legislative district lines should have been modified to reflect that growth. They claimed that they should be entitled to at least 17 more seats in the House of Representatives combined with the 39 seats they already held. Instead of making such adjustments, they argued, the legislators had protected their own seats (Austin American Statesman, June 14, 1991). After failing to persuade Governor Ann Richards to veto the bills (Richards let the bills become law without her signature), MALDEF, Texas Rural Aid and the Texas Civil Rights Project filed lawsuits on behalf of the coalition in federal and state district courts. They claimed the proposals diluted the voting strengths of Hispanic and Black Texans by not ensuring enough minority representatives to reflect their proportion of the state population. José Garza of Texas Rural Aid argued that to reflect the state population, Hispanics should have about 38 House and eight Senate seats instead of the 28 in the House and less than four in the Senate they would have under the adopted plan. The group also argued that the legislature should have used adjusted census figures rather than the original figures which undercounted minorities (San Antonio Light, June 18, 1991).

On August 22, 1991, State District Judge Mario Ramirez declared Texas' state legislative redistricting plans unconstitutional because they discriminated against minorities. The Judge further ruled that, "as it stands now officially, without adjustment, the 1990 Federal Census is an inaccurate count of the Texas population in general and to an even significantly greater extent, of the Hispanic and Black populations of the state" (S. A. News-Express, Aug. 23, 1991). The judge then ordered the state to draw up new plans based on adjusted census figures and submit them to him by September 30. The effect of Judge Ramirez' decision was postponed as Texas Attorney General Dan Morales appealed the ruling to the Texas Court of Appeals.

It is virtually impossible to ascertain the exact "political costs" to Hispanics of seats lost in Congress because all of the redistricting that took place at the state level for those positions was done in a very political climate, and there is no assurance that Hispanics would receive the equitable representation to which they were entitled. However, having seen how the U.S. Census figures are flawed and created an inequitable situation for Hispanics, one can now review how the redistricting process further denied Hispanics full representation even as it enabled them to increase their numbers in Congress.

THE REDISTRICTING PROCESS

Fifteen new U.S. House seats were allocated to states with large Hispanic populations after the 1990 Census, but even the most optimistic

Hispanic leaders were hoping for no more than half of that number to go to Hispanics. The redistricting process is one that is primarily governed by the partisan political climate of the legislatures of the individual states where the process occurs. In recent years, however, judicial review of the redistricting process and the guidelines set down in various Voting Rights Acts have increased the number of minority districts.

The 1975 amendments to the 1965 Voting Rights Act extend the provisions of the law to Spanish-Americans among other minorities and the 1982 amendments provide that "intent to discriminate" need not be proven in cases where redistricting processes show signs of discrimination. Although the 1982 amendments do not require racial quotas in redistricting, a judge or legislature could redraw voting districts to give a minority group minimum representation. Several court interpretations of the law have further strengthened the 1982 amendments by discouraging redistricting that dilutes minority voting strength and even encourages the creation of "minority-majority" districts (a district where a minority group is a majority). In the 1986 Supreme Court case of *Thornburg vs. Gingles,* the court interpreted the Voting Rights Act to require that House district lines not discriminate even unintentionally and even suggested that minority districts be drawn in areas where the minority group is large, geographically compact, and politically cohesive. The Thornburg case was widely interpreted as requiring mapmakers to design districts in which racial or ethnic minorities were a majority whenever the residential patterns made it possible (Huckabee, 1992). Because of these standards which facilitated court challenges to legislative-drawn redistricting plans that deleted minority voting strength of minorities, court involvement in the 1992 redistricting process was greater than ever before. One result was that the courts were less sensitive than state legislatures would have been to the interests of incumbent congressmen. All of these conditions then created a most favorable atmosphere for Hispanics, along with other minorities, to improve their representation in Congress. The following state-by-state analysis will summarize the redistricting process and the subsequent electoral circumstances that enabled Hispanics to gain new seats in the U.S. House of Representatives.

CALIFORNIA

The state of California continued its phenomenal growth rate in the decade of the 1980's increasing by almost 6 million and 25.7 percent between 1980 and 1990. As a result, it was allotted seven new seats in the U.S. House of Representatives. Hispanics accounted for over 3.1 million of California's new population, increasing by 69 percent from 4.5 to 7.7

million, so that by 1990, they comprised just over one-fourth (25.%) of California's population (U.S. Census, 1990). Consequently, Hispanics reasonably expected at least three, if not four, of California's seven new Congressional seats. Eventually, Hispanics ended up with a net gain of one new seat because one of two new Hispanic Congresspersons elected, Lucille Roybal-Allard, replaced her father, Congressman Edward Roybal, who retired from a seat that had long been regarded as an Hispanic enclave.

The redistricting process in California began with the Democratic-party controlled state legislature enacting a plan on September 17, 1991, which was then vetoed by Republican Governor Pete Wilson. The State Supreme Court, controlled by the Republican Party, then redrew House district lines to incorporate the seven new house seats. The new plan placed most of the "new" seats in areas of Republican strength such as Southern California, the Central Valley, and San Francisco's East Bay suburbs (C.Q., November 7, 1992). The plan had the effect of "packing" the Hispanic population into two contiguous districts in the Los Angeles metropolitan area.

One of the new districts created was the 30th District, which comprised a considerable part of Congressman Edward Roybal's old 25th district constituency. The district retained the largely Hispanic communities of Lincoln Heights, Boyle Heights, and El Sereno, and added new Hispanic immigrant neighborhoods such as Echo Park, East Hollywood, and Pico-Union along with Eagle Rock and Silver Lake. The district had a 61 percent Hispanic majority, but only 34 percent of the registered voters. Anglos made up 55 percent of the registered voters in the district (L.A. Times, May 28, 1992). The splitting of Roybal's 25th district also made it possible for him [Roybal] to leave part of his constituency to his top district aide, Henry Lozano, and part to his daughter, Lucille Roybal-Allard. Lozano immediately emerged as the favorite in the 30th district, but emerging primary opposition and family concerns led him to withdraw from the race. This opened the door to Democratic State Representative Xavier Becerra who was recruited by and promptly won endorsement from Roybal and fellow Congressman Esteban Torres. Becerra, a Stanford University educated lawyer, had been a state deputy attorney general and former legislative aide before being elected to the California State Assembly from Monterey Park, a Los Angeles suburban community. Becerra's chief primary opponent in a crowded ten-person Democratic Primary was Leticia Quezada, a Los Angeles school board member. Quezada won endorsement from Los Angeles City Councilman Richard Alatorre and State Senator Art Torres thus continuing the split between the two Hispanic camps consisting of Roybal, Esteban Torres, and County Supervisor Gloria Molina [who supported Becerra], and

Alatorre and Art Torres [who supported Quezada]. Quezada criticized Becerra as an "outsider" to the district while another opponent urged Becerra to finish his first term as assemblyman. Eventually aided by the high-powered endorsements, Becerra won a close victory in a low turnout [fewer than 30,000) primary. Becerra went on to win the general election over Republican Morry Waksbury with 59% of the vote.

The second new district created from part of Congressman Roybal's old 25th district was the 33rd Congressional District. This district, encompassing downtown Los Angeles, portions of Boyle Heights and East Los Angeles [which were in Roybals' district], also includes the southeast-area communities of Commerce, Vernon, Huntington Park, Bell, Bell Gardens, Maywood, Southgate and Cudahy. The district with its 84 percent Hispanic population has the largest concentration of any Latino district in the United States. In this district, Lucille Roybal-Allard, a California State Assemblywoman was regarded as a natural successor to her father. In addition to her family name and connections, Roybal had developed a reputation over three terms in the state assembly as an able community advocate and environmental activist who opposed an industrial incinerator and toxic waste recycling plant in the community of Vernon. Roybal won the primary with 74 percent of the vote over Frank Fernandez who got 17 percent and in the general election when she secured 63 percent of the vote to defeat Robert Guzman who got 30 percent (C.Q., January 16, 1992). Hispanic candidates also competed for three other Congressional seats but in those cases, the Republican drafted redistricting plan prevailed. Democrats Anita Perez-Ferguson in District 23 and Robert Bañuelos in District 46 each ran against incumbent Republicans but were defeated even though they drew over 40 percent of the vote. Republican Tony Valencia ran in District 50 and lost, receiving about 30 percent of the vote (S.W. Voter Research, 1992).

The victories by Becerra and Roybal-Allard, combined with two other Hispanic Congressmen Esteban Torrez and Matthew "Marty" Martinez, gave Hispanics four congresspersons from California which is encouraging, but when one considers that Hispanics make up one-fourth of California's population, that number is far short of the 13 seats which would give Hispanics three equitable shares of the largest single state congressional delegation.

TEXAS

Like California, Texas also saw a population growth [although not as dramatic] in the decade of the 1980's, increasing by 19.4 percent from 14.2 million to 17 million. Texas qualified for three new seats in Congress due to the increase, giving it a total of 30 Congresspersons. As in California, Hispanics accounted for a considerable number of Texas' population increase. Hispanics increased by 1.3 million [from 3 million to 4.3 million] or 45 percent in the period from 1980 to 1990 and now account for 25.5 percent of Texas' population (U.S. Census, 1990).

The Texas State Legislature meeting in a special session in the summer of 1991 produced a Congressional redistricting plan in August 25, 1991 that protected all 19 Democratic incumbents and gave Republicans only the eight seats they previously held. The three new seats were set aside for minorities with Blacks getting a new seat in Dallas and Hispanics getting two new Hispanic majority seats, one in Houston and the other in San Antonio. Signed by Governor Ann Richards on August 29, the new plan was approved by the U.S. Justice Department on November 18, despite pending federal court challenges.

Texas' new 29th Congressional District was called by some a "geraldomander" because its jagged lines zig-zagging across the city of Houston intentionally sought to encompass Hispanic enclaves in order to create a Hispanic majority (Suro, 1992). But the district also illustrates the futility of creating a minority-majority district without sufficient ethnic community mobilization and organizational planning. In Houston, the nation's fourth largest city, Hispanics are the largest of several minority groups who make up 28 percent of the 1.7 million population. This was clearly the motivation in creating the 29th District with its 60 percent Hispanic majority. However, because many of its primarily Mexican-American population are immigrant (non-citizens) young (only 55.4 percent of the voting age population) and or unregistered to vote, they only make up 31 percent of the voting population of the district.

Ben Reyes, Houston's first elected Hispanic Councilman and State Senator Gene Green, a lawyer and long-time state legislator, finished first and second respectively in a crowded March, 1992 Democratic primary. However, since neither candidate received a majority, a runoff election was held on April 14 which Green won by 186 votes. Reyes challenged the outcome in state district court, arguing that at least 430 runoff ballots were cast by voters who had voted in the Republican primary. Since such crossover voting is not allowed, District Judge John Delaney nullified the results and ordered a new runoff election which was held on July 28. Green won the new runoff election with 51.5 percent of the vote to Reyes' 48.5 percent and a margin of 1,132 votes. In addition to the low registration by Hispanics, Reyes was targeted by the National Rifle Association for his support of gun control legislation. The NRA sponsored a barrage of radio advertisements and direct mail notices that focused on Reyes' 1990 bankruptcy and other personal issues (C.Q. August

1, 1992). Green went on to handily defeat Clark Kent Ervin, a former White House aide in the November, 1992 General Election.

A second Hispanic-majority seat was the 28th District which encompassed part of San Antonio and surrounding areas. In this case, the scenario could not have been better scripted for an Hispanic candidate. Texas State Senator, Frank Tejeda, a San Antonio native, a Yale graduate, and a sixteen-year veteran of the state legislature, was elected with no major party opposition in either the primary or general election. His general election opponent, David Slatter, a Libertarian, provided only token opposition. Tejeda, a decorated Vietnam veteran, describes himself as a pro-business Democrat and the coalition of Hispanic and business interests cemented his easy victory (C.Q. November 7, 1992).

In addition to the 28th and 29th Districts, the new Texas Congressional districting map greatly altered the 23rd District, represented by incumbent Democratic Congressman Albert Bustamante. Bustamante, who was first elected in 1984, had received only token opposition in prior re-election bids and was secure enough to accept 21 new counties in a redistricting plan that gave him a sprawling district larger than New York state. The district spanned from San Antonio in the east, to El Paso in the west and from Odessa in the north, to Laredo in the south. About one-third of the 23rd district's constituents were new to the district and had not voted for Bustamante before. But the enlarged district was not the only reason responsible for Bustamante's problems in 1992. Bustamante was one of several House incumbents who fell victim to unfavorable publicity resulting from ethically questionable behavior. He was one of the Congressmen linked to the scandal involving overdrafts in the U.S. House Bank, and Bustamante's opponent, Republican Henry Bonilla, offered a new political twist when he reminded voters of Bustamante's *"cheques calientes"* (hot checks). In addition to the bank overdrafts, Bustamante also suffered negative publicity from an on-going investigation by a federal grand jury. His purchase of a new half-million dollar home in the exclusive Dominion neighborhood further angered many of his low-income constituents who questioned if Bustamante had forgotten his roots as a Mexican-American farm worker. Bustamante was subsequently convicted by a federal court of racketeering and accepting an illegal gift. Bonilla, a television executive, struck the perfect anti-incumbent theme in his criticism of "higher taxes and bounced checks" constantly reminding voters that he was the "new guy . . . running for office for the first time" (C.Q. October 10, 1992). Bonilla also benefitted from the recognition of his photogenic wife, Deborah Knapp, a popular anchorwoman in a local television station. In the end, the combination of the negative publicity and the enlarged district enabled Bonilla to defeat Bustamente to become Texas' fourth Hispanic Congressman but the only one who is a Republican.

FLORIDA

If the overall population and Hispanic population increases of California and Texas were impressive, they were surpassed by the State of Florida which saw an overall increase of 32.7 percent from 9.7 million to 12.9 million in the 1980's. The Hispanic population, made up predominantly of Cuban-Americans, increased by 83.4 percent from 858,000 to 1.6 million. Hispanics now constitute 12.2 percent of the state's population. Florida qualified for four additional seats in the U.S. House as a result of its increase, and the Hispanic population understandably sought one or two seats to join the one currently held by Congresswoman Ileana Ros-Lehtinen, the first Hispanic woman in Congress who was elected in 1989 (U.S. Census, 1990).

The Florida situation, however, differed markedly from that faced by Hispanics in other states. The Florida Legislature was confronted by a conflict between Blacks and Hispanics over the number of minority districts created and who should control them. The dilemma baffled even the academic community, as Susan MacManus, professor of government at the University of South Florida, noted in her work, *Reapportionment and Representation in Florida*, "If we go beyond these broad categories and get into these notions of group representation carried out to the limit, it could be very difficult to govern this country" (N.Y. Times, May 30, 1992).

While the rapid growth of Florida's Hispanics merited consideration, Black leaders pointed to the even larger Black population which accounted for 1.8 million residents that made up 13.6% of the population. Yet, Florida Blacks had not been represented in Congress by a Black Congressman since Reconstruction. State Representative James Burke, a Black Democrat from Miami, argued that Blacks had suffered more in the history of Florida than Hispanics and thus merited first consideration. Said Burke: "The question is whether the Hispanic community has been harmed the same way the Black community has . . . There is a priority and if you have only limited resources, you have to look at the community that has the longer hardship and history" (N.Y. Times, May 30, 1992).

Beyond the issue of race, the conflict reflected a traditional partisan dispute between Democrats and Republicans with each party wanting more seats for the minority group that votes for its candidates. Unlike other states where both Blacks and Hispanics are Democrats, in Florida most Hispanics (Cubans) identify with the Republican party, while Blacks still identify with the Democrats. Thus, the racial conflict over redistricting transcended into a partisan conflict with white Democratic legislators supporting Blacks and white Republican legislators supporting Hispanic claims.

Because the legislature was unable to develop an acceptable redistricting plan, a three-judge, U.S. federal district court panel approved a congressional redistricting plan on May 29, 1992 that created three predominantly Black districts and two Hispanic districts. Hispanics, however, were able to capitalize only on the 21st District which covers a fairly compact section of northeast Dade County (Miami) and has an Hispanic population in excess of 70 percent.

Lincoln Diaz-Balart, a Cuban-born lawyer whose family immigrated to the United States in 1960, won the 21st district seat by beating fellow Cuban and State Senator Javier D. Suoto in a bitter Republican primary that was both nasty and personal. Suoto, an anti-Castro resistance fighter, tried to portray Diaz-Balart as having family connections to the Cuban dictator, but the negative campaigning backfired when Diaz-Balart also stressed his opposition to Castro and promised to use his office to continue economic pressure on Castro's regime. Diaz-Balart captured the nomination with 69 percent to Suoto's 31 percent and because the Democrats had not contested the seat in the primary, Diaz-Balart was elected. In addition to his opposition to Cuba, Diaz-Balart is opposed to the North American Free Trade Agreement (NAFTA) because of Mexico's ties to Cuba and the potential competition of Mexican agricultural products to Florida. And while supporting the conservative spending cuts and no new tax-fiscal policies of Republicans, Diaz-Balart may side with Democrats on health, social welfare and migrant worker issues he favored as a state senator (C.Q., Jan. 16, 1992). Diaz-Balart, along with fellow Cuban Ileana Ros-Lehtinen and new Texas Congressman Henry Bonilla, will provide some conservative Republican flavor to the Democratic controlled Congressional Hispanic Caucus (CHC).

ILLINOIS

Just as the prospects for additional Hispanic Congressmen were improving in California, Texas, and Florida due to population increases and the acquisition of new congressional seats, the prospects for a Hispanic Congressman from Illinois paradoxically increased as that state was losing population and two Congressional seats.

Several developments and circumstances contributed to Hispanics achieving their first congressional seat from the Midwest. The first is that while Illinois' population was virtually stagnant, increasing by some 4,000 persons, the Hispanic population was increasing by 42.3 percent from 636,000 to 904,000 (U.S. Census, 1990). Moreover, a considerable part of the increase occurred in the Chicago area where Hispanics increased by about 29 percent and now constitute about one-fifth of the city's population.

Notwithstanding Illinois' loss of two congressional seats, Hispanic leaders in Chicago began to call for a Hispanic district after the 1990 census results were released. By May 1991, Hispanics had formed a Latino coalition known as the Illinois Latino Committee for Fair Redistricting to lobby for the Hispanic seat. The Latino coalition brought together the Midwest-Northeast Voter Registration Project, the Latino Institute and the Mexican-American Legal Defense and Education Fund (MALDEF). However, in March 1991, the prospects appeared to be dashed following a meeting of Illinois' Democratic Congressmen held in Washington, D.C. The Congressmen expressed opposition to a new Hispanic district because, they said, the Hispanic population was spread too thinly across Chicago making the creation of a compact and contiguous district too difficult. A more compelling reason was that no incumbent Democrat appeared willing to retire in order to give way to a Hispanic district. Congressmen Dan Rostenkowski, Frank Annunzio and Sydney Yates were rumored to be considering retirement, but all repeated intentions of seeking re-election in 1992. Nor were Congressmen Rostenkowski (powerful chairman of the House Ways and Means Committee) or Congressman William Lipinski, both harboring large Hispanic enclaves in their districts, willing to step aside or give up their Hispanic constituents to a new district. Rostenkowski's Northwest Chicago district was 42 percent Hispanic while Lipinski's Southwest Chicago district included 37 percent Hispanics (Chicago Tribune, March 30, 1991).

On May 1991, Illinois' Republican Congressmen presented a redistricting plan that would establish one new Hispanic and retain three Black congressional districts. The highly partisan plan would combine the districts of incumbents William Lipinski and Martin Russo into one southwest suburban district and Dan Rostenskowski's and Frank Annunzio's district into a northwest side district, thus forcing the incumbents to run against each other. The GOP plan was embraced by Republicans in the Illinois General Assembly (Chicago Tribune, May 21, 1991).

On May 29, the Latino Coalition unveiled a partial redistricting map that would create a new Hispanic Congressional district while preserving three Black districts in Chicago. The proposed district connected

Puerto Rican precincts from Rostenskowski's northwest side district with Mexican-Americans in Lipinski's and Martin Russo's southwest side districts. The two enclaves would be connected by a sliver along the lakeside district of Black Congresswoman Cardiss Collins. The proposed district would include 325,000 Hispanics, making them 63 percent of the population with 29 percent white and 6 percent Black (Chicago Tribune, May, 30, 1991).

Almost immediately, the Latino coalition map was criticized by both the incumbent Democratic and Black Congressmen. On May 30th, still another redistricting plan was proposed jointly by the leaders of Illinois' General Assembly, Senate President Phillip Rock and House Speaker Michael Madigan. Although their map rejected the Latino coalition map, it did create an alternative Hispano district by combining the two Hispanic enclaves through a corridor that runs through west suburban Oak Park, River Forest and Cicero (Chicago Tribune, June 1, 1991). Not to be outdone, Black leaders organized into a group known as the "Task Force for Redistricting for Maximum Black Political Representation," that offered a counter proposal with an Hispanic district that would connect the Hispanic enclaves through the far western suburbs. The Hispanic district would contain a 61.3 percent Hispanic majority while solidifying all three Chicago Black districts. The Latino coalition immediately rejected the Black Task Force plan and criticized its effort to "maximize the gains of one community at the expense of another" (Chicago Tribune, June 15, 1991). In succeeding days still other redistricting maps were offered by Black Congressmen and the Chicago urban league but they also were rejected by the Latino coalition.

Finally in mid-June, State Senate President Phillip Rock announced that in view of the conflicting interests and proposals, the Democratic majority in the Senate could not agree on a congressional districting plan that satisfied both incumbent Congressmen or Hispanic leaders and were giving up the effort of achieving a plan before the June 30th legislative deadline. The task of redistricting was thus left to a federal district court. The prospects of an Hispanic district seemed jeopardized if done by the court since some experts questioned whether a federal court would uphold an Hispanic district created by the gerrymandering necessary to link the two Hispanic enclaves in the northwest and southwest areas of Chicago. Federal Court guidelines have stressed the need for creating districts that are both "compact and contiguous." Not only were the two Hispanic enclaves separated by geography, but also by ethno-historical differences, with the northwest Latinos (living in Humboldt Park) constituting mainly Puerto Ricans and those of the southwest (living in Pilsen) constituting mainly Mexican-Americans (Chicago Tribune, June

20, 1991). Thus, as one political analyst pointed out, Hispanics in Chicago "do not live together . . . because they are not one community . . . To understate the case, these two groups do not form a community, even if their names and accents may sound alike to the rest of us." This pundit went on to point out that the entire exercise of guaranteeing a seat to an Hispanic Chicagoan "is based on the theory, widely assumed and rarely examined, that citizens can be ably represented only by someone of their own ethnicity. The word for this is segregation [which] has not historically been an advantage to members of a minority group" (Margolis, 1991).

With the redistricting process now shifting to the federal district court, a new minority coalition of Hispanic and Black leaders filed a lawsuit seeking the creation of one Hispanic district (with 64 percent Hispanics) and three Black districts ranging from 64 to 69 percent Black populations.

The impetus for a Hispanic district was further enhanced by a Republican redistricting lawsuit filed in the summer of 1991 and a compromise redistricting map filed by incumbent Democratic Congressmen in August, 1991. The Democratic map pitted six incumbents running against each other in three districts. They included Rep. Rostenkowski who faced Frank Annunzio and House Minority leader Robert Michel who would be opposed by Congressman Thomas Ewing (Chicago Tribune, Aug. 29, 1991).

In late 1991, the federal district court approved the plan drawn by Illinois Republicans which created the one Hispanic seat and retained three Black districts in Chicago. The new district described as "one of the most contrived-and misshapen-minority-majority districts carved in 1992" joins the northwest Puerto Rican community with the Mexican-Americans on the southwest by "a thin looped skein of white, ethnic neighborhoods that stretches west to the Cook-DuPage county line and back again" (C.Q., Jan. 16, 1992). Almost immediately following the release of the new Congressional redistricting map, several candidates announced their candidacy for the 4th Illinois Congressional district which was to be the first Hispanic Congressional district in the Midwest. Since the district was heavily Democratic party-oriented, attention focused on the Democratic primary whose winner would likely be elected. The first to announce was former Alderman Juan Soliz, a Mexican-American lawyer and former teacher who had also served one term in the Illinois House of Representatives. On December 8, 1991, Alderman Luis Gutierrez, a Puerto Rican, announced his candidacy and promised a career as a "commuter" Congressman who would retain close ties to his constituency. Gutierrez, the Chicago City Council's President pro-tempore and a close political ally of Mayor Richard Daley, emerged as the favorite (Chicago Tribune, Dec. 9, 1991). Although several others expressed an interest in the race, they dropped out when Gutierrez received Daley's endorsement and the prospect of gaining most of the district's white votes. The contest quickly evolved into a contest between candidates representing the two competing Hispanic sub-groups—Gutierrez, representing the northwest side Puerto Ricans and Soliz, representing the southwest side Mexican-Americans. Gutierrez, the better financed candidate with $100,000 in campaign funds launched a media blitz that included campaign ads in Spanish language television, radio and newspapers along with direct mailings in both English and Spanish. Soliz' more limited campaign ads were on English language television stations.

On March 5, 1992, a Chicago Tribune Poll showed Gutierrez with a large lead over Soliz among all voters in the district. Gutierrez received 40 percent support to Soliz' 22 percent. The ethnic sub-groups aligned as expected with 50 percent of the Mexican-Americans favoring Soliz and 23 percent backing Gutierrez. Meanwhile 70 percent of the Puerto Ricans supported Gutierrez to 30 percent for Soliz. Although Mexican-Americans outnumber Puerto Ricans in the district by 2 to 1, Gutierrez was favored because of the support he was receiving from non-Hispanics in the district who favored him by 32 percent to 17 percent for Soliz (Chicago Tribune, March 5, 1992). In the March 17, 1992 primary, Gutierrez emerged as the victorious candidate with 60 percent of the vote to Soliz' 40 percent. Although the better financing was a factor, the key to Gutierrez' victory was the endorsement of Mayor Daley and the support of the Cook County Democratic organization which enabled him to win a large share of the non-Hispanic vote.

In the general election, Gutierrez faced another Mexican-American political newcomer, Hildegarde Rodríguez-Schieman, a Republican. Gutierrez received 73 percent to Rodríguez-Schieman's 27 percent (C.Q., Jan. 16, 1992). In addition to making history as the Midwest's first Hispanic Congressman, Gutierrez faced the challenge in his first two years as Congressman of consolidating his support by unifying the Mexican-American and Puerto Rican enclaves into a single "district community."

NEW JERSEY

As in Illinois, Hispanics in New Jersey were able to secure their first seat in Congress even as the state was losing population and one seat in the U.S. House. While New Jersey's overall population showed a decline of

5 percent to 7.7 million in the 1990 census, its Hispanic population was rising by 50.4 percent to 740,000 (U.S. Census, 1990).

In its 1992 session, the New Jersey State Legislature, controlled by the Republican party, enacted a measure to give authority for congressional redistricting to a bipartisan redistricting commission. In March 1992, the commission released its new congressional district map which incorporated the bulk of retired Congressman Frank Guarini's old district into a new 13th district that is 43 percent Hispanic (N.Y. Times, April 8, 1992). In addition to comprising less than a majority in the new "Hispanic" district, Hispanics made up only 22 percent of its registered voters. The gerrymandering of the district is visible in the district which "snakes from the northern tip of North Bergen in Hudson County, covering parts of New Jersey's largest cities, including one-third of Newark and more than half of Jersey City, and reaches to Perth Amboy in Middlesex County" (Nieves, 1992).

The two overriding factors that led to the creation of New Jersey's 13th Congressional district were the tremendous growth of the Hispanic population even as the state was losing population and a seat in Congress and the coincidental retirement of long-time Democratic Congressman Frank J. Guarini. The commission was able to satisfy a new constituency while avoiding the dislocation of an incumbent Congressman. The combination of the two factors also thrust Robert Menendez, a Cuban-American who had been Mayor of Union City and a New Jersey State Senator, into the spotlight as a natural successor to Rep. Guarini and as New Jersey's first Hispanic Congressman. Menendez, the son of Cuban immigrants, was born in New York City but moved with his family to Union City, New Jersey, in his youth. At 19, Menendez organized a civic group that successfully agitated for a public referendum and the attendant publicity enabled him to win election to the Union City Board of Education at the age of 20, the youngest office holder in New Jersey history. After receiving a degree in urban studies and political studies from St. Peter's College in New Jersey, Menendez received a law degree from Rutgers University. In 1986, Menendez was elected Mayor of Union City, despite opposition from entrenched political machine, and in 1987 began service as State Assemblyman. In March 1991, while retaining his position as Mayor of Union City, he was appointed to the New Jersey State Senate, a position he held until his resignation in December, 1992, following election to Congress (Menendez, 1993).

Menendez is not only a Democrat, unusual for a Cuban, but also is a social liberal who advocates a tax and spend policy to stimulate economic growth. Menendez faced Jersey City lawyer, Robert P. Haney, Jr., in the Democratic primary but won easily with 69 percent of the vote.

Although he won in all cities in the district and received votes from all groups, his most overwhelming support came from the predominantly Hispanic communities such as Union City (75.6% Hispanic) where he got 84 percent of the vote and West New York (73.3% Hispanic) where he got 79.9 percent of the vote (Cong. District No. 13, 1992). In the November general election, Menendez faced a host of candidates including Republican Fred J. Theemling who had twice lost to Rep. Guarini. Although Theemling tried to cast Menendez as the insider candidate, Menendez nonetheless won a landslide victory again capturing close to 70 percent of the vote (C.Q., Jan. 16, 1992). Because of his impressive political background and his mainstream liberal Democratic philosophy, Menendez will likely emerge as one of the leading new figures in the Congressional Hispanic Caucus.

NEW YORK

The pattern of Illinois and New Jersey was repeated in the state of New York where the overall state population remained virtually unchanged (a 2.5 percent increase) while the Hispanic population increased by slightly over half a million or 33.4 percent. Hispanics now number 2.2 million or 12.3 percent of the state's population (U.S. Census, 1990). New York lost three seats in Congress due to reapportionment caused by the 1990 census figures, so the prospects for the addition of any Hispanic seats to the one they already had appeared remote. Leaders from the Puerto Rican community, who comprise the bulk of New York's Hispanic community, began to call for an Hispanic district shortly after the release of the 1990 census. The New York state legislature began to wrestle with the congressional redistricting issue in 1991, but after a year of study failed to arrive at a compromise. The main source of division was partisan, resulting from Republican party control of the state senate and Democratic Party control of the state assembly. By April, 1992 when it appeared that the legislature was deadlocked on the issue, the Puerto Rican Legal Defense and Education Fund (PRLDEF) took the initiative by filing a lawsuit in federal district court asking the court to assume jurisdiction over redistricting in view of the legislative deadlock. On April 7, a federal district court panel gave the state legislature a deadline of April 27 to either agree on a new plan or risk losing control of the process to the courts (N.Y. Times, April 8, 1992). Subsequently, three state supreme court referees prompted by a state court lawsuit originated by New York's Democratic Congressmen released a redistricting plan which created two Hispanic districts while preserving most incumbents' districts.

A federal court master, acting in response to the PRLDEF lawsuit, also proposed a redistricting map that created three Hispanic districts. That plan however, was criticized by incumbents and Black leaders who saw it as a threat to Black congressmen.

In June, 1992 when the legislature appeared on the verge of passing the redistricting bill proposed by the state court referee which created two Hispanic districts, the PRLDEF sought a federal court injunction that would invalidate any plan that did not create three Hispanic districts. Nonetheless, the legislature approved its plan on June 9, and Governor Mario Cuomo, although urging the U.S. Justice Department to add a third Hispanic district when it reviewed the plan, signed the measure (C.Q., June 13, 1992). In July, the U.S. Justice Department approved the redistricting plan indicating that its review found that "the redistricting legislation was neither designed to discriminate against minority voters nor does it have a retrogressive effect on their voting rights" (Washington Post, July 4, 1992). Of the two Hispanic majority districts, one from the South Bronx was tailored to favor the incumbent Democrat, José Serrano, the only Puerto Rican in Congress, who was elected in 1990. Serrano ran for re-election and was elected in 1992.

The second Hispanic majority district, the 12th, incorporates various Latino enclaves within its boundaries which run from Manhattan's lower East Side to a portion of Southwest Brooklyn, snaking along New York Bay, to north-central Brooklyn and including some Latino neighborhoods in Queens. Included are the neighborhoods of Williamsburg, Bushwick, Sunset Park, East New York, Corona, Elmhurst and Jackson Heights. Hispanics make up 58 percent of the population but only 49 percent of its registered voters. Democrats outnumber Republicans by 3 to 1 (C.Q., Jan. 16, 1992).

Several prominent Puerto Ricans entered the race including Ruben Franco, President and General Counsel for PRLDEF, Elizabeth Colon, the former executive director of the Association of Puerto Rican Executive Directors; Rafael Mondez, an assistant professor of psychology and organizer of the New Alliance Party; Eric R. Melendez, an engineer from Queens and Nydia M. Velazquez, a former New York City councilwoman and secretary of Puerto Rico's Department of Puerto Rican Community Affairs in the United States. However, an unexpected development quickly threatened the prospects for an Hispanic. Long time incumbent, Congressman Stephen J. Solarz (who had served nine terms in Congress) announced on July 8 that he would seek election from the 12th district. Solarz, whose Brooklyn district (which had been predominantly Jewish) was carved into six pieces, had considered running against fellow incumbent, Ted Weiss in the eighth district but decided against it when polls indicated that Weiss would win. Solarz entered the race with several advantages. In addition to his name recognition as an influential congressman, he had accumulated a $2 million "rainy day" campaign war chest. In addition, the four Hispanics in the race posed a possible splintering of the Hispanic vote (N.Y. Times, July 9, 1992). Solarz also carried negative baggage as one of the congressmen tarnished by the House Banking scandal. Solarz was one of the most heavy abusers of the overcharge privilege, having written 743 bad checks. Rather than focusing on the issues relevant to a poor Hispanic constituency, the Democratic Primary campaign evolved into a debate over whether a minority group can best be represented by one of their own ethnicity or by someone from a different ethnic group, in this case a well-heeled white incumbent with a large campaign fund. Some Hispanic leaders such as Bronx Borough President, Fernando Ferrer and Angelo Falcon, President of the Institute of Puerto Rican Policy, along with the candidates, denounced Solarz' candidacy and considered ways to focus support on one Hispanic candidate. However, neither of the four Hispanics was willing to withdraw from the race. In response, Solarz argued that the Voting Rights Act was designed to empower people to vote for representatives of their own choice and not to create a "form of apartheid . . . to transform Congress into the Lebanese Parliament, where different seats are set aside for different nationalities" (Washington Post, Aug. 21, 1992). Solarz insisted that the voters of the district should decide who could best serve their needs and that with his seniority and experience in Congress, he was more qualified than any of the other candidates in the race to represent the district.

To help carry the campaign to his adoptive constituents, Solarz hired two prominent Hispanics. Mickey Ponce, a Puerto Rican political expert, was hired as director of field operations and Rudy Garcia, metropolitan editor of Noticias del Mundo, a popular Spanish newspaper, was hired as press secretary and consultant on political advertisements. Soon the well-financed Solarz campaign featured Spanish-language television and radio commercials along with a direct-mail campaign targeting voters by age, ethnicity and occupation. Solarz himself learned a few Spanish phrases, delivered in his own heavy accent, to affirm his appeal to Hispanics (N.Y. Times, Aug. 21, 1992). Following their inability to convince each other to back out of the race, the Hispanic candidates resorted to "sniping" at each other by questioning the other's motives for running and feverishly trying to secure endorsements from organizations and influentials.

Among the five Hispanics, Nydia Velazquez was most successful in securing key endorsements from New York Mayor David Dinkins, the

Rev. Jesse Jackson, Ruth Messinger, Manhattan Borough President, and Dennis Rivera, President of the Local 1199 of the Drug, Hospital and Health Worker's Union. With those endorsements, Velazquez was able to build a coalition of Hispanic and Black voters that gave her 33 percent of the vote to Solarz's 27 percent and Ms. Colon's 26 percent in the September, 1992 primary. The remaining candidates had 14 percent between them (N.Y. Times, Sept. 16, 1992).

Following her primary victory, Velazquez went on to defeat Republican Angel Diaz with 77 percent of the vote in the November, 1992 General Election. Nydia Velazquez thus became the first Puerto Rican woman and the second Hispanic woman (following Ileana Ros-Lehtinen) elected to the U.S. Congress. Velazquez, born in Yabucoa, Puerto Rico, on March 28, 1953, to a sugar cane worker and his wife, was one of nine children. She received a B.A. from the University of Puerto Rico (Rio Piedras) and a Masters in Political Science from New York University. In 1984, Velazquez was appointed to the New York City Council and served until 1986 when she was appointed to serve the Commonwealth of Puerto Rico in the United States as National Director of the Migration Division and later as Head of Community Affairs for Puerto Ricans living in the United States. It was in the latter position that Velazquez became an activist leader of New York's Puerto Rican community and a close political ally of Mayor Dinkins and labor leader Rivera. Velasquez' greatest challenge will be to demonstrate that a Puerto Rican, born and educated in Puerto Rico and an officer in that government, can adapt her talents to represent the needs of her New York Puerto Rican constituency.

THE CONGRESSIONAL HISPANIC CAUCUS: PROSPECTS FOR THE 1990'S

In 1787, Anti-Federalist Robert Yates said that "the term representative, implies that the person or body chosen for this purpose should resemble those who appoint them" and also that "for an assembly to be a true likeness of the people of any country, they must be considerably numerous" (Yates, 1967). Yates pointed out that the United States, albeit young at the time, was made up of a number of different classes of people and that to have proper representation of them, all groups should have the opportunity of choosing their best informed to represent them. John Adams echoed those sentiments when he said that a representative legislature "should be an exact portrait, in miniature, of the people at large" (Adams, 1967). Whether Adams' and Yates' views can be seen as a reflection of the founding fathers' perception of the ideal "representative" or of the basis of representation in American constitutionalism, they do show that the founders appreciated the value of diversity among representatives in a legislative body.

If the U.S. Congress of today, were an "exact portrait, in miniature of the people at large" as Adam's conceived, there would be 30 Hispanics in the U.S. House of Representatives and 7 in the U.S. Senate. Obviously these numbers are not present.

The 103rd Congress welcomed the largest class of Hispanic congresspersons in history. Eight new Hispanic members entered the U.S. House of Representatives and their overall number increased from ten to seventeen. Counting the two non-voting members from Puerto Rico (Carlos Romero-Barcelo) and the Virgin Islands (Ron de Lugo), the Hispanics will number 19 in the House, the largest delegation of Hispanics ever. Nevertheless, Hispanics who constitute nine percent of the United States population are still underrepresented in the U.S. House with 4.4 percent of the membership. Hispanics have not been represented in the U.S. Senate since the defeat of Senator Joseph M. Montoya in 1976 (C.Q., Jan. 2, 1993).

Consequently, Hispanics can look at their numbers in Congress with some satisfaction and some disappointment. Indeed, the increasing numbers of Hispanics is encouraging but that the numbers are not greater and still far short of equitable representation has to be a disappointment.

It is somewhat difficult to evaluate the implications of the increased numbers of Hispanics in Congress for Hispanics as a whole because increased numbers alone do not always translate into greater power. It is also difficult to measure the benefit derived by the Hispanic group from the power and influence of one of their number because a congressperson represents a district constituency that may include Hispanics as well as other groups. Nor is it always possible to clearly identify issues and positions that are favorable to an ethnic group. What may be viewed as a benefit to one segment of the Hispanic community such as Mexican-Americans, may be seen as a detriment to another segment, such as the Cuban community. Consequently, any effort to measure the impact of change in representation of Hispanics in Congress is largely speculation. Having considered the pitfalls of such analysis, one may conjecture some observations about the prospects for Hispanics in the 1990's.

The increased number of Hispanics will undoubtedly enhance both the collective power of Hispanics operating as a group and the individual power of members resulting from their position in the House arena. To date, probably the greatest impact of Hispanic Congresspersons has been on an individual basis. The influence of the late U.S. Senator Dennis

Chavez (D./N.M.) over public works projects was legendary. In more recent times, Congressman E. "Kika" de la Garza (D./Tex.) and Henry Gonzales (D./Tx.) have wielded great power and influence as Chairs of the House Agriculture and House Banking, Finance and Urban Affairs Committee respectively. Both of these most senior Hispanic Congressmen retain their positions in the 103rd Congress. Three Hispanics now serve on the powerful House Appropriations Committee: Esteban Torres (D. Calif.), Ed Pastor (D. Az.) and José Serrano (D.N.Y.). Congressman Bill Richardson became the first Hispanic to serve in the House leadership heirarchy when he was selected as one of four chief deputy whips for the Democrats in the House.

The collective power of Hispanics in the House of Representatives has been channelled through the Congressional Hispanic Caucus and there is reason to expect that group will be more influential. In recent years, the Hispanic Caucus has been able to pass some legislation of concern to Hispanics and to influence others. The creation of the Cabinet Committee on Opportunities for the Spanish Speaking, the Hispanic Access to Higher Education Act intended to boost Hispanic enrollment in college, and the Birth Defects Registry Act, designed to track children with birth defects, were enacted as a result of the impetus of the caucus. And while the caucus was not able to prevent passage of the Immigration Reform and Control Act (IRCA), it was able to secure amnesty provisions and anti-discriminatory clauses contained in it.

The increased numbers will make the caucus "more visible and [it] will have a louder voice" as new member Frank Tejeda pointed out (C.Q., Jan. 2, 1993). Certainly the diversification of the caucus (both geographically and by cultural group) with new members from Illinois (Gutierrez) and New Jersey (Menendez) along with recent additions from Florida (Ros-Lehtinen) and Arizona (Pastor) as well as the new members from California, Texas, Florida and New York, will provide a greater ideological and regional mix that will more accurately reflect the diversity of America's Hispanic population. Until 1990, most Hispanics in Congress were Mexican-Americans from the Southwest. Today, they include Mexican-Americans from the Southwest and Midwest, Puerto Ricans from New York and Cubans from Florida and New Jersey.

The ideological and partisan division of the caucus will continue to be evident, with the Republicans from Florida (Ros-Lehtinen and Diaz-Balart) and Texas (Bonilla) more clearly juxtaposed to the remaining caucus members who are liberal to moderate Democrats. And, not all Hispanic Congressmen are members of the caucus. Henry Gonzales from Texas and Matthew "Marty" Martinez continue to boycott the caucus in the 103rd Congress.

Historically, the greatest difficulty of the caucus has been that its
members have pursued their own individual agendas whether based on
constituency interests, personal goals, ideological or other interests,
rather than pursuing a common agenda on Hispanic concerns. This will
probably continue to be an obstacle to unity along with natural differences that will emerge over specific issues.

Already, some issues such as the North American Free Trade Agreement (NAFTA), a Cuban trade embargo, Puerto Rican statehood and
Immigration Reform have created visible differences of opinion among
caucus members. Notwithstanding those partisan and ideological differences, the caucus members appear willing to engage in a common effort to seek consensus. As Solomon Ortiz (D. Texas) said, "There will be
some issues that divide us, but there are more issues like education, housing and jobs that unite us." The new Chairman of the caucus, José Serrano from New York, although a liberal Democrat, has promised to
"lead the caucus by consensus . . . on very emotional issues that we disagree on, we just won't go into them in the caucus" (C.Q., Jan. 2, 1993).

Serrano appears determined to make the position of caucus chair a
more activist one than has been the case before when caucus chairmen
regarded the position as a temporary/honorary one. Serrano has met several times with President Clinton and First Lady Hillary Rodham Clinton to discuss Hispanic concerns and health care reform. He also arranged caucus meetings with cabinet officers. Serrano has also worked
with Rep. Kweisi Mfume (D. Md.), Chairman of the Congressional
Black Caucus (CBC) to forge an alliance between the two minority caucuses and thus enhance possible future coalitions on civil rights or other
issues (Mulligan, 1993).

On July 22, 1993, President Clinton invited the dozen Democratic members of the caucus to the White House to discuss the proposed
budget and matters of mutual concern. The Democrats pledged continued support for the President's budget proposal in return for his support
of their agenda. Among critical items in the House version of the budget
bill, the members listed funding for empowerment zones in major cities,
earned income tax credits for the working poor, no automatic caps on
entitlements programs without a review and increased Medicare pay-
ments in Puerto Rico. They also expressed support for a Senate provision
that provides tax incentives for businesses operating in Puerto Rico. Caucus Chair Serrano also pointed out to the President some discriminatory
amendments added to the budget and other pending legislation such as
one amendment that cuts off federal funding to any agency that assists
undocumented workers. Although there was some disappointment that
Republican members of the caucus were excluded from the meeting, the

overall consensus was that the White House meeting which lasted 45 minutes was a historic precedent that reflected the growing collective influence of the Hispanic caucus (Gonzales, 1993).

In October 1993, the Caucus demonstrated its potential influence when they united in opposition to a provision in the $1 billion unemployment compensation bill which would partly finance the jobless benefits by cutting welfare payments to elderly immigrants. The threatened opposition by the Caucus caused the Democratic House leadership to search for an alternate method to finance the jobs bill (Albuquerque Journal, Oct. 3, 1993).

CONCLUSION

To politicians and journalists, ever focused on the present, the changes wrought by the 1990 census, the redistricting process and the 1992 elections may well suggest the long-awaited "awakening" of Hispanic political power in American politics. The political scientist, however, must take the longer view, evaluating the developments of the 1990's in the context of the past and reflect on its future implications. In retrospect, some of the developments reflect a repetition of past occurrences while others reflect new trends. In either case, several important conclusions can be drawn from the cases and events discussed in this paper.

First of all this study has demonstrated that Hispanics gained a substantial number of new seats in Congress. The seven new seats represent the largest single gain ever, bringing the number of Hispanic congresspersons to seventeen which is the greatest number ever. However, notwithstanding the gains and numbers, the advances were not as great as they could have been or should have been. Hispanics, it was shown, lost one and possibly two seats due to the census undercount, they lost potential seats in the redistricting process in the various states and they lost one seat (in Houston, Texas) in the 1992 elections.

It is also evident that the advances in number of Hispanics in Congress are primarily attributable to American legal processes (laws and court decisions/interpretations) rather than to the activism of the Hispanic community itself. The combined effect of the 1965 Voting Rights Act (and particularly the 1975 and 1982 Amendments) have established legal standards regarding redistricting and minority representation that have opened unprecedented opportunities for Hispanics and other minorities. Equally important have been federal court decisions in cases such as *Thornburg vs. Gingles* whose interpretations have fostered affirmative action in the creation of minority-majority districts. The vigilance of the U.S. Department of Justice and its strict adherence to the principles laid down in the Voting Rights Act has also been important. The significant increase in the Hispanic population in all the states cited in the study combined with the statutory guidelines and legal monitoring have forced states to create Hispanic districts.

While activism from Hispanic groups has not been the main impetus for change, it has been shown to contribute to the states' incentive to comply with federal legal guidelines. Hispanic activism, whether channeled through individual organizations such as MALDEF, PRLDEF, SWVREP or Latino Coalitions such as those which formed in Texas, Florida, Illinois and New York, were important forces in lobbying for the creation of Hispanic congressional districts. The litigation strategy as used in Illinois and New York along with media attention generated by Hispanic organizations generated pressure on the states to comply with federal rules.

The Hispanic community, it was shown, will usually close ranks to support a Hispanic candidate when a clear opportunity presents itself in a race between an Hispanic and non-Hispanic candidate. However, this is not always the case, and several Hispanic candidates can sometimes split the vote and enhance the prospects for a non-Hispanic as was the case in New York and Texas. In some cases, the Hispanic community is not fully organized or mobilized to take advantage of its position even if a Hispanic district is created. In several cases it was shown that the Hispanic population made up a substantial majority of a congressional district only to decline considerably in the proportion (to a slight majority or even a minority) of the registered voters. In Houston, Texas, the failure of the Hispanic community to register and vote for Ban Reyes enabled Gene Green to win the Hispanic district.

In their effort to secure greater representation, Hispanics are finding themselves in competition with African-Americans who are also seeking improvement or trying to retain past gains. In Illinois, Florida and New York, Hispanic efforts to secure a district were viewed as either challenging to or conflicting with Black districts. As demonstrated in Illinois, both groups are better served if they are able to cooperate rather than engage in an adversarial position. The Illinois case also presents a unique situation where two Hispanic sub-groups, Mexican-Americans and Puerto-Rican-Americans were combined into one district. Each group predictably supported their own candidate in the primary and joined ranks in the general election.

Finally, the Hispanic Congressional delegation is today a microcosm, a reflection of the diversity of the Hispanic people of the United States. Mexican Americans, Cubans and Puerto Ricans from different parts of the country and reflecting different partisan and ideological orientations are represented by the Hispanics in Congress. It is unlikely that all the members of the Hispanic caucus will achieve consensus on all or even the most important issues to Hispanics. It is more likely that the different personalities, partisanship and political ideologies, constituency interests and personal agendas of the individual members, will undermine the unity of the Hispanic caucus. However, the extent to which the individual members can rise above these differences and come together, on the basis of common cultural, linguistic and surname characteristics, will determine the collective future of Hispanics in American politics.

References

Adams, John, "Letter to John Penn," quoted in Hannah Pitkin, *The Concept of Representation* (Berkeley: University of California Press, 1967), p. 60.

"A Black-Hispanic Struggle Over Florida Redistricting." *The New York Times* (May 30, 1992), G:1.

"Black activists downplay rift with the Hispanics over remap plan." *Chicago Tribune*, (June 15, 1991), 2,4:1.

"Census Revisions Would Widen Political Gains of 3 Big States." *New York Times* (June 14, 1991).

"Congressional District # 13, New Jersey Election Results," 1992 and "The 13th Congressional District of New Jersey, Demographics," 1992. "Congressman Bob Menendez: A Short Biography." Information sheet provided by the Congressman's office, Washington, D.C., 1993.

"Court will get remap Rock says." *Chicago Tribune*, (June 20, 1991), 1,1:6. Also "Hispanic district becomes longer shot." *Chicago Tribune.* (June 23, 1991), 4,4:4.

"Democrat map sets up incumbent battles." *Chicago Tribune* (August 29, 1991), 2C, 2:3.

González, Christian and Patricia Guadalupe. "Clinton Courts Hispanic Caucus on Budget." *Albuquerque Journal* (August 4, 1993).

"GOP Dreams of a Comeback Via the New Map Dissolve." *Congressional Quarterly* (November 7, 1992), 3580.

"GOP Has Hope for New Plan." *Chicago Tribune* (May 21, 1991), 2C1:5.

"Green Squeaks by Reyes, This Time for Good." *Congressional Quarterly* (August 1, 1992), 2297.

"Gutierrez builds big lead thanks to non-Hispanics." *Chicago Tribune* (March 5, 1992), 1,1:4.

"Gutierrez vows to be 'commuter' congressman in Hispanic district." *Chicago Tribune* (December 9, 1991), 2C, 3.

"Hispanic Caucus wields new clout." *Albuquerque Journal* (October 3, 1993).

"Hispanic district alternative urged." *Chicago Tribune* (June 1, 1991), 1,5:5.

"Hispanic district plan hits roadblock." *Chicago Tribune* (March 30, 1991), 1:4.

"Hispanics Gain Members, Power." *Congressional Quarterly.* (January 2, 1993), 7.

"Hispanics Gain Members, Power." *Congressional Quarterly and Weekly Report* (51, No. 1, January 2, 1993), 7.

"Hispanic Map Plan Hard on Incumbents." *Chicago Tribune* (May 30, 1991), 2C6:3.

Huckabee, David C. "Congressional Districts: New Rules Produce Odd Shapes." *CRS Review:* Washington, D.C., Congressional Research Service (June-July, 1992), 16–19.

"Latino Redistricting Gains Big in U.S. Congress and State Assembly." *Southwest Voter Research Notes* (Vol. 6, No. 4, December, 1992), 6.

Margolis, Jon. "Gerrymander, meet dumbbell and the street-eating ooze." *Chicago Tribune* (June 25, 1991), 1,19:1.

"Menendez to seek Congressional Seat." *New York Times* (April 8, 1992), B 4:3.

Milligan, Susan. "The View From the Top." *Albuquerque Journal* (July 4, 1993), B–1. "Minority coalition calls for veto of redistricting bills." *Austin American Statesman* (June 14, 1991).

"New Members, New Districts;" *Congressional Quarterly.* (50, No. 14 November 7, 1992), 52.

"New York Districting Plan Approved." *Washington Post* (July 4, 1992), A 9:1.

"New York Legislators Pass New Map, But It Faces Legal Challenges." *Congressional Quarterly* (June 13, 1992), 1733.

Nieves, Evelyn. "A New House District Could Make History." *New York Times* (October 28, 1992).

"Race and Hispanic Origin." *1990 U.S. Census Profile* (No. 2, June, 1991), 4–5.

"Replacing Roybal: Key race for Latinos." *Los Angeles Times* (May 28, 1992), B1:2.

"Ruling Gives Deadline to Albany for Redrawing Districts." *New York Times* (April 8, 1992), B,5:1.

Russell, Joel. "The Political Event of the Decade." *Hispanic Business* (May, 1991), 40.

"Rep. Solarz Loses in a New District." *New York Times* (September 16, 1992), A–1:5.

"Solarz's Toughest Fight." *The Washington Post* (August 2, 1992), C:7.

"Solarz Will Run in District Tailored as Hispanic Seat." *New York Times* (July 9, 1992), B,3:1.

"State Redistricting plans ruled unconstitutional." *San Antonio Express-News* (August 23, 1991).

"Suits hit plans to redistrict." *San Antonio Light* (June, 18, 1991).

Suro, Robert. "Hispanic Politicians Seek a Recipe for Raw Numbers." *New York Times* (April 12, 1992), IV, 5:1.

Tabor, Mary B. W. "Loyalty and Labor: Nydia Marganta Velazquez." *New York Times* (September 17, 1992), B–6.

"The New Class: More Diverse, Less Lawyerly, Younger." *Congressional Quarterly and Weekly Report* (November 7, 1992), 7.

"The New Congress." *Congressional Quarterly* (January 16, 1992), 52.

" 'The New Guy' Trying to End Bustamante's Reign in 23rd." *Congressional Quarterly* (October 10, 1992), 3198.

"The Selling of Stephen Solarz." *The New York Times* (August 21, 1992), B–2:1.

"U.S. Won't Revise 1990 Census, Says Chief of Commerce." *New York Times* (July 16, 1991).

Vigil, Maurilio E. "Hispanics Gain Seats in the 98th Congress After Reapportionment." *International Social Science Review,* 59, No. 1 (Winter, 1984).

Yates, Robert. "Essays of 'Brutus' to the Citizens of the State of New York." (November 29, 1987), in Michael Kammen, *The Origins of The American Constitution.* New York: Viking Penguin, 1986, 322–324.

10. Latinos and Substantive Representation in the U.S. House of Representatives: Direct, Indirect, or Nonexistent?

Rodney E. Hero and Caroline J. Tolbert

REPRESENTATION, A CENTRAL ISSUE IN U.S. politics and governance, is a complex concept, having several dimensions.[1] How well individuals and groups are represented in governmental institutions, including legislative bodies, warrants attention in any case but may be especially important in regard to those historically underrepresented. Latinos, one of the fastest growing populations in the United States, comprise about 8% of the entire U.S. population and about a quarter of the population of such large states as California and Texas.[2] Yet, little attention has been given to representation or to other significant normative questions concerning Latinos in U.S. political science research (cf. Hero 1992, Meier and Stewart 1991). The dearth of research on Latinos extends to research on national institutions, such as Congress. Latino representation in Congress, particularly substantive representation is examined here.

Descriptive, or sociological, representation means essentially the "ability of groups to elect representatives with similar traits" (Welch and Hibbing [1984] 1988)—in the present case, being able to elect representatives of Latino background. Research consistently indicates a low degree of Latino descriptive representation at various levels and in various institutions of U.S. government (even controlling for non-citizenship;

Hero, Rodney E. and Caroline J. Tolbert. "Latinos and Substantive Representation in the U.S. House of Representatives: Direct, Indirect, or Non-Existent?" *American Journal of Political Science*, volume 39 (August, 1995): 640–652. Reprinted by permission of The University of Wisconsin Press.

see, e.g., Welch 1990, Meier and Stewart 1991, Browning, Marshall, and Tabb 1984, Hem 1992). Substantive representation means having a "representative with congruent policy views acting as an advocate" (cf. Welch and Hibbing 1988, 291–292). As with descriptive representation, research indicates little substantive representation of Latinos (cf. Browning, Marshall and Tabb 1984, Welch and Hibbing 1988, Meier and Stewart 1991).

The central focus of this paper is voting in the U.S. House of Representatives on issues defined as salient to Latinos. The analysis builds on earlier work on Latino representation in Congress (Welch and Hibbing 1988), yet goes beyond that work in several important respects. Welch and Hibbing studied the 93rd through 96th Congresses (1972–1980), using the conservative coalition score as the measure of substantive representation. The use of conservative coalition scores was based on their expectation that, with some exceptions, Latinos on the whole would "be more liberal than Anglos, more likely to favor government intervention in the marketplace and in protecting individual rights" (Welch and Hibbing 1988, 292; cf., however, Dyer and Vedlitz 1986; de la Garza et al. 1992, 84).

In this examination of substantive representation, the major dependent variable is how members of Congress voted "on issues of concern to Latino leaders," in the 100th Congress as determined by the Southwest Voter Research Institute, Inc. (SWVRI 1989). The SWVRI is a non-profit, nonpartisan organization that undertakes analyses regarding the interests of Mexican Americans/Latinos. The SWVRI scores represent "the extent to which votes [by Members of Congress] coincide with Hispanic state legislators' views on the issues" (SWVRI 1989).[3]

The SWVRI score addresses most of the concerns raised by Welch and Hibbing (1988, 294) regarding measures of Latino interests. The SWVRI scores are based on a *number* of votes ($n = 15$), and an *array* of issues,[4] including domestic social service measures (e.g., Housing, the Homeless, Civil Rights, Legal Services) and foreign policy questions seen as especially important to the Latino population (cf. Welch and Hibbing 1988, 294, 297; see Appendix).[5]

ANALYSIS

In addressing substantive representation of Latinos in the House during the 100th Congress (1987–88), two major questions are examined: (A) whether Representatives who are of Latino origin have distinctive patterns of roll-call voting, and (B) whether larger Latino populations (constituencies) have an effect on the voting behavior of their representatives (regardless of representatives' own ethnic backgrounds).[6] Other variables that might have an impact were also included: percent urban population in the district (*Congressional Districts in the 1980s*), percent black population in the district (*Almanac of American Politics 1990*), per capita income in the district (Cavanagh 1984), and representatives' party affiliation (cf. Welch and Hibbing 1988, 293–94).[7]

The Representatives included in the initial stages of the analysis are, in line with previous research, those whose districts have at least 5% Hispanic population (*n* = 115; cf. Welch and Hibbing 1988) and who had participated in at least 11 of the 15 votes selected by the SWVRI.[8] The mean SWVRI score for representatives from these 114 districts is 67.2 (ranging from 0 to 100; standard deviation = 41.2). Table 1 presents specific findings.

A. The Voting Patterns of Latino Representatives

Table 1 (Model 1A) shows that Latino representatives score 10 points higher on the SWVRI measure than non-Latinos. This level of difference is fairly close to Welch and Hibbing's finding that Hispanic representatives have "voting records . . . nearly 13 points [on a scale of 0 to 100] less conservative [or more liberal] than a non-Hispanic representative." In the Welch and Hibbing study (1988, 295), Hispanic representatives' scores were different from non-Hispanics at statistically significant levels; here they are not.

Welch and Hibbing also examined patterns within regions and found that Hispanic representatives from the southwest (Arizona, California, Colorado, New Mexico, and Texas) had conservative coalition scores 23 points less conservative (more liberal) than their non-Latino counterparts. Our study found that Latino representatives in the southwest differed from non-Latinos on the SWVRI score by only about 6.5 points in the 100th Congress (results not shown). This difference is, then, substantially less in 1987–88 than it had been during the 1970s.[9]

B. Latino Constituencies and Voting Patterns

Perhaps the small difference between Hispanic and Anglo members of Congress results because Anglo Representatives are also responsive to

TABLE 1

Impact of Hispanic US House Representative (Model 1A) and Percent Hispanic in Congressional District (Model 1B) on SWVRI Voter Score[a]

	MODEL 1A	MODEL 1B
Hispanic Representative	10.01	9.88
	(5.97)	(8.09)
Percent Hispanic in congressional district	—	0.01
		(0.19)
Percent urban	0.42***	0.04***
	(0.01)	(0.01)
Percent black	0.11	0.11
	(0.13)	(0.13)
Per capita income	0.07	0.07
	(0.08)	(0.09)
Political party	73.43***	73.42***
	(3.71)	(3.74)
(Constant)	−28.42**	−28.51**
	(10.89)	(11.55)
Adjusted R^2	.85	.85
Standard error	16.09	16.16
N =	114	114
F =	127.03***	104.88***

Note: Correlation diagnostics indicate no problems of multicollinearity. Pearson (*r*) correlation between percent Latino and party identification is .28; between percent Latino and percent urban is .06; and between percent Latino and per capita income is −.52. The correlation between percent urban and per capita income is .20; and between percent urban and party identification is .34. The correlation between per capita income and percent Democratic vote is −.38.
Entries are regression coefficients, standard errors in parenthesis.
* = .05 probability; ** = .01 probability; *** = .001 probability.

Hispanic constituents. Model 1B shows the impact of the percent Hispanic population in the district on Representatives' voting patterns (cf. Welch and Hibbing 1988, 295–296). Percent Hispanic in the district has no independent impact on SWVRI voter scores. The representatives' political party affiliation (coded Republican = 0, Democrat = 1) is clearly the most important variable in the analysis; percent urban in the district has a significant impact as well. These findings for districts with 5% or more Hispanics contrast with those of Welch and Hibbing, who found a weak (but statistically significant) relationship between percent Hispanic constituency and conservative coalition scores.

When only the southwest districts were analyzed, percent Hispanic among constituents again has no independent impact (results not shown). That is, patterns within regions concerning Hispanic substantive representation are similar to those for the nation as a whole. Again, this finding is somewhat different from that of Welch and Hibbing (cf. 1988, 295–97).

The evidence thus far suggests little or no Latino substantive representation in the 100th Congress. In contrast, Welch and Hibbing (1988, 297) claim that "in the U.S. House, Hispanics do not lack influence; they just lack the influence their numbers warrant." Almost a decade later, our evidence suggests a continued lack of substantive representation for Latinos.

While both this and the earlier study find weak to virtually nonexistent substantive representation, there are some differences in the findings. What might account for the differences? The different dependent variables used do not explain this because, as noted earlier, when the conservative coalition score is substituted for the SWVRI score, the findings remain essentially unchanged. Several possible explanations that are not mutually exclusive for the differences can be offered.

One explanation is that representatives' voting patterns were, simply, different in the 1970s than in 1987–88. There was, in fact, substantially greater partisan polarization in Congressional voting during the 1980s than the 1970s (Stone, Rapoport and Abramowitz 1990). This polarization may have led to greater support among Democrats, and less among Republicans, for policies salient to groups such as Latinos. Hence, what was partly explained in the 1970s by a factor such as "percentage Hispanic in the district," may have been subsumed by party affiliation during the 1980s; this is developed further below. Another, perhaps related, point is that the 100th Congress also differed from the congresses of the 1970s due to the 1980 reapportionment. The distribution of Latinos within House districts may have been altered in such a way and to an extent that produced different roll-call voting patterns.

Yet another explanation for the different findings may lie in an assumption, and related data aggregation, of the Welch and Hibbing study. Welch and Hibbing contend that "since members of Congress build distinct voting records in every Congress, we have treated each representative's record in each of these two-year periods as a unique case. Thus the total possible N for the project was 1,740 (4 [Congresses, 1972–80] X 435), even though the total number of individuals serving during these eight years was much lower" (1988, 298). Treating each representative's record in each two-year period as a unique case may not be entirely appropriate. One would expect a strong correlation between a Representative's voting pattern from one Congress to the next. What may have happened, then, is that due to the large number of cases, the relationships (and their statistical significance) reported by Welch and Hibbing were somewhat inflated by their assumption of uniqueness.

While Table 1 and related evidence provide virtually no indication of substantive representation for Latinos in the 100th Congress, other evidence confounds that. Specifically, the *outcome* of *every one* of the 15 votes used to calculate the SWVRI scores was congruent with the preferences of the Latino state legislators questioned by SWVRI. Thus, although the percentage of Latinos among constituents is not significantly related to higher SWVRI scores, all the votes included in the SWVRI scores were decided in the "preferred" direction. The implications of this deserve consideration.

INDIRECT SUBSTANTIVE REPRESENTATION?

Scholars contend that substantive representation may take different forms (Weissberg 1978). Representation can be "dyadic" (or "direct"), where the question is whether a direct link exists between the voting patterns of elected representatives and their constituents/interests. Dyadic representation has been the focus of the present study, to this point, and was likewise the focus for Welch and Hibbing. On the other hand, substantive representation may be "collective" or "institutional" or "virtual"; that is, legislatures may *collectively* represent the people "*as a whole*" (Weissberg 1978). This can also be viewed as indirect substantive representation.

A variation of collective representation is Hurley's (1989) concept of partisan representation that focuses "on how well the parties in Congress represent their rank-and-file identifiers." Hurley claims that individual legislators "may not be able to represent accurately the opinions of a district that is heterogeneous but the parties in Congress can and may respond to the distribution of opinion among their identifiers in the electorate. In this way district minorities receive representation. A Democrat living in a district represented by a Republican may find himself or herself at frequent odds with the district's own representative, but may have his or her view taken by the *majority* of Democrats in the *institution*" (Hurley 1989, 242, emphasis added).

Weissberg's and Hurley's arguments suggest, then, that substantive representation may occur in a collective or indirect partisan form, although it may not be directly predictable based on district characteristics, such as proportion of Latinos. While the concepts of collective

TABLE 2

*Impact of Percent Hispanic in Congressional District
on Vote for Democratic Congressional Candidate*

	All Districts	Districts with 5% plus Hispanic Population
Percent Hispanic in congressional district	0.18 (0.14)	0.45** (0.18)
Percent urban	0.26*** (0.08)	0.33* (0.17)
Percent black	0.40*** (0.10)	0.53** (0.17)
Per capita income	−0.36*** (0.08)	−0.16 (0.11)
(Constant)	69.37*** (6.34)	35.16** (14.84)
Adjusted R^2	.20	.31
Standard error	23.85	20.95
$N =$	424	114
$F =$	25.92***	13.88***

Entries are regression coefficients, standard errors in parenthesis.
* = .05 probability; ** = .01 probability; *** = .0001 probability.

and/or partisan representation cannot be tested here, those ideas do suggest that a focus on the institution "as a whole" is useful. Therefore, the previous analysis was extended to *all* House districts.

Data for the extended analysis indicate that House members who are themselves Hispanic have SWVRI scores about 10 points (9.59) higher than the overall average. Hispanic representatives within the southwestern states differ by almost 9 points from all other southwestern House members, controlling for other variables. The extended analysis does not alter findings reported in Model 1A of Table 1.

Model 1B was also extended to examine the relationship between percent Hispanic population and SWVRI scores for all House districts. When all districts are included, the percent Hispanic population in the district continues to have no measurable impact on Representatives' voter score. This provides additional evidence of limited to nonexistent indirect Hispanic representation. Party affiliation of the representative remains the most important variable. Other analysis (not shown) indicates that non-Latino House members from the southwest and from Florida have SWVRI scores 16 points *lower* than the overall average, while those from New York and New Jersey have scores almost 15 points *higher* than the general average (cf. Welch and Hibbing 1988, 296).

A final point worthy of consideration is raised by the concept of "partisan" (collective) substantive representation as well as by the consistent finding that party is the strongest predictor of SWVRI scores. While political party is a strong predictor of substantive representation, it may be that percent Latino in districts affects the level of electoral support for Democratic candidates (cf. de la Garza et al. 1992, 126). And that substantive representation occurs through party voting.

The relationship between percent Hispanic in a district and vote for Democratic candidate is examined in Table 2. The process outlined does seem to occur to a limited degree. Percent Latino in the district has a small (and statistically significant) impact on the vote for Democratic candidates in districts with 5% or more Hispanic population. There is no significant impact when all districts are considered; this is hardly surprising given that Latino proportions are, of course, small when the other districts are included.

CONCLUSION

The study finds little or no direct or indirect substantive representation of Latinos in the U.S. House. Even with the doubling of the number of Latinos in the U.S. House during the 1980s, Latino descriptive representation in the late 1980s was well below parity in Congress. Initial analysis indicated that the differences in voting patterns between Latino and non-Latino House members are not significant, and appear less different than they had been during the 1970s. Additionally, the relationship between the size of Latino constituencies and direct or "dyadic" substantive Congressional voting patterns in the 100th Congress appears no stronger, and, perhaps weaker, than indicated in research from the 1970s.

On the other hand, the roll-call votes deemed to be most important to Latinos were all decided consistent with Latino preferences. Thus, the concept of "collective" or indirect substantive representation, and a specific variant of that, partisan representation, was discussed and the analysis was extended to all districts. Percent Hispanic in district is related, albeit weakly, to the vote for Democrats in those districts with 5% or more Hispanics (but not when all districts are considered).

Overall, dyadic-direct substantive representation of Latinos in the 100th Congress was limited, and less than in the 1970s. Any substantive representation that does occur does so in a collective and/or partisan form and results mostly from Democrats and generally comes from Representatives *outside* the southwest, except for those who are themselves Latino. Even Representatives who are of Latino origin may be affected more by factors such as party affiliation and levels of district urbanization. The absence of descriptive and/or substantive (dyadic) representation of Latinos, as Latinos, in Congress mirrors their descriptive *under*representation at virtually all levels and in all institutions of American government.

The finding that Congress may substantively represent Latinos, albeit only collectively, should not be overlooked. This study is the first to find evidence of indirect substantive representation regarding Latinos. This finding is important both theoretically and normatively. At the same time, whether this collective-partisan representation "compensates" fully or partly for the essential absence of direct substantive representation is itself a theoretical and normative issue that deserves future attention. At this juncture, however, several points might be briefly noted.

The evidence examined in this and the previous study (Welch and Hibbing) only focused upon roll-call votes *actually taken,* of course. There could be issues of concern to Latinos that were not the subject of floor votes in Congress. The collective-partisan representation on House floor votes therefore actually taken says nothing about whether other, perhaps more significant, Latino concerns were placed "on the agenda" *in the first place* (cf. SWVRI 1989, 8; Hall and Wyman 1990).

Finally, while collective-partisan processes is a form of substantive representation, its indirectness and unpredictability may make the achievement of *accountability* difficult. A brief look at the Senate data on the SWVRI scores indicates little or no relationship to percent Latino in the state; and only 6 of the 15 votes used to calculate the Senate SWVRI scores had outcomes that were congruent with Latino preferences. Collective or substantive representation seems weak to nonexistent in the Senate as well. These and related issues underscore the need for further empirical and normative assessment of Latinos and U.S. democracy.

APPENDIX

House Votes Used to Create SWVRI Scores for the 100th Congress

H01 Contra Aid Passage of H.J. Res. 175, to block $40 million in aid to the Nicaraguan contras until the Reagan administration accounted for the money provided thus far. Passed 230 to 196. 3/11/87 Hispanic Leadership poll favored a "yea" vote.

H02 *Star Wars* Bennett (D-Fla.) amendment to H.R. 1748 (FY 1988 Defense Authorization) to reduce spending for Star Wars by $500 million. Adopted 219 to 199. 5/12/87 Hispanic Leadership Poll favored a "yea" vote.

H03 *Housing* Gray (D-Ill.) amendment to H.R. 4 (Community Development Act) to lower from 30% to 23% of income the rent elderly tenants pay in subsidized housing. Adopted 284 to 137. 6/10/87 Hispanic Leadership Poll favored a "yea" vote.

H04 *Housing* Passage of H.R. 4 (Housing and Community Development Act) authorizing $10.6 billion for federally assisted housing, and $5.2 billion for other housing programs. Passed 285 to 120. 6/11/87 Hispanic Leadership Poll favored a "yea" vote.

H05 *Legal Services* Shumway (R-Calif.) amendment to H.R 2763 (FY 1988 Justice Department Appropriations) to delete the Legal Services Corporation's $305.5 million appropriation. Rejected 127 to 282. 7/1/87 Hispanic Leadership Poll favored a "nay" vote.

H06 *Catastrophic Health Insurance* Passage of H.R. 2470, to expand Medicare benefits to protect elderly and disabled people from the costs of catastrophic illness. Passed 302 to 127. 7/22/87 Hispanic Leadership Poll favored a "yea" vote.

H07 *Central American Refugees* Passage of H.R. 618, to suspend for two years the U.S. government's planned deportation of Salvadoran and Nicaraguan refugees. Passed 237 to 181. 7/28/87 Hispanic leadership favored a "yea" vote.

H08 *Occupational Health* Passage of H.R. 162. to require notification of workers exposed to toxic chemicals or other workplace hazards that mean a potentially high risk of disease. Passed 225 to 186. 10/15/87 Hispanic Leadership Poll favored a "yea" vote.

H09 *Welfare Reform* Passage of H.R. 1720. Family Welfare Reform Act, requiring states to provide education and training to put long-term welfare recipients to work, and replacing the existing AFDC program with a Family Support Program. Passed 230 to 194. 12/16/87 Hispanic Leadership Poll favored a "yea" vote.

H10 *Contra Aid* Passage of H.J. Res. 444, approving President Reagan's request for $36.2 million in weapons and humanitarian aid for the Nicaraguan contras. Rejected 211 to 219. 2/3/88 Hispanic leadership favored a "nay" vote.

H11 *Civil Rights* Vote to override President Reagan's veto of S. 557, Civil Rights Restoration Act. Veto overridden 292 to 133. 3/22/88 Hispanic Leadership Poll favored a "yea" vote.

H12 Amnesty Passage of H.R. 4222, extending the amnesty program for eligible illegal aliens from May 4, 1988 to November 30, 1988. Passed 213 to 201. 4/20/88 Hispanic Leadership Poll favored a "yea" vote.

H13 Star Wars Bennett (D-Fla) amendment to H.R 4264 (FY 1989 Defense Authorization) to reduce funding for Star Wars by $600 million. Adopted 223 to 195. 5/4/88 Hispanic Leadership Poll favored a "yea" vote.

H14 Plant Closings Notification Passage of S. 2527, requiring employers to give 60 days notice of plant closings. Passed 286 to 136. 7/13/89 Hispanic Leadership Poll favored a "yea" vote.

H15 Homeless Passage of H.R. 4352 (McKinney Homeless Assistance Act) authorizing $642 million to help house, feed and care for the homeless. Passed 333 to 80. 8/3/88 Hispanic Leadership Poll favored a "yea" vote.

NOTES

1. Individuals can obtain the data and documentation necessary to replicate the analysis from the authors. The data used were compiled from several sources noted in the references.

2. There has been considerable debate regarding the proper name or label to use regarding this population. Some observers prefer "Hispanic," others "Mexican American," "Chicano," etc. For reasons that need not be discussed, "Latino" will generally be used here.

3. The SWVRI scores were developed in the following way. All Latino state legislators in the country were mailed a questionnaire in January 1989. Twenty issues considered by the 100th Congress in 1987 and 1988 were included in the poll. The state legislators were asked to indicate how they would have voted on each issue; "don't know" responses were permitted.

Those issues with more than 75% in agreement, either in favor or against, were deemed to have a "Latino position." This decision rule resulted in 15 votes in the House (and 15 votes in the Senate) used to create a Latino (SWVRI) support score.

A composite score—ranging from 0 to 100—was given to each member of Congress indicating the percent agreement with Hispanic state legislators' views. If the member was absent or did not vote on a particular issue, a "?" is shown, but that issue was not figured into the composite score (SWVRI 1990).

For the analysis undertaken in the present paper, Representatives were included only if they had actually voted on at least 11 of the 15 votes selected by SWVRI. That threshold was chosen to assure that members who participated on just a few of the votes were not included.

4. Several problems with the use of roll-call votes have been raised

(Fleisher and Bond 1992, 527; Hall and Wayman 1990, 801–802). Probably the major concern is that roll-call votes reflect strategic, as well as policy, goals. Acknowledging possible shortcomings, roll-call votes are nonetheless a central component of the legislative and representative process.

5. The SWVRI scores also include other votes that some observers may not deem directly relevant to Latino interests. These votes should not be discounted, for at least two reasons. To assume that Latino interests are only (directly) affected by, and that Latinos only have concerns about, issues that have explicit Latino dimensions is empirically questionable and normatively suspect. Also the scant previous research that has been published on our central question (i.e., Welch and Hibbing) did not examine votes chosen with specific attention to Latino concerns that the SWVRI votes have.

As it turns out, SWVRI scores are highly correlated with conservative coalition scores for the 100th Congress ($r = -.85$). To further assure that any differences in findings between the present research and the previous study are not due to the different dependent variables, the analyses of substantive representation *were also* undertaken with U.S. House members' conservative coalition scores. When this was done, the *major findings* discussed later *were not altered*.

6. In 1987–88 there were 10 Latino members of the U.S. House, up from five during the 1970s (the period of the Welch and Hibbing study, cf. 1988, 291, 298). In 1987–88, 2% of U.S. House members were Latinos, while 6.4% of the nation's population was of Hispanic origin. Thus, Latinos are represented just about one-third (.36) of what parity predicts, which was similar to the .44 ratio for blacks (cf. Grofman and Handley 1989, 444.)

All but one, i.e., nine of the ten, of the Latinos in the 100th Congress were Democrats—the exception was Manuel Lujan, Republican of New Mexico's District 1. There were no Hispanics in the Senate during the 100th Congress, and there had been none since 1976. Latinos are not only underrepresented from the standpoint of descriptive representation in the House, the districts represented by Latino members of the House are distinctive. These districts are more urban than for the nation as a whole, averaging 88.1% urban to about 74% for all House districts. The House seats held by Hispanic congressmen also have larger Hispanic populations (an average of 49.4%) than is the case for the nation as a whole (6%). Finally, the House districts represented by Hispanics have substantially lower levels of per capita income than those represented by non-Hispanics. Using a per capita income index that "standardizes" the average district to 100, the average for districts represented by Latinos is 74 (Cavanagh 1984).

7. There is surprisingly little correlation between the independent variables; see note to Table 1.

8. The 5% threshold approximates the national average for Latinos (7% to 10%); it also reduces the number of Congressional districts from 435 to 114. A higher threshold of 10% would reduce the number of districts below a level for reliable estimates.

9. With a "pooled" data set (discussed later) Welch and Hibbing also

examined the Hispanic(s) (of whom there was only one in each Congress) vs. non-Hispanic members of Congress from the New York–New Jersey area. Such an examination is not undertaken here because of the absence of a similar data set.

REFERENCES

Almanac of American Politics, 1990. 1989. Washington, DC: National Journal.

Browning, Rufus P., Dale Rogers Marshall, and David H. Tabb. 1984. *Protest is Not Enough: The Struggle of Blacks and Hispanics for Equality in Urban Politics.* Berkeley: University of California Press.

Cavanagh, Thomas E., ed. 1984. *The JCPS Congressional District Fact Book.* Washington, DC: Joint Center for Political Studies.

de la Garza, Rodolfo O., Louis DeSipio, F. Chris Garcia, John Garcia, and Angelo Falcon. 1992. *Latino Voices: Mexican, Puerto & Cuban Perspectives on American Politics.* Boulder: Westview Press.

Dyer, James A., and Arnold Vedlitz. 1986. "The Potential for Minority Coalition Building." Presented at the annual meeting of the Southern Political Science Association.

Fleisher, Richard, and Jon R. Bond. 1992. "Assessing Presidential Support in the House II: Lessons from George Bush." *American Journal of Political Science* 36:524–41.

Grofman, Bernard, and Lisa Handley. 1989. "Preconditions for Black and Hispanic Congressional Success." *American Politics Quarterly* 17:436–45.

Hall, Richard L., and Frank W. Wayman. 1990. "Buying Time: Moneyed Interests and the Mobilization of Bias in Congressional Committees." *American Political Science Review* 84:797–820.

Hero, Rodney E. 1992. *Latinos and the U.S. Political System: Two-tiered Pluralism.* Philadelphia: Temple University Press.

Hurley, Patricia A. 1989. "Partisan Representation and the Failure of Realignment in the 1980s." *American Journal of Political Science* 33:240–61.

Meier, Kenneth J., and Joseph Stewart, Jr. 1991. *The Politics of Hispanic Education.* Albany: State University of New York Press.

Southwest Voter Research Institute. 1989. "The 100th Congress: How They Voted on Issues of Concern to Latino Leaders." *Southwest Voter Research Notes* 3:1.

Stone, Walter J., Ronald B. Rapoport, and Alan I. Abramowitz. 1990. "The Reagan Revolution and Party Polarization in the 1980s." In *The Parties Respond: Changes in the American Party System,* ed. L. Sandy Maisel. Boulder: Westview Press.

Weissberg, Robert. 1978. "Collective vs. Dyadic Representation in Congress." *American Political Science Review* 72:535–47.

Welch, Susan. 1990. "The Impact of At-Large Elections on the Representation of Blacks and Hispanics." *Journal of Politics* 52:1050–76.

Welch, Susan, and John R. Hibbing. 1984. "Hispanic Representation in the U.S. Congress." *Social Science Quarterly* 65 2:328–35. Reprinted in F. Chris Garcia, ed. 1988. *Latinos and the Political System.* Notre Dame: University of Notre Dame Press.

PART IV

Outputs from the Political System: Issues and Policies

MUCH OF THE "payoff" for pursuing power through political participation comes as outputs or outcomes of the political system in the form
of the resulting governmental policies. Although the reasons for participating in politics are manifold, the central objective of most participants
is to affect government's allocation of goods, values, and resources; that
is, to have policy that is considered favorable enacted or to have policy
proposals that are judged unfavorable stopped.

Many Latinos who are engaged in pursuing political power in the
U.S. political system do so because they want the system to be on their
side of particular issues or policies. As the system produces policy outputs and outcomes, Latinos seek to influence the enactment of some public policies and the defeat of others. What issues are those to which Latinos give high priority, that is, are on the "Hispanic agenda"?

Several of these issues are shared by many other Americans in similar socioeconomic straits. Compared to the average Anglo American,
Latinos are more poorly educated, suffer greater unemployment, under-
employment, and poverty: they have lower incomes, lower home ownership rates, more substandard housing; health care is typically inferior;
and crime victimization more common. These and other concerns about
security and well-being on the Latino agenda are shared with substantial
portions of the non-Latino community. They may serve as points of political mobilization.

There are also issues which have a disproportionate impact on Latinos because they are culturally distinct ethnics. Anti-discrimination
and pro-opportunity policies such as affirmative action are examples of
issues that are of a less inclusive nature. Even more so are culturally
specific policies such as the protection of the Spanish language from attacks such as English-only policies. Immigration policies are increasingly

279

of interest to Latinos because they incorporate elements of all three types—socioeconomic, discriminatory, and cultural.

Education is high on the agenda of Latino public policy issues. Various opinion surveys, including the Latino National Political Survey, have indicated the primary and perennial priority that Latinos attribute to improved quantity and quality of their education. It is common knowledge that a good education accrues to the advantage of those who experience it, but Latinos traditionally have received inferior and/or inappropriate educational services. Additionally, this area is generally one of the most important and controversial of all public policies, making it a prime focus of Latino politics. For example, there has been debate about the efficacy and wisdom of bilingual education for years. Other continuing points of concern have included: the representation of Latinos in positions of influence within the educational system, such as teachers, principals, administrators, and school board members; the issues of equal access to educational opportunities; the persistently high drop out rate; and desires for a culturally relevant education.

In their research piece, Luis Fraga, Kenneth Meier, and Robert England have examined the relationship between Hispanic representation on school boards and public policy outputs that affect Hispanic students. Surveying several large urban school districts, they analyze the relationship between Hispanic representation on school boards and the employment of Hispanic teachers and the impact that Hispanic teachers have on the educational environment of Latino students. The educational environment for many Hispanic students is characterized as one of "second generation discrimination," which is a manifestation of institutional discrimination that is more subtle than the more familiar overt discrimination. Outside of the schools, educational inequality also continues. The representation of Hispanics on school boards is still proportionately below their number in the general population, and even though great gains have been made over the last decade, the relative discrepancy may continue to grow as many school districts are experiencing tremendous increases in their Latino school-age populations. At-large elections have been instrumental in keeping the proportion of Latino school board members down; however, successful court challenges are increasing the number of single member, districted school board elections. The authors conclude that Hispanics remain in a subordinate political position and thus are unable to affect educational policy to their benefit to any significant extent. They call for increased political attention to public education, as they see successes in this arena as being extremely important to the betterment of the Latino community.

Latinos on the whole remain on the lower rungs of the economic and employment ladder. Unemployment is generally much higher among Latinos than non-Latinos, often twice that of the general majority population. And even when employment is at a comparable rate, such as in some sectors of the public service, Latinos remain over-represented in lower level jobs and under-represented in the higher paying, managerial, supervisory, and administrative ranks. In their study of Hispanic employment at the local level in the five Southwestern states,[1] Susan Welch, Albert Karnig, and Richard Eribes found that there had been an increased representation from 1973 to 1978 in the level of Hispanic employment to the point where Latinos were only slightly underrepresented in overall numbers. However, a less positive finding was that Hispanic males were paid less than Anglo males at each level of employment and that Hispanics were clustered in the lower levels of the public work force. Moreover, Hispanic females were in an even more depressed position. Additionally the authors found a negative correlation between black and Latino public employment; the higher the level of black employment, the lower the proportion of Latino employment. Other studies have shown that competition between blacks and Latinos for public employment may work against coalition politics. Types of city government may or may not be a factor affecting levels of Hispanic municipal employment. The effects of the structural forms of local governments and the presence of Latinos in city councils on Latino employment levels are not yet clear.[2]

Another public policy issue which concerns Latinos is that of immigration. There has been considerable speculation about the status and effects of recent immigration into the United States, particularly from Mexico and other Latin American countries. In his article, "The Engine of Latino Growth: Latin American Immigration and Settlement in the United States," Louis DeSipio examines and analyzes the reality of the patterns of immigration from some of the settlement issues arising from those conditions. Latino immigrants are characterized by many dimensions of diversity, including national origin, but generally possess low levels of education and income. However, since they are very much involved in the labor force, they are neither impoverished nor reliant on needs-based social welfare programs. While predominantly Spanish-speaking, most also speak or are learning English. With the exception of non-citizens, almost all are very attached to the U.S. and intend to make it their permanent home. Between 80 and 95 percent plan to naturalize, although these intentions are often not realized. The relatively low rate of naturalization is attributed to recent residence, sociodemographic patterns, and the administrative process. Recently, there has been some added incentives to naturalize, including increasingly restrictive immigration legislation being considered by Congress, and some Latino organizations such as NALEO have organized naturalization efforts. These are seen as inadequate, especially in light of the great potential for empowerment through community mobilization by Latino leaders and organizations towards naturalization.

Another major public policy debate over the last few decades has been that regarding language. The debate has been primarily over the use of Spanish relative to the use of English. This political battle is particularly salient to the Latino community, as it involves arguably the most important symbolic manifestation of the Hispanic culture—the Spanish language. The Latino National Political Survey has verified that Hispanics feel very strongly about the protection and promotion of their language. This and other studies show that non-Hispanics are equally as strongly opposed to several aspects of the use of the Spanish language. Ronald Schmidt, in "Latinos and Language Policy: The Politics of Culture," provides an overview of this political cultural battle. He organizes his overview into three major themes: (1) the debate over bilingual education; (2) linguistic access policies, such as the involvement of language minorities in elections and in the use of Spanish in other public business such as the provision of governmental services; and (3) the continuing battle over "official English" language policy. These policies can be understood through the utilization of three distinctive philosophical perspectives: linguistic pluralism, assimilationism, and nationalism. Citing evidence from the Latino National Political Survey, Schmidt demonstrates that it is the pluralist approach which is most favored by the rank and file Latino. The Latino populace in the United States generally favors bilingualism and biculturalism, seeking to protect the Spanish language, but not to the exclusion of English. Latinos strongly support the learning of English, but also favor government action and public policies which maintain and promote the Spanish language.

There is another policy, or more precisely, a cluster of policies which have become increasingly controversial over the past decade or so, and in the mid-1990s seemed to be on the way to becoming the most hotly debated and controversial public policy issue in which U.S. Hispanics have a direct and immediate, tangible as well as symbolic, stake. From the mid-1960s until the mid-1990s, governments have established policies in all branches and at all levels which can be included under the umbrella term "affirmative action." Although there is a wide variation in the specifications of these affirmative action statutes, judicial decisions, rules, and regulations, in general, they encourage or require public sector organizations (and those private ones which are associated with governments) to actively pursue the inclusion of previously excluded or disadvantaged groups. Such policies are a form of compensatory treatment which encourages governmental agencies and organizations under the regulation of government to take positive and affirmative steps to give an advantage to previously disadvantaged groups. "Federally protected groups" which are afforded this preferential treatment include women, African Americans, Hispanic Americans, Asian Americans and Pacific Islanders, Native Americans, and Alaskan Natives. Over 160 policies just at the federal level promote the recruiting, hiring, or retention of these protected minorities. In some cases, federal contracts require "set asides," a specified percentage of the number or amount of contracts to be awarded exclusively to minority-owned enterprises. Such affirmative action also extends into education, not only in the form of targeted recruitment, retention, and promotion of faculty and staff, but also to the recruitment and retention of students as well as the provision of special scholarship and fellowship funds.

Opposition to such policies increased through the 1980s and became quite vehement in the late 1980s and early 1990s as non-protected groups, particularly white males, railed against what they called "reverse racism" with very vocal expressions of opposition. After the Congressional elections of 1994, when Republican victories were attributed in large part to "angry white males" who were disturbed at, among other things, what they saw as discrimination against them, governmental officials, particularly the victorious Republicans, contended that they would abolish affirmative action programs. In the mid-1990s, legislation was introduced in several states including California, calling for the abolition of any such preferential treatment programs. Republican aspirants for the 1996 presidential nomination promised to abolish preferential treatment programs. Proponents of such programs sought backing in constitutional dictates and the American philosophical tenets of equality, fairness, and "color blind justice."

Without a doubt, this issue is of major importance to Latinos, as many of their advancements have been facilitated by affirmative action programs. Even with such programs, measures of socioeconomic and political success in the mid-1990s still documented that Latinos as well as other disadvantaged groups had not yet attained parity. Proponents of the continuation of affirmative action argue that the elimination of such programs would not only halt the incremental progress that has been made, but would allow the system to slip back into its traditional mode of "institutional racism." This political debate will give expression to the full range of Hispanic politics and perhaps place an emphasis on effective *coalitional* politics, since it may provide a clear catalyst for cooperation among those minority groups which have been helped by such programs. The following article on "Latinos and Affirmative Action" initiates an exploration of the possible impact of this issue on Latino political strategies. To do this it presents a brief background of the development and status of such programs, the arguments for and against affirmative action, the analysis of relevant survey data, and the various possibilities for coalitional policies which may ensue from the discourse and activities surrounding this issue.

While most of the policy issues which are the subject of Latino political activity are in the domestic arena, there has also been some concern expressed about foreign policy issues, and most particularly about United States relations with Latin America. In *Latinos and the Political System,* Armando Rendon explained that Latinos have been mainly concerned with their own "survival" in the United States, but that as betterment is obtained domestically, Latinos will increasingly turn their attention to relations with the Latin American countries. He surmised that as Latinos turned their attention to foreign affairs, they would play a much more important part in international relations in the Western hemisphere. A closer relationship among Latinos of all national origins within the Americas was forecast.[3]

However, this speculative view is challenged in the article by Rodolfo de la Garza and his LNPS colleagues on "Mexican, Puerto Rican, and Cuban Foreign Policy Perspectives." The investigators use data from the Latino National Political Survey to empirically test two competing hypotheses of the foreign policy perspectives of Latinos: a culturalist perspective and the "structural" formulation. On the basis of their survey evidence, the authors conclude that the three largest Latino groups in the United States do *not* share similar views either with regard to their identity as Latinos or with regard to their interest in Latin America. Instead, each group's main homeland identification is with that of their own national origin, as is each group's interest in Latin America, rather than with the region in general. Only the foreign born, and especially those who have not been naturalized, are even a little attentive to homeland politics, while native born and naturalized Latinos are overwhelmingly oriented more towards U.S. politics and policies. The authors conclude by stating that Latinos do not view Latin America through a single lens, that it is difficult to identify a single foreign policy issue that would galvanize attitudes among this population, and that Latinos would most likely be involved in foreign policy the way other Americans are, that is "intermittently and only when it clearly affects their daily lives."

It should be noted that issues such as immigration and NAFTA (the North American Free Trade Agreement) which have been very salient in the 1990s are those kinds of "foreign policy" issues which may activate and mobilize various Latino groups toward participation in foreign policy issues.[4]

NOTES

1. Susan Welch, Albert Karnig, and Richard Eribes, "Changes in Hispanic Employment in the Southwest," *Western Political Quarterly* 36, no. 4 (December 1983): 660–73; reprinted in *Latinos and the Political System,* ed. F. Chris Garcia (Notre Dame, Ind.: University of Notre Dame Press, 1988), 411–25.

2. See, for example, Kenneth R. Mladenka, "Barriers to Hispanic Employment Success in 1,200 Cities," *Social Science Quarterly* 70 (June 1989): 391–407.

3. Armando B. Rendon, "Latinos: Breaking the Cycles of Survival to Tackle Global Affairs," in *Ethnicity and U.S. Foreign Policy,* rev. ed., ed. Abdul Aziz Said (Praeger, 1981); reprinted in *Latinos and the Political System,* 441–59.

4. For an optimistic exposition of this view and the more general role of Latinos in U.S. foreign policy, see "Latinos, Global Change, and American Foreign Policy," report of the New America Global Dialogue Conference, October 7–9, 1994, sponsored by the Stanley Foundation in collaboration with the Tomas Rivera Center (Muscadine, Iowa: Stanley Foundation, 1991).

11. Hispanic Americans and Educational Policy: Limits to Equal Access

Luis Ricardo Fraga, Kenneth J. Meier, and Robert E. England

ALTHOUGH HISPANIC AMERICANS are the nation's second largest and fastest growing minority, they have received little attention in the political science literature. Hispanics have many of the same political and economic disadvantages that blacks do; but compared to blacks, we know little about their access to political power and the effect of public policies on them. This research examines the access of Hispanics to equal educational opportunity in U.S. urban school districts. We will first establish education's crucial role in determining economic and social opportunities for Hispanics and link these to political representation. We will then test several hypotheses. First, the level of Hispanic representation on urban school boards will be assessed, including a look at the relationship between selection plans, population, and representation. Second, one form of bureaucratic representation, Hispanic access to teaching positions, will be related to school board representation and Hispanic population. Third, educational policy will be linked to school board representation, teacher representation, Hispanic political resources, and social cleavages in the school district. Specifically, this paper will examine the determinants of second-generation educational discrimination—the post-desegregation acts that limit equal access to education. In

"Hispanic Americans and Educational Policy: Limits to Equal Access" by Luis Ricardo Fraga, Kenneth J. Meier, and Robert E. England in *Journal of Politics* Volume 48:4, pp 850–876; by permission of the authors and the University of Texas Press.

most cases data on Hispanics will be contrasted with data on blacks and Anglos.[1]

HISPANICS AND EDUCATION

The history of Hispanics in America is replete with numerous instances of discrimination. Mexican-Americans have been denied rightful title to their land (Acuña, 1981, pp. 2–120; Barrera, 1979, pp. 1–30). Immigration policies often have been designed to aid Anglo landowners at the expense of Hispanic workers (Gamio, 1971; Samora, 1971; Bustamante, 1976; Cárdenas, 1975). Efforts of workers to unionize have been discouraged (Galarza, 1977; Gómez-Quinoñes, 1972; García, 1975). To prevent remedial action in these areas by government, the right to vote has been restricted by legislation, English-only ballots, gerrymandering, at-large elections, and exclusionary slating practices (U.S. Commission on Civil Rights, 1975; Carrión, 1983, pp. 129–307; Davidson and Fraga, 1984; Fraga, 1984; Schaeffer, 1984, pp. 321–3, 331–2).

Nowhere has public policy been more detrimental to the development of Hispanics, however, than in education. Education in America is viewed as the key to upward political, social, and economic mobility (McPartland and Braddock, 1981). If individuals are denied access to quality education, then access to political power, social status, and good jobs is also limited. Despite the American ideal of equal educational opportunity, access to public education has historically been limited on the basis of race and ethnicity (Weinberg, 1977).

Both educational history and current policy clearly demonstrate that Hispanics have been denied equal access to education. Segregation of Hispanic students, particularly in California and Texas, began in the late 1800s (Fernández and Guskin, 1981, p. 112). The quality of education in these segregated schools was far below that in mainstream Anglo schools (Weinberg, 1977, pp. 144–6; San Miguel, 1982, p. 702). Although *de jure* segregation of Hispanics was outlawed when federal courts in the late 1940s declared that Hispanics were "whites," (San Miguel, 1982, p. 708; Alcalá and Rangel, 1972), *de facto* segregation has continued.

De facto segregation was furthered by two methods. Assignment systems based on assessments of language deficiencies or other individual needs, which were on their face not based exclusively upon race or ethnicity, were used to separate Hispanics from Anglos. In addition, desegregation plans often paired Hispanic and black schools but allowed Anglo students to remain in all-Anglo schools (San Miguel, 1982, p. 710).

In *Cisneros v. Corpus Christi Independent School District* (324 F. Supp. 599, S.D. Tex., 1970), the courts recognized Hispanics as a separate ethnic group. This recognition allowed Hispanics to seek legal relief from segregated school systems. Because legal and policy processes move slowly, however, most Hispanics still attend segregated schools (Brown et al., 1980, p. 48; see also Orfield, 1981, p. 190; Bullock, 1980, p. 599).[2]

Equally detrimental to Hispanic students is inequitable school financing. State funding formulas often used factors such as teacher qualifications which restricted funds allocated to predominantly Hispanic districts (Weinberg, 1977, p. 163). In addition, the largest source of locally generated revenues for public school expenditures comes from the property tax. Predominantly Hispanic school districts tend to be large central city school districts which, on a per capita basis, have a lower property tax base (see *San Antonio Independent School District v. Rodríguez*, 411 U.S. 1, 1973).

Segregation and funding decisions together can create an overall pattern of educational inequity for many Hispanic students. Other educational policy practices, however, can have as severe an impact on quality education for Hispanics. These practices are termed "second-generation school discrimination." In general, second-generation school discrimination concerns those efforts to keep educational opportunities racially separate within schools (see Rodgers and Bullock, 1972; Stewart and Bullock, 1981). Three practices have been specifically identified by the Office of Civil Rights as potentially discriminatory: ability grouping, suspensions, and tracking. These practices may appear on the surface to be normal, good educational practices; but on closer examination, they can have a deleterious impact on minority students.

Ability Grouping

Ability grouping is using intellectual ability as a criterion to assign students to different classes or different groups within a class. Ability grouping includes assignment of students to advanced, enriched, or honors classes as well as the assignment of students to special education or remedial education classes. Although ability grouping has a long tradition in education that predates efforts to desegregate schools, it has two similarities with efforts to segregate students. First, students are grouped with those racially similar to themselves and separated from those who are different. Second, status is accorded to some groups; advanced placement classes are perceived as better than regular classes; regular classes are perceived to be better than special education classes, etc.

These actions, even if taken for valid educational reasons, can counteract the intent of integration, equal educational opportunity for all groups (McConahay, 1981).

Ability grouping has been criticized by a variety of desegregation scholars because it separates minority students from Anglos (see Smith and Dziuban, 1977, p. 54; McConahay, 1981, p. 47; Epps, 1981, p. 103). Rather than teaching the minority student, he or she is diagnosed as having intellectual or linguistic problems and shunted off to a special education, EMR, or in the case of Hispanics, bilingual class (Fernández and Guskin, 1981). Such criticism is reinforced by the empirical findings concerning ability grouping. The U.S. Commission on Civil Rights (1976, p. 129) reviewed a series of studies and concluded that *ability grouping actually had negative effects on low-ability groups* and that the results on high-ability groups were inconclusive. Because minority students were generally segregated into the lower-ability groups (Eyler, et al., 1981, p. 221), grouping reduced the self-esteem of minority students, produced resentment among racial groups, contributed to discipline problems and dropouts, and resulted in inferior education due to the low teacher expectations (Rosenbaum, 1976; U.S. Commission on Civil Rights, 1976). In short, ability grouping provided few of the benefits claimed by its proponents and resulted in racial resegregation harmful to minority students.

Suspensions

Suspensions are a second tactic that can be used to resegregate school systems. By disciplining minority students more severely and more frequently than Anglo students, school systems can push students out of school (Children's Defense Fund, 1974, p. 130). The literature reveals a clear pattern of disproportionate suspensions for many minority students (U.S. Commission on Civil Rights, 1976; Arnez, 1978; Kaeser, 1979). According to Eyler, Cook, and Ward (1983, p. 42), research results concerning Hispanic suspensions are mixed. In some districts Hispanics are disproportionately suspended; but in school districts with large Hispanic enrollments, the Hispanic suspensions ratio tends to be slightly lower than the Anglo ratio.

Tracking and Educational Attainment

Differences in ability grouping and discipline often coexist with differences in tracking. Children in high-ability groups generally choose or are counseled to choose a college preparatory track. Students in low-ability groups select or are counseled into vocational or general tracks (Eyler et al., 1981, p. 222). Because minority students are disproportionately placed in low-ability groups, they are less likely to be prepared for further education after high school.

A separate manifestation of the tracking phenomenon for Hispanics can be bilingual education programs. While bilingual programs are in theory a form of ability grouping, Hispanics may be pulled out of regular classes and placed exclusively in a bilingual education program. Such one-way maintenance programs can be equivalent to the establishment of a dual education system (Eyler et al., 1983, p. 137). Research also suggests (1) that children are placed in bilingual education programs based on their ethnicity rather than their English proficiency and (2) that transfers out of bilingual programs are rare, thus creating a "Hispanic track" in the school (Eyler et al., 1983, pp. 139–140).[3]

The end result of racial differences in ability grouping, suspensions, and tracking can be differentials in educational attainment (Eyler et al., 1983; Fernández and Guskin, 1981). Students assigned to lower-ability groups are more likely to perceive that education is futile (U.S. Commission on Civil Rights, 1976). Students disciplined disproportionately are likely to leave school (Children's Defense Fund, 1974). Students placed in vocational tracks are less likely to receive the best education the district can offer (Eyler et al., 1981). If minorities are discriminated against in ability grouping, discipline, and tracking, then they will be more likely to drop out of school or if they finish school will be less likely to go on to post-secondary education (McPartland and Braddock, 1981).

Because segregation, funding decisions, and second generation discrimination create an overall pattern of educational inequity, many Hispanic students do not receive the same quality education that Anglo students do. The purpose of this research is to investigate why. The history of Hispanic Americans suggests that educational inequities may be linked to political inequities between Anglos and Hispanics. Educational policy is a direct product of the political process (Weinberg, 1977). At the school district level, elected or appointed public officials set the major parameters of educational policy. Teachers, in turn, are the primary implementors of these educational policies. As such they serve as bureaucrats within the educational system who daily exercise substantial discretion in the application of educational policy to students. A lack of representation among political decision makers and subsequent access to the education bureaucracy may well be the reasons why educational policies do not benefit Hispanics. To the linkage between political representation, access to the bureaucracy, and policy impact, we now turn.

HYPOTHESES AND METHODS

We hypothesize that the number of Hispanic school board representatives in a district is due to the nature of the board election/selection plan and the Hispanic population in the district. School boards that elect members from single-member districts are more likely to have more Hispanic representatives than will school districts with at-large elections or appointive selection. We also hypothesize that increased levels of Hispanic school board representation and large Hispanic populations enhance the number of Hispanic teachers who are employed in a district. Lastly, we hypothesize that the combination of Hispanic school board representation and Hispanic teachers works to limit the second-generation school discrimination faced by Hispanic students. We also anticipate that Hispanic social and political resources and the social class differentiation between Hispanics and Anglos can serve to limit such discrimination. Theoretical justifications for these hypotheses are presented below.

THE SAMPLE

To assess these relationships, an elaborate data set was constructed from several sources. Data on school board representation were merged with data on Hispanic teachers, data on educational policy outputs, and census data for the school district.[4] The data requirements limited this study to major urban districts with a minimum of 25,000 students. Because many urban school districts have few Hispanic students, the study was further limited to those districts with 5 percent or more Hispanic enrollment. A total of 35 urban school districts met these criteria and had available data (see appendix A). We are confident that these school districts are fairly representative of the Hispanic educational experience; these districts contain 35 percent of all Hispanics residing in the U.S. in 1980. Unlike most research on Hispanics, our sample includes districts populated by Puerto Ricans, Cuban Americans, and other Hispanics as well as those populated by Chicanos.

REPRESENTATION

Although black representation in political institutions has been well studied, similar research on Hispanics is meager. Representation in most studies generally is defined in simple descriptive terms; a group is "adequately represented" if that group's percentage composition of the city council, bureaucracy, or other institution is the same as its population percentage. By this definition, blacks are underrepresented on city councils (Robinson and Dye, 1978; Karnig, 1976) and overrepresented on central city school boards (Welch and Karnig, 1978; Robinson and England, 1981).

Representation levels for Hispanics are generally lower than those for Blacks. Both Taebel (1978, p. 145) and Karnig and Welch (1979, p. 469) found that Hispanics held approximately 44 percent of the city council seats that would be expected given their population percentage. Welch and Hibbing (1984, p. 328) found an even lower level of Hispanic representation in the U.S. Congress. Most minority representation studies rely solely on this proportionality view of representation, a view that Pitkin (1967) calls descriptive representation (for exceptions see Meier and England, 1984; Welch and Hibbing, 1984; Harmel, Hamm and Thomspon, 1983; Bullock and MacManus, 1981). Proportionality is essentially a passive form of representation because someone is considered representative merely by being something (black, Hispanic, Anglo) rather than by doing something. Pitkin argues that representation should be viewed as an activity, as "acting in the interests of the represented." Many other scholars of representation have attempted to link active and passive representation by advocating a variety of representation definitions (see Eulau and Karps, 1977).

The linkage between passive representation (minority access to elected positions) and active representation (public policies that favor minority interests), has been made infrequently for black representatives and hardly at all for Hispanics. Much research on black representation uses expenditures or employment as indicators of public policy (Welch and Karnig, 1980; Dye and Renick, 1981; Eisinger, 1982a, 1982b). Expenditure measures are difficult to link to minority interests. A wealth of case-study literature avoids this difficulty but has problems of generalizability (see Keller, 1978; Levine, 1974; Nelson, 1972; Poinsett, 1979; Stone, 1971; Keech, 1968). The only empirical studies of active representation for blacks using neither expenditure nor employment data are Meier and England's (1984) analysis of second-generation discrimination against black students and Browning, Marshall and Tabb's (1984) assessment of ten California cities. The single nonemployment study of Hispanic representation and public policy finds that congressional districts with more Hispanics have members of Congress who vote less conservatively (Welch and Hibbing, 1984).

REPRESENTATION LEVELS

Engstrom and McDonald (1981) demonstrate that under certain conditions an effective way to measure passive representation is to regress the proportion of seats held by a group on the group's share of the total population. If the intercept of this regression is fairly close to zero, then the slope can be interpreted as a measure of representational equity.[5] Perfect proportional representation exists when the slope is 1.0.

The linkage between population and representation is also affected by the method of selection. Much litigation and substantial research have addressed the relationship between at-large elections and minority representation. At-large elections force minority candidates to run citywide races so that minorities must often run in an electorate with an Anglo majority. In elections with substantial racial vote polarization, minority candidates are at a clear structural disadvantage. At-large races further limit minority candidates because they require greater campaign resources than smaller district elections do.

A massive literature has shown that at-large elections result in lower levels of black representation (for a summary, see Karnig and Welch, 1982; Davidson and Korbel, 1981). Only three studies have failed to show the detrimental impact of at-large elections (Cole, 1974; MacManus, 1978; and Welch and Karnig, 1978; but see Engstrom and McDonald, 1981). Only two studies examine the impact of at-large city council elections on Hispanics. Taebel (1978, p. 151) found that at-large elections hindered Hispanic representation, but Karnig and Welch (1979, p. 474) did not. The different results may be a function of different samples (Karnig and Welch, 1979).

The seats-population regression for Hispanic school board members is shown in table 1.[6] The population slope can be interpreted as follows: for every increase of one percent in Hispanic population, Hispanics attain .774 percent more school board seats when selection plan is held constant. In other words, Hispanics hold 77 percent of the school board seats that one would expect given their school district population.[7]

Because the selection plan variables were entered as dummy variables, they have a unique interpretation. The slopes show the difference in representation between at-large and ward elections, and appointive and ward selections. At-large election plans reduce Hispanic representation on school boards by 2.6 percent relative to single-member district election. Similarly an appointive plan reduces Hispanic representation by 6.3 percent relative to the level of representation with single-member districts. Although the small number of districts with ward

TABLE 1

The Determinants of Hispanic School Board Representation

Independent Variable	Slope	Beta	T-Score
% Hispanic Population	.774	.82	7.91
At-Large Election Plan	−2.635	−.10	.78
Appointed Selection	−6.316	−.19	1.51
Intercept = 1.6 R^2 = .69 F = 23.0			
n = 35			

and appointive plans limits the statistical significance of our findings,[8] they are in the anticipated direction. At-large elections and appointive selection plans reduce levels of Hispanic representation on school boards even when one controls for the size of the Hispanic population.

The modest negative impact of at-large elections on Hispanics compared to the larger impact on blacks can be explained. Hispanics are not as residentially segregated as blacks; Lopez (1981, p. 54) found a residential segregation index of 70.7 percent for blacks and 42.9 percent for Hispanics in fifty-eight southwestern cities. The greater dispersion of Hispanics mitigates some of the impact of at-large elections because they are not as concentrated in only some sections of the city. Nonetheless at-large elections do limit Hispanic representation.

ACCESS TO THE BUREAUCRACY: TEACHERS

One indirect policy output of minority access to elected positions is minority access to government employment. Dye and Renick (1981, p. 484) found that city council representation was associated with greater Hispanic employment in administrative, professional, and protective jobs. Representation had no impact on lower level government jobs. Welch, Karnig, and Eribes (1983, p. 669), on the other hand, discovered no relationship between city employment and Hispanic representation on the city council.

Greater minority employment in a school district may also result from greater minority representation on the school board. Bureaucratic positions, however, are more important than just as a source of jobs. Bureaucrats can also perform representative functions and advocate the interests of Hispanics in day-to-day policy decisions (see the vast literature

TABLE 2

The Determinants of the Percent Hispanic Teachers

Independent Variable	Slope	Beta	T-Score
% Hispanic Population	.274	.72	5.96
% Hispanic on School Board	.096	.23	1.98
Intercept = −.759 R^2 = .85 F = 86.6			
n = 34			

on representative bureaucracy, Meier and Nigro, 1976; Saltzstein, 1979). In terms of educational policy, perhaps the most important bureaucrats are teachers. Teachers serve as role models for Hispanic students, and make day-to-day decisions that affect them (Thomas and Brown, 1982, p. 168); some scholars rate the teacher as the most important variable in the student's school environment (Smith and June, 1982, p. 232).

Table 2 shows the relationship between the proportion of Hispanic teachers and both Hispanic population and Hispanic representation on the school board. Both measures are significantly related to the number of Hispanic teachers. For each additional one percent of Hispanic population the percentage of Hispanic teachers increases by .27; in other words, Hispanics have only slightly more than one-fourth the number of teachers one would expect based on population alone. Equally important in table 2 is that Hispanic school board representation also has a positive impact. A one percent increase in Hispanic school board representation results in a .096 percent increase in teachers. No other variables including Hispanic community education or income are significantly related to the proportion of Hispanic teachers.[9]

The low level of Hispanic representation among teachers is surprising when compared to the proportion of black teachers. Blacks were over-represented by 16 percent. In raw numbers, the average school district in this study has 4.2 percent Hispanic teachers and 15 percent black teachers even though the minorities' population figures are fairly equal. Why blacks are more successful in gaining access to teaching positions is not clear. Blacks have better representation on school boards (107 percent versus 77 percent), but this difference is minor compared to the difference in teachers (116 percent versus 27 percent, data not shown). The potential labor pool for black teachers might be slightly larger; the median education level for blacks in these school districts is 10.7 years compared to 9.3 for Hispanics. Again this difference is not nearly large enough to explain the huge difference in teachers. One other factor that may explain the lack of Hispanic teachers is the absence of Hispanic institutions of higher education. When blacks were denied access to white educational institutions, they could become teachers (normally in black schools) by attending black educational institutions such as Fisk, Morehouse, and Grambling. Hispanics have no similar institutions (Olivas, 1983, p. 116).

POLICY IMPACT: SECOND-GENERATION DISCRIMINATION

Although Hispanic access to school board seats and teaching positions (passive representation) is important in and of itself, such access is more important if it has policy implications (active representation). If Hispanic school board members and teachers act in the interests of the Hispanic community, then educational policies should be more beneficial to Hispanic students. We need to know if it matters to the Hispanic student whether or not he/she attends school in a district where Hispanics are represented in policy-making and policy-implementing positions. This study uses several indicators of second-generation educational discrimination as policy outcome measures.[10]

Three separate measures of ability grouping for students are available: number of students assigned to advanced classes, number of students assigned to special education classes, and number of students assigned to classes for the educable mentally retarded (EMR classes).[1] For each grouping, a "representation ratio" is calculated. For example, for the students assigned to advanced classes, the ratio is the proportion of Hispanic students in advanced classes divided by the proportion of Hispanic students in the school district. This ratio equals 1.0 when Hispanics have access to these classes in exact proportion to their numbers. When Hispanics are assigned to proportionately fewer advanced classes, the ratio is less than one. When Hispanics are assigned to more advanced classes than their students proportions, the ratio is greater than one.

To indicate discipline differentials, a ratio is created using the number of students suspended for one or more days. Similar to the ability grouping ratios, the proportion of suspended students who are Hispanic is divided by the proportion of Hispanic students in the district. Finally, three indicators of educational attainment are used based on the number of students who drop out of school, the number of students who go to college, and the number of students who attend vocational schools.[12] A representation ratio is created for each of these measures.

TABLE 3

Mean Educational Policy Ratios by Race of Student

POLICY RATIO	HISPANICS	BLACKS	ANGLOS
Advanced Classes	.49*	.53*	1.50
Special Education	.90	1.24*	.93
EMR Classes	1.06*	2.12*	.59
Suspensions	.98	1.81*	.93
Vocational School	.31*	.89*	1.52
Attending College	.36*	.40*	2.01
Dropouts	2.02*	1.42*	.77
Teacher Ratio	.27*	.98	1.19

*Significantly different from Anglos at .01 or less.

If second-generation educational discrimination is used against Hispanic students as it is against black students (see Meier and England, 1984), then we would expect the ratios to be less than one for advanced classes, college attendance, and post-secondary vocational enrollments. The ratios should be greater than one for special education, EMR classes, suspensions, and dropouts.

Table 3 displays the mean policy ratios for Hispanics, blacks, and Anglos. Similar to blacks, Hispanics are significantly underrepresented in advanced classes, post-secondary vocational school enrollment, and college attendance. Both blacks and Hispanics are also overrepresented in EMR classes and in dropouts. Unlike blacks, however, Hispanics are not overrepresented in special education classes or in suspensions.

Although both blacks and Hispanics faced similar educational inequities, the patterns are different. Blacks are clearly affected more by ability grouping than Hispanics. They are overrepresented by 24 percent in special education classes, overrepresented by 112 percent in EMR classes, and underrepresented by 47 percent in advanced classes. Hispanics have severe problems only in access to advanced classes.[13]

The striking numbers in table 3, however, are for the educational attainment indicators. The Hispanic dropout rate is 60 percent worse than the black dropout rate and almost three times as high as the Anglo rate. Hispanics are less likely to attend college and significantly less likely than blacks to attend post-secondary vocational schools.

The results of table 3 suggest different patterns of second-generation discrimination for Hispanic and black students. Black students are more likely to be punished by negative ability grouping and disproportionate discipline. The result is a lower educational attainment. The process for Hispanics is more subtle. Hispanics are similarly denied access to advanced classes and funneled into EMR classes, but they are not subjected to greater discipline. Their educational attainment, however, suffers even more than blacks.

Discrimination is only one possible explanation for the ratios presented in table 3. One could make an argument, though not an easy one, that these figures represent differences in educational potential. One strong argument against this view is the interrelationship of the indicators. School districts that disproportionately group black students in lower-ability groups also do this to Hispanic groups. The correlation between the Hispanic and black indices is .48 for EMR classes, .64 for special education classes, and .25 for advanced classes, and .26 for suspensions. In addition, the indices are internally consistent with each other. EMR classes, special education classes, suspensions, and dropouts are positively correlated for both Hispanics and blacks. Similarly, advanced classes, college attendance, and vocational school enrollments are also positively correlated.[14]

SECOND-GENERATION DISCRIMINATION: AN EXPLANATION

Even though second-generation discrimination against Hispanic students is fairly prevalent, it varies substantially from district to district. School dropout rates range from a low of 1.16 to a high of 5.42; similarly college attendance rates range from .03 to 1.08. In some school districts, therefore, Hispanic students achieve equity in educational opportunity. The important question is, why do some school districts provide greater educational equity to Hispanics than others?

Representation

One explanation for the treatment of Hispanic students concerns our earlier discussion of the relationship between passive and active representation. If school board members and teachers are effective advocates for Hispanic students, then second-generation discrimination should be lower in school districts with greater Hispanic representation in policy-making and policy-implementing positions. Two measures of representation are used: the percentage of the school board controlled by Hispanics and the percentage of Hispanic teachers. We hypothesize that a greater percentage of Hispanic school board members and a greater percentage of Hispanic teachers will result in lower levels of second generation discrimination.

The raw percentage rather than a representation ratio is used for two reasons. First, influence on the school board is a function of votes, not representation ratios. Hispanic board members should be better able to attain their goals if they have 40 percent of the seats in a district 60 percent Hispanic than if they have 10 percent of the seats in a district that is 5 percent Hispanic. Similarly the percentage of Hispanic teachers increases the probability that a Hispanic student will come into contact with a Hispanic teacher. Second, each of our policy measures already contains the proportion of the Hispanic student body as a denominator. Using a similar measure for school board members and teachers, therefore, would divide both the independent and dependent variables by essentially the same number. Such a procedure can create relationships as an artifact of the division process (Uslander, 1976).

Resources

Representation is not the only determinant of public policy. The ability to affect policies issued by the school board or implemented by the school system should be a function of Hispanic political resources. Compared to blacks, Hispanics have not developed as strong a political, economic and organizational infrastructure (see Karnig, 1979; Fernández and Guskin, 1981). Traditional measures for political resources such as other elected officials, businesses owned, social organizations founded, etc. are difficult to find for Hispanics and generally show few resources.[15] Two potential resources measures will be used—education and income (on the importance of education, see Sigelman and Karnig, 1977). Since education and income levels may be directly related to some of the policy indicators, both measures were turned into ratios that compared Hispanics to Anglos (see Karnig, 1979). The measures are the ratio of Hispanic median education to Anglo median education and the ratio of Hispanic median income to Anglo median income.

These two measures not only reflect the relative potential resources of the Hispanic and Anglo communities, but they also reflect the potential social differences between the two groups. Giles and Evans (1985; 1986) have argued that if a minority is similar to the majority, the majority will be less threatened by the demands of the minority and more likely to grant the minority access to majority institutions. Giles and Evans (1986) contend that discrimination is less likely against middle-class blacks than against lower-class blacks because middle-class blacks share many of the values of middle-class whites. They imply that class has much to do with discrimination. Feagin (1980) presents a similar argument.

The argument of Giles, Evans, and Feagin is directly applicable to Hispanics. Hispanics, especially those who physically resemble Anglos, can be assimilated into Anglo institutions easier than blacks because they may be able to "pass" for Anglos. Hispanic students with higher incomes and from families with high education levels, under the Giles-Evans-Feagin hypothesis, are less likely to be perceived as a threat to the Anglo community. We hypothesize, therefore, that the higher the ratio of Hispanic income and education to Anglo income and education, the lower the resistance of the Anglo community and the education establishment to equal treatment for Hispanic students.

Social Class

The final political explanation for second-generation discrimination is also related to the Giles-Evans-Feagin power thesis. If the school district as a whole is fairly wealthy and the Hispanic community is fairly poor, then the standardized tests used to classify students will racially differentiate between Anglos and Hispanics. In such a community, these tests may also be accorded more legitimacy. In combination the tests provide teachers and administrators with "objective" reasons for separating Hispanic students from Anglos.

If the school district itself, however, has a large proportion of poor Anglos, then use of such standardized criteria will funnel a great many Anglos into similar programs. If discrimination is an explanation for the differences in Hispanic educational equity, then we would expect such measures as special education to be used less for Hispanics when the district poverty level for Anglos is high.[16]

Second-generation discrimination in this view is based both on race and class. Given a homogeneous middle-class Anglo community, Hispanics are differentiated from Anglos by both race and class. Discrimination might be a function of either. If the Anglo community is heterogeneous, then educational policy may be used to limit opportunities of poor whites also.

Findings

The relationships between the five independent variables and the seven policy ratios are shown in table 4. For the ability grouping indicators, the

TABLE 4

Impact of Hispanic Representation on Educational Policy

Hispanic Policy Ratio	Board Members	Hispanic Teachers	Education Ratio	Income Ratio	Poverty	R^2	F
Special Education	.22	.08	−.40*	−.18	−.23	.35	2.7
EMR Classes	.22	.34	−.10	−.47*	−.70	.52	5.5
Advanced Classes	.03	−.03	.02	.13	.45*	.17	1.1
Suspensions	−.31	.41	−.19	−.09	−.41*	.17	1.8
College Attendance	−.25	.45*	.30*	.51*	.05	.61	7.7
Dropouts	.10	−.47*	−.35*	−.45*	−.16	.61	8.0
Vocational Training	−.20	.14	−.05	.35	.03	.14	.7

*$p<.05$
n = 31
All coefficients are standardized regression coefficients.

regression equation predicts fairly well for special education (R^2 = .35) and EMR classes (.52) but not for advanced classes (.17). For EMR classes two significant relationships exist. Strong negative relationships exist between EMR placement of Hispanics and both Anglo poverty and the Hispanic/Anglo income ratio. As predicted, school districts with higher levels of Anglo poverty funnel fewer Hispanics into EMR classes; in addition, in school districts where Hispanic income is closer to Anglo income, Hispanics are less likely to be placed in EMR classes.

For special education, the only significant relationship is for the Hispanic/Anglo education ratio, but the interpretation is the same as for EMR classes. In school districts where Hispanic education levels approach Anglo levels, Hispanics are less likely to be placed in special education classes. For advanced classes, the single significant relationship is poverty. As predicted, as poverty increases, the proportion of Hispanic students who are admitted to advanced placement classes increases.

The relationship between the independent variables and suspensions is disappointing. Only one variable is significantly related to the suspension ratio, and the overall level of explanation is low (R^2 =.17). As predicted, the proportion of Hispanics suspended decreases in school districts with higher levels of Anglo poverty.

The most striking findings are for educational attainment. The proportion of Hispanic teachers is positively related to Hispanics going on to college and negatively related to dropouts. Both relationships are significant; for dropouts, the teacher measure has the greatest impact of any variable and for college attendance, the second greatest impact. Both the education and income ratios are also significant in these regressions. The closer that Hispanic income and education levels are to those of the Anglo community, the more likely Hispanic students are to go to college and the less likely they are to drop out. In both cases the five variables explain over three-fifths of the variation. Vocational school enrollments are unrelated to any of the independent variables.

The results of table 4 offer some promise for improving the educational experience of Hispanic students. Of the seven indicators of educational equity, clearly college enrollments and dropout rates are the most important. Both represent policy outcomes, the end result of the policy process, rather than outputs, a preliminary impact. If Hispanic students can be kept in school, they are better off even if ability grouping and disciplinary practices are discriminatory. Both these measures are significantly related to the proportions of Hispanic teachers.

The promising nature of these findings is that the number of Hispanic teachers is a variable that can be manipulated by other policy actors in the short run, whereas income and education levels probably cannot. By instituting special recruitment programs or reliance on special scholarship programs, more Hispanics can be encouraged to become teachers. Hispanic activists can focus public attention on the equity of the teacher recruitment process. The net result should be improved educational opportunities for Hispanic students. Affirmative action in this context can have a double benefit, first by providing more opportunities for Hispanic teachers and second by improving the educational environment for Hispanic students.

The relationship between Hispanic representation and educational policy toward Hispanics is significantly different from the relationship for Blacks. Meier and England (1984, p. 399) found that school board membership had a significant impact on black enrollments in EMR classes and advanced classes. The proportion of black teachers similarly had strong simple correlations with ability grouping and discipline (Meier, 1984, p. 257). Neither variable was significantly related to the educational attainment of black students.

This raises the question of why Hispanic representation on school boards appears to be unrelated to educational policy toward Hispanics. Three reasons can be suggested. First, even though ten percent of the school board seats in these districts are held by Hispanics, in many districts Hispanics lack representation. In 17 of the 35 districts, not a single Hispanic serves on the school board. Although the proportion of Hispanic teachers may be less than the proportion of school board members in the average school district, every school district in the sample has some Hispanic teachers. Second, Hispanic school board members are not without a role in the educational process examined in this article. Hispanic school board members were significantly related to the proportion of Hispanic teachers. If Hispanic school board members do nothing more than assist in gaining additional teaching positions for Hispanics (e.g., by promoting affirmative action plans), they will play a role in limiting educational inequities for Hispanic students. Third, all Hispanic school board members might not be equally effective in representing the needs of the Hispanic community. Six of the school districts in the sample have appointive school boards; in such cases Hispanic board members are appointed by non-Hispanic politicians. In addition, in at-large cities, Hispanic school board members must be acceptable to a majority of the city. In such circumstances the Anglo power structure has been known to select and run a token Hispanic candidate (Davidson and Fraga, 1984; Fraga, 1984) or to prevent Hispanic candidates from running (Fuentes, 1984, p. 132).

An indirect assessment of the quality of Hispanic school board representation under different types of selection plans can be made by examining the policy indicators for districts using each selection plan. These figures are shown in table 5. Although the small number of school districts with other than at-large selection plans limits generalizations, an interesting pattern results. For five of the seven policy indicators Hispanic students in school districts with ward or mixed election systems are better off than Hispanics in districts with at-large elections.

Although definitive conclusions are impossible with the present

TABLE 5

Educational Policy Measures under Different School Board Plans

	SELECTION PLAN		
Hispanic Policy Ratio	At Large	Ward/Mixed	Appointive
Advanced Classes	.46	.47	.64
Special Education	.91	.92	.83
EMR Classes	1.15	.92	.83
Suspensions	1.01	1.24	.61
Vocational Training	.30	.45	.22
Attending College	.38	.46	.20
Dropouts	2.09	1.82	1.96

data, the results suggest that perhaps the type of Hispanic school board member selected in an at-large system is less effective in representing Hispanic interests. District and mixed selection plans appear to produce Hispanic school board members that can better represent the Hispanic community. The findings for appointive members are inconclusive. Given the limited number of school districts in our data set, these speculations about the quality of representation should be considered as hypotheses rather than firm conclusions (see Wald and Sutherland, 1982). Nonetheless, they are consistent with the findings of Meier and England (1984) regarding the effectiveness of black representation.

CONCLUSION

This study allows us to draw several conclusions regarding Hispanics and educational policy. Hispanics have been unable to elect school board members in numbers anywhere near their percentage in the population. This is partly due to the use of at-large elections in many school districts. Because the proportion of Hispanic teachers is related to both Hispanic population and Hispanic school board members, Hispanics are significantly underrepresented among teachers also. The findings suggest that Hispanics are in a subordinate political position and are thus unable to affect educational policy to their benefit.

One impact of educational policy, second-generation discrimination, was investigated in depth. Although some evidence of ability grouping exists, the data reveal much lower levels of educational attainment for Hispanics. Consistent with the above conclusion, we found that these differences in educational attainment are related to the lack of Hispanic political influence, particularly as translated through the lack of Hispanic teachers. Denial of equal educational opportunities, therefore, is substantially a function of unequal political resources.

All our findings, however, are not pessimistic. Two important institutional characteristics, structures of school board representation and levels of bureaucratic representation, can be manipulated to improve Hispanic access to educational opportunities. More Hispanic school board members can increase the number of Hispanic teachers, and more Hispanic teachers can contribute to higher educational achievement for Hispanic students. We do not mean to imply that these elements of public education in the United States can be changed easily. Historical evidence supports the view that subordinate racial minority group access to educational opportunities have always required a level of political influence

APPENDIX A

School Districts Included in the Analysis

District	COMPOSITION OF STUDENT BODY		
	% Hispanic	% Black	% Anglo
Amarillo	8	8	84[a]
Austin	24	17	59
Boston	12	44	40
Chicago	15	60	23
Corpus Christi	60	6	34
Dade County (Miami)	32	29	39
Dallas	12	44	44
Denver	30	21	47
El Paso	60	3	37
Ft. Worth	14	34	52
Fresno	30	10	60
Gary	8	80	12
Hartford	30	50	20
Houston	23	44	33
Lansing	10	18	70
Las Vegas	5	12	80
Los Angeles	35	25	34
Lubbock	28	12	60
Milwaukee	5	42	51
Newark	21	68	11
New York	30	40	30
Oklahoma City	5	31	59
Orange County (Orlando)	5	25	70
Paterson	29	52	17
Philadelphia	6	62	31
Pueblo	40	2	57
Racine	8	17	75
Salt Lake City	18	1	80
San Antonio	67	16	12
San Bernadino	24	16	58
San Diego	15	15	64
San Jose	24	2	72
Stockton	12	3	82
Tucson	33	5	61
Worchester	7	5	88
Mean all Districts	22.4	26.2	49.8
Standard Deviation	16.1	21.4	22.4

Mean Population Residing in all Districts   786,094
Mean Percent Hispanic Population   14.5
Mean Percent Black Population   15.3

a. Percentages may not add up to 100 because district contains significant numbers of other racial groups.

at legislative, executive, and judicial levels which itself is inhibited by the educational process. Our study suggests, however, that minority group leaders would do well to concentrate a large part of their efforts on making such substantive changes within the educational system of the United States. The enhanced position in America of Hispanics and other subordinate racial minority groups may well depend on such successful efforts.

NOTES

We would like to thank F. Chris Garcia, Susan Welch, Joseph Stewart, Michael Olivas, Lee Sigelman, Chandler Davidson, and Charles Bullock for comments on an earlier draft of this manuscript.

1. This research uses the term "Anglo" to denote non-Hispanic whites. This Southwestern term is more precise than the commonly used term "whites," in that Hispanics are clearly excluded from the group.

2. For the 35 school districts in our sample, the segregation of blacks and Hispanics is relatively equal. For blacks 52.9 percent of students would need to be moved so that all schools had an equal racial balance; for Hispanics, the percentage is 50.5.

3. We do not imply that a properly designed bilingual education program has no benefit for Hispanic or Anglo students. A well-designed program that is intended to provide a transition to learning in English and also emphasizes the qualities of Hispanic culture would benefit both Hispanic and Anglo students. If a bilingual education program is used to eliminate Hispanics from the regular classroom, however, it has little value.

4. The data on Hispanic teachers are from the U.S. Office of Civil Rights, "Student Trend Data," and were supplied by Professor Franklin Wilson of the University of Wisconsin. School board representation data are from a survey conducted in 1978; see Robinson and England (1981). Hispanics were identified by school administrators; we assume individuals were identified by Spanish surname. Other data sources are listed in notes 11 and 12.

5. The sample size must be fairly large so that a few extreme cases do not distort the regression. An intercept different from zero has substantive implications. An intercept significantly less than zero indicates a threshold effect below which Hispanics would receive no representation. A positive intercept would indicate a bias in favor of Hispanic representation. In our case, the intercept was not statistically different from zero.

6. Engstrom and McDonald (1981) argue that selection plans are interactive with population, not additive as we present them here. We disagree with Engstrom and McDonald. Engstrom and McDonald (1981, p. 348) do not operationalize a true interactive model but rather calculate three separate regres-

sions between black population and city council seats, one for each type of selection plan. This process forces an interactive interpretation without determining if the additive model is superior. The correct procedure would be to estimate the following equation:

$$Y = a + b_1x_1 + b_2X_2 + b_3X_3 + b_4X_1X_2 + b_5X_1X_3$$

where X_1 is the percent minority population, X_2 is a dummy variable for at large selection plans, and X_3 is a dummy variable for appointive selection plans, and the b's are regression coefficients.

The relationship is interactive only if b_4 and b_5 are significant. We operationalized this model, and these slopes were not significant; the model added no additional explained variation to that found in table 1. Collinearity in this regression, in fact, makes all five coefficients unstable. In a subsequent work, Engstrom and McDonald (1982, note 6) admit that the interactive model is not superior empirically to the additive model.

7. Since these 35 school districts have large Hispanic populations, one would expect that representation is better in these districts than in other school districts. Using a sample of 168 school districts associated with the SMSAs as of 1970, the corresponding slope was .679. We also ran additional analysis to determine if the slope for this equation was too low because Hispanic voters have lower levels of turnout. Although no registration figures by race are available for these districts, we tried two surrogates, native-born Hispanics and Hispanics over the age of 18. In both cases the level of explanation was significantly worse. In addition, the regression coefficient declined rather than increased.

8. Our "sample" includes 22 at-large districts, six appointive districts, and seven districts with ward or mixed election. All school board members elected in mixed systems were elected from a ward, not at-large.

9. We also ran this equation using the percent of Hispanics with four or more years of college. This variable was not significant when entered into the equation in table 2.

10. Good policy indicators for assessing the relationship between passive and active representation must have two characteristics. First, they must be phenomena the school board members and teachers can affect. Second, they must be directly linked to the Hispanic community so that board members and teachers recognize decisions that are in the interests of the Hispanic community. Expenditure figures that are normally used (see Welch and Karnig, 1980, for the best of this analysis) fail to meet either criteria. School system expenditures are often limited by property values, state appropriations, and federal aid formulas—forces largely outside the control of the local school district. In addition, if the focus is educational equity within a school district, then the level of expenditures is often irrelevant; the distribution of expenditures is far more important.

11. The data on special education, EMR classes, and advanced classes are taken from the U.S. Office of Civil Rights, *Elementary and Secondary School*

Civil Rights Survey: School Year 1976–77 (Washington, D.C.) These data
were provided by Professor Joseph Stewart, Jr., of West Virginia University.
The data for advanced classes were a combination of data for advanced placement classes and classes for the gifted. The suspensions data are from the same
source.

12. The data on dropouts, college attendance, and vocational training
were taken from the National Center for Education Statistics, *Social and Economic Characteristics of U.S. School Districts, 1970* (Washington, D.C., 1975).
All data are for the school district, not the city in which the school district is
located.

13. Although we have no conclusive evidence, we speculate that this pattern occurs for two reasons. First, even large districts have only limited resources
available for EMR and special education classes. The large ratios for blacks indicate that many of the classroom slots are filled by black students (43 percent of
the total). Given that some Anglo students must also be placed in these classes on
objective criteria, this leaves fewer positions that Hispanics can fill. A second reason why Hispanics might not fare as poorly as blacks on these measures is that
a discriminatory school district has another option for segregating Hispanic students; they can be placed in bilingual education programs. The correlation between Hispanic assignment to bilingual education programs and the ability
grouping measures are −.28 for special education and −.23 for EMR classes. The
negative relationships indicate that bilingual education is used more when other
disadvantaged classes are used less. This finding is consistent with the hypothesis
that special education classes, EMR classes, and bilingual education classes can
be used as substitutes for each other.

14. For Hispanics 16 of the 21 policy intercorrelations are in the correct
direction. Such a pattern could occur by chance only four times in 1000 tries. For
blacks, 18 of the 21 correlations are in the correct direction; the probability of
this result is less than 1 in 1000.

15. We attempted to measure Hispanic resources in other ways including
the number of Hispanic elected officials and the number of Hispanic-owned businesses. In the case of elected officials, too few other elected officials were
identified to provide a meaningful measure. In terms of businesses, the Census
Bureau does not report the number of Hispanic-owned businesses if there are
fewer than 100 such establishments within a city. For ten of our cities this was
the case.

16. If such programs were nondiscriminatory, then the level of Anglo
poverty should not affect the proportion of Hispanics assigned to these programs. Objective need for placement of Hispanics in such programs cannot in
any logical way be linked to Anglo poverty. Such a relationship suggests discrimination even if all persons assigned to special education programs objectively belong in them because it would imply that Hispanics who need to be in these
classes are shut out of them so that Anglos can receive the benefits of this instruction.

REFERENCES

Acuña, Rodolfo. 1981. *Occupied America: A History of Chicanos,* 2d ed. New York: Harper and Row.

Alcalá, Carlos M., and Jorge C. Rangel. 1972. Project Report: De Jure Segregation of Chicanos in the Texas Public Schools. *Harvard Civil Rights—Civil Liberties Law Review* 7:307–391.

Arnez, Nancy L. 1978. Implementation of Desegration as a Discriminatory Process. *Journal of Negro Education* 47:28–45.

Barrera, Mario, 1979. *Race and Class in the Southwest: A Theory of Racial Inequality.* Notre Dame, Ind.: University of Notre Dame Press.

Brown, George H., Nancy L. Rosen, S. T. Hill, and Michael A. Olivas. 1980. *The Condition of Education for Hispanic Americans.* Washington: National Center for Education Statistics.

Browning, Rufus P., Dale R. Marshall, and David H. Tabb. 1984. *Protest Is Not Enough: The Struggle of Blacks and Hispanics for Equality in Urban Politics.* Berkeley, Calif.: University of California Press.

Bullock, Charles S., III. 1980. The Office of Civil Rights and Implementation of Desegregation Programs in the Public Schools. *Policy Studies Journal,* 8: 597–615.

Bullock, Charles S., III, and Susan A. MacManus. 1981. Policy Responsiveness to the Black Electorate. *American Politics Quarterly* 9:357–368.

Bustamante, Jorge. 1976. Structural and Ideological Conditions of the Mexican Undocumented Immigration to the United States. *American Behavioral Scientist* 19:364–376.

Cárdenas, Gil. 1975. United States Immigration Policy Toward Mexico: An Historical Perspective. *Chicano Law Review* 2:66–89.

Carrión, A. M. 1983. *Puerto Ricans: A Political and Cultural History.* New York: Norton.

Children's Defense Fund. 1974. *Children Out of School in America.* Washington, D.C.: Children's Defense Fund of the Washington Research Project.

Cole, Leonard A. 1974. Electing Blacks to Municipal Office: Structural and Social Determinants. *Urban Affairs Quarterly* 10:17–39.

Davidson, Chandler, and Luis Ricardo Fraga. 1984. Nonpartisan Slating Groups in an At-large Setting. Pp. 119–144 in Chandler Davidson, *Minority Vote Dilution.* Washington, D.C.: Howard University Press.

Davidson, Chandler, and George Korbel. 1981. At-large Elections and Minority-Group Representation. *Journal of Politics* 43:982–1005.

Dye, Thomas R., and James Renick. 1981. Political Power and City Jobs: Determinants of Minority Employment. *Social Science Quarterly* 62:475–486.

Eisinger, Peter K. 1982a. Black Employment in Municipal Jobs. *American Political Science Review* 76:330–392.

———. 1982b. The Economic Conditions of Black Employment in Municipal Bureaucracies. *American Journal of Political Science* 26:754–771.

Engstrom, Richard L., and Michael D. McDonald. 1981. The Election of Blacks to City Councils. *American Political Science Review* 75:344–354.

———. 1982. The Underrepresentation of Blacks on City Councils. *Journal of Politics* 44:1088–1105.

Epps, Edgar G. 1981. Minority Children: Desegregation, Self-evaluation, and Achievement Orientation. Pp. 85–106 in Willis D. Hawley, *Effective School Desegregation: Equity, Quality, and Feasibility.* Beverly Hills, Calif.: Sage.

Eulau, Heinz, and Paul D. Karps. 1977. The Puzzle of Representation: Specifying Components of Responsiveness. *Legislative Studies Quarterly* 2:233–254.

Eyler, Janet, Valerie Cook, Rachel Thompkins, William Trent, and Leslie Ward. 1981. Resegregation: Segregation Within Desegregated Schools. Pp. 210–329 in Christine Rossell et al., *Assessment of Current Knowledge About the Effectiveness of School Desegregation Strategies.* Nashville, Tenn.: Vanderbilt University, Institute of Public Policy.

Eyler, Janet, Valerie Cook, and Leslie Ward. 1983. Resegregation: Segregation Within Desegregated Schools. Pp. 126–162 in Christine H. Rossell and Willis D. Hawley, eds., *Consequences of School Desegregation.* Philadelphia: Temple University Press.

Feagin, Joe R. 1980. School Desegregation: A Political-Economic Perspective. Pp. 25–50 in W. G. Stephan and Joe R. Feagin, *School Desegregation: Past, Present and Future.* New York: Plenum Press.

Fernández, Ricardo, and Judith T Guskin. 1981. Hispanic Students and School Desegregation. Pp. 107–140 in *Effective School Desegregation.* See Epps, 1981.

Fraga, Luis Ricardo. 1984. *Nonpartisan Slating Groups: The Role of 'Reformed' Parties in City Electoral Politics.* Ph.D. dissertation, Rice University.

Fuentes, Luis. 1984. Puerto Ricans and New York City School Board Elections: Apathy or Obstructionism? Pp. 127–138 in James Jennings and Monte Rivera, *Puerto Rican Politics in Urban America.* Westport, Conn.: Greenwood Press.

Galarza, Ernesto. 1977. *Farm Workers and Agri-business in California.* Notre Dame, Ind.: University of Notre Dame Press.

Gamio, Mario. 1971. *Mexican Immigration to the United States.* New York: Dover.

Garcia, Mario T. 1975. Racial Dualism in the El Paso Labor Market, 1880–1920. *Aztlán* 6:197–218.

Giles, Michael W., and Arthur S. Evans. 1985. External Threat, Perceived Threat, and Group Identity. *Social Science Quarterly* 66:50–66.

Giles, Michael W., and Arthur S. Evans. 1986. The Power Approach to Intergroup Hostility. *Journal of Conflict Resolution* 30: 469–485.

Gómez-Quinoñes, Juan. 1972. The First Steps: Chicano Labor Conflict and Organizing, 1900–1920. *Aztlán* 3:13–49.

Harmel, Robert, Keith Hamm, and Robert Thompson. 1983. Black Voting Cohesion and Distinctiveness in Southern Legislatures. *Social Science Quarterly* 64:183–192.

Kaeser, Susan C. 1979. Suspensions in School Discipline. *Education and Urban Society* 11:465–486.

Karnig, Albert K. 1979. Black Resources and City Council Representation. *Journal of Politics* 41:134–149.

Karnig, Albert K., and Susan Welch. 1979. Sex and Ethnic Differences in Municipal Representation. *Social Science Quarterly* 60:465–481.

———. 1982. Electoral Structure and Black Representation on City Councils. *Social Science Quarterly* 63:99–114.

Keech, William R. 1968. *The Impact of Negro Voting.* Chicago: Rand McNally.

Keller, Ernest. 1973. The Impact of Black Mayors on Urban Policy. *The Annals* 439:40–52.

Levine, Charles H. 1974. *Racial Conflict and the American Mayor.* Lexington, Mass.: Lexington Books.

Lopez, Manual Mariano. 1981. Patterns of Interethnic Residential Segregation in the Urban Southwest. *Social Science Quarterly* 62:50–63.

McConahay, John B. 1981. Reducing Racial Prejudice in Desegregated Schools. Pp. 252–63 in *Effective School Desegregation.* See Epps, 1981.

MacManus, Susan A. 1978. City Council Election Procedures and Minority Representation. *Social Science Quarterly* 59:153–161.

McPartland, James M., and Jomills H. Braddock. 1981. Going to College and Getting a Good Job: The Impact of Desegregation. In *Effective School Desegregation.* See Epps, 1981.

Meier, Kenneth J. 1984. Teachers, Students, and Discrimination: The Policy Impact of Black Representation. *Journal of Politics* 46:252–263.

Meier, Kenneth J., and Robert E. England. 1984. Black Representation and Educational Policy: Are They Related? *American Political Science Review* 78: 392–403.

Meier, Kenneth J., and Lloyd G. Nigro. 1976. Representative Bureaucracy and Policy Preferences. *Public Administration Review* 36:458–470.

Nelson, William. 1972. *Black Politics in Gary.* Washington: Joint Center for Political Studies.

Olivas, Michael A. 1983. Research and Theory on Hispanic Education: Students, Finance and Governance. *Aztlán* 14:111–146.

Orfield, Gary. 1981. Housing Patterns and Desegregation Policy. Pp. 185–221 in *Effective School Desegregation.* See Epps, 1981.

Pitkin, Hannah F. 1967. *The Concept of Representation.* Berkeley, Calif.: University of California Press.

Poinsett, Alex. 1970. *Black Power Gary Style.* Chicago: Johnson.

Robinson, Theodore P., and Thomas R. Dye. 1978. Reformism and Black Representation on City Councils. *Social Science Quarterly* 59:133–141.

Robinson, Theodore P., and Robert E. England. 1981. Black Representation on Central City School Boards Revisited. *Social Science Quarterly* 62:495–502.

Rodgers, Harrell R., and Charles S. Bullock, III. 1972. *Law and Social Change.* New York: McGraw-Hill.

Rosenbaum, James E. 1976. *Making Inequality: The Hidden Curriculum of High School Tracking.* New York: John Wiley.

Saltzstein, Grace Hall. 1979. Representative Bureaucracy and Bureaucratic Responsibility. *Administration and Society* 10:465–475.

Samora, Julian. 1971. *Los Mojados: The Wetback Story.* Notre Dame, Ind.: University of Notre Dame Press.

San Miguel, Guadalupe. 1982. Mexican-American Organizations and the Changing Politics of School Desegregation in Texas, 1945–1980. *Social Science Quarterly* 63:701–715.

Schaefer, Richard T. 1984. *Racial and Ethnic Groups.* 2d ed. Boston: Little-Brown.

Sigelman, Lee, and Albert K. Karnig. 1977. Black Education and Bureaucratic Employment. *Social Science Quarterly* 57:858–863.

Smith, Elsie J., and Lee N. June. 1982. Role of the Counselor in Desegregated Schools. *Journal of Black Studies* 13:227–240.

Smith, Marzell, and Charles D. Dziuban. 1977. The Gap Between Desegregation Research and Remedy. *Integrateducation* 15:51–55.

Stewart, Joseph, and Charles S. Bullock, III. 1981. Implementing Equal Education Opportunity Policy. *Administration and Society* 12:427–446.

Stone, Chuck. 1971. *Black Political Power in America.* New York: Dell.

Taebel, Delbert 1978. Minority Representation on City Councils. *Social Science Quarterly.* 59:142–152.

Thomas, Gail E., and Frank Brown. 1982. What Does Educational Research Tell Us About School Desegregation Effects? *Journal of Black Studies* 13:155–174.

U.S. Commission on Civil Rights. 1975. *The Voting Rights Act: Ten Years After.* Washington, D.C.: U.S. Government Printing Office.

———. 1976. *Fulfilling the Letter and Spirit of the Law: Desegregation of the Nation's Schools.* Washington, D.C.: U.S. Government Printing Office.

Uslander, Eric M. 1976. The Pitfalls of Per Capita. *American Journal of Political Science* 20:125–133.

Wald, Kenneth D., and Carole Sutherland. 1982. Black Public Officials and the Dynamics of Representation. Pp. 239–253 in Laurence W. Moreland, Todd A. Baker, and Robert P. Steed, *Contemporary Southern Political Attitudes and Behavior.* New York: Praeger.

Weinberg, Meyer. 1977. *A Chance to Learn: The History of Race and Education in the United States.* London: Cambridge University Press.

Welch, Susan, and John R. Hibbing. 1984. Hispanic Representation in the U.S. Congress. *Social Science Quarterly* 65:328–335.

Welch, Susan, and Albert K. Karnig. 1978. Representation of Blacks on Big City School Boards. *Social Science Quarterly* 59:162–172.

———. 1980. *Black Representation and Urban Policy.* Chicago: University of Chicago Press.

Welch, Susan, Albert K. Karnig, and Richard Eribes. 1983. Changes in Hispanic Local Public Employment in the Southwest. *Western Political Quarterly* 36: 660–673.

12. The Engine of Latino Growth: Latin American Immigration and Settlement in the United States

Louis DeSipio

IMMIGRATION AND SETTLEMENT ARE THE two anchors of what is often referred to more simply as immigration. Immigration is the process by which nationals of one country move to another land. This process can be temporary—what a tourist does on a visit to another country—or permanent—when a national of one country moves to another country intending to reside in that nation permanently. Settlement, on the other hand, is not a single act—crossing a border—but instead a process during which short- and, particularly, long-term immigrants adapt to the new nation. Settlement is a more complicated process from an analytical perspective. It involves all aspects of this transition—economic and social adaptation, acculturation, and political transition. Yet, despite its complexity, it is by far the less studied of the two anchors.

The study of immigration and settlement has long been central to understanding the United States. Throughout much of the nation's history immigration has driven national growth and served as a key element in the nation's mythology of itself. As such, immigration has been a topic of national pride. Periodically through U.S. history, however, immigration and immigrants have been targets of national concern. These waves of support for and opposition to immigration have tended to cloud scholarship about the appropriate levels of immigration and the process of immigrant settlement. In the early 1990s, the United States is again in a period of active and at times vitriolic debate about the consequences and costs of immigration (Simon 1989; Borjas 1990; Fuchs 1990; Bouvier and Grant 1994; Brimelow 1995). This controversy often obscures our understanding of who is moving to the United States and whether these immigrants are adapting to permanent life here.

In this chapter, I examine Latin American immigrants along several dimensions. I begin by exploring historical and contemporary patterns of immigration from Latin America including the numbers of Latin American immigrants, their countries of origin, and the various statuses under which they have entered the United States. I also examine settlement issues focusing particularly on those characteristics, attitudes, and behaviors that are raised by scholars and polemicists who oppose current levels of immigration. I look at the socioeconomic characteristics of Latin American immigrants, particularly educational characteristics, economic and labor force participation, and use of social welfare services. With this foundation, I look at several measures of civic awareness and civic attachment including the ultimate measure of immigrants' political attachment: naturalization. For both immigration and naturalization, I look at efforts in Congress and in the public policy community to reshape the questions of who may immigrate and what opportunities these immigrants have to become U.S. citizens.

LATIN AMERICAN IMMIGRATION

Over the past thirty years, Latin Americans have made up the largest share of immigrants to the United States (U.S. Immigration and Naturalization Service [hereafter INS] 1994). Their overall share is steadily growing (see table 1). Although this pattern will likely change before the end of the decade, Latin Americans have constituted the majority of all immigrants from 1991 to 1993.

While Latin American immigration of this magnitude is a recent occurrence, Latin Americans have long been part of the stream of immigrants to the United States. It is important to recognize that the composition of this immigration stream has changed over time. One of the most important changes was the revisions made to U.S. immigration law in 1965. As I will suggest, this law created the foundation for the volume of today's immigration as well as for the concerns that many policymakers and citizens have expressed. As a result, I divide my discussion of this topic into pre- and post-1965 immigration. Recognizing its importance, I discuss the numbers of immigrants from Latin America, their share of the immigrant stream, and their countries and regions of origin within Latin America. For both eras, though particularly in the latter era, I also examine the immigrant status on which these immigrants entered the United States.

TABLE 1

Immigration to the United States 1821-1993, by Region of Origin.

IMMIGRATION PERIOD	TOTAL IMMIGRATION	LATIN AMERICA IMMIGRATION	PERCENT LATIN AMERICAN
1821-1830	143,439	9,287	6.5
1831-1840	599,125	19,800	3.3
1841-1850	1,713,251	20,746	1.2
1851-1860	2,598,214	15,411	0.6
1861-1870	2,314,824	12,729	0.5
1871-1880	2,812,191	20,404	0.7
1881-1890	5,246,613	33,663	0.6
1891-1900	3,687,564	35,661	1.0
1901-1910	8,795,386	182,662	2.1
1911-1920	5,735,811	401,486	7.0
1921-1930	4,107,209	592,201	14.4
1931-1940	528,431	51,319	9.7
1941-1950	1,035,039	10,457	0.1
1951-1960	2,515,479	605,681	24.1
1961-1970	3,321,677	1,193,645	35.9
1971-1980	4,493,314	1,618,884	36.0
1981-1990	7,338,062	3,111,760	42.4
1991-1993	3,705,436	1,913,081	51.5

Notes: This table reports on immigrants to permanent resident status. No reliable source of data exists on annual levels of undocumented immigration. The 1991-1993 category includes immigrants from earlier decades who legalized their status under the Immigration Reform and Control Act of 1986.
Source: Author's compilation based on U.S. Immigration and Naturalization Service 1994: Table 2.

Immigration from Latin America before 1965

Latin Americans have been part of U.S. immigration from its first years. During the 1820s, the first decade in which the government recorded entrances, immigrants from Latin America made up 6.5 percent of all immigrants. Although they did not reach this share of immigration for another ninety years, the numbers of Latin American immigrants increased throughout the 1800s.

Beginning in the first decade of this century, the numbers of Latin American immigrants increased rapidly. Nearly 200,000 came in the first decade of this century. This number doubled in the 1910s and increased by almost 200,000 more in the 1920s. These figures probably underestimate true levels of immigration because many entrances along southern borders went unrecorded (Sanchez 1993, chapter 2).

With the Depression, immigration from all parts of the world declined. Latin American immigration followed this pattern, declining to slightly more than 50,000 in the 1930s and 10,000 in the 1940s. Again, these numbers are not accurate reflections of the true levels of migration. The 1930s figures neglect the mass deportation and voluntary returns of Mexican immigrants and U.S. citizens of Mexican ancestry.

The reported immigration levels for the 1940s and 1950s are also somewhat misleading. Beginning in 1942, the U.S. government established the Bracero Program. Designed initially as a short-term guest worker program to provide labor to U.S. agricultural interests to remedy labor shortages during World War II, it lasted until 1964. During its twenty-two–year history, the Bracero Program admitted over 4.6 million Mexican nationals for temporary work in the United States. The Bracero Program gave rise to the initial patterns of seasonal agricultural migration that led to the rapid growth in undocumented migration from Mexico (and, subsequently, from other parts of Latin America) beginning in the 1960s (Calavita 1992).

The "Braceros" (as these immigrants were called) were the leading edge of a steady increase in immigration from Latin America beginning in the 1950s. That decade saw the highest level of Latin American immigration for a ten-year period. Yet, it was only the beginning. Latin American immigration grew from 605,681 in the 1950s to 1,193,645 in the 1960s. Although these levels pale by comparison to contemporary levels of immigration, this post-war period is important for several reasons. Beginning with the 1950s, Latin Americans came to represent a large and steadily increasing share of total immigration. Second, the Bracero Program initiated the migration patterns that led to the contemporary flow of undocumented immigrants, particularly from Mexico.

Immigration from Latin America after 1965

As I have indicated, contemporary patterns of Latin American immigration began in the 1950s. The patterns, however, would not have been able to continue without a statutory change enacted in 1965. In that year, Congress amended the Immigration and Nationality Act in a manner that altered the priorities of U.S. immigration and opened the door to large-scale U.S. immigration to non-Europeans, most of whom had been at a severe disadvantage in access to U.S. immigration prior to 1965. Although Latin Americans (and other residents of the Western Hemisphere) were not explicitly disadvantaged under the pre-1965 law, the new law created the conditions for a rapid increase in overall immigration. This increase in immigration, particularly from Asia, offered an environment in which immigration from Latin America could continue to increase with only minimal scrutiny for many years.

When Congress reexamined the foundation of U.S. immigration law in 1965, it sought to reverse the exclusionary aspects of the then-existing law. The 1965 act abolished the quota system that limited immigration mostly to Northern and Western Europeans. In its place, Congress established a preference system that awarded visas on a first-come, first-served basis. The preferences in the new law were for immediate family members of U.S. citizens and permanent residents, and for persons with job skills that were in short supply in the United States. Immigrants who could meet these preferences were eligible for immigration subject to two numerical limitations. Congress limited annual preference immigration to 290,000 worldwide and 20,000 from any country. Congress also established a category of immigrants not subject to numerical limitation—immediate relatives of U.S. citizens.

The 1965 law has been amended several times, but is the foundation for today's law. The law is notable for several reasons. First, it makes family unification the cornerstone of immigration eligibility. Today, more than two-thirds of immigrants obtain their visas because they have family members already residing in the United States. Second, despite the limits on immigrants from individual countries, the 1965 law exempted immediate family members of U.S. citizens (spouses, parents, and minor children) from these limits. Combined, these exemptions make the countries that have sent the most immigrants over the past two decades the ones most eligible to send immigrants in the coming years. Prospective emigrants in these countries are the most likely to have relatives in the United States who can sponsor their immigration. As a result, several countries dominate the flow of immigrants. In 1992, for example, seven countries saw 25,000 or more of their nationals migrate to the United States: the (former) Soviet Union, China, India, the Philippines, Vietnam, Mexico, and the Dominican Republic (U.S. INS 1993, Table 2).

The impact of the 1965 act has been nothing short of profound. The number of immigrants to permanent residence has increased steadily. The 1950s, the last decade before the change in the law, saw 2.5 million immigrants. In the 1960s, this number grew to 3.3 million. In the 1970s and 1980s, nearly 4.5 and 7.4 million people immigrated to permanent residence, respectively.[1] At current rates, this number will increase again in the 1990s, to approximately 10 million. The major sources of the immigration are Latin America and Asia. While Western Hemisphere immigration was not numerically limited prior to 1965, it is inconceivable that this flow from the Americas would have reached today's levels absent

TABLE 2

Estimated Undocumented Immigrant Population,
by Country of Origin, October 1992.

Top 20 Countries of Origin, 1992

COUNTRY OF ORIGIN	POPULATION
1. Mexico	1,321,000
2. El Salvador	327,000
3. Guatemala	129,000
4. Canada	97,000
5. Poland	91,000
6. Philippines	90,000
7. Haiti	88,000
8. Bahamas	71,000
9. Nicaragua	68,000
10. Italy	67,000
11. Honduras	61,000
12. Colombia	59,000
13. Ecuador	45,000
14. Jamaica	42,000
15. Dominican Republic	40,000
16. Trinidad and Tobago	39,000
17. Ireland	36,000
18. Portugal	31,000
19. Pakistan	30,000
20. India	28,000
Other countries	618,000
Total	3,379,000

Undocumented Immigrants by Region of Origin, 1992

		%
Total Latin America of Top 20	2,050,000	60.7
Total Europe of Top 20	225,000	6.7
Total Non-Spanish-Speaking Caribbean of Top 20	240,000	7.1
Total Asia of Top 20	148,000	4.4
Canada	97,000	2.9
Other countries	618,000	18.3
Total	3,379,000	

Source: U.S. Immigration and Naturalization Service 1994: Table O.

a significant increase in immigration from other parts of the world. The 1965 act permitted this increase and linked family unification to immigrant visa access.

The true level of current immigration from Latin America is somewhat lower than table 1 indicates. These figures include foreign nationals who achieved permanent status under the provisions of the Immigration Reform and Control Act (IRCA) of 1986. These immigrants are recorded as having arrived in the year in which they receive their legalized status and we know this not to be the case. If the IRCA legalization beneficiaries are removed so that we just examine the approximately 750,000 immigrants who received permanent resident visas in 1992, Asia replaces Latin America as the region sending the most immigrants. Slightly more than 45 percent of these new immigrant visas went to Asians, 26 percent went to Latin Americans, and 19 percent went to Europeans (U.S. INS 1993, Table 8). If the patterns from 1992 remain throughout the decade, approximately 2 million new Latin American immigrants will arrive during the decade as permanent residents.

Undocumented Immigration

Needless to say, immigrants to permanent residence do not account for all immigrants to the United States. Among immigrants who establish a long-term residence, the other large group is the undocumented. Their numbers are necessarily somewhat more difficult to estimate. It is safe to say, however, that their numbers are large and probably growing. Several indirect measures suggest this. First, IRCA offered the opportunity to legalize to undocumented immigrants who had been resident in the United States for approximately four years at the time of the bill's passage. Despite this limitation to long-term residents and extensive documentation requirements, more than two million formerly undocumented residents of the United States received permanent resident status under this program. An additional one million individuals with shorter periods of undocumented residence who had worked in agriculture for specified periods of time also received permanent resident status through the Special Agricultural Worker (SAW) provisions of IRCA. A second indicator is an estimate by the INS of the number of undocumented immigrants residing in the United States in October 1992. It placed the number at approximately 3.4 million (U.S. INS 1994, Table O). Estimates from the early 1980s indicate that the number of undocumented immigrants increases by between 100,000 and 300,000 per year (Passel and Woodrow 1985).

Undocumented immigrants are heterogeneous in origin and in migration patterns. While many cross one of the U.S. land borders without a visa, as many as one-third enter the United States on a non-immigrant visa (such as a tourist or student visa) and then stay after its expiration. Their origins are also diverse. According to the INS calculation of undocumented immigrants residing in the United States in October 1992, approximately 70 percent of undocumented immigrants come from the Americas (see table 2). The single largest country of origin is Mexico, which alone accounted for almost 40 percent of undocumented immigrants.

Sources of Latin American Immigration

Immigration from Latin America is diverse in its origins. Although this immigration has been driven by the experiences of Mexican immigrants for most of the twentieth century, immigrants from other parts of Latin America were the majority of immigrants in the nineteenth century and have become an increasing share of contemporary Latin American immigrants.

As I suggested earlier, the first decade of this century marked an important turning point for Latin American immigration. It was in this decade that immigration from the Americas began to become a large number of overall immigration. This period also saw a change in the origins of immigrants from Latin America. Although the federal government did not carefully monitor immigration from the Americas prior to 1917, it is safe to say that the major source of Latin American immigration in the nineteenth century was the Caribbean. Beginning in 1910, Mexico began to dominate immigration from the Americas, as it has continued to do. Neither Central nor South America provided many immigrants to the United States before the 1950s. This influence of Mexican immigrants has grown in recent years, though in some ways this is an artifact of the legalization program for long-term undocumented immigrants. In the 1950s, the first decade for which there are reliable country-specific immigration data, Mexicans made up almost half of Latin American immigrants (see table 3). By the early 1990s, Mexicans made up more than two-thirds of Latin American immigrants. The Caribbean and South American shares of the immigrant flow have declined slightly and the Central American share has grown.

If the immigrants who attained permanent resident status under IRCA are excluded to present a picture of those permanent residents who arrived in the current year, Mexico's share of Latin American immigra-

TABLE 3

*Regions and Countries of Origin of Immigrants
from Latin America, 1951-1993.*

Region	1951-1960	1961-1970	1971-1980	1981-1990[1]	1991-1993[1]
Latin America and the Caribbean	605,681	1,193,645	1,618,884	3,111,760	1,913,081
Mexico	49.5%	38.0%	39.6%	53.2%	67.4%
Spanish-Speaking Caribbean[2]	18.1%	30.2%	33.8%	16.9%	10.8%
Central America	7.4%	8.5%	8.3%	15.0%	11.9%
South America	15.1%	21.6%	18.3%	14.8%	9.9%
Other America[3]	9.9%	1.6%	0.1%	0.0%	0.0%
Countries	1951-1960	1961-1970	1971-1980	1981-1990[1]	1991-1993[1]
Mexico	299,811	453,937	640,294	1,655,843	1,288,693
Cuba	78,948	108,536	264,863	144,578	33,340
Dominican Republic	9,897	93,292	148,135	252,035	128,834
El Salvador	5,895	14,992	34,436	213,539	99,794
Argentina	19,486	49,721	29,897	27,327	11,296
Colombia	18,048	72,028	77,347	122,849	44,754
Ecuador	9,841	36,780	50,077	56,315	24,684

Notes:

[1] Data from the 1980s and early 1990s include immigrants legalized under the Immigration Reform and Control Act of 1986.

[2] Caribbean data includes some who immigrated from the English-speaking Caribbean.

[3] This is a residual category used by the Immigration and Naturalization Service to account for immigrants that INS records do not clearly account for. As INS recordkeeping has improved, the category has been used much less frequently.

Source: Author's compilation based on U.S. Immigration and Naturalization Service 1994: Table 2.

tion drops considerably, with the other regions of Latin America increasing their share. Of the current immigration to permanent residence, Mexico makes up 43 percent, the Spanish-speaking Caribbean and Central America approximately 20 percent each, and South America 18 percent.

Although it is difficult to predict the future course of immigration, this pattern of a slow decline in Mexico's share of Latin American immigration is likely to continue. Adding to this likelihood, a recent agreement between the United States and Cuba assures an increasing number of Cuban immigrants in the coming years. Further, ongoing legislative efforts to restrict or cap the numbers of family members who can enter the United States outside of numerical limitations will, if implemented, have the greatest impact on Mexican immigration. One caveat to this is necessary. The figures reported here for the country and regional shares of Latin American immigration do not include undocumented immigrants. As I suggested earlier, Mexico is the single largest source of this immigrant stream. Thus, while it is not possible to predict with certainty, it seems likely that Mexico will continue to dominate Latin American immigration, though its share of the total will decline.

Congressional Efforts to Restructure Immigration

These patterns of immigration that I have identified may soon experience another change. At this writing, Congress is considering proposals that will make major changes to U.S. immigration law. While it is not possible to predict precisely the outcome of these Congressional debates, I discuss some of the major proposals and indicate how changes such as these would influence migration from the Americas. Congress has voted to separate its consideration of legal and undocumented immigration and I follow that model.

At the beginning of the Congressional session, it seemed likely that Congress would reduce the number of immigrants from the current level of approximately 800,000 annually to approximately 500,000 annually. This immigration level, unlike the targets in the current law, would be a firm limit with no exceptions for immediate family members. Were firm limits to be established, fewer immigrants from Latin America would be eligible to immigrate. Somewhat unexpectedly, Congress has moved away from a discussion of the volume of legal immigration and, instead, has focused most of its attention on the characteristics desired of permanent resident immigrants and on control of undocumented immigrants.

Congress has used the period of consideration about a new immigration law, however, to potentially change who will be eligible to immigrate. Since the early 1900s, the immigration law has prohibited the immigration of individuals likely to become a "public charge." This standard was never defined and is difficult to enforce. Under the current law, the U.S. citizen or permanent resident who petitions for the immigration of a foreign national formally promises to sponsor that individual, reducing the likelihood that he or she will become dependent on government services. The courts, however, have interpreted this sponsorship as voluntary. The proposed immigration legislation would change this standard and make this sponsorship legally binding. Equally importantly, to assure that the sponsorship had some meaning, the proposed legislation would require that the combined income of the sponsor's family and the immigrant equal between 1.25 (in the Senate bill) and 2 (in the House bill) times the federal poverty line for a family of that combined size. Thus, for a family of four seeking to sponsor an immigrant, the sponsor would have to have an income of approximately $32,000 (in 1995 dollars) under the legislation passed in the House of Representatives. Were this proposal to become law, particularly in the form passed in the House, it would place a class dynamic into immigration eligibility that has been absent since 1965. Its likely impact would be to reduce the number of immigrants from the two largest Latin American sending countries—Mexico and the Dominican Republic—and to reduce Latin American immigration relative to Asian immigration.

Congress is also seeking to limit immigrant eligibility for federal social welfare programs such as Supplemental Security Income and Medicaid. Not only could the sponsor's income be taken into account to determine eligibility (for ten years in the Senate bill or until naturalization in the House bill), but also the immigrant could be deported as a public charge if he or she were determined to be eligible for one of these programs. What evidence exists indicates that immigrants have low rates of social welfare program use (Pachon and DeSipio 1994). The one exception is Supplemental Security Income, a program for the elderly poor, which already denies immigrants access until they have resided in the United States for five years. While these proposals would probably have less impact on Latin American immigration than the sponsorship requirements, they might potentially slow the process of immigrant adaptation and settlement and adversely affect immigrants from Latin America who tend to be poorer than immigrants from other parts of the world.

Congress has focused its attention more precisely on undocumented immigration and seems more likely to pass legislation this year. The core of proposals follows a recent pattern in Congressional as well as executive policy in this area—appropriate more money for the border patrol. Congress is proposing to hire an additional 1,000 border patrol agents annually for the next five years, increasing the border patrol from 5,175 to 10,000 by the year 2000. The legislation also funds a fourteen-mile "triple fence" in San Diego, increases the criminal penalties for smuggling undocumented aliens into the United States and using false documents to get a job, and creates a pilot program through which employers could verify the work eligibility of new employees. As I indicated these provisions concerning undocumented immigrants are much more likely to become law than those addressing immigration to permanent residence. Increasing the size of the border patrol will undoubtedly have some impact on short-term undocumented immigrants, such as those going to day jobs in U.S. border cities, but will probably have much less impact on undocumented immigrants seeking long-term residence in the United States. As a result, its greatest impact will be felt among residents of U.S.-Mexican border cities. Over time, increased enforcement may reduce the incentives to undocumented migration, but enforcement efforts to date have had little impact.

SOCIOECONOMIC STATUS OF IMMIGRANTS FROM LATIN AMERICA

For analysts of contemporary immigration, one of the greatest concerns is that today's immigrants are less likely than their predecessors to have the skills, education, and interests to succeed in the United States (Borjas 1990). While it would be impossible and inaccurate to compare today's immigrants, or more narrowly today's Latin American immigrants, to immigrants who arrived at the turn of the century or in the years before the reform of the immigration law in 1965, it is now possible to present a portrait of contemporary immigrants. This portrait is facilitated by the availability of two surveys of the Latino[2] political values, attitudes, and behaviors and immigration and naturalization experiences—the National Latino Immigrant Survey (NLIS)[3] and the Latino National Political Survey (LNPS).[4] These surveys, conducted in 1988 and 1989–1990, respectively, provide baseline data for a discussion of the socioeconomic condition of Latino immigrants that serves as a necessary background to a discussion of their civic attachment and civic participation.[5]

The history of immigration from the Americas suggests an important factor that must be understood prior to this discussion of Latino immigrant sociodemographic characteristics. I have already suggested the diversity of Latino immigrants in terms of origin. A second diversity is temporal; immigrants from Latin America have had different immigration patterns and as a result, different histories in the United States. With the exception of Cubans, the majority of immigrants from the Americas have arrived in the past twenty-five years. Cubans and Mexicans, however, have sizable immigrant populations who arrived in the 1960s and before (68 percent and 46 percent, respectively). These early immigrants from Mexico are somewhat different than those who followed and are, for example, much more likely to work in agriculture. These varying immigration histories must be kept in mind while considering the sociodemographic conditions of Latino immigrants.

In the discussion that follows, I assess Latino educational attainment, linguistic patterns, labor force participation, and economic status. I focus on these characteristics because they, in addition to being descriptive in their own right, serve as background to the discussion of civic attachment and civic participation in the final section. Throughout this discussion, I speak broadly of the characteristics of Latino immigrants. I will, however, indicate where there is significant variation between Latino national-origin groups.

Latino Immigrant Educational Attainment

Like many immigrants who preceded them, Latino immigrants have relatively low levels of formal education. More than 60 percent of Mexican immigrants, for example, have eight or fewer years of schooling and just 30 percent have earned high school degrees or have post–high school education. On average, Cuban immigrants have slightly higher levels of education—38 percent have eight or fewer years of education and 49 percent have completed high school or gone beyond high school.[6] By the standards of the U.S.-born population, these educational attainment rates are rather low. Among the U.S.-born population, the average level of educational attainment is slightly more than twelve years. Although the data are not easily available, the average educational attainment among the U.S.-born with comparable ages and urban residence to most immigrants from Latin America would be even higher. The average levels of education for Mexican immigrants are also low by the standards of immigrants generally (Schoeni, McCarthy, and Vernez 1996).

The majority of the educational capital comes with the immigrant at the time of immigration. Among NLIS respondents, the majority received their final year of formal education abroad. Just one-quarter of Dominicans, for example, received formal schooling in the United States.

Since arriving in the United States, many Latino immigrants have supplemented their formal education with classes in either English or U.S. history and civics. Although classes in these subjects prepare immigrants for the naturalization exam, they report that for the most part they took them for other reasons.

Latino Immigrant Linguistic Patterns

The language world of Latino immigrants is dominated by Spanish, but is not by any means exclusively driven by Spanish. As the findings on

English courses should indicate, Latino immigrants are learning English and many are comfortable with their English-language skills.

At home, Latino immigrants live in an almost exclusively Spanish world. The majority speak only Spanish at home. If the share that speaks more Spanish than English is added, the share of Spanish-dominant households rises to more than three-quarters. These high rates of Spanish exclusivity and predominance hold for all national-origin groups.

Outside of the home, Latino immigrants report much higher rates of English-language use. The majority of working Latino immigrants, for example, report that speaking English is either very or somewhat important for their jobs. Among Central Americans and South Americans, more than 80 percent report the importance of English for their employment.

Latino immigrants report varied levels of English-language skills. The majority of Mexican and Dominican immigrants evaluate their English-language abilities (speaking, listening comprehension, writing, and reading) as not well or not at all. Among Central Americans and South Americans, on the other hand, the majority rate their abilities as well or very well. It is important to note that few immigrants report that they have no English-language abilities. According to the NLIS, the share of the Latino immigrant population that believes that they have no abilities in English range from 5 percent among South Americans and 6 percent among Central Americans to 16 percent among Cubans, 19 percent among Mexicans, and 25 percent among Dominicans.

Latino Immigrant Labor Force Participation

The relatively lower levels of formal education among Latino immigrants compared to the Latino and non-Latino U.S.-born and their weak English-language skills might indicate potential difficulties in the workforce. In fact, the opposite is the case. Overall Latino immigrants show higher rates of labor force participation than do U.S.-born Latinos or non-Latinos. Nearly 70 percent of foreign-born Mexicans, for example, are workers. These high rates of labor come despite higher than average rates of temporary unemployment. Overall, more than 90 percent of Latino immigrants have worked since their arrival in the United States.

Latino immigrants are concentrated in the less-skilled ranks of the U.S. labor force with the highest concentrations in three categories of jobs—service (18.3 percent); technical, sales, and administrative support (16.7 percent); and operator, fabricator, and laborer (16.1 percent). One occupational category that employs few Latino immigrants deserves special note. Relatively few Latino immigrants work in agricultural labor. Mexican immigrants, however, are the exception. Approximately 17 percent of Mexican immigrants work in agriculture.

Among Latino immigrants not in the labor force, the most common reason is work in the home. Seventy percent of Mexican immigrants and one-third of Cuban immigrants who do not work are homemakers. Few Mexican immigrants and approximately 43 percent of Cuban immigrants who do not work are retired.

Latino Immigrant Economic Conditions

Despite their concentration in low-skill occupations, Latino immigrants are not, for the most part, living in poverty. Instead, Latino immigrants tend to live in households with multiple workers and use these multiple earnings to build a livelihood that could be described as working poor or lower middle class. In contrast to the claims of many critics of immigration, Latino immigrants are not large-scale users of social welfare services. Although Latino immigrant household poverty rates decline with longer periods of residence in the United States, a recent study of immigrants to California found that the earning gap between households headed by Mexican or Central American immigrants and households headed by a U.S.-born individual remains persistent over time, unlike the experiences of immigrants from other parts of the world. In other words, the relative disadvantage that one would expect during the first years after immigration remains throughout the immigrant's life for many Mexican and Central American immigrants (Schoeni, McCarthy, and Vernez 1996).

Latino immigrant households had average incomes of between $18,000 and $19,000 per year in 1988. These average incomes were consistent across national-origin groups, with the exception of Dominican respondents to the NLIS who had average incomes of approximately $14,000 annually in 1988. These averages were lower than those for U.S.-born Latinos ($21,000) and for U.S.-born non-Hispanic whites ($28,000) in that year, but were well above the poverty line ($12,500).

These Latino immigrant household incomes are built to a large degree on multiple wage earners. Fully one-third of Mexican and Cuban immigrant households had three or more wage earners. Among married couple households, more than 70 percent saw both spouses working.

Average incomes can mask the experiences of people or households at the extremes. Each of the Latino national-origin groups had a significant share of their co-nationals living in poverty, including 45 percent of

Dominicans, 25 percent of Mexicans, and approximately 20 percent of Cubans, Central Americans, and South Americans. Despite these poverty rates, a small minority of Latino immigrants receive social welfare benefits. As might be expected from the data presented above, Dominicans are the most likely to receive benefits with approximately one-quarter reporting that they receive Medicaid, food stamps, housing assistance, or help from some other need-based government program. Mexicans and Central Americans are the next most likely to receive program assistance with approximately 10 percent of the immigrant populations receiving some sort of aid.

An Overview of Latino Immigrant Sociodemographic Conditions

These various social indicators offer evidence of a growing Latino immigrant integration to the U.S. society. As I will indicate in the final section, this attachment has a political scope, but here it is important to note its economic and linguistic dimensions. Economically, Latino immigrants are neither overwhelmingly successful nor overwhelmingly disadvantaged. They, on average, bring relatively low levels of education to the United States and work in the less-skilled professions. These disadvantages have not relegated Latino immigrants to poverty, however. High rates of labor force participation and high numbers of working household members catapult average Latino household earnings to a level near that of the Latino U.S.-born. Contrary to popular notions, few Latino immigrants rely on needs-based social welfare programs. Linguistic adaptation to the United States, or more specifically to English, offers a second indicator of Latino immigrant acculturation. Although almost all Latino immigrants speak Spanish at home, a large share and the majority of some national-origin groups report that their English skills are good or very good. The need for English-language skills at work seems to be a force driving the acquisition of English. As I will suggest, these various employment, income, and English-language skills come together as factors that predict the likelihood of an immigrant making the transition to U.S. citizenship through naturalization.

CIVIC ATTACHMENT AND CIVIC PARTICIPATION
AMONG LATIN AMERICAN IMMIGRANTS

The final indicator of immigrant settlement that I examine involves political identities and political behaviors. To explore this question of civic attachment, I examine several attitudinal measures and one much more formal indicator—naturalization. I examine these themes more thoroughly in DeSipio (1996). The LNPS and the NLIS indicate that Latino immigrants develop an attachment to the United States and to U.S. political values relatively quickly after their arrival. This attachment, however, does not lead many Latino immigrants to a formal attachment to the United States through naturalization. Thus, non-citizenship reduces the ability of Latino immigrants to act on the attachment they feel to the United States and reduces the political power of Latinos more generally. After demonstrating that Latino immigrants have developed an attitudinal attachment to the United States, I suggest some factors that may be deterring them from making this attachment formal.

Latino Immigrant Attachment to the United States

The great majority of Latino immigrants reported that they intended to make the United States their permanent home. Regardless of national origin, more than 95 percent of NLIS respondents reported that they "presently plan to make the United States their permanent home."

This reported intention to reside here permanently was reinforced by a series of positive attitudes toward life in the United States. Overwhelmingly, immigrants reported that life is better here and that they expect their children's lives to be better than their own. This attachment and expectation for a better life was true of each of the national-origin groups.

The LNPS offers a final indication of this attachment. Nearly 80 percent of the Cuban immigrants and almost two-thirds of the Mexican immigrants with five or more years of residence reported either an extremely strong or very strong love for the United States. At the other extreme, just 11 percent of Mexicans and 4 percent of Cuban citizen-eligible immigrants reported "not very strong" love of the U.S.

Emerging Political Attachment to the United States

The intention to live in the United States and attachment to it was tempered, however, by the political reality of non-citizenship. Among the non-citizens, the dominant political allegiance remained to the country of origin. Despite their non-citizenship, more than one third of each of the national-origin groups and nearly half of the Dominican immigrants already were more connected to the United States.

As this discussion should imply, Latino immigrants seek to make their attachment to the United States more formal. Among NLIS respondents, between 82 and 95 percent of each national-origin group had applied for or planned to apply for U.S. citizenship. Among respondents who had not yet naturalized, 78 percent of Cuban immigrants, 79 percent of Mexican immigrants, 93 percent of Dominican immigrants, and 81 percent of other Latino immigrants intended to apply for citizenship in the future.

Among non-citizens in the NLIS, approximately 60 percent of each of the national-origin groups reported that naturalizing was "very important." At the other extreme, between 3 percent of Mexican immigrants and 6 percent of Cuban immigrants felt the converse, that naturalizing was "not at all" important.

With the high levels of intent to remain permanently in the United States, the strong love for the United States, and the considerable interest in naturalization, one might expect that Latinos are quick to naturalize once they achieve statutory eligibility. The reality is quite different. Among the immigrant groups comprising a major share of the immigrant pool, Latinos are consistently among the slowest to naturalize. Until the mid-1980s, Cuban Americans proved the exception to this rule. Today, however, they are among the slowest to naturalize.

This gap between interest in naturalization and U.S. citizenship rates is somewhat more complicated than this discussion suggests. Many Latinos initiate the naturalization process but fail to become citizens. According to the NLIS, between 38 and 51 percent of the non-citizens had begun to naturalize in some concrete manner, but had not yet completed the process. This gap indicates that a large share of Latino immigrants desire U.S. citizenship, but are not actively pursuing it.

Naturalization and the Latino Community

Why is there such a gap between Latino immigrant interest in U.S. citizenship and successful naturalization? The first is perhaps the most obvious, but also the most often overlooked in the scholarship on naturalization—the longer the residence in the United States, the higher the likelihood of naturalization. The second explanation relates to the individual characteristics of immigrants. Certain sociodemographic traits, immigration characteristics, and associational patterns have been found to increase the likelihood of immigrant naturalization. Finally, a third explanation has to do with the administration of naturalization. Many immigrants who are interested in seeking U.S. citizenship and who have taken behavioral steps toward achieving that goal are deterred by the INS's administration of the program. While none of these factors alone explains the gap between attachment to the United States and low levels of citizenship attainment, they should present a picture of immigrant populations with higher levels of interest in joining the polity than raw naturalization rates would suggest.

The initial scholarship on naturalization posited that cultural differences among various nationalities influenced Americanization potential. Southern and Eastern Europeans (the "new" immigrants at the turn of the century) were assumed to be less able to become Americans than were Northern and Western Europeans. Beginning in the 1920s, however, scholars more carefully began to examine the propensity to naturalize and found that length of residence explained most differences in nationality and regional naturalization rates (Gavit 1971 [1922]). On average, nationalities that had been in the United States for the longest average periods had the highest naturalization rates. Thus, nationality or cultural differences explained little, at least for turn-of-the-century immigrants.

Thus, the first wave of naturalization scholarship raised a second-level question that analysts continue to grapple with today: what factors distinguish immigrants who naturalize from those who do not? Although there is no comprehensive study of immigrants nationally, several recent studies (each relying on different pools of immigrants) have identified clusters of factors—sociodemographic characteristics, attitudinal and associational traits, and immigration characteristics—that supplement length of residence as a predictor of naturalization.

All naturalization scholars to some degree look at the sociodemographic characteristics of immigrants. These include such factors as income, white collar employment, professional status, home ownership, years of schooling, and English-language abilities (Barkan and Khokolov 1980; Portes and Mozo 1985; Jasso and Rosenzweig 1990; Yang 1994; DeSipio 1996). The married are more likely to naturalize than the unmarried and women more likely than men. Immigrants who arrived as young children are more likely to naturalize than are people who arrived in the United States as teenagers or adults. A review of the sociodemographic data presented in the second section of this chapter should suggest that Latino immigrants are at a disadvantage when it comes to the traits that predict successful naturalization; low wages, low levels of education, and lower English skills are all factors that discourage naturalization and the Latino immigrant population has a large share with each of these traits.

Other scholars find attitudinal and associational variables, such as roots in the United States, attitude toward life in the United States, and social identification as an American, to be positive predictors of naturalization (García 1981; Portes and Curtis 1987). Immigrants who associate mostly with non-citizens are less likely to naturalize (DeSipio 1993). Immigrant community attitudes also influence naturalization. Jones-Correa (1994) finds that an "ideology of return [to the home country]" discourages naturalization.

The last category of variables relates to characteristics at the time of immigration that shape the settlement experience. Positive factors include visa categories, with immigrants who entered as refugees and skilled workers more likely to naturalize than other immigrants (Jasso and Rosenzweig 1987, 1990). Emigration for political reasons (whatever the formal source of the immigrant visa) also increases naturalization's likelihood (Portes and Mozo 1985; Jasso and Rosenzweig 1990). Considering these other factors found to have a positive influence on naturalization, a counterintuitive finding by one scholar is that the higher the home country's GNP, the lower the likelihood of naturalization (Yang 1994).

This study of characteristics at immigration has also returned the scholarship to a consideration of national and regional origin. Jasso and Rosenzweig (1987) find that immigrants from Mexico are less likely than average, controlling for other immigration-related factors, to naturalize. Portes and Mozo (1985) find that immigrants from Canada and Mexico are less likely to naturalize than nationals of other countries, controlling for sociodemographic factors. Finally, controlling for sociodemographic, associational, and immigration-related factors, DeSipio (1993) finds that among Latinos, Cubans and Dominicans are more likely than Mexicans to begin the naturalization process and to become U.S. citizens.

Because there is no comprehensive survey data on immigrant naturalization, it is not possible to say how these factors interact nor to assess their relative influence on naturalization. That said, these individual differences account for part of the gap between immigrant attachment to the United States and successful naturalization. Each of the factors discussed so far varies from individual to individual. The final deterrent to naturalization influences some nationalities more than others and some geographic areas more than others. The administration of naturalization is highly decentralized, which results in differential treatment of applicants from INS district office to INS district office.

The impact of this administrative inconsistency is difficult to measure precisely, but two outcomes are likely, each of which discourages interested Latino immigrants from pursuing citizenship. First, immigrants from different countries and regions have different administrative denial rates (DeSipio and Pachon 1992). This, in part, may reflect different immigrant skill and education levels, but also reflects variation in office practice. Overall, applicants from Latin America, the Spanish- and English-speaking Caribbean, and Africa have higher than average denial rates. Second, some INS offices have higher-than-average-rates of unsuccessful applicants. Offices at the high end of the spectrum for administrative denials—Miami, Newark, and San Jose—and the low end—Boston and Denver—have a sufficient mix of immigrants that immigrant characteristics alone cannot explain the variation. The variety of experiences of individual naturalization applicants who go before the INS may, in turn, lead to confusion in immigrant populations which could discourage some interested immigrants from seeking naturalization.

In sum, naturalization is far from automatic among immigrants interested in becoming U.S. citizens. The statutory requirements and bureaucratic administration make naturalization seem a difficult goal for many immigrants.

Latino Community Organizational Efforts to Promote Naturalization

Until recently, there have been few organized efforts to promote naturalization in the Latino community. Two exceptions are efforts in the Miami Cuban-American community to naturalize large numbers in the late 1970s and 1980s (Portes and Mozo 1985) and the recent efforts by the National Association of Latino Elected Officials to coordinate a national U.S. citizenship education and promotion campaign (NALEO Educational Fund 1985; Pachon 1991).

The first occurred within the Cuban-American community. As its focus shifted and its self-perception changed from that of an exile to an immigrant community in the mid-1970s, Cuban-American leaders in Miami promoted naturalization. They presented U.S. citizenship as a tool to accomplish political ends as well as to sever political ties with the Cuban government. They also recognized that many of the exiles would not return to Cuba, even if Castro fell. Naturalization served the Cuban-American leadership's national political ends by giving it increased leverage in Washington to promote the overthrow of Castro and Cuban communism as well as its local ends to garner local political power in Miami and Dade County. This political power was increasingly important to ensure the continued growth of Cuban economic power in the region.

This Cuban-American naturalization promotion had the desired impact. Naturalization rates among early Cuban immigrants are among the highest of any immigrant group (Portes and Mozo 1985). This high rate of naturalization has translated into local and national political influence (Moreno and Warren 1992; Grenier et al. 1993).

To some extent, community-wide mobilization toward naturalization has declined in recent years. This probably reflects the combined impacts of declining immigration in the 1970s (reducing the pool), a change in composition of the Cuban immigrant and refugee pool (with the Mariel boatlift), and the ability to increase the electorate through the mobilization of U.S.-born Cuban Americans.

The other exception to the pattern of limited Latino interest in encouraging and assisting naturalization is, to date, more diffuse than the efforts in the Cuban-American community, but in the end much more ambitious. Beginning in 1985, the National Association of Latino Elected Officials[7] initiated a research and demonstration project on the causes of low naturalization rates in the Latino communities. In addition to research, the project advocated before Congress and the executive branch to raise the salience of naturalization, promoted its importance nationally and before Latino leaders, and established a national toll-free telephone number to provide citizenship information to applicants. By 1987, this project research led to the development of a prototype citizenship service center in East Los Angeles. The U.S. citizenship center tested several models for the delivery of direct citizenship services while promoting U.S. citizenship to immigrants in California and nationwide. The most efficient and effective model—mass citizenship workshops followed by individual assistance in completing the application, supplemented, if necessary, by civics and history classes—is now being implemented by coalitions including NALEO and local community service organizations in California, Texas, Illinois, and New York and on an irregular basis in Arizona and Florida.

NALEO's success has caused other national and local Latino organizations to recognize the importance of naturalization and the need for administrative reform and direct citizenship assistance (National Council of La Raza 1991). NALEO's initiatives have also spurred community groups to conduct on-going citizenship promotion and assistance activities. One of these operates with active support from the Chicago Democratic party.

Increasing Interest in Naturalization among Immigrants

The increase in Latino community resources to promote naturalization and assist immigrants seeking citizenship could not have come at a better time. Between 1994 and early 1996, several changes in policy and in immigrant-state relations occurred that spurred unprecedented demand for naturalization. This increase in interest has also spurred the beginnings of a backlash in the larger society that may lead to Congressional efforts to change naturalization law.

The incentive structure surrounding naturalization changed dramatically for many immigrants between 1994 and 1996. In this period, the annual number of applications for naturalization surged from approximately 350,000 per year to between 800,000 and 1,000,000 annually. Although INS was ill-equipped to handle this new demand initially, it promises to process 1,000,000 applications in FY 1995 and expects to handle at least 800,000 annually in 1996 and 1997. It is not yet possible to determine how many of these new citizenship applicants are from Latin America and the Caribbean. If patterns from previous years continue, however, it is safe to say that between one-third and two-fifths are Latino.

Why has demand for naturalization increased so dramatically? Four factors combined to encourage many long-term residents to seek citizenship (DeSipio forthcoming). First, California's Proposition 187 demonstrated that many in the United States sought to limit the rights of immigrants. While 187 primarily targeted the undocumented, many permanent residents reacted to its anti-immigrant rhetoric (NALEO Educational Fund 1993). By naturalizing, they protected their rights as individuals and gained the vote as a tool to express their opinions. Second, Republican Congressional leadership's "Contract with America" proposed reductions in government program benefit eligibility for permanent residents. Again, naturalization offered protections. Third, the INS required that "green cards" issued before 1980 be replaced. The replacement procedure required both an application and a fee. This fee was just $25 less than the fee for naturalization and for many the application process was no more difficult. As I have suggested, these long-term permanent residents are the immigrants most likely to want to naturalize. Finally, at about this same time, approximately 2.6 million immigrants became eligible for citizenship. These were the recipients of legalization under the Immigrant Reform and Control Act of 1986 and represented the largest single pool of naturalization-eligible immigrants ever to attain citizenship eligibility at one time. Many of these legalization beneficiaries had completed some of the knowledge-based requirements for citizenship when they applied for permanent residence and, thus, had a streamlined citizenship application. Combined, these four factors increased demand for naturalization and raised the salience of U.S. citizenship both within the immigrant communities (probably spurring even more applications) and in the citizen population.

While many have embraced the new citizens, there is also the beginning of a backlash against the surge in naturalization (Chávez 1996; Miller 1996a, 1996b). These concerns focus on two dimensions of naturalization. First, some argue that the requirements for naturalization are too few and these new citizens cheapen the meaning of citizenship. Although not as often articulated, the second concern relates to the potential political power of the naturalized. As they are concentrated in a few states, the newly naturalized could influence the outcome of close local elections. So, it is argued, ethnic leaders spur naturalization among the unprepared as a way for expanding the ethnic leader's political power. These concerns have not resulted in Congressional action, and they may never be taken seriously enough to have any real impact on naturalization law. Should they, however, and should Congress increase the barriers to citizenship, the Latino community will pay a political price. As I will indicate in the conclusion, naturalization offers an opportunity for Latino empowerment that is perhaps richer than traditional strategies such as voter registration.

CONCLUSION

Despite the low levels of U.S. citizenship among Latino immigrants, many have developed a psychological attachment to the United States and have made behavioral steps toward naturalization. These preliminary efforts to become U.S. citizens, however, end in frustration for many. Despite this frustration, the non-citizens offer a rich pool of immigrants who have demonstrated an engagement with government that would make for good citizens. Thus, Latino empowerment strategies must tap this need.

Clearly interest in U.S. citizenship alone does not assure naturalization. Many Latino immigrants have been impeded in accomplishing their goal. I believe that there are two broad explanations for this failure. First, the administration of naturalization is ill-designed to assist the average applicant from Latin America. While the statutory requirements are relatively minimal and while most potential applicants could meet them without too much study, the administrative requirements and procedures deter many from applying and others from completing the process. Second, with the exception of the Cuban-American community, Latino leaders and organizations as well as non-ethnic political and community leaders have failed until recently to promote naturalization or to assist immigrants interested in pursuing U.S. citizenship.

The historical results of this neglect of naturalization are evident in the low rates of naturalization among those Latinos who have expressed interest in or pursued U.S. citizenship. A wide-scale Latino community mobilization, even if just targeted at those who have expressed some concrete interest in naturalization, could reverse these trends, particularly if it were to build on the demand that has appeared in all immigrant communities over the past two years.

Similar factors distance the non-naturalized from naturalization as distance the non-voter from voting. Two fundamental differences, however, distinguish these types of civic non-participation. First, the non-voters have had many opportunities and encouragements to register. Yet, many stay away from the polls, whether through decision, indecision, or ignorance. Few Latino non-citizens, with the exception of Cuban Americans, on the other hand, have had much encouragement or assistance to naturalize. Second, since the mid-1970s and probably before, few non-voters have experienced personal discouragement in their effort to exercise the franchise. Thus, their decision not to vote is private. Although there are costs associated with registering and voting, today these can be overcome with a minimum of effort. Non-citizens contemplating naturalization, however, face more active discouragement. Dealing with INS is intimidating. The application form is not sensitive to the education levels of many of its users. Confusion abounds about the risks in failing the exam. Applicants have few places to turn to get assistance when they have questions or concerns. Finally, unlike voter registration or voting, applying for naturalization can take months, even a year or more in some cases. Thus, the reward—naturalization—which many reported they have sought or would like to seek is often in the long-term future.

A complete empowerment strategy based on naturalization could incorporate the desires for citizenship among the 5,000,000 to 6,000,000 Latinos currently eligible. The desire is there among immigrants. The numbers to have a significant impact, perhaps an impact as great as registering every non-voter, are there. What have been lacking, however, are the leadership and the resources to assist these potential new citizens and voters.

NOTES

1. Immigration data for the 1980s and the 1990s as well as for individual years beginning in 1988 include beneficiaries of legalization through the Immigration Reform and Control Act (IRCA) of 1986. Although recorded as entering permanent residence in the late 1980s and early 1990s, most of these individuals

actually arrived in the United States prior to January 1, 1982, either in an un-documented status or by overstaying non-permanent visas.

2. I use the terms 'Latino' and 'Hispanic' interchangeably to refer to residents of the United States who trace their ancestry to the Spanish-speaking regions of Latin America and the Caribbean.

3. The primary focus of the NLIS was Latino immigrant attitudes towards and experiences with naturalization. As a result, the sample includes permanent resident Latino immigrants with the five years of residence necessary for naturalization. The NLIS includes 1636 respondents. Survey methodology and descriptive findings are published in Pachon and DeSipio (1994).

4. The LNPS sample included the three largest Latino national-origin groups—Mexican Americans, Puerto Ricans, and Cuban Americans—as well as a control group of non-Hispanic whites in thirty-eight cities and two rural counties nationwide (García et al. 1989). The sample included 3,415 respondents including more than 2,800 Latinos. Survey methodology and descriptive findings appear in de la Garza et al. (1992).

5. The limitations of each data set should be noted. The NLIS examines Latino immigrants eligible for naturalization. As a result, it excludes undocumented immigrants and permanent resident immigrants with fewer than five years of residence (three, if married to a United States citizen). The LNPS examines the three dominant Latino national-origin groups—those of Mexican, Puerto Rican, and Cuban origin. As a result, it cannot speak to the experiences of Latino immigrants from other parts of Latin America and the Caribbean.

6. Educational attainment rates for Dominicans, Central Americans, and South Americans cannot be directly compared to these figures. Among these other Latino populations eligible for U.S. citizenship, who I would hypothesize have more education on average than their co-ethnics, show widely divergent rates of education. The share of the Dominican, Central American, and South American populations with eight or fewer years of education are 57, 35, and 20 percent, respectively. The rates with high school degrees and beyond are 33, 50, and 55 percent, respectively.

7. I was a staff member of the NALEO Educational Fund during the U.S. Citizenship project.

REFERENCES

Barkan, E. R., and N. Khokolov. 1980. "Socioeconomic Data as Indices of Naturalization Patterns in the United States: A Theory Revisited." *Ethnicity* 7.

Borjas, George J. 1990. *Friends or Strangers: The Impact of Immigrants on the U.S. Economy.* New York: Basic Books.

Bouvier, Leon F., and Lindsey Grant. 1994. *How Many Americans? Population, Immigration, and the Environment.* San Francisco: Sierra Club Books.

Brimelow, Peter. 1995. *Alien Nation: Common Sense about America's Immigration Disaster.* New York: Random House.

Calavita, Kitty. 1992. *Inside the State: The Bracero Program, Immigration, and the I.N.S.* New York: Routledge.

Chávez, Linda. 1996. "New Citizens Getting Off Too Easily." *USA Today* (July 3).

de la Garza, Rodolfo O., Louis DeSipio, F. Chris García, John A. García, and Angelo Falcón. 1992. *Latino Voices: Mexican, Puerto Rican, and Cuban Perspectives on American Politics.* Boulder, Colo.: Westview Press.

DeSipio, Louis. 1995. "Are We Incorporating the Next Generation? Citizenship and Naturalization Among U.S. Immigrants." Paper prepared for presentation at the Western Political Science Association, Portland, Oregon.

DeSipio, Louis. 1996. *Counting on the Latino Vote: Latinos as a New Electorate.* Charlottesville, Va.: University Press of Virginia.

DeSipio, Louis. Forthcoming. "After Proposition 187 the Deluge: Reforming Naturalization Administration While Making Good Citizens." *Harvard Journal of Hispanic Policy* 9.

DeSipio, Louis, and Harry P. Pachon. 1992. "Making Americans: Administrative Discretion and Naturalization." *UCLA Chicano/Latino Law Review* 12 (Spring): 52–66.

Fuchs, Lawrence H. 1990. *The American Kaleidoscope: Race, Ethnicity, and the Civic Culture.* Hanover, N. H.: University Press of New England.

García, F. Chris, John A. García, and Angelo Falcón. 1989. "Studying Latino Politics: The Development of the Latino National Political Survey." *PS: Political Science and Politics* 22: 848–852.

García, John A. 1981. "Political Integration of Mexican Immigrants: Explorations into the Naturalization Process." *International Migration Review* 15 (4): 608–625.

Gavit, John Palmer. 1971 [1922]. *Americans by Choice.* New York: Harper Brothers.

Grenier, Guillermo J., with Fabiana Invernizzi, Linda Salup, and Jorge Schmidt. 1993. "Los Bravos de la Politica: Politics and Cubans in Miami." In *Barrio Ballots: Latino Politics in the 1990* Elections, ed. Rodolfo O. de la Garza, Martha Menchaca, and Louis DeSipio. Boulder, Colo.: Westview Press.

Jasso, Guillermina, and Mark R. Rosenzweig. 1985. "What's in a Name? Country of Origin Influences on the Earnings of Immigrants in the United States." Economic Development Center, University of Minnesota. *Bulletin* #85–4 (June).

Jasso, Guillermina, and Mark R. Rosenzweig. 1990. *The New Chosen People: Immigrants in the United States.* New York: Russell Sage Foundation.

Jones-Correa, Michael. 1994. "Between Two Nations: The Political Life of Latin American Immigrants in New York City." Doctoral dissertation, Princeton University.

Miller, John J. 1996a. "The Naturalizers." *Policy Review: The Journal of American Citizenship* 78 (July-August).

Miller, John J. 1996b. "Dumbing Down Naturalization." *Georgetown Immigration Law Journal* 10 (1): 55–57.

Moreno, Dario, and Christopher Warren. 1992. "The Conservative Enclave: Cubans in Florida." In *From Rhetoric to Reality: Latino Politics in the 1988 Elections,* ed. Rodolfo O. de la Garza and Louis DeSipio. Boulder, Colo.: Westview Press.

NALEO Educational Fund. 1985. *Proceedings of the First National Conference on Citizenship and the Hispanic Community.* Washington, D.C.: NALEO Educational Fund.

NALEO Educational Fund. 1993. "The Unheard Voice of One Out of Every Four Californians: What Do Immigrants Think about Anti-Immigrant Rhetoric?" Los Angeles: NALEO Educational Fund.

National Council of La Raza. 1991. *Unlocking the Golden Door: Hispanics and the Citizenship Process.* Washington, D.C.: National Council of La Raza Policy Analysis Center.

Pachon, Harry P. 1991. "U.S. Citizenship and Latino Participation in California." In *Racial and Ethnic Politics in California,* ed. Byran O. Jackson and Michael B. Preston. Berkeley: Institute of Governmental Studies Press.

Pachon, Harry, and Louis DeSipio. 1994. *New Americans by Choice: Political Perspectives of Latino Immigrants.* Boulder, Colo.: Westview Press.

Passel, Jeffrey S., and Karen A. Woodrow. 1985. "Growth of the Undocumented Alien Population in the United States, 1979–1983, as Counted in the Current Population Survey and the Decennial Census." Paper presented at the Population Association of America Meeting.

Portes, Alejandro, and John Curtis. 1987. "Changing Flags: Naturalization and Its Determinants among Mexican Immigrants." *International Migration Review* 21, no. 2 (Summer): 352–372.

Portes, Alejandro, and Rafael Mozo. 1985. "The Political Adaptation Process of Cubans and Other Ethnic Minorities in the United States: A Preliminary Analysis." *International Migration Review* 16 (1).

Sanchez, George J. 1993. *Becoming Mexican American: Ethnicity, Culture, and Identity in Chicano Los Angeles, 1900–1945.* Berkeley: University of California Press.

Schoeni, Robert F., Kevin F. McCarthy, and Georges Vernez. 1996. *The Mixed Economic Progress of Immigrants.* Santa Monica, Calif.: Rand Corporation.

Simon, Julian L. 1989. *The Economic Consequences of Immigration.* Cambridge, Mass.: Basil Blackwell, Inc.

U.S. Bureau of the Census. 1993. *The Foreign-Born Population in the United States. 1990 Census of Population.* 1990CP-3-1. Washington, D.C.: U.S. Government Printing Office.

U.S. Immigration and Naturalization Service. 1993. *1992 Statistical Yearbook of the Immigration and Naturalization Service.* Springfield, Va.: National Technical Information Service.

U.S. Immigration and Naturalization Service. 1994. *1993 Statistical Yearbook of the Immigration and Naturalization Service.* Springfield, Va.: National Technical Information Service.

Yang, Philip Q. 1994. "Explaining Immigrant Naturalization." *International Migration Review* 28 (3): 449–477.

13. Latinos and Language Policy: The Politics of Culture

Ronald Schmidt, Sr.

FEW CONTROVERSIAL POLICY ISSUES are more closely associated with the U.S. Latino community than language policy. For at least three decades, Latino political activists have been vigorously engaged with the issue of language policy at every level of government and in a variety of ways. Similarly, public commentaries about language policy—from radio talk show debates to testimony before public officials to advocacy broadsides to academic treatises—make frequent references to a close connection between this policy issue and U.S. Latinos.

A brief look at the demographics of language in the U.S. shows why this association between language policy and Latinos should occasion little surprise. The 1990 Census found that Spanish-speakers constituted a numerical majority (54.4%) of the nearly 32 million U.S. residents (14% of the U.S. population) whose usual language was not English. The next most numerous language group was that of French-speakers, who numbered less than 10 percent of Spanish-speakers, 1.7 million compared to 17.3 million (Wiley, forthcoming, chap. 2).

The vast majority of U.S. Spanish-speakers, in turn, have roots in Latin America (especially Mexico) or the Caribbean (especially Puerto Rico and Cuba), coming from the same national-origin groups that constitute some 80 percent of the still-emerging U.S. ethnic group labeled as "Latino" or "Hispanic" (de la Garza et al. 1992, 7). Further, the growth pattern for Latino communities over the last several decades suggests that the demographic basis for the close connection between Latinos and U.S. language policy will continue into the foreseeable future (Crispell 1992). Indeed, while the nation as a whole experienced a 40 percent increase in non–English-speakers from 1979 to 1989, there was a 65 per-

343

cent increase in Spanish-speakers during the same decade (Wiley, forth-coming, chap. 2). At the same time, it is important to note that most U.S. Latinos are bilingual, as only 8.4 percent of Spanish-speakers reported to the 1990 Census that they were non-English speaking (Wiley, forthcoming, chap. 2).

The purpose of this essay is to provide an overview of this important and complex relationship between contemporary language policy and the Latino communities of the United States. What are the specific policy issues that confront Latinos, Latino public officials, and other public policymakers in relation to language in the contemporary political arena? What are the stakes in these conflicts, for Latinos and for the country as a whole? Where do the Latino publics stand on these issues? What is the future of the politics of language in the U.S., and what are the implications for Latinos? These are the questions to be addressed in this essay.

THE POLITICS OF LANGUAGE: AN OVERVIEW

Three specific policy issues dominate the contemporary debate over language policy in the United States. The first issue to emerge, in the 1960s, was that of how best to educate non–English-speaking students in the public schools, most of whom were (and remain today) Latino youngsters. The second controversy, which became prominent in the 1970s, is actually a complex of issues that I will label "linguistic access" to civil and political rights. And the third issue emerged at the end of the 1970s as a backlash against the first two forms of language policy: the demand that English be made the sole "official" language of the United States and its states and localities. The issues are overlapping and interrelated in that they feed upon and influence each other, but they can be described separately.

1. Language in Education: The Role of Bilingual Education

Latinos have played a prominent role in this policy issue from the outset of its reemergence as a political question in the 1960s. Though several local school districts (most notably in Texas and south Florida) adopted bilingual education programs earlier, it was the U.S. Congress' adoption of The Bilingual Education Act in 1968 as an amendment (Title VII) to the Elementary and Secondary Education Act that first nationalized the issue. The law's primary sponsor, Senator Ralph Yarborough (D-Tex), was particularly interested in providing federal support for local bilingual education programs in south Texas that were aimed at stemming the relatively high drop-out rates and low educational attainment rates of Latino students (Lyons 1990).

Initially a small demonstration grant program, the federal bilingual act was given a considerable boost in 1974 when the U.S. Supreme Court decided unanimously (in *Lau v. Nichols*) that teaching students in a language they do not understand is a violation of the Civil Rights Act of 1964. On the strength of this decision by the Court, the U.S. Office of Education's civil rights unit in 1975 issued guidelines (known as the "Lau Remedies") that strongly encouraged local school districts to establish bilingual education programs for their "Limited English Proficient" (LEP) students. Subsequently, more than half of the states adopted laws that required or permitted bilingual education instruction in the public schools, and most states made use of Title VII funds.

Political controversy grew apace with the expansion of bilingual education programs. The initial controversy was over the definition and aims of bilingual education. Though the options were numerous, the political controversy over this question eventually settled down to two alternatives: *transitional* vs. *maintenance* bilingual education. The intent of the former approach is strictly assimilative and temporary, using the students' home language in the classroom only until they master English well enough to be "mainstreamed" into English-only classes. The idea is to use the students' native languages in subjects other than language so they won't fall behind while they are mastering English. Once that goal is reached, the "bilingual" aspect of the students' education is over.

The "maintenance" version of bilingual education, on the other hand, aims to produce a *bi*lingual adult. That is, while it too insists that LEP students must master English, it additionally wants the students to achieve mastery of their home languages (Spanish in the case of Latino youngsters). Among bilingual education teachers (as represented by NABE, for example) and language experts (see, e.g., Cummins 1989), the maintenance version was strongly favored. Most Latino political activists and lobbying organizations (e.g., National Council of La Raza, LULAC, MALDEF) also supported bilingual outcomes for bilingual education. Successive legislative revisions left no doubt by the end of the 1970s, however, that maintenance bilingual education had little support among elected officials, as state and federal legislation was increasingly specific in mandating a transitional approach.

By the early 1980s the debate had shifted to a new question:

whether bilingual education should be mandated at all. Critics of on-going (mostly transitional) bilingual education programs had reached the conclusion that it should be replaced with approaches (such as "English immersion") that did not rely on the "crutch" of students' home languages. Citing disputed evaluation research faulting the effectiveness of bilingual education, they mounted a campaign to give local school districts the flexibility to devise and implement their own approaches to the education of LEP students, thus avoiding the strictures of the "Lau Guidelines."

These critics of bilingual education found a friendly hearing among the educational officials of the Reagan Administration, particularly after William Bennett became Secretary of Education in 1983. Bennett, an articulate and insistent proponent of cultural assimilation in U.S. education policy, launched a strong campaign to eliminate the federal "bias" in favor of bilingual approaches to LEP education. In the political fray that followed, proponents of a maintenance approach to bilingual education—including Latino organizations and activists—found themselves in the ironic position of having become the leading supporters of *any* version of federally mandated bilingual education, even the transitional approach.

With many Congressional Democrats supporting a continuation of federal support for bilingual education, a compromise bill to extend the federal program was approved in 1988, in which 75 percent of Title VII funds were "set aside" for "transitional bilingual education programs" with the remaining 25 percent to be used for experimental programs at the local level (including both English immersion and maintenance bilingual education). Subsequently, both Presidents George Bush and Bill Clinton appointed educational administrators who were committed to retaining a federal commitment to bilingual education. Whether the Republicans controlling the 104th Congress would mount a new attack on Title VII programs remains unclear as of this writing. At state and local levels, meanwhile, vocal and unresolved political conflicts over bilingual education continued into the mid-1990s, with Latinos continuing to play a major part in the controversies.

2. "Linguistic Access" Policies

In the 1970s the second language policy issue arose, that of linguistic access to political and civil rights. The central aim of these policies is to remove language as a barrier to full participation in the arenas of civil society. The most controversial access question has been voting rights for citizens of the United States who are not literate in English. Early in the 1970s, several Latino political organizations (led by MALDEF, the Mexican American Legal Defense and Education Fund) began to mount an eventually successful lobbying campaign to persuade Congress to amend the Voting Rights Act of 1965 to include protections for "language minorities."

Following testimony organized primarily by MALDEF, Congress found in its 1975 Extension of the Act " . . . that voting discrimination against citizens of language minorities is pervasive and national in scope" (U.S. Commission on Civil Rights 1981, 120). This finding was based upon the conjunction of widespread educational discrimination against Latinos (resulting in low English-literacy rates among Latinos) and the provision of ballots and election materials only in English. As a remedy, the Voting Rights Act was amended to require that registration forms, ballots, and election materials in a language other than English must be provided if more than 5 percent of the voters in an election district spoke the same non-English language and if the English illiteracy rate in the district was greater than the national illiteracy rate (Leibowitz 1982, 7–9). Though diluted for a period during the Reagan and Bush Administrations, in 1992 the linguistic access provisions of the law were strengthened so that non-English ballots and election materials are now triggered by the presence of only 10,000 U.S. citizen speakers of a language minority group, a change that increased the number of covered counties in the U.S. from 197 to 256 (Ross 1992).

As noted above, the underlying logic of language policies of this type is that access to political and civil rights should not be denied because of a language barrier. Accordingly, Latino activists (along with other language minority activists) have applied the same logic to other arenas of civil society, in addition to the right to vote: to public social services (Obledo and Alcala 1980), to full understanding of courtroom proceedings (Piatt 1990), and to protection against employment discrimination under the guise of linguistic uniformity rules (Mydans 1990).

Each of these applications of the logic of linguistic access rights remains fundamentally unsettled and controversial (see, e.g., Savage 1994), but the most controversial certainly remains that of so-called "bilingual ballots." Opponents in many states were (and are) incensed that U.S. citizens might be allowed to vote in languages other than English, and that their tax dollars are used to print election materials in non-English languages. A voter initiative in California's 1984 general election, directing the governor to send a letter to President Reagan expressing the state's opposition to ballots in languages other than English, for example, won by nearly a two-to-one margin.

3. The Campaign for an "Official English" Language Policy

Both bilingual education and non-English ballots were important stimulants to the emergence of the third focus of language policy controversy. By the end of the 1970s many citizens had become alarmed at what they considered to be the "bilingualization" (and particularly the "Latinization") of U.S. society and public policy, and out of that alarm came the campaign to adopt English as the sole "official" language of the United States and its states and local communities. The Official English Movement—known to its detractors and to some supporters as the "English-Only" Movement—formally began on a national level on April 27, 1981, when Senator S. I. Hayakawa (R-California) introduced into the Senate a proposed amendment to the U.S. Constitution that would have designated English as the sole "official" language of the United States. Hayakawa's proposal received little support in the Senate, but it was subsequently joined by a similar measure in the House of Representatives. Though the Congress continued to show little interest in the issue, a proposed "official English" amendment has been introduced into each Congress since 1981. Whether it will gain greater support in the Republican-controlled 104th Congress was unclear as of this writing.

Meanwhile, in 1983 Hayakawa (by then retired from the Senate) joined forces with John Tanton, a physician and political activist, to organize a nationwide lobbying group known as "U.S. English." Tanton previously had been president of Zero Population Growth and had also been a founder of the Federation for American Immigration Reform (FAIR), a group dedicated to limiting immigration to the United States. Through continuous national direct-mail and advertising campaigns, U.S. English claimed a membership of 400,000 by 1990, and was joined in 1987 by another nationwide lobbying group known as "English First."

In their literature, both organizations attacked bilingual education policies and "bilingual" ballots and called for the designation of English as the sole "official" language. Though unsuccessful thus far in Congress, the campaign has won some important votes at the state and local levels. By lopsided margins, for example, mostly symbolic state voter initiatives for official English were successful in three states with large concentrations of Latinos: California (1986), Colorado (1988), and Florida (1988). A hotly contested measure with far-reaching and substantive implementation language was narrowly approved by voters in Arizona (1988). Victories were achieved as well in several notable local elections, including Miami (1980) and San Francisco (1984). By 1990 a total of seventeen states had designated English as their sole official language through either voter initiative or legislative action (Marshall 1989; Mydans 1990).

Meanwhile, however, opposing political activists—among whom Latinos were quite prominent—organized a new counter-offensive. In 1987 a national coalition of civil rights and educator groups was formed establishing the "English Plus Information Clearinghouse" (EPIC) in Washington, D.C. to lead the fight against the English Only movement. As denoted by its title, the aim of EPIC is to support the mastery of English by all residents of the U.S. plus the retention and/or learning of other languages (Henry 1990, 32). This coalition has claimed successes in turning back official English campaigns in several states (including Texas), and it supported a successful suit by Latino litigants overturning Arizona's 1988 official English initiative (*Yniguez and Gutierrez v. Mofford* et al. 1990). Like the other two issue-areas of contemporary language policy, then, the campaign for an official English policy remains unresolved and the subject of political controversy.

THE ARGUMENTS AND THE STAKES

What is at stake for Latinos in these three areas of language policy controversy, and what is at stake for the U.S. polity as a whole? Do the choices in these conflicts really make a difference for the life chances and well-being of Latinos? One of the most fruitful ways to get at these questions is to examine the arguments of the activists most intensely involved. As will be seen, underlying each of the three issues of language policy are relatively set positions staked out by partisans in these political conflicts. For purposes of this essay, the positions will be described as "pluralism," "assimilationism," and "Latino nationalism." Further, though there are important differences among supporters of each of these positions, their distinguishing characteristics in this essay are as follows:

"Pluralists" support a language policy aiming at a *bi*lingual population and a polity which supports rights of both English-speaking and non–English-speaking residents to publicly interact with each other and with the government in the Spanish language;

"Assimilationists," in contrast, want virtually all public language domains to be exclusively English and they therefore support a language policy which aims at an early and efficient language *shift* to English;

Latino "nationalists," finally, believe that the only way to ensure the survival of the Spanish language and Latino cultures in the U.S. is to use language policy to support Spanish-*dominant* language domains in public spaces of the society.

1. The Case for Linguistic Pluralism

Most supporters of the Official English movement have articulated the language policy alternatives for the United States as between linguistic "assimilation" and linguistic "separatism" (denoted in this essay as "Latino nationalism"). Among Latino political activists, however, the most prominent language policy position is a third alternative: that of linguistic pluralism. The fundamental *premise* of pluralist language policies is that multiple languages and language groups is the "natural" condition of most countries in the world today, including the United States (Wardhaugh 1987). The boundaries of most independent countries do not coincide neatly with the boundaries between linguistic groups. From this perspective, Latino pluralists stress that in the United States the Spanish language has roots just as deep and just as legitimate as the English language. In large areas of what is now the U.S., including the entire Southwest and Puerto Rico, Spanish was the principal language of public discourse prior to these territories being forcibly incorporated into the U.S. through conquest and annexation. Moreover, the Spanish language never "died" in these areas; Spanish-speaking communities have remained continuously visible (and audible) in various parts of the U.S. from the time of their annexation to the present. As Josè Càrdenas succinctly put it in a 1977 critique of a critical report on bilingual education: "My ethnic culture is a part of this American culture" (Càrdenas 1977, 77).

Given the premise of the U.S. as a multilingual nation, the primary *claim* of linguistic pluralists is that justice requires tolerance of and respect for the rights of all language groups, including linguistic minorities. Just what these rights are is a complex question for which there are a variety of "pluralistic" answers. In brief, however, there are two primary language rights that are stressed by Latino pluralists: the right to non-discrimination and the right to "cultural reproduction."

In its briefest formulation, the first of these rights—the right to non-discrimination—means that the equal rights and opportunities guaranteed under U.S. law (especially the Civil Rights Act of 1964) and the U.S. Constitution (especially the Fourteenth Amendment) must include *linguistic* rights and opportunities. Denying Spanish-speakers ac-

cess to voting materials, to ballots, to social services, to educational opportunities, or to equal employment opportunities is a clear violation of
these rights. What is at stake here is equal access to rights and opportunities accorded to all Americans, equal access which is prevented by a
language barrier. This line of argument has played a prominent role in
much of the litigation over language policy in this country (see, e.g., *Lau
v. Nichols* 1971; Liebowitz 1982; Piatt 1990).

Dissatisfied with the incompleteness of the "non-discrimination"
logic of the preceding paragraph, however, many Latino pluralists argue
in addition for the second language right noted above, the right to "cultural reproduction" as a *public* right. The dissatisfaction stems from the
fact that the courts and most lawmakers have accepted the linguistic non-
discrimination argument only insofar as Latinos (and other language minorities) are not fluent in English. Thus, the Supreme Court's famous
Lau decision is premised on a *language barrier* faced by the linguistic
minority. Similarly, so-called "bilingual ballots" were adopted by Congress only because educational discrimination had prevented language
minorities from becoming literate in English. The assumption in both
cases is that English is the "real" language of the United States and that
speaking another language is a "handicap," a barrier that must be overcome.

From a pluralist perspective, the problem with this formulation is
that there is no long-term *public* protection for the language minority's
right to cultural reproduction. While they see non-discrimination as an
important aspect of language rights, many Latino pluralists want public
support for cultural reproduction as well. What is at stake from this perspective is the *survival* of Latinos as ethnolinguistic groups and their
right to expect public cultural institutions (e.g., public schools) to enable
and support their cultural reproduction over time. That is, as full, tax-
paying members of U.S. society, Latinos have a right to expect that institutions such as the public schools will help to maintain and further develop *their* language and culture just as it does the language and culture
of the dominant Anglo group.

A good example of this line of argument is Eduardo Hernandez-
Chavez' case for a "maintenance" version of bilingual education (1984).
Like other pluralists, Hernandez-Chavez seeks to make clear the neces-
sity for Latinos and other language minority students to learn English:

For language minority children in the United States, strong English
proficiency in all domains is essential. English proficiency is indispensable in today's world for advanced academic training. Participating adequately in business, commerce, or the occupational mar-

ket without a full command of English would be extremely difficult
for an individual. And the use of English for interethnic relations
in most situations is natural and appropriate and thus very important. (Hernandez-Chavez 1984, 171).

Nevertheless, it is *equally important* that education for language minority students aim for the development of "full cognitive academic abilities
in the native language" (Hernandez-Chavez 1984, 172).

Underlying this argument for genuine bilingualism as the goal of
public education is Hernandez-Chavez' conviction that there is a "deep
need to revitalize ethnolinguistic communities in the United States; to
give them a measure of self-determination in one of the most important
areas of modern life; and, ultimately, to build the capacity of these communities for self-sufficiency" (Hernandez-Chavez 1984, 179). This is so
because full and equal participation in U.S. society means not that language minorities try to become indistinguishable from the white majority, but rather that "they strengthen themselves from within—culturally,
socially, politically, and economically" (Hernandez-Chavez 1984, 170).

This need to revitalize the capacity of Latino communities to repro-
duce themselves, in turn, must be buttressed by recognition of the right
to ethnic self-determination in U.S. policy. Hernandez-Chavez argues
that members of language minority groups have the *political* right to define their own educational interests as members of the U.S. polity. This
right entails their freedom to maintain distinctive linguistic and cultural
ties through *public* institutions such as the schools: "Education for language minority children . . . must serve the true interests of minority
groups rather than the interests of the majority group—interests as defined by the minority communities themselves, not as they are perceived
by majority group educators or scholars" (Hernandez-Chavez 1984, 178).
If this democratic right were fully realized, Hernandez-Chavez is convinced that "the goals of education would surely change from an emphasis on mainstreaming and assimilation to cultural pluralism and ethnolinguistic solidarity" (Hernandez-Chavez 1984, 178).

In short, then, pluralists aim for a polity in which the multiplicity
of ethnolinguistic groups is taken as the benchmark for a healthy and
democratic society. Members of component groups in such a society
should be enabled by language policy to participate equally in the public
spaces of civil society without having to give up their cultural and linguistic identities. While pluralists acknowledge English as the *lingua
franca* of U.S. society, they also insist on the right to participate in U.S.
society as Spanish-speakers and to public support for the reproduction of
their language and culture in public institutions.

To put this position in perspective, it is useful to note the similarity of the Latino pluralist argument with the vision of a pluralistic Canada formulated several decades ago by the Canadian Royal Commission on Bilingualism and Biculturalism. The Commission argued that Canada's language policy should aim toward an egalitarian polity in which

> everybody has the same access to the various benefits of a society without being hindered by [sic] his cultural identity. Thus, it is not enough for members of a minority group to have access to the same activities, institutions, and benefits as the members of the majority group; that simply requires an absence of discrimination against individuals as such. The equality to which we refer requires that a person who engages in some activity or associates with some institution need not renounce his own culture, but can offer his services, act, show his presence, develop, and be accepted with all his cultural traits. (Canada, Royal Commission 1973, 5).

This vision of a political community in which the members of an ethnolinguistic minority group may participate fully and equally in the institutions of civil society without shedding their cultural traits is one which most Latino pluralists may recognize as very similar to their own. And it is toward the realization of this vision that Latino linguistic pluralists have worked in their efforts on behalf of a "maintenance" version of bilingual education, in support of various linguistic access measures, and against the campaign to make English the sole official language in the United States

2. The Case for an Assimilationist Policy

While most Latino political activists have supported a pluralistic language policy, there are others who argue on behalf of an assimilationist approach. And the arguments of Latino linguistic assimilationists differ from those of both Latino pluralists and non-Latino assimilationists. Most non-Latino assimilationists stress the dangers of a "Latinization" of the nation, and especially the deep political conflicts they predict will result from a permanent linguistic pluralism. Former U.S. Senator (and co-founder of U.S. English) S. I. Hayakawa, for example, articulated the case for an assimilationist language policy as follows:

> The ethnic chauvinism of the present Hispanic leadership is an unhealthy trend in present-day America. It threatens a division perhaps more ominous in the long run than the division between

blacks and whites. Blacks and whites have problems enough with each other, to be sure, but they quarrel with each other in the same language. Even Malcolm X, in his fiery denunciations of the racial situation in America, wrote excellent and eloquent English.

But the present politically ambitious "Hispanic Caucus" looks forward to a destiny for Spanish-speaking Americans separate from that of Anglo-, Italian-, Polish-, Greek-, Lebanese-, Chinese-, Afro-Americans and all the rest of us who rejoice in our ethnic diversity, which gives us our richness as a culture, and the English language, which keeps us in communication with each other to create a unique and vibrant culture. (Hayakawa 1985, 11–12)

Latino advocates of linguistic assimilation, in contrast, may acknowledge the dangers of pluralism for "national unity," but their primary stress is on the benefits of assimilation for Latinos themselves. Latino proponents make two fundamental arguments for linguistic assimilation as being in the interest of Latinos. The *first* argument is that only assimilation offers the hope of greater equality in U.S. society, whereas policies of linguistic pluralism reinforce obstacles to Latino mobility. To the extent that Latinos cling to their language and culture, the argument goes, they will hold themselves back from full equality in U.S. society. To the extent that the state encourages linguistic and cultural pluralism, it will be guilty of perpetuating a caste-like ethnic inequality in U.S. society with Latinos as victims. The stakes, for this argument, are centered on social mobility and equality for Latinos in U.S. society.

The basic *premise* of this argument is that the United States is *not*, in truth, a multilingual society in any meaningful egalitarian sense. English is the dominant language of the country and has been so from the beginning. All "newcomer" groups, however incorporated into the U.S., have had to adapt to this reality. Moreover, nearly all contemporary U.S. Latinos are themselves *immigrant* newcomers, or the descendants of immigrants, for whom adapting to the U.S. culture is an important, necessary, and legitimate self-transformation. It cannot be viewed as an unjust imposition—an act of "conquest"—for the United States to ask voluntary immigrants, or the children of those immigrants, to adapt to the language and culture of the country.

Linguistic access measures, such as bilingual ballots or bilingual public services, only encourage Latino newcomers to resist adapting to the linguistic reality of the United States and, as a consequence, keep a significant number of Latinos from successful social, economic, and political mobility. Bilingual education is also faulted because it is not believed by assimilationists to be successful in enabling Latino youngsters to quickly master English, thereby keeping them from effective social mobility in U.S. society (see, e.g., Porter 1990).

The case for linguistic and cultural assimilation as necessary for Latino self-interest is perhaps most powerfully made by writer Richard Rodriguez (1982). In his poignant autobiography, for example, Rodriguez stresses the alienation and estrangement felt by the immigrant non–English-speaking child, who never feels that he or she truly *belongs* in this country. Rodriguez believes that pain is inevitable in childhood, and he eloquently articulates the special pain of loss that occurred in his family when he and his siblings lost their ability to speak fluently in the language of the family. Nevertheless, Rodriguez believes that the sacrifice was necessary and valuable, because *only* by truly "owning" the public language of the United States (a transformation which could not occur, he is convinced, without giving up the "private" language of his family) was it possible for him to feel that he truly *belonged* as an American in the United States:

> Only when I was able to think of myself as an American, no longer an alien in *gringo* society, could I seek the rights and opportunities necessary for full public individuality. The social and political advantages I enjoy as a man result from the day that I came to believe that my name, indeed, is *Rich-heard Road-ree-guess*. . . . I celebrate the day I acquired my new name. Those middle-class ethnics who scorn assimilation seem to me filled with decadent self-pity, obsessed by the burden of public life. Dangerously, they romanticize public separateness and they trivialize the dilemma of the socially disadvantaged. (Rodriguez 1982, 19, 27)

In short, assimilationists argue that language minority children cannot become truly *equal* in their own hearts and minds while bearing the linguistic and cultural marks of "difference" in the English-dominant society of the United States. Only by claiming an English-language cultural identity of their own—which cannot happen so long as they cling to the "private" cultures of their families—will Latinos be placed on a path toward genuine social equality.

The *second*, and somewhat different, argument stressed by Latino assimilationists is that to the extent Latinos want to retain their ethnic language and culture, they should do so *privately*. Like religion, ethnic language and culture should be kept in the private sector—away from government support, control, and interference—through a sort of "wall of separation." In keeping with Rodriguez' interpretation, Spanish is viewed as a fundamentally "private" language in the United States. Accordingly, those who find it valuable for their personal lives should work privately to maintain and support it. This, as Linda Chavez (former executive director of "U.S. English") has explained, is what other ethnic immigrant groups have done, and it is what Latinos should do as well:

> If Hispanic parents want their children to be able to speak Spanish and know about their distinctive culture, they must take the responsibility to teach their children these things. Government simply cannot—and should not—be charged with this responsibility. . . . The best way for Hispanics to learn about their native culture is in their own communities. Chinese, Jewish, Greek, and other ethnic communities have long established after-school and weekend programs to teach language and culture to children from these groups. Nothing stops Hispanic organizations from doing the same. (Chavez 1991, 164)

Employing the language of liberal individualism, Chavez argues that government interference in the reproduction of ethnic culture is dangerous to the healthy diversity of Latino cultures: "Government bureaucracies given the authority to create bicultural teaching materials homogenize the myths, customs, and history of the Hispanic peoples of this hemisphere, who, after all, are not a single group but many groups" (Chavez 1991, 164). In this argument, then, the stakes are understood in terms of *freedom,* the private freedom from governmental domination.

In the face of what they view as the strength of these two arguments, Chavez and other assimilationists argue that those Latino activists who are seeking to promote a bilingual, bicultural polity in the U.S. are acting only to promote their own selfish material and political interests, pyramiding their own power at the expense of the Latino-origin publics of the United States (Chavez 1991, 61). Thus, Chavez and others work to convince Latinos to reject these "self-appointed" leaders in favor of linguistic assimilation and the freedom to prosper as *individuals* in U.S. society.

3. The Case for a Nationalistic Language Policy

Latino opponents of assimilation typically respond to the above argument by asserting that assimilationists ignore important aspects of U.S. society. Most centrally, the idea that Latinos can simply "melt" into an "individualistic" society where everyone is judged on their "merits" is an unrealistic fantasy that ignores the realities of U.S. *racism.* Instead, leaving behind language and cultural group leaves one stripped of the cultural supports that might provide protection and nurturance in an indifferent and competitive (at best) or hostile and anti-Latino (at worst) environment. Further, the liberal individualistic mythology of Linda Chavez and her cohorts ignores the fact that the state cannot be "neutral" in matters of language and culture. Teaching *only* English in the public schools *necessarily* operates to advantage some and to disadvantage other groups who must bear an unfair and unequal cost in order to maintain their supposedly "non-American" language and culture privately.

While many pluralists would agree with the foregoing response to assimilationism, some critics of assimilation go further to critique as well the assumptions of a pluralistic policy. *Latino nationalists* represent the most prominent of these critics of both assimilation and pluralism, though their argument is in agreement with portions of each of the previous two positions. Like pluralists, for example, nationalists agree that it is important—and should be the public policy goal of the United States—to help preserve and further develop the Latino language and cultures in this country. Requiring Latinos to give up who they are in order to be considered fully "American" is not the path to either true equality or freedom, but the path to cultural genocide.

Like assimilationists, on the other hand, the nationalists are very aware of the unequal power position of the two principal languages of the United States. English is recognized as an extraordinarily powerful language that is poised to overwhelm and eclipse other languages in North America, including Spanish. Without attention to the maintenance of linguistic boundaries to protect Spanish-dominant linguistic domains, the greatest likelihood is that Spanish-speakers will assimilate through language shift into English by the third generation on U.S. soil (see, e.g., Veltman 1983; Fishman 1985). This is so because English is the language of power and opportunity under present conditions, so that all the incentives for upwardly mobile Latinos operate to undermine the preservation of the Spanish language and Latino cultures. Hernandez-Chavez alluded to this reality in a revealing footnote in his argument for bilingual education when he noted the "ambivalence felt in many Chicano communities toward other Chicanos who have attained middle-class status. They are perceived," he writes,

> as assimilated *agringados* who, having rejected the values of the ethnic community, accept Anglo-American ways.
>
> At the same time, parents exhibit a very natural aspiration for their children to achieve educational and economic mobility and regard the learning of English as the means to do so. *No contradiction is seen because there is little recognition of the extent of decul-*

*turation that is required by the educational and economic systems
in order to achieve a substantial amount of mobility.* The belief exists that assimilation is a personal choice, unrelated to upward mobility and the characteristics that must be acquired to attain it.
(Hernandez-Chavez 1978, 547, emphasis added)

Under present conditions, in short, social mobility for Latinos in U.S.
society requires a high degree of deculturation.

It is precisely for this reason that *quebecois* nationalists in Canada
decided several decades ago to reject the pluralist policy of the Canadian
Federal government. Because of their control over economic opportunities in overwhelmingly English-speaking North America, Canadian English-speakers held much more power and influence—even in Quebec—
than did the French-speaking *quebecois*. Under those conditions, they
reasoned, a policy that purports to give linguistic "equal opportunity" to
individual speakers of both French and English would inevitably result
in more and more people adopting English—the language of power—as
their primary language rather than French (see e.g., Brazeau and Cloutier
1977, 222–23). In an attempt to stem that tide, accordingly, Quebec's
Bill 101 restricted some language freedoms in schools, workplaces, and
public signs in an attempt to preserve that province as a French-domi-
nant language domain in English-dominant North America.

Among U.S. Latinos, however, few political leaders have worked for
a nationalistic language policy. Indeed, this writer has found only two
Latino authors who have argued for a policy of Spanish-dominant language domains in the United States (excluding Puerto Rico): Ray Castro
(1976) and Mario Barrera (1988). Though both authors urge policies
supporting Spanish-dominant enclaves in majority Latino areas, neither
goes so far as to seek a policy restricting individual linguistic freedoms
along the lines of Quebec's Bill 101. Thus the Latino nationalist option
remains relatively underdeveloped in the United States, at least in comparison with other multilingual countries.

LATINO PUBLICS AND LANGUAGE POLICY

Having surveyed the battlegrounds over U.S. language policy and the
rhetorical weapons deployed by Latino political activists, we next examine the position of the Latino publics on this issue. To what extent do
rank-and-file Latinos support the three language policy positions outlined above? The most extensive data source yet available for Latino public opinion is that generated by the Latino National Political Survey (de

la Garza et al. 1992). A review of the LNPS data published thus far indicates that the Latino publics are in substantial agreement with political activists on the subject of language policy. That is, most Latinos in the U.S. support a pluralistic language policy, rejecting both the assimilationist position and that of the nationalists.

This is evident from the responses to several survey questions regarding language policy, reported separately for each of the three most significant national-origin Latino groups (i.e., Mexicans, Puerto Ricans, Cubans; see de la Garza et al. 1992, 96–100). That the Latino publics are not attracted by the *nationalist* cause is evident from their responses to questions on language use and language and history schooling. Over 90 percent of each national-origin group of respondents, for example, agreed that all citizens and residents of the U.S. should learn English (see table 1). Similarly, fewer than 10 percent of each respondent group believed that the primary purpose of bilingual education should be "to maintain Spanish language/culture" (see table 5). Finally, another question attempting to gauge support for a nationalist approach to public education (on the "type of history students should study") resulted in fewer than 3 percent of each respondent group supporting more schooling in the history of the country of origin than of the United States. Majorities of Mexican- and Cuban-origin respondents believed that the preponderance of schooling should be in U.S. history, while a 71 percent majority of Puerto Rican respondents favored equal treatment of U.S. and Puerto Rican history (see table 3).

If most Latino National Political Survey respondents were not nationalists, they were not *assimilationists* either. Indeed, most respondents from each national-origin group clearly rejected assimilationist language policies. Majorities of each national-origin group, for example, rejected the proposition that English should be the official language of the United States, a staple position for the linguistic assimilation movement and one that almost 80 percent of LNPS' Anglo respondents favored (see table 2). Similarly, fewer than 15 percent of each Latino respondent group chose "to learn English" as the primary objective of bilingual education programs (see table 2). And fewer than 28 percent of each national-origin Latino group favored a policy of allowing employers to impose English-only rules in the workplace (see table 8).

Instead, clear majorities of each Latino national-origin group favored policies that are best understood as *pluralist*. That is, rejecting both English-only and Spanish-only policies, LNPS respondents strongly supported policies promoting *bi*lingualism—not only as a transitional "crutch" but as the objective of public policy. Thus, not only do the Latino publics oppose English-only official language and workplace lan-

guage rules, but they strongly support bilingual education and the provision of public services in Spanish. Over 90 percent of each respondent
group favored public services provision in Spanish (see table 7) and at
least 80 percent of each group supported bilingual education policies (see
table 4). Further, strong majorities (at least 70 percent) of each group
favored a maintenance approach to bilingual education by supporting
"to learn two languages" as the primary objective of this form of schooling (see table 5). Equally striking is the finding that a majority of each
respondent group was willing to be taxed more in order to ensure the
continuance of bilingual education programs (see table 6).

In short, the LNPS data indicates decisively that the three major
national-origin Latino groups are strongly supportive of a pluralistic approach to U.S. language policy, rejecting policies of both assimilation and
Latino nationalism. Contrary to the assertions of Linda Chavez and others, then, there appears to be a strong congruence between the policy
positions advocated by most Latino political leaders and activists and the
preferences of their ethnic publics.

LATINOS, LANGUAGE, AND THE FUTURE

What is the future of the politics of language for the Latino community?
In regard to preferences, there is little reason to expect Latinos to turn
away from their support for a bilingual, pluralistic language policy in the
near future. Together with continued relatively high levels of international migration from Latin America to the U.S., the on-going development and expansion of Spanish language and bilingual institutions (e.g.,
radio and television stations, marketing campaigns, newspapers and
magazines, etc.) provide structural support for possible long-term bilingualism for Latinos in this country, particularly if U.S. governments expand the provision of bilingual education and public services in step with
the expected expansion of Latino electoral clout over the next generation.

The fact that Latinos overwhelmingly support a pluralist, rather
than a nationalist approach to language policy could help to allay the
fears of those who perceive these groups to be rejecting assimilation in
favor of a nationalist policy of "separatism." Ironically, however, the apparent inability of many assimilationists to recognize the very existence
of (not to say Latino support for) this third, pluralist alternative provides
the greatest likelihood for the transformation of Latino support for pluralism into support for a nationalistic approach. In the formulation of
anthropologist George Scott, this is so because " . . . the degree of an eth-

nic group's identity will vary in direct proportion to the amount of opposition encountered by the group; the greater the opposition, the
greater the degree of identity, and conversely, the lesser the amount of
opposition, the lesser the degree of identity" (Scott 1990, 163).

Put differently, opposition to Latino desires to preserve and maintain their linguistic and cultural heritage, expressed through strident
policies demanding assimilation, seems more likely to drive Latinos toward a more defensive nationalistic posture than would broad consensual support for a bilingual, pluralistic policy. This is particularly the
case insofar as "racial" hostility and discrimination continue to affect
Latinos and shape their perceptions regarding the possibility of social
assimilation in U.S. society.

Given the processes of public opinion formation in contemporary
U.S. politics, however, there is little reason to expect assimilationist leaders, or the broader voting public, to adopt a more complex understanding of language policy than the typical dichotomy between "assimilationist" or "separatist" alternatives. Finding a way to win the support
of non-Latinos for a third, English *Plus* alternative remains one of the
most daunting political challenges for Latino and other linguistic pluralists in the years ahead.

TABLE 1

U.S. Citizens and Residents Should Learn English, by National Origin

CITIZENS AND RESIDENTS OF THE U.S. SHOULD LEARN ENGLISH	MEXICAN	PUERTO RICAN	CUBAN
Strongly Agree	251	142	79
	29.1%	25.0%	25.6%
Agree	537	386	206
	62.3%	67.7%	66.8%
Disagree	62	32	19
	7.2%	5.6%	6.1%
Strongly Disagree	12	10	5
	1.4%	1.7%	1.6%
Total	862	569	309
	100.0%	100.0%	100.0%

Source: de la Garza et al. 1992, 98

TABLE 2

English as the Official Language, by National Origin

English Should Be the Official Language	Mexican	Puerto Rican	Cuban	Anglo
Strongly Agree	116	66	33	198
	13.7%	12.1%	10.7%	45.6%
Agree	262	200	89	147
	30.7%	36.8%	29.3%	33.7%
Disagree	334	223	145	75
	39.2%	41.2%	47.5%	17.3%
Strongly Disagree	140	54	38	15
	16.4%	10.0%	12.4%	3.4%
Total	852	543	304	435
	100.0%	100.0%	100.0%	100.0%

Source: de la Garza et al. 1992, 97

TABLE 3

What Type of History Students Should Study, by National Origin

Type of History	Mexican	Puerto Rican	Cuban
Only U.S. history	68	29	49
	7.8%	4.9%	15.7%
More U.S. than RG history*	403	122	159
	46.1%	20.8%	50.9%
U.S. history and RG history equally	398	418	103
	45.4%	71.6%	32.9%
More RG than U.S. history	6	15	2
	0.7%	2.6%	0.5%
Only RG history	2	1	0
	0.2%	0.1%	0.0%
Total	875	585	312
	100.0%	100.0%	100.0%

Source: de la Garza et al. 1992, 100.

*RG is "respondent's group."

TABLE 4

Attitude toward Bilingual Education, by National Origin

ATTITUDE TOWARD BILINGUAL EDUCATION	MEXICAN	PUERTO RICAN	CUBAN
Strongly Support	321	232	100
	37.1%	39.7%	32.3%
Support	368	278	174
	42.5%	47.5%	56.1%
Feel Uncertain	113	42	19
	13.0%	7.2%	6.1%
Oppose	46	23	6
	5.3%	3.9%	1.9%
Strongly Oppose	18	10	11
	2.1%	1.7%	3.5%
Total	866	585	310
	100.0%	100.0%	100.0%

Source: de la Garza et al. 1992, 99.

TABLE 5

Objective of Bilingual Education, by National Origin

OBJECTIVE OF BILINGUAL EDUCATION	MEXICAN	PUERTO RICAN	CUBAN
To learn English	119	67	32
	14.7%	11.9%	10.3%
To learn two languages	569	415	240
	70.3%	73.6%	77.3%
To maintain Spanish language/culture	74	45	15
	9.1%	7.9%	4.9%
Other	48	37	23
	5.9%	6.6%	7.5%
Total	809	564	310
	100.0%	100.0%	100.0%

Source: de la Garza et al. 1992, 99.

TABLE 6

Willingness To Be Taxed for Bilingual Education, by National Origin

WILLING TO PAY MORE TAXES FOR BILINGUAL EDUCATION	MEXICAN	PUERTO RICAN	CUBAN
No	266	174	142
	31.0%	30.0%	45.9%
Yes	592	406	167
	69.0%	70.0%	54.1%
Total	858	580	309
	100.0%	100.0%	100.0%

Source: de la Garza et al. 1992, 99.

TABLE 7

Attitude toward Public Service Provision in Spanish, by National Origin

PUBLIC SERVICES SHOULD BE PROVIDED IN SPANISH	MEXICAN	PUERTO RICAN	CUBAN	ANGLO
Strongly Agree	197	154	85	59
	22.9%	26.5%	28.1%	13.7%
Agree	579	390	202	244
	67.3%	67.2%	66.4%	56.9%
Disagree	71	31	15	85
	8.3%	5.4%	5.0%	19.8%
Strongly Disagree	14	5	2	41
	1.6%	0.9%	0.5%	9.6%
Total	861	580	304	429
	100.0%	100.0%	100.0%	100.0%

Source: de la Garza et al. 1992, 97

NOTE

An earlier version of this essay was presented at the 1995 annual meeting of the Western Political Science Association in Portland, Oregon. The author thanks F. Chris Garcia, Paula McClain, Terry Wiley, and Adela de la Torre for helpful comments on that earlier draft, though, of course, not all of their suggestions were followed.

TABLE 8

Attitudes toward Requiring English in the Workplace, by National Origin

BUSINESSES CAN REQUIRE ENGLISH DURING WORKING HOURS	MEXICAN	PUERTO RICAN	CUBAN	ANGLO
Strongly Agree	58	19	18	84
	6.7%	3.4%	5.8%	19.4%
Agree	198	122	65	150
	23.1%	21.8%	21.3%	34.6%
Disagree	459	332	166	155
	53.5%	59.1%	54.2%	35.8%
Strongly Disagree	144	88	57	44
	16.7%	15.7%	18.8%	10.2%
Total	859	561	306	433
	100.0%	100.0%	100.0%	100.0%

Source: de la Garza et al. 1992, 98.

REFERENCES

Barrera, Mario. 1988. *Beyond Aztlan: Ethnic Autonomy in Comparative Perspective.* New York: Praeger.

Brazeau, Jacques, and Edoard Cloutier. 1977. "Interethnic Relations and the Language Issue in Contemporary Canada: A General Appraisal." In *Ethnic Conflict in the Western World,* ed. Milton J. Esman. Ithaca: Cornell University Press.

Canada, Royal Commission on Bilingualism and Biculturalism. 1973. *Bilingualism and Biculturalism: An Abridged Version of the Royal Commission Report.* Canada: McClelland and Steward Limited, in cooperation with the Secretary of State Department and Information Canada.

Cardenas, Jose. 1977. "Response I." In *Language, Ethnicity, and the Schools: Policy Alternatives for Bilingual-Bicultural Education,* ed. Noel Epstein. Washington, D.C.: Institute for Educational Leadership, George Washington University.

Castro, Ray. 1976. "Shifting the Burden of Bilingualism: The Case for Monolingual Communities." *The Bilingual Review* 3, no. 1 (January-April): 3–30.

Chavez, Linda. 1991. *Out of the Barrio: Toward a New Politics of Hispanic Assimilation.* New York: Basic Books.

Crispell, Diane. 1992. "The Nation of New Immigrants." *The Numbers News* (American Demographics, Inc.) 12 (no. 8): 1.

Cummins, James. 1989. *Empowering Minority Students.* Sacramento: California Association for Bilingual Education.

de la Garza, Rodolfo O., Louis DeSipio, F. Chris Garcia, John Garcia, and Angelo Falcon. 1992. *Latino Voices: Mexican, Puerto Rican, & Cuban Perspectives on American Politics.* Boulder: Westview Press.

Fishman, Joshua. 1985. "The Ethnic Revival in the United States: Implications for the Mexican-American Community." In *Mexican Americans in Comparative Perspective,* ed. Walker Connor. Washington, D.C.: The Urban Institute Press.

Hayakawa, S. I. 1985. *One Nation . . . Indivisible? The English Language Amendment.* Washington, D.C.: The Washington Institute for Values in Public Policy.

Henry, Sarah. 1990. "English Only: The Language of Discrimination." *Hispanic: The Magazine For and About Hispanics* (March): 28–32.

Hernandez-Chavez, Eduardo. 1984. "The Inadequacy of English Immersion Education as an Educational Approach for Language Minority Students in the United States." *Studies on Immersion Education.* Sacramento: California State Department of Education.

Kloss, Heinz. 1977. *The American Bilingual Tradition.* Rowley, Mass.: Newbury House.

Leibowitz, Arnold H. 1982. *Federal Recognition of the Rights of Minority Language Groups.* Rosslyn, Va.: National Clearinghouse for Bilingual Education.

Lyons, James J. 1990. "The Past and Future Directions of Federal Bilingual Education Policy." *The Annals of the American Academy of Political and Social Science* 508 (March): 66–80.

Marshall, David F. 1989. "Up-date and Implications for English Teachers of English Only Legislation." Paper presented to the National Conference of Teachers of English (November).

Mydans, Seth. 1990. "Pressure for English-Only Job Rules Stirring a Sharp Debate Across U.S." *New York Times* (August 8): A10.

Obledo, Mario, and Carlos Alcala. 1980. "Discrimination against the Spanish Language in Public Service: A Policy Alternative." In *Politics and Language: Spanish and English in the United States,* ed. D. J. R. Bruckner. Chicago: University of Chicago Center for Policy Study.

Piatt, Bill. 1990. *Only English?, Law and Language Policy in the United States.* Albuquerque: University of New Mexico Press.

Porter, Rosalie Pedalino. 1990. *Forked Tongue: The Politics of Bilingual Education.* New York: Basic Books.

Rodriguez, Richard. 1982. *Hunger of Memory: The Education of Richard Rodriguez, An Autobiography.* Boston: David R. Godine.

Ross, Michael. 1992. "Senate OKs Bill to Expand Voter Language Aid." *Los Angeles Times* (August 8): A1, A11.

Savage, David G. 1994. "High Court Lets English-Only Job Rules Stand." *Los Angeles Times* (June 21): A1, A14.

Scott, George M. 1990. "A Resynthesis of the Primordial and Circumstantial Approaches to Ethnic Group Solidarity: Towards an Explanatory Model." *Ethnic and Racial Studies* 13, no. 2 (April): 147–71.

U.S. Commission on Civil Rights. 1981. *The Voting Rights Act: Unfulfilled Goals.* Washington, D.C.: U.S. Government Printing Office.

Veltman, Calvin. 1983. *Language Shift in the United States.* Berlin: Mouton.

Wardhaugh, Ronald. 1987. *Languages in Competition: Dominance, Diversity, and Decline.* Oxford: Basil Blackwell.

Wiley, Terrence G. (forthcoming). *Language, Literacy, and Diversity in the United States.* Washington, D.C. and McHenry, Ill.: Center for Applied Linguistics and Delta Systems.

14. Latinos and the Affirmative Action Debate: Wedge or Coalition Issue?

F. Chris Garcia

IN EARLY 1995 a public policy issue forged into the forefront of the American political agenda, an issue that was of special importance to Latinos. That issue was the profusion of programs known collectively as "Affirmative Action." Although the concept of affirmative action and the many programs embodied under that generic label have been somewhat controversial from its inception, the breadth and intensity of the debate over the concept and its application increased significantly in the 1980s. It became one of the most salient and hotly debated issues following the 1994 Congressional election and seemed to be a primary issue as the 1996 presidential election approached.

This issue has substantial direct implications for Latinos, along with other ethnic and racial groups, because these programs have provided very significant substantive benefits for Latinos and have embodied important supportive symbolic messages. Some of the discourse on this issue must focus on why these special programs are justifiable for specially designated groups, which groups should be protected, and why.

One of the consequences of such a debate, which would be particularly significant to Latinos, may be a clearer understanding of their "ambivalent" ethnic or racial status. Peter Skerry has posed this question of "ambivalence" in dichotomous terms with regard to Mexican Americans.[1] He asks if Latinos are more similar to African Americans and Native Americans in that they are oppressed racial "victims" of a strongly discriminatory society which has for generations engaged in systematic racial oppression often sanctioned by law, including slavery and genocide. Or alternatively, are Latinos more similar to white Catholic ethnic immigrants who came to this country voluntarily and who were subject to varying degrees of discrimination, but eventually have progressed and been incorporated into the core culture?

More directly, the affirmative action debate also has significant strategic implications for Latino politics. Does the controversy over affirmative action provide a salient issue at the national level which may provide an optimal opportunity to activate and unify Latinos, or is it more likely to even further fragment Latino groups from each other and from coalitions with potential allies?

What Is "Affirmative Action"?

The concept of affirmative action first needs to be clarified. Several interpretations are possible, and certainly any particular interpretation of the concept can lead to different debates and conclusions. However, in general it is agreed that affirmative action embodies the idea that special extraordinary and positive efforts must be made by organizations to provide extra opportunities for members of *groups* previously excluded from those opportunities, that is, certain historically disadvantaged groups are consequently entitled to advantages. The concept usually includes various kinds of "preferential treatment" or "compensatory consideration" for members of defined "target groups." The most common areas of preferential or compensatory treatment are in the areas of education, employment, and the awarding of government contracts.

In education, generally this means that schools, and most particularly colleges and universities, take special positive action in the recruitment of faculty, staff, and students from the defined disadvantaged groups. In universities, searches to fill new positions must proceed on the basis of special efforts to seek out and recruit candidates from protected groups and advance their candidacies at every possible stage of the hiring process. Academic units are urged to hire qualified members of protected groups for faculty and staff positions. Once hired, special considerations may also be given to them in promotion, tenure, and other advancement processes. Students from protected groups are also sought out through special recruitment "outreach" efforts. Often specially designated scholarships and fellowships are available to them; additionally, support units such as special "services" programs as well as special group "studies" academic programs are available.

Similar advantaged treatment is accorded in the area of non-academic employment. Typically in both academic and non-academic organizations, if federal monies are involved, the organization comes under the provisions of federal affirmative action guidelines. Employers and labor unions are encouraged to recruit, train, retain, and promote members of the federally targeted groups. The goal often is to have an organization that "looks like America" or like a particular state or city in its racial, ethnic, and gender proportions—a kind of ethnic or gender group–based proportional representation.

The other major area of affirmative action is special "set aside" programs. Typically a certain percentage of government contracts, say 10 percent, must be set aside for awarding only to minority or women owned or operated businesses. Another variation involves awarding monetary bonuses to federal contractors who subcontract at least 10 percent of their contract amount to disadvantaged business enterprises.

To assess the implications of affirmative action for national politics in general, but more particularly for Latinos in national politics, we must first examine briefly the history of affirmative action programs, their development, and their application. Then the arguments for and against such programs will be presented. The opinions of the general public and those of Latinos will be examined. Various alternatives for resolving the tensions and conflicts in affirmative action programs will be examined. Finally, we will look at the possible resolution of this controversy and its implications for Latinos and Latino politics, most particularly with regard to potential political coalition strategies.

BACKGROUND AND DEVELOPMENT
OF AFFIRMATIVE ACTION PROGRAMS

It may come as a surprise that there is no national affirmative action law. Instead there are over 160 federal programs based on various regulations, executive orders, court decisions, and sections of legislation which together comprise a loosely integrated federal affirmative action policy. These programs range from mild, vague statements of intention to detailed and specific mandates enforceable through legal sanctions.

The concept of affirmative action emerged from the civil rights era of the 1950s and early 1960s and exploded after the civil disturbances of the mid and late 1960s. In the late 1950s and early 1960s there was considerable national activity around the provision of full civil rights for previously excluded groups, with a focus on African Americans. The Civil Rights Acts of 1957 and 1960 had been passed in attempts, albeit rather ineffectual, to promote equal opportunity in the exercise of the franchise.

In 1964 the most comprehensive and far-reaching piece of national legislation since the constitutional amendments of the post–civil war era passed. This was the Civil Rights Act of 1964, which outlawed discrimination in the areas of housing, employment, education, and public accommodations. One of the earliest statutory uses of the phrase "affirmative action" is contained in one provision of that legislation. Exercising strong leadership on behalf of its passage was Democratic President Lyndon Johnson, who before he became president (following the assassination of President John Kennedy on November 22, 1963) reportedly had a conversation with James Farmer, the former head of the Congress on Racial Equality (CORE). Farmer had urged Johnson to consider a policy that would provide "compensatory preferential hiring" for African Americans. It is reported that Vice President Johnson replied, "Yes, it is a good idea, but don't call it compensatory. Call it 'affirmative action'." In 1965, President Johnson issued Executive Order 11,246 which called for "affirmative action" among federal contractors, including universities receiving federal funds, to recruit and hire people from all previously excluded groups. The purpose was to make up for America's legacy of slavery and segregation by directing employers to pay special attention in hiring for jobs where they had fewer minorities than would be expected given the pool of available candidates. In 1968 the regulation was expanded to include women.

President Johnson had argued strongly that simply ending discrimination, as the 1964 Civil Rights Act was intended to do, would not bring blacks into the American mainstream. At a speech at Howard University in 1965, he said, "You do not take a person who, for years, has been hobbled by chains and liberate him, and bring him to the starting line of a race and then say 'you are free to compete with all the others,' and still justly believe that you have been fair." His many Great Society social programs, including the War on Poverty, were part of the effort to remove the handicaps in that race towards achievement and parity. The idea was to give individuals who suffered from a legacy of *group*-based discrimination and its consequent disadvantaging effects a new *equality of opportunity* to acquire the requisites necessary to compete on an equal footing. Another major piece of national legislation promoted by the Johnson Administration was the Voting Rights Act of 1965 which was designed to extend full electoral and representational rights to individual members of excluded groups. This later developed into a very important "affirmative action" program in the electoral sphere that provided dramatic boosts towards Latinos electing other Latinos to office.

Although the name "affirmative action" and some minor actions towards this goal began in that period, it was actually under the Republican administration and presidency of Richard Nixon that the first major manifestations of such a policy occurred. In 1969 President Nixon announced the Philadelphia Plan. Promulgated by Labor Secretary George Schultz, this plan required that companies doing business with the federal government set up goals and timetables for the hiring and promotion of African Americans in craft union jobs. (Some critics have charged that the Philadelphia Plan was actually intended as a conscious effort to drive a wedge between the Democratic constituencies of blacks and organized labor, which at that time was primarily white and outwardly exclusionary.)

Another noteworthy action during the Nixon Administration was a regulation which defined the categories of minorities who were to receive compensatory preferences. Included were African Americans, Asians and Pacific Islanders, *Hispanics,* Native Americans and Alaskan Natives, and women. While initially much of the civil rights activity and compensatory policies had been directed at African Americans, now a much broader "official" definition of minorities, including "Hispanics," became officially ensconced in federal law.[2]

With Nixon, the emphasis shifted from providing individuals with an equal opportunity to succeed to preferential treatment which would produce *equality of results* for particular groups.[3] This shift coincided with the era of the Chicano Movement, a heightened period of political consciousness and activism, which was at its apex from the mid-1960s to the mid-1970s. The unprecedented attention given to the status and plight of Mexican Americans, especially the farm workers, and other Hispanics caught the attention of the national Republicans. Chicanos were pressing their claims and demands for parity and equality as a distinctive ethnic/racial group employing tactics which were very similar to the activities of the African Americans. In some areas of the Southwest a new separate Chicano "third" party, *El Partido de la Raza Unida,* had enjoyed some successes, usually at the expense of the Democratic party. Republicans did not let pass the opportunities afforded them to weaken the traditional Hispanic loyalty to the Democratic party. Allegedly, they even clandestinely supported Raza Unida activities. In any case, including Hispanics as benefactors of a racial preference program was strategically smart, irrespective of whether or not it was ethically motivated.

Other important affirmative action milestones included court decisions in the 1970s and 1980s. One of the most definitive was the 1978 *Bakke* case concerning admission to the medical school at the University of California, Davis. A white student applicant, Alan Bakke, had challenged the admission of ethnic minority students who had lower test scores than he did. The court ruled that the affirmative action provisions which allowed this were permissible. Since race had been a factor in the exclusion of minorities' access to professional schools, race could now be used as a positive (but not "decisive") factor in their acceptance. However, the court stressed that there could be no establishment of numerical quotas; only a broad concept of goals and timetables was permissible.

The Supreme Court in *Bakke* and other decisions in the 1970s had ratified race-conscious remedies, but it did not choose to deal with the point that there was a fundamental tension or even a contradiction between the actual wording of the 1964 Civil Rights Act and that laws' underlying philosophical concern with the disadvantaged situation of minorities. Title VII, Section 703(j), of the 1964 Civil Rights Act plainly bans preferences by race, gender, ethnicity, and religion in business and government. Obviously at that time the provision was meant to forbid continuing the advantages of white males and to prevent discrimination against people of color, women, and other disadvantaged minorities. Thus in attempting to reconcile the literal mandate for colorblindness with the intent to advance opportunities for colored groups, Justice Harry Blackmun in the *Bakke* case enunciated the quintessential paradox that "in order to get beyond racism, we must first take account of race."

Federal affirmative action programs proliferated during the 1980s and increasingly in the policies of state and local governments. For example, contract "set aside" programs existed among almost 300 cities and counties in the 1980s. By the mid-1990s, federal affirmative action plans included more than twenty set-aside provisions, about fifty requirements for affirmative action goals based on race or gender, and roughly forty racial or gender preferences. However, as affirmative action's legal status was being strengthened by courts' decisions during the decade (until the Supreme Court's 1988 term), its political support was deteriorating. Increasingly through the 1980s, pollsters detected submerged anger among whites, especially white men, who grumbled that they were the victims of racial discrimination, that affirmative action preferential programs were "reverse racism," and that racism was antithetical to the American values of equality and fairness and was in violation of civil rights legislation. It has not gone unnoticed that there is an irony here in that many of the people who were complaining about reverse racism and calling for colorblindness had not previously evidenced any concern when the "victims" were ethnic and racial minorities. Exclusion and discrimination on the basis of a *group's* color or other visible features, *regardless of an individual's "qualifications,"* had been practiced for 300 years of this country's history. In addition, over the years many of the routine procedures and practices of many major American institutions regularly and systematically put members of distinctive racial or cultural groups at a permanent disadvantage, a condition termed "institutional racism" or "institutional discrimination." This institutional bias is so ingrained and unnoticed that some contend that perhaps the only way which this subtle form of discrimination can be countered is to have institutional policies which make positive assets of color, race, ethnicity, or gender.

The debate over affirmative action policies and practices increased most strongly in the 1994 congressional election in which Republicans took over majority control of the United States House of Representatives and the United States Senate, as well as a majority of governorships in the states and majority control of many state legislatures. The key bloc vote (in terms of total numbers) providing conservative Republicans with electoral support was said by many analysts to be that of "angry white males." Among other things with which they were purportedly upset was what they perceived to be "reverse racism;" they felt discriminated against and excluded from the benefits which the recipients of affirmative action programs were receiving.

A new chapter in the status of affirmative action programs may have begun with two important decisions rendered by the United States Supreme Court in June 1995. While through the 1970s and 1980s the Supreme Court generally had been supportive of several disputed affirmative action programs, especially at the federal level, Republican-appointed changes in the composition of the Court increasingly presaged a conservative shift. On June 12, 1995, in the case of *Adarand Construction v. Pena,* the Court let it be known that, at a minimum, federal affirmative action programs would henceforth be under very strict judicial scrutiny. The case involved the awarding of a federal highway contract (including a $10,000 federal bonus payment) to a company using an Hispanic-owned "disadvantaged" subcontractor over the white-owned Adarand business, even though the latter's bid to the contractor was $1,700 lower. Adarand sued in Federal District Court in Colorado, challenging the constitutionality of the set-aside program. It lost, appealed to the 10th Circuit Court of Appeals, lost again, and appealed to the highest Court.

Writing for the five-person majority, Justice Sandra Day O'Connor ruled that federal programs classifying people by race, even for an ostensibly benign purpose such as expanding opportunities for members of minorities, are presumably unconstitutional. Such an approach could violate the basic principle of the Fifth Amendment of the Constitution, which guarantees the equal protection of "persons, not groups." Programs of racial group preference "must be subject to the most searching judicial scrutiny" and can be upheld only if they are "narrowly tailored" to accomplish a "compelling governmental interest."

Neither this particular program nor federal affirmative action programs in general were held unconstitutional. The case was remanded back to the U.S. District Court for review under these new "strict scrutiny" standards. Proponents of affirmative action found some solace in Justice O'Connor's recognition that "the unhappy persistence of both the practice and the lingering effects of racial discrimination against minorities in this country is an unfortunate reality, and government is not disqualified from acting in response to it. . . . " As a last resort, a limited program of preferences could be justified to remedy a clear pattern of "prior discrimination" against minorities.

The somewhat ambiguous ruling meant among other things that while courts may be directed towards applying stricter standards, it will be left to the more political branches of government, the executive and the legislative, to consider and reconsider, to devise, structure, and administer, the multitude of affirmative action programs in many areas at all levels in both the private and public sector, depending upon the specific circumstances of the situation.

ADVANTAGES AND DISADVANTAGES OF AFFIRMATIVE ACTION

In assessing the benefits and successes of affirmative action, there can be little doubt that the thirty years of affirmative action programs from 1965 to 1995 have produced many tangible successes.[4] Previously excluded and disadvantaged groups have been provided opportunities which otherwise would have been much slower in coming, if ever at all. Faculty, staff, and student bodies of our nation's colleges and universities are much more diversified than previously. Although the "Hopwood" decision rendered by the Fifth Circuit U.S. Court of Appeals on March 18, 1996 indicated that multicultural diversity is not adequate reason to give preferential admission to the University of Texas law school, it is not clear that this position will be upheld by the Supreme Court. Other Court decisions have proclaimed the domain of higher education as a special area in which extraordinary efforts to enhance diversity is especially desirable and necessary. In the employment sector not only have minority and women's employment been significantly increased, but their advancement into higher-paying, more authoritative positions has been noticeable. Not only can women and ethnic professionals, managers, and administrators serve as role models, once in positions of authority they are uniquely positioned to counteract any manifest insititutional racism, thus having a positive "multiplier effect" on their organizations and their communities.[5] Even if those affirmative action employment programs under the aegis of public law are diminished, many private employers have found that employing and advancing women and ethnic minorities are good business practices and are likely to continue some variation of promoting diversity in their work forces. Set-aside programs for minority firms have provided contracts to minority business enterprises which otherwise would have been disadvantaged and probably would have been eliminated from competition with well-established and well-connected contractors. Although the *Adarand* case and related actions by government may portend the end of contract set asides, increased educational and employment opportunities may serve as functional substitutes for minority business contract "quotas." Hispanics, long the nation's "invisible minority," have been officially recognized in all these affirmative action programs and now are found in noteworthy positions of education, government, and private enterprise.

For all the achievements of affirmative action programs, there seem to be, at least in the mid-1990s, significant if not equivalent disadvantages. In fact, the affirmative action concept was intended to be temporary. It was conceived to provide preferential treatment for a limited time to members of groups that had historically been excluded in order to give members of those groups the boost they needed toward parity. At some point, although that specific point was very unclear, enough opportunity through compensatory programs would have been provided that those programs would no longer be needed. Minorities and women could then compete at an equal opportunity level with members of the white majority. What seems to have not been considered was (a) how programs which provide benefits, once institutionalized, develop inertia and a life of their own in support of their internal and external clientele, and (b) more importantly, what would be the status of affirmative action programs if racism and ethnocentrism continued in seeming perpetuity to operate to the disadvantage of distinctive ethno-racial groups (a point to which we shall return).

Perhaps the most formidable argument mustered against affirmative action programs at this point is that they may have reached a point where they seem to be doing as much or more overall harm than good. It is clear that while a majority of the American public supports the general idea of equal opportunity, especially on an individual basis, and is generally opposed to racial, ethnic, and gender discrimination, it is equally evident that virtually any specification of programs that imply preferential treatment to a group, or which smack of quotas or "reverse discrimination" are likewise opposed. While Americans do support programs which eliminate or compensate for proven cases of discrimination, they are opposed to what they perceive as a general group entitlement plan regardless of specific circumstances. Yet it must also be noted that some other group preference plans and practices have been perceived as justifiable and seem generally acceptable. One thinks, for example, of veterans' preferences in education and employment and special admissions for students with special non-academic (e.g., athletic or alumni) characteristics.

The overall effect of publicity given to such programs by spokespersons opposing them seems increasingly to set group against group and to increase and heighten the disuniting of America, with factions divided along race and ethnicity becoming increasingly suspicious and hostile toward each other. Because of some apocryphal stories of the abuse and misapplication of affirmative action, even some persons formerly supportive of the goals of the programs have been turned against them, and even worse may feel themselves victimized with a resultant resentment against the members of groups benefiting from the programs. Anyone concerned with the common good must carefully consider any approach which extracts this high an overall cost. Fewer leaders and spokespersons have explained the positive outcomes of affirmative action programs, not only for the immediate beneficiaries, but also for the good of the nation.

In addition to the practical consideration of its harmful effect on the unity of this nation, there is also a philosophical argument that is made in opposition, that the U.S. Constitution should be "colorblind," and that the Declaration of Independence emphasizes individual freedom, not group entitlement. Positions should be obtained and advancement made based on individual merit, not on group membership. An individual should not be given special advantage simply because he or she is identified or claims to be a member of one of the special federally protected groups. Such group preference violates the basic concept of fairness and equality among individuals, long a basic principle of American society. It is an injustice to persons who do not qualify for these programs to be rejected regardless of their individual qualifications. However, it is seldom recalled that the people who are accorded affirmative action are members of groups who were excluded not because of their qualities as individuals but solely because of their *group* characteristics.

Moreover, some contend that affirmative action is also demeaning to members of minority groups who will be perceived as being in whatever positions they attain simply because they are members of these protected groups regardless of their individual merit or qualifications.[6]

Another shortcoming increasingly pointed out by opponents of affirmative action is that its implementation in terms of group categorization is sometimes so broad as to appear virtually mindless. From the perspective of reparation or corrective justice, it does not make sense that *all*

Latinos, African Americans, Asians, American Indians, and women are in need of, or deserve, special protection and assistance regardless of any other of their characteristics or their particular situation. To define rights exclusively in ethnic, racial, or gender terms is narrow-minded at best and can be ludicrous in the extreme. Should the daughter of a Cuban physician be given preferential admission status to law school over that of the son of an impoverished coal miner from Appalachia? Should a recent immigrant from Mexico be afforded the same advantages as a third- or fourth-generation Mexican American? It should be recalled that the driving principle of affirmative action initially was to compensate for past injustices done to members of a *group suffering from a long legacy of discrimination* that handicapped succeeding generations. For example, Mexican Americans in the Southwest have for generations been working hard and paying taxes to support their public institutions, including universities and colleges, and yet until very recently were never given an equal opportunity to attend and benefit from these institutions. Puerto Ricans' labor and other resources have been exploited since they were conquered and became colonial subjects in 1898; they still are not accorded the full rights of citizenship.

The same argument can be made, of course, for the other distinctive (or, as courts have used the term, "cognizable") ethnic and racial minorities with a long history in the United States. African Americans are the most well-known example, with their history of slavery and outright, officially sanctioned racial segregation and discrimination. The American government's policy of genocide towards the Native Americans, the taking of their lands, and their forced separation from mainstream society is also another very obvious manifestation of the kinds of histories of racial discrimination which were meant to be remedied by affirmative action programs.

It is significant that the heyday of affirmative action programs, that is, the 1970s and 1980s, was also the decades of noticeably increasing volumes of immigration, particularly of Asians and Hispanics, the two fastest-growing ethnic groups in the United States. Much of the new composition of American immigration results from the decision in 1965 to get rid of the McCarran Act national quota system which was driven by racist assumptions. However, should these post-1965 immigrants and their children be eligible for affirmative action benefits? They are, and maybe they should be, but the same rationale cannot then apply. American laws have discriminated against Asian immigrants throughout their history here, most notably the internment in relocation centers for the Japanese Americans during World War II and the Chinese Exclusion Acts. It is also true that Latinos, particularly the Mexican Americans in much of the Southwest, have a long history of discrimination, often backed by state action, until the various civil rights laws of the 1960s. But it is not unreasonable to pose the question: why should immigrants who have come to America voluntarily in the last three decades qualify for affirmative action? This is not to say that immigrants do not make valuable contributions to the United States and that this country does not need to rethink and improve its immigration laws, including the humane treatment of immigrants. To the contrary, both positions are eminently evident. But the rationale for compensatory treatment for a long-standing history of exclusion of certain groups does not apply to immigrants coming to the United States during the last generation or two. Lyndon Johnson's description of the crippling effects of racist discrimination in this country's past can be justifiably recalled when judging who should be eligible for any kind of compensatory programs.

Individual white men also maintain that they should not pay for the racist sins of a white power structure of generations past. More generally, the American sense of fair play is offended when any specific individual is rejected or excluded for reasons having nothing to do with his or her own character or abilities. An oft-cited example of this misapplication of remedies for past group rights and wrongs to individual cases is exemplified by the New Jersey case of *Taxman v. Piscataway*. A white teacher, Sharon Taxman, and a black teacher, Debra Williams, were both hired on the same day with equal qualifications to teach business education at Piscataway High School. When fiscal exigency forced the board to reduce the number of teachers in 1989, instead of utilizing a method of chance selection, the black teacher was retained in the name of departmental racial diversity. The school itself had twice the percentage of black teachers eligible to teach in that county. Several lessons, good and bad, can be learned from this instance currently being litigated before the U.S. Supreme Court. These include the questionable practice of levying heavy costs for a nation's legacy on *specific individuals* (very different than enhancing opportunity for members of a long-disadvantaged group), and the way in which the wish to increase diversity and promote multiculturalism has become conceptually tangled with affirmative action.

Another argument against affirmative action programs made especially by white males is that they are now a disadvantaged group and that all the positions and resources have gone to ethnic and racial minorities and women. This may be the perception, but the facts and figures do not verify this contention or perception. Most economists say that there are few statistical justifications for such white anger with affirmative action. The top occupational and professional positions in this society are still

overwhelmingly held by white males. White males make up about 43 percent of the labor force but hold about 95 percent of senior management
jobs. Non-Hispanic white males, who make up 33 percent of the population, comprise 80 percent of all tenured college faculty, 77 percent of
the U.S. Congress, 92 percent of all state governors, and 90 percent of all
newspaper editors. The percentage of Latino managers and professionals
has risen only slightly between 1973 and 1993, to 4 percent. The percentages of Latino graduates from colleges and universities have increased slightly; Latino ownership of businesses still constitutes less than
1 percent of the nation's total; Latinos receiving doctorates in the nation's colleges and universities equal about 2 percent or so. Very few major institutions are headed by CEOs, administrative authorities, or boards
from any ethnic or racial minority.

Affirmative action programs directed towards government contracts are relatively small in dollar terms. The Small Business Act Section
8(a) program, which covers about half of all federal minority contracting
involved only about 2.7 percent of all government procurement, about
$4.9 billion in 1994. (However it has also been noted that in 1994, 25
percent of all federal procurement dollars awarded to small businesses
went to "minority" businesses, and that minorities own 9 percent of the
businesses in this country.)

It seems that, with the possible exception of racial set-asides in government procurements and contracts, the "quotas" that affirmative action critics complain about exist more in political rhetoric than in reality.
It is true that there sometimes are established goals and timetables, but
typically organizations are required only to make good-faith efforts to
meet them. For example, during the 1970s, firms that had goals of increasing minority participation by 10 percent actually achieved only the
1 percent level.

However, as is well known, it is not the reality of the situation, the
statistics and the numbers, but the perceptions of such programs that
often bring an issue to the public agenda and usually are most important
in its resolution. Any program which is seen as not fair is not going to be
accepted by many for very long. And there are constant stories of decisions and policies which seem to be senseless and unfair, and these provide opponents of affirmative action with tools to mobilize the opposition. Certain instances and cases do not serve to advance the cause of
affirmative action. For example, the California Civil Rights Initiative had
its source in reactions to the recruiting of minority faculty members,
which upset two professors sufficiently to initiate the CCRI. When the
California state legislature passed a bill (not signed by Governor Wilson)
that would have mandated quotas in the proportion of minority admis-

sions and graduates to be equal to those existing in the population of California, two professors were driven to propose the Initiative. The *Piscataway* case with regard to termination of employment cited above also shows the irrational or at least arbitrary way in which programs can be administered. While argument can be made (as the school authorities did) that such discrimination against majority individuals and for racial minority individuals can be justified on the grounds of promoting the multicultural diversity of public institutions, this is in many ways a different argument toward a different objective. These kinds of decisions do tend to heighten the intensity against what are seen as affirmative action type decisions.

IMPLICATIONS FOR COALITIONS AMONG LATINOS AND NON-LATINOS

That affirmative action could become a major issue, if not *the* major issue in the late 1990s, has great implications for Latinos and Latino politics as well as for the politics and status of other "minority" groups. It certainly has immediate, direct, and multiple implications for Latino politics, and *coalition* politics in particular. As a focus for coalition politics, affirmative action might mobilize two major types of alliances: (1) an intra-Hispanic coalition pulling together Latinos of varying backgrounds, or (2) a coalition of Latinos with certain non-Hispanic groups. Ostensibly, affirmative action could serve as an issue that would consolidate most Latinos regardless of national origin or socioeconomic status. Since the typical policy makes no distinctions among Hispanics, all can benefit from inclusion in the protected group category. Affirmative action would seem to be a policy around which all of the incredibly diverse groups termed "Latinos" could be mobilized.[7] Also, since other ethnic and racial minorities, particularly African Americans, Asians and Pacific Islanders, and Native Americans and Alaskan natives, are federally protected under the affirmative action rubric, the issue would seem to provide an ideal vehicle for cross-ethnic/racial group coalitions. Another potential member group of such a pro-affirmative action coalition would be white women, another of the federally protected groups, who number 52 percent of the population and have vastly more resources than all the ethnic-racial groups combined. Potentially then, affirmative action could be the ideal issue to activate and mobilize a liberal or progressive coalition at the national level as well as at state and local levels.

However, there are also possibilities that affirmative action could further aggravate societal divisions, that is, become an even greater "wedge issue." Most obviously, it could divide (and already has to some extent divided) those groups who benefit from the affirmative action programs from those who do not, those who are excluded primarily being white males. Leaders of the Democratic party have been particularly concerned about this issue being a wedge which would further drive apart the mainly liberal coalition that has made up the Democratic party since the New Deal, and perhaps even deliver the death blow to that party's grand coalition. Although it is true that ethnic/racial minorities have supported the Democratic party nationally in very high proportions and that women recently have given a slight edge to the Democrats in national elections, the Democrats cannot win congressional and presidential elections without substantial support from white males. Although the party has lost some support from that group over the past few decades, white males who are liberal in their economic positions, members of labor unions, and generally those who are of the working, lower socioeconomic classes have also been a mainstay of the national Democratic party. Affirmative action could conceivably be that wedge issue that would completely and permanently break away these white male elements of the Democratic coalition.

ATTITUDES TOWARDS AFFIRMATIVE ACTION

Various public opinion surveys confirm that it was not only white males that did not approve of affirmative action in the early 1990s, but that most Americans oppose *specific* affirmative action programs that give preference to, or set quotas for, minorities and women in contracts, jobs, hiring, promotions, and college admissions.[8] A March 1995 Washington Post/ABC News Poll indicated that these were opposed by 75 percent of all United States adults.[9] The 75 percent included 81 percent of whites and 46 percent of African Americans. Approximately, some 25–30 percent would totally abolish such programs, and about half would change them. Other surveys showed that similar numbers, between 70 and 90 percent of whites and a majority of non-whites nationally, also opposed preferential and quota programs and had for a period of several years.

Politicians seeking to take advantage of this wave of public opinion reacted demonstrably. Republican presidential candidate Phil Gramm announced that upon being elected president he would by executive order abolish affirmative action programs. Pat Buchanan also voiced his disapproval, as did Lamar Alexander. Senator Robert Dole, who had supported some civil rights and affirmative action programs in the past, asked the Congressional Reference Service to conduct an extensive, detailed survey of the existing federal programs in order to review these for their fairness and effectiveness. In June 1995 presidential aspirant and Governor of California Pete Wilson abolished those affirmative action programs in the state which he could by way of executive order. President Bill Clinton first announced he would recommend specific changes in the nation's affirmative action programs, but then instead decided to initiate a task force review of affirmative action to develop broad goals for potential revisions rather than making detailed modifications himself. Many commentators saw this as an apparent bid by the president, concerned about the 1996 elections, to appeal to disaffected white males who increasingly have been voting Republican. On March 3, 1995, President Clinton in describing the Affirmative Action Task Force's work said, "I want to know what these programs are exactly. I want to know whether they are working. I want to know whether there is some other way we can reach any objective without giving a preference by race or gender in some of these programs." His political dilemma was that the president risked losing his electoral foundation, the white liberals, women, and ethnic minorities without whose support he would not have been elected in 1992. For example, Hispanics had cast 62 percent of their presidential votes for Clinton, a "minority" (43 percent) president among the general electorate. However, he also was aware of the tide of opposition growing against affirmative action especially among white males and that some substantial level of electoral support is needed from this large and resourceful group.

On July 19, 1995, the much anticipated report was presented to the president who on that date made a major television address to the nation as well as some satellite-fed remarks directed to the convention of the National Council of La Raza meeting in Dallas. In essence the president affirmed his support of the principles of and continued necessity for governmental affirmative action programs. In his national telecast he remarked: "We should reaffirm the principle of affirmative action and fix the practices. We should have a simple slogan: Mend it, but don't end it." At the same time, he opposed programs which incorporated quotas, created preferences for unqualified individuals, created reverse discrimination, or continued even after its purposes have been achieved.[10]

Bob Dole reacted to the president's position by responding that "This is not a difficult issue: Discrimination is wrong, and preferential treatment is wrong too." However after Bob Dole became the GOP presidential nominee, little more rhetorical opposition was vocalized by him until late in the campaign. Then, in what some saw as a desperate bid to challenge Bill Clinton for California's 54 electoral votes, Dole came out in support of the state's anti-affirmative action referendum, Proposition 209. The legislation he supported, the Equal Opportunity Act, primarily prohibits the federal government from granting or requiring preferences, but does little to affect private sector preferential treatment (which seems to have become good business policy) nor education's drive towards diversity.

In California, which often provides harbingers of things to come across the rest of the nation, an anti-affirmative action measure was introduced into the state legislature, and it was also proposed through direct initiative by voters' petition signatures as a November 5th ballot referendum. This proposed statewide legislation, called the California Civil Rights Initiative, was put before the voters in 1996. The CCRI would prohibit the state or localities from using "race, sex, color, ethnicity or national origin as a criterion for either discriminating against, or granting preferential treatment to, any individual or group in . . . public employment, public education, or public contracting." When this proposed initiative was placed before the registered voters of the state by the *Los Angeles Times* Poll in March 1995, 66 percent of all voters favored the CCRI, 26 percent opposed, and 8 percent did not know. Particularly useful for our purposes, this survey included oversamples of groups affected most by the policy and reported their opinions on the CCRI, as well as on other affirmative action items. This survey question was part of an extensive series of polls and articles produced by the *Los Angeles Times* in February and March 1995. These studies are notable for their depth of exploration, the March survey utilizing both a national and a California sample, and most noteworthy, for including significant samples of Latinos, blacks, and Asians and reporting those groups' opinions.[11] Seventy-one percent of whites favored the CCRI, as did 54 percent of Asians and a slight majority (52 percent) of Latinos. The only group which was opposed, and slightly at that, were blacks, with 48 percent opposing and 45 percent favoring the amendment.

A statewide survey by the *Los Angeles Times* in mid-July 1996 revealed that 59 percent of registered voters would support the CCRI. But when the voters were told that it would "effectively eliminate state-run affirmative action programs" an additional 11 percent opposed it. At this point, after considerable discourse in Latino communities about the CCRI, 42 percent of the Latinos disapproved and 45 percent approved.[12]

Proposition 209 became a hotly debated and well-publicized issue during the fall 1996 campaign. Opposition against the measure continued to increase, especially among ethnic groups. In the *Los Angeles Times* survey conducted October 17–21, the close division among Latinos evidenced in the July survey was found again, but this time with positions reversed, as 42 percent of Latino voters opposed the amendment, and 38 percent favored it. When Californians cast their ballots on this measure on November 5th, it was approved by 54 percent of all the voters. However, in a record turnout for Latinos, including many new citizens, 76–78 percent voted against it. A similar proportion of African Americans also opposed the CCRI, as did 61 percent of Asians and a majority of women—52 percent. Sixty-three percent of whites and 61 percent of males voted in favor of the referendum.

The all-inclusive, ambivalent wording of the initiative and the duplicated wording of the survey question makes a definitive interpretation problematic at best. At the least, the Proposition 209 poll data evidences perhaps a minimally consensual issue position among Hispanics, but one that changed considerably over a period of several months. Some more clues may now be available for further understanding intragroup or intergroup Latino coalition formation, particularly around various perceptions of the ideas involved in affirmative action. However, precise and in-depth understanding and its many implications must await further analysis.

Opinion survey researchers must be especially careful when polling on a highly charged and loosely defined topic such as affirmative action. Indeed, as pollsters examined this issue more fully, it became evident that the specific question wording was a paramount consideration.[13] When items used words connoting fairness or compensation for exclusion or past injustices, the public seem to favor such programs. However, when wording suggested *preferential* treatment or *quotas* for groups, the opinion is typically negative.

We will examine some of the questions posed by the *Los Angeles Times* in its March 1995 poll about and to Latinos on affirmative action–related items. Comparisons with the other groups sampled will provide some insight into whether this issue may serve as a basis for intergroup coalition or as a wedge that could drive them even further apart.

When a question was asked about the "conditions for Hispanics in America," Latinos' assessments were very similar to that of whites, as 52 percent of Latinos and 56 percent of whites thought that "Hispanics . . . ability to get adequate housing, and education, and job opportunities, and social acceptance by whites" was good or very good. A slight majority (52 percent) of blacks felt that the condition of Hispanics is bad. However, big majorities of all groups, including 67 percent of Hispanics, agree that we are not close to "eliminating discrimination against racial and ethnic minorities in America once and for all."

Each respondent in this national sample was also asked "Have you, yourself, ever been discriminated against because of your race or ethnic background when you were seeking a job or educational opportunity, or have you never been discriminated against?" The only group from whom a majority had experienced discrimination was the blacks, 52 percent of whom answered in the affirmative. A similar proportion of Latinos (53 percent) reported that they had *not* experienced discrimination, while 45 percent said they had. Interestingly, 16 percent of white women and 21 percent of white men also reported personal discrimination on account of their race or ethnicity. When asked whether they had "ever been a victim of reverse discrimination," agreement came from 28 percent of the white men, 22 percent of blacks, 21 percent of Latinos, and 14 percent of white women.

Small proportions of each group reported receiving "job or educational opportunities as part of an affirmative action program," — 17 percent of Latinos, 16 percent of blacks, 6 percent of white women, and 1 percent of white men.

The *Los Angeles Times* general question on affirmative action was: "Generally speaking, are you in favor of affirmative action programs designed to help minorities get better jobs and education, or are you opposed to them—or haven't you heard enough to say?" This benevolently worded item, with its reference to assistance and betterment, drew support from big majorities of Latinos (77 percent), 76 percent of blacks, and only a plurality of whites, 45 percent. Twenty percent of the latter group "did not know." Among whites, there was a large gender gap as a majority of white women (54 percent) favored such programs, while among white men only 35 percent agreed and 47 percent opposed. At this general level, there is consensual support among those "minorities" that affirmative action programs are designed to help.

The introduction of the use of "quotas" in affirmative action programs greatly affected the responses. Respondents were asked how they felt about affirmative action programs that used quotas, about programs that did not use quotas, or if they opposed all affirmative action items. Affirmative action programs without quotas were supported by a plurality of all groups. Attaching quotas separated the whites, both men and women, from the blacks and Latinos. Thirty-nine percent of blacks and 35 percent of Latinos favored programs with quotas, while only 12 percent of white men and 21 percent of white women did so. And all groups thought that affirmative action programs "end up using quotas" at least occasionally and often more than that.

The idea of "preferential" treatment also separated the racial/ethnic minorities from the whites, including white women. Even in a carefully qualified question ("Because of past discrimination, should qualified minorities receive preference over equally qualified whites in such matters as getting into college or getting jobs?"), 74 percent of white women and 82 percent of white men rejected preferential treatment. Latinos and blacks were closely divided, with only slightly more opposed than supportive.

Numerical goals and timetables for hiring and percentage set asides for contracts revealed similar patterns. At least three-fourths of blacks favored them, as did about two-thirds of Hispanics. A plurality of white women (48 percent) were in favor, but a majority of white men were opposed.

In the area of education, the question was posed: "When deciding who will be admitted, should public universities consider only a student's academic record or should some students be admitted in an attempt to balance the student body by looking at geographic location, ethnicity or gender as well as academic record?" The most common pattern of positions emerged, whites oppose considerations other than academic record (men, 62 percent, women, 57 percent); blacks favor balancing admission decisions by taking into consideration geography, ethnicity, or gender (51 percent); and Latinos are in between, divided at 42 percent for each position.

With regard to Latinos, the most focused question was "Do you think affirmative action programs designed to help Hispanics get better jobs and education go too far these days, or don't they go far enough, or are they just about adequate now?" The largest segment of Latinos (45 percent) felt the programs were adequate now, followed by 39 percent who felt that they don't go far enough, with only 5 percent saying they go too far. A 41 percent plurality of blacks felt these programs were inadequate; 35 percent judged them adequate. The largest group of white women (39 percent) said that programs for Hispanics were adequate; 24 percent felt they go too far. Among white men a slight plurality (38 percent) thought affirmative action for Hispanics goes too far, and 36 percent thought they were adequate.

The key policy proposal question provided three options about the preferred stance on affirmative action: whether affirmative action needs to be continued because discrimination is still common, whether affirmative action has simply gone on too long even though discrimination is still common, or whether affirmative action is no longer needed because discrimination has largely been eliminated. This item produced a clear distinction between whites and the racial/ethnic groups on whether affirmative action needs to be continued. Seventy-five percent of blacks and 64 percent of Latinos felt that affirmative action needs to be continued, while only 45 percent of white women and only 32 percent of white men agreed. At least half the whites thought the time had come to discontinue these programs (50 percent of the women and 61 percent of the men). A large proportion of the opponents thought that discrimination was still common but that this approach toward remedies had gone on too long; 21 percent of the white males felt that "discrimination has been largely eliminated."

From these survey data, one can infer that there might be a basis for a coalition between Latinos and blacks on this issue. The nation's two largest ethnic/racial minority groups were in substantial agreement on many aspects of affirmative action, including the need for its continuation and the benefits accruing from some of its specific programs. White women were somewhat more ambivalent; a large proportion was generally supportive, but they seemed to be much more doubtful about specific programs. White men are most in opposition. At least one out of five were strongly opposed to any form of affirmative action, and much larger proportions, often a majority, did not favor any kind of preferential or quota system. Yet about one-third of white men did seem to support the idea.

The numerical size of the ethnic/racial minority electorate is relatively small, combined perhaps 15–20 percent of the electorate. To be successful, therefore, there must be a high degree of consensus among them not just on the concept, but on what the parameters of specific programs will be. This latter point, which programmatic approaches are utilized to promote the cause, is particularly important to a very large proportion of the electorate, the white women. At the electoral level, they are the "swing" element that holds the key to the balance of power. If the affirmative action approach is to continue, specific programs could be devised, or continued, that would attract the support of a coalition of unified Latinos and blacks, a fraction of white males, and most crucially, a majority of white women. The attitudinal foundations are there for such an approach by enlightened political leadership. Before proceeding with a further analysis of the strategic ramifications of affirmative action for Latinos, let us examine more closely the arguments made for and against affirmative action, with emphasis on their application to Latinos.

POSSIBLE ALTERNATIVES AND REFORMS

Given that affirmative action has become a major issue on the public agenda, that programs are being scrutinized, and that reform (if not elimination) is in the works, what possible modifications may ensue? One of the most common suggestions, supported by some leaders in both the liberal and conservative camps, has been that the economic status of an individual should be a consideration in determining whether that individual should be eligible for preferential treatment regardless of ethnicity or race.[14] On March 3, 1995 President Clinton said, "I want us to emphasize need-based programs where we can because they work better and have a bigger impact and generate more support." Affirmative action programs could then be opened up to economically disadvantaged white people. Some feel that it is difficult to justify the government's providing special privileges to racial minorities of the upper-middle or upper class, while impoverished or subsistence-level working-class whites are not eligible for similar preferential treatment. This violates most American's concepts of justice and fairness. It does not make sense to have the children of an Argentinean immigrant millionaire be given preference in admission to a college or university or in a job application over the sons or daughters of an impoverished white Appalachian miner. Some kind of "means testing" might be utilized. However, giving preference to the poor in job hiring or promotions in and of itself does not seem to be the optimal approach; providing job training and additional training to enhance their levels of employability would be more acceptable. Incorporating economic criteria in decisions about college admissions may be more reasonable. In fact a Field Poll of Californians in May 1995 revealed that half (50 percent) of the voters would accept giving some weight to economic need in making college admissions decisions between two otherwise equal applicants. However, a majority (64 percent) would not give it weight in job or promotions candidacies.[15]

Although its implementation might be somewhat difficult, perhaps eligibility for inclusion into a program of affirmative action should include components of history and economics as well as race and ethnicity. Many of our social programs already are economic need-based, and admission to college, recruitment, retention, and advancement in education and employment could logically and rightfully be applied to the economic underclass of our society. Moreover, because of the continuing clustering of most of the federally protected racial and ethnic groups at the bottom of the economic ladder, that is, in the lowest-paid jobs and in the ranks of the impoverished, an emphasis on economic criteria would inevitably have a disproportionately favorable impact upon racial and ethnic minorities without unjustifiably giving "successful" individuals from those groups yet additional advantages.

On the other hand people can alter and in the United States many have changed, their economic position substantially over time. This may happen within one generation and is more likely to happen over two or three. In contrast, race is relatively immutable, and when it does change (as with the children of inter-racial marriage), its vestiges are seldom completely eradicated. A class-related style of dress or mannerism is much easier to conceal or change than are those physical differences which Americans perceive as important "racial" distinctions. Persons of distinctive phenotype or physiognomy may likely be treated differentially, even after they have achieved middle-class or professional status.

If affirmative action programs were to be eliminated completely, where would that leave federally protected groups? What programs, if any, then might take their place? Assuming that the American public still believes in equality of opportunity and fairness and is opposed to discrimination, any new programs and policies which are devised *must be based on the admission that prejudice and racism still exist in this country.* It is true that individual prejudice seemed to be declining and tolerance was increasing, especially over the past fifty years or so (at least until the 1980s). However, undeniable as it is that some individual prejudice continues, more importantly, *institutional* racism is still enmeshed in the everyday fabric of this society. Many of our major institutions, such as corporations, lending institutions, government agencies such as the FBI and schools[16] still perpetuate inherent biases in them which subtly, but regularly and continually, operate to the disadvantage or exclusion of certain groups, particularly ethnic or racial groups such as Latinos, African Americans, and Native Americans, regardless of the individual abilities or potentials of members within those groups. Thus, any reformed affirmative action programs or their replacements must proceed on the assumption that racism still exists and is not acceptable. Deep and long-term ethnic and racial discrimination cannot be eliminated without ethnic- and race-conscious solutions. Therefore, perhaps one approach might be to increase anti-discrimination monitoring and stiffen the penalties for discrimination. Much closer scrutiny of individual discrimination and institutional racism must be employed and sanctions and punishment for discrimination must be increased. The statutory basis for anti-discrimination exists; now its implementation must be revived and improved. For example, the 1991 Civil Rights Act provides sanctions if employers' practices have a "disparate impact" on minority applicants thereby discouraging employers from returning to discriminatory practices and encouraging them to keep in place some kind of affirmative action plans to reflect proportionality.

If preferential programs are to be continued, albeit on a reformed basis, it seems that at least one major adjustment is necessary, and perhaps more. If race and ethnicity are to be continued as major criteria, then it must be made clear as to the status of *immigrants.* If some racial and ethnic groups are to be given preferential treatment on the basis of compensation for a history of discrimination, then only those groups who have had such a disadvantaged legacy in this country can qualify for those programs. This cannot be determined solely on the basis of national origin, but must also take into consideration the history in the United States of the ancestral groups of those individuals potentially eligible for such programs. However, such considerations are fraught with difficulties.

IMPLICATIONS FOR UNITY OR DIVISION

As the debate over eliminating or modifying affirmative action intensifies, this issue can either be divisive or integrative in its impact on Latinos. Currently, all Latinos regardless of socioeconomic class, national origin, or generational history in the United States are eligible for special benefits because of their categorical membership in the federally protected, designated group "Hispanics." Thus, all Latinos conceivably could have a major stake in the outcome of this debate, and this issue can serve as a policy around which Latinos of many different backgrounds can mobilize.[17]

But it can also serve as a wedge issue among Hispanics, most particularly if proposed reforms should include considerations of ancestral generation or economics. For example, how far back in history should Latinos have resided in the United States in order to validly claim that their background, including that of their ancestors, was so subject to discrimination and exclusion that they qualify for preferential benefits now? Some have suggested that perhaps only those with an ancestral presence in this country prior to 1965 can rightfully claim inclusion. A large percentage (30–35 percent) of Mexicans residing in the U.S. and Mexican Americans are foreign-born. Should they be entitled to affirmative action benefits? There is little disagreement that they should be entitled to protection against discrimination and perhaps even to improved treatment as immigrants, but that is not the question here.

What should be the situation for Puerto Ricans? They have been subject to colonial domination and in many cases exploitation, both economic and political, for centuries, regardless of whether they currently reside on the island or on the mainland; the case for affirmative action for them seems fairly clear. In contrast is the case of Cuban Americans. With the exception of a fairly small percentage of Cubans, most contemporary Cuban Americans trace their ancestry in the United States to the 1960s at the earliest. In general, they have not endured a legacy of discrimination and exclusion comparable to that of Mexican Americans and Puerto Ricans. Additionally, as many have pointed out, Cubans are political refugees who have been treated extremely well by the federal government. Some estimate that just from 1962 to 1976 some $2 billion of direct assistance and perhaps as much as $4 billion of special governmental aid was given to Cuban Americans as political refugees from a communist country.[18]

Latino immigration continues at a voluminous and increasing pace from all of Latin America to the United States. As the laws of affirmative action policies are currently implemented, Nicaraguan refugees or Dominican immigrants of last week, as a result of their inclusion in the "Hispanic" category, are entitled to the same affirmative action benefits as a Mexican American or Puerto Rican whose ancestors in the United States were not only subject to exploitation, but to *generations* of discrimination including state-sanctioned segregation, separate and not usually equal laws, formal and informal prejudice, and intimidation and violence including beatings and lynchings.

How do Latinos of varying sociodemographic characteristics, such as socioeconomic class or generational status, feel about affirmative action? The only extant data which allows for such analysis comes from the Latino National Political Survey conducted in late 1989 through early 1990. In the course of the in-person interviews, respondents were handed a card on which was printed two extreme statements on affirmative action at the end points of a five-point scale. They were asked to indicate where along that continuum between the two polar statements they would place themselves. At one extreme was the statement that "the government should establish quotas in college admissions and job hiring to ensure [respondents' own group] representation." At the other extreme was the statement that "college admission and job hiring should be based strictly on merit." The Anglo cohort subsample in the survey was also presented this item with the wording of the question referring to "Hispanics."

For purposes of analyzing their responses, the middle position (point three on the five-point scale) was eliminated, and the two positions on each side, merit (1 and 2) and quotas (4 and 5), are each collapsed and combined into a dichotomized total response of (a) those favoring the merit position and (b) those favoring quotas. [See table 1]

Among Anglos, 91 percent favored merit, while only 9 percent favored quotas. Among the Latinos, the Cuban position was most similar to the Anglos, although not quite as lopsided towards merit, 73 percent of Cubans favored the "strict merit" position and 27 percent favored affirmative action quotas. Mexican-American responses and those of Puerto Ricans were distinctive from those of Cubans and Anglos and resembled

TABLE 1

Positions on Merit Versus Quotas, by Ethnic Group

	ANGLOS	MEXICANS	P. RICANS	CUBANS	TOTAL
Favors Merit:	320	531	201	397	1,449
	91.4%	52.7%	49.3%	73.1%	73.1%
Favors Quotas:	30	476	207	146	859
	8.6%	47.3%	50.7%	26.9%	37.2%
TOTAL N=	350	1,007	408	543	2308

Chi-Square = 223.16 Significance = .00000 DF = 3
Tau with "Preference" dependent = .096

each other. Both groups were closely divided in their positions, a slight majority of Mexicans (53 percent) took the merit side of the argument compared to 47 percent on the quota side; 49 percent of the Puerto Ricans favored the merit side compared to a very slight majority of 51 percent on the side of quotas.

Although one must be careful not to generalize too much from this one strongly worded item, it is one indication of several possible implications for Latino coalitional or "wedge" politics. It is obvious that again there are major differences on this issue between whites and many of the Latinos, with more than nine out of ten whites favoring admission and job hiring based strictly on merit. Cubans take a distinctive position between that of whites and that of Mexicans and Puerto Ricans, with a large majority of Cubans favoring the merit position. Mexicans and Puerto Ricans are close in their views on this issue, but are distinct from those of Cubans and especially from those of whites. However, it should be noted that Mexicans and Puerto Ricans are themselves each closely divided on this issue. Mexicans tend to be slightly more in favor of the merit position and Puerto Ricans slightly more disposed towards the quota side. So there definitely are some differences among national-origin groups as well as divisions within each group.

One might conclude from this and other evidence that while there may be some potential for transnational "Latino" mobilization around this issue, it is just as likely that the issue could be a wedge issue, even among Latinos, certainly between different national-origin groups, perhaps between different generations, and possibly between Latinos of varying socioeconomic status. These possibilities were pushed a little further using the LNPS survey item. Various socioeconomic variables were examined to see whether they had differential impacts on the opinions of these groups on this issue.

Some measures of socioeconomic status or immigration generation did prove to be significant for all the cultural groups. Among Anglos, age was the most significant factor among all the socioeconomic variables relative to their position on the merit versus quotas question. The greater the age, the more the opposition to this affirmative action remedy. Among Mexicans, the most significant variables affecting their positions were income (those in the lowest-income classes were by far the most in favor of government quotas) and to a lesser extent, education (those with both the least and the most education were most supportive of quotas), and age (the greater the age, the greater the proportion in favor of the merit position). Among Puerto Ricans, increased income and education were correlated with changing majority support from quotas to merit, and increased income also had the same, if a lesser, effect towards merit. Only among Puerto Ricans did gender make a significant difference, with 55 percent of the females leaning towards quotas and 56 percent of the males favoring merit. None of the traditional socioeconomic indicators seemed to be particularly significant among Cubans; all sociodemographic groupings favored the merit side, although opposition to quotas decreased somewhat among those with relatively less education and income.

A coalition based on their majority support of quotas would only include low-income (under $20,000 household income annually) Mexicans and Puerto Ricans. Low-income Cubans and Anglos still favor the merit position. This income-based, pro-affirmative action Latino coalition includes 54 percent of the Mexican and 70 percent of the Puerto Rican population.

Nativity/generation (place of birth and immigration generation in the mainland U.S.) is significant for Puerto Ricans and Mexicans on this issue of affirmative action. A majority of those born in Mexico or Puerto Rico in both groups favored the quota approach, while larger majorities of U.S.-born Mexican Americans and mainland-born Puerto Ricans preferred the merit system. Very small proportions of Cubans, whether born in Cuba (28 percent) or in the U.S. (14 percent) were in favor of the quotas.

From this limited evidence, the creation of a coalition of Latinos around at least this one major approach to affirmative action would be problematic to say the least. Simply on the basis of national origin, only half of Puerto Ricans and slightly less than half of Mexicans have supportive attitudes on this issue. Very few Cubans agree with them. Economic means testing or qualifying on the basis of place of nativity would further deplete the ranks of Latinos supporting this coalition. Mexicans and Puerto Ricans who have relatively higher incomes and are U.S. or mainland born are not very supportive.

In light of this analytical evidence from the LNPS survey that support for affirmative action is very divided among these Latino groups, indicating the possibility of a wedge among Latinos, let us return to the idea of coalitions with like-minded non-Latinos. Among the federally protected groups, almost nothing is known about the attitudes of Native Americans on this issue, while limited surveys tell us that Asian Americans are generally not very supportive of affirmative action programs. On the other hand, all evidence indicates that African Americans are the strongest and most consensual supporters of affirmative action.[19] The March 1995 Los Angeles Times national survey also revealed that African Americans are the only group from which a majority felt that " . . . conditions for Hispanics in America . . . their ability to get adequate housing, and education, and job opportunities and social acceptance by whites . . . are bad." Black Americans also were the only group among whom a plurality (41 percent) felt that "affirmative action programs designed to help Hispanics to get a better job and education" didn't go far enough. On a question specifically on quotas in affirmative action programs, the distribution of opinions of blacks and Latinos were virtually identical. So there seems to be a favorable basis of opinions for a coalition of a large proportion of African Americans and a portion of Latinos on this issue.

How about a coalition of supportive Latinos and women, the other major (and by far the largest) federally protected group? Sixty percent of all women and 54 percent of white women are generally in favor of affirmative action programs. Women are more sympathetic to the disadvantaged condition of Latinos than are men (a 14 percent gender gap, according to the *Los Angeles Times* poll), although they are ambivalent about whether affirmative action programs for Hispanics are adequate now, have gone too far, or haven't gone far enough. All evidence indicates that a substantial portion of women would be resourceful members of a coalition supporting many aspects of affirmative action.

Perhaps Latinos might be part of a cross-cultural coalition of men and women constructed around a liberal political ideology. One problem is that self-identified "liberals" are a relatively small proportion of the electorate, averaging about 25 percent over the past several years. Another difficulty is that Latinos are not uniformly or even predominantly liberal in their political ideologies. The Latino National Political Survey revealed that Mexicans include about the same proportion of liberals as do Anglos. Similarly, Puerto Ricans had about the same percentage of liberals, while Cubans were overwhelmingly conservative.

The political ideology proffered by the survey respondents seemed to make a major difference in the attitudes of only two of the four LNPS cultural groups towards affirmative action. As might be expected, among Anglos, increasing conservatism was associated with increasing support for the merit position. Among Mexican Americans, those who were liberal tended to support the quota option. However, among Puerto Ricans and Cubans political ideology did not seem to have any significant relationship. Thus it is not clear that a shared liberal ideology would be sufficient to form an attitudinal basis for an intergroup coalition on affirmative action, much less a coalition that is numerically large enough to exercise much influence.

One of the major concerns among Democratic politicians and political activists is that such an issue as affirmative action may break up the Democratic party coalition that includes ethnic/racial minorities and liberal whites, particularly lower income whites, and white women. Women have been slightly more identified with the Democrats; Democrats usually receive 60–80 percent of the Hispanic vote in national elections; African Americans typically give 80–90 percent of their support to Democrats. However, our analysis showed very little correlation between party identification and ethnicity on the issue of affirmative action. In fact, no significant correlation emerged between the party identification of Anglos, Mexicans, Puerto Ricans, and Cubans and their positions on this item. While the opinion on affirmative action might be virtually the same among each of the groups composing each party, the effects on each party would be significantly different. The Democratic party has in its base much larger proportions of those groups which are more divided on the issue, Latinos and women. Republicans have a less ethnically diverse, more homogeneous coalition; their base is composed of a much larger proportion of groups that are united in their opposition to affirmative action, namely white males.

In conclusion, as a coalition issue either for Latinos or for the Democratic party, affirmative action is at least problematic. Almost all but one of the groups (the Cubans) whom these policies directly benefit are divided among themselves. One must conclude that Latinos are ambivalent and divided on this important issue. National origin, economic status, and nativity/generation are some of the characteristics of Latinos that cleave them on this issue. Most in favor of affirmative action among Latinos are those who have the lowest socioeconomic status and are the most recent immigrants to mainland U.S.A. These Latinos, being among the least incorporated into this society, are probably also those most in need of assistance. Yet affirmative action programs to assist them, particularly those involving quotas, are not finding much support, even among other Latinos. Those Latinos most likely to participate in politics, who have the highest levels of income and education, and have the deepest roots in this society, are the least convinced about the preferential treatment approach to helping the minorities. Latinos are great supporters of governmental involvement in problem solving. They fully realize that discrimination against Latinos is a major problem. Most Latinos also realize that affirmative action programs have operated to their benefit. It is also very likely that Latinos would like to help society's disadvantaged, including new residents and citizens. However, some of the specific approaches utilized in affirmative action are not considered the optimal way to combat discrimination and assist the needy.

Latinos' positions on affirmative action and its specific programs will be shaped and changed as the public discourse continues. Specific proposals on reforming these policies in assisting disadvantaged groups will have differential impacts on Latinos, depending on the specifics of the proposals and the characteristics of the particular Latinos. While at the most general and symbolic level it attracts support from Latinos, as soon as specifics are introduced the effects on Latino reactions will be as varied as the Latino population is diverse. Unless great care is taken and wisdom is exercised, there is a great potential for this becoming a wedge issue among Latinos. However, with careful and judicious refinement of these programs, Latinos could be very supportive.

Affirmative action is just as likely to be a wedge issue among the general population. It would be very easy and regrettable for public leaders to employ heated rhetoric in this discussion. It might be tempting for some to play one group off against another for political gain. If some elements do mobilize around this issue, conflicting positions might just harden and intensify and cause more hostility and antagonism among ethnic and racial groups. If not handled with care and responsibility this issue could actually become a wedge issue not only for Latinos, but on a much larger scale. This is an issue which may not only wedge apart the Democratic coalition, but more importantly the general populace of this country.

In the area of affirmative action, as in others, it seems that what is good for the United States in general is also what is good for Latinos. Hopefully, Latinos who have suffered from a legacy of discrimination and exclusion and have not had the same opportunity to succeed as other Americans will not disproportionately lose out again as affirmative action programs and policies are modified. As usual the situation with Latinos is much more complex than it is with, for example, African Americans or Native Americans, primarily because of the diversity of the Latino experience in the United States. In any proposed reformulations of these policies, distinctions will have to be made, and differential applications of the policy will need to make distinctions between those Latinos who are most in need and most justly deserving of various kinds of assistance, and those who are less so.

As is the case with other distinctive minorities, both personal and institutional discrimination will continue to be an unfortunate fact of life for Latinos. It is essential that the oftentimes ineffective and inefficient administration and enforcement of the laws against discriminatory treatment be improved. The continuation of the subtle, less detectable, and more widespread occurrences of inherent institutional discrimination may be the most intractable problem of bias for most Latinos. Perhaps the strongest argument for the continuation of affirmative action programs into the indefinite future is that some kinds of affirmative action approaches are still needed to provide the necessary counterbalance to continuing unfair treatment. Rather than the traditional justification based on compensation, perhaps the strongest argument for affirmative action programs is that they may serve as one of the few effective programs of *countervailing bias* for offsetting the hidden and subtle biases found in the everyday operations of most of this nation's institutions.

It is unlikely that many affirmative action programs will remain unscathed over the next few years. In fact some of these programs possibly have progressed to the point that they seem to be doing almost as much harm as they are good, since they do seem to be increasing racial antagonism and divisiveness,[20] and policies which increase prejudice and ethnocentrism are certainly not good for this nation or its people, including Latinos. While there is no doubt that affirmative action programs have done much in promoting the parity of previously disadvantaged and excluded people, additional solutions and new approaches must now be debated, formulated, proposed, and incorporated into public policies and programs designed to counter all forms of unfair discrimination against any groups.

In the long run some adjustments in affirmative action programs in congruence with Americans' beliefs in equality, fairness, and justice, and that are specifically formulated to provide or keep open equal opportunity in those situations where it is demonstrably needed, cannot help but benefit those Latinos who have been precluded from sharing the American dream. If our political leaders and political activists are judicious in dealing with the debate over affirmative action, both Latinos and non-Latinos could come through this point of public controversy in mutually improved situations. President Clinton has said that "our institutions benefit from diversity" that "affirmative action has been good for America" and that "if properly done, affirmative action can help us come together, go forward and grow together. It is in our moral, legal and practical interest to see that every person can make the most of his life. In the fight for the future, we need all hands on deck and some of those hands still need a helping hand."[21] The goal of any reformed programs should be a national community in which there is lessened hostility between the groups, increased opportunity for all of those who need it, and an overall feeling of enhanced well being, cooperation, and even mutual respect, all prerequisites for an increasingly heterogeneous nation.

NOTES

Special thanks for their assistance with several aspects of this article are extended to Elliott Barkan, the late John Brennan, Sandra Garcia, Ronald

Schmidt, Scotty Shea, and Joseph Stewart. Their insights and perspectives were most welcome when writing on a highly complex and emotion-laden subject. The inclusion of any and all statements and misstatements is solely the responsibility of the author.

1. Peter Skerry, *Mexican Americans: The Ambivalent Minority* (New York: The Free Press, 1993).

2. Perhaps the most comprehensive elaboration of the history of the early affirmative action period is Hugh Davis Graham's *The Civil Rights Era: Origins and Development of National Policy, 1960-1972* (New York: Oxford University Press, 1990).

3. This thesis forms the basis for a comprehensive exposition of the development of affirmative action policies and practices in Herman Belz' *Equality Transformed: A Quarter Century of Affirmative Action* (New Brunswick: Transaction Publishers, 1991).

4. For several specific examples of such achievements see the White House document, "Affirmative Action Review: A Report to the President," July 19, 1995.

5. The "multiplier effect" occurs when well-positioned beneficiaries of affirmative action in addition to serving as role models, act to assist others of their identity groups in achieving well-being and also to inhibit discrimination against them. A well-organized and well-documented discussion of many aspects of affirmative action including the "multiplier effect" is found in Paul Brest and Miranda Oshige, "Affirmative Action for Whom?" *Stanford Law Review* (May 1995): 855-900.

6. For extended discussions of this and other negative implications for individuals from protected groups written by some of them, see Stephen L. Carter, *Reflections of an Affirmative Action Baby* (New York: Basic Books, 1991); Ruben Navarrette, *A Darker Shade of Crimson: Odyssey of a Harvard Chicano* (Cambridge: Harvard University Press, 1993); Thomas Sowell, *Preferential Policies: An International Perspective* (New York: W. Morrow, 1990); and also Shelby Steele, *The Content of Our Character: A New Vision of Race in America* (New York: St. Martin's Press, 1990).

7. Felix M. Padilla has theorized that Latino ethnicity has its origin in common cultural characteristics but is fortified and activated by Latinos' exclusion from the larger society and by political mobilization which itself is catalyzed by certain governmental or public policies; see his *Latino Ethnic Consciousness: The Case of Mexican Americans and Puerto Ricans in Chicago* (Notre Dame, Ind.: University of Notre Dame Press, 1985).

8. For a review of poll trends on affirmative action and some analysis of some of their features such as question wording, see Charlotte Steeh and Maria Krysan, "The Polls—Trends: Affirmative Action and the Public, 1970-1995," *Public Opinion Quarterly* 60, no. 1 (Spring 1966): 128-158.

9. *Washington Post*/ABC News Poll of 1,524 adults, March 16-19, 1995.

10. See three White House documents dated July 19, 1995: "Memorandum for Heads of Executive Departments and Agencies," "Remarks by the Presi-

dent on Affirmative Action" (11:40 a.m. EDT), and "Remarks by the President in Satellite Feed to La Raza Convention in Dallas, Texas" (2:16 p.m. EDT).

11. Thanks go to the late Mr. John Brennan, Director of the *Los Angeles Times* Poll and Mr. Rob Cioe for providing details and elaborations of their surveys. For the reports on the CCRI, see the *Los Angeles Times* issues of February 19, 20, and 21, 1995. For the more general surveys on affirmative action employing a national and a California sample, see published reports in the *Los Angeles Times,* March 29 and 30, Part A, page 1, 1995.

12. *The Los Angeles Times* poll released July 21, 1996 by courtesy of Mr. Ray Enslow.

13. Steeh and Krysan, "The Polls—Trends," 129–135. See also Jim Norman, "America's Verdict on Affirmative Action is Decidedly Mixed," *The Public Perspective* (June-July 1995): 20–25.

14. A major proponent of class-based affirmative action is Richard D. Kahlenberg. See his articles, "Class Not Race," *The New Republic* (April 3, 1995) and "Equal Opportunity Critics," *The New Republic* (July 17 and 24, 1995): 20–25.

15. Field Institute Poll by Mark DiCamillo and Mervin Field. This was a statewide survey of 744 California voters conducted May 16–22, 1995. Doctor Elliott Barkan, Professor of History, California State University-San Bernardino, who assisted in the development of the questions asked in this survey, provided the author with the detailed information on this poll.

16. For an extensive exposition of the continuing biases of schools against Hispanics in the subtler forms of "second-generation discrimination," see Kenneth J. Meier and Joseph Stewart, Jr., *The Politics of Hispanic Education* (Albany: State University of New York Press, 1990).

17. In fact affirmative action employment cases are used as illustrations of factors leading toward mobilizing Latinos as a politicized transnational interest group in Padilla, *Latino Ethnic Consciousness.*

18. T. D. Allman, *Miami: City of the Future* (New York: Atlantic Monthly Press, 1987).

19. The March 1995 *Los Angeles Times* Poll; Affirmative Action Results. The University of Chicago's continuing General Social Survey has shown African Americans to be the most ardent, long-term supporters of affirmative action. These and other poll results are presented and analyzed in the unpublished paper by Stephen Earl Bennett, Alfred J. Tuchfarber, Andrew Smith, and Eric Rademacher, "Americans' Opinions About Affirmative Action," Institute for Policy Research, University of Cincinnati, March 1995. The March 1995 *Los Angeles Times* survey confirmed a continuation of this trend.

20. In their experimentation with racial attitudes, Sniderman and Piazza found that racial antagonism increased significantly among those subjects who were presented with the concept of affirmative action. See Paul M. Sniderman and Thomas L. Piazza, *The Scar of Race* (Cambridge, Mass.: Belknap Press of Harvard University Press, 1993).

21. "Remarks by the President on Affirmative Action," July 19, 1995.

15. Mexican, Puerto Rican, and Cuban Foreign Policy Perspectives: A Test of Competing Explanations

Rudolfo O. de la Garza, Jerome Hernandez,
Angelo Falcon, F. Chris Garcia,
and John Garcia

THIS PAPER EXAMINES THE foreign policy orientations of Mexicans, Puerto Ricans, and Cubans in the United States. Specifically, it analyzes the attachment these groups have for Latin America and how salient Latin American politics and U.S foreign policy toward Latin America are to these three groups.

Ethnic groups have a long contentious relationship with American foreign policy makers. On the one hand, policy makers like to think of foreign policy as non-partisan and, in some sense, above politics.[1] Consequently, it has historically been the arena least affected by the interest group involvement that characterizes domestic politics.[2] Nonetheless, ethnic groups have, with varying success, long sought to influence U.S. policy toward their respective "homelands."[3] Indeed, in what surely is an overstatement, two distinguished scholars have asserted that such efforts have become "the single most important determinant of American foreign policy."[4]

LATINO FOREIGN POLICY VIEWS

There are two competing formulations of Latino[5] foreign policy views. One, which we label the "cultural" perspective, argues that because of cultural commonalities emanating from Latin America and shared experiences as immigrants and minorities in this nation, Hispanics in the United States constitute a Latin American diaspora. As such, Latinos are especially interested in the politics of Latin America and in U.S. policy toward the region.[6] Hence, in line with this view, issues such as the Panama Canal treaty and U.S. policies toward Latin America in general "hold the community's attention."[7]

This culturalist perspective is the source of wildly divergent political claims. Liberal critics of U.S. foreign policy argue that given how interested Hispanics are in Latin America, Latinos will use their increased political clout to become the vanguard for developing a new approach to Latin America that will "support a more humane and sensible approach to foreign policies."[8] Others invoke Hispanic attachment to Latin America to substantiate the charge that Latinos pose an irredentist or separatist threat to the nation.[9] This argument is then used to mobilize support for restricting immigration and making English the nation's official language.

However, the accuracy of the culturalist formulation is unknown; moreover it derives from untested premises. First, it assumes that distinct Hispanic national-origin groups in the United States constitute a Latin American diaspora analogous to a national diaspora, that is, "a people with common national origin who reside outside a claimed or an independent home territory."[10] According to this formulation, the "home country" includes all of Latin America rather than the "home" countries for each national-origin group, e.g., Mexico for Mexican Americans. Second is the assumption that U.S. policy toward Latin America and politics internal to Latin America are highly salient to U.S. Latinos. Third, it assumes that Latinos have a distinctive attachment to Latin America and a unique view of U.S. policy toward the region that is independent of factors such as national origin, levels of integration into American society, socioeconomic status, and political differences rooted in home-country politics. In sum, the culturalist formulation is that U.S. Latinos share a distinct interest in and particular affection for all of Latin America.

An alternative viewpoint which we label the "structural" formulation, differs in four fundamental ways from the culturalist formulation. First, it argues that Latinos of different national origins do not constitute a single ethnicity because such disparate groups do not share the kinds of historical experiences within which ethnic identities are couched.[11] Survey results support this argument. Mexicans, Puerto Ricans, and Cubans overwhelmingly prefer national-origin labels to pan-ethnic labels;

moreover, among Cubans and Puerto Ricans, the native born prefer "American" to pan-ethnic labels.[12]

Second, the structural formulation views Hispanic national-origin groups in the United States as separate and distinct "emergent ethnicities."[13] Such ethnicities are rooted in historical ties to specific Latin America countries but have evolved primarily in response to American socioeconomic and political processes. Their historical origins notwithstanding, therefore, they are products of American society and are principally oriented toward American issues. Because it lacks the historical roots that national-origin ethnicities have, a pan-ethnic identity will reflect even more strongly its American influences. Thus, those who share in this identity will focus on American issues to an even greater extent than do Mexicans or Cubans. The results of the first study to analyze "Latino" ethnicity illustrate this. After noting the differences in Mexican and Puerto Rican ethnicities and specifying the conditions under which the two groups came together as "Latinos," the study concluded that " . . . it is safe to say that at this time in history the kind of Latino ethnic identity and consciousness described in this study may have relatively little to do with Latin America. It seems clear that this group identification is largely a phenomenon of American urban life. . . . "[14]

A third major difference is that the structural perspective does not assume that Latin American issues are salient to all or most Latinos in the United States, i.e., the Latin American diaspora. Instead, it assumes that sociodemographic and ethnic characteristics determine which issues will be salient, how salient they will be, how issues will be viewed, and whether, in fact the nominal members of the diaspora actually identify as members of the group.[15] Thus, the structuralist perspective is compatible with the conceptualization of the diaspora as consisting of three segments:

1. 'core members' or organizing elites who are intensively active in diasporic affairs;
2. 'rear guard members,' or past diaspora activists who have drifted away; and,
3. 'silent members' or those whom diaspora elites, host governments, or home governments consider as potential recruits for diasporic politics.[16]

The silent members may be thought of as an "imagined community" that exists primarily in the minds of ethnic and non-ethnic elites.[17] Some silent members may identify with the symbols of the old country without maintaining an interest in its domestic or foreign politics, and still others may not identify in any way as members of the diaspora or with home-land symbols or issues. Those who do not identify in any way with the homeland are probably a small segment of the silent group.[18]

It is important to note that, because of the tenuous existence of a "Latin American" ethnicity, the proportion within each of these catego-ries probably differs for the Latin American diaspora compared to any specific national-origin diaspora. It is especially likely that the core elite of the former is much smaller in relative and absolute terms than it is for the latter, and that the "silent members" constitute almost all of the Latin American diaspora. Thus, the Latin American diaspora may be an excellent example of how elites invoke an "imagined community" to ad-vocate for particular policy preferences.

The final major difference between the structuralist and the cultu-ralist approaches is that the former assumes that at all levels within the diaspora there may be significant differences in how the homeland is viewed. Thus, even those focused on homeland politics will not necessar-ily be interested in or supportive of the same issues or positions.[19] This is evident among Puerto Ricans, Mexicans, and, most powerfully, Cu-bans.[20] Consequently, even a mobilized diaspora may be politically irrele-vant if it is more or less equally divided in its views of a particular policy.

This paper tests the culturalist and structuralist formulations in three ways. First, it analyzes each group's affect for Latin American countries as compared to other countries. Second, it examines the extent to which Mexicans, Puerto Ricans, and Cubans are attentive to politics in the United States versus politics in their respective "home countries." Third, it evaluates whether these Hispanic national-origin groups have a distinct and cohesive view of U.S. policy toward Latin America.

DATA

The data analyzed here are from the Latino National Political Survey (LNPS), a nationally representative sample of 1,546 Mexicans, 589 Puerto Ricans, and 682 Cubans (see table 1). Together, these groups con-stitute over 80 percent of all Hispanics in the continental United States, and the sample analyzed here is representative of more than 90 percent of the nation's Mexican, Puerto Rican, and Cuban-origin populations. Those Mexicans, Puerto Ricans, and Cubans not represented in the sam-ple fall into two categories: those who reside in states in which the popu-lation was less than 5 percent Hispanic, and those who reside in census tracts with less than 3 percent Hispanics even if they reside in states that

TABLE 1

LNPS Sociodemographic and Ethnic Characteristics

	Mexican %	P.R. %	Cuban %
Gender			
Male	52.2	44.4	49.0
Female	47.8	55.6	51.0
Sample Size (N)	1546	589	679
Age Group			
18–24	22.7	20.4	12.7
25–34	31.2	28.8	18.9
35–50	27.3	31.7	27.2
51–65	13.5	12.6	24.2
66+	5.3	6.5	17.0
Sample Size (N)	1544	589	674
Education			
0–8 yrs.	39.7	30.1	33.3
9–12 yrs.	16.8	21.8	13.5
HS Degree	36.1	37.0	33.0
Post HS education	7.4	11.1	20.2
Sample Size (N)	1542	586	673
Employment status			
Temporary labor	10.9	12.1	7.0
Unemployed	24.0	37.8	31.8
Employed	65.1	51.1	61.2
Sample Size (N)	1542	588	678
Nativity			
Foreign Born	50.5	65.7	86.5
Native Born	49.5	34.3	13.5
Sample Size (N)	1546	589	679
Citizenship			
Yes	56.8	99.6	45.9
No	43.2	0.4	54.1
Sample Size (N)	1546	589	679
Language			
English	29.8	20.7	6.8
Bilingual	30.6	45.1	27.6
Spanish	39.6	34.2	65.6
Sample Size (N)	1545	588	677

Table 1 continued on next page

Table 1 continued

	Mexican %	P.R. %	Cuban %
Racial Identification			
Non-latino	51.4	62.3	95.3
Latino	48.6	37.7	4.7
Sample Size (N)	1463	563	672
Religion			
Catholic	77.4	65.2	77.7
Protestant	11.9	22.3	13.7
Other	10.7	12.6	8.6
Sample Size (N)	1543	589	679
Household Income			
0–12,999	28.1	45.5	29.3
13,000–19,999	18.1	17.0	18.1
20,000–29,999	20.7	17.3	19.9
30,000–39,999	15.4	11.5	12.2
40,000–49,999	8.6	4.1	4.4
50,000+	9.1	4.6	16.1
Sample Size (N)	1434	543	615

met the 5 percent threshold.[21] A respondent is defined as a member of one of these populations if she, one parent, or two grandparents were solely of Mexican, Puerto Rican, or Cuban ancestry.

LNPS initially sampled these three groups as distinct populations rather than as a single population that could be aggregated under a single label such as "Hispanic" or "Latino" to avoid the implication of cultural homogeneity or political unity inherent in such labels.[22] The individual groups will be identified as Mexicans, Puerto Ricans, and Cubans.

Over 97 percent of all interviews were completed between August 1989 and February 1990. Respondents had the choice of being interviewed in English or Spanish, and 60 percent chose Spanish.

Concept Operationalization and Analysis

The independent variables used in the analysis are divided into sociodemographic measures and ethnic indicators. The former includes gender, religious affiliation, household income, education, occupation, and age. The ethnic indicators are national origin, nativity, self-rated language competence, and racial self-identification, characteristics generally associated with ethnicity. National origin identifies an individual's historical nationality. Nativity specifies country of birth and is central to understanding how ethnicities evolve.[23] Language competence is the cultural characteristic considered most central to ethnic maintenance and reproduction.[24] Here, language competence was measured by combining responses to two questions asking what language is usually spoken at home, and the respondent's overall ability in English and Spanish.

Although ethnicity is rooted in these objective characteristics, it also includes a subjective component.[25] Here, racial self-identification is used to tap that subjective dimension. LNPS operationalized racial identification with the following item: "Do you consider yourself white, black, or something else?" Those who answered something else were asked to indicate what that was, and only those who responded referring to Spanish or Latin American–origin labels or to "brown" colors were categorized as "Latino referents." The reason for this was to differentiate those who have begun to identify with a new racial category (i.e., a Latino race) from those who define themselves with historically established racial categories such as black or white. Therefore, those who identified as black were grouped with white identifiers as "non-Latino" identifiers. It must be emphasized that placing respondents in this category does not suggest that they are not Latinos. It merely indicates that, whatever their national origin, they do not define themselves *racially* as "Latinos."

Racial identity is particularly appropriate as an indicator of the subjective aspect of Latino ethnicity because it reflects the on-going evolution in their ethnicity. Latinos are "racially" mixed, that is, they include whites, blacks, Indians, and combinations of these and other groups such as Asians. Nonetheless, racial identity has historically been a divisive issue in Mexico, among Mexicans in the United States, in Cuba, among Cubans in the United States, and among Puerto Ricans on the mainland and in Puerto Rico.[26] In addition to the impact of these legacies, Latino racial self-identification might also be affected by the increased saliency of ethnicity in the United States in recent years.[27] For example, among the Spanish-origin population, it is argued that this ethnic revival has manifested itself with an increasing preference for self-identifying racially with labels such as Hispanic, mestizo or raza, or with colors such as brown, rather than with either black or white.[28]

ANALYSIS

Our analysis tests the following propositions:

1. Mexicans, Puerto Ricans, and Cubans have high and equal affect for all of Latin America.
2. Political issues in Latin America have high saliency for Mexicans, Puerto Ricans, and Cubans.
3. Mexicans, Puerto Ricans, and Cubans have a distinct and cohesive view of U.S. policies toward Latin America.
4. Differences in sociodemographic and ethnic characteristics (national origin, language ability, nativity, and racial self-identification) have no impact on foreign policy perspectives.

To the extent that the culturalist formulation is correct, the results should support these hypotheses. If the structuralist formulation is correct, the results should counter these hypotheses.

I. HIGH AND EQUAL AFFECT FOR LATIN AMERICA

The first issue we examine is affect for ten nations. Using a "feeling thermometer" scale, respondents were asked to rank their fondness for Mexico, Puerto Rico, Cuba, Nicaragua, Venezuela, Russia, Israel, Japan, Britain, and the United States.

The responses to these question lend no support to the culturalist formulation but are strongly consistent with the structuralist formulation. As Table 2 illustrates, Latinos are neither uniformly positive about all Latin America, nor do they agree in their affect for Latin American countries. All three groups are most positive about the United States. Mexicans and Puerto Ricans then rank their respective "homeland" second, while Cubans rank Puerto Rico above Cuba. However, in no case does a majority of any Latino group rank more than one Latin American country positively. In addition, in several cases respondents ranked non–Latin American countries above Latin American nations. Indeed, Britain was the third most positively ranked nation among Mexicans and Cubans, and among Puerto Ricans it ranked higher than Nicaragua and Cuba.

The respondents were also grouped according to nativity, language use, and racial identification. By far, the United States received the highest score when respondents were grouped according to these three ethnic indicators, regardless of their respective categories. Other significant patterns associated with these ethnic measures are: the foreign born have

TABLE 2

Percent With Positive* Feelings toward Countries by Ethnic Indicators

COUNTRY	NATIONAL ORIGIN			NATIVITY	
	Mexican	Puerto Rican	Cuban	Foreign Born	Native Born
Mexico					
%	70.8	44.7	26.9	54.7	55.0
N	1539	577	670	1735	1051
Puerto Rico					
%	41.1	90.0	60.2	61.4	48.4
N	1441	586	672	1674	1024
Cuba					
%	17.5	18.5	49.2	30.5	17.7
N	1450	577	672	1671	1028
Venezuela					
%	40.1	41.8	41.9	42.2	33.1
N	1393	566	657	1637	979
Nicaragua					
%	21.5	24.8	14.7	22.7	17.1
N	1438	569	662	1653	1016
Russia					
%	17.6	13.7	9.2	12.3	18.5
N	1445	571	667	1650	1032
Japan					
%	35.8	35.9	44.8	38.5	36.0
N	1439	569	652	1639	1021
Israel					
%	28.2	31.3	31.6	30.5	28.4
N	140	566	645	1605	1011
Britain					
%	44.2	38.3	55.3	42.9	50.2
N	1422	556	645	1615	1008
United States					
%	95.0	94.5	96.2	94.6	96.1
N	1541	586	677	1747	1058

Table 2 continued on next page

Table 2 continued

COUNTRY	LANGUAGE			RACIAL IDENTIFICATION**	
	English	Bilingual	Spanish	Non-Latino	Latino
Mexico					
%	51.5	53.7	57.5	48.5	65.7
N	627	916	1238	1723	948
Puerto Rico					
%	45.6	61.9	58.0	58.6	53.2
N	621	900	1175	1684	901
Cuba					
%	15.8	25.3	30.9	27.4	22.6
N	621	904	1171	1685	903
Venezuela					
%	30.4	38.8	43.0	39.0	38.5
N	599	868	1146	1634	877
Nicaragua					
%	16.4	20.1	23.0	17.7	25.3
N	620	886	1161	1670	888
Russia					
%	22.6	15.7	9.5	12.9	17.1
N	623	902	1155	1680	893
Japan					
%	37.9	39.6	35.7	37.8	37.3
N	621	897	1140	1658	891
Israel					
%	31.1	29.3	29.3	29.5	30.8
N	617	882	1116	1632	880
Britain					
%	55.9	43.7	41.6	46.7	43.8
N	620	872	1130	1643	870
United States					
%	95.9	96.1	94.1	96.7	93.1
N	629	925	1247	1738	950

* A score >50 degrees indicates a warm or positive evaluation. Reported here are the percentages of respondents who rated each country at 51 degrees or higher.

** Respondents who self-classified their racial identification as black or white are classified as Non-Latino on this characteristic.

higher affect than the native born for the Latin American countries. However, both foreign and native born report higher affect for Britain and Japan than for Venezuela, Cuba, and Nicaragua. English monolinguals and bilinguals express lower affect for Latin America than do Spanish monolinguals. Even among the latter, however, Britain ranks higher than Nicaragua and only slightly below Venezuela. Those who identify racially in terms of Latino referents are more positive toward Latin America than are non-Latino identifiers. Again, however, even among Latino identifiers, Britain ranks higher than most Latin American countries, and Japan also does better than Nicaragua, Cuba, and Venezuela.[29]

To further examine our first hypothesis, we analyzed the extent to which these scores indicated that respondents viewed these countries so similarly that they could be considered a single entity. The first test included all Latin American countries with the exception of each group's respective homeland. The homeland was excluded in order to examine affect for the region in general. The results indicate that the respondents do view these distinct countries similarly enough to suggest that they perceive the countries as constituting a Latin American entity.[29]

To test the validity of this finding, we then analyzed our respondents' affect scores for all the countries listed in Table 2 to compare ratings of Latin American and non–Latin American countries. If respondents rate the Latin American countries differently than non–Latin American countries, this would indicate that they view these countries as part of a "Latin American" entity such as the culturalist formulation predicts.

The results indicate that while Mexican, Puerto Rican, and Cuban responses all reflect something of a distinct orientation toward Latin America, no two national-origin groups respond identically to all Latin American countries. Moreover, in no case does a group's Latin American dimension include all the Latin American countries. For our purposes, what is most significant is that the Latin American countries listed in Table 2 do not constitute a discrete affective dimension for Mexicans, Puerto Ricans, or Cubans.[30]

Puerto Ricans are the most likely to view Latin American countries distinctively. Their responses indicate that they view Nicaragua, Cuba, Venezuela, and Mexico similarly; however, they relate to Israel much as they do to these four countries. Even more significantly, they relate to Puerto Rico as they do the United States rather than as they do to Latin American countries. This may be because they see both the United States and Puerto Rico as their countries of origin.

Cubans relate to these ten countries along three dimensions, and none qualifies as Latin American. The first dimension includes only Cuba, reflecting the continued intensity of the refugee experience. The remaining two dimensions that characterize Cuban views appear to have an ideological rather than a Latin American basis. Democratic countries (Great Britain, Japan, Puerto Rico, Israel, Venezuela, and the United States) make up the second dimension. The third consists of Russia, Nicaragua, and Mexico. Mexico may be included with these two because it has been openly supportive of left-wing governments.

Mexicans manifest a "Latin American" dimension that includes only Mexico, Puerto Rico, and Nicaragua. Their views of Cuba are negatively associated with their views of the United States and fall along a separate second spectrum. This suggests that the positive evaluation Mexicans have of the United States is related to the negative view they have of Cuba. Mexican views of Venezuela fall along the dimension that includes Japan, Great Britain, Israel, and Russia.

Because respondents' attitudes evidenced no distinct Latin American dimension that includes all Latin American countries and only these countries, respondents' affect for each country was analyzed to measure the independent effect each of the four ethnic indicators listed in Table 2 has on attitudes toward each country.[31] Our results indicate that:

1. Each national-origin group is significantly more positive toward its home country than are the other two groups.
2. The only countries regarding which there are no statistically significant differences associated with national origin are the United States and Venezuela.
3. The groups differ regarding non–Latin American countries: Puerto Ricans are less positive toward Britain than Mexicans, while Cubans are more positive; there are no statistically significant differences regarding Japan; Puerto Ricans are less positive than Mexicans toward Israel; Cubans and Puerto Ricans are less positive than Mexicans toward Russia.
4. The foreign born have higher affect than the native born for Mexico, Puerto Rico, and Venezuela, but nativity has no effect on attitudes toward Nicaragua and Cuba.
5. Latino self-identifiers have higher affect than non-Latino self-identifiers for all Latin American countries except Venezuela.
6. English monolinguals and bilinguals have lower affect for Mexico and Cuba than the Spanish monolinguals, but language ability is not related to attitudes toward Venezuela.
7. The country for which respondents express the highest affect is the United States.

Together, these results contradict the culturalist formulation but support the structuralist perspective. They indicate that respondents do not view Latin American countries as if they constitute a distinct region to which they are particularly attached, and that differences in national origin, nativity, language competence, and racial self-identification influence how Latin American countries are viewed.

II. High Saliency for Latin American Politics

The second hypothesis tested concerns Latino interest in Latin American *vs.* U.S. politics. The structuralist argument expects these groups to be much more involved with politics in the United States than in Latin America because both the native and foreign born have more of a stake in U.S. than in Latin American politics. Few of the native born are likely to be personally affected by Latin American affairs. Political attentiveness is unlikely absent such a stake. Also, most immigrants come with the intent to stay.[32] Therefore, even though they may have greater connections to Latin American affairs, the foreign born too are likely to be focused on U.S. developments because it is here where their future is being determined.

The culturalist perspective predicts widespread attention to Latin American issues. This interest, according to this view, is rooted in attachments that exist independently of any material or other direct personal involvement with specific developments.

Our indicator of interest in Latin American politics is interest in homeland politics compared to interest in U.S. politics. Our assumption is that if respondents express little or no interest in homeland issues, it is unreasonable to expect them to be interested in the politics of other Latin American countries or of the region in general. We asked our respondents whether they were more concerned with the government and politics in their homeland, the U.S., or both.

As Table 3 illustrates, from one-third to almost half of each national-origin group follows homeland politics to some degree. However, those who do so are primarily the foreign born and Spanish dominant, most of whom are foreign born. Furthermore, only 2 percent of U.S. citizens of Mexican origin are primarily interested in Mexican politics, and only an additional 8 percent are equally interested in both Mexican and U.S. issues. Even among Cuban-origin citizens who are overwhelmingly foreign born, only 4 percent are primarily focused on Cuba while 77 percent focus primarily on U.S. issues. Clearly, these results suggest that homeland politics are salient only to a very small group of these Latinos,

TABLE 3

Interest in U.S. or Homeland Politics by Ethnic Indicators

Political Focus	NATIONAL ORIGIN			NATIVITY	
	Mexican	Puerto Rican	Cuban	Foreign Born	Native Born
U.S.	67.6%	55.3%	63.4%	50.6%	85.6%
Both	22.4	30.0	27.4	34.3	10.6
Homeland	10.0	14.7	9.2	15.1	3.8
Total N	1445	547	639	1619	1012

	LANGUAGE			RACIAL IDENTIFICATION	
	English	Bilingual	Spanish	Non-Latino	Latino
U.S.	89.2	73.2	43.7	65.7	61.0
Both	8.4	21.4	36.9	24.1	27.1
Homeland	2.4	5.4	19.4	10.2	11.9
Total N	598	891	1141	1620	902

	NATIONAL ORIGIN BY CITIZENSHIP					
Political Focus	Mexican		Puerto Rican		Cuban	
	Citizen	Non Citizen	Citizen	Non Citizen	Citizen	Non Citizen
U.S.	89.5	37.6	55.4	NA	76.5	51.6
Both	8.2	42	30	NA	19.8	34.2
Homeland	2.4	20.4	14.6	NA	3.7	14.2
Total N	837	608	545		303	336

almost all of whom are immigrant non-citizens. Further analysis confirmed these patterns.[33]

Together, these results directly refute the culturalist formulation. They indicate that attention to homeland policy public is much smaller than the culturalist formulation predicts. Moreover, interest in the homeland is not independent of distinctive ethnic characteristics as the culturalist formulation predicts but instead is significantly affected by differences in national origin, language competence, and nativity.

III. U.S. POLICIES TOWARDS LATIN AMERICA

Next we analyzed attitudes toward specific issues related to U.S. policy vis-à-vis Mexico, Puerto Rico, and Cuba. The culturalist formulation

TABLE 4

Cause of Mexican Economic Problems by Ethnic Indicators

Cause of Mexican Problems	NATIONAL ORIGIN			NATIVITY	
	Mexican	Puerto Rican	Cuban	Foreign Born	Native Born
1. Corruption & inefficiency	84.2	82.5	93.0	87.7	83.0
2. Corruption & US Policies	9.8	9.2	4.2	7.0	10.5
3. US Policies	6.1	8.3	2.9	5.3	6.5
Total N	1438	487	578	1541	962

	LANGUAGE			RACIAL IDENTIFICATION	
	English	Bilingual	Spanish	Non-Latino	Latino
1. Corruption & inefficiency	82.7	86.8	86.8	87.6	82.3
2. Corruption & US Policies	11.6	6.9	7.8	7.6	10.5
3. US Policies	5.7	6.3	5.4	4.9	7.2
Total N	582	826	1092	1534	861

posits that Latinos, regardless of nativity, language ability, and racial self-identification would oppose U.S. Latin American foreign policy. The structuralist argument is that attitudes will vary depending on ethnic characteristics.

First we examined perceptions concerning Mexican economic problems. The survey was conducted during the nadir of U.S.-Mexico relations[34] and while Mexico was still reeling from economic collapse and charges of rampant governmental corruption and incompetence. Yet, whether they were grouped by national origin, nativity, language competence, or racial self-identification, over 80 percent of Latino respondents said Mexican "governmental corruption and inefficiency," was the source of Mexico's economic problems. Fewer than 20 percent blamed it on U.S. policies exclusively or in combination with Mexican corruption.

Again, these results were then analyzed to determine how each ethnic characteristic independently affected these results.[35] The results are mixed. First, after controlling for all other independent variables, differences in national origin significantly affect Latino responses. While

Mexicans and Puerto Ricans do not differ, Cubans are more likely than Mexicans to explain Mexico's problems in terms of Mexican governmental corruption and inefficiency. Second, nativity, racial identification, and language ability have no statistically significant independent effect on respondents' explanations of Mexico's internal problems. The former result refutes the culturalist formulation, but the latter does not. These patterns, however, must be interpreted with the recognition that over 80 percent of all respondents blamed Mexico's problems on Mexican corruption and inefficiency. Stated differently, the clearest and predominant finding contradicts the culturalist formulation.

The second issue examined is whether Puerto Rico should be a state, a commonwealth, or an independent nation. We define the culturalist position as supporting independence. Independence is what Puerto Ricans expected following the Spanish-American War, and for some this is the only way for Puerto Rico to protect its cultural and historical identity. From the culturalist perspective, to support either commonwealth status or statehood is to accept options that demean Puerto Rico's national identity. The structuralist formulation would argue that self-interest rather than nationalism would determine how the issue is viewed. Thus, although Puerto Rico experiences severe economic problems,[36] it is much better off than its Caribbean neighbors. Therefore, it would appear to be in Puerto Rico's interests to maintain its close ties to the United States, either as a state or as a commonwealth.

Overall, as Table 5 indicates, by majorities ranging from 83 to 94 percent, Latinos favor statehood or commonwealth over independence, the option preferred by the culturalist formulation. It is especially noteworthy that, when grouped by national origin, only 4 percent of Puerto Ricans on the mainland support independence. This pattern remains when respondents are grouped according to nativity, language competence, and racial self-identification. These results overwhelmingly contradict the culturalist prediction.

The third question asked concerned whether the United States should establish diplomatic relations with Cuba. The culturalist position supports recognition because non-recognition is a hostile act infringing on the sovereign rights of a nation and reflects continuing efforts by the United States to overthrow Cuba's revolutionary government. Table 6 illustrates that the majority of respondents, whether grouped by national origin or other ethnic characteristics oppose recognition.

Further analysis produces similar results. After controlling for all other characteristics, national-origin differences remain. Puerto Ricans and Cubans are more likely than Mexicans to oppose recognizing Cuba, and Cubans are the most opposed to recognition. The native born are

TABLE 5

Support for Status of Puerto Rico by Ethnic Indicators

Puerto Rican Status	NATIONAL ORIGIN			NATIVITY	
	Mexican	Puerto Rican	Cuban	Foreign Born	Native Born
1. Statehood	22.3	27.2	28.6	23.4	27.4
2. Commonwealth	60.3	69.2	65.3	68.5	55.5
3. Independence	17.3	3.6	6.2	8.1	17.0
Total N	1265	561	550	1469	908
	LANGUAGE			RACIAL IDENTIFICATION	
	English	Bilingual	Spanish	Non-Latino	Latino
1. Statehood	29.2	28.8	19.6	26.3	22.9
2. Commonwealth	54.1	59.9	71.4	63.5	63.3
3. Independence	16.7	11.3	9.1	10.2	13.8
Total N	524	832	1017	1469	811

also more likely than the foreign born to oppose recognizing Cuba. Differences in a respondent's racial identification or language ability had no statistically significant effect on this question.[37]

The final test to determine Latino foreign policy perspectives examines attitudes toward Central American issues. The survey was completed when this region was a major area of United States concern. The LNPS asked two questions which had been previously asked of the nation at large:

> Which do you think is the greater cause of unrest in Central America today: subversion from Cuba, Nicaragua, and the Soviet Union, or poverty and lack of human rights in the area?

> Some people think that the U.S. government should be more involved in the internal affairs of Central American countries. Others think it should be less involved in this area. Do you think that the U.S. should be more involved or less involved?[38]

We define the culturalist perspective as explaining the region's problems in terms of poverty and human rights, and as favoring less U.S. involvement in the area. The responses provided some support for this view particularly with regard to the source of problems. As described in Table 7, more than 75 percent of Mexicans and 68 percent of Puerto

TABLE 6

Should U.S. Recognize Cuba, by Ethnic Indicators

Recognize Cuba	NATIONAL ORIGIN			NATIVITY	
	Mexican	Puerto Rican	Cuban	Foreign Born	Native Born
No	51.5	59.5	66.0	56.6	57.7
Yes	48.5	40.5	34.0	43.5	42.3
Total N	1252	485	627	1479	886
	LANGUAGE			RACIAL IDENTIFICATION	
	English	Bilingual	Spanish	Non-Latino	Latino
No	53.4	58.5	57.5	59.5	53.7
Yes	46.6	41.5	42.5	40.5	46.3
Total N	516	802	1042	1496	774

Ricans agreed that poverty and human rights violations were responsible for Central American unrest, while 58 percent of Cubans blamed communist subversion. The majority of respondents within all the ethnic categories also supported the culturalist position.

A 1988 *Times Mirror* national survey produced similar results. It found that 61 percent of the U.S. population cited poverty and human rights as the cause of the problems, 18 percent thought these and communist subversion were the cause, and only 19 percent attributed the problems exclusively to communist subversion. It seems, then, that the nation as a whole shared the culturalist position. Thus, on this issue, it may be meaningless to define such views as reflective of a distinct "Latino" perspective.

There are, however, differences among Latinos regarding involvement in Central America. While two-thirds of Mexican respondents agreed that the U.S. should be *less* involved in Central America, 57 and 76 percent respectively of Puerto Ricans and Cubans favored *more* involvement. Also, while majorities of foreign born and Spanish monolinguals supported increased involvement, majorities of native born and English monolinguals supported decreased involvement. Racial self-identification also affected attitudes, with Latino self-identifiers favoring a decreased U.S. presence in the area and non-Latino self-identifiers supporting the opposite position.

Analyzing the independent effects of the ethnic indicators on these

TABLE 7

Cause of Unrest in Central America, by Ethnic Indicators

Cause of Unrest	NATIONAL ORIGIN			NATIVITY	
	Mexican	Puerto Rican	Cuban	Foreign Born	Native Born
Communist subversion	23.2	320	57.5	37.6	25.1
Poverty & Human Rights Abuses	76.8	68.9	42.5	62.4	74.9
Total N	1316	467	518	1405	897
	LANGUAGE			RACIAL IDENTIFICATION	
	English	Bilingual	Spanish	Non-Latino	Latino
Communist subversion	22.4	29.8	40.4	38.3	24.1
Poverty & Human Rights Abuses	77.6	70.2	59.6	61.7	75.9
Total N	533	767	999	1400	810

responses again reveals patterns that strongly refute the culturalist formulation. Cubans and Puerto Ricans are much more likely than Mexicans to explain Central American problems in terms of communist subversion; bilinguals and English speakers are more likely than the Spanish dominant to explain these problems in terms of poverty and human rights abuses, as are Latino identifiers relative to non-Latino identifiers. There are no statistical differences in how native and foreign born view these problems.[39]

CONCLUSION

This analysis has examined competing explanations of Mexican, Puerto Rican, and Cuban foreign policy attitudes. The culturalist formulation perceives U.S. Hispanics (including these three largest Latino groups and other Latin American–origin individuals) as a unified Latin American diaspora, and argues that they maintain a high level of interest in Latin American politics and U.S. policy toward the region. Furthermore, it asserts that these groups have a substantially homogeneous and typically critical view of U.S. policies toward Latin America.

TABLE 8

Level of U.S. Involvement in Central America by Ethnic Indicators

US Involvement Should:	NATIONAL ORIGIN			NATIVITY	
	Mexican	Puerto Rican	Cuban	Foreign Born	Native Born
Increase	39.6	57.1	75.5	55.9	45.4
Decrease	60.4	42.9	24.5	44.1	54.6
Total N	1490	551	655	1667	1029
	LANGUAGE			RACIAL IDENTIFICATION	
	English	Bilingual	Spanish	Non-Latino	Latino
Increase	43.7	51.1	56.6	54.8	46.3
Decrease	56.3	48.9	43.4	45.2	53.7
Total N	611	903	1178	1682	907

The structuralist formulation disputes this. Instead, it argues that these issues activate a small core group consisting principally of elites, who then create an imagined community which they proclaim shares these elite concerns. The structuralist perspective further notes that rather than having homogeneous views, differences in national origin, nativity, language competence, and racial self-identification produce variations in Hispanic perspectives on these issues. Finally, the structuralist formulation suggests that to the extent there is interest in Latin America, it focuses on specific national-origin homelands rather than the region in general. Even here, however, the attachments are principally cultural and symbolic and do not constitute for most of the group an ongoing interest either in homeland politics or in U.S. policies toward the homeland.

The results of this analysis support the structuralist argument and diminish the culturalist perspective on virtually every count. While Latinos express strong attachment to their "homelands," there is no evidence that they have high affect for Latin America as a whole. Indeed, they express higher affect for several non–Latin American countries than for selected Latin American countries.

Similarly, there is no evidence that Latin American politics are especially salient for these groups. Indeed, the foreign born, and especially those who have not naturalized, are the only segment of these populations that is even somewhat attentive to homeland politics. The native born and naturalized immigrants are overwhelmingly oriented toward U.S. politics and policies. If particular national-origin groups do not follow politics in their ancestral homelands, it is difficult to imagine that they would pay attention to events in other countries or the region as a whole.

Furthermore, it is clear that, contrary to the culturalist formulation, ethnic differences among Latinos affect foreign policy concerns. Most notable are the differences among the national-origin groups. Puerto Ricans and Cubans regularly differ from Mexicans in terms of the saliency of issues and the policy alternatives they favor. Other ethnic factors such as language ability and nativity also systematically affect foreign policy attitudes.

In conclusion, then, it seems clear that those who claim that foreign policy issues are especially salient to the Latino populace, and that they have a distinct view on such issues are mistaken. There is no question that many Latino elites are particularly interested in Latin American issues, but even they are not of one voice regarding policy.

It is also clear that several ethnic characteristics affect how foreign policy issues are viewed. After controlling for socioeconomic and demographic factors, ethnic indicators have independent effects on policy preferences and affinities. Moreover, the patterns they produce strongly suggest that these effects are a function of an identity created within the United States rather than being purely reflective of home country cultures and identifications. Therefore, those concerned about how these groups view foreign policy should begin by recognizing that their views are primarily the products of American socialization experiences.

Finally, these results clearly indicate that Latinos do not view Latin America through a single lens. Moreover, it is difficult to identify any single foreign policy issue that will galvanize attitudes among this population in the way that South African and Israeli issues have galvanized African American and Jewish American attitudes. For example, the North American Free Trade Agreement (NAFTA) was an issue that "Hispanic" leaders claimed was an issue around which all Hispanics would rally. Yet, it split the Hispanic Congressional Caucus almost evenly, with all but one Mexican American supporting it, while the Cuban and Puerto Rican representatives all opposed it.

Given all this evidence, we should expect Latinos to engage foreign policy the way other Americans do, that is, intermittently and only when it clearly affects their daily lives. It is idealistic to expect that they would be more active than their fellow citizens. It is unreasonable to expect they will speak with only one voice, and it is irresponsible to charge that they will pursue national interests other than those of this nation.

NOTES

This paper is a product of the Latino National Political Survey which was funded by the Ford Foundation, the Rockefeller Foundation, the Stanley Foundation, and the Tinker Foundation.

1. Charles Mathias, "Ethnic Groups and Foreign Policy," *Foreign Affairs* (Chicago: Council on Foreign Relations, 1981), 975–98.

2. Alejandro Quester, "The Rise of Ethnicity: Determinants of Ethnic Perceptions among Cuban Exiles in Miami," *American Sociological Review* 49 (June 1978): 383–97; Barr Hughes, *The Domestic Context of American Foreign Policy* (San Francisco: Freeman Press, 1978).

3. Mohammed E. Ahrari, ed., *Ethnic Groups and U.S. Foreign Policy* (New York: Greenwood Press, 1987).

4. Nathan Glazer and Daniel P. Moynihan, eds., *Ethnicity: Theory and Practice* (Cambridge, Mass.: Harvard University Press, 1975).

5. We use the terms 'Latino' and 'Hispanic' interchangeably for stylistic reasons.

6. A. B. Rendon, "Latinos: Breaking a Cycle of Survival to Tackle Global Affairs," in *Ethnicity and U.S. Foreign Policy,* ed. Abult Aziz Said (New York: Praeger, 1981); Irene Rothenberg, "Mexican American Views of U.S. Relations with Latin America," *Journal of Ethnic Studies* 6 (Spring 1978): 72–86.

7. Maria de los Angeles Torres, "Latinos and U.S. Policies toward Latin America: A Case Study of the 1988 Presidential Campaign," *Latino Studies Journal* 1 (September 1990): 19; Irene Rothenberg, "Chicanos, the Panama Canal Issue, and the Reagan Campaign: Reflections from 1976 and Projections for 1980," *Journal of Ethnic Studies* 7 (Winter 1980): 37–50.

8. De los Angeles Torres, "Latinos and U.S. Policies toward Latin America"; Rendon, Latinos: Breaking a Cycle of Survival."

9. See Lawrence H. Fuchs, *The American Kaleidoscope: Race, Ethnicity, and the Civic Culture* (Hanover: University Press of New England, 1991), 255–56.

10. Yossi Shain, "The Role of Diasporas in the U.S. in the Restructuring of the "New World Order'," paper presented at MIT Center of International Migration on the Security and Stability of States, December 1991.

11. Anthony Smith, *The Ethnic Revival in the Modern World* (Cambridge: Cambridge University Press, 1981).

12. Rodolfo O. de la Garza, L. DeSipio, F. C. Garcia, J. Garcia, and A. Falcon, *Latino Voices: Mexican, Puerto Rican, and Cuban Perspectives on American Politics* (Boulder, Colo.: Westview Press, 1992), 40.

13. Eugene E. Roosens, *Creating Ethnicity: The Process of Ethnogenesis*

(Newbury Park, Calif.: Sage, 1989); William Yancey et al., "Emergent Ethnicity: A Review and Reformulation," *American Sociological Review* 41 (June 1976), 391–403.

14. Felix M. Padilla, *Latino Ethnic Consciousness: The Case of Mexican Americans and Puerto Ricans in Chicago* (Notre Dame, Ind.: University of Notre Dame Press, 1985), 144.

15. See Rodolfo O. de la Garza, "Chicano-Mexican Relations: A Framework for Research." *Social Science Quarterly* 63 (March 1989)" 115–130; de la Garza et al., *Latino Voices*, 11.

16. In Shain, "Role of Diasporas in the U.S.," 13–14.

17. Benedict Anderson, *Imagined Communities: Reflections on the Origins and Spread of Nationalism* (New York: Versco, 1983).

18. Shain, "Role of Diasporas in the U.S.," 14.

19. Ibid., 10.

20. For Puerto Ricans, see Angelo Falcon, "The 'Divided Nation' Thesis Comes Home to Roost: The Puerto Rican Diaspora in the United States and the Proposed Puerto Rican Status Referendum, " in *Colonial America: The Struggle for Puerto Rican Independence,* ed. Edwin Melendez (Boston: South End Press, forthcoming); for Mexicans, de la Garza, "Chicano-Mexican Relations," and R. O. de la Garza and C. Vargas, "Paisanos, pochos, o aliados politicos?" *Revista Mexican de Sociologia* 2 (April-June 1991): 185–206; for Cubans, see Damian J. Fernandez, "From Little Havana to Washington, D.C.: Cuban-Americans and U.S. Foreign Policy," in *Ethnic Groups and U.S. Foreign Policy,* ed. Mohammed E. Ahrari (New York, Greenwood Press, 1987) and de los Angeles Torres, "Latinos and U.S. Policies toward Latin America."

21. For a complete description of the sample, see R. de la Garza et al., *Latino Voices.*

22. Frank D. Bean and Marta Tienda, *The Hispanic Population of America* (New York: Russell Sage Foundation, 1987).

23. Rodolfo Alvarez, "The Psycho-Historical and Socioeconomic Development of the Chicano Community in the United States," in *The Mexican American Experience,* ed. R. O. de la Garza, F. Bean, C. Bonjean, R. Romo, and R. Alvarez (Austin: University of Texas Press, 1985); Alejandro Portes, "The Rise of Ethnicity."

24. Susan E. Keefe and Amando M. Padilla, *Chicano Ethnicity* (Albuquerque: University of New Mexico Press, 1987).

25. Frederick Barth, ed., *Ethnic Groups and Boundaries* (New York: Little, Brown, 1969).

26. Earl Shorris, *Latinos: The Bibliography of the People* (New York: N. W. Norton, 1992), 149–50, 161, 163–64; for Mexicans in Mexico, see Guillermo Bonfil Batalla, *Mexico Profundo: Una Civilizacion Negada* (Mexico, D.F.: Editorial Grijalbol. S.A., 1987) and Michael Meyer and William L. Sherman, *The Course of Mexican History* (New York: Oxford University Press, 1983), 203–17; for Mexicans in the U.S., see Guadalupe San Miguel, Jr., Let All of Them Take Heed: *Mexican Americans and the Campaign for Educational*

Equality in Texas, 1910–1981 (Austin: Center for Mexican Studies, 1987); for Cubans in Cuba, see Carlos Moore, *Castro, the Blacks and Africa* (University of California, Los Angeles: Center for African American Studies, 1988) 21, and Jorge I. Dominguez, *Cuba: Order and Revolution* (Cambridge, Mass.: Belknap Press, 1978), 8; for Puerto Ricans, see Clara E. Rodriguez, *Puerto Ricans: Born in the U.S.A.* (Boston: Unwin Hyman, 1989), 49–56, and U.S. Commission on Civil Rights, *Puerto Ricans in the Continental United States: An Uncertain Future* (Washington, D.C.: 1976).

27. Harold Issacs, *Idols of the Tribe: Group Identity and Political Change* (Cambridge, Mass.: Harvard University Press, 1975); Nathan Glazer, *Affirmative Discrimination: Ethnic Inequality and Public Policy* (New York: Basic Books, 1975).

28. Clara E. Rodriguez, "Race, Culture, and Latino 'Otherness' in the 1980 census," *Social Science Quarterly* 73 (December 1992).

29. The results produced a Cronbach's alpha coefficient of 0.7709, 0.7451, and 0.6421, respectively for Mexicans, Puerto Ricans, and Cubans.

30. The data were analyzed using a factor analysis consisting of a maximum likelihood extraction with an oblique rotation. After an initial analysis, only those dimensions with eigenvalue scores greater than one were selected to construct a model of how the ten countries were related. Three factors explaining 36.7, 43.3, and 39.5 percent respectively of the total group variance met this criterion for the Mexican, Puerto Rican, and Cuban subsamples. In each case too little of the total variance in how all ten countries are perceived was accounted for us to confidently accept any of these models. Nonetheless, the patterns illustrate distinct country groupings.

31. The analysis consisted of OLS regression on the four ethnic and eight sociodemographic variables. Since racial self-identification may correlate highly with the other ethnic variables in the equation, we tested two regression models, one with three ethnic indicators excluding racial self-identification and the other with all four. Overall the results of the two analyses did not differ significantly. Therefore we only report the results of the second. For complete details of the analysis, contact the principal author.

32. De la Garza et al., *Latino Voices*, 44.

33. The analysis used a logistic regression in which the dependent variable was dichotomized into those who focus exclusively on U.S. politics vs. all others. For complete details, contact the principal author.

34. Robert A. Pastor and Jorge G. Castaneda, *Limits to Friendship: The United States and Mexico* (New York: Vintage Books, 1989).

35. The analysis consisted of logistic regression in which the dependent variable was dichotomized into internal corruption and inefficiency versus U.S. policies or U.S. policies and internal corruption. For complete details, contact the principal author.

36. National Council of La Raza, *Poverty Project Newsletter* 4, no. 4 (Winter 1993): 3.

37. Responses were analyzed using a multivariate OLS regression. The

equations tested are the same as those used previously. For complete details, contact the principal author.

38. Norman Ornstein, Andrew Kohut, and Larry McCarthy, *The People, the Press, and Politics* (Reading, Mass.: Addison-Wesley, 1988).

39. The analysis consisted of OLS regressions as described previously.

PART V

Feedback:
Outcomes, Prospects,
and Conclusions

THE POLITICAL SYSTEM OF THE United States is an ever-changing dynamic set of inter-relationships. We have examined how one significant portion of the United States population—Americans of Latino/Hispanic ancestry—have been pursuing power within the American political system. Unfortunately, the framework of the presentation may imply that this relationship is a static one, one that occurs in discrete stages, when in fact, this is not the case.

Every time a political decision is made, it immediately has "feedback" effects throughout the entire political system. There are a multitude of reactions to a new policy, which may be implemented to a greater or lesser extent or completely ignored. Its implementation has significant ramifications for the rest of the system as well as for Latino politics specifically. As the system accommodates and adjusts to a new policy, an *outcome*, or policy-relevant conditions, begins to take shape. Latinos may either benefit or lose from the new policy. This not only affects the way Latinos then think about government, but as they and others react, it also shapes their new inputs into the system. The outcomes of governmental decisions not only affect new inputs into the system, but they also have direct effects on the decision makers themselves. Thousands of decisions made each day by all branches of government at national, state, and local levels produce varying outcomes which give the political environment new shapes and which in turn cause reactions that influence the political activities of all those who participate in politics. Latino politics through the "Decade of the Hispanics" and the decade of "recognition and diversity" produced many major and visible outcomes, and these in

427

turn are affecting the politics of Latinos as they head into the twenty-first century.

In what situation did Latinos find themselves in the early 1990s? What is the condition of Latinos in the United States political system in the decade of the 1990s? Latinos certainly had gained many more resources than were possessed before the "movement" period of the 1960s and early 1970s. Moreover, most indicators evidenced some additional progress during the 1980s although there also were contradictory indications of some slippage. Their economic status generally was somewhat improved, as were their educational levels. However this measurement of change in status is severely confounded by the increased diversity in national-origin composition and immigration of Latinos. There were about 7 million more Latinos in the United States in 1990 compared to 1980. Latinos increasingly gained expertise and experience in areas of leadership and organization, although relatively few of them had yet gained very influential, much less powerful, positions in some of our major institutions. These accomplishments made many Latinos a little more optimistic about their future.

Yet any optimism must be tempered by the fact that some aspects of the national and world environment were changing to the disadvantage of Latinos. Trends in the technologization and globalization of the economy posed heightened obstacles for Latinos as well as other segments of the workforce which serve primarily as sources of unskilled and semiskilled labor. The United States is very much affected by these international forces. In this country, inequalities in income and wealth were growing. A pervasive anxiety, cynicism, or even anger manifested itself in hostility towards immigrants, in particular towards Latinos both north and south of the border, and in a greater animosity towards nonwhite people and others seeking to overcome their disadvantaged status and attain economic and political equality. Some detected a trend towards a conservative or even reactionary political and social atmosphere in the 1994 Republican sweep of the elections and the policy programs proposed in the GOP "Contract With America."

In spite of these caveats, the pursuit of power through the political activities of Latinos did produce some beneficial outcomes for Latinos. Any objective perusal of the indicators of social, political, and economic well-being would show some significant improvements for Latinos over the past three decades. It is true, however, that these gains have been far from comprehensive or radical. They have not altered substantially the basic distribution of power between Latinos and core culture society. There have been few major institutional reforms aimed at eliminating the institutional racism still prevalent in American society, although there have been some, such as affirmative action programs and voting rights protections. Nor for that matter, have all or even most of the needs and demands of the Latino people been met. In fact, the improvements have been piecemeal, slow, and relatively minor. It may be that the advancements have been just substantial enough to mitigate further demands and deplete much of the energy from major mobilization movements. It may be that incremental changes are all that can be expected, and that cumulatively over more decades or even generations, they will total to a very significant change in the status of Latinos. In any case, it is accurate to say that Latino politics have produced some gainful outcomes, and these advances should be recognized. However, much remains to be done.

One related question is how Latinos should best employ their relatively limited political resources to have maximum impact on the political system. A variety of styles and strategies will be needed, depending upon the time and circumstances. The rapidly increasing numbers of Latinos in this country will assuredly heighten recognition and potential, yet for many years to come, Latinos will remain a national numerical minority and a numerical minority in all states with the possible exception of California and New Mexico.

Two major ways to maximize Latino impact on the policy-making process are: 1) through alliances and coalitions and 2) through organization. Particularly in large urban settings, organizational bases are very important; institutions such as labor unions and churches seem to offer significant opportunities as organizational bases. Additionally, alliances need to be sought with other like-minded groups, perhaps most logically, with other disadvantaged minorities, whether they are coalitions among different Latino national-origin groups, with other ethnic or racial minorities, with ideologically compatible white men or women, or with any or all of those with low or deteriorating economic situations.

It is not clear that electoral politics or even conventional politics will produce the kinds of equality and parity which some Latinos seek. In the 1990s, there is great disaffection as well as increasing cynicism and alienation even from groups which have purportedly held the balance of power in this society, such as the white middle class. Therefore, the goals of Latino politics, regardless of styles and strategies, are to exercise meaningful control over a significant portion of their lives, in other words, empowerment. Probably both public and private sector structural arrangements would have to be altered radically to empower most if not all of the people in American society. It is most probable that just electing people to office, having access to decision makers, and engaging in patronage politics will not by themselves bring about the kinds of changes sought by Latinos and other disaffected and disempowered people. In order to obtain empowerment, a multitude of varying political strategies must be employed, including electoral participation. But, electoral participation must be more than just a short-term means in itself, but must be an intermediate strategy that will lead to further structural and policy victories, that is, to more favorable policy outcomes and institutional reforms.

What are likely to be the parameters of Latino politics in the remaining few years of the twentieth century and the first decade of the twenty-first? Some possibilities are less ambiguous than others. First, Latinos do have many more resources than ever before. Latinos' economic status has been improved; significant educational and social gains have been obtained; there is a growing cadre of Latinos with good education, training in community and large-scale organizations, and leadership experience in a variety of settings. Although the 1980s decade seemed to be a period of retrenchment in America, and the 1990s a period of increased conservatism and even reactionism, that does not mean that Latinos can allow the years around the turn of the century to be a period of regression. Latinos who are concerned with the situation have renewed their efforts and worked as hard as in the past. Through the 1980s, their tactics took more conventional and traditional forms, since political tactics that were used successfully in the late 1960s and early 1970s were either ignored or brought forth negative reactions from the majority culture in the 1980s rather than producing sympathetic understanding and support. The economic situation has become a tight one with little or no slack to afford majority culture people the luxury of supporting causes that do not serve their own immediate interest. Competition not cooperation, egocentrism rather than social concern, and ethnocentrism rather than toleration of diversity seem to be descriptive of the 1990s as it was of the 1980s.

In light of this situation, it seems wise for Latinos to use a variety of tactics in pursuing their political, social, and economic goals. Doubtless, attempts to increase Latino influence in electoral politics will be continued and strengthened. Voter registration and get-out-the-vote drives continue to be important and necessary, but certainly not sufficient, for the attainment of at least one form of basic political power. Efforts should be continued to recruit candidates for public office and other leadership positions who are at one and the same time both genuinely concerned with the needs of the Latino people and who still are at least minimally acceptable to the core culture. However, the limitations as well as the benefits of accommodation politics have increasingly been realized. Either a new mode of electoral politics such as that which leads to empowerment of the Latino communities must be employed, or else other political strategies must be used.

Increased efforts should be made to improve the electoral process through a judicious relationship with political parties. More pressure must be exerted on the Democratic party to be responsive to a group most of which has long been its staunch supporter. As for the Republican party, although it continues to make some pronouncements about increased Latino affiliation based on a shared conservative ideology, it does not seem able to shed its conservative, elitist, and ethnocentrist values which preclude the party's acceptance of Latinos (with the exception of Cubans) or Latinos' needs to any meaningful degree. Meanwhile the hope for a successful "third" independent party or for an imminent major realignment of the current parties, which had seemed to become slim in the 1970s and 1980s, increased in the 1990s. The support for Ross Perot in the 1992 presidential campaign, a major trend in support away from the two establishment parties, and an increase in proclaimed "independent" status among the electorate may presage some new party coalitions. Conceivably, a third "reform" party could recruit Latinos to its cause as a way of exerting pressure on both major parties and on other established institutions. However, the experience with the Ross Perot "independent" candidacy in 1996 eliminates some possibilities in this regard. To be successful at the national level, such a party would probably function more as a kind of electorally oriented pressure group rather than a group which actually could capture many major public offices. Economic class–oriented minor parties could continue to remind the dominant institutions in America about the enduring hardships Latinos and others have undergone in this capitalistic system. All of these minor parties can pose challenges to and contribute innovative alternatives to the consensus-constrained, majority-oriented, approaches of the major parties.

Whether involving political parties or more specific interest groups, *coalition* politics must be one of the major strategies of any relatively powerless minority group, particularly at levels above the communities in which Latinos are the majority. Latinos will continue to explore alliances with other reform-minded groups. Other ethnic groups of color such as Native Americans and Blacks remain potential allies since many of the problems of the Latinos are shared by these other disadvantaged groups. A coalition based on socioeconomic status which transcends race and ethnicity may have the greatest potential of all in these times of high and increasing economic inequality. Renewed labor unions and reformed religious organizations also could become very appropriate institutional

allies for challenging the historical exclusivity of major American institutions.

　　With regard to alliances, it is not entirely clear that the various nationality groups within the "Latino" rubric actually constitute a cohesive
"community." Certainly, Mexican Americans, Cuban Americans, Puerto
Ricans, and other Spanish ancestry groups have much in common. Yet it
is also evident that there are significant differences between each of these
groups' historical, demographic, and socioeconomic circumstances. Although it is often done, one cannot speak with complete confidence
about a Latino political community as if it were a unified reality rather
than an abstract goal. Indeed, the Latino National Political Survey demonstrated that at the turn of the decade Mexicans, Puerto Ricans, and
Cubans, though perceiving themselves to be similar culturally, did not
perceive themselves to have much in common politically. A further elaboration of this research plus much additional investigation is needed
to clarify the precise parameters of political and cultural identifications
within and among Latino groups, how these groups feel about themselves and other Latino groups, as well as their identification with the
United States political community. Similarities and differences in their
attitudes towards various governments and their other political values
and opinions on issues must be further delineated and analyzed. Further
investigation into fundamental cultural and political orientations also is
needed before the term "Latino" or "Hispanic" is completely meaningful. At this point it seems likely that there may in fact be a sufficient basis
for unity and cooperation among these groups to at least allow one to
speak generally of Latino politics. The resultant information could provide leadership with optimal opportunities to pursue power successfully.

　　Latinos can continue to support traditional Hispanic "interest-
group organizations" that have become increasingly concerned with political, economic, and educational advancement. Increased levels of education and income should allow more support through donations and
memberships for these long-standing associations, such as LULAC and
the GI Forum. Other associations such as NALEO, the National Council of La Raza, MALDEF, and the Congressional Hispanic Caucus are
also increasingly in the forefront of representing the views of Latinos to
national leaders in Washington. This kind of interest-group activity is
important since it remains essential that the media, national political
authorities, and federal bureaucracies continue to be reminded of the
increasing presence and plight of the nation's second largest ethnic minority.

　　It will probably be at the local community level where most of Latino involvement in interest-group politics will take place. Those issues

which are at the top of many Latino agendas are very conducive to the activation of issue-oriented community interest groups. The political resources gained over the past three decades by Latinos, such as education, leadership training, organizing skills, and other material resources can be employed effectively to exert pressure on community politicians and other local decision makers.

Successful political outcomes still will be difficult to achieve. The time and effort required will be substantial, and the opposition will continue to be widespread and powerful. For example, public support for such programs as affirmative action and bilingual education is, to put it mildly, not what it was in the 1960s and 1970s. In fact, opposition to preferential treatment programs seems to be at an all time high and headed for a critical situation. Another dramatic, if short-sighted, manifestation of this is the "English only" movement.

Another major consideration is the continuing influx of immigrants, a great proportion of whom are from Latin America. This has engendered xenophobic as well as economic opposition to Latinos, whether immigrants or not. Not only is the issue a divisive one among Anglos, it also has posed considerable ambivalence among the Latino population. Latino immigration has, however, provided an increasing population base for favorable policy decisions in the areas of redistricting and reapportionment. It has also allowed spokespersons to point out both the great potential inherent in large numbers and the political and socioeconomic inequities amplified by the large numbers of unskilled, impoverished, poorly educated foreign-born Latinos. Some students of Latino politics have surmised that the impact of the immigration issue is so great that it is changing the essence of Latino politics from one of citizen civil rights to that of immigration policy and the status of immigrants.

Some observers feel that the 1990s will be characterized by a reaction against many of the features of American society which began with the New Deal and continued unevenly into the 1980s. The Republican sweep in the 1994 elections is interpreted as an expression of the people's having enough of the following: big, corrupt, unresponsive, and unaccountable government, especially at the federal level; a mindless bureaucracy; high taxes; sensationalist, irresponsible media; inadequate education; the disintegration of families; lagging patriotism; special, favorable treatment of special interest groups, especially racial and ethnic minorities; a lack of a feelings of mutual responsibility and community; and many other signs of a failing society—one that has lost its historical moorings in traditional values and institutions.

Some potential bright spots for Latinos in U.S. politics do exist.

Perhaps the most significant are the demographic reports which, although varying in details, agree that Latinos are the fastest growing minority group in the United States. Sheer force of numbers can be an extremely valuable political resource. One traditional way that population resources can be used to affect policies is through elections where numbers are of utmost importance. Latinos historically have registered and voted in much lower numbers than non-Hispanics, with the exceptions of Cubans and Mexican Americans in a few areas in the Southwest. In the 1980s, major efforts were made to register Latinos by organizations such as the Southwest and Midwest Voter Registration Education Projects, and notable increases were the result. In the 1990s, major efforts are being made by organizations such as NALEO, the National Association of Latino Elected Officials, to naturalize large numbers of immigrants, since naturalization is not only a prerequisite to the citizen's right to the franchise but also seems to enhance the rates of participation in elections. The Latino population is much younger than the national average, and thus an increase in Latino registration and participation in the future is more likely on that basis alone, as the population matures. In summation, Latinos are not only the fastest growing minority in population, but also in voter registration.

Some victories have been won in court decisions which have struck down multi-member, at-large electoral districts. Boosted by the burgeoning Latino population, fair redistricting may continue to allow Latinos to have more and more opportunities to elect representatives of their choice at all levels of government. The increase in Latino elected officials over the past two decades has been dramatic and offers opportunities for many more advances. Another positive sign is the new recognition of the importance of Latin America, including Mexico, in United States policy considerations, and the consequent possible roles that Latinos can play in the relationship between Latin America and the United States.

Some of these foregoing points and others have been brought forth in a symposium on "Latino Politics in the 1990s" sponsored by and printed in the *National Political Science Review.* In this symposium, organized and introduced by the author, several scholars of Latino politics were asked to present their perspectives on the future of Latino politics, more particularly in the 1990s. The introduction to the symposium includes a summation or exposition of each of the author's views on significant aspects of Latino politics.

There is no doubt that the United States is undergoing a Latinization or Hispanicization, the cumulative effects of which will eventually be a major transformation of the social, economic, and political institutions of the United States. In a society in which distinctive ethnic minorities are projected to become the majority midway through the twenty-first century, Latinos likely will constitute the largest proportion of those. In fact, over the last three or four decades it has become most apparent that Latinos are a large and significant group in the American political system, and it has been recognized that they have potential for substantial political and economic power. The leaders of our society and much of the attentive public have come to recognize the significance of the situation. The increased growth, diversity, and dispersion of Hispanics of many national origins into all areas of the United States will increasingly open the eyes and minds of many more Americans.

As they have throughout their history, Latinos will persist and persevere in their efforts to better their lives and to create in the United States a social and political environment conducive to the realization of these goals. Latinos' efforts towards achieving equality will continue and inexorably will lead to that achievement. Political, social, and economic progress will continue to be made. The path may be long, arduous, and uneven but the belief of the vast majority of Americans in the basic concepts of liberty and justice, equality and prosperity, in addition to Latinos' historical determination, diligence, and perseverance, inevitably will result in a society in which equality and justice are much closer to being realities for all U.S. citizens, including Latinos.

16. Symposium I:
Latino Politics in the 1990s
Introduction

F. Chris Garcia

THE DECADE OF THE 1980s was heralded as being "the Decade of the Hispanics." However, as the 1980s drew to a close, it was evident that, although some minor gains had been made, Latinos by and large were disappointed in the changes that had occurred over the past ten years. The most notable gains seem to have been made in Latino political representation. At the end of the decade there were more elected and appointed public officials of Hispanic origin than there had been at any time in U.S. history. However, socioeconomic data pointed to only minimal gains, and even some regression, in areas such as employment, income, education, housing, and health. In addition to these objective indicators of well-being, there was also a widespread feeling among Latinos that the achievement of Latino political empowerment and equal status was still a long way off. This was particularly frustrating since relatively large advances, initiated in the late 1960s and early 1970s, had led to great expectations for the 1980s; yet progress toward equal opportunity and parity had leveled off. This was all the more disturbing in light of demographic projections that indicated that there had been and would continue to be a tremendous increase in the proportion of Latinos in the U.S. society—a phenomenon that was projected to continue through at least the next two or three decades.

Consequently, as Latinos entered the 1990s, most assessments of the 1980s were tinged with disappointment. Some of the hopefulness expressed for the 1990s revealed an optimism that did not seem to be based on any particular new information about the system, nor did it seem to be based on possibly more successful strategies or innovative conceptual approaches. No careful analyses provided a solid foundation for sanguine expectations. There was only a hope that things would be better, perhaps simply and somehow inevitably because there would be more Latinos in society, and eventually the dominant society would have to deal with a large proportion of its population in a more benevolent and egalitarian manner. Social and political observers agreed that more, and more effective, organization and mobilization were necessary, since these are general elements in political success, but why this had not occurred sooner and why the 1990s would be particularly supportive or promotive of these was not clearly spelled out.

It is true that during the 1980s successful legal challenges to many local at-large electoral systems (with the courts declaring them null and void) have resulted in some additional Latino representation from Latino areas. In some areas, electoral participation rates improved. However, there was also some evidence indicating that Latino participation in some cases had declined. Latinos were still significantly underrepresented, holding less than 1 percent of the nation's elective offices though comprising 9 percent of the population.

A few advances were made due to the successful lobbying in Washington by national Latino advocacy organizations, such as the National Council de la Raza and the National Association of Latino Elected Officials. Yet, organizations such as the Mexican American Legal Defense and Education Fund (MALDEF) and the League of United Latin American Citizens (LULAC) also experienced several internal problems that may diminish their effectiveness.

The main thrust of Latino politics in the 1980s had been electoral and litigational, but it is not clear how much more can be done in these areas to increase the well-being of the Latino communities. Certainly, higher electoral participation among Latinos would mean that the group would have more influence, and litigation could continue to redress personal and organizational injustices. However, both of these strategies may be approaching a point of diminishing returns without the addition of some new conceptualizations, strategies, and approaches for Latino politics in the 1990s.

It is to add some expert perspectives to this dialogue over Latino politics in the 1990s that the participants in the Latino politics symposium direct their analyses and musings. It is always risky business for anyone to go on public record with projections for the future, and social scientists have not been particularly adept at making accurate long-term projections. However, these symposium papers present some perceptive analyses of and challenging ideas about past and current approaches to Latino politics, along with some likely scenarios for their future.

There are common threads found running through most of these papers. There must be some new synthesis, or at least a restructured dialectic, that will produce something very different and more successful than Latino politics have produced in the past. More of the same probably will not suffice to make any significant difference. Perhaps as a precondition, Latinos need to look inward and resolve some internal contradictions and inconsistencies. Perhaps a new collective consciousness under the label of Hispanic or Latino is needed in order to transcend, at least partially, the great heterogeneity of the Latino population. Some new associations and coalitions must be formed, some at the attitudinal level, others taking organizational forms. Some of these will be within the Latino communities themselves, perhaps emphasizing some common Hispanic cultural ties as symbolic rallying points. The danger of such an approach, of course, is that attachments that tie Latino communities together along cultural lines may further estrange those groups that otherwise might be allies but that do not share these cultural manifestations. So perhaps a variety of strategies and approaches must be employed, depending not only upon the political players, but also upon the stage, (that is, the area and circumstances) and the particular issue at hand. Rudy de la Garza examines some of these "endogenous" factors that will affect future Latino political success, especially the naturalization of the burgeoning Latino immigrant population.

It may very well be, as Luis Fraga posits, that as Latinos strive for greater equality, the distinctiveness of the Latino culture must necessarily be diminished. Conversely, as cultural ties weaken, an important political resource may be lost. In any case, new coalitions and associations must be formed. Certainly ad hoc coalitions on certain kinds of issues, particularly in urban areas, may include other racial minorities, particularly African Americans. James Jennings details how distinctive ethnic and racial minorities must work together to advance common interests and must work hard to diminish sources of conflict. Otherwise, it is likely that the position of a great proportion of disadvantaged minorities will deteriorate further.

Latinos must not be prejudicially opposed to any alliance that will advance common interests; principled pragmatism must be the guiding precept. Luis Fraga sees Latinos working together with certain elements of the core cultural majority. In that interplay between minorities and majorities, which will involve compromise and negotiation toward

finding a common ground for action, the perception of the public interest can be broadened to include both Latino and Anglo special interests.

Issues around which interests may coalesce may include pressing
domestic concerns such as education; economic well-being, including
health care and housing; the reduction of crime; and control of the drug
problem. These are issues that will be high on the nation's agenda and
will not be distinctive to any one ethnic group. If the U.S. economy continues to deteriorate or even show signs of weakness, then nonminority
as well as minority citizens will increasingly be seeking new ways to
maintain or improve their situation. In the past, hard times have often
meant that the more secure majority has been even more resistant to
sharing benefits with minorities. However, due to the increasing economic inequities and the deterioration of the middle class, the changing
demographic composition of our society, and the attainment of some positions of security and influence by Latinos, such exclusion or repression
can no longer occur so easily. A new, constructive, positive approach to
shared interests and shared approaches to new common problems must
be the result, or all segments of society will suffer.

Some domestic issues will call for particular approaches; others
will call for different strategies. In order to be most effective, Latinos will
have to engage in a great deal of internal assessment and evaluation. Perhaps some issues that Latinos have tried to push onto the public agenda
will have to become more a responsibility of the Latino communities
themselves. For example, bilingual education in the nation's public
schools may have to assume the form of a transitional pedagogy if it is to
be publicly supported; its function as language maintenance may have to
be supported by the Latino community through the establishment of its
own language and cultural educational institutions. As Ron Schmidt observes, education may be at the top of the agenda for the nation and
for Latinos. The nation's public school systems are approaching a crisis
stage. It is very possible that a major reformulation of their structure,
support, and operation will occur in the 1990s. Latinos will find many
allies among other minority groups, as well as among the majority, who
will be anxious to participate in an improved reformulation of education.

Joining education as a priority issue will be our economic condition. The last part of the 1980s and the first part of the 1990s provided
strong evidence that the economic situation of many Americans was
worsening. The gap between rich and poor was growing. Middle- and
lower-income Americans of all races and ethnic groups found themselves
in increasingly dire straits and were more and more critical of traditional
political institutions and processes. Faith and trust in government was

diminishing rapidly. Indeed, low-income, core-culture Americans seemed to be less enthusiastic about the efficacy of themselves and their political institutions, as well as less optimistic about their future economic and political status, than are Latinos. Many Latinos are actually more enthusiastic about the possibilities of becoming a part of the system and reaping its benefits in the future (that is, being upwardly mobile) than are non-Latinos.

In this stage of internal reassessment and introspection, Latinos must give considerable attention not only to which issues to approach in what manner and to various possibilities for coalitions and alliances, but also to their own organizational situation, including the problem of leadership. Considerable thought, time, and effort must be spent on organizing resources, such as money, motivation, knowledge, and population, in the most effective manner possible. Considerable resources must also be directed to the building of a leadership cadre and to the support of these key persons in a renewed and revitalized organizational base. Latinos can neither afford the luxury of being internally divisive or nonsupportive of their leaders, nor can they be relatively unskilled in organizational activities.

In the international arena, as Cold War tensions and concern with Eastern Europe and the Soviet Union decrease, perhaps more and more of our foreign policy will be focused on the Third World areas of Asia, Africa, and Latin America. At the same time, demographic projections are that many of the new citizens of the United States will come from these latter areas. There are opportunities as never before for the United States to play a new role in a new world order characterized by peace and international understanding. As the United States becomes more and more a microcosm representative of the global population, Latinos can play a unique and significant role in relations with Latin America. However, Latinos in the United States must be major players in the politics of the United States before an international role will be appropriate.

Apparently, the 1990s will be a period of increased internationalization and globalization of politics, with the confrontation between communist and noncommunist ideologies being less significant. Democratic ideology and practice, which involves considerations of equality and the incorporation of all significant populations, will be the focus of both national and international politics in the 1990s.

Maria Torres sees democratization and incorporation coming in both the United States and Latin America and hopes that the United States will adopt a less threatening international posture. This will allow a normalization and reform of politics in Latino communities here and in Latin America.

The new Latino politics of coalitions and alliances, the strengthening of organizational bases, more internal mutual support and self-responsibility, the reexamination of the strategic and long-range importance of cultural politics, the critically differentiated approaches toward various issues, and a new and enlightened internationalism—all will have not only practical implications, but also major significance for the scholarly investigations of Latino politics. In fact, as Rodney Hero points out, Latino scholars now should incorporate newer theoretical approaches and/or use new analytical techniques that can contribute to our understanding of Latino politics in the future and can also help Latino political practitioners be more clear about their own purposes and objectives.

New approaches by scholars of Latino politics and new strategies developed by Latino political practitioners must go hand in hand as never before; that is, they must be in a symbiotic relationship in order to proceed intelligently and effectively into and through the 1990s. Smart and wise Latino politics, in its reformulated manifestations, will advance not only the well-being and happiness of Latinos, but should also have salutary effects on all Americans and indeed on all democracies, increasingly a larger and larger portion of the global community.

Self-Determination, Cultural Pluralism, and Politics

Luis Fraga

HISTORICALLY, LATINO POLITICS HAVE been distinct from much mainstream politics in three fundamental respects. First, they have been anti-status quo. In this regard they have been a politics that have promoted change in policies, procedures of election, and overall access to governmental decision making. At times this focus on change has been antisystem, although most often the type of change advocated has been one that attempted to push American political practice to live up to reasonable interpretations of America's own political promise (Acuña, 1972; Garcia and de la Garza, 1978; Shockley, 1974). Second, they have been egalitarian. That is, the central focus of the calls for change has been to include Latino interests equal to those of middle- and upper-class Anglos, and at times African Americans, in politics (Browning, Marshall, and Tabb, 1984). This has been demonstrated most clearly in the calls for policy parity by Latino political leaders in areas such as voting, education, housing, employment, and criminal justice. Third, Latino politics have very often focused on maintaining a distinct "cultural community." The elements of this community include the Spanish language and pride in distinct origins, family relationships, celebrations, food, and, to an extent, religion. This cultural distinctiveness of Latino communities has been used to enhance popular mobilization, establish candidate credibility, and, most notably, to limit assimilation as an unquestioned goal and strategy in politics (Rendon, 1971; Acuña, 1972).

The continued presence of Latino communities in the United States with distinct political interests has been due largely to their lack of opportunity to advance within society. The barriers to advancement are well known and include discrimination, segregation, and violence. One

442

of the primary promoters of these barriers has been an exclusionary political-economic system that has allowed, if not promoted, separation from the mainstream. The lack of self-determination which Latino communities have been allowed to exercise, has enhanced the presence of cultural pluralism in the United States.

A Latino politics of the 1990s will be very distinct from its predecessors, in that the three dimensions described above will no longer be as compatible with each other. In fact, the very success, especially since the 1970s, of Latino politics in realizing both system modification and greater equality today threatens the maintenance of a cultural community with clearly distinct political interests. And it has been this sense of a distinct culture that has been the inspiration for many of the efforts directed at change and equality. Greater opportunities for the free exercise of self-determination threaten cultural pluralism for Latinos more than exclusion and exploitation ever could.

However, this disjunction between cultural maintenance and change-oriented egalitarianism can be reconciled. It will require, however, a recognition of the limits of interest-group politics and its focus on policy parity, and a much broader understanding of community that explicitly includes the public interest. It will require the attainment of what I shall term the *informed public interest*. The attainment of that reconciliation is the fundamental challenge to Latino politics in the 1990s.

To develop these concerns, I shall focus on two major criticisms that have been levied upon contemporary Latino politics and that should become even more severe in the 1990s. Each of these criticisms flows from an understanding of the major change that has occurred in the recent past in American political development. That change is the enhancement of access by African Americans and certain language minorities, including Latinos, to the system of governance through greater formal representation resulting from alterations in the systems of election and representation through the Voting Rights Act. For the six states of Arizona, California, Florida, New Mexico, New York, and Texas, the number of Latino elected officials has increased from a total of 1,185 in 1973, to an estimated 3,321 in 1989 (NALEO, 1990). This is an increase of just over 280 percent. Although the 1989 figure is still substantially below population parity, it is a dramatic increase.

An impassioned argument is made by Thernstrom (1987) and other critics of the development of the Voting Rights Act that the imposed inclusion of minority communities in formal representation leads to several undesirable consequences for the polity. The major consequence worthy of consideration is that imposed representation of racial and ethnic communities institutionalizes, and thus makes permanent, ethnic and ra-

cial conflict within the regime. Minority and nonminority representatives, the argument continues, participate within a system of representation where an incentive system has been designed to reward ethnically
and racially exclusive rather than inclusive, constituency service. Cooperation and compromise, to the extent that they occur, represent aberra-
tions in the structured legislative process. As a result, ethnicity and race
continue to be dimensions through which both legislators and the public
evaluate public policy. The elimination of ethnocentrism and racism in
American society becomes even less likely.

This argument, which laments the structural changes that have led
to greater representational equity for Latinos, is misguided in several respects. The transformation of the representational regime, which has
given Latinos more of an opportunity to select their first-choice candidates to office, simply reflects identified cleavages within the polity. It neither initiates nor causes these divisions. Nonetheless, it can perpetuate
their presence. To the extent that such perpetuation is achieved, it merely
reflects underlying divisions within the society that have existed for many
decades. It is irrational to think that a constituency will continue to identify its political interests as distinctive from a majority solely because of
its representation. The constituency will identify its interests consistent
with its understanding of reality. That reality is one where ethnicity and
race are relevant in assessing the costs and benefits of public policy. Denying racial and ethnic cleavages does not eliminate them.

Moreover, the proponents of this argument are misguided in their
implicit understanding of the representation of Latino interests as largely
primordial, or, at least, inconsistent with a properly evolving polity (see
the critical discussion in Rothschild, 1981). Although ethnic divisions
can result in considerable violence, as has been demonstrated recently in
countries as varied as Sri Lanka, the Soviet Union, Hungary, and Yugo-
slavia, this is unlikely to be the case for Latinos in the United States today. Contemporary ethnic representation in a polity as developed as the
United States is more likely to be as sophisticated and appropriately strategic as the representation of any other interest, such as those organized
by industry, labor, or region. To conclude otherwise requires that one assume that the Latino representative does not have the capacity to distinguish between advocacy and policy success in a majoritarian legislature.
If the representative of a Latino constituency is to provide for his or her
community, he or she must be more than an instigator of conflict. The
representative must be able to convince representatives of other constituencies that his or her plan also serves their constituencies' interests in an
effort to secure the necessary number of legislative votes to achieve initial
enactment. Latino ethnic representation, when that representation is a

minority of the interests represented in a legislature, must and can adapt to the requisites of legislative success in the modern polity. Coalition building, compromise, and the force of legislative argument and legislative politicking are the means to such success. Majoritarian legislative decision making provides no guarantees to any minority; Latino ethnic interests are no exception.

Notice the implication of the argument thus far. Because of the system modification that has provided greater representational equity to Latinos, and in order to serve the needs of Latino communities, the representative of these communities must begin a process of redefining his or her community's interests in terms that are convincing to representatives of other constituencies. What is suggested is that the representative must begin a process of politically redefining the Latino community.

Herein lies the disjunction between greater opportunity for self-determination and the maintenance of traditional cultural communities. A strong argument is made by some critics of the representatives of minority communities that this enhanced ethnic and racial formal representation has been largely symbolic and very minimally beneficial to the larger mass of the most materially disadvantaged and opportunity-disadvantaged African Americans and Latinos (see Reed, 1988). At least three major disadvantages result. First, ethnic and racial communities develop a false sense of hope that these representatives will be able to provide them with beneficial public policies. At best the representatives can provide some public policies that largely benefits middle-class elements in minority communities, such as greater municipal employment, appointment to boards and commissions, more favorable minority-firm contracting, or the pursuit of capital-directed economic growth with a faith in the benefits of "trickle down." Second, the larger Anglo community develops a false sense that real progress has been made. As a result, they either become complacent, and assume that no further access to governance need be gained by ethnic and racial communities, or accept no responsibility for developing constructive solutions to the social and economic conditions confronted by many minority communities. Third, these ethnic and racial representatives are inhibited from developing the necessary class focus in their policy analysis and advocacy, which is necessary if any real systemic change is to occur that will benefit most African Americans and Latinos. Geographically based ethnic and racial representation inhibits this interethnic class focus.

The response to these critics provides the reconciliation of the disjunction between greater self-determination and the maintenance of a distinct cultural community. The above critical analysis makes two errors. One, it incompletely understands benefits to ethnic and racial communities in terms of material parity. Material parity, of course, should be an ultimate standard with which to measure the status of segments of the population. However, there exists a prior stage in the conceptualization of material progress for minority communities. That stage is one where the public interest is broadened to include the interests of minority communities. An exclusive focus on material parity suggests a zero-sum understanding of benefit. The public interest described here understands benefit to be mutually satisfactory to minority and nonminority communities. This *informed public interest* understands viability. Minority and nonminority communities must be allowed to appreciate that not all problems for which changes may be sought are within the purview of government. This informed public interest is beyond interest group politics. Parity is an insufficient justification for the receipt of favorable policy. The informed public interest begins to make progress toward a more inclusive discourse of politics that requires all demand making to be stated and justified in terms that are acceptable to the broader, longer-term interests of the regime.

The analysis also misunderstands the nature of the community within ethnic and racial groups. How can a Latino politics that expects mainstream politics to change (that is, to adapt, evolve, and accommodate) to incorporate Latino interests not have the same expectations of change (that is, again adaptation, evolution, and accommodation) of itself? A Latino political community, like Latino culture, is not static. The 1990s will be the time when a reconsideration of the dimensions of that community will be possible. And as suggested, the major dimension to be reconsidered is the one that addresses the *sense of purpose* of the group. As a way of constructively surviving the threatening actions of mainstream society, Latinos have appropriately placed a high priority on maintaining their cultural distinctiveness. However, what has always been absent in this strategy of maintenance was a clear goal that justified the maintenance beyond maintenance. The attainment of an informed public interest can provide that purpose by requiring both representatives of Latino communities and scholars and intellectuals of Latino politics to ground their calls for policy benefit in terms consistent with the needs of the larger community.

In the end, the 1990s will be the time when Latino communities, largely through their elected representatives, will begin to outline, through self-determination, the dimensions of that public interest. It is expected that this informed public interest is likely to take Latino representatives and their constituencies away from understandings of the traditional virtues of their ethnic communities. If Latinos do not do this through self-determination, it is likely that it will be done to them by others. A change in the nature of Latino communities is inevitable. Through an understanding of purpose that contributes directly to an enlightened general polity, the preservation of a worthy Latino community is inevitable as well.

REFERENCES

Acuña, Rodolfo. 1972. *Occupied America.* San Francisco: Canfield Press.

Browning, Rufus P., Dale Rogers Marshall, and David H. Tabb. 1984. *Protest Is Not Enough.* Berkeley: University of California Press.

Garcia. F. Chris, and Rodolfo O. de la Garza. 1978. *The Chicano Political Experience.* North Scituate, MA: Duxbury Press.

National Association of Latino Elected Officials (NALEO). 1990. *1989 Roster of Hispanic Elected Officials.* Washington, DC: NALEO Educational Fund.

Reed, Adolph, Jr. 1988. "The Black Urban Regime: Structural Origins and Constraints." *Comparative Urban and Community Research,* 1:138–89.

Rendon, Armando B. 1971. *Chicano Manifesto.* New York: Macmillan Publishing Co.

Rothschild, Joseph. 1981. *Ethnopolitics.* New York: Columbia University Press.

Shockley, John Staples. 1974. *Chicano Revolt in a Texas Town.* Notre Dane, IN: University of Notre Dame Press.

Thernstrom, Abigail M. 1987. *Whose Votes Count?* Cambridge, MA: Harvard University Press.

Latino Politics: A Futuristic View

Rodolfo O. de la Garza

DEMOGRAPHERS PREDICT THAT, given current reproductive and immigration trends, Latinos will be the nation's largest minority group by the year 2010. Understandably, Latino leaders often use these projections to assert that Latinos will be a formidable political force in the future. Making such claims is much easier than realizing them, however, and if they unrealistically raise expectations, such assertions may have negative consequences.

Rather than rely exclusively on demographic projections to estimate future Latino political influence, it is useful to consider the effects of additional factors that, given our current understanding of Latinos and American society, will affect the political future of Latinos. These additional factors may be broken down into endogenous and exogenous categories; that is, those factors that Latinos are in a position to influence substantially and those that are largely beyond their influence. The major exogenous factors are immigration, national and state-level conditions, party competition, legal decisions, and national shifts in public opinion. The principal endogenous factors include Latino organizations, naturalization and the political incorporation of immigrants, development of a pan-national origin identity, relations with blacks, and patterns of electoral participation.

It should be obvious that the line between these categories is not fixed, and that today's exogenous factors could become endogenous in the future. Moreover, endogenous variables are not necessarily more significant than are the exogenous to future Latino political influence. For example, continued large-scale illegal immigration and prolonged economic recession could give rise to substantial increases in anti-Latino sentiments among the general public, which could become manifest in public policy and party platforms. Court decisions, particularly regarding affirmative action, reapportionment, and redistricting, could dramatically increase or decrease Latino political clout. Changes in levels of party competitiveness could similarly alter Latino political influence. If, for example, Anglo identification with the Democratic party continues to diminish, resulting in expanding Republican hegemony, Latinos, who in sizeable majorities identify themselves as Democrats, may find themselves increasingly influential within a party whose influence continuously declines.

As has been noted, however, such developments are essentially beyond Latino control. Therefore, the remainder of this paper will examine those factors that will affect future Latino political power and that they can directly influence.

LATINO ORGANIZATIONS

Although several Latino organizations have long histories, their presence as national organizations and as participants in national policymaking is a recent phenomenon. The beginnings of their effective presence in Washington can be traced to the Carter years of 1976–1980 (de la Garza, 1984). Ironically, it was also during those years that their combined presence and influence reached its apogee. The Reagan administration ushered in a less-hospitable political environment and sharply reduced the programs with which many of these organizations were involved. Since then, Latino organizational presence in Washington has declined in terms of both the number of organizations still active and the size of their staffs. Today, players include the National Council de la Raza (NCLR), the National Association of Latino Elected Officials (NALEO), Aspira, the National Puerto Rican Coalition, the Mexican American Legal Defense and Education Fund (MALDEF), the Congressional Hispanic Caucus, the League of United Latin American Citizens (LULAC), and the National Coalition of Hispanic Health and Human Services Organizations (COSSMO). While some of these may have an important impact on specific issues (NCLR and, to a lesser extent, NALEO seem to have influence on a wide range of issues), overall it is difficult to discern their collective influence on policy. For example, Senator Moynihan's 1988 welfare reform reflects attention to the conditions of the black community but not to the situation of Latinos, suggesting that these organizations were unable to affect the shaping of this key legislation. Similarly, although Latino organizations did influence key aspects of the Immigration Reform and Control Act (IRCA) of 1986, IRCA was enacted despite vigorous protestations by NCLR and others that it would result in anti-Latino discrimination (de la Garza, 1991).

All of these organizations have limited autonomy because of virtual dependency on funding sources, such as the corporate world, foundations, and federal contracts, that are beyond their control. Corporate donations are of diminishing utility since these are disproportionately from the alcohol and tobacco industry, both of which are under increasing attack for targeting minority populations now that Anglo America is becoming abstemious (Maxwell and Jacobson, 1989). Foundations are neither reliable nor permanent sources of funds, and their support diminishes as their priorities shift or as political conditions change (Oppenneimer-Nicolau and Santiestevan, 1990). The once-vibrant National Association of Chicanos in Higher Education became moribund when it lost foundation funds. The Southwest Voter Registration Project has suffered substantial declines in funding despite undeniably significant achievements and continued patterns of electoral participation. As noted previously, changes in federal priorities between the Carter and Reagan administrations affected service organizations similarly. To the extent that these shortcomings are overcome, that is, as Latino organizations increase the support they receive from their own constituents, their individual and collective influence will increase. This is a principal reason why the Cuban American National Foundation, a newcomer to the Latino world of organizations but one that receives its funds primarily from its members, is so effective (Moreno, 1990). Cubans, it must be recognized, are more affluent than other Latino groups. Nonetheless, there is no doubt that the expanded Mexican American and Puerto Rican middle and upper-middle class has resources with which to increase substantially the support it provides Latino organizations. The continued absence of such support points either to a major weakness in the collective commitment to Latino issues from the Latino community or to an indictment of Latino organizations for their inability to tap that commitment.

It would also seem especially important for Latino organizations to develop an effective unified umbrella organization, so that Latino views would be continuously and effectively voiced on a wide range of issues. This would be possible so long as the organization focused on domestic issues toward which Latinos of various national origins share a general consensus (Pachon and DeSipio, 1990). Such an organization could function without threatening the individual identities of its membership. At present, while there is increased cooperation among the several key groups, the possibility of formal institutionalized collaboration is uncertain.

Another institutional void that Latinos need to fill is in the area of research organizations. There is currently nothing for Latinos like the Joint Center for Political Studies, which speaks out regularly and authoritatively from an intellectual perspective on black political and economic issues. The Tomas Rivera Center and the National Council de la Raza have fledgling efforts in this regard, but both suffer from the suspicion that their product reflects their role as advocacy groups. The Inter-University Program for Latino Research is also a fledgling organization that may evolve to play the kind of role described here. However it comes into being, such an organization is essential if Latinos are to be in a position to influence policy.

Relatedly, there is no mechanism for an ongoing dialogue between the Latino intelligentsia and Latino political leaders. The recent appearance of popular publications that appeal to mass Latino audiences notwithstanding, there is no magazine such as *The New Republic* or the *Nation* where issues are raised and debated. There are few newspapers with editorial pages that systematically include columns on Latino issues and Latino perspectives of national and international issues. There are also no national radio or television programs that voice these views. Without such outlets, it will remain difficult for Latinos to develop, clarify, and communicate their arguments to themselves and to the nation at large.

NATURALIZATION AND THE POLITICAL INCORPORATION OF IMMIGRANTS

For decades, Latino citizens did nothing to stimulate naturalization among Latino immigrants. Now, led by NALEO, organizations are recognizing that this is the most untapped segment of the potential Latino electorate, and they have initiated naturalization and political incorporation campaigns. As recently as 1980, Mexicans did not rank among the top ten immigrant groups in terms of naturalization rates. Since 1985, they have ranked among the top three (Immigration and Naturalization Service, 1988:92).

As naturalization and incorporation efforts continue, the number of Latino voters will increase dramatically. In 1988, there were more Latinos ineligible to vote because of noncitizenship than there were Latino voters (NALEO, 1989a:v). However, Latino immigrants cite the desire to vote in U.S. elections as a principal reason for naturalizing. More significantly, 81 percent of Latino naturalized citizens register to vote, compared to 70 percent of the nation at large (NALEO, 1989b). Thus, initiatives focusing on mobilizing naturalized immigrants into electoral politics are likely to enjoy substantial success.

It should be noted that naturalization efforts will affect the several Latino groups of different origin differently. As native-born citizens, Puerto Ricans find them irrelevant. Cubans will be decreasingly affected since immigration from Cuba has slowed dramatically, and it is likely that those who came and wanted to naturalize probably have already done so. The population of Mexican origin, especially in the Southwest where it is concentrated, will be most affected since it makes up approximately 65 percent of the total Latino population nationally. In the Southwest it constitutes over 90 percent. Central Americans are another group that could be specifically targeted for significant results. These differential impacts could increase the role that Mexican Americans play in national Latino initiatives.

DEVELOPMENT OF A NATIONAL IDENTITY

Preliminary results from the Latino National Political Survey (LNPS) indicate that traditional labels of national origin such as "Mexican American," "Puerto Rican" and "Cuban" are overwhelmingly preferred to inclusive terms such as "Hispanic" or "Latino." Furthermore, more LNPS respondents prefer to identify as "American" than as "Latino," and only slightly more prefer "Hispanic" to "American." Relatedly, when asked if all Hispanics/Latinos are very similar or not very similar culturally, significantly more selected the latter. Even more noteworthy is the fact that respondents overwhelmingly agree that the political interests of Cubans, Mexican Americans, and Puerto Ricans are not very similar (de la Garza et al., 1990).

Rhetoric aside, much is yet to be done if the several national-origin groups are to develop a shared identity that may be accommodated under one label such as "Hispanic" or "Latino" (Garcia and Garza, 1990; Ortiz and Brownstein-Santiago, 1990). Many factors, such as geographical dispersion, history, and policy preferences impede the creation of such an identity. There is also considerable resistance in some quarters to its growth. Noteworthy leaders of the several national-origin groups, for example, have protested against such an identity. It should not be assumed, therefore, that such an identity will evolve automatically. Without such an identity, it will be difficult for Latino leaders to maximize their potential political clout as they need it. For such an identity to become real, therefore, leaders may have to develop specific strategies to win over their respective constituencies.

RELATIONS WITH BLACKS

The quality of Latino-black relations will have an important impact on the political status of Latinos in the future. While it is often claimed that Latinos and blacks are part of a rainbow coalition that will lead to a majority-minority dominant coalition, there is also evidence that major issues may divide the two (Perspectives, 1980; Chaves, 1990). These include

1. Resentment among many blacks over Latino access to affirmative action programs that blacks believe were designed for them (Changing Relations Project Reports,[1] 1990).
2. Tensions because of the perception that immigration results in job displacement and the reallocation of public resources to Latinos rather than to blacks.
3. Tensions resulting from Latino population growth that produces Latino majorities in schools that previously had black majorities, administrators and staff. Latino demands for curricular reform and staffing changes thus become Latino-black competitions. Similar results occur because of the Latinization of police forces and the all-too-frequent charges of police brutality against Latino cops by blacks. Miami and Houston in particular are experiencing these situations.
4. Battles over reapportionment and redistricting. Population is the foundation for allocating legislative seats. The number of state legislative seats is fixed, while the number of congressional seats allocated to each state may vary slightly as a result of the census. Given that, in cities with substantial Latino and black populations, these groups often live in juxtaposition and that Latino population growth greatly exceeds black population growth, any increase in legislative seats designed to accommodate the growth of the Latino population could come at the expense of blacks (see O'Hare, 1989).

Mutually satisfactory responses to these issues would obviously benefit both groups. Such outcomes will not be easily achieved, and Latino and black leaders will therefore need to be diligent to avoid the divisiveness that could result from exacerbating these differences.

Patterns of Electoral Participation

Latino political futures will greatly differ depending on whether the following patterns change or are maintained:

1. Latino, especially Mexican American and Puerto Rican, voters turnout at rates far lower than rates for whites or blacks. In 1988, 62, 54, and 46 percent of eligible Anglo, black, and Latino adults voted, respectively. Latino influence will remain minimal so long as this trend continues.
2. Mexican Americans and Puerto Ricans vote solidly Democratic. This will increase their influence within the Democratic party but may decrease their overall influence if the Democratic party continues to decline in influence. In other words, Mexican Americans and Puerto Ricans may play key roles in selecting the Democratic nominees for statewide and national office, but that is of little benefit when those candidates lose the general election.
3. Younger, more affluent Mexican American voters switch to the Republican party or become independents (Garcia, 1987:13), as evidenced by the increase in high-level appointments by former President Reagan and President Bush and by Republican governors in key states such as Texas and California. Ironically, however, in Florida, Cuban support for the Republican party may liberalize the party on domestic policy; that is, Cuban support may move it toward increased support for social spending and opposition to nativist language policies (Moreno, 1990). If this trend also develops among Mexican American Republicans, it could push both parties to respond more positively to Latino domestic policy concerns.

Conclusion

These factors suggest that the opportunity exists for Latinos to significantly improve their political status, but they also point out obstacles that could limit such gains. At present, the factor most likely to increase Latino political clout is naturalization. Ironically, a second positive trend is in the increased bipartisanship of Latinos. The most serious problems have to do with Latino electoral turnout and black-Latino relations. The former is a long-standing problem that has not significantly improved despite eliminating the barriers, such as English-only ballots, strict registration requirements, and at-large election systems, that have been used to explain low rates of electoral participation.

In conclusion, Latinos are in a position to increase their political clout in the 1990s. The extent to which they do so will depend on factors beyond population growth. Latino leaders would therefore do well to focus on those factors and forego population-based predictions that, if taken seriously, could have negative effects. After all, Latinos are unlikely to mobilize if they believe that numbers alone will make them politically powerful.

NOTES

1. The Changing Relations Projects was a two-year ethnographic study of relations between established residents and immigrants in six cities. Rodolfo O. de la Garza is a member of the project Board. Contact him for further information regarding the project.

REFERENCES

Changing Relations Project Reports. 1990. See note 1.

Chavez, Linda. 1990. "Rainbow Collision." *The New Republic,* 19 November, pp. 14–16.

de la Garza, Rodolfo O. 1984. "And Then There Were Some: The Role of Chicanos as National Political Actors, 1967–1980." *Aztlan,* 15, no. 1 (Spring): 1–24.

———. 1991. "Immigration Reform as a Civil Rights Issue: A Mexican American Perspective." In Gillian Peele and Bruce Cain, eds., *Developments in American Politics.* London: Macmillan Education Limited.

de la Garza, Rodolfo O., Angelo Falcon, F. Chris Garcia, and John Garcia. 1990. Unpublished results from the Latino National Political Survey.

Garcia, F. Chris. 1987. "Comments on Papers Presented on the Panel on Latinos and the 1984 Election." In R. O. de la Garza, ed., *Ignored Voices: Public Opinion Polls and the Latino Community.* Austin, TX: Center for Mexican American Studies, University of Texas.

Garcia, John, and Mlita Garza. 1990. "Common Experiences Meld Diverse Hispanic Groups." *Hispanic Link,* 24 September, p. 3.

Immigration and Naturalization Service Statistical Yearbook, 1988. Washington, DC: Immigration and Naturalization Service.

Maxwell, Bruce, and Michael Jacobson. 1989. *Marketing Disease to Hispanics.* Washington, DC: Center for Science in the Public Interest.

Moreno, Dario, 1990. "The Political Empowerment of Cuban-Americans." Paper presented at Inter-University Program for Latino Research Conference, San Luis Obispo, May 25–26.

Moreno, Dario, and Nicol Rae. Forthcoming. "The Conservative Enclave: Cubans in Florida." In R. O. de la Garza and Louis DeSipio, eds., *Latinos and the 1988 Election.* Austin, TX: Center for Mexican American Studies, University of Texas.

National Association of Latino Elected and Appointed Officials (NALEO). 1989a. *National Roster of Hispanic elected Officials.* Washington, DC.

———. 1989b. 7 September. Press Release.

O'Hare, William P. 1989. *Redistricting in the 1990s: A Guide for Minority Groups.* Washington, DC: Population Reference Bureau.

Oppenneimer-Nicolau, Siobhan, and Henry Santiestevan. 1990. *From the Eye of the Storm.* Washington, DC: Hispanic Policy Development Program.

Ortiz, Vilma, and Cheryl Brownstein-Santiago. 1990. "Unifying Label Vital for Latino Empowerment." *Hispanic Link,* 17 September, p. 3.

Pachon, Harry, and Louis DeSipio. 1990. "Latino Legislators and Latino Caucuses." *New Directions for Latino Public Policy Research,* Working Paper no. 11. IUP/SSRC Committee for Public Policy Research on Contemporary Hispanic Issues, The Center for Mexican American Studies, University of Texas at Austin.

Perspectives, pp. 12–18. 1980. Washington, DC: U.S. Commission on Civil Rights.

Latino Politics in the 1990s:
A View from California

Ronald J. Schmidt

THE AIM OF THIS ESSAY is to identify and articulate some of the key challenges facing Latino politics in the United States for the next decade. For several decades a central preoccupation of those political scientists who had a special interest in the Latino populations of the United States has been the problem of "empowerment": Why do Latinos not have a power position in the United States political economy commensurate with their numbers? How do they get their "fair share"? This essay stands within that tradition of enquiry, and it argues that the 1990s will be a crucial decade for Latinos because of the inexorable working out of demographic and economic changes that have been in motion for at least twenty-five years. The essay will focus primarily on California—partly because this state has by far the largest number of Latinos (34 percent of Latinos in the United States, according to the Census Bureau in 1988), and partly because the forces highlighted herein are most advanced in California and may, therefore, be harbingers for the future of Latino politics generally.

The *demographic* story underlying this analysis has been often repeated: it is a story of the unprecedented and explosive growth of the Latino population. There is not space to repeat the story here. Suffice it to say that Latinos are experiencing the greatest numerical increase of any ethnic group in the nation (a 34 percent growth rate in the 1980s, according to the Census Bureau, compared to 7 percent growth rate for the population as a whole), and demographers expect that early in the next century it will be the largest minority group in our population (Houston, 1988; Valdivieso and Davis, 1988).

In California, as elsewhere in the Southwest, Latinos have been the

largest minority ethnic group for some time, and demographers expect
that the 1990 census will show that 25 percent of the state's population
is Latino. A recent report, moreover, predicts that the population in California will be 30 percent Latino by 2000, that Anglos will lose their majority status by the end of the century, and that Anglos and Latinos will
constitute roughly equal portions of the state's population about twenty
years later (Roderick, 1990).

In addition to the sheer numbers, it is politically important to note
that the growth stems almost equally from two sources: massive immigration, and relatively high birth rates in the Latino population. These
sources of growth are important politically because, in addition to ensuring that a significant portion of the Latino population will be ineligible
to vote (as noncitizens), both together ensure that this population will
be relatively young. Thus in 1988 the median age in the United States
was 32.2 years, compared to only 25.5 years for Latinos (Valdivieso and
Davis, 1988:3).

It is a truism in political science that young people have a significantly lower rate of participation in politics than do their elders, and
several recent surveys of American youth indicate that this is an even
more pronounced pattern with the present generation of young adults
(Oreskes, 1990). This may help to account for the fact that voters in recent California elections have had a median age over 50, and it is estimated that it will reach 60 by the end of the century (Walters, 1990:17).
These demographic realities may also help to account for the fact that in
the 1986 statewide elections in California, Anglos made up 57 percent of
the population but 85 percent of the electorate, while Latinos composed
almost 25 percent of the population and only 6 percent of the voters
(Walters, 1989). The point to be emphasized, in any case, is that one of
the principal challenges for Latino empowerment in the 1990s will continue to be the huge task of political incorporation—not only the incorporation of Latino immigrants but of a whole generation of the young as
well.

The second change to be highlighted here in relation to Latino empowerment is economic. Both conservative (Phillips, 1990) and liberal
(Zeitlin, 1990) political analysts have recently emphasized that one of the
most important changes in the U.S. political economy in the last decade
was significant growth of economic inequality and a decline of the middle class as a proportion of the U.S. population. Latinos, along with the
African-American population, have been particularly affected by these
economic changes. A 1989 report issued by the National Council of La
Raza found a significant drop in Latino family income in the 1980s, and
a concomitant increase in the proportion of Latinos living below the pov-

erty line. Most discouraging was the finding that poverty increased among married-couple Latino families, from 13.1 percent to 16 percent (Davis, 1989).

And once again this phenomenon seems to be particularly pronounced in California, where publicists and analysts routinely refer to the state's developing "two-tier" economy or to the emergence within the state of a "Third-World" economy of enlarging rich and poor classes and a declining middle class (Leigh, 1990; Tietz and Shapira, 1989; Ong et al., 1989). This phenomenon has been particularly significant in its impact on Latinos in California. Recent studies on Southern California's economy, where the concentration of Latinos is highest, have found substantial increases in below-poverty-level wages for full-time workers. Not surprisingly, therefore, Latinos made up 64 percent of Los Angeles county's low-wage, full-time workers in 1987, but 34 percent of the county's population (Ong et al., 1989:36). Similarly, in 1986–1987 Chicano males in Los Angeles County had average earnings equal to only 61.4 percent of Anglo male earnings, lower than those of any other racial or ethnic group (Ong et al., 1989:90).

In summary, the economic changes of the past decade have not been kind to the Latino community in California or nationally. As was true of the United States population as a whole, the 1980s brought upper-scale Latinos increased prosperity, but the growing number of Latinos at the bottom of the economic scale found themselves with a decreasing proportion of the nation's wealth. By 1988, in fact, the Tomas Rivera Center had convened a conference to analyze the question of whether William J. Wilson's analysis of the "underclass" could be used accurately to understand the large and growing impoverished segment of the Latino population.

The point to be emphasized here is that the intersection of the two changes highlighted above—the demographic and the economic—has immense political importance for Latinos, and increasingly, for the nation as a whole. Taken by themselves, as noted above, the demographic changes in the community represent an enormous challenge of political incorporation. Yet those changes cannot be taken alone, for the deterioration of the Latino community's economic position poses equally serious political challenges. That is, just as youthfulness and noncitizenship affect the power position of the Latino community, so too does its economic base. For it is also a truism in political science that low-income groups—particularly those not organized into unions or other such associations—play a lesser role in politics and wield far less power than do the more affluent (Wolfinger and Rosenstone, 1980). Without the intervention of other political factors, then, the intersection of the demo-

graphic and economic changes described above may be expected to reduce the power position of Latinos in the United States over the next
decade, despite their increasing numerical importance in the general
population.

Latino political elites (and indeed all who are concerned about the
well-being of the nation), then, face some serious questions of strategy
and policy. Challenges to minority vote dilution such as gerrymandering
or citywide elections, will continue to be important, as will support for
various forms of ethnic-preference policy (for example, affirmative action hiring, minority set-aside programs for contractors, or broadcasting
licenses). The data presented above, however, lead me to argue that these
efforts—by themselves—will be insufficient to change the power position of the Latino community in the decade ahead. The maturation of a
huge generation of Latino youths—many of whom are poor, many of
whom are not citizens of the United States, most of whom can be expected to have little impulse toward political participation—represents a
demographic and economic wave likely to overwhelm the effects of even
successful law suits to counter vote dilution and to sustain ethnic-preference policies.

What are the implications of these data, then, for a strategy of empowerment for Latinos? First, the generation of Latino youths represents
an enormous pool of human resources and political potential that cannot
be allowed to go waste (see Hayes-Bautista, Schink, and Chapa, 1988 for
a related analysis). This means that public education must remain at the
top of the Latino policy agenda and must be moved to the top of the
national agenda generally. The evidence is overwhelming that educational attainment is the single most important variable in determining
rates of political participation (Wolfinger and Rosenstone, 1980:23–30)
and in determining the occupational tier of a given worker in our increasingly two-tier economy (Leigh, 1990). Yet during the 1980s Latinos continued to fall farther behind the population as a whole in levels of educational attainment (Houston, 1988).

Again, however, even successful educational reform is not sufficient
to rectify the problem of Latino empowerment in the United States political economy. For there are structural changes in both the political and
economic sectors that need to be addressed as well. After all, the transformation of California's economy toward a Third-World pattern is not
simply a function of low educational attainment among the recent immigrant population. Rather, structural changes in global economic relationships, abetted by the policies of the past two Republican administrations,
have been instrumental in the decline of the middle class and in the im-

poverishment of low-wage workers. Growth sectors in the past several decades have been in low-wage and high-wage service occupations, while the manufacturing sector, which provided a toehold into the middle class for many Latinos in the previous generation, has suffered a decline. A serious effort at coming to grips with the subject of Latino empowerment, then, will require a political strategy that addresses questions of economic class and inequality (see Torres, 1988 for an elaborated analysis of this point).

Structural changes in the nation's political system, finally, must also be addressed on the Latino agenda for the 1990s. A century ago, the last great wave of immigrants to this country was incorporated into the polity through political party machines with a strong motive to encourage immigrants to become citizens and to vote (Buenker, 1978). Today, however, the process of becoming a citizen is no longer under the control of the party machines nor, indeed, are there party machines in the same sense. In "reformed" states like California, political parties can scarcely be said to exist at all, outside the legislature or the minds of potential voters when they register for primary elections. Without effective party organizations, politicians bent on winning election are far more fixated on raising the enormous sums necessary to pay for their advertising campaigns than they are in recruiting young people, immigrants, or the poor into the political system.

Still, numbers count in electoral political regimes. Given the political motivation and organizational base, the vast number of Latinos *can* be converted into large numbers of votes, which *can* be converted into political power and a transformed policy agenda. The point is that the same demographic data—large numbers of youth and recent migrants to the United States—presently resulting in lower political participation rates could be converted into the Latino community's greatest political asset. The task is to build the organizational and programmatic bases from which these incorporation and conversion processes can be mounted. Ultimately, this is the primary challenge for Latino politics in the 1990s.

REFERENCES

Buenker, John D. 1978. *Urban Liberalism and Progressive Reform.* New York: W. W. Norton & Co., Inc.
Davis, Kevin. 1989. "Latino Poverty Grew over Decade, Study Finds." *Los Angeles Times,* 16, December A28.

Hayes-Bautista, David E., Werner O. Schink, and Jorge Chapa. 1988. *The Burden of Support: Young Latinos in an Aging Society.* Palo Alto: Stanford University Press.

Houston, Paul. 1988. "Census Bureau Says More Latinos Finish Education." *Los Angeles Times,* 7, September, I14.

Leigh, Nancey Green. 1990. "What Happened to the American Dream? Changing Earning Opportunities and Prospects of Middle-Class Californians, 1967–1987." *California History* 68, no. 4 (Winter 1989/90): 240–47.

Ong, Paul, et al. 1989. *The Widening Divide: Income Inequality and Poverty in Los Angeles.* Los Angeles: UCLA School of Architecture and Urban Planning.

Oreskes, Michael. 1990. "Profiles of Today's Youths: Many Just Don't Seem to Care." *New York Times,* 28, June pp. A1, 11.

Phillips, Kevin. 1990. "Reagan's America: A Capital Offense." *New York Times Magazine,* 17, June 26–28, 40, 64.

Roderick, Kevin, 1990. "Californians: 30 Million and Counting." *Los Angeles Times,* 16, May pp. A1, 16.

Teitz, Michael B., and Philip Shapira. 1989. "Growth and Turbulence in the California Economy." In Rodwin and Sazanami, eds., *Deindustrialization and Regional Economic Transformation: the Experience of the United States.* Winchester, MA: Unwin and Hyman.

Torres, Rodolfo D. 1988. *Latinos in the U.S. Economy: A Critique and Reformulation of Theories of Income Inequality and Policy Alternatives.* New York: Centro de Estudios Puertorriquenos, Hunter College, City University of New York.

Valdivieso, Rafael, and Cary Davis. 1988. "U.S. Hispanics: Challenging Issues for the 1990s." *Population Trends and Public Policy,* no. (December): 1–16.

Walters, Dan. 1989. "The 'New' California." A keynote speech presented to the Conference on "Envisioning California," Sacramento, February.

———. 1990. "California: A State of Change." Pp. 1–18 in Walters, ed., *California Political Almanac, 1989–90 Edition.* Santa Barbara: Pacific Data Resources.

Wolfinger, Raymond E., and Steven J. Rosenstone. 1980. *Who Votes?* New Haven: Yale University Press.

Zeitlin, Maurice. 1990. "U.S. Misery in Inequality: Ignoring the Grim Truths." *Los Angeles Times,* 20, May pp. M4, 8.

Will Cuba Be Next? What about Miami?

Maria Torres

A DECADE AGO, as thousands of people jammed the Peruvian Embassy in Havana trying to leave Cuba, Cuban-American newspapers and radio stations heralded the downfall of Fidel Castro.

Today, again, Cuba watchers are debating whether Castro will last beyond this year. Some are arguing that this time tougher U.S. measures against Cuba will guarantee his downfall.

U.S.-Cuban relations frame the contours of Cuban-American politics. For Cuban Americans, their future is intimately tied to the successful resolution of thirty years of conflict.

Aging Cuban-American organizations have set up military training camps, as they have for the last thirty years every time it looked like the Revolution was faltering. Added to the exiles' arsenal are government committees studying ways of quickening Cuba's government's demise and bracing for the imminent impact that such changes will bring to south Florida. Miami's Police Department has contingency plans for the night of festivities once Castro falls. Self-anointed presidential hopefuls, such as Jorge Mas Canosa, have hired experts, including Milton Friedman, to concoct economic and political plans for their future governments.

There is no doubt that Cuba's government is at a crossroads. A critical part of its international economic and political frame of reference is in flux. All over the world, state-controlled planned economies are decentralizing and privatizing. One-party political structures are giving way to multi-party representation. The ideological and practical aspects of these changes are beginning to have a profound impact on Cuban society.

Nevertheless, at least two important facts differentiate the Cuban situation. First, Cuba's government came to power through a popular

463

revolution, a factor not present at least in the case of the nations of Eastern Europe. Second, since the first U.S. incursion into Cuban politics in 1898, Cubans have perceived the United States as an intruder—much like Poles viewed the Soviets—and viewed Castro, like Walesa, as the person who unshackled his people from their oppressor.

These two facts in and of themselves do not guarantee the survival of the present government. They do, however, continue to frame the political debate in Cuba. This is especially true after the U.S. invasion of Panama, which served as an unsettling reminder to Cubans of the available political alternatives in Latin America.

The changes in Eastern Europe are an important impetus for debate in Cuba, but beyond the backdrop of the East/West view is a more critical challenge to the system from inside: that posed by Cuba's younger generations. Most people in Cuba today were born after the Revolution. Their educational, social, and, in most cases, economic standing are a result of the successes of the Revolution. While the majority of Cubans may have had harder lives without the Revolution, they have no life experience with which to internalize this distinction. Thus, they have become a catalyst for change.

Most of these young people have a stake in the present-day system, so they seek not to overthrow or substantively change the regime, but merely to participate in its future in a more democratic fashion. They do not rule out the possibilities of direct elections of the members of the National Assembly or of the president, and they are enthusiastic about Gorbachev's reforms.

Generational pressure is also a growing reality in the Cuban-American community in the United States, as its younger members are increasingly disinclined to support attempts to take over the island. Most believe that change will occur in Cuba through internal processes. They are curious about their parents' homeland, but more concerned with their lives in the United States. Increasingly they advocate for a more democratic culture in their own community.

Both in Cuba and in the Cuban-American community, debate about the future of Cuba or U.S.-Cuban relations is extremely difficult.

In Cuba, while broad discussions are taking place within the confines of the party, in public people are rallied into a unified position allowing little room for debate or dissent. Human rights activists are accused of being agents of the United States government and are jailed under laws that prohibit the right of assembly and criticism.

Last year the FBI named Miami the capital of U.S. terrorism, after eighteen bombs went off in the homes and businesses of Cuban-Americans working to better relations with Cuba. Hard-line organizations, such as the Cuban-American National Foundation, accuse those who support better relations with Cuba of being agents of the Castro government. They throw their repressive weight around in Washington and in Cuban-American communities throughout the United States. Recent examples of this occurred when Foundation members successfully lobbied State Department officials to deny visas to the world-famous Cuban Orquesta Aragon, who was to perform in a city-sponsored event in Chicago. They were also involved in urging Treasury Department agents to break into the home of Ramon Cernuda, director of a Miami-based Museum of Cuban Art, in the middle of the night to confiscate his paintings, because some had been painted by artists living in Cuba. The courts found that Cernuda's constitutional rights had been violated, and many were deeply troubled about the antidemocratic nature of the political culture propagated by conservative exiles.

It is interesting to note that there is a debate about a more democratic culture between generations of Cubans on both sides of the Florida Straits. Aggressive U.S. policies toward Cuba have had the effect of furthering the position of the antidemocrats on the island and in the United States.

Meaningful political and economic openings in relations with Cuba occurred during the Carter administration, when policies were aimed at negotiating with the Cuban government rather than at attacking the regime. Political prisoners were released, elections were held, and free peasant and craft markets flourished.

It seems clear that the United States needs a more productive alternative to the thirty-year-old, unsuccessful, policy of harsh posturing and an economic embargo aimed at strangling the island government—TV Marti being the latest example. Simply opening up relations and encouraging exchanges would be a more engaging and constructive approach. Removing Cuba's most notorious external threat would inevitably contribute to opening the political space on the island. It would also allow the Cuban-American community to rid itself of its obsession with overthrowing the current Cuban government. And this would help Cuban-Americans to normalize their politics.

The only ones who would object to such an approach are those who are not really concerned with economic and political progress in Cuba or in the Cuban-American community, but who, rather, are interested in holding on to their own power—whether in Havana or Miami.

Questions and Approaches in Understanding Latino Politics: The Need for Clarification and Bridging

Rodney E. Hero

UNDERSTANDING "Latino Politics in the 1990s" is an important task both in terms of actual, practical politics, and in terms of how those politics are studied. There are a number of significant issues that have, to this point, affected the *study of* Latino politics and that are likely to continue to do so into the 1990s. Several issues that seem particularly significant regarding research approaches and questions about Latino politics will be noted and addressed in this discussion. The comments offered below also seek to underscore the need for conceptual clarification and theoretical bridging. That is, it appears that names or labels, concepts, and the like have been used ambiguously or too casually in the study of Latino politics. Also, the literature on mainstream politics and cognate research on Latino politics have not been brought together adequately.

Major questions that require more careful attention in the study of Latino politics include definitions of the phenomena and of descriptions of the theoretical approaches, assumptions, and questions that underlie scholarly (and popular) efforts to understand and comprehend Latino politics. It can be noted at the outset that the very notion of Latino politics implies separate and distinctive social and political phenomena that are neither simple nor easily understood. But, to a considerable degree, these matters have not been well understood or have not been adequately accounted for in much, perhaps most, research and discussion. This, then, is one area where the study of Latino politics raises important theoretical and empirical questions that are closely interrelated.

Individual self-identification is a major issue, which has ostensible

implications for group behavior as well as for group political and social cohesiveness (Lampe, 1982). Ethnic identification is often taken for
granted in much social science research, and political science research
has probably taken this issue for granted to a greater degree than other
social science disciplines (cf., however, Garcia, 1981). The subtlety and
complexity of identification issues and processes have been recognized
and debated extensively (Munoz, 1989; Acuña, 1988; Garcia, 1981). It
has been increasingly perceived that identity is itself an issue or "problematic" worthy of attention; that it may, indeed should, be seen as a
dependent variable and not solely as an independent variable. The creation and use of particular labels (such as "Mexican American," "Chicano," "Latino," or "Hispanic") is not just a simple act of naming.
Rather, it situates or constitutes individuals and groups. There is, in
short, a political and/or social construction of ethnicity that must be understood as part of the study of Latino politics. But that has not influenced how issues of Latino politics are studied. The simple, easy acceptance and use of official group designations, particularly the Census
Bureau's term "Hispanics," needs to be understood as itself political.
Inattentiveness to this may also introduce theoretical and methodological
imprecision into research.

Studies of Latino politics also raise questions concerning appropriate theories or explanations, theories that have broader implications for
the understanding of American politics. Despite considerable questioning
and criticism, much if not most of the research on Latino politics has
implicitly followed a pluralist or behavioralist approach (cf. Garcia and
de la Garza, 1977). By and large, the assumption has been that Latinos
are like most other ethnic groups, and are but one of a number of groups
that compete with other groups for political influence on a relatively
equal basis. Therefore, the focus has been on traditional, conventional
questions of "normal" politics, even though, the notion of a Latino politics implies significant differences. There are reasons to question the ade-
quacy of such an interpretation for Latino politics, even in pluralism's
modified forms (see, for example, Manley, 1983 on "neopluralism" and
"pluralism I and II").

There have been few analyses that consciously incorporate alternative perspectives on Latino politics such as "coalitional bias" or "systemic power" interpretations (Stone, 1986, 1980; cf. Flores, 1989).
Coalitional bias suggests that in day-to-day governance all groups are not
looked upon as equally desirable coalition partners, and that ethnic
or racial and social-class status are often intertwined, serving as cues to
what groups are more or less desirable, more or less socially and politically important. Systemic power arguments alert scholars to the sig-

nificant ways in which power is exercised through the "logic of situations" and indirectly, not just in readily apparent and direct ways. Better understanding of contemporary minority politics requires attention to these possibilities.

Similarly, much of the research has focused on a number of political research issues that gained prominence in the 1960s; primary among these is the impact of governmental structure—particularly district versus at-large elections—on the election of Latinos to city council positions (Bullock and MacManus, 1989; Hero and Beatty, 1989). These are not unimportant questions (Meier, Stewart, and England, 1989). But the substantive significance of the election of "ethnics" to city councils and to mayoral positions—where Latino election has occurred most frequently—may have been overstated historically (Wolfinger, 1974; Erie, 1985). And those elections seem increasingly less significant in light of broader social developments, and related theorizing, in the 1980s.

There have been a number of scholars—from rather different ideological perspectives—who have pointed to major alterations and changes in the status of urban governments. Peterson (1981) has argued that cities should avoid redistributive policies, presumably those policies most germane to Latinos and other disadvantaged groups, and stress developmental policies; allocational policies are a third type. Building on Peterson's arguments, Sharp (1990) has contended that urban politics are bifurcated between allocational policies—which include such matters as police patrol allocations, snow removal, trash collection—and developmental politics. Allocational policies tend to have high levels of visibility and controversy, and, to a considerable degree, allocational policies may reflect an overall pluralistic pattern of power. Developmental policies, which are presumably at the heart of urban governmental concerns, most often have low visibility and conflict and exhibit an elitist pattern of power, dominated by banking, corporate, and development interests. Redistributive policies, Sharp implies, are, at most, peripheral. Others who question the role of contemporary cities are Gottdiener (1987), who has written of the "decline of urban politics," and Kantor (1988), who writes of the "dependent city" (also see Elkin, 1987).

To be sure, these interpretations have been challenged; nonetheless, they cannot be ignored, and they have had a major impact on thinking and analysis of urban politics. Yet much of the mainstream research, particularly what might be called the "empirical/behavioral" work, has either not acknowledged or has not adequately accounted for this. There have been a number of studies that have examined the impact of various elements of local governments' electoral structure on the election of Latinos, but with little or no attention to the theorizing about urban government during the 1980s. Thus, the important question of what urban elections, and, indeed, urban politics more generally, mean as an avenue for the political and social mobility of Latinos in the coming decade has yet to be squarely faced, theoretically or practically.

At another level, issues of Latino politics need to be considered in light of broader themes of American democratic politics. Hochschild (1988, 1984), for instance, has suggested that the African-American situation in the United States is not simply an exception or anomaly but may in some ways be necessary or symbiotic to the workings of the American political system. Are Latino politics also symbiotic, or are they an exception? Hochschild's questions are important, and her work has pursued these issues from the standpoint of school desegregation policies (1984). Later work has addressed less visible but equally significant aspects of these issues: issues of "second generation discrimination" in the educational arena, that is, the discrimination that may occur after formal desegregation and that manifests itself in such institutional practices as ability grouping, disciplinary policies, and educational outcomes. Analyses of institutions and their potential biases need to be given greater attention. Institutions and policies that appear to facilitate and enable group advancement may, in the course of "normal" practices, also constrain and impede individual and group development. These are themselves political issues and have larger political implications.

There are a number of relatively specific issues that require attention and need to be linked to other literature as well. It has long been suggested, for instance, that Latino interest groups function differently than do mainstream interest groups; they tend to be multifunctional and have several other unique characteristics (Vigil, 1987). At the same time, scholars have argued that interest group activities in the United States have been supplemented or supplanted by "issue networks" (Heclo, 1978). Research in state politics has indicated that minority groups may now have a presence in state politics, but that that presence is not necessarily to be equated with power (Thomas and Hrebenar, 1990). What do, or might, these arguments mean for Latino interest groups and Latino politics? And, in the many analyses of political culture in the American states (spawned Elazar's work [1984]), the significance of Latinos to political culture has hardly been considered. Bridges need to be built here.

It is often implied in much of the research on Latinos (and other minority groups) that their only interests or goals are for redistributive policies (see, for example, Browning, Marshall, and Tabb, 1984). The possibility that groups such as Latinos may have political values and perspectives that can broaden or modify social and political discourse and debate is thus precluded, virtually by definition. At the same time, this heavy emphasis on redistributive issues draws attention away from the ways in which Latinos are affected by other, nonredistributive policies. This social-psychological and policy segmentation obscures, rather than clarifies and links, Latino politics with larger political and policy processes.

If there is to be advancement in the study of Latino politics in the 1990s the approaches, and their associated assumptions, need to be questioned, understood, and addressed. Following that, the linkage of Latino politics research with and to research in other issues in American politics is necessary. In the absence of attention to these concerns, our understanding of Latino politics and of the broader American political system will be incomplete or inadequate.

References

Acuña, Rodolfo. 1988. *Occupied America.* New York: Harper and Row.
Browning, Rufus P., Dale Rogers Marshall, and David H. Tabb. 1984. *Protest Is Not Enough.* Berkeley, CA: University of California Press.
Bullock, Charles S., III, and Susan A. MacManus. 1989. "Structural Features of Municipalities and the Incidence of Hispanic Councilmembers." Paper presented at the annual meeting of the Southwestern Political Science Association.
Elazar, Daniel J. 1984. *American Federalism: A View from the States.* New York: Harper and Row.
Elkin, Stephen. 1987. *City and Regime in the American Republic.* Chicago: University of Chicago Press.
Erie, Steven. 1985. "Rainbow's End: From the Old to the New Urban Ethnic Politics." Pp. 249–75 in Lionel Maldonado and Joan Moore, eds., *Urban Ethnicity in the United States: New Immigrants and Old Minorities.* Beverly Hills, CA: Sage.
Flores, Henry, 1989. "The Selectivity of the Capitalist State: Chicanos and Economic Development." *Western Political Quarterly,* 42 (June): 377–96.
Garcia, F. Chris, and Rodolfo O. de la Garza. 1977. *The Chicano Political Experience: Three Perspectives.* Duxbury.
Garcia, John. 1981. "Yo Soy Mexicano . . . : Self-Identity and Sociodemographic Correlates." *Social Science Quarterly,* 62 (March): 88–98.
Gottdiener, M. 1987. *The Decline of Urban Politics.* Newbury Park, CA: Sage.
Heclo, Hugh. 1987. "Issue Networks and the Executive Establishment." In Anthony King, ed., *The New Political System.* Washington, DC: American Enterprise Institute.
Hero, Rodney E., and Kathleen M. Beatty. 1989. "The Elections of Federico Pena

as Mayor of Denver: Analysis and Implications," *Social Science Quarterly,* 70 (June): 300–10.

Hochschild, Jennifer. 1988. "The Double-Edged Sword of Equal Opportunity." In Ian Shapiro and Grant Reeher, eds., *Power, Inequality, and Democracy.* Boulder, CO: Westview.

———. 1984. *The New American Dilemma: Liberal Democracy and School Desegregation.* New Haven: Yale University Press.

Kantor, Paul, with Stephen David. 1988. *The Dependent City: The Changing Political Economy of Urban America.* Boston: Scott, Foresman.

Lampe, Philip. 1982. "Ethnic Labels: Naming or Name Calling?" *Ethnic and Racial Studies,* 5 (October): 542–48.

Manley, John. 1983. "Neopluralism: A Class Analysis of Pluralism I and Pluralism II." *American Political Science Review,* 77 (June): 368–83.

Meier, Kenneth, Joseph Stewart, Jr., and Robert England. 1989. *Race, Class, and Education: The Politics of Second Generation Discrimination.* Madison, WI: University of Wisconsin Press.

Munoz, Carlos, Jr. 1989. *Youth, Identity, Power: The Chicano Movement.* New York: Verso.

Peterson, Paul. 1981. *City Limits.* Chicago: University of Chicago Press.

Sharp, Elaine B. 1990. *Urban Politics and Administration: From Service Delivery to Economic Development.* New York: Longman.

Stone, Clarence. 1980. "Systemic Power in Community Decision Making." *American Political Science Review,* 78 (December): 978–90.

———. 1986. "Race, Power, and Political Change." Pp. 200–222 in Janet K. Boles, ed., *The Egalitarian City.* New York: Praeger.

Thomas, Clive S., and Ronald J. Hrebenar. 1990. "Interest Groups in the States." Pp. 123–58 in V. Gray, H. Jacob, and R. Albritton. eds., *Politics in the American States.* 5th ed. Glenview, IL: Scott, Foresman.

Vigil, Maurilio. 1987. *Hispanics in American Politics.* Lanham, MD: University Press of America.

Wolfinger, Raymond. 1974. *The Politics of Progress.* Englewood Cliffs, NJ: Prentice-Hall.

Blacks and Latinos in the American City in the 1990s: Toward Political Alliances or Social Conflict?

James Jennings

THE SOCIAL AND POLITICAL relationships between blacks and Latinos in the big cities of America will be one of the most pressing issues for urban politics in the 1990s. This development represents a new and major challenge to mayoral leadership. The demography that characterizes the American city, the social and economic similarities between blacks and Latinos, and national and international political trends underlie the importance of evolving social relationships between blacks and Latinos in urban settings. As political economist Kenneth M. Dolbeare asks,

> What will it mean, for example, to have predominantly black and Hispanic populations in almost all the major cities, with nearly all-white surrounding suburbs? . . . Is it reasonable to expect working coalitions between Hispanics and blacks? We know that there is a high potential for new minority political power, but not much about its prospects for realization. (Dolbeare, 1986:14).

As further suggested by political scientist Rufus P. Browning and his colleagues, raising this question is justified by focusing on blacks and Latinos in particular because "Blacks and Latinos are the two largest minority groups in the United States, composing 18.1 percent of the national population in 1980 and much larger proportions in many states and cities" (Browning et al., 1990:6).

It is clear that the bigger American cities and key electoral states are becoming increasingly populated by blacks *and* Latinos, and also in some

472

TABLE 1.

Rate of Increase in Population Growth by Race and Ethnicity, 1980–1990

	% Increase
White	6.2
Black	12.7
American Indian, Eskimo, and Aleut	18.9
Latino	34.0
Asian or Pacific Islander	70.3

Source: Rafael Valdivieso and Cary Davis "U.S. Hispanics: Challenging Issues for the 1990s" Population Reference Bureau, Inc., Washington D. C., December 1988.

cities, by people of Asian descent. In 1980, for example, there were twenty-six cities across the United States that had 100,000 or more inhabitants and where blacks and Latinos *each* comprised at least 10 percent of the total population (U.S. Department of Commerce, 1989: Table 39). The number of cities where a combined black and Latino proportion has reached or exceeded 20 percent increased between 1980 and 1990. Furthermore, the population of communities of color are growing much more rapidly than is the white population. Table 1 shows the rate of increase in population growth for major groups between 1980 and 1990.

The growth illustrated in Table 1 for Latinos is taking place in urban areas. In 1985 there were at least forty-four Metropolitan Statistical Areas with at least 100,000 Latinos residing in them; it is important to note that these geographical areas are also those where the black population is rapidly increasing in numbers (Word, 1989).

These figures suggest that the growth of the Latino population has created vast political potential for this group. A large proportion of the Latino population is concentrated in nine states that contain 40 percent of the congressional seats in the United States, as well as three-quarters of all the electoral votes needed to elect a president. While Latinos only comprised 7.3 percent of the total U.S. population in 1985, they comprised 15 percent or more of the population in the following states: California, Texas, Arizona, and New Mexico. In the following states Latinos comprised between 7.5 and 15 percent of the total statewide population: Colorado, New York, Florida, and New Jersey. The total electoral votes in all of these states is 169, more than half of what is needed to elect a president (270) (Bureau of the Census, 1988). And the electoral votes will increase for these states, precisely due to the growth of the Latino,

TABLE 2.

Growth of Latino Voting-Age Population: 1970–1980

STATE	NUMBER OF HISPANICS (1980)	%GROWTH
Arizona	265,688	+88
California	2,775,170	+11
Colorado	204,301	+70
Florida	629,292	+130
Illinois	379,208	+73
New Jersey	307,321	+85
New Mexico	292,714	+82
New York	1,061,852	+35
Texas	1,756,971	+82

Source: Hispanic Policy Development Project, *The Hispanic Almanac* (New York: 1984).

Asian, and black populations, after legislative reapportionment based on the 1990 Census.

Table 2 illustrates the growth of the Latino voting-age population between 1970 and 1980, in the major growth states for Latinos.

In some of the bigger states in this list, however, the black percentage of the total voting-age population is also high and continuing to increase. In 1980, in California, for example, blacks made up 7.5 percent of the voting-age population, in Florida it was 10.8 percent, in Illinois it was 13.6 percent, in New Jersey it was 11.7 percent, in New York it was 13.1 percent, and in Texas it was 11.0 percent. In all of these big states the black proportion of the total voting-age population has increased since 1980 (see Joint Center for Political Studies, 1985). Both blacks and Latinos are part of a broad demographic and, possibly therefore, political and social transformation of the United States. The nature of this transformation will be partially dependent on the political relationships between these two groups.

The query posed by Dolbeare implies that blacks and Latinos can be approached monolithically; this is not true. There are major social and economic differences within the overall Latino community that should not be overlooked in investigating relationships between blacks and Latinos. As the Latino population continues to grow, social and economic differences within and between various Latino groups may become more prominent and salient as political issues (see for example, Nelson, 1919; Garcia, 1989; for some discussion regarding the possibility of political differentiation within a Latino community, see Jennings, 1989). While the median age for Mexican Americans, or Chicanos, was 23.6 years in

1989, for Cubans it was 41.4 years! The labor force participation for Puerto Ricans in this year was 54.2 percent, but for Chicanos it was 67.8 percent, and for Cubans it was 62.3 percent. There are also significant differences between Puerto Ricans, Chicanos, Cubans, and persons from countries in Central and South America regarding unemployment rates, poverty, percent of female-headed households, median income levels, and occupational characteristics (U.S. Department of Commerce, 1990, also McKay, 1985). Some of these differences may explain how relationships between blacks and Latinos evolve in different urban settings.

The growth of both black and Latino populations in cities is generally associated with increasing levels of poverty compared to whites in the United States. Blacks and certain sectors of the Latino population are experiencing increasing social and economic problems that seem to show the need for greater amounts of economic assistance and resources, as well as greater attention on the part of urban mayoral leadership. But despite significant social and economic similarities between blacks and some groups of Latinos, it is quite possible that a cleavage will emerge between these two communities of color. The kind of cleavage suggested here is different than discussed in earlier works focusing on urban political or mayoral leadership. Political scientist Clarence N. Stone describes one focus of some of these earlier works:

> Banfield, in particular in his work with James Q. Wilson, talked about urban conflict primarily in terms of a cleavage between a provincial and tradition-minded ethos linked to machine politics and a cosmopolitan and modern-minded ethos linked to good government reform. This cleavage, rather than class or racial conflict, was the focus of Banfield and Wilson's understanding of city politics (Stone, 1988:138).

In 1968, the Kerner Commission identified major political and social cleavages in urban America along racial and class lines; this report focused on the economic chasm between the haves and the have-nots (National Advisory Commission on Civil Disorders, 1968). The continuing prominence of this kind of economic cleavage was again recognized in a twenty-year review of the Kerner Commission's findings (Harris and Wilkins, 1988). But the cleavage between haves and have nots, while continuing to characterize urban politics, will now become even more complex as it is impacted by the particular political and social relationships between blacks and Latinos—generally, two "have-not" groups.

Many social and political issues that urban mayors have to try to resolve are now colored by the political relationships between blacks and Latinos. For example, in places like Miami and Houston conflict between police and community reflects, in part, ethnic division and hostility between blacks and Latinos. In both these cities, instances of police brutality have involved Latino officers abusing black residents. In the area of education, there are instances both of political conflict and of cooperation between blacks and Latinos in cities like Chicago and New York. Electoral redistricting struggles in places like Los Angeles and Boston have, to a certain degree, reflected black and Latino political solidarity. Police and community relations, education, and redistricting are but a few issues that have always confronted the mayor's office; today, these same issues become even more complex and pressing as a result of the growth and political maturing of two communities of color, neither of which has been accepted or integrated fully into the higher echelon of private and corporate wealth in urban America.

Due to the lower social and economic status of blacks and Latinos and their particular political needs, at least two scenarios are possible in projecting an answer to Dolbeare's query. One scenario is characterized by political conflict between blacks and Latinos, as may have been the case at various times in cities like Miami, New York City, and Detroit. But the other scenario is one of blacks and Latinos joining to push a common political agenda, as was witnessed in the Harold Washington mayoral campaigns in Chicago, the Mel King mayoral campaign in Boston in 1983, and the David Dinkins mayoral victory in New York City. Both scenarios can have a major impact on the political direction of the American city. One writer suggests further, and in stronger terms, that acting together politically these two groups actually have the power to significantly influence the direction of the American economy at a national level. (Gallegos, 1986). But even though the coalitions among communities of color can have a significant impact in these areas, as political scientist Rodney E. Hero stated, "Those coalitions . . . probably are not as simply created, or maintained, as it sometimes appears" (Hero, 1989:349).

The mayor of a big city can assist in building a common political front between blacks and Latinos, or the mayor can seek short-term political advantages by encouraging one group to act as an electoral counterweight to the other group. There was some evidence of the latter response at the national level when Ronald Reagan and the Republican party attempted to mold the Latino electorate as a political counterweight to loyal black Democrats. There are also local instances of mayors attempting to utilize one group of black or Latino citizens to counter the political influence of the other group. Former mayors Kevin White in Boston, and Edward Koch in New York City were accused of attempting such strategies at various times during their administrations.

The implications for each of these scenarios are significant for the overall politics and economic direction of the American city. If conflict between blacks and Latinos becomes the political norm, then we should not expect much progress toward a public policy that responds to the economic and social needs of the poverty-level and working-class strata in each of the communities. The major reason for this claim is that the political influence of one group seeking social changes may be countered or dampened by that of the other group. If blacks, Latinos—and people of Asian descent—do support common political agendas and coalitions, however, then it may mean that have-not interests could develop stronger platforms by which to challenge actors representing and benefiting from the economic and wealth status quo in urban America.

FURTHER RESEARCH

Several questions and issues should be explored in order to investigate further some of the possibilities suggested in this brief essay. First, what is the history of black and Latino political relationships in different cities and regarding various policy issues? What conditions or factors lead either to political cooperation or competition between blacks and Latino activists? Under what conditions have multiracial coalitions led to the election of black, Latino, or Asian candidates? What characteristics are found in those places where black and Latino political cooperation has been evident? What politics or social tools or processes contribute to cooperation or competition, and what is the role of the mayor in the American city as far as this question is concerned? And what kinds of demands upon government will emerge as a result of political collaboration between blacks and Latinos? Will these demands be different than the traditional benefits sought from local government? These questions will become more significant and important as both blacks and Latinos continue to numerically dominate an increasing number of American cities.

REFERENCES

Browning, Rufus P., et al. 1990. *Racial Politics in American Cities*. New York: Longman Publishers.

Dolbeare, Kenneth M. 1986. *Democracy at Risk: The Politics of Economic Renewal*. New Jersey: Chatham House Publishers.

Gallegos, William. 1986. "The Sunbelt Strategy and Chicano Liberation." *Forward*. 5 (Spring): 1–32.

Garcia, F. Chris, ed. 1989. *Latinos in the U.S. Political System.* Notre Dame, IN: University of Notre Dame Press.

Harris, Fred R., and Roger W. Wilkins. 1988. *The Quiet Riots: Twenty Years after the Kerner Report.* New York: Pantheon Books.

Hero, Rodney E. 1989. "Multiracial Coalitions in City Elections Involving Minority Candidates: Some Evidence from Denver." *Urban Affairs Quarterly,* 25, no. 2 (December): 342–351.

Jennings, James. 1989. "Future Directions for Puerto Rican Politics." In Garcia, 1989.

Joint Center for Political Studies. 1986. *Black Elected Officials: A National Roster, 1985.* Washington, DC.

Mckay, Emily G. 1985. "A Demographic Summary of Hispanic Americans." Washington DC: National Council of La Raza.

National Advisory Commission on Civil Disorders. 1968. *Report.* Washington, DC: Government Printing Office.

Nelson, Dale C. 1979. "Ethnicity and Socioeconomic Status as Sources of Participation: The Case of Ethnic Political Culture." *American Political Science Review,* 73 (December): 1024–38.

Stone, Clarence N. 1989. "Paradigms, Power, and Urban Leadership." In Bryan D. Jones, *Leadership and Politics.* Lawrence, KS: University Press of Kansas.

U.S. Department of Commerce. Bureau of the Census. 1988. "The Hispanic Population in the United States: March 1988 (Advance Report)." Current Population Reports, P-20, no. 431. Washington, DC: Government Printing Office.

———. 1989. *Statistical Abstract of the U.S., 1989.* Table 39. Washington, DC: Government Printing Office.

———. 1990. "The Hispanic Population in the United States: March 1989." Current Population Reports, P-20, no. 444. Washington, DC: Government Printing Office.

Word, David L. 1989. "Population Estimates by Race and Hispanic Origin for States, Metropolitan Areas, and Selected Counties: 1980 to 1985." U.S. Department of Commerce, Bureau of the Census, Current Population Reports P-25, no. 1040-Rd-1. Washington, DC: Government Printing Office.